THE RADICAL WILL

Randolph Bourne

THE RADICAL WILL

Selected Writings
1911 - 1918

Preface
by Christopher Lasch

Selection and Introductions
by Olaf Hansen

Pluto Press

Unit 10 Spencer Court, 7 Chalcot Road,
London NW1 8LH

01-722 0141

URIZEN BOOKS • NEW YORK

Introduction & Prefatory Notes (c) 1977 by Olaf Hansen
Preface (c) 1977 by Christopher Lasch
(c) 1977 Urizen Books, Inc. New York
The Prayer of a Materialist, A Sociological Poet, The Scientific Manager, A Little Thing of Brunnellechis, Practics vs. Product, Suffrage and Josella, Chivalry and Sin, The Night Court, Pageantry and Social Art, The Disillusionment, The Artist in Wartime, The Doctrine of the Rights of Man are published here for the first time, and are so published with the kind permission of Columbia University which is the owner of the original manuscripts.
ISBN — 0-916354-00-8 (cloth)
0-916354-01-6 (paper)

Library of Congress Cataloging in Publication Data

Bourne, Randolph Silliman, 1886-1918.
   The Radical Will:
   Randolph Bourne (Selected Writings 1911-1918)

   Bibliography: p.
   Includes index.
     1. Political science--Collected works. I. Hansen,
Olaf   II. Title.
JA93.B68A36 1976   320.5'092'4   76-8495
ISBN 0-916354-00-8
ISBN 0-916354-01-6 pbk.

Contents

Preface

by Christopher Lasch

The search for new forms of thought, which engaged so many American intellectuals in the period immediately preceding the First World War, sprang from a pervasive sense that the material transformation of American society required a new politics and a new culture. Older forms of thought, rooted in social conditions now superceded, appeared to have exhausted their capacity to organize or make sense of experience. The growth of industrial "trusts," the rise of the labor movement, and the growing dominance of organizations over individuals undermined the historic foundations of individualism. The trend toward monopoly and the corporations' demand for state intervention in the economy made classical liberalism obsolete. The emergence of the United States as a world power appeared to require a new foreign policy, one that repudiated earlier traditions of isolationism, opposition to standing armies, and limited government. The "new immigration" from southern and eastern Europe, the rounding out of America's continental empire, and the creation of a new empire abroad condemned the "genteel tradition" of American culture—a provincial culture based on the spiritual ascendancy of New England—to obsolescence.

Dissatisfaction with older traditions produced a broad-based cultural revolt. Indeed the emergence of an American intelligentsia, a new social stratum the importance of which Randolph Bourne was one of the first to glimpse, cannot be understood except as the product of this ferment—this struggle to come to grips with a rapidly changing society and to find ways of describing it as accurately as possible, of controlling its new energies, or alternately of releasing their liberating potential. Pragmatic philosophy, progressive education (which centered on the demand that the schools explain the "realities of modern life"), the Chicago school of sociology, the Chicago school of architecture, Theodore Roosevelt's New Nationalism, the new liberalism articulated by the founders of *The New Republic,* and the "new paganism" of *The Masses,* all originated, whatever their differences, in a deliberate rejection of older traditions and reflected the belief that a new society needed new modes of thought. Similarly the attempt to renew American letters, which rallied briefly around *Seven Arts,* rested on the belief that the United States required not only a literature but a music, architecture, painting, and philosophy commensurate with its transformation from an English colony into a sprawling, polyglot, cosmopolitan power. Just as Theodore Roosevelt and other imperialists wanted a military establishment and a foreign policy to match America's status as a newly arrived world power, so Van Wyck Brooks appeared to be demanding a culture that would reflect "America's coming-of-age"; but unlike Roosevelt, he saw the nation's economic maturity not as the foundation of imperialist adventures abroad but as providing the leisure and the freedom from purely material preoccupations that would permit the development, at last, of a thriving indigenous culture.

A major issue in this multifaceted cultural protest—an issue on the resolution of which much would depend—was whether cultural experimentation would crystallize around conceptions of a new nationalism or whether it would transcend the character of a merely national revival and develop a broader vision of liberation and renewal. A related issue was whether the new culture—the culture of "modernism"—should merely reflect new "realities" or simultaneously subject them to criticism. Should urban architecture, for example, "reflect the realities of the machine age" or provide forms designed to humanize it, to release modern technology from its historically constricting capitalist form? The writers associated with *Seven Arts,* although they formulated a more promising version of the "American renaissance" than any other group of intellectuals in this period, never managed to resolve either question. On the one hand, their call for a renewal of American letters could mean that American art had to be judged by European standards; that it had to be a critical art; and that although it grew out of American experience (instead of imported English traditions) it had to achieve a certain distance from that experience. Van Wyck Brooks and James Oppenheim, editor of *Seven Arts,* were careful to dissociate themselves from William Dean Howells's dictum that art should reflect social reality. According to Brooks, this view "denied the fundamental fact of artistic creation: that the reality of the artist's vision is something quite different from the apparent reality of the world about him."

On the other hand, many articles in *Seven Arts* seemed to call precisely for an art reflective of the sweep and turmoil of American life. Whereas Brooks in his early writings had no intention of demolishing genteel culture only to set up popular culture in its place (a popular culture itself modeled on the genteel tradition), many of his followers drew a simplistic contrast between literary culture and the culture of the folk, celebrating the crude vitality of the one, deploring the "curling wisp of incense" of the other. In his essay, "On Creating a Usable Past," Brooks himself sanctioned the literary nativism that was to guide the work of Constance Rourke, Gilbert Seldes, and Lewis Mumford, and which eventually came to guide his own work as well. Having denied in an early work that it was possible "deliberately to *establish* an American tradition," he now invited just such an attempt: a search for buried treasure, for a submerged American popular culture counter to the genteel official culture.[1]

Of all the writers associated with this promising movement in American letters, only Randolph Bourne outgrew its origins and limitations. By identifying the revolt against provincialism with the ideal of a "trans-national America," he attempted to rule out a retreat into higher forms of provincialism. "Whatever American nationalism turns out to be, it is certain to become something utterly different from the nationalism of twentieth-century Europe"—"not a nationality but a trans-nationality." Trans-national America (as the term makes clear) implied not the idea of a melting pot but rather a federation of cultures which would eventually result in a culture beyond nationalisms of every kind; not the ethnic pluralism advocated by recent spokesmen of the "ethnic revival" but a culture beyond ethnicity; not a glorification of ethnic consciousness in its existing state of parochialism but a genuine cosmopolitanism. The immigrants who interested Bourne were not the immigrants of the urban ghettos but the "acclimatized" sons of immigrants he met at Columbia, in whose presence, he wrote, the American provincial breathed "a larger air" and felt himself "citizen of a larger world." The literary culture of New England stood condemned, in Bourne's eyes, not because it stifled popular culture but because its academic dominance—now happily beginning to weaken, he thought—prevented "the creation of a proletarian man of letters." Like his Italian contemporary, Antonio Gramsci, Bourne saw that the emancipation of the working class and the democratization of society depended in part on the emergence of working-class intellectuals—men and women whose origins made them "oblivious to the repressions of that tight little society in which [the native American] so provincially grew up." Like Gramsci, Bourne wanted this "younger intelligentsia" not to confirm the masses in their superstitions but to attack "stale and familiar attitudes" in every form.

Unlike Brooks and many of his followers, Bourne never exalted popular culture over "high culture." He attacked the "Americanization" of the immigrants precisely because the breakdown of immigrant cultures created "cultural outlaws, without taste, without standards but those of the mob." His defense of diversity did not deny the need for an "impelling integrating force." It was because the "colonial" culture of the Anglo-American elite failed to provide such a unifying force, according to Bourne, that American society was dissolving into "detached fragments of people," who became "the flotsam and jetsam of American life, the downward undertow of our civilization with its leering cheapness and falseness of taste and spiritual outlook, the absence of mind and sincere feeling which we see in our slovenly towns, our vapid moving pictures, our popular novels, and in the vacuous faces of the crowds on the city street."

Bourne was less beguiled by false promises of cultural liberation than his contemporaries because he had a better understanding of the political dimension of prewar debates about American culture. He saw the enemy not as the "genteel tradition" but as the hegemony of the Anglo-American ruling class and the class system itself. In his eyes, the problem of cultural renewal remained inseparable from the problem of social change. The enthusiasm with which most intellectuals threw themselves into justification of the war soon confirmed the accuracy of this assessment: ostensibly liberating ideologies, formerly associated with progressivism, now enlisted in the service of the state. Thanks to the support of the intellectuals, the state made war in the name of social progress and cultural regeneration. Lacking a critique of the dominant forms of social relations, the critique of the "genteel tradition" collapsed into a mindless celebration of practicality, action, power, and war. No one foresaw this collapse more clearly than Bourne or analyzed it with such precision.

Neither his awareness of the connections between culture and politics, so unusual among critics of his time, nor his attacks on the "significant classes" made Randolph Bourne a Marxian socialist, any more than his search for a national culture made him a literary nationalist in the style of the later Van Wyck Brooks. Bourne's early death, together with the variety of his interests and the eclectic, undogmatic character of his thought, invites rival attempts to claim him for a particular tradition and to see him alternately as an early spokesman for the revolt of youth, a forerunner of the "proletarian" critics of the thirties, or as an anarchist attempting to revive a preindustrial type of organic community. A new generation of American Marxists, more attuned than their predecessors to the interplay of economics and culture, mind and society, subjectivity and objectivity, will find in Bourne a kindred spirit and may therefore be tempted to assimilate him to one or another tradition of Marxism; or failing that, to condemn him precisely for neglecting the one body of thought which could have given his ideas theoretical coherence.

The understanding of American radicalism and its history has suffered from a recurrent tendency either to force it into European categories or to make its very resistance to this procedure the basis of a general condemnation of the American Left. Olaf Hansen's introduction to the present collection not only criticizes this tendency but clarifies the intellectual problem from which it springs; for while the absence of a Marxian tradition has had profound effects on American intellectual life, according to Hansen, merely deploring its absence does little to explain those effects. Such an approach also leads to a neglect of the real achievements, both practical and theoretical, of American radicalism. Without exaggerating those achievements or the "convergence" between American radicalism and Marxism, we need to "concentrate," in Hansen's words, "on those intellectual efforts which come nearest to fulfilling their promise as an equivalent to the explanatory scope and coherence of [European] Marxist thought."

Europeans have sometimes appreciated American thinkers more than those thinkers have been appreciated at home; Americans have repeatedly learned from Europeans how to reach sound judgments not only of the shortcomings of their own culture but of its virtues. Such an experience played a part in launching the fruitful work of Brooks and of Randolph Bourne himself; and it is therefore fitting that a European intellectual, Olaf Hansen, should now present to an American audience the most comprehensive collection of Bourne's writings. It is doubly fitting that the appearance of this collection coincides with the first beginnings of a new movement in American criticism and theory—a movement shaped, at least in part, in the spirit of the Frankfurt School and of what was perhaps its nearest American equivalent, the movement of intellectual renewal of which Bourne was the most courageous and clearsighted exponent.

NOTE

1. Van Wyck Brooks, *The Wine of the Puritans: A Study of Present-Day America* (New York, 1909), p. 134.

Introduction

AFFINITY AND AMBIVALENCE

by Olaf Hansen

One of the most fascinating and yet disturbing aspects of American intellectual history in the twentieth century is the absence of an established Marxist tradition. This absence itself has left, however, a definite mark. Key terms of radical thought have gradually changed their meaning while being confronted with their counterparts in the Marxist tradition. At the same time this tradition has shown a remarkable adaptability.

If we can nowadays observe tendencies of convergence between the two lines of radical thought, a convergence due mainly to the decreasing urgency of the economic aspects of Marxism, at least in the industrialized countries of the West, we should remember that there have been periods when Marxist thought had above all a kind of negative attraction for the radical American intellectual. The American radical intellectual who was at the same time as much drawn to Marxist philosophy as he felt provoked to react against it followed the ambivalent pattern of a recurring paradox. Components of Marxism were taken out of context, developed a certain influence and then were swiftly discarded as inadequate for the solution of a present or impending crisis.

Intellectual energies were then directed toward the construction of viable alternatives, which by necessity were not alternatives to a genuine Marxist philosophy—which had not been dealt with in the first place—but usually were efforts to reconstruct modes of native radicalism. Hence, the American radical intellectual, more often than not, appeared to wind up in a position of original affinity to Marxism. He established his answers to a cultural or political crisis by reacting against something he tried to do without: the explanatory value of critical theories deriving their basic tenets from the Hegelian-Marxist matrix.

Original affinity often meant that in order to arrive at a unified concept of reality intellectuals adopted the moral indignation they found articulated in Marxist thought, adding to it their own humanistic social philosophy. Another common stance emphasized the scientific character of Marxism and incorporated it into a positivistic philosophy where science and rationality were almost identical terms.

Occasionally the result of such efforts was a rather stale mixture of various trivialized intellectual concepts which nonetheless revealed the political reality of capitalism.

In the history of American intellectual radicalism, we find a wealth of contributions concerning the social character of the world of common experience. We miss, however, an equal richness of theoretical explication, complementary concepts capable of analyzing the world of common experience from the perspective of more general interpretations.

Stating the obvious is easier, of course, than accounting for it. One must ask how it is possible that the most influential coherent philosophy of the nineteenth and twentieth centuries never established itself in the United States. We may come to some understanding by discussing texts in the radical tradition wherein the quest for an alternative originality worked at its creative best.

Rather than trace the meandering path of antidialectical thinking within the American radical tradition from decade to decade, and follow it through the pitfalls of various attempts to pragmatize Marx, seeing him as a "scientist" of future revolutions, or simply "americanizing" him, as the slogan went in the thirties, one should concentrate on those intellectual efforts which come nearest to fulfilling their promise as an equivalent to the explanatory scope and coherence of Marxist thought. Such examples show the persistent rejection of Marxism creating new affinities to it, the attempt to differ producing analogies which again demand a comparison with their opposites, thus affording us through their incongruity a perspective on the particular quality of the culture which produced one and prevented the other.

To analyze the avoidance of a Marxist stance by looking at the most original attempts to create an alternative, should also provide insights into the common roots of a Marxist mode of thought. Theodor W. Adorno's statement that John Dewey's philosophy was above all characterized by its latent dialectical qualities, the implications of which Dewey himself tried to overlook, can be systematically generalized if we look at the Hegelian elements of Pragmatism at large. It is these hidden dialectical elements of Pragmatic philosophy and of course the sociological and philosophical dimensions added by George Herbert Mead and Josiah Royce which provide the matrix for the most successful concepts of a social and cultural criticism which rejeçts the Marxist approach while taking a similar point of departure and arriving at structurally analogous results. This partial likeness of analytical insights as compared to rather strict differences where ideology is concerned has produced a conflict which in turn is responsible for an iconographic mode of expression within the American radical intellectual tradition, for a habit of thought with a considerable aesthetic substance of its own. If it occasionally seems that a lack in terminology is more than compensated for by relying on the cognitive persuasion of images, we can nevertheless detect the dialectical edge of abstract thought in the peculiar blend of the political and the poetic of which these images consist.

It would be a fascinating task to write a history of the rejection of Hegelian-Marxist thought in this country. Starting with the refutation of dialectical thinking by William James and John Dewey, the latter being a complex case of ambivalent attitudes, one would have to discuss the influence of neo-Hegelian thought by looking at Josiah Royce and his influential English contemporary F. H. Bradley and at the relationship of this particular kind of idealism with the pragmatic philosophy and social psychology of the same period. Having thus established the outlines of a general intellectual disposition, one could follow the course of important debates, the New Historians' discussion about the importance of economic forces as historical determinants and Charles Beard's final rejection of the Marxist temptation; Max Eastman's violent debate with Sydney Hook in the thirties, a debate of special interest, as both its participants had been students of John Dewey; Thurman Arnold's discussion with Sydney Hook about the symbolic character of politics and the latter's critical appraisal of the nature of dialectical thought; and last but not least Edmund Wilson's elaborate attempt to deal with Marxism, *To The Finland Station,* a book which sums up in grandiose fashion the sentiments of one decade anticipating those of the next.

There are further examples, but another, possibly more productive, way of reconstructing the past focuses on single events instead of following the development of many until they form a historical continuum. To concentrate on one person's intellectual activities as a paradigmatic expression of the social and cultural contradictions of his time allows for a detailed reconstruction of the ideological cross-currents of the day and of the use that was made of them. Given the right person, who undoubtedly has to be both broad in the scope of his intellectual engagements and sufficiently thorough, we have a chance to watch the crucial process of common experience being turned over in a private mind only to be reconstructed through vision and analysis as an interpreted common experience become part of the public social consciousness.

RANDOLPH BOURNE

When we come to deal with the decade before the United States' entry into World War I, if we look for a social and cultural critic who fulfills the described expectations as a catalyst of intellectual currents, our attention is immediately drawn to the figure of Randolph Bourne.

Randolph Silliman Bourne, whose career as a man of letters covered less than a decade, became the legendary hero of his time immediately after his premature death in 1918. He was a likely candidate for that role, despite the fact that *all* the crucial books of that particularly productive period of intellectual history had been written, not by him, but by his contemporaries. Walter Rauschenbusch's *Christianity and the Social Crisis* appeared in 1907 when Bourne was twenty-one. The year 1909 saw both Van Wyck Brooks' *The Wine of the Puritans* and Herbert Croly's *The Promise of American Life.* Four years later, in 1913, Walter Lippmann published *A Preface to Politics,* which was followed by *Drift and Mastery,* about which Bourne was to comment enthusiastically "There is a book one would have given one's soul to have written."

YOUTH AND EDUCATION

Born in 1886 in Bloomfield, New Jersey, Randolph Bourne emerged as a critic of culture and society at a relatively late stage of his development. Six years elapsed between his graduation from high school in 1903 and his entering Columbia

by means of a scholarship. How he spent these six years remains in the dark, but it was a profoundly frustrating time for
Bourne as he constantly looked for work without the hoped-for
results. Paul Rosenfeld, one of Bourne's closest friends, gives
the following account of Bourne's precollege days:

> It was difficult for Bourne to make his way unaided to the uni-
> versity; and, at the conclusion of high-schooling he took the
> first position of secretary to some moneyed drearies, then of
> musical proofreader in a pianola-record factory; then of ac-
> companist to a toreador singing-master in Carnegie Studios
> who euchered him of his pay.

The echoes of those days are clearly audible in the tone and
subject matter of Bourne's essays "The Handicapped" and
"Exploitation." Bourne did not, however, come from a poor family. He grew up in comfortable surroundings, even though the
financial problems of his immediate family demanded continuous assistance from a well-to-do uncle. Piano lessons, frequent
visits to the opera and the opportunity to read at his leisure
made for an education of more than average middle-class standards.

His diary-notes of the year 1901, when Bourne was fifteen,
show a wide-ranging interest in the political and cultural events
of the day combined with an almost precocious capacity of
emotion and sensibility. Nothing in the following lines betrays the
exasperations and hardships he must have suffered, unless one
takes exactly this as evidence of the desperate effort to be just
like anybody else.

Saturday, Feb. 9, 1901
I found that Mrs. Griffin had a ticket for Stanton for the
Symphony this afternoon when I got up there, and that Aunt
Fan wanted to see me and had one for me. I took a car down
there and found that she wanted me to stay in, take lunch
with her and then go up to Carnegie Hall. I did not like this
thing. Right there before some of the Gymnasium girls, she
unbuttoned my coat, looked all over it, inspected my collar, to
see whether it was clean, examined my necktie, made me
hold out my hands to see if they or my nails were clean,
made me open my mouth to see if my teeth were clean, and

then brushed me off after making comments about things in general. I think it was one of the most disgusting, ill-bred, rude things to do. I am not going through it again, it is mortifying.

Then went down to the Studio where Miss Perkins was practising. She is every inch a lady, and I wish that she were Aunt Fan. I'm sure she'd never do a thing like that or tell my mother, her sister, that it would be better for them if their mother should die, then she wouldn't have to take care of her. Miss Perkins has just bought a beautiful set of Scott's works, published by an Edinburgh firm, in leather, with etchings and illustrations. I began "Quentin Durward." When I read it three years ago I thought it one of the best books I had ever read.

The lunch was very dainty and lovely, of course, only I was not much taken with "the little maid," Pauline, a big strapping German of about fifty, who has such a "sweet spirit" and is "so attentive" and whom we have served up regularly for Sunday night Supper. She didn't know how to set the table, and was extremely slow in serving things. The studio is, on the whole, a very nice little place. The concert, I enjoyed very much. My seat was in the dress circle, but I could see very well. I was rather disappointed by the first number on the programme. It seemed rather disconnected in character and not at all pretty. Mrs. Toedt sang very well, and some charming songs, 4b, being especially sweet. The Beethoven larghetto was perfect, and one of the best I've heard by an orchestra, smooth, melodious, and played so well. The march was very good, too.

Bourne's childhood, much like the rest of his life, was far from normal. After what he once referred to as a "terribly messy birth" his face, mutilated by the forceps, remained misshapen, twisted in an awkward angle. At the age of four, he contracted spinal tuberculosis and was left a dwarfed hunchback. Bourne's shocking physical appearance and its sharp contrast to his intellectual charisma have been the subject of numerous anecdotes which helped to create the Bourne legend. The difference, however, between anecdote and legend is a question of historical texture: from its very beginning the Bourne legend had been patterned upon a consciousness of intellectual crisis, an awareness of social collapse and last but not least upon the question of guaranteeing social cohesion. As early as 1919, a year after Bourne's death, Waldo Frank in *Our America* went to the heart of the Bourne legend with his appraisal of Bourne's capacity to analyze the underlying connections between discordant forces in society.

The best significance of Randolph Bourne lies in the joining, through his work, of the political and the cultural currents of advance. Brooks holds aloof from the transience of affairs. Our most sensitive poets and novelists do likewise. The crassness of the American world is too much for them. . . . Bourne, almost alone, embraced the two. More than any of our fellows, he pointed the path of fusion which American leadership must take. His political discussions were actually lit by a spiritual viewpoint. They took into account the content of the human soul, the individual soul, the values of *being*.

Frank's opinion, inspired by a dualistic view of the world, was soon to be replaced by others of similar dichotomous persuasion. In 1930, Seward Collins opened his attack against the antihumanists of the Left by referring to Randolph Bourne (and Van Wyck Brooks) as the original source of present evils. Michael Gold on the other hand was convinced that Randolph Bourne, had he lived, would have become the Great American Critic—after the Marxist fashion of that time, of course. All these characterizations of Bourne rest upon the negative or positive fascination with his ability to combine heterogenous points of view, thus emphasizing to the point of projection his propensity for avoiding the restrictions of intellectual compartmentalization.

Bourne's early death helped to create another aspect of his legend, an aspect expressed in the repeated question of how he would have developed had he lived into the following decades. The question makes sense, of course, only when seen as a formula to express opinions about the potentialities of the past as a disguise of the hopes for the future. That these hopes should be projected onto Bourne is worth noticing, since it reveals the quality of his work in more than one way. On the one hand, we learn how Bourne stood out among his contemporaries and how quickly, in public memory, he became the representative of the political promises made by the rebellious young intellectuals of the prewar years, promises only Bourne had kept. Thus, as early as 1921, Harold Stearns in *America and the Young Intellectual* felt obliged to rescue Bourne from the fate of being misinterpreted by Van Wyck Brooks, who was suspected of playing down the real scope of Bourne's political interest.

It is sensibility moving in a rather rarefied atmosphere of ideas and subtle evocations, explaining too, his constant fear that our younger writers will be drawn away from the true spirit of culture into the more or less irrelevant vortex of politics and sociology. For example, Randolph Bourne in the "History of a Literary Radical" spoke of living down "the new orthodoxies of the classics," and in his introduction to that book Mr. Brooks interprets that to mean that had Bourne lived, his interest would have "concentrated more and more on the problem of evoking and shaping an American literature"—an interpretation that I think clearly incorrect.

Looking once more at Michael Gold, we learn on the other hand that in 1926, when among cultural and literary critics socialistic ideas had become one of the key issues, Bourne is still remembered as the great hope of the past, against whose shadow one measures the stature of contemporaries. Under the headline "America Needs A Critic," the reader of the *New Masses* was told:

> Waldo Frank is not the critic. He has a dark huge Whitman-like emotion about America . . . Mystics cannot run locomotives, or explain the Machine Age to us. . . . Van Wyck Brooks started out to be that critic. . . . But he is lost up the blind alley of Freud . . . Max Eastman was the finest candidate, a true artist and scientist, but the victim of an anomaly. He was a poet with old-fashioned tendencies, and so faced backwards. . . . Edmund Wilson is a force, but is bogged in formalism, and never drives clean to the great mark. V. F. Calverton has a wide, scholarly knowledge of the new criticism, but is undeveloped in esthetic insight or emotion. . . . Randolph Bourne might have grown into the critic we need. He knew how great mass changes create the new artist, the new thoughts. He studied the international working-class move-

ment. He was undaunted in the storms of history, and accepted the fact that capitalism must change. In his mind the world was one—and he examined all the political and economic facts, along with every other fact in a period, when he discussed literature.

The portrait drawn by Michael Gold is surprisingly adequate, even though it makes Bourne look a little too much like a synthesis of Gold's own contemporaries.

Bourne did indeed try to assimilate the most divergent facets of the culture and society he knew; the reason for his fame, however, was his will to differ, was a kind of intellectual obstinacy in which his contemporaries saw moral greatness as well as rational maturity. Although Bourne undoubtedly shared the convictions held by other members of the *Seven Arts* group—to the same extent that he owed a great number of opinions to his contemporaries—he differed from all of them in the sense of being an exemplary intellectual, at home with the contradictions of the world around him, relying on analysis rather than on rationalizations or ideologies. He believed in the necessity of creative vision, yet he did not subscribe to utopianism. He was convinced that each new generation had the choice of a political and historical fresh start, but he did not resort to a full-fledged cult of the young. He had a decided inclination to the concrete. His criticism of the growing degradation of social values, his polemics against the downfall of pragmatic philosophy, his essays on education and politics all rely on a relentless analysis of tangible experience rather than on the abstract logic of preconceived ideas. Bourne, in other words, was used to dealing with culture and society as something to be lived with. He did not treat them as removed objects of abstract analysis.

Croly and Bourne

If one likes to conceive of history as a drama, and tries to look for a suitable opponent to the position held by Bourne, the obvious choice would have to be Herbert Croly.

The difference between those two men, especially when seen against their common background, helps illuminate the intellectual tensions characteristic of their time. Both of them shared the prevailing sense of crisis as well as the corresponding sense of need for an alternative to a downward tendency they saw in American culture and politics. Neither of them believed that an answer to the disruptive forces in society and the resulting degeneration of cultural values could be found within the ideological framework of traditional progressivism. The ordinary notions of reform and uplift had to be replaced by more fundamental efforts of analysis. In a letter to Bourne, written at an early stage of their relationship, Croly tried to describe the general direction of future criticism.

I believe also that a certain amount of conscious patriotism in our critical standard is necessary in order to enable us to have the effect which we should like to have upon the actual practice of the arts in this country. We have to be thoroughly critical, but there must be also a positive impulse behind this criticism. . . . In the present chaos of artistic standards and practice, I do not see how it will be possible to do any authoritative writing on these subjects, except on the basis of social standards.

The theme is a familiar one, even if Croly lays considerable stress on the importance of patriotism, more, at least, than the formula of a desirable national, democratic culture usually implied. At the time of Croly's letter, however, Bourne was hardly aware, or at least did not show that he was, of the fundamental differences of intellectual and ethical temperament which would later separate him from Croly. When *The New Republic* was founded, he wanted a position of potential influence and showed some disappointment when he was not offered the coveted post as editor of the art section. He was asked instead to write about education and town-planning—a subject close to the heart of Croly, who had displayed a life-long interest in architecture.

Mutual respect and efforts from Croly's side to make Bourne feel at ease among the members of the inner circle of *The New Republic* could not cover up the deeply rooted differences between the two men. Even the personal dissimilarities were striking. Croly, the famous author of *The Promise of American Life,* was pathologically shy, his extreme reticence having become as notorious as the lofty and involved style of his writing. Bourne, on the other hand, whose early essays had been praised for their lucidity, was already known as a brilliant conversationalist, eager to socialize. Both of them shared a sense of crisis as well as the conviction that it was the intellectual's task to set things right. The idea of intellectual leadership appealed to both, though in a totally different fashion. Croly's attitude was best summed up in the words of Edmund Wilson:

> It was still possible for Herbert Croly to feel that the United States was a kind of mystical entity—something isolated, self-contained and self-perpetuating—that could be counted on to solve its own problems and eliminate its own disease.

Bourne's attitude was of course far less mystical. His sociological and aesthetic sensibilities were based on a thorough academic education, a far less eclectic one than Croly's. As both men had been influenced by Josiah Royce, the different use they made of their common source is revealing. In *The Promise of American Life,* Croly relies above all on Royce's philosophy of loyalty when discussing the relationship between the individual and society, adding an elitist dimension, however, by explicitly referring to Santayana's concept of a "social aristocracy." Bourne's favorite theme in Royce's philosophy was that of the "Beloved Community," a notion which Bourne tried to radicalize by complementing its idealistic implications with ideas taken from interactionist behaviorism on one hand and socialist politics on the other.

In keeping with these differences they arrived at diametrically opposed concepts of a harmonious social order. The contrast of their visions was a paradigm of political alternatives faced by those intellectuals who had been disappointed in their belief in their society as a culturally cohesive context. Croly conceives of a better society by relying on both instrumental reason and social technology as means of planning the organic society which would come to be a living social order by an act of faith on the part of every single citizen. The philosophy of order underlying Croly's theory of the state leads him into a dilemma which remains unsolved, ideology filling the gap between the two horns of his dilemma.

His proposal of a dominating social order guided by strong leadership through an all but totalitarian power of the administrative organs of the state can only be conceived as a democratic one if the individual by his or her own decision agrees to the place one occupies in the social hierarchy. The reverberations of the Hegelian echo, clearly audible in Royce's philosophy of loyalty, cannot be missed in the final pages of Croly's *Promise of American Life,* where to be loyal means both to be true to oneself and to the state. Neither can one overlook the militancy in Croly's description of a powerful state which by the very force of its existence guarantees the identity of its subjects, a stance which has great affinities to conservative interpretations of the Hegelian theory of state, not to mention the fascist models patterned upon them.

If Croly's proposal for an integrated society bordered on a totalitarian solution, Bourne's argument points in the opposite direction. Familiar with the various socialist schools of his time, he developed an early penchant for the more individualistic socialist persuasions, at one time putting his hope on the syndicalist Industrial Workers of the World. He had been an active member of the Intercollegiate Socialist Society during his college days and was sent to the Second International in Vienna as a delegate of that organization. He shunned, however, what he had identified as the dogmatic elements in Marxism, steering equally clear of the bourgeois traces he detected in the social philosophy of the Fabians, whose meetings he had attended during his brief stay in England.

From the start, Bourne's socialism incorporated two vital elements: the belief in man's unquenchable need for an organic social order allowing for his individual freedom and an extreme sensitivity to existing injustices inflicted on the individual by a repressive society. Bourne was not inclined to let matters rest with an abstract identification of capitalism and repression but recognized authoritarian tendencies in both the bourgeois and socialist camps.

Bourne's aversion to all forms of authoritarian intervention into the free and creative development of the individual forced him to conceive of a good society in terms of the unalienated self-fulfillment it allowed its subjects. That these would bear out all the hopes he attached to them as the vital force in the formation of a future harmonious society was his firm conviction in 1914 when he wrote in a letter to a friend:

> The world universal seems to begin to take form as social; your spiritual man is my social man, vibrating in camaraderie

with the beloved society, given new powers, lifted out of himself, transformed through the enriching stimulation of his fellows,—the communion of saints,—into a new being, spiritual because no longer individual. This malady *hunger,* thwarted and unsatisfied by the chaos of a society split up into separate, mutually uncomprehending groups. In this era of communications, our knowledge by description has infinitely outrun our capacity for knowledge by acquaintance, and it is in the effort that the soul makes to stretch its social consciousness out to the limits of its command of the resources and knowledge of the world, *to feel and assimilate and sympathize with what it knows, that we have the agonies of spiritual strain.*

Obviously, the spiritual strain Bourne mentioned demanded a relief by more practical consequences than those concepts which had produced it in the first place. Hence Bourne's critical comments on the limitations of Royce's idealism.

From my interpretation, I can only get the peculiar sense of life that you speak of, by sweeping ideally past the barriers, or identifying myself with the "Beloved Community" that Royce speaks about. And this seems too much like appeasing my social hunger by bread of foam.

Bourne knew only too well the illusory nature of any attempt to find a material equivalent to his utopian dreams of a "complete social consciousness" which would turn the world into a "Kingdom of Heaven."

His alternatives lay elsewhere, one being the effort to make practical use of theoretical knowledge. With a certain daring and at the risk of being misunderstood, Bourne applied his understanding of social psychology to a description of potential social harmony, drawing on both the interactionist theories of identity-formation and its macrocosmic consequences. The result is a utilitarian version of philosophical and psychological insights whose appeal is enhanced at once by their seemingly practical simplicity and metaphorical overtones. We know that Bourne had always been ill at ease with the separation of academic knowledge from the world of everyday life, his firm conviction being that rationality could not be compartmentalized—true only

in the realm of academic discussion and disposable in the practical affairs of the day. In a letter written from Columbia, he
complained about the double standards he had observed there
as a student.

> I am a little vexed with Columbia just now, so am not a good
> judge of what she means to others. I feel myself growing a
> little stale here, and am in trouble over some impassioned let-
> ters I wrote to the college daily protesting against the poor
> treatment of the scrub women, and the low ages of the chil-
> dren employed around the campus. With all its "sweetness
> and light," Columbia, like other Universities too, I suppose,
> does not hesitate to teach Social Ethics in the class-room and
> exploit its labor force on the side. Any one who points out the
> inconsistency is denounced as a sentimental idealist and a
> crank.

Extending, however, his inclination for the concrete into the
fields of social psychology and philosophy enabled him to break
down the barrier between theory and practice, and provided him
furthermore with a key to the practical implications of theory itself. His later criticism of John Dewey's instrumentalist version of
Pragmatism shows that Bourne occasionally knew more about
the practical consequences of philosophic arguments than did
their authors.

It was his early ambition to add a utilitarian dimension to
idealistic reason without losing its inherent truths. A comparison
between a passage taken from Royce's essay "Self-
Consciousness, Social Consciousness and Nature" with an
analogous version of the same idea by Bourne may demonstrate
his procedure. Royce had written:

> This whole customary popular and philosophical opposition
> between a man's self-consciousness as if it were something
> primitive and lonely, and his social consciousness, as if it
> were something acquired apart from his self-consciousness
> through intercourse with his fellows, is false to human na-
> ture. . . . On the contrary, I am conscious of myself, on the
> whole, as in relation to some real or ideal fellow, and apart
> from my consciousness of my fellows I have only secondary
> and derived states and habits of self-consciousness.

In his essay, "The Excitement of Friendship," Bourne did not hesitate to personalize abstract philosophical reasoning and add to it a touch of urgency.

> The persons, causes, and books that unlock the prison of my intellectual torpor I can justly call my friends, for I find that I feel toward them all the same eager joy and inexhaustible rush of welcome. . . . The speaker whom I hear, the book that I read, the friend with whom I chat, the music that I play, even the blank paper before me, which subtly stirs me to cover it with sentences that unfold surprisingly and entice me to follow until I seem hopelessly lost from the trail—all these shall be my friends as long as I find myself responding to them, and no longer. They are all alike in being emergencies that call upon me for instant and definite response.

As a second strategic alternative chosen to avoid the trap of utopianism—this apart from his reliance on current theoretical knowledge—he used the past as both an explanatory model and a satirical image, a usage he had adopted from Thorstein Veblen. He thus draws on the past when evoking the idea of a harmonious universe, but he also likes to point out residues of obsolete habits in present society in order to denounce them. The look backward into an intangible past has a certain melancholy quality that is only saved from the danger of escapist sentimentality by its expressed use as a metaphor. Bourne uses the past in order to understand the present, not to look away from it.

> What the primitive man had easily, through the compactness of his society, and what every compact group gets easily,— the exaltation of the individual by concerted social expression of the common desires, ideas and ideals,—we are reaching out for with great pain and striving, thwarted and perplexed by the barriers of class, codes, institutions, which have served their little local purpose and now straddle the ways along which we are feeling for a complete social consciousness which must eventually raise the whole world to a Kingdom of Heaven. But ah! there is the stern realization that these barriers are here, impeding the realization of life.

Using past and future as metaphors *against* the present allows him to fix a critical eye on the world around him. As a third alternative, he identified the utopian with the concrete, thereby incorporating the ·concrete into visionary schemes. He turned himself into a wry observer of political and cultural affairs, sometimes participating, but more often taking the role of the ironic commentator. His moral seriousness was never to be doubted. Irony for Bourne was not a pose but an almost ethical way of cognition, the only one in fact, he believed which allowed for complete honesty. If Bourne's early essays dealing with the problems of an ironic or experimental way of life occasionally have a slight sophomoric ring to them, with all their emphasis on intellectual excellence, his essay "The Life of Irony" has to be read as a mature document of Bourne's position in a world he saw characterized by absurd contradictions. The ironic attitude was a mere reflex of the general state of affairs, Bourne claimed, to which the observer had nothing to add but a radical will of his own, a will not to distort but to expose.

> Absurdity is an intrinsic quality of so many things that they only have to be touched to reveal it. The deadliest way to annihilate the unoriginal and the insincere is to let it speak for itself. Irony is this letting things speak for themselves and hang themselves by their own rope. Only, it repeats the words after the speaker, and adjusts the rope. . . . The ironical method might be compared to the acid that develops a photographic plate. It does not distort the image, but merely brings clearly to the light all that was implicit in the plate before. . . . Similarly the ironist insists always on seeing things as they are. He is a realist whom the grim satisfaction of see-. ing the truth compensates for any sordidness that it may· bring along with it. Things as they are, thrown against the background of things as they ought to be,—this is the ironist's vision.

His dealing with the ironist's vision of the world allowed him to perceive the aesthetic consciousness underlying the ironic perspective, a discovery at which he arrived by a conclusion *ex negativo*, criticizing the facile mode of aestheticism. Aesthetic consciousness and ironic perspective, Bourne claimed, were justified only as expressions of social awareness, based on a compassionate view of reality, thus transcending the dichotomy of optimistic and pessimistic judgments.

The kind of aesthetic irony that Pater and Omar display is a paralyzed, half-seeing, half-caring reflection on life,—a tame, domesticated irony with its wings cut, an irony that furnishes a justification and a command to inaction. It is the result not of exquisitely refined feelings, but of social anaesthesia. . . . The ironist has no right to see beauty in things unless he really cares. The aesthetic sense is harmless only when it is both ironical and social.

His belief in the possible reconciliation of reality's extreme contradictions through the ironist's viewpoint was to be shaken only when any justification in seeing "something beautiful and joyous even in the most hapless" had ceased to exist. Bourne did not realize that his description of the chink in the ironist's armor as the fear of "a shrinkage of his environment, a running dry of experience" would eventually prove to be devastatingly correct.

The turmoil of the United States' entry into World War I was not needed to turn Bourne into a bitter critic of the deprivations and injuries inflicted upon the individual by society. His angry statements on behalf of the younger generation, his enthusiastic declarations of its independence from conventional restraints imposed upon it in the name of conformism and tradition were only in part optimistic appraisals of the young middle-class intelligentsia he knew. Bourne was certainly convinced nevertheless that the younger generation would change the world for the better, going so far as seeing its members as representatives of a coming cosmopolitanism which would break down the barriers and inhibitions of cultural provincialism.

His elaborate descriptions of the younger generation's struggle for freedom have, however, an edge of doubt, even when Bourne seems most enthusiastic about future developments. It was not, after all, a conflict between two generations he tried to analyze, but the possibilities of an uninhibited development of the individual in an authoritarian society. Social developments, when analyzed from an anti-authoritarian viewpoint, had taken a turn for the worse and were destructive of individual self-fulfillment and collective cultural expression alike. This had so captivated Bourne's attention that he ran the risk of conceiving

of the individual in almost anachronistic terms. Youth was
gradually turned into a metaphor serving as a contradistinction
to the community of philistines as well as to more tangible forms
of social constraint. In fact, the involuntary dialectics of Bourne's
radical defense of the individual entailed a negation of what he
tried to vindicate, the individual's capacity for an unalienated
development of identity and personality. Whenever his descriptions of the blunting effect of social norms on creative, personal
growth became especially "lurid," as he once called it, he was
forced to concede that under the given circumstances the individual has become a virtually unthinkable notion.

In such instances, where Bourne follows his own logic of
analysis to the extreme, we detect the dark undercurrent to his
ardent optimism, realizing that his convictions about the potential strength of the individual are more than equaled by his skepticism of social control and his fear that social cohesion would
always be maintained at the cost of the individual. In order to
understand Bourne's deeply rooted resentment against the social and psychological constraints of the individual, we have to
turn to the late fragment "Old Tyrannies." It is an extremely sar-
castic version of his opinion of the world and the individual's
place in it. The Bourne we meet is not the optimist, not the enthusiastic ideologist of youthful insurrection. What we get instead
is a pessimistic, even bitter look at the futility of the individual's
efforts to struggle for his freedom against dominant forces of his
surroundings. Man, the fragment claims, is a prisoner from the
day of his birth, a victim already at the very moment of his creation.

> You are a helpless victim of your parents' coming together.
> There is denied you even the satisfaction of knowing that they
> created you, in their own bungling fashion, after some man-
> ner of a work of art, or of what they imagined an adequate
> child should be. On the contrary, you may be merely an ac-
> cident, unintentioned, a species of catastrophe in the life of
> your mother, a drain upon the resources that were none too
> great already. And your parents have not only not conceived
> you as a work of art, but they are wholly incapable after you
> are born of bringing you up like a work of art.

The process of growing up, the gradual development of intellectual faculties, only enhance the precarious equilibrium between

the individual's quest for freedom and the inhibitive tendencies of the world around him. In the end, all that remains is the knowledge of having fought a lost battle: under the illusion of having manipulated the world he has been manipulated himself—to the extent of corruption. Not only has the individual proved to be helpless against the influence of the integrating forces in society, he has also, by actively participating in the destruction of his own potential freedom, lost the moral dignity of the victim. Describing this process, Bourne renounces both the idea of individual moral responsibility and the notion of an autonomous subject, capable of responsible conduct.

> So you have never overtaken the given. Actually you have fallen farther and farther behind it. You have not affected the world you live in; you have been molded and shaped by it yourself. Your moral responsibility has been a myth, for you were never really free enough to have any responsibility. While you thought you were making headway, you were really being devoured.

In the process of unraveling the individual's fate, Bourne conceives of the individual's history as a continuous path toward his own destruction, a figure of thought which is developed in an undialectical fashion, based on an uncompromising vision of dominant social control. Indeed, Bourne radicalizes his view of the necessary process of socialization to such an extent that he cannot avoid the conclusion of seeing the internalization of social norms as the very beginning of the individual's extinction.

> We live almost entirely a social life, that is, a life as a constituted unit in society, rather than a free and personal one. Most people live a life which is little more than a series of quasi-official acts. Their conduct is a network of representations of the various codes and institutions of society. They act in such a way in order that some institutional or moral scripture may be fulfilled, rather than that some deep personal direction of growth should be realized . . . . The normal, or the common relation between society and the individual in any society that we know of is that the individual scarcely exists.

Bourne's hyperbolic description of the social system as virtually annihilating all possibilities of successful individuation serves as a dramatic background to his more sober analysis of those realms where social control is especially enforced against violations of societal norms. Singling out as social taboos the respect of property, norms of sexual behavior, and the sanctity of the institutions of the state, Bourne concentrates on central elements of other theories of society without developing one of his own. Moreover, this line of thought shows that his criticism of culture and society includes other sources aside from those he had tapped in the context of pragmatic philosophy. It is also obvious that the loose connection of his central topics is indicative of a theoretical deficiency. In fact, Bourne's readings in sociology, which included virtually all established American and French authors of his time, had never resulted in a firm theoretical or methodological conviction, the only exception being his decided inclination for social psychology. Thus, he drew heavily on such authors as E. A. Ross who had occupied a prominent place on his academic reading-lists or on Gustave Le Bon whose theory of mass behavior had impressed him. Bourne's eclectic reading provided him with more insights into the nature of society than he could possibly have integrated into a stringent, logical formula, if he had ever wished to do so in the first place. As a result, we meet in Bourne's essays an aesthetic bent more often than not as the consequence of his trying to describe the undescribable. Accordingly, after having stated that the individual hardly exists, Bourne finishes his argument on a telling note of ambivalence. Having doubted the possibility of successful individuation, he writes:

> We all enter as individuals into an organized herd-whole in which we are as significant as a drop of water in the ocean, and against which we can about as much prevail. Whether we shall act in the interests of ourselves or of society is, therefore, an entirely academic question.

The feelings about the individual's nonexistence stand in contrast to Bourne's emphatic insistence on the relevance of the very problem he denounced as academic, and are contradicted by the style and rhetoric of his own account. This ambivalence makes sense as an expression of Bourne's freedom from the restrictions of theoretical order; he can cross the barriers of analytical logic and follow his ideas to the extreme point of their inherent negation. Truth is thus established in the process of gradually eliminating the balance between the normal and the exception, shifting it around until we look at the normal as the exception. We know of course that individuals exist, but following Bourne, we ought to be surprised at the fact that they do. We also know that man is not a work of art, but Bourne's telling us that he should be seen as one focuses our attention on the precarious position of civilization between the two extremes, nature and art. In the last instance, truth for Bourne is the possibility of insight rather than the probability of analysis.

Bourne's aesthetic stance prevents him from suggesting alternatives to social predicaments whose general character does not allow for specific corrections. Instead, he approaches the objects of his criticism with a kind of mimetic capacity, assimilating their inherent contradictions into his style of description and eventually into his conception of their very nature. Under Bourne's insistent, almost evil stars, the factual seems to crumble, layer after layer of the habitual withers away until we are left with the unresolvable paradox of existence. Had Bourne been more of a mystic, these gloomier aspects of his intellectual disposition would have considerably blurred his critical intentions.

The young Bourne's maxim to see "things as they are, thrown against the background of things as they ought to be," prevented him from overt pessimism. He developed instead a method of contradistinctive analysis. His ambition to describe, with the called-for élan, the difference between what is and what ought to be works to his advantage when he inveighs against the dangers of social coercion or against the herd-instinct in general, one of his favorite targets. The method of dramatically opposing two states of being has its disadvantages, however, when the question arises of how things ought to be, in which case Bourne is occasionally given to an ahistorical evocation of a kind of *status quo ante*. At work here is another implicit dialectical turn in Bourne's method: his all-embracing attention to concrete phenomena of everyday life leaves no room for the development of piecemeal solutions, nor does it call for the construction of utopian alternatives. In fact, Bourne manages instead to show us quite literally how things ought to be by referring to their ideal state of being. By negative association with the development of their present state, we are forced to imagine such as an almost platonic idea antecedent to all possible developments.

The described figure of thought represents the conservative element of Bourne's radicalism, which remains an implicit motive of his cultural criticism. His glance into the past is essentially a melancholy gesture, an expression of despair over the hopelessness of things as they are.

In his early years, however, Bourne knew how to turn despair into fury, easily transferring his skepticism into scorn. His vehement attacks on the social pressures directed against the young generation became indictments of both the family as a place of repression and the conformistic demands of society in general. Bourne, articulating the sentiments of many, soon became the spokesman of rebellious youth in what looked like just another generational conflict. There was more at stake, though, at least for Bourne, who looked back with disappointment at *Youth and Life,* a collection of his early essays. He had, after all, tried to achieve more than a polemic analysis of generational differences, seeing in the family above all a complex example of group behavior at large. The family, Bourne had argued, could be analyzed like any other group in society, exerting the same kind of pressure and leaving hardly any room for an uninhibited development of its members. "The average family is about as well mated as any similar group would be, picked out at random from society," he had written, seeing at work in the family the same pressures youth would meet in the world.

> The family is a little microcosm, a sheltered group where youth feels all those currents of influence that sway men in their social life. Some of them are exaggerated, some perverted, but they are most of them there in that little world. . . . Family life thus not only presses upon its youth to conform to its customs and habits and to the opinions of the little social world in which it lives, but also drags its youth down with its claims, and warps it by its tension of uncongeniality, checks its spontaneity by its lack of appreciation, and injures its soul by friction and misunderstanding.

At the heart of his argument lay the conviction that social groups of any kind were above all characterized by a tendency to seek self-stabilization by exerting pressure on their members, a tendency which Bourne held to be true for society in general.

The secret ambition of the group seems to be to turn out all its members as nearly alike as possible. It seeks to create a type to which all new adherents shall be molded. Each group, then, that we have relations with is ceaselessly working to mold us to its type and pattern. It is this marvelous unseen power that a group has of forming after its own image all that come under its influence, that conquers men. It has the two instincts of self-preservation and propagation strongly developed, and we tend unthinkingly to measure its value in terms of its success in the expression of those instincts. Rather should it be measured always in terms of its ability to create and stimulate varied individuality. This is the new ideal of social life.

Bourne's realization that the influence of the family was gradually diminishing, that members of the younger generation were breaking away from traditional ways of life, did not result in an optimistic appraisal of a future freedom. Instead, he complained that the young rebels of his time had more often than not simply exchanged old authorities for new ones and occasionally even renounced the benefits of familial life without gaining anything instead. Bourne did indeed take his notion seriously that the family was a microcosm of society, stating that an escape from it only too often meant a clash with more direct forms of social coercion. What had been true for the family was also true, of course, for political groups.

The principal object of every organization, as every youth soon discovers who feels dissatisfaction with the policies of church, club, college, or party, is to remain true to type. Each is organized with a central vigilance committee, whose ostensible function is direction, but whose real business is to resist threatening change and keep matters as they are. The ideal is smoothness; every part of the machine is expected to run along in its well-oiled groove. Youths who have tried to introduce their new ideas into such organizations know the weight of this fearful resistance.

The only alternative Bourne had to offer was the development of a new philosophy of social behavior based on a radical negation of existing social conditions but not content merely with such negation. Lacking a unified theory of society, for better and for worse, he had to look for a source of this new philosophy within the society he described as a virtually closed system of repression. In his early writings his hopes seem to rest upon the young generation, although he is well aware of the fact that this hope implies some wishful thinking. Accordingly, his statements about the role of youth in the development of a new social philosophy and a corresponding way of life are made as hopeful assumptions, implicitly expressing doubt about their eventual fulfillment.

> The emancipation of the spirit is insufficient without a new means of spiritual livelihood to take its place. The youth of today cannot rest on their liberation; they must see their freedom as simply the setting free of forces within themselves for a cleaner, sincerer life, and for radical work in society. The road is cut out before them by pioneers; they have but to let themselves grow out in that direction.

Later, after the political course of events had frustrated most of Bourne's hopes, he would significantly exchange "youth" for an even less tangible group of people, talking in a letter to Van Wyck Brooks about the "malcontents" who would be susceptible to a new social consciousness.

Bourne's hope for a more communal social philosophy, which would be the preliminary step to the establishment of an organic social order, was based on more than just his belief in the dissatisfaction of a rebellious few. His undialectic attacks against the various manifestations in society of the herd-instinct were complemented by clear insights into the dialectical nature of social experience as its opposite. He knew well enough that the proper socialization of experience required a reciprocity of perspectives which could be achieved in small groups, but he was uncertain how such single achievements could be so effectively generalized as to be·socially relevant. Just as he had used his concept of the herd-instinct as discriminatory evidence when discussing the negative aspects of social groups, so he wanted to employ its counterpart, social hunger, as proof of his conviction that out of the experience of small political groups there would eventually grow a communal whole.

I see the social movement with all its manifestations,—
feminism, socialism, social religion, internationalism, etc.,—
slowly linking the chains of social consciousness, and thus
transforming the individual persons, the individual groups, lifting them to a higher level, giving them a more abundant
sense of sympathy and unanimity. . . . There is the reconciliation to make between this glorified sense of sociality, and the
blind, senseless operation of "hard instinct" under which social groups first seemed to me to operate.

Bourne had no definite political strategy to offer. He took for
granted, however, the convincing character of the interactionist
model of social experience in both political and ethical re-
spects. Trying to develop a political equivalent to Royce's notion
of the "beloved community" on the one hand and believing on
the other that a political solution could only be achieved with the
assistance of enlightened individuals whose quest for "personal
salvation" was not that of a complacent elite, he arrived at a
conception of middle-class radicalism which would be the
source of many ambivalences in his later work.

It was one thing to look for an aesthetic correlative of political
convictions by studying examples of social consciousness and
holding them up to reality. It was a different one altogether to
look for a political agent who in his activities would blend the
political and aesthetic realms of life. Bourne had used the term
friend as a metaphor for a sympathetic generalized other. He
would soon realize that it was more difficult to locate political
groups who could fill that role.

Before he had to deal with the more concrete aspects of political life, however, he had a chance of broadening his view by
taking his convictions to Europe and testing them against a different cultural background. Bourne's journey to Europe was indeed a major step in his development. It was an event he turned
into a veritable *Bildungsreise,* meeting literary celebrities, visiting
political headquarters of socialist parties and studying architecture and town-planning on his way through Great Britain, France,
Italy, Germany, and Denmark. It was the year before Europe
went to war and emotions ran high in the various countries,
which did not keep Bourne from relishing every moment of his
grand tour. In fact, it is surprising what little notice he took of the
growing war-hysteria, his letters betraying hardly any awareness

of the events to come. He seemed to have been preoccupied with satisfying his social and aesthetic interests, cramming as much as he possibly could into every day.

In Great Britain, he visited the Fabian offices which then were run by Sydney and Beatrice Webb, attended readings by Bernard Shaw and G. K. Chesterton, met H. G. Wells and Havelock Ellis. He heard Sylvia Pankhurst speak and enjoyed meetings of left-wing socialists because of their contrast to philanthropic socialism, which he scorned about as much as he disliked the liberal intellectuals he had met.

> The social conscience does not seem to have touched England at all, except in the shape of Christian philanthropy of the type of the poor old Oxford people who are bringing classical education into the slums and attempting to "raise the people" by means of Plato and Burne-Jones and Rossetti. Toynbee Hall, a reproduction of an Oxford College, with dining-hall decorated in pale Pre-Raphaelite figures, and library and living-room and bed-rooms copied bodily from the sheltered, quietistic retreats of Oxford,—the whole set in the midst of the slum of Whitechapel, is one of the most marvellous demonstrations of the futility of the English mind that I know. But the average intellectual liberal seems to be a very complacent sort of person, quite convinced that England is getting along all right, very impatient with theorists and extremists of all sorts, busy and happy and uncritical just like our American friends.

His opinion of English culture and society in general was low. He disliked what he came to refer to as the "English solution" to social and spiritual conflicts, a solution which worked by simply ignoring the unpleasant. "If happiness is the absence of spiritual conflict," he wrote of the Englishman, "he should be the happiest man in civilization." Despite his aversion to a great number of aspects of the English way of life, an aversion that was to reach a climax when, in his essays after the outbreak of World War I, he was to deplore the Anglo-Saxon influence in the United States, he admired the English middle-class socialist. As always, Bourne felt more desperate about the social problems at hand, as he wrote in a letter home, but he was awed by their learning and by the ease with which they addressed a working-class audience.

> The middle-class Socialists are many of them hardheaded people, thoroughly saturated with economics and history, and used to addressing working-class audiences without a trace of that patronage which one might expect. These radicals are much superior to our rather childish people, who talk with a bravado as if they were doing the most desperate thing in the world to be Socialists at all. These people over here take the thing much more naturally and coolly, and have much more of a standing. The Socialist speaking and writing seems to me on a much higher plane than at home, much more direct and definite and intellectual. At the same time it is thoroughly seasoned with revolt.

Despite such occasional favorable impressions, Bourne had developed a definite dislike of what he experienced as Anglo-Saxon complacency and "pulled down the curtain on England with a resolve," as he wrote from France.

Although it took him longer to make personal acquaintances in France, he immediately had the impression of "breathing a freer, more congenial air." Bourne attended some summer courses offered at the Sorbonne, again visited political headquarters and attended the rallies of various parties always searching for the "aggressively socialist type." He struck up a friendship with a young French girl, whose portrait he drew in a sketch titled "Mon Amie," which was published in *The Atlantic Monthly*. His most important acquaintance, however, was with Jules Romains, in whom he saw a "gallicised Whitman." Bourne wrote an unpublished article on a book of poems by Romains, *La Vie Unanime,* an article in which he admired the unanimistic school of poetry for its blend of the spiritual with the sociological.

This interpretation of Jules Romains' poetry is above all interesting for what it reveals about Bourne himself. For the first time he established a connection between sociological and aesthetic arguments, claiming that the coming new social consciousness needed an artistic expression of its own. Again he also tries to legitimize the new social consciousness by referring to a mythical past, when there was unity between nature and the individual, and group-life was the only form of social existence.

The first religion, the first feeling and thinking, originated not at all in the fear and awe experienced before the powers of nature, or in the desire to explain the mysteries of things, but rather in an intense social consciousness, in a mystical sense of the unity and power of living things, non-human as well as human. It was the group that came first, the collective thinking and feeling that was the first reality. The Group-Will, the Group-Desire, the Group-Action, were the first gods, the reverberation of these collective representations was the first thinking, and only very slowly did the individual mind and consciousness and logical thought emerge from this fused and intense tribal life.

The modern equivalent to ancient group-life, according to Bourne, are the "liberating forces of democratic camaraderie," the very opposite to that other aspect of modern mass-society, the herd-instinct. For once, Bourne was convinced that ultimately the social instincts would prevail over the "compressing forces of conventionality," and he looked with some expectations at the manifestations of twentieth-century city-life.

Who can walk the lighted streets of a city at night and watch the flowing crowds, the shining youthful faces, the eager exhilaration of the sauntering life, or who can see the surge of humanity on a holiday or Sunday, without feeling the strange power of this mass-life? This mysterious power of the city which sucks out the life of the countryside, which welds individuals into a co-operative life, is not this the basal force of the age, and does it not suggest the stirrings of a new civilization, socialized and purified? In this garish, vulgar, primitive flow of Broadway, are not new gods being born?

Bourne's hope for the new gods was based far more on his enthusiasm for Romains' poetry than on a belief in any inherent forces within the masses themselves. He did not even fully adopt all the current aesthetic interpretations of the mass as a metaphor for a new primitivism or a coming functional social order, discarding the futurist movement in Italy as a mere reaction against traditional art-forms. What really fascinated Bourne was the particular blend of the poetic with the sociological which he found realized in *La Vie Unanime,* a unity of poetic expression and sociological thought which appealed to his own desire to eliminate the barriers between the realms of aesthetic and cognitive experience. It is not surprising then that Bourne should see in Romains a modern Walt Whitman, just the kind of poet he hoped for in the United States.

But he is a Whitman industrialized, and, if I may say it, sociologized; for besides the push of industrial invention and energy that throbs through his poetry, there is a strong intellectual fibre running through him, the fibre of sociological science which Whitman of course could not have. To us Americans this poetry—and one sees so clearly the same drift in many of our very young writers at home—should come as a fulfilment of Whitman, who, prophetic before his time, was submerged in our cult of an individualistic capitalism. That day, however, is definitely over; we are breaking our idols, and are ready for a new worship.

It is obvious that with all his interest in politics, Bourne was yet convinced that aesthetic experience was the most adequate way of realizing what a society based on a new sense of sociality would be all about.

Going one step further, he not only saw art as an expression of potential freedom but claimed that the development of aesthetic sensitivity in itself should be seen as a political act, a conclusion at which he arrived when dealing with the social importance of architecture and town-planning. For good reasons he saw no difference between the aesthetic and the professional side of both fields, knowing that his belief in a synthesis of the creative aspects of aesthetic expression and those of its skillful implementation could be demonstrated best if he claimed the expressive and the instrumental elements in the "civic arts" to be one. With this concept of a socially conscious aesthetic sensitivity in the background, he could also talk about taste being a political category, having thus bridged the gap between the individual and the social relevance of aesthetic experience.

Any general improvement in taste means a demand for a rise in the standard of living, and this rise is *the* great fulcrum, I am convinced, in social progress. Until people begin really to *hate* ugliness and poverty and disease, instead of merely pity-

ing the poor and the sick, we shall not have, I fear, any great
social advance. I am immensely interested in civic art, town-
planning and kindred movements over here, and shall use all
my opportunities to study them. Architecture, with communal
art, landscape gardening, etc.—I am almost ready to believe
is the King of the arts, because of its completely social nature.

Bourne's interest in architecture and town-planning dominated
the rest of his time in Europe. Switzerland appealed to him as
a perfect example of the kind of organic society he had always talked about, where the cultural and political affairs could
be understood and contemplated by its citizens. He was awed
by the water-power projects and praised the fact that civic planning in Switzerland took into account future developments, a
kind of planning he sorely missed in the United States.

The two weeks Bourne spent in Germany were completely devoted to visiting examples of town-planning, civic art and
garden-cities, his studies taking him to Ulm, Nuremberg, and
Dresden where he saw the new slaughterhouse which he
thought to be characteristically German. He also studied the restoration plans in Rothenburg, seeing it as a "little laboratory of
medieval and modern town-planning" and admiring the "policy
and spirit of a typical little German municipality." Taken by the
results of the municipal planning he had studied, he was quite
willing for a time to put up with what he described as a process
of decision-making which was "undemocratic in political form,
yet ultra-democratic in policy and spirit, scientific, impartial, giving the populace—who seemed to have no sense of being
excluded from 'rights'—what they really wanted. . . ." Bourne
was soon to see the other side of a society, however, which he
saw characterized by a profound sympathy between the people
and their government, when in Berlin he witnessed the outbreak
of the war and watched the Kaiser, a "prim, staccato-voiced,
helmeted figure, a very symbol of war," speak to a hysterical
crowd in front of his palace.

Had Bourne not realized by then that the very aspects of the
twentieth-century mass-society which he had thought to be indicative of a growing new social consciousness had turned in the
very opposite direction, he did so when in Sweden he met with
the eminent socialist Karl Hjalmar Branting, later prime minister

of Sweden. Socialist hopes in Europe had been crushed, though it was not evident during those first weeks of the war to what extent. Upon his return to the United States, Bourne left behind the shattered dreams of an international socialist alliance and his belief in the younger generation as a political force.

World War I

The promise of the "renaissance of the twentieth century" which he thought he had witnessed in Europe was not to be fulfilled. Bourne came back to a United States whose cultural maturity he doubted more than before. More than ever, Bourne wanted his voice to be heard and he used whatever chances he had as a contributor to *The New Republic*. His preoccupation with problems of progressive education gave him an excellent chance to hold forth about the unseverable ties which existed between the educational process and culture as a whole. True Deweyite that he was, he stressed that real learning did not consist in adopting certain skills or in digesting prepared bits of knowledge but was a process of habit formation where the aim was to "learn how to learn." Dewey's argument that "in learning habits, it is possible for man to learn the habit of learning" was the source of Bourne's conviction that the success of progressive education could be measured by the degree to which it enabled the student to participate actively in the political and cultural affairs of the world around him. Only if the activities in the schoolroom enabled the student to apply his intelligence elsewhere could education guarantee the growth of a socialized intelligence which—in the long run—would not leave society unaffected. The positive appraisals of the educational projects of William Wirt, also a follower of John Dewey, whose schools in Gary Bourne had visited, were based above all on his conviction that here, for the first time in the history of progressive education, one could observe how school life and communal affairs were fully integrated.

Notwithstanding his intense interest in education, Bourne devoted a considerable amount of his attention to other fields as well, writing occasional literary reviews, brief essay-portraits, some of them satirical, and short pieces on architecture and town-planning. He had to realize, however, that his concern about the possible integration of various intellectual and artistic

activities into a national cultural whole was threatened by a diffe-
rent kind of national unity, established by coercion and not by
the democratic spirits of creative individuals, as he had hoped.
Universal military service was a much discussed issue and
Bourne realized that its introduction would be a kind of perverted version of the national unity he had thought of. It seems
like a suggestion of future developments that in 1916 we find in
The New Republic side by side an essay by John Dewey about
American culture and education and one by Bourne titled "A
Moral Equivalent for Universal Military Service," reminiscent of
William James' thesis about the "moral equivalent for war." It is
a telling difference of emphasis which characterizes the two essays. Their basic concern is virtually identical, both of them
wondering how a national culture can be achieved. Where
Dewey can still look into the future, optimistically describing the
effects of true learning on the development of a democratic culture, Bourne is already concentrating on political developments
which would eventually supersede any discussion about a truly
democratic culture. As Bourne had done in the past, Dewey still
believed that educational theory was a central factor in the creation of a culture which would not be the possession of one
class, as Dewey's argument went.

> The beginning of a culture stripped of egoistic illusions is the
> perception that we have as yet not culture: that our culture is
> something to achieve, to create. . . . To transmute a society
> built on an industry which is not yet humanized into a society
> which wields its knowledge and its industrial power in behalf
> of a democratic culture requires the courage of an inspired
> imagination. . . . It is as elements in this heroic undertaking
> that current tendencies in American education can be ap-
> praised. Since we can neither beg nor borrow a culture with-
> out betraying both it and ourselves, nothing remains save to
> produce one. . . . It is for education to bring the light of sci-
> ence and the power of work to the aid of every soul that it
> may discover its quality. For in a spiritually democratic soci-
> ety every individual would realize distinction. Culture would
> then be for the first time in human history an individual
> achievement and not a class possession. . . . Our public edu-
> cation is the potential means for effecting the transfiguration
> of the mechanics of modern life into sentiment and imagina-

tion. . . . To bring to the consciousness of the coming generation something of the potential significance of the life of today, to transmute it from outward fact into intelligent perception, is the first step in the creation of a culture.

Bourne in the meantime had drawn a different line of defense,
opposing not only a backward tendency in education or an avoidance of the present, both of which Dewey feared, but a development where the "craving for unity of sentiment" would be
answered by a new militaristic trend. As an active member of
the American Association for International Conciliation and editor
of two pamphlets published under its auspices, Bourne was
aware of the implications of the growing nationalism he observed.

All around us we feel a very genuine craving for unity of sentiment, for service, for some new national lift and broadening
which shall keep us out of the uneasy pettiness into which
the American conscience has threatened to fall. In our hearts
we know that to crystallize this desire into a meaningless sentiment, or into a piling-up of armaments or a proscribing of
alien cultures, would not satisfy us. We want action, but we
do not want military action. Even the wildest patriots know
that America could have to go through the most pernicious
and revolutionary changes to accept the universal military
service which they advocate.

Education, Bourne pointed out, was the only form of "conscription" to which Americans had ever agreed. Thus, it seemed only
adequate to direct the growing demand for national unity into
that direction. He suggested therefore a national educational
service, which he not only saw as a peaceful alternative to military conscription but claimed to be a logical consequence of the
public school system. He realized that such a service would
have to avoid any competition with other forms of unskilled labor
or industry. Once more, he envisioned an "army of youth" attacking the social and cultural ills of the country.

What we need is a service which shall not so much do the
old work of the world as create new demands and satisfy
them. This national service could do the things which need to

be done, but which are not now being done. It could have for its aim the improvement of the quality of our living. Our appalling slovenliness, the ignorance of great masses in city and country as to the elementary technique of daily life—this should be the enemy of the army of youth. I have a picture of a host of eager young missionaries swarming over the land, spreading the health knowledge, the knowledge of domestic science, of gardening, of tastefulness, that they have learned in school.

Such a service would provide apprentices for communal services in town and country, as many schools and colleges are already actually providing. Food inspection, factory inspection, organized relief, the care of dependents, playground service, nursing in hospitals—all this would be a field for such an educational service.

Bourne's suggestion for a practical alternative to universal military service was a last effort to evoke the traditional values of pragmatic meliorism against the political currents of the day. He followed, however, the course of events, dealing in book reviews with the question of "Americanization," a slogan which significantly enough had replaced the plea for a national culture. It is easy to detect in Bourne's reviews of even minor works the outline of future arguments, since he obviously picked certain books to make a point which he probably could not have otherwise discussed. The pro-Wilson stance of *The New Republic's* editors balanced precariously between what Croly had once referred to as the power of the word, that is to say, diplomacy, over against the power of the sword. The step was about to be taken that would lead from a spirit of preparedness into an all-out military armament. Seen in this light, Bourne's book reviews are subtle studies in the art of literary partisanship. He harbored no illusions about the growing strength of the pro-allies sentiments among the wealthy and influential Americans of Anglo-Saxon stock and was quick to make a distinction between this nativisim and what he tried to see as true Americanism. Thus his review of a book by Frances A. Kellor, *Straight America,* is turned into an indictment of the "ruling class which needs democratizing," and a plea for "cooperative Americanism" instead of chauvinistic unity. In anticipation of later essays, Bourne claimed that a "cooperative Americanism" could not be patterned upon the European model but had to rely on functioning communities instead of on nebulous patriotism. Repeating some of his own ideas, Bourne in the guise of a book review managed to hold a position which had become unpopular among the less radical intellectuals of *The New Republic.*

Miss Kellor makes a noble and eloquent plea for an Americanism which is much broader than the "nativism" of the Anglo-Saxon, but she yokes it to a program which is almost necessarily nativistic in its implications. It is notorious that the conception of national unity which includes military service, belligerent defense of American rights, is one held largely by the staunchly nativistic element. The men and women of goodwill who are working for practical Americanization in social reorganization and genuine economic and educational assimilation of the immigrant are mostly in the other camp. They are not content with an "industrial mobilization" which is a mere war measure. They believe that any form of national service should be far more fundamentally educational than anything the so-called "civic training camps" can provide. They believe that America and its ideal of the future are still in the making, and that a premature cohesion on a basis of belligerent self-protection would defeat that slow learning to live together which a wise and modern Americanism involves.

Bourne's evocation of the "men and women of goodwill" was a futile gesture and betrayed both a certain amount of political innocence and an overestimation of the intellectual's role in politics. His disappointment with the failure of the socialist and working-class movements in Europe to prevent the war had led Bourne to a renewed emphasis of the importance of intellectual leadership. The young radical, he claimed, had to be fiercely intellectual, providing the labor movement with a coherent philosophy.

The young radical today is not asked to be a martyr, but he is asked to be a thinker, an intellectual leader. So far as the official radicals deprecate such an enterprise they make their movement sterile. Yet how often when attempts are made to group radicals on an intellectual basis does not some orthodox elder of the socialist church arise and solemnly denounce such intellectual snobbishness.

Bourne's argument was not intended to promote intellectual snobbery. He wanted to say that the young intellectuals had good reason to rely on their own judgment instead of trying to assimilate the view of political groups. Such emphasis on intellectual self-reliance was not just the result of Bourne's rising concern about the political development in general. His former uneasiness over the growing isolation of critical intellectuals from the mainstream of American culture and politics had momentarily given way to a new optimism. The founding of *The Seven Arts* had provided him with a platform from which to preach to his countrymen. The editors of the magazine, James Oppenheim, Waldo Frank, and Van Wyck Brooks, also seemed to constitute an intellectual ambience which supported his hopes that a combination of political analysis and poetic vision could be achieved. As it turned out, it was Bourne, who—in his reaction to John Dewey's essays in *The New Republic* on the question of conscientious objection—became so preoccupied with politics that the more moderate views of his co-editors hardly helped to influence the image of the magazine. It eventually folded when its chief supporter withdrew her assistance on account of Bourne's antiwar essays.

After Dewey had taken his stand, Bourne indeed reacted quickly and with a vengeance. He did not simply attack his former teacher's personal opinion but claimed the breakdown of an entire philosophical system, namely Dewey's instrumentalistic version of Pragmatism. Bourne, like so many of his generation, had once believed that Dewey's philosophy was the only way to harmonize the idea of progress and the hope for its social and moral control. Dewey's claim that one could only discuss the question of progress by taking a particularistic approach, looking at specific means and ends, was exactly what had once attracted Bourne, as it seemed the only "scientific" way of dealing with social problems. He had also endorsed what was known in philosophical terms as the experimentalist criterion, popularizing its implications in his early essays.

We should remember that the fascination of Dewey's thought was based above all on its ambivalencies, turning epistemological and metaphysical questions into methodological ones while retaining idealistic overtones at the same time. It was of course the methodical in Dewey and his related inclination to discuss general values in practical terms of possible lines of action which had made his version of Pragmatism so popular. The attempt to combine scientific method and moral judgment in a concept of social technology and identifying intelligence with the results of its application was not, however, as Bourne had come to realize, a suitable approach to master a large-scale crisis such as the United States' entry into World War I. The opposite was true. Dewey's philosophy, with its tendency to translate existing reality into method, demanded reason and intelligence as a necessary condition in order to show the hoped for results.

Dewey's philosophy is inspiring enough for a society at peace, prosperous and with a fund of progressive goodwill. It is a philosophy of hope, of clear-sighted comprehension of materials and means. Where institutions are at all malleable, it is the only clue for improvement. It is scientific method applied to "uplift." But this careful adaptation of means to desired ends, this experimental working out of control over brute forces and dead matter in the interests of communal life, depends on a store of rationality, and is effective only where there is strong desire for progress. It is precisely the school, the institution to which Dewey's philosophy was first applied, that is of all our institutions the most malleable. And it is the will to educate that has seemed, in these days, among all our social attitudes the most rationally motivated. It was with education, and almost education alone, that seemed susceptible to the steady pressure of an "instrumental" philosophy. Intelligence really seemed about to come into conscious control of an institution, and that one of the most potent in moulding the attitudes needed for a civilized society and the aptitudes needed for the happiness of the individual.

Bourne's criticism is, of course, also a renunciation of his own former beliefs, being directed against the attempts to use education as a paradigm for moral and social developments within society. He had also realized that the convergence of his own idealistic convictions and Dewey's moral stance had fooled him into believing that a discussion of values was unnecessary since there existed a tacit understanding about the general direction of progress.

Even if Bourne's criticism of Dewey is not fully justified, since Dewey had stated his moral and social aims often enough, it points out a weak spot in his philosophy. Dewey's tendency to identify—in the name of scientific and practical thought—the existent with the normative had already caused Charles S. Peirce to make some caustic remarks to the extent that Dewey was on the verge of regarding "logic" as a natural history of thought. Bourne came to a similar conclusion when, attacking the intellectuals at large, he pointed out that their thought had become a mere rationalization of what was going on. He was referring, of course, to those liberal intellectuals who had subscribed to a pragmatistic approach to politics, thinking especially of the liberals at *The New Republic*. If Dewey had become his key target, it was only because he realized that a new class of young technocrats had been influenced by instrumentalistic thought and had turned it into an ideology of visionless efficiency. Bourne did not single out Dewey alone. He attacked Herbert Croly and Walter Lippmann, among others, finally talking about an intellectual class which had guided the nation into a war nobody had wanted. It is not the exaggeration alone which throws a light on Bourne's feelings about the responsibility of the intellectuals but his insight that the mass of the population would be unable to resist the political course of events even if they wanted to. The more Bourne analyzed what he considered the treason of the intellectuals, the more he learned about their precarious position in the social system and about this system itself.

> Our resources in men and materials are vast enough to organize the war-technique without enlisting more than a fraction of the people's conscious energy. Many men will not like being sucked into the actual fighting organism, but as the war goes on they will be sucked in as individuals and they will yield. There is likely to be no element in the country with the effective will to help them resist. They are not likely to resist of themselves concertedly. . . . It is unlikely that enough men will be taken from the potentially revolting classes seriously to embitter their spirit. Losses in the well-to-do classes will be sustained by a sense of duty and of reputable sacrifice. From the point of view of the worker, it will make little

difference whether his work contributes to annihilation overseas or to construction at home. Temporarily, his condition is
better if it contributes to the former. We of the middle classes
will be progressively poorer than we should otherwise have
been. Our lives will be slowly drained by clumsily levied taxes
and the robberies of imperfectly controlled private enterprises. But this will not cause us to revolt. There are not likely
to be enough hungry stomachs to make a revolution.

He eventually concluded that a "semi-military State-socialism"
would be the result of the United States' participation in the war.
This, of course, was the exact opposite of his own vision of a
cooperative or trans-national America.

In a letter from London in 1913, Bourne had already complained about American loyalty to Anglo-Saxon civilization, a
loyalty which he considered to be a "great mistake." Three
years later, he used Mary Antin's book, *The Promised Land,* as
an occasion to inveigh against the melting-pot ideology, which
he wanted to see replaced by higher ideals. His criticism was
directed above all against "the ruling class, descendent of those
British stocks which were the first permanent immigrants," a ruling class he accused of dictating the terms of Americanization
without the consent of the governed.

Americanization on the terms of a reactionary ruling class,
Bourne claimed, not only meant physical exploitation but also
entailed the destruction of the national cultures of immigrants.
Instead of a "detritus of cultures" Bourne wished to see a
peaceful competition of various cultures which would result in a
cosmopolitan "federation of cultures, turning America into the
first "international nation." The cosmopolitan ideal, he elaborated, did not mean that its supporters believed in a "policy of
drift." The opposite was the case: they too wanted an integrated
America.

But they do not want one which is integrated only for domestic economic exploitation of the workers or for predatory
economic imperialism among the weaker peoples. They do
not want one that is integrated by coercion or militarism, or
for the truculent assertion of a mediaeval code of honor and
of doubtful rights. They believe that the most effective integration will be one which coordinates the diverse elements and

turns them consciously toward working out together the place of America in the world-situation.

Once again, Bourne's suggestions end on a note which reminds the reader of his intellectual indebtedness to Josiah Royce, who had discussed similar ideas in his book *Race Questions, Provincialism, and Other American Problems*. Lacking a political agent for the implementation of his program, Bourne could only appeal to the "younger intelligentsia" to provide the groundwork for a cosmopolitan American culture.

All our idealisms must be those of future social goals in which all can participate, the good life of personality lived in the environment of the Beloved Community.

Bourne's opinions about the political realities of American society were far from optimistic, though, as he had realized, there existed even in peacetime a powerful potential for conflict between what he called the "significant classes" and those enlightened few who believed that America's future was as a social democracy. If he had once hoped that one might fulfill the American promise by keeping the United States out of the war in Europe while waging a continuous battle against the philistines of the older generation, he was soon convinced that he had to reckon with more aggressive political forces. Bourne eventually came to the conclusion that the whole organization of national life was a thinly disguised warfare between the ruling "significant classes" and the rest of the governed. The latency of this conflict he stated became manifest in the dominance of the State in times of crisis: the State as an institution of potential coercion had always been present, even if its influence was not felt during periods of relative stability. Bourne had begun to develop these ideas immediately after his return from Europe, even if at first he had kept them hidden underneath a rhetoric of political reform and poetic vision. Throughout his published and unpublished work of the time preceding the United States' entrance into World War I, we find, however, bitter stabs at the political power of the "significant classes" which can at random direct "the entire nation's strength in a moment to any cause or movement that seems to advance their will or their private class sense of honour or justice," a notion which Bourne would elaborate in his famous "Fragment on the State."

The significance, however, of this fragment lies not so much in its assessment of the political power of the mighty and the influential, but in Bourne's description of how, in a time of crisis, loyalty to the State is maintained among the governed. These passages turn the fragment into a study of the totalitarian potential of the bourgeois state. Bourne adds significance to the verdict by pointing out that the political reality of totalitarianism, in its manifest form an exception for the middle class, is the everyday experience of the working classes.

The members of the working classes, that portion at least which does not identify itself with the significant classes and seek to imitate it and rise to it, are notoriously less affected by the symbolism of the State, or, in other words, are less patriotic than the significant classes. . . . They live habitually in an industrial serfdom, by which, though nominally free, they are in practice as a class bound to a system of machine-production the implements of which they do not own, and in the distribution of whose product they have not the slightest voice, except what they can occasionally exert by a veiled intimidation which draws slightly more of the product in their direction. From such serfdom, military conscription is not so great a change.

Bourne, for obvious reasons, does not discuss in his fragment the feasibility or even possibility of revolution. His insight into the opportunism of the intellectuals in the face of political pressure and his pessimism about the political abilities of the working-class left him without a suitable revolutionary force on which to put his hopes. The fragment, as it stands, does not try to disguise the fact that Bourne saw no alternative to the situation he analyzed. It is also quite obvious that Bourne's vision of the "Beloved Community" had been superseded by the grim specter of totalitarian society.

If Bourne's unfinished treatise on the State leaves the reader guessing as to what his development might have been had he pursued his analysis of the totalitarian tendencies in bourgeois society, his career as a literary critic is less enigmatic. After the demise of *The Seven Arts,* Bourne was forced to express his views on the war in the form of book-reviews written for *The New Republic,* and in a more explicit tone, for *The Dial.* This did not mean, though, that he used his literary criticism as a mere vehicle to smuggle in alien contents where he was supposed to restrict himself to aesthetic judgments.

Bourne's literary criticism, on the contrary, had always been integrated into his view of the world at large. He had never tried to separate his activities as a literary critic from his role as a critic of culture and society. His convictions about the important role of the critic urged him, however, to insist on the difference between art as expression and criticism as analysis. It is the young Deweyite, of course, who in the name of clarity and method attacks Spingarn for having confused the functions of criticism and art.

> The normal function of criticism is to react upon Art, as the normal function of human life is to react upon the world. . . . To reduce criticism and art to the same terms is to destroy completely the vital meaning of either. . . . They have separate functions, and their life together must not be an irresponsible abandonment of rational control, but a constant mutual guidance and checking of the other.

Mutual guidance on which terms, one may ask, as Bourne never subscribed to one particular school of criticism. Neither did he focus his attention on specific art forms. Instead, he used his critical reviews as a means of describing how in various ways artistic creativity prevailed over the restrictions of common experience. If we can detect a continuous interest in Bourne's literary criticism, it is the effort to look for an aesthetic correlative for what he had once called social hunger. He obviously assumed that underlying the patterns of socially standardized sensitivity there was a barely controlled urge for creativity, which, once it was set free, would have a considerable social impact.

If Bourne, in a letter to Van Wyck Brooks, called for the desperate spiritual outlaws with a lust to create, this did not mean that his hopes for an outburst of creativity rested entirely on the young intellectuals. Just as he had once seen the rise of "social man" as a general development, so he believed that there existed a common tendency toward creative expression in conflict with the repressive functions of the social system. As a result, the creative urge had a revolutionary potential exactly where it was most suppressed: among the working classes.

An outbreak of creativity also meant the creation of a new symbolic order, based on the kind of social consciousness he had defined as a necessary condition of an organic society which would be modeled on the idea of the "beloved community." In analogy to his conviction that the old concepts of individualism had to give way to a new, more socialized breed of individuals, he believed that the traditional separation within the arts would be superseded by more collective ways of artistic expression.

The individual is transcended. The jealous old individual arts with their formal techniques and their tight little categories of critical norms get broken up. . . . The solitary artist bores. We like group-art. And we are tired of seeing artistic expression stereotyped, sophisticated, artificially segregated into subjects. We want to get expressiveness in some sort of thick whole, not by making the arts imitate each other, but by making them co-operate and blend until the spectator forgets what each art is contributing to the joy of the whole.

Bourne saw the transcendence of the individual in the arts as an expression of the same process in reality. He had realized that artistic expression was not to be understood by looking at its results alone, but was part of the symbolic environment of man. His emphasis on the social importance of art was based on the insight that changes within this environment could not be effected by means of social engineering alone, but involved a reinterpretation of the cultural system itself. An acknowledgment of the existence of repressed creativity was a first step in the direction of such a reinterpretation. Creativity had to be seen as both a general source of rebellion against an "over-repressed and mechanicalized world" and as a specific potential of protest within different class contexts.

Bourne accordingly looked for the rise of social art in various camps, discussing contemporary pageants and their impact on the workers as well as the theater of Jacques Copeau. In every case what he looked for was the same, the realization of "culture as living effort, a driving attempt both at sincere expression and the comprehension of sincere expression wherever it was found." When Bourne talks about the "new class-consciousness of poets," he means their growing awareness of the necessity to create a culture which can be used, a culture which allows the participation of all the people not just a chosen few. In view of Bourne's early identification of society as a vast conspiracy against the individual, it is not surprising that he should eventually see a similar opposition between society and the artist. Again, Bourne's attack on society is rather too dramatic to do justice to the artists involved relationship with society, but then, as so often, he tries to drive home merely one aspect of the whole truth and does not want to distract from the point he is trying to make. His undialectical concept of society as the deadly enemy of the artist is both a rhetorical device and the result of his identifying the dialectic with the aesthetic in the image of a harmonious community. His criticism of society is specified only where he discusses the bourgeois category of good taste, a reminder of course that the genteel tradition was still very much on his mind.

> "Society," we say, whether it be in the form of the mob or the cultivated dinner-circle, is the deadly enemy of the literary artist. Literary promises can be seen visibly fading out in the warm beams of association with the refined and the important. And social glamor was never so dangerous as it is today when it is anxious to be enlightened and liberal. Timidity is still the reigning vice of the American intellect, and the terrorism of "good taste" is yet more deadly to the creation of literary art than is sheer barbarism. The literary artist needs protection from the liberal audience that will accept him though he shock them, but that subtly tame him even while they appreciate.

Bourne's aversion to the educated middle-class audience needed the relief of a counterimage. In his early years, he had drawn upon the topos of the "beloved community" in describing the possibilities of mutual understanding among those friends whose identity-forming discourse he had taken as a model of the new social consciousness he sought. He refers once more to this idea of perfect understanding when he claimed (in a critical assessment of H. L. Mencken's invectives against bourgeois society) that the ideal audience an artist seeks is an audience of total comprehension. As he had done before, Bourne used the ideal as a normative guide for his judgments of reality.

Mr. Mencken's mode of critical attack thus plays into the hands of the philistines, demoralizes the artist, and demoralizes his own critical power. Why cannot Demos be left alone for a while to its commercial magazines and its mawkish novels? All good writing is produced in serene unconsciousness of what Demos desires or demands. It cannot be created at all if the artist worries about what Demos will think of him or do to him. The artist writes for that imagined audience of perfect comprehenders. The critic must judge for that audience too.

As the critical reference to Demos makes clear, Bourne did not intend to conceive of social art or of democratic culture as a mass-culture in the modern sense of that term. The meaning of social art was based upon its counterfactual nature which owed itself to an imaginary anticipation of the free movement of intellect between the factual and the ideal. Mass culture would have been much too exact a reproduction of the factual. Indeed, Bourne took a rather pessimistic view of mass cultural manifestations, deploring both their cheap sentiments and their vulgar taste.

Insisting on the importance of artistic imagination, Bourne had no great sympathy for sociological fiction which did not "fuse life into artistic form," as he put it in a review of a novel he criticized despite its "anticapitalistic sentiments" which he approved. Sociological fiction, he claimed, had to be judged on the basis of sociological pertinency and not as a literary art. His criticism of the genre did not imply that he objected to its subject matter. The opposite was true, as is demonstrated in a polemical review of a novel by H. G. Wells, whom he criticized for having "almost forgotten that there ever was such a thing as a proletarian," a reproach which was not meant as a plea for a "proletarian novel" but simply as a demand for a broader poetic vision.

Bourne was not preoccupied with the problem of proletarian art, despite the recurrent mention he makes in his reviews of topics which two decades later would be discussed under the label of proletarian aesthetics. Literary partisanship meant, for

Bourne, describing the conditions under which individuals live, fighting their struggle for self-conscious individualism against the maiming forces of an alienating economical and psychical surrounding. He tried to discover in literature the imaginative transformation of the social individual into a fictional self whose image could then be held up against the restrictions of the material world. If the idealistic concept of the Beloved Community could not be secularized by means of instrumentalistic reason, its truth should at least be preserved in the truth of fiction.

What Van Wyck Brooks once remarked of Bourne's writing in general is certainly true for his literary criticism: it is "a sort of corpus, a text full of secret ciphers, and packed with meanings between the lines." The writings must be read as an effort to establish a critical standard which onto the aesthetic object the possibility of its secularization. He took the idea of culture seriously, in a thoroughly worldly fashion, which gave his poetic vision a materialistic edge and prevented him from succumbing to the utopian fallacy.

Randolph Bourne's significance as a creative critic of culture can best be summed up in the words Charles H. Cooly used to describe the role of the artist:

> The "significance" of an artist means, I suppose, his contribution to a culture of which his work is a part, so that to understand it you must understand *him*.

Bourne's quest for a rational community had this significance. He wanted to be a citizen of this world without giving up his vision of how much better a place it might be. His contribution to the attainment of such hopes was a radical analysis of the world's shortcomings.

1
Youth and Life:
In Search of a Radical Metaphor

I want to see independent, self-reliant progressive generations, not eating each other's hearts out, but complementing each other and assuming a spiritual division of labor; I want the father and mother besides raising the children to lead independent lives of their own (this "I have nothing to live for but my children" that one hears so much is most demoralizing, I think), to add their own life-works of art to the great picture-gallery of personality of the past.

RANDOLPH BOURNE

Youth and Life: In Search of a Radical Metaphor

The early Bourne, so the legend goes, was mainly a publicist and spokesman for rebellious youth. Because this evokes the idea of an ever recurring generational conflict, it is much too general to do justice to the very precise themes of Bourne's early writings and, at the same time, neutralizes their critical content. It is certainly true that Bourne has to be seen in the context of that "innocent rebellion" H. F. May spoke of. It is also true that Bourne's early articles in the *Atlantic Monthly* dealing with the problem of a life style appropriate to the younger generation were widely read. But in spite of his interest in European youth movements, particularly socialist ones, Bourne was at no time merely the prophet of a youth cult. It should be said at the outset that youth was for Bourne a metaphor expressing the necessity of a socio-critical, intellectually unyielding attitude toward reality. Its goal was both the restoration of the individual and the improvement of the public weal. Bourne did not feel that the freedom to be eccentric guaranteed individualism. What he demanded was the successful realization of the self in social interaction. He was not interested in a post-romantic concept of autonomy but in an identity attained in the struggle against socialization. His concentration on the *faits sociaux* derives from this motive. It was a concentration marked by a nonpositivist, esthetically mediated sensibility and made Bourne one of the eminent figures of his time.

What characterizes Bourne and distinguishes him from contemporaries such as Van Wyck Brooks, the early Waldo Frank, and James Oppenheim is his gift for extremely detailed argument sharpened through contact with social reality. It was not so much a general despair over the inadequacy of American culture that motivated him. To a much greater measure than is true of a man such as Brooks, his judgments were based on experience. His texts testify to a marked subjectivity but his thinking is less governed than Brooks' by themes which are already part of the literary domain. One need only compare the early texts included here with "The Soul: An Essay Toward a Point of View" by Brooks. The differences are apparent. Where Brooks searches the past for models ". . . great souls of history who had shown men how to be true to themselves . . ." Bourne focuses much more on the future, on the possibility of attaining this very goal. That he avails himself of the philosophical and historical knowledge of his time for background shows that Bourne had a greater command of intellectual traditions.

In part, the difference between Bourne and Brooks can certainly be explained biographically. Because he was a cripple, tne evaluation of, and the coming to terms with reality demanded a considerable measure of analytical insight and sensibility from Bourne. He described this in his essay "The Handicapped—By One of Them," which first appeared anonymously in the *Atlantic Monthly,* in 1911. But more important than this biographical particularity was another of Bourne's qualities. Through a critical synthesis, he could discover connections where his contemporaries merely saw irreconcilable opposites. Waldo Frank has properly emphasized this aspect of Bourne's thought although his own organicism fundamentally differs from Bourne's preference for the concrete. Yet they both share the Whitmanesque background, particularly the anti-institutional impulse of *Democratic Vistas.* But in contrast to Frank, Whitman remains a relatively unreconstructed background in Bourne, and this also applies to Bergson and Nietzsche although their influence is clearly recognizable. What is of central importance, however, are reflections dealing with the socio-psychological conditions of the possibility of individuality, and it is these which give Bourne's position its originality. His insights result as much from a study of William James and Josiah Royce as from Le Bon and Bosanquet. In addition, he was familiar with the socio-psychological work of E. A. Ross, Charles Cooley, and W. I. Thomas. The knowledge that social groups tend toward self-stabilization and that this results in pressures exerted on group members has its counterpart in the conviction that individuality arises in the successful interaction with counter force. In the tension of this opposition, Bourne develops a double-sided ar-

gument whose undialectical structure allows him to emphasize
both its positive and negative aspects.

But beyond these two trains of thought, he develops a third
position by virtue of which neither negation nor utopia are left as
the only abstract alternatives. This is the position of irony not
only as a cognitive method but as a way of life. Irony makes it
possible to endure contradictions critically and patiently without
losing oneself to them. "Things as they are, thrown against the
background of things as they ought to be—this is the ironist's
vision" ("The Life of Irony"). Bourne stuck to this vision even
when the gap that had to be bridged became such as to compel him to substitute polemics for irony. An example of this is the
late fragment "Old Tyrannies." Written at the same time as the
treatise on the state, it testifies to the continuity of Bourne's
thought, its evident resignation notwithstanding.

The texts that follow demonstrate the various fundamental aspects of Bourne's early thought. They show that he is not interested in proclaiming a preconceived view about the role of
the younger generation, nor in assuming that it exists as a real
entity that might be socially and politically effective. Youth and
Life are metaphors of an intellectual construct whose critical and
radical tenor defines a space that has to be filled with political
content. In this respect, Bourne was much less metaphysically
inclined than certain representatives of European youth movements of the time. Youth does not guarantee a new beginning
but merely its possibility, which Bourne sought to demonstrate
through a combination of critical analysis and symbolic and
metaphorical evocation. The concise imagery and intellectual
precision of Bourne's observations result from the conjunction of
these two levels of argument.

"The Prayer of a Materialist" and "Sabotage" both appeared
in the *Columbia Monthly* under the pseudonym Aurelius Bloomfield, the first in February, 1911, the second in November, 1913.
For almost a year, Bourne was also editor of the Monthly (1911/
1912). These two texts should be seen as expressions of
Bourne's early interest in questions of socialism and problems
concerning the reconcilability of scientistic materialism and religious and spiritual experience. It may be said with some plausibility that "Sabotage" owes its existence to the impression the
strike of textile workers in Paterson made on him. That he followed the strike and its effects with great attention is evident in

his text "Pageantry and Social Art" which refers to the famous "pageant" in Madison Square Garden that owed much to John Reed's direction. Bourne's interest in socialism intensified during his student days. He became a member of the Intercollegiate Socialist Society, and when he went to Europe in 1913/14 it was this developing interest which guided his perceptions.

Except for the last text and "The Experimental Life," all those that follow appeared in the *Atlantic Monthly* during the period from 1911 to 1915. Most of them were reprinted in the volume *Youth and Life* (1913), some in a revised version.

Bourne's first contribution to the *Atlantic Monthly,* "The Two Generations," had been written as a reaction to an article which had appeared in that publication and had made critical comments about the younger generation. But Bourne gained the respect of Ellery Sedgwick, the editor of the journal. Suddenly, he had the chance to develop and generalize this thought. It is clearly noticeable that Bourne searches for patterns of thought that may be given a wider applicability, and that he found them increasingly in the writings of John Dewey, William James, Josiah Royce and, last but not least, in Bergson. Already in the essay "The Handicapped," there is a suggestion that the biographically substantiated subjectivity perceives itself as the medium of statements about society and does not view itself solipsistically as an object for its own reflections. In essays such as "Youth," "The Life of Irony," and "The Experimental Life," we note a quality which differs from the somewhat laborious search for an adequate form of expression that characterizes the early writings in the *Columbia Monthly.* Strongly influenced by William James, Bourne not only accepted the multiplicity of possible experiences but discovered that an unprejudiced reaction to them was the condition that makes identity possible. In this sense, his comments entitled "Youth" are marked by a double-sided argument, typical of Bourne. While he turns to a younger generation as an audience, the term "youth" also contains the promise that "to keep one's reactions warm and true is to have found the secret of perpetual youth." It is the sustained struggle with reality that assures this result. It would be going too far to call Bourne a disciple of William James although he did write in a letter dating from 1913: "My enthusiasm for James is really comparatively recent, for two years ago when I was studying a philosophy course with a wonderful teacher, the best we have here who, by the way, suggested several of the titles of my essays, I was a rank materialist and took great delight in lacerating a rather tender and green young man whose delight was in Emerson and Plato, whom I despised." It would be more accurate to say that Bourne combines diverse elements in his reflections. Some are traditional and become apparent in the influence of Emerson, Thoreau, and Whitman. Others are contemporary, such as Dewey's experimentalism and the idealist interactionism of Josiah Royce. Thus "The Excitement of Friendship" and "The Experimental Life" complement each other in the same way that "The Dodging of Pressures" is placed in a more critical perspective by "The Life of Irony" which points to the pressures against which ironic distance has to prevail.

The fragment "Old Tyrannies" has an importance all its own. Particularly when contrasted with the optimism of the early essays, it turns out to be one of Bourne's most pessimistic texts. But it does show how decisively Bourne also took hold of the negative aspects of his thought, how he could also probe the individual's lack of freedom that results from socialization, in spite of his faith in its powers of resistance.

Sources of first publication

"The Handicapped"	*Atlantic Monthly,* September,1911
"The Prayer of a Materialist"	*Columbia Monthly,* February,1911
"Sabotage"	CM., November, 1913
"Youth"	AM., April, 1912
"The Excitement of Friendship"	AM., December, 1912
"The Dodging of Pressures"	*Youth and Life* (1913)
"The Life of Irony"	AM., March, 1913
"The Experimental Life"	*Youth and Life* (1913)
"This Older Generation"	AM., September, 1915
"Old Tyrannies"	*Untimely Papers* (1919)
"The Mystic Turned Radical"	AM., February, 1912

THE HANDICAPPED

It would not perhaps be thought, ordinarily, that the man whom physical disabilities have made so helpless that he is unable to move around among his fellows can bear his lot more happily, even though he suffer pain, and face life with a more cheerful and contented spirit, than can the man whose deformities are merely enough to mark him out from the rest of his fellows without preventing him from entering with them into most of their common affairs and experiences. But the fact is that the former's very helplessness makes him content to rest and not to strive. I know a young man so helplessly deformed that he has to be carried about, who is happy in reading a little, playing chess, taking a course or two in college, and all with the sunniest goodwill in the world, and a happiness that seems strange and unaccountable to my restlessness. He does not cry for the moon.

When one, however, is in full possession of his faculties, and can move about freely, bearing simply a crooked back and an unsightly face, he is perforce drawn into all the currents of life. Particularly if he has his own way in the world to make, his road is apt to be hard and rugged, and he will penetrate to an unusual depth in his interpretation both of the world's attitude toward such misfortunes, and of the attitude toward the world which such misfortunes tend to cultivate in men like him. For he has all the battles of a stronger man to fight, and he is at a double disadvantage in fighting them. He has constantly with him the sense of being obliged to make extra efforts to overcome the bad impression of his physical defects, and he is haunted with a constant feeling of weakness and low vitality which makes effort more difficult and renders him easily fainthearted and discouraged by failure. He is never confident of himself, because he has grown up in an atmosphere where nobody has been very confident of him; and yet his environment and circumstances call out all sorts of ambitions and energies in him which, from the nature of his case, are bound to be immediately thwarted. This attitude is likely to keep him at a generally low level of accomplishment unless he have an unusually strong will, and a strong will is perhaps the last thing to develop under such circumstances.

That vague sense of physical uncomfortableness which is with him nearly every minute of his waking day serves, too, to make steady application for hours to any particular kind of work much more irksome than it is even to the lazy man. No one but the deformed man can realize just what the mere fact of sitting a foot lower than the normal means in discomfort and annoyance. For one cannot carry one's special chair everywhere, to theatre and library and train and schoolroom. This sounds trivial, I know, but I mention it because it furnishes a real, even though usually dim, "background of consciousness" which one had to reckon with during all one's solid work or enjoyment. The things that the world deems hardest for the deformed man to bear are perhaps really the easiest of all. I can truthfully say, for instance, that I have never suffered so much as a pang from the interested comments on my personal appearance made by urchins in the street, nor from the curious looks of people in the street and public places. To ignore this vulgar curiosity is the simplest and easiest thing in the world. It does not worry me in the least to appear on a platform if I have anything to say and there is anybody to listen. What one does get sensitive to is rather the inevitable way that people, acquaintances and strangers alike, have of discounting in advance what one does or says.

The deformed man is always conscious that the world does not expect very much from him. And it takes him a long time to see in this a challenge instead of a firm pressing down to a low level of accomplishment. As a result, he does not expect very much of himself; he is timid in approaching people, and distrustful of his ability to persuade and convince. He becomes extraordinarily sensitive to other people's first impressions of him. Those who are to be his friends he knows instantly, and further acquaintance adds little to the intimacy and warm friendship that he at once feels for them. On the other hand, those who do not respond to him immediately cannot by any effort either on his part or theirs overcome that first alienation.

This sensitiveness has both its good and bad sides. It makes friendship that most precious thing in the world to him; and he finds that he arrives at a much richer and wider intimacy with his friends than do ordinary men with their light, surface friendships, based on good fellowship or the convenience of the moment. But on the other hand this sensitiveness absolutely unfits him for business and the practice of a profession, where one must be "all things to all men," and the professional manner is indispensable to success. For here, where he has to meet a constant stream of men of all sorts and conditions, his sensitiveness to these first impressions will make his case hopeless. Except with those few who by some secret sympathy will seem to respond, his deformity will stand like a huge barrier between his personality and other men's. The magical good fortune of attractive personal appearance makes its way almost without effort in the world, breaking down all sorts of walls of disapproval and lack of interest. Even the homely person can attract by personal charm. But deformity cannot even be charming.

The doors of the deformed man are always locked, and the key is on the outside. He may have treasures of charm inside, but they will never be revealed unless the person outside cooperates with him in unlocking the door. A friend becomes, to a much greater degree than with the ordinary man, the indispensable means of discovering one's own personality. One only exists, so to speak, with friends. It is easy to see how hopelessly such a sensitiveness incapacitates a man for business, professional, or social life, where the hasty and superficial impression is everything, and disaster is the fate of the man who has not all the treasures of his personality in the front window, where they can be readily inspected and appraised.

It thus takes the deformed man a long time to get adjusted to his world. Childhood is perhaps the hardest time of all. As a child he is a strange creature in a strange land. It was my own fate to be just strong enough to play about with the other boys, and attempt all their games and "stunts," without being strong enough actually to succeed in any of them. It never used to occur to me that my failures and lack of skill were due to circumstances beyond my control, but I would always impute them, in consequence of my rigid Calvinistic bringing-up, I suppose, to some moral weakness of my own. I suffered tortures in trying to learn to skate, to climb trees, to play ball, to conform in general to the ways of the world. I never resigned myself to the inevitable, but overexerted myself constantly in a grim determination to succeed. I was good at my lessons, and through timidity rather than priggishness, I hope, a very well-behaved boy at school; I was devoted, too, to music, and learned to play the piano pretty well. But I despised my reputation for excellence in these things, and instead of adapting myself philosophically to the situation, I strove (and have been striving ever since) to do the things I could not.

As I look back now It seems perfectly natural that I should have followed the standards of the crowd, and loathed my high marks in lessons and deportment, and the concerts to which I was sent by my aunt, and the exhibitions of my musical skill that I had to give before admiring ladies.[1] Whether or not such an experience is typical of handicapped children, there is tragedy there for those situated as I was. For had I been a little weaker physically, I should have been thrown back on reading omnivorously and cultivating my music, with some possible results; while if I had been a little stronger, I could have participated in the play on an equal footing with the rest. As it was, I simply tantalized myself, and grew up with a deepening sense of failure, and a lack of pride in what I really excelled at.

When the world became one of dances and parties and social evenings and boy-and-girl attachments—the world of youth—I was to find myself still less adapted to it. And this was the harder to bear because I was naturally sociable, and all these things appealed tremendously to me. This world of admiration and gayety and smiles and favors and quick interest and companionship, however, is only for the well-begotten and the debonair. It was not through any cruelty or dislike, I think, that I was refused admittance; indeed they were always very kind about inviting me. But it was more as if a ragged urchin had been asked to come and look through the window at the light and warmth of a glittering party; I was truly in the world, but not of the world. Indeed there were times when one would almost prefer conscious cruelty to this silent, unconscious, gentle oblivion. And this is the tragedy, I suppose, not only of the deformed, but of all the ill-favored and unattractive to a greater or less degree. The world of youth is a world of so many conventions, and the abnormal in any direction is so glaringly and hideously abnormal.

Although it took me a long time to understand this, and I continue to attribute my failure mostly to my own character, trying hard to compensate for my physical deficiencies by skill and cleverness, I suffered comparatively few pangs, and got much better adjusted to this world than to the other. For I was older, and I had acquired a lively interest in all the social politics; I would get so interested in watching how people behaved, and in sizing them up, that only at rare intervals would I remember that I was really having no hand in the game. This interest just in the ways people are human has become more and more a positive advantage in my life, and has kept sweet many a situation that might easily have cost me a pang. Not that a person with my disabilities should be a sort of detective, evil-mindedly using his social opportunities for spying out and analyzing his friends' foibles, but that, if he does acquire an interest in people quite apart from their relation to him, he may go into society with an easy conscience and a certainty that he will be entertained and possibly entertaining, even though he cuts a poor enough social figure. He must simply not expect too much.

Perhaps the bitterest struggles of the handicapped man come when he tackles the business world. If he has to go out for himself to look for work, without fortune, training, or influence, as I personally did, his way will indeed be rugged. His disability will work against him for any position where he must be much in the eyes of men, and his general insignificance has a subtle influence in convincing those to whom he applies that he is unfitted for any kind of work. As I have suggested, his keen sensitiveness to other people's impressions of him makes him more than unusually timid and unable to counteract that fatal first impression by any display of personal force and will. He cannot get his personality over across that barrier. The cards seem stacked against him from the start. With training and influence something might be done, but alone and unaided his case is almost hopeless. At least, this was my own experience. We were poor relations, and our prosperous relatives thought they had done quite enough for us without sending me through college, and I did not seem strong enough to work my way through (although I have since done it). I started out auspiciously enough, becoming a sort of apprentice to a musician who had invented a machine for turning out music-rolls. Here, with steady work, good pay, and the comfortable consciousness that I was "helping support the family," I got the first pleasurable sensation of self-respect, I think, that I ever had. But with the failure of this business I was precipitated against the real world.[2]

It would be futile to recount the story of my struggles: how I besieged for nearly two years firm after firm, in search of a permanent position, trying everything in New York in which I thought I had the slightest chance of success, meanwhile making a precarious living by a few music lessons. The attitude toward me ranged from "You can't expect us to create a place for you," to, "How could it enter your head that we should find any use for a man like you?" My situation was doubtless unusual. Few men handicapped as I was would be likely to go so long without arousing some interest and support in relative or friend. But my experience serves to illustrate the peculiar difficulties that a handicapped man meets if he has his own way to make in the world. He is discounted at the start: it is not business to make allowances for anybody; and while people were not cruel or unkind, it was the hopeless finality of the thing that filled one's heart with despair.

The environment of a big city is perhaps the worst possible that a man in such a situation could have. For the thousands of seeming opportunities lead one restlessly on and on, and keep one's mind perpetually unsettled and depressed. There is a poignant mental torture that comes with such an experience— the urgent need, the repeated failure, or rather the repeated failure even to obtain a chance to fail, the realization that those at home can ill afford to have you idle, the growing dread of encountering people—all this is something that those who have never been through it can never realize. Personally I know of no particular way of escape. One can expect to do little by one's own unaided efforts. I solved my difficulties only by evading them, by throwing overboard some of my responsibility, and taking the desperate step of entering college on a scholarship. Desultory work is not nearly so humiliating when one is using one's time to some advantage, and college furnishes an ideal environment where the things at which a man handicapped like myself can succeed really count. One's self-respect can begin to grow like a weed.

For at the bottom of all the difficulties of a man like me is really the fact that his self-respect is so slow in growing up. Accustomed from childhood to being discounted, his self-respect is not naturally very strong, and it would require pretty constant success in a congenial line of work really to confirm it. If he could only more easily separate the factors that are due to his physical disability from those that are due to his weak will and character, he might more quickly attain self-respect, for he would realize what he is responsible for, and what he is not. But at the beginning he rarely makes allowances for himself; he is his own severest judge. He longs for a "strong will," and yet the experience of having his efforts promptly nipped off at the beginning is the last thing on earth to produce that will.

Life, particularly if he is brought into harsh and direct touch with the real world, is a much more complex thing to him than to the ordinary man. Many of his inherited platitudes vanish at the first touch. Life appears to him as a grim struggle, where ability does not necessarily mean opportunity and success, nor piety sympathy, and where helplessness cannot count on assistance and kindly interest. Human affairs seem to be running on a wholly irrational plan, and success to be founded on chance as much as on anything. But if he can stand the first shock of disillusionment, he may find himself enormously interested in discovering how they actually do run, and he will want to burrow into the motives of men, and find the reasons for the crass inequalities and injustices of the world he sees around him. He has practically to construct anew a world of his own, and explain a great many things to himself that the ordinary person never dreams of finding unintelligible at all. He will be filled with a profound sympathy for all who are despised and ignored in the world. When he has been through the neglect and struggles of a handicapped and ill-favored man himself, he will begin to understand the feelings of all the horde of the unpresentable and the unemployable, the incompetent and the ugly, the queer and crotchety people who make up so large a proportion of human folk.

We are perhaps too prone to get our ideas and standards of worth from the successful, without reflecting that the interpretations of life which patriotic legend, copybook philosophy, and the sayings of the wealthy give us are pitifully inadequate for those who fall behind in the race. Surely there are enough people to whom the task of making a decent living and maintaining themselves and their families in their social class, or of winning and keeping the respect of their fellows, is a hard and bitter task, to make a philosophy gained through personal disability and failure as just and true a method of appraising the life around us as the cheap optimism of the ordinary professional man. And certainly a kindlier, for it has no shade of contempt or disparagement about it.

It irritates me as if I had been spoken of contemptuously my-

self, to hear people called "common" or "ordinary," or to see
that deadly and delicate feeling for social gradations crop out,
which so many of our upper-middle-class women seem to have.
It makes me wince to hear a man spoken of as a failure, or to
have it said of one that he "doesn't amount to much." Instantly I
want to know why he has not succeeded, and what have been
the forces that have been working against him. He is the truly
interesting person, and yet how little our eager-pressing, onrush-
ing world cares about such aspects of life, and how hideously
though unconsciously cruel and heartless it usually is.

Often I had tried in arguments to show my friends how much
of circumstance and chance go to the making of success; and
when I reached the age of sober reading, a long series of the
works of radical social philosophers, beginning with Henry
George, provided me with the materials for a philosophy which
explained why men were miserable and overworked, and why
there was on the whole so little joy and gladness among
us—and which fixed the blame. Here was suggested a goal,
and a definite glorious future, toward which all good men might
work. My own working hours became filled with visions of how
men could be brought to see all that this meant, and how I in
particular might work some great and wonderful thing for human
betterment. In more recent years, the study of history and social
psychology and ethics has made those crude outlines sounder
and more normal, and brought them into a saner relation to
other aspects of life and thought, but I have not lost the first
glow of enthusiasm, nor my belief in social progress as the first
right and permanent interest for every thinking and truehearted
man or woman.

I am ashamed that my experience has given me so little
chance to count in any way toward either the spreading of
such a philosophy or toward direct influence and action. Nor do
I yet see clearly how I shall be able to count effectually toward
this ideal. Of one thing I am sure, however: that life will have little meaning for me except as I am able to contribute toward
some such ideal of social betterment, if not in deed, then in
word. For this is the faith that I believe we need today, all of
us—a truly religious belief in human progress, a thorough social
consciousness, an eager delight in every sign and promise of
social improvement, and best of all, a new spirit of courage that

will dare. I want to give to the young men whom I see—who, with fine intellect and high principles, lack just that light of the future on their faces that would give them a purpose and meaning in life—to them I want to give some touch of this philosophy—that will energize their lives, and save them from the disheartening effects of that poisonous counsel of timidity and distrust of human ideals which pours out in steady stream from reactionary press and pulpit.

It is hard to tell just how much of this philosophy has been due to my handicaps. If it is solely to my physical misfortunes that I owe its existence, the price has not been a heavy one to pay. For it has given me something that I should not know how to be without. For, however gained, this radical philosophy has not only made the world intelligible and dynamic to me, but has furnished me with the strongest spiritual support. I know that many people, handicapped by physical weakness and failure, find consolation and satisfaction in a very different sort of faith— in an evangelical religion, and a feeling of close dependence on God and close communion with him. But my experience has made my ideal of character militant rather than long-suffering.

I very early experienced a revulsion against the rigid Presbyterianism in which I had been brought up—a purely intellectual revulsion, I believe, because my mind was occupied for a long time afterward with theological questions, and the only feeling that entered into it was a sort of disgust at the arrogance of damning so great a proportion of the human race. I read T. W. Higginson's *The Sympathy of Religions* with the greatest satisfaction, and attended the Unitarian Church whenever I could slip away. This faith, while it still appeals to me, seems at times a little too static and refined to satisfy me with completeness. For some time there was a considerable bitterness in my heart at the narrowness of the people who could still find comfort in the old faith. Reading Buckle and Oliver Wendell Holmes gave me a new contempt for "conventionality," and my social philosophy still further tortured me by throwing the burden for the misery of the world on these same good neighbors. And all this, although I think I did not make a nuisance of myself, made me feel a spiritual and intellectual isolation in addition to my more or less effective physical isolation.

Happily these days are over. The world has righted itself, and

I have been able to appreciate and realize how people count in a social and group capacity as well as in an individual and personal one, and to separate the two in my thinking. Really to believe in human nature while striving to know the thousand forces that warp it from its ideal development—to call for and expect much from men and women, and not to be disappointed and embittered if they fall short—to try to do good with people rather than to them—this is my religion on its human side. And if God exists, I think that He must be in the warm sun, in the kindly actions of the people we know and read of, in the beautiful things of art and nature, and in the closeness of friendships. He may also be in heaven, in life, in suffering, but it is only in these simple moments of happiness that I feel Him and know that He is there.

Death I do not understand at all. I have seen it in its cruelest, most irrational forms, where there has seemed no excuse, no palliation. I have only known that if we were more careful, and more relentless in fighting evil, if we knew more of medical science, such things would not be. I know that a sound body, intelligent care and training, prolong life, and that the death of a very old person is neither sad nor shocking, but sweet and fitting. I see in death a perpetual warning of how much there is to be known and done in the way of human progress and betterment. And equally, it seems to me, is this true of disease. So all the crises and deeper implications of life seem inevitably to lead back to that question of social improvement, and militant learning and doing.

This, then, is the goal of my religion—the bringing of fuller, richer life to more people on this earth. All institutions and all works that do not have this for their object are useless and pernicious. And this is not to be a mere philosophic precept which may well be buried under a host of more immediate matters, but a living faith, to permeate one's thought, and transfuse one's life. Prevention must be the method against evil. To remove temptation from men, and to apply the stimulus which shall call forth their highest endeavors—these seem to me the only right principles of ethical endeavor. Not to keep waging the age-long battle with sin and poverty, but to make the air around men so pure that foul lungs cannot breathe it—this should be our noblest religious aim.

Education—knowledge and training—I have felt so keenly my lack of these things that I count them as the greatest of means toward making life noble and happy. The lack of stimulus has tended with me to dissipate the power which might otherwise have been concentrated in some one productive direction. Or perhaps it was the many weak stimuli that constantly incited me and thus kept me from following one particular bent. I look back on what seems a long waste of intellectual power, time frittered away in groping and moping, which might easily have been spent constructively. A defect in one of the physical senses often means a keener sensitiveness in the others, but it seems that unless the sphere of action that the handicapped man has is very much narrowed, his intellectual ability will not grow in compensation for his physical defects. He will always feel that, had he been strong or even successful, he would have been further advanced intellectually, and would have attained greater command over his powers. For his mind tends to be cultivated extensively, rather than intensively. He has so many problems to meet, so many things to explain to himself, that he acquires a wide rather than a profound knowledge. Perhaps eventually, by eliminating most of these interests as practicable fields, he may tie himself down to one line of work; but at first he is pretty apt to find his mind rebellious. If he is eager and active, he will get a smattering of too many things, and his imperfect, badly trained organism will make intense application very difficult.

Now that I have talked a little of my philosophy of life, particularly about what I want to put into it, there is something to be said also of its enjoyment, and what I may hope to get out of it. I have said that my ideal of character was militant rather than long-suffering. It is true that my world has been one of failure and deficit—I have accomplished practically nothing alone, and can count only two or three instances where I have received kindly counsel and suggestion; moreover it still seems a miracle to me that money can be spent for anything beyond the necessities without being first carefully weighed and pondered over—but it has not been a world of suffering and sacrifice, my health has been almost criminally perfect in the light of my actual achievement, and life has appeared to me, at least since my more pressing responsibilities were removed, as a challenge and an arena, rather than a vale of tears. I do not like the idea of helplessly suffering one's misfortunes, of passively bearing one's lot. The Stoics depress me. I do not want to look on my life as an eternal making the best of a bad bargain. Granting all the circumstances, admitting all my disabilities, I want too to "warm both hands before the fire of life." What satisfactions I have, and they are many and precious, I do not want to look on as compensations, but as positive goods.

The difference between what the strongest of the strong and the most winning of the attractive can get out of life, and what I can, is after all so slight. Our experiences and enjoyments, both his and mine, are so infinitesimal compared with the great mass of possibilities; and there must be a division of labor. If he takes the world of physical satisfactions and of material success, I at least can occupy the far richer kingdom of mental effort and artistic appreciation. And on the side of what we are to put into life, although I admit that achievement on my part will be harder relatively to encompass than on his, at least I may have the field of artistic creation and intellectual achievement for my own. Indeed, as one gets older, the fact of one's disabilities fades dimmer and dimmer away from consciousness. One's enemy is now one's own weak will, and the struggle is to attain the artistic ideal one has set.

But one must have grown up, to get this attitude. And that is the best thing the handicapped man can do. Growing up will have given him one of the greatest, and certainly the most durable satisfaction of his life. It will mean at least that he is out of the woods. Childhood has nothing to offer him; youth little more. They are things to be gotten through with as soon as possible. For he will not understand, and he will not be understood. He finds himself simply a bundle of chaotic impulses and emotions and ambitions, very few of which, from the nature of the case, can possibly be realized or satisfied. He is bound to be at cross-grains with the world, and he had to look sharp that he does not grow up with a bad temper and a hateful disposition, and become cynical and bitter against those who turn him away. But grown up, his horizon will broaden; he will get a better perspective, and will not take the world so seriously as he used to, nor will failure frighten him so much. He can look back and see how inevitable it all was, and understand how precarious and problematic even the best regulated of human affairs may be. And if he feels that there were times when he should have been able to count upon the help and kindly counsel of relatives and acquaintances who remained dumb and uninterested, he will not put their behavior down as proof of the depravity of human nature, but as due to an unfortunate blindness which it will be his work to avoid in himself by looking out for others when he has the power.

When he has grown up, he will find that people of his own age and experience are willing to make those large allowances for what is out of the ordinary which were impossible to his younger friends, and that grown-up people touch each other on planes other than the purely superficial. With a broadening of his own interests, he will find himself overlapping other people's personalities at new points, and will discover with rare delight that he is beginning to be understood and appreciated—at least to a greater degree than when he had to keep his real interests hid as something unusual. For he will begin to see in his friends, his music and books, and his interest in people and social betterment, his true life; many of his restless ambitions will fade gradually away, and he will come to recognize all the more clearly some true ambition of his life that is within the range of his capabilities. He will have built up his world, and have sifted out the things that are not going to concern him, and participation in which will only serve to vex and harass him. He may well come to count his deformity even as a blessing, for it has made impossible to him at last many things in the pursuit of which he would only fritter away his time and dissipate his interest. He must not think of "resigning himself to his fate"; above all he must insist on his own personality. For once really grown up, he will find that he has acquired self-respect and personality. Grown-upness, I think, is not a mere question of age, but of being able to look back and understand and find satisfaction in one's experience, no matter how bitter it may have been.

So to all who are situated as I am, I would say—Grow up as fast as you can. Cultivate the widest interests you can, and cherish all your friends. Cultivate some artistic talent, for you will find it the most durable of satisfactions, and perhaps one of the surest means of livelihood as well. Achievement is, of course, on the knees of the gods; but you will at least have the thrill of trial, and, after all, not to try is to fail. Taking your disabilities for granted, and assuming constantly that they are being taken for granted, make your social intercourse as broad and as constant as possible. Do not take the world too seriously, nor let too many social conventions oppress you. Keep sweet your sense of humor, and above all do not let any morbid feelings of inferiority creep into your soul. You will find yourself sensitive enough to the sympathy of others, and if you do not find people who like you and are willing to meet you more than halfway, it will be because you have let your disability narrow your vision and shrink up your soul. It will be really your own fault, and not that of your circumstances. In a word, keep looking outward; look out eagerly for those things that interest you, for people who will interest you and be friends with you, for new interests and for opportunities to express yourself. You will find that your disability will come to have little meaning for you, that it will begin to fade quite completely out of your sight; you will wake up some fine morning and find yourself, after all the struggles that seemed so bitter to you, really and truly adjusted to the world.

I am perhaps not yet sufficiently out of the wilderness to utter all these brave words. For, I must confess, I find myself hopelessly dependent on my friends, and my environment. My friends have come to mean more to me than almost anything else in the world. If it is far harder work for a man in my situation to make friendships quickly, at least friendships once made have a depth and intimacy quite beyond ordinary attachments. For a man such as I am has little prestige; people do not want to impress him. They are genuine and sincere, talk to him freely about themselves, and are generally far less reticent about revealing their real personality and history and aspirations. And particularly is this so in friendships with young women. I have found their friendships the most delightful and satisfying of all. For all that social convention that insists that every friendship between a young man and woman must be on a romantic basis is necessarily absent in our case. There is no fringe around us to make our acquaintance anything but a charming companionship. With all my friends, the same thing is true. The first barrier of strangeness broken down, our interest is really in each other, and not in what each is going to think of the other, how he is to be impressed, or whether we are going to fall in love with each other. When one of my friends moves away, I feel as if a great hole had been left in my life. There is a whole side of my personality that I cannot express without him. I shudder to think of any change that will deprive me of their constant companionship. Without friends I feel as if even my music and books and interests would turn stale on my hands. I confess that I am not grown up enough to get along without them.[3]

But if I am not yet out of the wilderness, at least I think I see the way to happiness. With health and a modicum of achievement, I shall not see my lot as unenviable. And if misfortune comes, it will only be something flowing from the common lot of men, not from my own particular disability. Most of the difficulties that flow from that I flatter myself I have met by this time of my twenty-fifth year, have looked full in the face, have grappled with, and find in nowise so formidable as the world usually deems them; no bar to my real ambitions and ideals.

1. Compare Randolph Bourne: "Diary for 1901," *Twice-A-Year* V, VI (1940/ 41) pp. 89-98.
2. Compare "What is Exploitation?" Aside from the work described here, Bourne earned his living with the previously mentioned music lessons and as accompanist in the studios of Carnegie Hall. Bourne, for financial reasons, was unable to go immediately to college after his graduation. It was not until 1909 that he was able to enroll at Columbia College, and then only with the help of a scholarship.
3. Compare "The Excitement of friendship."

The Prayer of a Materialist

O World, which hast out of the dim vastness of Eternity and the ceaseless whirl of myriads of clashing atoms, evolved marvelously my consciousness, the one ultimate Reality, the reality which gives me power to recognize thy reality—I worship thee. I love thy music, colors, friendships, inspirations, strivings, satisfactions, ironies; but above all I love Matter, the stuff in which all these move and have their being. When I think, O World, of thy myriads of centuries, of countries, of environments, of species, of infinitely varied combinations and forms of matter, I am awed at the stupendous wonder of my being. Not in words can my fervent thankfulness be expressed, O World, but in a throbbing sympathy with thy heart, an understanding which binds the whole of me to thee. I am a part of the world; nothing can destroy me. If my consciousness shall at thy behest be transformed into some other mode of motion, I shall still exist, as all Energy forever exists. I am safe in thy hands. O World of Matter; I trust thee with an utter, an abandoning trust to carry me through the Eternity of the Future as thou hast carried me through the Eternity of the Past. And trusting thee, I do not ask the Why of things. I am content to know thee as thou callest to be known.

I recognize no vice but ignorance of thee, no crime but disobedience to thy laws. I do not need to punish or be punished by artificial chastisements; thou punishest relentlessly, irrevocably, infraction of thy laws, for disobedience of thee is its own punishment. With a pitying sympathy pardon our ignorance, for thou greatly sufferest because of it. Thou bearest through the centuries the long travail of suffering and death, the toll not only of disobedience but of helpless ignorance of thee. And it is thou who sufferest along with us. Pardon our laziness, our perversity, which will not see, which makes us chase the *phantoms* of a dream-world of the supernatural, of the spiritual, of the sentimental, while all around us lies the power and the glory of Matter and Energy which will make us free for ever more. Not out of wickedness but out of ignorance of thee springs all the evil with which the old earth festers—premature death, sickness, hatred, exploitation, poverty, sordidness—out of ignorance of thy healing power, thy creative strength, O Matter. Only by thee, not by reliance upon Spirit, shall evil be banished from the world. Only by learning thy mechanical laws, by discovering and applying thy forces, working on thy matter, O World, shall we slough off the evil from thee.

Thou grantest us, O World, fullest privilege to utilize, to exploit thee; thou exultest with joy at our feeble beginnings of this we call our Wonder-Age. Thy exhaustless store of power and mechanism lies ready in thee for the hand of Man to develop, to adapt rationally, and distribute, and enjoy. With such utilization thyself, O World, will at last be realized, the purposes revealed, thy final end achieved. And to Man is given the ineffable joy of being thy agent, of realizing himself in thy realization, of co-operating as part of thee in thy unfoldings. Then shall every man's life be rich and full and free, each beautiful personality developed to its highest potency in a life of warm, intimate inter-course with his fellows; then shall life be long and joyous, end-ing only when it has run its full course, and consciousness, un-hastening but unreluctant, serene and content, shall ebb slowly away. Then shall the earth be beautiful again, and men be happy, as they could not be when the spectre of poverty stalked the streets of earth. Then will all men worship thee, O World of Matter, as I worship thee now, and will glory in thy perfection and beauty.

Grant me, O World of Matter, that I may have my infinitesimal part in this great realization. Grant that what little there is of me may be dynamic towards the great end. Grant that I may know thee intimately in one of thy many aspects, and that I may add something of the knowledge of thee to the human store, some-thing that will slough off some of the evil which still clings to thee. Grant that my consciousness shall not go out before I have achieved something, O World, in the way of teaching my fellows about thee. And if my power is infinitesimal in the midst of so vast a world, at least let me be luminous in the tiny sphere where thou hast placed me. And when my light shall go out, take me, O World of Matter, to thy kindly bosom, knowing well that nothing can harm me in thee.

Sabotage
                                              I.

Into your machines, O my masters, you have knotted and kneaded our lives.

You have caught our early dawn and streaked it over with murky clouds of soot,

You have staled the freshness of our morning, and dried the dew of our limpid misty youth with the inexorable blatant roaring mechanics of your routine.

You have taken our flesh and our heart's blood, and with the cunning artifice of the sculptor have plastered and daubed us into your metal looms.

Our ambitions, our desires, our loves and gloomy fears, you have drawn out one by one into fine-spun threads, and tied our souls to your clashing wheels and whirling spindles,

And little pieces of our lives stick quivering to all their joints and frames—

Lost dead strains of our effort, lost and dead to us but still quick and alive in the subtlety of our adaptation,

Quick and alive in the skill of our muscles which rivets us even more tightly to the steel whose prisoners we are.

From the mystical touch of our labor, from the blood which we have poured so freely through their creaking metal veins,

Your machines have received life, received thought, have created;

We have been to them as gods and have breathed life into their dull clay.

But base and drabbled gods—

For over us, O my masters, turns ever your iron wheel of the world, the wheel of ownership, the wheel of exploitation,

And we who breathed the soul of life are in our turn drained of our soul of life,

As the machines spring into creation, we living bodies deaden—deaden—deaden—

Our muscles, tense, quick, sure, become the lifeless nerves, the deeply-channelled reflex

Through which the great thought and purpose of the machine expresses its conscious self.

We are the cogs, we are the levers, we are the machines, at which these metal monsters work.

We are their food, their body's nourishment,

We are one flesh with them—tangled, coiled, metabolized, inextricably knotted,
Into your machines, O my masters, you have knitted and kneaded our lives.

II.

But see! now as the dim confused cry of revolt sounds far without the factory walls,
As we strain to hear the wild sweet cruel words that bid us cease from labor—
Slowly ebbs back the blood into our veins, ebbs back from the vital triumphant lusty machines that have long dominated us.
We are men again, we strain to tear ourselves from the suffocating embrace,
We wrench ourselves from the fusion which has killed us.
From this blended body we strive to tear our bodies, from this tangled soul we strive to tear our souls.
And in the wrenchings what veins of the machine are opened! what sinews tear! what tender nerves are ripped asunder!
We wrestle and sweat to escape, and in the mad struggle what of the firmest tissues are broken! what of the strongest fibres are rent!
See! this bolt! it comes away with me—it is part of me—
I am ground into it, with the grindings of winter daybreaks and feverish August afternoons.
See! this handle! it cleaves to me as I tear myself away—it is a part of me—
It is I that have given it life—it loves me—it pulls and tears after me, and what if in its pulling it tears and kills the vital bowels of the machine.
See! we workers and our machines, we are all of one wondrous fabric—one thread of us do you pull, and the whole great sheet unravels,
We cannot help, O my masters; it was not we that knit us into the warp and woof of your machines—
It was not we that drained off our power and our passion into the cold lifeless steel, and thrust the remorseless drive and clank into our own sinews and muscles,
It was not we that kneaded our lives into the brick and steel.
What if in our wrenchings old moralities crumble, and the "Thou Shalt Nots" of our masters become as fine powder?

It was not we that stood on Sinai, or wrought the iron lock of ownership.

Curse yourselves, O my masters, as we pull and strain, and the great domineering machines lie wounded and stricken at our feet.

Curse yourselves, but in us dawns the mad hope, the wild certainty of the day when we both shall live!

The day when new free sweet moralities shall arise, and in the healing touch of brotherhood, the machines—into which, O my masters, you have knotted and kneaded our lives—shall be, not flesh of our body, but docile nerves and sinews of our will!

YOUTH

I

How shall I describe Youth, the time of contradictions and anomalies? The fiercest radicalisms, the most dogged conservatisms, irrepressible gayety, bitter melancholy—all these moods are equally part of that showery springtime of life. One thing, at least, it clearly is: a great, rich rush and flood of energy. It is as if the store of life had been accumulating through the slow, placid years of childhood, and suddenly the dam had broken and the waters rushed out, furious and uncontrolled, before settling down into the quieter channels of middle life. The youth is suddenly seized with a poignant consciousness of being alive, which is quite wanting to the native unquestioning existence of the child. He finds himself overpoweringly urged toward self-expression. Just as the baby, born into a "great, blooming, buzzing confusion," and attracted by every movement, every color, every sound, kicks madly in response in all directions, and only gradually gets his movements coordinated into the orderly and precise movements of his elders—so the youth suddenly born into a confusion of ideas and appeals and traditions responds in the most chaotic way to this new spiritual world, and only gradually learns to find his way about in it, and get his thoughts and feelings into some kind of order.

Fortunate the young man who does not make his entrance into too wide a world. And upon the width and depth of that new world will depend very much whether his temperament is to be radical or conservative, adventurous or conventional. For it is one of the surprising things about Youth that it can so easily be the most conservative of all ages. Why do we suppose that youth is always radical? At no age are social proprieties more strictly observed, and Church, State, law, and order, more rigorously defended. But I like to think that youth is conservative only when its spiritual force has been spent too early, or when the new world it enters into is found, for some reason, to be rather narrow and shallow. It is so often the urgent world of pleasure that first catches the eye of youth; its flood of life is drawn off in that direction; the boy may fritter away his precious birthright in pure lightness of heart and animal spirits. And it is only too true

that this type of youth is transitory. Pleasure contrives to burn itself out very quickly, and youth finds itself left prematurely with
the ashes of middle age. But if, in some way, the flood of life is
checked in the direction of pleasure, then it bursts forth in
another—in the direction of ideals; then we say that the boy is
radical. Youth is always turbulent, but the momentous difference
is whether it shall be turbulent in passion or in enthusiasm. Nothing is so pathetic as the young man who spends his spiritual
force too early, so that when the world of ideals is presented to
him, his force being spent, he can only grasp at secondhand
ideals and moldy formulas.

This is the great divergence which sets youth not only against
old age, but against youth itself: the undying spirit of youth that
seems to be fed by an unquenchable fire, that does not burn
itself out but seems to grow steadier and steadier as life goes
on, against the fragile, quickly tarnished type that passes relentlessly into middle age. At twenty-five I find myself full of the
wildest radicalisms, and look with dismay at my childhood
friends who are already settled down, have achieved babies
and responsibilities, and have somehow got ten years beyond
me in a day. And this divergence shows itself in a thousand different ways. It may be a temptation to a world of pleasure, it
may be a sheltering from the stimulus of ideas, or even a sluggish temperament, that separates traditional and adventurous
youth, but fundamentally it is a question of how youth takes the
world. And here I find that I can no longer drag the traditional
youth along with me in this paper. There are many of him, I
know, but I do not like him, and I know nothing about him. Let
us rather look at the way radical youth grows into and meets the
world.

From the state of "the little child, to whom the sky is a roof of
blue, the world a screen of opaque and disconnected facts, the
home a thing eternal, and 'being good' just simple obedience to
unquestioned authority," one steps suddenly into that "vast
world of adult perception, pierced deep by flaring search-lights
of partial understanding."

The child has an utter sense of security; childhood is unconscious even that it is alive. It has neither fears nor anxieties because it is incorrigibly poetical. It idealizes everything that it
touches. It is unfair, perhaps, to blame parents and teachers, as

we sometimes do in youth, for consciously biasing our child minds in a falsely idealistic direction; for the child will infallibly idealize even his poorest of experiences. His broken glimpses and anticipations of his own future show him everything that is orderly, happy, and beautifully fit. He sees his grown-up life as old age, itself a sort of reversed childhood, sees its youth. The passing of childhood into youth is, therefore, like suddenly being turned from the cozy comfort of a warm fireside to shift for one's self in the world. Life becomes in a moment a process of seeking and searching. It appears as a series of blind alleys, all equally and magnificently alluring, all equally real and possible. Youth's thirst for experience is simply that it wants to be everything, do everything, and have everything that is presented to its imagination. Youth has suddenly become conscious of life. It has eaten of the tree of the knowledge of good and evil.

As the world breaks in on a boy with its crashing thunder, he has a feeling of expansion, of sudden wisdom and sudden care. The atoms of things seem to be distintegrating around him. Then come the tearings and the grindings and the wrenchings, and in that conflict the radical or the poet is made. If the youth takes the struggle easily, or if his guardian angels have arranged things so that there is no struggle, then he becomes of that conservative stripe that we have renounced above But if he takes it hard—if his struggles are not only with outward material conditions, but also with inner spiritual ones—then he is likely to achieve that gift of the gods, perpetual youth. The great paradox is that it is the sleek and easy who are prematurely and permanently old. Struggle brings youth rather than old age.

In this struggle, thus beset with problems and crises, all calling for immediate solution, youth battles its way into a sort of rationalization. Out of its inchoateness emerges a sort of order; the disturbing currents of impulse are gradually resolved into a character. But it is essential that that resolution be a natural and not a forced one. I always have a suspicion of boys who talk of "planning their lives." I feel that they have won a precocious maturity in some illegitimate way. For the most of us youth is so imperious that those who can escape the hurly-burly and make a sudden leap into the prudent, quiet waters of life seem to have missed youth altogether. And I do not mean here the hurly-burly of passion so much as of ideals. It seems so much better, as well as more natural, to expose one's self to the full fury of the spiritual elements, keeping only one purpose in view—to be strong and sincere—than to pick one's way cautiously along.

The old saying is the truest philosophy of youth: "Seek ye first the Kingdom of God, and all these things shall be added unto you." How impossible for a youth who is really young to plan his life consciously! This process that one sometimes sees of cautiously becoming acquainted with various ideas and systems, and then choosing deliberately those that will be best adapted to a concerted plan, is almost uncanny. This confidence in one's immunity to ideas that would tend to disarrange the harmony of the scheme is mystifying and irritating. Youth talks of "getting" or ",accepting" ideas! But youth does not get ideas—ideas get him! He may try to keep himself in a state of spiritual health, but that is the only immunity he can rely upon. He cannot really tell what idea or appeal is going to seize upon him next and make off with him.

We speak as if falling in love were a unique phase in the life of youth. It is rather the pattern and symbol of a youth's whole life. This sudden, irresistible seizure of enthusiasm that he cannot explain, that he does not want to explain, what is it but the aspect of all his experience? The youth sees a pretty face, reads a noble book, hears a stirring appeal for a cause, meets a charming friend, gets fired with the concept of science, or of social progress, becomes attracted to a profession—the emotion that fixes his enthusiasm and lets out a flood of emotion in that direction, and lifts him into another world, is the same in every case. Youth glories in the sudden servitude, is content to let the new master lead wherever he will; and is as surprised as any one at the momentous and startling results. Youth is vulnerable at every point. Prudence is really a hateful thing in youth. A prudent youth is prematurely old. It is infinitely better, I repeat, for a boy to start ahead in life in a spirit of moral adventure, trusting for sustenance to what he may find by the wayside, than to lay in laboriously, before starting, a stock of principles for life, and burden himself so heavily for the journey that he dare not, and indeed cannot, leave his pack unguarded by the roadside to survey the fair prospects on either hand. Youth at its best is this constant susceptibility to the new, this constant eagerness to try experiments.

It is here that youth's quarrel with the elder generation comes in. There is no scorn so fierce as that of youth for the inertia of older men. The lack of adjustment to the ideas of youth's elders and betters, one of the permanent tragedies of life, is certainly the most sensational aspect of youth. That the inertia of the older people is wisdom, and not impotence, is a theory that you will never induce youth to believe for an instant. The stupidity and cruelties of their management of the world fill youth with an intolerant rage. In every contact with its elders, youth finds them saying, in the words of Kipling:

We shall not acknowledge that old stars fade and alien planets arise,
That the sere bush buds or the desert blooms or the ancient well-head dries,
Or any new compass wherewith new men adventure 'neath new skies.

Youth sees with almost passionate despair its plans and dreams and enthusiasms, that it knows so well to be right and true and noble, brushed calmly aside, not because of any sincere searching into their practicability, but because of the timidity and laziness of the old, who sit in the saddle and ride mankind. And nothing torments youth so much as to have this inertia justified on the ground of experience. For youth thinks that it sees through this sophism of "experience." It sees in it an all-inclusive attempt to give the world character, and excuse the older generation for the mistakes and failures which it has made. What is this experience, youth asks, but a slow accretion of inhibitions, a learning, at its best, not to do again something which ought not to have been done in the first place?

Old men cherish a fond delusion that there is something mystically valuable in mere quantity of experience. Now the fact is, of course, that it is the young people who have all the really valuable experience. It is they who have constantly to face new situations, to react constantly to new aspects of life, who are getting the whole beauty and terror and cruelty of the world in its fresh and undiluted purity. It is only the interpretation of this first collision with life that is worth anything. For the weakness of experience is that it so soon gets stereotyped; without new situations and crises it becomes so conventional as to be practically unconscious. Very few people get any really new experience after they are twenty-five, unless there is a real change of environment. Most older men live only in the experience of their youthful years.

If we get few ideas after we are twenty-five, we get few ideals after we are twenty. A man's spiritual fabric is woven by that time, and his "experience," if he keeps true to himself, consists simply in broadening and enriching it, but not in adding to it in arithmetical proportion as the years roll on, in the way that the wise teachers of youth would have us believe.

But few men remain quite true to themselves. As their youthful ideals come into contact with the harshnesses of life, the brightest succumb and go to the wall. And the hardy ones that survive contain all that is vital in the future experience of the man—so that the ideas of older men seem often the curious parodies or even burlesques of what must have been the cleaner and more potent ideas of their youth. Older people seem often to be resting on their oars, drifting on the spiritual current that youth has set going in life, or "coasting" on the momentum that the strong push of youth has given them.

There is no great gulf between youth and middle age, as there is between childhood and youth. Adults are little more than grown-up children. This is what makes their arrogance so insulting—the assumption that they have acquired any impartiality or objectivity of outlook, and have any better standards for judging life. Their ideas are wrong, and grow progressively more wrong as they become older. Youth, therefore, has no right to be humble. The ideals it forms will be the highest it will ever have, the insight the clearest, the ideas the most stimulating. The best that it can hope to do is to conserve those resources, and keep its flame of imagination and daring bright.

Therefore, it is perhaps unfair to say that the older generation rules the world. Youth rules the world, but only when it is no longer young. It is a tarnished, travestied youth that is in the saddle in the person of middle age. Old age lives in the delusion that it has improved and rationalized its youthful ideas by experience and stored-up wisdom, when all it has done is to damage them more or less—usually more. And the tragedy of life is that the world is run by these damaged ideals. That is why our ideas are always a generation behind our actual social conditions. Press, pulpit, and bar teem with the radicalisms of thirty years ago. The dead hand of opinions formed in their college days clutches our leaders and directs their activities in this new and strangely altered physical and spiritual environment. Hence grievous friction, maladjustment, social war. And the faster society moves, the more terrific is the divergence between what is actually going on and what public opinion thinks is actually going on. It is only the young who are actually contemporaneous; they interpret what they see freshly and without prejudice; their vision is always the truest, and their interpretation always the justest.

Youth does not simply repeat the errors and delusions of the past, as the elder generation with a tolerant cynicism likes to think; it is ever laying the foundations for the future. What it thinks so wildly now will be orthodox gospel thirty years hence. The ideas of the young are the living, the potential ideas; those of the old, the dying or the already dead. This is why it behooves youth to be not less radical, but even more radical, than it would naturally be. It must be not simply contemporaneous, but a generation ahead of the times, so that when it comes into control of the world, it will be precisely right and coincident with the conditions of the world as it finds them. If the youth of today could really achieve this miracle, they would have found the secret of "perpetual Youth."

II

In this conflict between youth and its elders, youth is the incarnation of reason pitted against the rigidity of tradition. Youth puts the remorseless questions to everything that is old and established—Why: What is this thing good for? And when it gets the mumbled, evasive answers of the defenders, it applies its own fresh, clean spirit of reason to institutions, customs, and ideas, and finding them stupid, inane, or poisonous, turns instinctively to overthrow them and build in their place the things with which its visions teem.

This constant return to purely logical activity with each generation keeps the world supplied with visionaries and reformers, that is to say, with saviors and leaders. New movements are born in young minds, and lack of experience enables youth eternally to recall civilization to sound bases. The passing generation smiles and cracks its weather-worn jokes about youthful effusions; but this new, ever-hopeful, ever-daring, ever-doing, youthful enthusiasm, ever returning to the logical bases of religion, ethics, politics, business, art, and social life—this is the salvation of the world.[1]

This was the youthful radicalism of Jesus, and his words sound across the ages "calling civilization ever back to sound bases." With him, youth eternally reproaches the ruling generation—"O ye of little faith?" There is so much to be done in the world; so much could be done if you would only dare! You seem to be doing so little to cure the waste and the muddle and the lethargy all around you. Don't you really care, or are you only fainthearted? If you do not care, it must be because you do not know; let us point out to you the shockingness of exploitation, and the crass waste of human personality all around you in this modern world. And if you are fainthearted, we will supply the needed daring and courage, and lead you straight to the attack.

These are the questions and challenges that the youth puts to his elders, and it is their shifty evasions and quibblings that confound and dishearten him. He becomes intolerant, and can see all classes in no other light than that of accomplices in a great crime. If they only knew! Swept along himself in an irrationality of energy, he does not see the small part that reason plays in the intricate social life, and only gradually does he come to view life as a "various and splendid disorder of forces," and exonerate weak human nature from some of its heavy responsibility. But this insight brings him to appreciate and almost to reverence the forces of science and conscious social progress that are grappling with that disorder, and seeking to tame it.

Youth is the leaven that keeps all these questioning, testing attitudes fermenting in the world. If it were not for this troublesome activity of youth, with its hatred of sophisms and glosses, its insistence on things as they are, society would die from sheer decay. It is the policy of the older generation as it gets adjusted to the world to hide away the unpleasant things where it can, or preserve a conspiracy of silence and an elaborate pretense that they do not exist. But meanwhile the sores go on festering just the same. Youth is the drastic antiseptic. It will not let its elders cry peace, where there is no peace. By its fierce sarcasms it keeps issues alive in the world until they are settled right. It drags skeletons from closets and insists that they be explained. No wonder the older generation fears and distrusts the younger. Youth is the avenging Nemesis on its trail. "It is young men who provided the logic, decision, and enthusiasm necessary to relieve society of the crushing burden that each generation seeks to roll upon the shoulders of the next."

Our elders are always optimistic in their views of the present, pessimistic in their views of the future; youth is pessimistic toward the present and gloriously hopeful for the future. And it is this hope which is the lever of progress—one might say, the only lever of progress. The lack of confidence which the ruling generation feels in the future leads to that distrust of machinery, or the use of means for ends, which is so characteristic of it today. Youth is disgusted with such sentimentality. It can never understand that curious paralysis which seizes upon the elders in the face of urgent social innovations; that refusal to make use of a perfectly definite program or administrative scheme which has worked elsewhere. Youth concludes that its elders discountenance the machinery, the means, because they do not really believe in the end, and adds another count to the indictment.

Youth's attitude is really the scientific attitude. Do not be afraid to make experiments, it says. You cannot tell how anything will work until you have tried it. Suppose "science confined its interests to those things that have been tried and tested in the world," how far should we get? It is possible that your experiments may produce by accident a social explosion, but we do not give up chemistry because occasionally a wrong mixture of chemicals blows up a scientist in a laboratory, or medical research because an investigator contracts the disease he is fighting. The whole philosophy of youth is summed up in the word Dare! Take chances and you will attain! The world has nothing to lose but its chains—and its own soul to gain!

III

I have dwelt too long on the conflicts of youth. For it has also its still places, where it becomes introspective and thinks about its destiny and the meaning of its life. In our artificial civilization many young people at twenty-five are still on the threshold of activity. As one looks back, then, over eight or nine years, one sees a panorama of seemingly formidable length. So many crises, so many startling surprises, so many vivid joys and harrowing humiliations and disappointments, that one feels startling old; one wonders if one will ever feel so old again. And in a sense, youth at twenty-five is older than it will ever be again. For if time is simply a succession of incidents in our memory, we seem to have an eternity behind us. Middle-aged people feel no such appalling stretch of time behind them. The years fade out one by one; often the pressure of life leaves nothing of reality or value but the present moment. They enjoy almost a new babyhood, while youth has constantly with it in all its vividness and multifariousness that specious wealth of abrupt changes, climaxes, and disillusions that have crowded the short space of its life.

We often envy the sunny noon of the thirties and forties. These elders of ours change so little that they seem to enjoy an endless summer of immortality. They are so placid, so robust, so solidly placed in life, seemingly so much further from dissolution than we. Youth seems curiously fragile. Perhaps it is because all beauty has something of the precarious and fleeting about it. A beautiful girl seems too delicate and fine to weather a long life; she must be burning away too fast. This wistfulness and haunting pathos of life is very real to youth. It feels the rush of time past it. Only youth can sing of the passing glory of life, and then only in its full tide. The older people's lament for the vanished days of youth may be orthodox, but it rings hollow. For our greatest fears are those of presentiment, and youth is haunted not only by the feeling of past change, but by the presentiment of future change.

Middle age has passed the waters; it has become static and placid. Its wistfulness for youth is unreal, and a forced sentimentality. In the same breath that it cries for its youth it mocks at youth's preoccupation with the thought of death. The lugubrious harmonies of young poets are a favorite joke. The feeling of the precariousness of life gives to the young man an intimate sense of its preciousness; nothing shocks him quite so much as that it should be ruthlessly and instantly snatched away. Middle age has acclimated itself to the earth, has settled down familiarly in it, and is easily befooled into thinking that it will live here forever, just as, when we are settled comfortably in a house, we cannot conceive ourselves as ever being dislodged. But youth takes a long time to get acclimated. It has seen so many mysteries and dangers about it, that the presence of the Greatest Mystery and the Greatest Danger must be the most portentous of things to it. It is this sense of the preciousness of his life, perhaps, that makes the boy so impatient of discipline. Youth can never think of itself as anything but master of things. Its visions are a curious blend of devotion and egotism. Its enthusiasm for a noble cause is apt to be all mixed up with a picture of itself leading the cohorts to victory. The youth never sees himself as a soldier in the ranks, but as the leader, bringing in some long-awaited change by a brilliant *coup d'état*, or writing and speaking words of fire that win a million hearts at a stroke. And he fights shy of discipline in smaller matters. He does not submit willingly to a course of work that is not immediately appealing, even for the sake of the glorious final achievement. Fortunate it is for the young man, perhaps, that there are so many organs of coercion all ready in the world for him—economic need, tradition, and subtle influence of family ambition—to seize him and nail him fast to some profession or trade or activity, before he is aware, or has time to protest or draw back!

It is another paradox of youth that, with all its fine enthusiasm, it should accomplish so little. But this seeming aimlessness of purpose is the natural result of that deadly fear of having one's wings clipped by discipline. Infinitely finer, it seems to youth, is it to soar freely in the air, than to run on a track along the ground! And perhaps youth is right. In his intellectual life, the young man's scorn for the pedantic and conventional amounts almost to an obsession. It is only the men of imagination and inspiration that he will follow at all.

But most of these professors, these lawyers, these preachers—what has been their training and education, he says, but a gradual losing of the grip of life, a slow withdrawing into an ideal world of phrases and concepts and artificial attitudes? Their thought seems like the endless spinning out of a spider's web, or like the camel living upon the fat of his own hump. The youth fears this sophistication of thoughts as he would fear losing his soul. And this seeming perversity toward discipline is often simply his refusal to let a system submerge his own real and direct reactions to his observation and experience.

And yet as he studies more and more, and acquires a richer material for thought, a familiarity with words, and a skill in handling them, he can see the insidious temptation that comes to thinking men to move all their spiritual baggage over into that fascinating unreal world. And he admires almost with reverence the men who have been able to break through the terrible crust, and have got their thinking into close touch with life again; or, best of all, those who have kept their thinking constantly checked up with life, and are occupied with interpreting what they see about them. Youth will never be able to see that this is not the only true and right business of thought.

It is the glory of the present age that in it one can be young. Our times give no check to the radical tendencies of youth. On the contrary, they give the directest stimulation. A muddle of a word and a wide outlook combine to inspire us to the bravest of radicalisms. Great issues have been born in the last century, and are now loose in the world. There is a radical philosophy that illuminates our environment, gives us terms in which to express what we see, and coordinates our otherwise aimless reactions.

In this country, it is true, where a certain modicum of free institutions, and a certain specious enfranchisement of the human spirit have been achieved, youth may be blinded and drugged into an acquiescence in conditions, and its enthusiasm may easily run into a glorification of the present. In the face of the more urgent ideals that are with us, it may be inspired by vague ideas of "liberty," or "the rights of man," and fancy it is truly radical when it is but living on the radicalisms of the past. Our political thought moves so slowly here that even our radicalism is traditional. We breathe in with the air about us the belief that we have attained perfection, and we do not examine things with our own eyes.

But more and more of the clear-sighted youth are coming to see the appalling array of things that still need to be done. The radical young man of today has no excuse for veering round to the conservative standpoint. Cynicism cannot touch him. For it is the beauty of the modern radical philosophy that the worse the world treats a man, the more it convinces him of the truth of his radical interpretation of it. Disillusion comes, not through hard blows, but by the insidious sappings of worldly success. And there never was a time when there were so many radical young people who cared little about that worldly success.

The secret of life is then that this fine youthful spirit should never be lost. Out of the turbulence of youth should come this fine precipitate—a sane, strong, aggressive spirit of daring and doing. It must be a flexible, growing spirit, with a hospitality to new ideas, and a keen insight into experience. To keep one's reactions warm and true is to have found the secret of perpetual youth, and perpetual youth is salvation.

1Bourne here refers to Earl Barnes, *Where Knowledge Fails* (1907).

THE EXCITEMENT OF FRIENDSHIP[1]

My friends, I can say with truth, since I have no other treasure, are my fortune. I really live only when I am with my friends. Those sufficient persons who can pass happily long periods of solitude communing with their own thoughts and nourishing their own souls fill me with a despairing admiration. Their gift of autostimulation argues a personal power which I shall never possess. Or else it argues, as I like to think in self-defense, a callousness of spirit, an insensitiveness to the outside influences which nourish and sustain the more susceptible mind. And those persons who can shut themselves up for long periods and work out their thoughts alone, constructing beautiful and orderly representations of their own spirits, are to me a continual mystery. I know this is the way that things are accomplished, that "monotony and solitude" are necessary for him who would produce creative thought. Yet, knowing well this truth, I shun them both. I am a battery that needs to be often recharged. I require the excitement of friendship; I must have the constant stimulation of friends. I do not spark automatically, but must have other minds to rub up against, and strike from them by friction the spark that will kindle my thoughts.

When I walk, I must have a friend to talk to, or I shall not even think. I am not of those who, like Stevenson, believe that walking should be a kind of vegetative stupor, where the sun and air merely fill one with a diffused sense of well-being and exclude definite thought. The wind should rather blow through the dusty regions of the mind, and the sun light up its dark corners, and thinking and talking should be saner and higher and more joyful than within doors. But one must have a friend along to open the windows. Neither can I sympathize with those persons who carry on long chains of reasoning while they are traveling or walking. When alone, my thinking is as desultory as the scenery of the roadside, and when with a friend, it is apt to be as full of romantic surprises as a walk through a woodland glen. Good talk is like good scenery—continuous yet constantly varying, and full of the charm of novelty and surprise. How unnatural it is to think except when one is forced to do it, is discovered when one attempts to analyze one's thoughts when alone. He is a rare genius who finds something beyond the mere visual images that float through his mind—either the reflection of what he is actually seeing, or the pictorial representations of what he has been doing or what he wants or intends to do in the near or far future. We should be shocked to confess to ourselves how little control we have over our own minds; we shall be lucky if we can believe that we guide them. Thinking, then, was given us for use in emergencies, and no man can be justly blamed if he reserves it for emergencies. He can be blamed, however, if he does not expose himself to those crises which will call it forth. Now a friend is such an emergency, perhaps the most exciting stimulus to thinking that one can find, and if one wants to live beyond the vegetative stupor, one must surround one's self with friends. I shall call my friends, then, all those influences which warm me and start running again all my currents of thought and imagination. The persons, causes, and books that unlock the prison of my intellectual torpor I can justly call my friends, for I find that I feel toward them all the same eager joy and inexhaustible rush of welcome. Where they differ it shall be in degree and not in kind. The speaker whom I hear, the book that I read, the friend with whom I chat, the music that I play, even the blank paper before me, which subtly stirs me to cover it with sentences that unfold surprisingly and entice me to follow until I seem hopelessly lost from the trail—all these shall be my friends as long as I find myself responding to them, and no longer. They are all alike in being emergencies that call upon me for instant and definite response.

The difference between them lies in their response to me. My personal friends react upon me; the lecturers and books and music and pictures do not. These are not influenced by my feelings or by what I do. I can approach them cautiously or boldly, respond to them slowly or warmly, and they will not care. They have a definite quality, and do not change; if I respond differently to them at different times, I know that it is I and not they who have altered. The excitement of friendship does not lie with them. One feels this lack particularly in reading, which no amount of enthusiasm can make more than a feeble and spiritless performance. The more enthusiasm the reading inspires in one, the more one rebels at the passivity into which one is forced. I want to get somehow at grips with the book. I can feel the warmth of the personality behind it, but I cannot see the face as I can the face of a person, lighting and changing with the iridescent play of expression. It is better with music; one can get at grips with one's piano, and feel the resistance and the response of the music one plays. One gets the sense of aiding somehow in its creation, the lack of which feeling is the fatal weakness of reading, though itself the easiest and most universal of friendly stimulations. One comes from much reading with a sense of depression and a vague feeling of something unsatisfied; from friends or music one comes with a high sense of elation and of the brimming adequacy of life.

If one could only retain those moments! What a tragedy it is that our periods of stimulated thinking should be so difficult of reproduction; that there is no intellectual shorthand to take down the keen thoughts, the trains of argument, the pregnant thoughts, which spring so spontaneously to the mind at such times! What a tragedy that one must wait till the fire has died out, till the light has faded away, to transcribe the dull flickering remembrances of those golden hours when thought and feeling seemed to have melted together, and one said and thought what seemed truest and finest and most worthy of one's immortalizing! This is what constitutes the hopeless labor of writing—that one must struggle constantly to warm again the thoughts that are cold or have been utterly consumed. What was thought in the hours of stimulation must be written in the hours of solitude, when the mind is apt to be cold and gray, and when one is fortunate to find on the hearth of the memory even a few scattered embers lying about. The blood runs sluggish as one sits down to write. What worry and striving it takes to get it running freely again! What labor to reproduce even a semblance of what seemed to come so genially and naturally in the contact and intercourse of friendship!

One of the curious superstitions of friendship is that we somehow choose our friends. To the connoisseur in friendship no idea could be more amazing and incredible. Our friends are chosen for us by some hidden law of sympathy, and not by our conscious wills. All we know is that in our reactions to people we are attracted to some and are indifferent to others. And the ground of this mutual interest seems based on no discoverable principles of similarity of temperament or character. We have no time, when meeting a new person, to study him or her carefully; our reactions are swift and immediate. Our minds are made up instantly—"friend or non-friend." By some subtle intuitions, we know and have measured at their first words all the possibilities which their friendship has in store for us. We get the full quality of their personality at the first shock of meeting, and no future intimacy changes that quality.

If I am to like a man, I like him at once; further acquaintance can only broaden and deepen that liking and understanding. If I am destined to respond, I respond at once or never. If I do not respond he continues to be to me as if I had never met him; he does not exist in my world. His thoughts, feelings, and interests I can but dimly conceive of; if I do think of him it is only as a member of some general class. My imaginative sympathy can embrace him only as a type. If his interests are in some way forced upon my attention, and my imagination is compelled to encompass him as an individual, I find his ideas and interests appearing like pale, shadowy things, dim ghosts of the real world that my friends and I live in.

Association with such aliens—and how much of our life is necessarily spent in their company—is a torture far worse than being actually disliked. Probably they do not dislike us, but there is this strange gulf which cuts us off from their possible sympathy. A pall seems to hang over our spirits; our souls are dumb. It is a struggle and an effort to affect them at all. And though we may know that this depressing weight which seems to press on us in our intercourse with them has no existence, yet this realization does not cure our helplessness. We do not exist for them any more than they exist for us. They are depressants, not stimulators, as are our friends. Our words sound singularly futile and halfhearted as they pass our lips. Our thoughts turn to ashes as we utter them. In the grip of this predestined antipathy we can do nothing but submit and pass on.

But in how different a light do we see our friends! They are no types, but each a unique, exhaustless personality, with his own absorbing little cosmos of interests round him. And those interests are real and vital, and in some way interwoven with one's own cosmos. Our friends are those whose worlds overlap our own, like concentric circles. If there is too much overlapping, however, there is monotony and a mutual cancellation. It is, perhaps, a question of attitude as much as anything. Our friends must be pointed in the same direction in which we are going, and the truest friendship and delight is when we can watch each other's attitude toward life grow increasingly similar; or if not similar, at least so sympathetic as to be mutually complementary and sustaining.

The wholesale expatriation from our world of all who do not overlap us or look at life in a similar direction is so fatal to success that we cannot afford to let these subtle forces of friendship and apathy have full sway with our souls. To be at the mercy of whatever preordained relations may have been set up between us and the people we meet is to make us incapable of negotiating business in a world where one must be all things to all men. From an early age, therefore, we work, instinctively or consciously, to get our reactions under control, so as to direct them in the way most profitable to us. By a slow and imperceptible accretion of impersonality over the erratic tendencies of personal response and feeling, we acquire the professional manner, which opens the world wide to us. We become human patterns of the profession into which we have fallen, and are no longer individual personalities. Men find no difficulty in becoming soon so professionalized that their manner to their children at home is almost identical with that to their clients in the office. Such an extinction of the personality is a costly price to pay for worldly success. One has integrated one's character, perhaps, but at the cost of the zest and verve and peril of true friendship.

To those of us, then, who have not been tempted by success, or who have been so fortunate as to escape it, friendship is a lifelong adventure. We do not integrate ourselves, and we have as many sides to our character as we have friends to show them to. Quite unconsciously I find myself witty with one friend, large and magnanimous with another, petulant and stingy with another, wise and grave with another, and utterly frivolous with another. I watch with surprise the sudden and startling changes in myself as I pass from the influence of one friend to the influence of some one else. But my character with each particular friend is constant. I find myself, whenever I meet him, with much the same emotional and mental tone. If we talk, there is with each one some definite subject upon which we always speak and which remains perennially fresh and new. If I am so unfortunate as to stray accidentally from one of these well-worn fields into another, I am instantly reminded of the fact by the strangeness and chill of the atmosphere. We are happy only on our familiar levels, but on these we feel that we could go on exhaustless forever, without a pang of ennui. And this inexhaustibility of talk is the truest evidence of good friendship. Friends do not, on the other hand, always talk of what is nearest to them. Friendship requires that there be an open channel between friends, but it does not demand that that channel be the deepest in our nature. It may be of the shallowest kind and yet the friendship be of the truest. For all the different traits of our nature must get their airing through friends, the trivial as well as the significant. We let ourselves out piecemeal it seems, so that only with a host of varied friends can we express ourselves to the fullest. Each friend calls out some particular trait in us, and it requires the whole chorus fitly to teach us what we are. This is the imperative need of friendship. A man with few friends is only half-developed; there are whole sides of his nature which are locked up and have never been expressed. He cannot unlock them himself, he cannot even discover them; friends alone can stimulate him and open them. Such a man is in prison; his soul is in penal solitude. A man must get friends as he would get food and drink for nourishment and sustenance. And he must keep them, as he would keep health and wealth, as the infallible safeguards against misery and poverty of spirit.

If it seems selfish to insist so urgently upon one's need for friends, if it should be asked what we are giving our friends in return for all their spiritual fortification and nourishment, the defense would have to be, that we give back to them in ample measure what they give to us. If we are their friends, we are stimulating them as they are stimulating us. They will find that they talk with unusual brilliancy when they are with us. And we may find that we have, perhaps, merely listened to them. Yet through that curious bond of sympathy which has made us friends, we have done as much for them as if we had exerted ourselves in the most active way. The only duty of friendship is that we and our friends should live at our highest and best when together. Having achieved that, we have fulfilled the law.

A good friendship, strange to say, has little place for mutual consolations and ministrations. Friendship breathes a more rugged air. In sorrow the silent pressure of the hand speaks the emotions, and lesser griefs and misfortunes are ignored or glossed over. The fatal facility of women's friendships, their copious outpourings of grief to each other, their sharing of wounds and sufferings, their half-pleased interest in misfortune—all this seems of a lesser order than the robust friendships of men, who console each other in a much more subtle, even intuitive way—by a constant pervading sympathy which is felt rather than expressed. For the true atmosphere of friendship is a sunny one. Griefs and disappointments do not thrive in its clear, healthy light. When they do appear, they take on a new color. The silver lining appears, and we see even our own personal mistakes and chagrins as whimsical adventures. It is almost impossible seriously to believe in one's bad luck or failures or incapacity while one is talking with a friend. One achieves a sort of transfiguration of personality in those moments. In the midst of the high and genial flow of intimate talk, a pang may seize one at the thought of the next day's drudgery, when life will be lived alone again: but nothing can dispel the ease and fullness with which it is being lived at the moment. It is, indeed, a heavy care that will not dissolve into misty air at the magic touch of a friend's voice.

Fine as friendship is, there is nothing irrevocable about it. The bonds of friendship are not iron bonds, proof against the strongest of strains and the heaviest of assaults. A man by becoming your friend has not committed himself to all the demands which you may be pleased to make upon him. Foolish people like to test the bonds of their friendships, pulling upon them to see how much strain they will stand. When they snap, it is as if friendship itself had been proved unworthy. But the truth is that good friendships are fragile things and require as much care in handling as any other fragile and precious things. For friendship is an adventure and a romance, and in adventures it is the unexpected that happens. It is the zest of peril that makes the excitement of friendship. All that is unpleasant and unfavorable is foreign to its atmosphere; there is no place in friendship for harsh criticism or faultfinding. We will "take less" from a friend than we will from one who is indifferent to us.

Good friendship is lived on a warm, impetuous plane; the long-suffering kind of friendship is a feeble and, at best, a half-hearted affair. It is friendship in the valley and not on the breezy heights. For the secret of friendship is a mutual admiration, and it is the realization or suspicion that that admiration is lessening on one side or the other that swiftly breaks the charm. Now, this admiration must have in it no taint of adulation, which will wreck a friendship as soon as suspicion will. But it must consist of the conviction, subtly expressed in every tone of the voice, that each has found in the other friend a rare spirit, compounded of light and intelligence and charm. And there must be no open expression of this feeling, but only the silent flattery, soft, and almost imperceptible.

And in the best of friendships this feeling is equal on both sides. Too great a superiority in our friend disturbs the balance, and casts a sort of artificial light on the talk and intercourse. We want to believe that we are fairly equal to our friends in power and capacity, and that if they excel us in one trait, we have some counterbalancing quality in another direction. It is the reverse side of this shield that gives point to the diabolical insight of the Frenchman who remarked that we were never heartbroken by the misfortunes of our best friends. If we have had misfortunes, it is not wholly unjust and unfortunate that our friends should suffer too. Only their misfortunes must not be worse than ours. For the equilibrium is then destroyed, and our serious alarm and sympathy aroused. Similarly we rejoice in the good fortune of our friends, always provided that it be not too dazzling or too undeserved.

It is these aspects of friendship, which cannot be sneered away by the reproach of jealousy, that make friendship a precarious and adventurous thing. But it is precious in proportion to its precariousness, and its littlenesses are but the symptoms of how much friends care, and how sensitive they are to all the secret bonds and influences that unite them.

Since our friends have all become woven into our very selves, to part from friends is to lose, in a measure, one's self. He is a brave and hardy soul who can retain his personality after his friends are gone. And since each friend is the key which unlocks an aspect of one's own personality, to lose a friend is to cut away a part of one's self. I may make another friend to replace the loss, but the unique quality of the first friend can never be brought back. He leaves a wound which heals only gradually. To have him go away is as bad as having him pass to another world. The letter is so miserable a travesty on the personal presence, a thin ghost of the thought of the once-present friend. It is as satisfactory as a whiff of stale tobacco smoke to the lover of smoking.

Those persons and things, then, that inspire us to do our best, that make us live at our best, when we are in their presence, that call forth from us our latent and unsuspected personality, that nourish and support that personality—those are our friends. The reflection of their glow makes bright the darker and quieter hours when they are not with us. They are a true part of our widest self; we should hardly have a self without them. Their world is one where chagrin and failure do not enter. Like the sundial, they "only mark the shining hours."

1.In 1910 Bourne had already written an essay on a similar theme in the *Columbia Monthly:* "Some Aspects of Good Talk."

THE DODGING OF PRESSURES

For a truly sincere life one talent is needed—the ability to steer clear of the forces that would warp and conventionalize and harden the personality and its own free choices and bents.[1] All the kingdoms of this world lie waiting to claim the allegiance of the youth who enters on the career of life, and sentinels and guards stand ready to fetter and enslave him the moment he steps unwarily over the wall out of the free open road of his own individuality. And unless he dodges them and keeps straight on his path, dusty and barren though it may be, he will find himself chained a prisoner for life, and little by little his own soul will rot out of him and vanish. The wise men of the past have often preached the duty of this open road, they have summoned youth to self-reliance, but they have not paid sufficient heed to the enemies that would impede his progress. They have been too intent on encouraging him to be independent and lead his own life, to point out to him the direction from which the subtle influences that might control him would come. As a result, young men have too often believed that they were hewing out a career for themselves when they were really simply offering themselves up to some institutional Moloch to be destroyed, or, at the best, passively allowing the career or profession they had adopted to mold and carve them. Instead of working out their own destiny, they were actually allowing an alien destiny to work them out. Youth enters the big world of acting and thinking, a huge bundle of susceptibilities, keenly alive and plastic, and so eager to achieve and perform that it will accept almost the first opportunity that comes to it. Now, each youth has his own unique personality and interweaving web of tendencies and inclinations, such as no other person has ever had before. It is essential that these trends and abilities be so stimulated by experience that they shall be developed to their highest capacity. And they can usually be depended upon, if freedom and opportunity are given, to grow of themselves upward toward the sun and air. If a youth does not develop, it is usually because his nature has been blocked and thwarted by the social pressures to which every one of us is subjected, and which only a few have the strength or the wisdom to resist. These pressures come often in the guise of good fortune, and the youth meets them halfway, goes with them gladly, and lets them crush him. He will do it all, too, with so easy a conscience, for is not this meeting the world and making it one's own? It is meeting the world, but it is too often only to have the world make the youth its own.

Our spiritual guides and leaders, then, have been too positive, too heartening, if such a thing be possible. They have either not seen the dangers that lurked in the path, or they have not cared to discourage and depress us by pointing them out. Many of our modern guides, in their panegyrics on success, even glorify as aids on the journey these very dangers themselves, and urge the youth to rely upon them, when he should have been warned not to gaze at all on the dazzling lure. The youth is urged to imitate men who are themselves victims of the very influences that he should dodge, and doctrines and habits are pressed upon him which he should ceaselessly question and never once make his own unless he is sure that they fit him. He will have need to be ever alert to the dangers, and, in early youth at least, would better think more of dodging them than of attaining the goal to which his elders tempt him. Their best service to him would be to warn him against themselves and their influence, rather than to encourage him to become like them.

The dangers that I speak of are the influences and inducements which come to youth from family, business, church, society, state, to compromise with himself and become in more or less degree conformed to their pattern and type. "Be like us!" they all cry, "It is easiest and safest thus! We guarantee you popularity and fortune at so small a price—only the price of your best self!" Thus they seduce him insidiously rather than openly attack him. They throw their silky chains over him and draw him in. Or they press gently but ceaselessly upon him, rubbing away his original roughness, polishing him down, molding him relentlessly, and yet with how kindly and solicitous a touch, to their shape and manner. As he feels their caressing pressure against him in the darkness, small wonder is it that he mistakes it for the warm touch of friends and guides. They are friends and guides who always end, however, by being masters and tyrants. They force him to perpetuate old errors, to keep alive dying customs, to breathe new life into vicious prejudices, to take his stand against the saving new. They kill his soul, and then use the carcass as a barricade against the advancing hosts of light. They train him to protect and conserve their own outworn institutions when he should be the first, by reason of his clear insight and freedom from crusted prejudice, to attack them.

The youth's only salvation lies, then, in dodging these pressures. It is not his business to make his own way in life so much as it is to prevent some one else from making it for him. His business is to keep the way clear, and the sky open above his head. Then he will grow and be nurtured according to his needs and his inner nature. He must fight constantly to keep from his head those coverings that institutions and persons in the guise of making him warm and safe throw over his body. If young people would spend half the time in warding away the unfavorable influences that they now spend in conscientiously planning what they are going to be, they would achieve success and maintain their individuality. It seems, curiously enough, that one can live one's true life and guarantee one's individuality best in this indirect way—not by projecting one's self out upon the world aggressively, but by keeping the track clear along which one's true life may run. A sane, well-rounded, original life is attained not so much by taking thought for it as by the dodging of pressures that would limit and warp its natural growth. The youth must travel the straight road serenely, confident that "his own will come to him." All he must strive for is to recognize his own when it does come, and to absorb and assimilate it. His imagination must be large enough to envisage himself and his own needs. This wisdom, however, comes to too many of us only after we are hopelessly compromised, after we are encrusted over so deeply that, even if we try to break away, our struggles are at the expense of our growth. The first duty of self-conscious youth is to dodge the pressures, his second to survey the world eagerly to see what is "his own." If he goes boldly ahead at first to seek his own, without first making provision for silencing the voices that whisper continually at his side, "Conform!"—he will soon find himself on alien ground, and, if not a prisoner, a naturalized citizen before he has time to think.

Nor is this a mere invitation to whimsicality and eccentricity. These epithets, in our daily life, are somewhat loosely used for all sorts of behavior ranging from nonconformity to pure freakishness. If we really had more original, unspoiled people in the world, we should not use these terms so frequently. If we really had more people who were satisfying their healthy desires, and living the life that their whole inner conscience told them was best, we should not find eccentric or queer the self-sustaining men and women who live without regard to prejudice. And all real whimsicality is a result rather of the thwarting of individuality than of letting it run riot. It is when persons of strong personality are subjected to pressures heavier than they can bear that we get real outbursts of eccentricity. For something unnatural has occurred, a spontaneous flow and progress has been checked. Your eccentric man par excellence is your perfectly conventional man, who never offends in the slightest way by any original action or thought. For he has yielded to every variety of pressure that has been brought to bear upon him, and his original nature has been completely obscured. The pressures have been, however, uniform on every side, so that they have seemingly canceled each other. But this equilibrium simply conceals the forces that have crushed him. The conventional person is, therefore, not the most natural but the most unnatural of persons. His harmlessness is a proof of his tremendous eccentricity. He has been rubbed down smooth on all sides like a rock until he has dropped noiselessly into his place in society. But at what a cost does he obtain this peace! At the cost of depersonalizing himself, and sacrificing his very nature, which, as in every normal person, is precious and worthy of permanence and growth. This treason to one's self is perhaps the greatest mistake of youth, the one unpardonable sin. It is worse than sowing one's wild oats, for they are reaped and justice is done; or casting one's bread upon the waters, for that returneth after many days. But this sin is the throwing away in willfulness or carelessness the priceless jewel of selfhood, and with no return, either of recompense or punishment.

How early and insidious is the pressure upon us to conform to some type whose fitness we have not examined, but which we are forced to take strictly on authority! On the children in the family what a petty tyranny of ideas and manners is imposed! Under the guise of being brought up, how many habits of doubtful value we learned, how many moral opinions of doubtful significance we absorbed, how many strange biases that harass and perplex us in our later life we have fastened upon our minds, how many natural and beautiful tendencies we were forced to suppress! The tyranny of manners, of conventional politeness, of puritanical taboos, of superstitious religion, were all imposed upon us for no reason that our elders could devise, but simply that they in turn had had them imposed upon them. Much of our early education was as automatic and unconscious as the handing down of the immemorial traditions in a primitive savage tribe. Now, I am far from saying that this household tradition of manners and morals is not an excellent thing for us to acquire. Many of the habits are so useful that it is a wise provision that we should obtain them as naturally as the air we breathe. And it is a pressure that we could not, at that age, avoid, even if we would. But this childhood influence is a sample of true pressure, for it is both unconscious and irresistible. Were we to infringe any of the rules laid down for us, the whole displeasure of the family descended upon our heads; they seemed to vie with each other in expressing their disapproval of our conduct. So, simply to retain our self-respect, we were forced into their pattern of doing things, and for no other reason than that it was their pattern.

This early pressure, however, was mild in comparison with what we experienced as we grew older. We found then that more and more of our actions came insensibly but in some way or other before this court of appeal. We could choose our friends, for instance, only with reservations. If we consorted with little boys who were not clean, or who came from the less reputable portions of the town, we were made to feel the vague family disapproval, perhaps not outspoken, but as an undercurrent to their attitude. And usually we did not need flagrantly to offend to be taught the need of judicious selection, for we were sensitive to the feeling that we knew those around us would entertain, and so avoided the objectionable people from a diffused feeling that they were not "nice." When we grew old enough to move in the youthful social world, we felt this circle of tyranny suddenly widen. It was our "set" now that dictated our choices. The family pressure had been rather subtle and uneasy; this was bold and direct. Here were the most arbitrary selections and disqualifications, girls and boys being banned for no imaginable reason except that they were slightly out of the ordinary, and our little world circumscribed by a rigid public opinion which punished nonconformity by expulsion. If we tried to dodge this pressure and assert our own privileges of making lovers and friends, we were soon delivered an ultimatum, and if we refused to obey, we were speedily cast out into utter darkness, where, strange to say, we lacked even the approbation of the banned. Sometimes we were not allowed to choose our partners to whom we paid our momentary devotions, sometimes we were not allowed to give them up. The price we paid for free participation in the parties and dances and love affairs of this little social world of youth was an almost military obedience to the general feeling of propriety and suitability of our relationships with others, and to the general will of those in whose circle we went. There was apt to be a rather severe code of propriety, which bore especially upon the girls. Many frank and natural actions and expressions of opinion were thus inhibited, from no real feeling of self-respect, but from the vague, uncomfortable feeling that somebody would not approve. This price for society was one that we were all willing to pay, but it was a bad training. Our own natural likings and dislikings got blunted; we ceased to seek out our own kind of people and enjoy them and ourselves in our own way, but we "went with" the people that our companions thought we ought to "go with," and we played the games and behaved generally as they thought we ought to do.

The family rather corroborated this pressure than attempted to fortify us in our own individuality. For their honor seemed to be involved in what we did, and if all our walk in life was well pleasing to those around us, they were well pleased with us. And all through life, as long at least as we were protected under the sheltering wing of the family, its members constituted a sort of supreme court over all our relations in life. In resisting the other pressures that were brought to bear on us, we rarely found that we had the family's undivided support. They loved, like all social groups, a smoothly running person, and as soon as they found us doing unconventional things or having unusual friends they were vaguely uneasy, as if they were harboring in their midst some unpredictable animal who would draw upon them the disapproving glances of the society around them. The family philosophy has a horror for the "queer." The table board is too often a place where the eccentricities of the world get thoroughly aired. The dread of deviation from accepted standards is impressed upon us from our youth up. The threat which always brought us to terms was—"If you do this, you will be considered queer!" There was very little fight left in us after that.

But the family has other formidable weapons for bringing us to terms. It knows us through and through as none of our friends and enemies know us. It sees us in undress, when all our outward decorations of spirit and shams and pretenses are thrown off, and it is not deceived by the apologies and excuses that pass muster in the world at large and even to our own conscience. We can conceal nothing from it; it knows all our weakest spots and vulnerable feelings. It does not hesitate to take shameless advantage of that knowledge. Its most powerful weapon is ridicule. It can adopt no subtler method, for we in our turn know all its own vulnerabilities. And where the world at large is generally too polite to employ ridicule upon us, but works with gentler methods of approbation and coldness, our family associates feel no such compunction. Knowing us as they do, they are able to make that ridicule tell. We may have longings for freedom and individuality, but it is a terrible dilemma that faces us. Most men would rather be slaves than butts; they would rather be coralled with the herd than endure its taunts at their independence.

Besides the pressure on a youth or girl to think the way the family does, there is often the pressure brought upon them to sacrifice themselves for its benefit. I do not mean to deprecate that perfectly natural and proper desire to make some return for the care and kindness that have been lavished upon them. But the family insistence often goes much further than this. It demands not only that its young people shall recompense it for what it has done for them, but that they do it in the kind of work and vocation that shall seem proper to it. How often, when the youth or girl is on the point of choosing a congenial occupation or profession, does the family council step in and, with the utmost apparent goodwill in the world, dictate differently! And too often the motives are really policy or ambition, or, at best, sheer prejudice. If the youth be not persuaded, then he must bear the brunt of lonely toil without the sympathy or support of those most dear to him. Far harder is the lot of the young woman. For there is still so much prejudice against a girl's performing useful work in society, apart from her God-given duty of getting married, that her initiative is crushed at the very beginning. The need of cultivating some particular talent or interest, even if she has not to earn her living, seems to be seldom felt. Yet women, with their narrower life, have a greater need of sane and vigorous spiritual habits than do men. It is imperative that a girl be prevented from growing up into a useless, fleshly, and trivial woman, of the type one sees so much of nowadays. Even if a girl does marry, a few intellectual interests and gifts and tastes will not be found to detract from her charm or usefulness. The world never needed so much as it does today women of large hearts and large minds, whose home and sphere are capable of embracing something beyond the four corners of their kitchen. And the world can get such women only by allowing them the initiative and opportunity to acquire varied interests and qualities while they are young.

The family often forges sentimental bonds to keep it living together long after the motive and desire have departed. There is no group so uncongenial as an uncongenial family. The constant rubbing together accentuates all the divergencies and misunderstandings. Yet sometimes a family whose members are hopelessly mismated will cling together through sheer inertia or through a conscientious feeling of duty. And duty to too many of us is simply a stimulus to that curious love for futile suffering that form some of the darker qualities of the puritan soul. Family duty may not only warp and mutilate many a life that would bloom healthily outside in another environment, but it may actually mean the pauperization of the weaker members. The claims of members of the family upon each other are often overwhelming, and still more often quite fictitious in their justice. Yet that old feeling of the indissolubility of the family will often allow the weak, who might, if forced to shift for themselves, become strong, to suck the lifeblood from the stronger members. Cooperation, when it is free and spontaneous and on a basis of congeniality, is the foundation of all social life and progress, but forced cohesion can do little good. The average family is about as well mated as any similar group would be, picked out at random from society. And this means, where the superstition of indissolubility is still effective, that the members share not only all the benefits, but also all each others' shortcomings and irritations. Family life thus not only presses upon its youth to conform to its customs and habits and to the opinions of the little social world in which it lives, but also drags its youth down with its claims, and warps it by its tension of uncongeniality, checks its spontaneity by its lack of appreciation, and injures its soul by friction and misunderstanding.

This family pressure upon youth is serious, and potent for much good and evil in his later life. It is necessary that he understand how to analyze it without passion or prejudice, and find out just how he can dodge the unfavorable pressure without injury to the love that is borne him or the love that he bears to the others. But let him not believe that his love is best shown by submission. It is best shown by a resolute determination and assertion of his own individuality. Only he must know, without the cavil of a doubt, what that individuality is; he must have a real imaginative anticipation of its potentialities. Only with this intuition will he know where to dodge and how to dodge. It is true that the modern generation seems to be changing all this. Family cohesion and authority no longer mean what they did even twenty years ago. The youth of today are willful, selfish, heartless, in their rebellion. They are changing the system blindly and blunderingly. They feel the pressure, and without stopping to ask questions or analyze the situation, they burst the doors and flee away. Their seeming initiative is more animal spirits than anything else. They have exploded the myth that their elders have any superhuman wisdom of experience to share with them, or any incontrovertible philosophy of life with which to guide their wandering footsteps. But it must be admitted that most have failed so far to find a wisdom and a philosophy to take its place. They have too often thrown away the benefits of family influence on account of mere trivialities of misunderstanding. They have not waited for the real warpings of initiative, the real pressure of prejudice, but have kicked up their heels at the first breath of authority. They have not so much dodged the pressure as fled it altogether. Instead of being intent on brushing away the annoying obstacles that interfered with the free growth of their own worthier selves, they have mistaken the means for the end, and have merely brushed off the interferences, without first having any consciousness of that worthier self. Now of course this is no solution. It is only as they substitute for the authority that they throw off a definite authority of their own, crystallized out of their own ideals and purposes, that they will gain or help others to gain. For lack of a vision the people perish. For lack of a vision of their own personalities, and the fresh, free, aggressive, forward, fearless, radical life that we all ought to lead, and could lead if we only had the imagination for it, the youth of today will cast off the narrowing confining fetters of authority only to wander without any light at all. This is not to say that this aimless wandering is not better than the prison-house, but it is to say that the emancipation of the spirit is insufficient without a new means of spiritual livelihood to take its place. The youth of today cannot rest on their liberation; they must see their freedom as simply the setting free of forces within themselves for a cleaner, sincerer life, and for radical work in society. The road is cut out before them by pioneers; they have but to let themselves grow out in that direction.

I have painted the family pressures in this somewhat lurid hue because they are patterns of the other attacks which are made upon the youth as he meets the world. The family is a little microcosm, a sheltered group where youth feels all those currents of influence that sway men in their social life. Some of them are exaggerated, some perverted, but they are most of them there in that little world. It is no new discovery that in family life one can find heaven or one can find hell. The only pressure that is practically absent in the family is the economic pressure, by which I mean the inducements, and even necessities, that a youth is under of conforming to codes or customs and changing his ideals and ideas, when he comes to earn his livelihood. This pressure affects him as soon as he looks for an opening, as he calls it, in which to make his living. At that time all this talk of natural talents or bents or interests begin to sound faraway and ideal. He soon finds that these things have no commercial value in themselves and will go but a short way toward providing him with his living. The majority of us "go to work" as soon as our short "education" is completed, if not before, and we go not by choice, but wherever opportunity is given. Hence the ridiculous misfits, the apathy, the restlessness, and discontent. The world of young people around us seems too largely to be one where both men and girls are engaged in work in which they have no interest, and for which they have no aptitude. They are mournfully fettered to their work; all they can seem to do is to make the best of it, and snatch out of the free moments what pleasure and exhilaration they can. They have little hope for a change. There is too much of a scramble for places in this busy, crowded world, to make a change anything but hazardous. It is true that restlessness often forces a change, but it is rarely for the better, or in the line of any natural choice or interest. One leaves one's job, but then one takes thankfully the first job that presents itself; the last state may be worse than the first. By this economic pressure most of us are sidetracked, turned off from our natural path, and fastened irrevocably to some work that we could only acquire an interest in at the expense of our souls.

It is a pressure, too, that cannot easily be dodged. We can frankly recognize our defeat, plunge boldly at the work and make it a part of ourselves; this course of action, which most of us adopt, is really, however, simply an unconditional surrender. We can drift along apathetically, without interest either in our work or our own personalities; this course is even more disastrous. Or we can quietly wait until we have found the vocation that guarantees the success of our personalities; this course is an ideal that is possible to very few. And yet, did we but know it, a little thought at the beginning would often have prevented the misfit, and a little boldness when one has discovered the misfit would often have secured the favorable change. That self-recognition, which is the only basis for a genuine spiritual success in life, is the thing that too many of us lack. The apathy comes from a real ignorance of what our true work is. Then we are twice a slave—a prey to our circumstance and a prey to our ignorance.

Like all discoveries, what one's work is can be found only by experiment. But this can often be an imaginative experiment. One can take an "inventory of one's personality," and discover one's interests, and the kind of activity one feels at home with or takes joy in. Yet it is true that there are many qualities which cannot be discovered by the imagination, which need the fairy touch of actual use to develop them. There is no royal road to this success. Here the obstacles are usually too thick to be dodged. We do not often enough recognize the incredible stupidity of our civilization where so much of the work is uninteresting and monotonous. That we should consider it a sort of triumph that a man like Mr. John Burroughs should have been able to live his life as he chose, travel along his own highroad, and develop himself in his own natural direction, is a curious reflection on our ideals of success and on the incompleteness of our civilization. Such a man has triumphed, however, because he has known what to dodge. He has not been crushed by the social opinion of his little world, or lured by specious success, or fettered by his "job," or hoodwinked by prejudice. He has kept his spirit clear and pure straight through life. It would be well for modern youth if it could let an ideal like this color their lives, and permeate all their thoughts and ambitions. It would be well if they could keep before them such an ideal as a pillar of fire by day and a cloud by night.

If we cannot dodge this economic pressure, at least we can face it. If we are situated so that we have no choice in regard to our work, we may still resist the influences which its uncongeniality would bring to bear upon us. This is not done by forcing an interest in it, or liking for it. If the work is socially wasteful or useless or even pernicious, as so much business and industrial work today is, it is our bounden duty not to be interested in it or to like it. We should not be playing our right place in society if we enjoyed such a prostitution of energies. One of the most insidious of the economic pressures is this awaking the interest of youth in useless and wasteful work, work that takes away energy from production to dissipate in barter and speculation and all the thousand ways that men have discovered of causing money to flow from one pocket to another without the transference of any fair equivalent of real wealth. We can dodge these pressures not by immolating ourselves, but by letting the routine work lie very lightly on our soul. We can understand clearly the nature and effects of this useless work we are doing, and keep it from either alluring or smothering us. We can cultivate a disinterested aloofness toward it, and keep from breathing its poisonous atmosphere. The extra hours we can fill with real interests, and make them glow with an intensity that will make our life almost as rich as if we were wholly given over to a real lifework. We can thus live in two worlds, one of which is the more precious because it is one of freedom from very real oppression. And that oppression will seem light because it has the reverse shield of liberty. If we do drudgery, it must be our care to see that it does not stifle us. The one thing needful in all our work and play is that we should always be on top, that our true personality should always be in control. Our life must not be passive, running simply by the momentum furnished by another; it must have the motive power within itself; although it gets the fuel from the stimulation of the world about it, the steam and power must be manufactured within itself.

These counsels of aloofness from drudgery suggest the possibilities of avoiding the economic pressures where they are too heavy completely to dodge, and where the work is an irrevocable misfit. But the pressures of success are even more deadly than those of routine. How early is one affected by that first pressure of worldly opinion which says that lack of success in business or a profession is disgraceful! The one devil of our modern world is failure, and many are the charms used by the medicine men to ward him away. If we lived in a state of society where virtue was its own reward, where our actions were au- tomatically measured and our rewards duly proportioned to our efforts, a lack of success would be a real indication of weakness and flaw, or, at best, ill-preparation. But where business success is largely dependent on the possession of capital, a lucky risk, the ability to intimidate or deceive, and where professional suc- cess is so often dependent upon self-assertion or some irrele- vant but pleasing trait of personality, failure means nothing more than bad luck, or, at most, inability to please those clients to whom one has made one's appeal. To dodge this pressure of fancied failure and humiliation is to have gone a long way to- ward guaranteeing one's real success. We are justified in adopt- ing a pharisaical attitude towards success—"Lord, I thank thee that I have not succeeded as other men have!" To have judged one's self by the inner standards of truth to one's own personal- ity, to count the consciousness of having done well, regardless of the corroboration of a public, as success, is to have avoided this most discouraging of pressures.

It is even doubtful whether business or professional success, except in the domain of science and art, can be attained without a certain betrayal of soul. The betrayal may have been small, but at some point one has been compressed, one has yielded to alien forces and conformed to what the heart did not give as- sent to. It may be that one has kept silent when one should have spoken, that one has feigned interests and enthusiasms, or done work that one knew was idle and useless, in order to achieve some goal; but always that goal has been reached not spontaneously but under a foreign pressure. More often than not the fortunate one has not felt the direct pressure, has not been quite conscious of the sacrifice, but only vaguely uneasy and aware that all was not right within him, and has won his peace only by drugging his uneasiness with visions of the final triumph. The pressure is always upon him to keep silent and conform. He must not only adopt all the outward forms and ceremonies, as in the family and social life, but he must also adopt the traditional ideals.

The novice soon finds that he is expected to defend the citadel, even against his own heresies. The lawyer who finds anomalies in the law, injustice in the courts, is not encouraged to publish abroad his facts, or make proposals for reform. The student who finds antiquated method, erroneous hypotheses in his subject, is not expected to use his knowledge and his genius to remodel the study. The minister who comes upon new and living interpretations for his old creeds is not encouraged to speak forth the truth that is in him. Nor is the businessman who finds corrupt practices in his business encouraged to give the secrets away. There is a constant social pressure on these "reformers" to leave things alone.

And this does not arise from any corrupt connivance with the wrong, or from any sympathy with the evildoers. The cry rises equally from the corrupt and the holy, from the men who are responsible for the abuses and those who are innocent, from those who know of them and those who do not. It is simply the instinctive reaction of the herd against anything that savors of the unusual; it is the tendency of every social group simply to resist change. This alarm at innovation is universal, from college presidents to Catholic peasants, in fashionable club or sewing circle or political party. On the radical there is immediately brought, without examination, without reason or excuse, the whole pressure of the organization to stultify his vision and force him back into the required grooves. The methods employed are many: a warning is issued against him as being unsound and unsafe; his motive is to make trouble, or revenge himself on the directors for some slight; finally he is solemnly pilloried as an "enemy of the people." Excellent reasons are discovered for his suppression. Effective working of an organization requires cooperation, but also subordination; in the interests of efficiency, therefore, individual opinion cannot be allowed full sway. The reputation of the organization before the world depends on its presenting a harmonious and united front; internal disagreements and criticisms tend to destroy the respect of the public. Smoothness of working is imperative; a certain individual liberty must, therefore, be sacrificed for the success of the organization. And if these plausible excuses fail, there is always the appeal to authority and to tried and tested experience. Now all these reasons are simply apologies brought up after the fact to justify the first instinctive reaction. What they all mean is this, and only this: He would unsettle things; away with him!

In olden times, they had sterner ways of enforcing these pressures. But although the stake and dungeon have disappeared, the spirit of conservatism does not seem to have changed very much. Educated men still defend the hoariest abuses, still stand sponsor for utterly antiquated laws and ideals. That is why the youth of this generation has to be so suspicious of those who seem to speak authoritatively. He knows not whom he can trust, for few there are who speak from their own inner conviction. Most of our leaders and molders of public opinion speak simply as puppets pulled by the string of the conservative bigotry of their class or group. It is well that the youth of today should know this, for the knowledge will go far toward steeling him against that most insidious form of pressure that comes from the intellectual and spiritual prestige of successful and honored men. When youth sees that a large part of their success has been simply their succumbing to social pressure, and that their honor is based largely on the fact that they do not annoy vested interests with proposals or agitations for betterment, he will seek to discover new standards of success, and find his prophets and guides among the less fortunate, perhaps, but among those who have retained their real integrity. This numbing palsy of conservative assent which steals over so many brilliant and sincere young men as they are subjected to the influence of prestige and authority in their profession is the most dangerous disease that threatens youth. It can be resisted only by constant criticism and candid vigilance. "Prove all things: hold fast to that which is good," should be the motto of the intellectual life. Only by testing and comparing all the ideals that are presented to one is it possible to dodge that pressure of authority that would crush the soul's original enthusiasms and beliefs. Not doubt but convention is the real enemy of youth.

Yet these spiritual pressures are comparatively easy to dodge when one is once awake to them. It is the physical pressure that those in power are able to bring to bear upon the dissenter that constitutes the real problem. The weak man soon becomes convinced of his hardihood and audacity in supposing that his ideas could be more valuable than the running tradition, and recants his heresies. But those who stick stiff-neckedly out are soon crushed. When the youth is settled in life, has trained for his profession and burned his bridges behind him, it means a great deal to combat authority. For those in power can make use of the economic pressure to force him to conformity. It is the shame of our universities that they are giving constant illustrations of this use of arbitrary power, directed usually against non-conformity in social and political opinion. Recent examples show the length to which even these supposedly enlightened institutions are willing to go to prevent social heresy in their midst. Often such harsh measures are not needed. A subtle appeal to a man's honor is effective. "While you are a member of a society," it is said, "it is your duty to think in harmony with its ideals and policies. If you no longer agree with those ideals, it is your duty to withdraw. You can fight honorably for your own ideas only from the outside." All that need be said about this doctrine, so fair and reasonable on the surface, is that it contains all the philosophic support that would perpetuate the evil of the world forever. For it means attacking vested evil from the weakest vantage point; it means willfully withdrawing to the greatest distance, shooting one's puny arrows at the citadel, and then expecting to capture it. It means also to deny any possibility of progress within the organization itself. For as soon as dissent from the common inertia developed, it would be automatically eliminated. It is a principle, of course, that plays directly into the hands of the conservators. It is an appeal to honor that is dishonorable. Let it seduce no man's sincerity!

The principal object of every organization, as every youth soon discovers who feels dissatisfaction with the policies of church, club, college, or party, is to remain true to type. Each is organized with a central vigilance committee, whose ostensible function is direction, but whose real business is to resist threatening change and keep matters as they are. The ideal is smoothness: every part of the machine is expected to run along in its well-oiled groove. Youths who have tried to introduce their new ideas into such organizations know the weight of this fearful resistance. It seems usually as if all the wisdom and experience of these elders had taught them only the excellence of doing nothing at all. Their favorite epithet for those who have individual opinions is "troublemakers," forgetting that men do not run the risk of the unpopularity and opprobrium that aggressiveness always causes, for the sheer love of making trouble. Through an instinct of self-preservation, such an organization always places loyalty above truth, the permanence of the organization above the permanence of its principles. Even in churches we are told that to alter one's opinion of a creed to which one has once given allegiance is basely to betray one's higher nature. These are the pressures that keep wavering men in the footpaths where they have once put their feet, and stunts their truer, growing selves. How many souls a false loyalty has blunted none can say; perhaps almost as many as false duty! In the dodging of these pressures many a man finds the real spiritual battle of his life. They are a challenge to all his courage and faith. Unless he understands their nature, his defeat will bring despair or cynicism. When the group is weak and he is strong, he may resist successfully, press back in his turn, actually create a public opinion that will support him, and transfuse it all with his new spirit and attitude. Fortunate, indeed, is he who can not only dodge these pressures but dissolve them! If he is weak and his efforts are useless, and the pressure threatens to crush him, he would better withdraw and let the organization go to its own diseased perdition. If he can remain within without sacrifice to his principles, this is well, for then he has a vantage ground for the enunciation of those principles. Eternal vigilance, however, is the price of his liberty.

The secret ambition of the group seems to be to turn out all its members as nearly alike as possible. It seeks to create a type to which all new adherents shall be molded. Each group, then, that we have relations with is ceaselessly working to mold us to its type and pattern. It is this marvelous unseen power that a group has of forming after its own image all that come under its influence, that conquers men. It has the two instincts of self-preservation and propagation strongly developed, and we tend unthinkingly to measure its value in terms of its success in the expression of those instincts. Rather should it be measured always in terms of its ability to create and stimulate varied individuality. This is the new ideal of social life. This is what makes it so imperative that young men of today should recognize and dodge the pressures that would thwart the assertion of this ideal. The aim of the group must be to cultivate personality, leaving open the road for each to follow his own. The bond of cohesion will be the common direction in which those roads point, but this is far from saying that all the travelers must be alike. It is enough that there be a common aim and a common ideal.

Societies are rarely content with this, however; they demand a close mechanical similarity, and a conformity to a reactionary and not a progressive type. If we would be resolute in turning our gaze toward the common aim, and dodging the pressure of the common pattern, our family, business, and social life would be filled with a new spirit. We can scarcely imagine the achievement and liberation that would result. Individuality would come to its own; it would no longer be suspect. Youth would no longer be fettered and bound, but would come to its own as the leaven and even leader of life. Men would worship progress as they now worship stagnation; their ideal in working together would be a living effectiveness instead of a mechanical efficiency.

This gospel is no call to ease and comfort. It is rather one of peril. The youth of this generation will not be so lightly seduced, or go so innocently into the bonds of conservatism and convention, under the impression that they are following the inspired road to success. Their consciences will be more delicate. They know now the dangers that confront them and the road they are called on to tread. It is not an easy road. It is beset with opportunities for real eccentricity, for selfishness, for willfulness, for mere bravado. It would be surprising, after the long premium that has been placed on the pattern, not to see a reaction in favor of sheer freakishness. Many of our modern radicals are examples of this reaction. Yet their method is so sound, their goal so clear and noble, their spirit so sincere, that they are true pioneers of the new individuality. Their raciness is but the raciness of all pioneers everywhere. And much of their irresponsibility is a result of that intolerable pressure against which they are revolting. They have dodged it, but it dogs them and concentrates itself sullenly behind them to punish them for their temerity. The scorn of the world hurts and hampers them. That ridicule which the family employed against deviation is employed in all large social movements against the innovators. Yet slowly and surely the new social ideal makes its way.

It is not a call to the surrendering of obligations, in family or business or profession, but it is a call to the criticism of obligations. Youth must distinguish carefully between the essential duties and the nonessential, between those which make for the realization of the best common ideals, and those which make merely for the maintenance of a dogma or unchallenged superstition. By resisting the pressures that could warp, do we really best serve society; by allowing our free personality to develop, do we contribute most to the common good. We must recognize that our real duty is always found running in the direction of our worthiest desires. No duty that runs roughshod over the personality can have a legitimate claim upon us. We serve by being as well as by doing. It is easy to distort this teaching into a counsel to unbridled selfishness. And that, of course, is the risk. But shall we not dare to take the risk? It may be also that in our care to dodge the pressures, we may lose all the inestimable influences of good that come along mixed in with the hurtful. But shall we not take the risk? Our judgments can only grow by exercise; we can only learn by constantly discriminating. Self-recognition is necessary to know one's road, but, knowing the road, the price of the mistakes and perils is worth paying. The following of that road will be all the discipline one needs. Discipline does not mean being molded by outside forces, but sticking to one's road against the forces that would deflect or bury the soul. People speak of finding one's niche in the world. Society, as we have seen, is one vast conspiracy for carving one into the kind of a statue it likes, and then placing it in the most convenient niche it has. But for us, not the niche but the open road, with the spirit always traveling, always criticizing, always learning, always escaping the pressures that threaten its integrity. With its own fresh power it will keep strong and true to the journey's end.

[1] One might think that this essay was written under the influence of Emerson's "Self-Reliance." Compare:

The objection to conforming to usages that have become dead to you is that it scatters your force. It loses your time and blurs the impression of your character. If you maintain a dead church, contribute to a dead Bible-society, vote with a great party either for the government or against it, spread your table like base housekeepers—under all these screens I have difficulty to detect the precise man you are: and of course so much force is withdrawn from your proper life. But do your work, and I shall know you. Do your work, and you shall reinforce yourself. A man must consider what a blind-man's-buff is this game of conformity.

It is clear, however, that Bourne's arguments derive from his own experience rather than from a contemplation of intellectual history and tradition. With respect to Bourne's own family, compare John A Moreau: *Randolph Bourne—Legend and Reality* (1966). Also compare John Dewey: "Self-Realization as the Moral Ideal," *Philosophical Review,* II, November, 1893.

THE LIFE OF IRONY

I could never, until recently, divest myself of the haunting feeling that being ironical had something to do with the entering of the iron into one's soul. I thought I knew what irony was, and I admired it immensely. I could not believe that there was something metallic and bitter about it. Yet this sinister connotation of a clanging, rasping meanness of spirit, which I am sure it has still in many people's minds, clung about it, until one happy day my dictionary told me that the iron had never entered into the soul at all, but the soul into the iron (St. Jerome had read the psalm wrong), and that irony was Greek, with all the free, happy play of the Greek spirit about it, letting in fresh air and light into others' minds and our own. It was to the Greek an incomparable method of intercourse, the rub of mind against mind by the simple use of simulated ignorance and the adoption, without committing one's self, of another's point of view. Not until I read the Socrates of Plato did I fully appreciate that this irony—this pleasant challenging of the world, this insistent judging of experience, this sense of vivid contrasts and incongruities, of comic juxtapositions, of flaring brilliances, and no less heartbreaking impossibilities, of all the little parts of one's world being constantly set off against each other, and made intelligible only by being translated into and defined in each others' terms—that this was a life, and a life of beauty, that one might suddenly discover one's self living all unawares. And if one could judge one's own feeble reflection, it was a life that had no room for iron within its soul.

We should speak not of the Socratic method but of the Socratic life. For irony is a life rather than a method. A life cannot be taken off and put on again at will; a method can. To be sure, some people talk of life exactly as if it were some portable commodity, or some exchangeable garment. We must live, they cry, as if we were about to begin. And perhaps they are. Only some of us would rather die than live that puny life that they can adopt and cover themselves with. Irony is too rich and precious a thing to be capable of such transmission. The ironist is born and not made. This critical attitude towards life, this delicious sense of contrasts that we call irony, is not a pose or an amusement. It is something that colors every idea and every feeling of the man who is so happy as to be endowed with it.

Most people will tell you, I suppose, that the religious conviction of salvation is the only permanently satisfying coloring of life. In the splendid ironists, however, one sees a sweeter, more flexible and human principle of life, adequate, without the buttress of supernatural belief, to nourish and fortify the spirit. In the classic ironist of all time, irony shows an inherent nobility, a nobility that all ages have compared favorably with the Christian ideal. Lacking the spur of religious emotion, the sweetness of irony may be more difficult to maintain than the mood of belief. But may it not for that very reason be judged superior, for is it not written, He that endureth unto the end shall be saved?

It is not easy to explain the quality of that richest and most satisfying background of life. It lies, I think, in a vivid and intense feeling of aliveness which it gives. Experience comes to the ironist in little darts or spurts, with the added sense of contrast. Most men, I am afraid, see each bit of personal experience as a unit, strung more or less loosely on a string of other mildly related bits. But the man with the ironical temperament is forced constantly to compare and contrast his experience with what was, or what might be, or with what ought to be, and it is the shocks of these comparisons and contrasts that make up his inner life. He thinks he leads a richer life, because he feels not only the individual bits but the contrasts besides in all their various shadings and tints. To this sense of impingement of facts upon life is due a large part of this vividness of irony; and the rest is due to the alertness of the ironical mind. The ironist is always critically awake. He is always judging, and watching with inexhaustible interest, in order that he may judge. Now irony in its best sense is an exquisite sense of proportion, a sort of spiritual tact in judging the values and significances of experience. This sense of being spiritually alive which ceaseless criticism of the world we live in gives us, combined with the sense of power which free and untrammeled judging produces in us, is the background of irony. And it should be a means to the truest goodness.

Socrates made one mistake—knowledge is not goodness. But it is a step towards judging, and good judgment is the true goodness. For it is on judgment impelled by desire that we act. The clearer and cleaner our judgments then, the more definite and correlated our actions. And the great value of these judgments of irony is that they are not artificial but spring naturally

out of life. Irony, the science of comparative experience, compares things not with an established standard but with each
other, and the values that slowly emerge from the process, values that emerge from one's own vivid reactions, are constantly
revised, corrected, and refined by that same sense of contrast.
The ironic life is a life keenly alert, keenly sensitive, reacting
promptly with feelings of liking or dislike to each bit of experience, letting none of it pass without interpretation and assimilation, a life full and satisfying—indeed a rival of the religious life.

The life of irony has the virtues of the religious life without its
defects. It expresses the aggressive virtues without the quiescence of resignation. For the ironist has the courageous spirit,
the sympathetic heart and the understanding mind, and can
give them full play, unhampered by the searching introspection
of the religious mind that often weakens rather than ennobles
and fortifies. He is at one with the religious man in that he hates
apathy and stagnation, for they mean death. But he is superior
in that he attacks apathy of intellect and personality as well as
apathy of emotion. He has a great conviction of the significance
of all life, the lack of which conviction is the most saddening feature of the religious temperament. The religious man pretends
that every aspect of life has meaning for him, but in practice he
constantly minimizes the noisier and vivider elements. He is essentially an aristocrat in his interpretation of values, while the
ironist is incorrigibly a democrat. Religion gives a man an intimacy with a few selected and rarified virtues and moods, while
irony makes him a friend of the poor and lowly among spiritual
things. When the religious man is healing and helping, it is at
the expense of his spiritual comfort; he must tear himself away
from his companions and go out grimly and sacrificingly into the
struggle. The ironist, living his days among the humbler things,
feels no such severe call to service. And yet the ironist, since he
has no citadel of truth to defend, is really the more adventurous.
Life, not fixed in predestined formulas or measurable by fixed,
immutable standards, is fluid, rich and exciting. To the ironist it
is both discovery and creation. His courage seeks out the
obscure places of human personality, and his sympathy and
understanding create new interests and enthusiasms in the other
minds upon which they play. And these new interests in turn
react upon his own life, discovering unexpected vistas there,
and creating new insight into the world that he lives in. That

democratic, sympathetic outlook upon the feelings and thoughts and actions of men and women is the life of irony.

That life is expressed in the social intercourse of ourselves with others. The daily fabric of the life of irony is woven out of our critical communings with ourselves and the personalities of our friends, and the people with whom we come in contact. The ironist, by adopting another's point of view and making it his own in order to carry light and air into it, literally puts himself in the other man's place. Irony is thus the truest sympathy. It is no cheap way of ridiculing an opponent by putting on his clothes and making fun of him. The ironist has no opponent, but only a friend. And in his irony he is helping that friend to reveal himself. That half-seriousness, that solemn treatment of the trivial and trivial treatment of the solemn which is the pattern of the ironist's talk is but his way of exhibiting the unexpected contrasts and shadings that he sees to be requisite to the keenest understanding of the situation. The ironist borrows and exchanges and appropriates ideas and gives them a new setting in juxtaposition with others, but he never burlesques or caricatures or exaggerates them. If an idea is absurd, the slightest change of environment will show that absurdity. The mere transference of an idea to another's mouth will bring to light all its hidden meaninglessness. It needs no extraneous aid. If an idea is hollow, it will show itself cowering against the intellectual background of the ironist like the puny, shivering thing it is. If a point of view cannot bear being adopted by another person, if it is not hardy enough to be transplanted, it has little right to exist at all. This world is no hothouse for ideas and attitudes. Too many outworn ideas are skulking in dark retreats, sequestered from the light; every man has great sunless stretches in his soul where base prejudices lurk and flourish. On these the white light of irony is needed to play. And it delights the ironist to watch them shrivel and decay under that light. The little tabooed regions of well-bred people, the "things we never mention," the basic biases and assumptions that underlie the lives and thinking of every class and profession, our second-hand dogmas and phrases— all these live and thrive because they have never been transplanted, or heard from the lips of another. The dictum that "the only requisites for success are honesty and merit," which we applaud so frantically from the lips of the successful, becomes a ghastly irony in the mouth of an unemployed workingman. There would be a frightful mortality of points of view could we have a perfectly free exchange such as this. Irony is just this temporary borrowing and lending. Many of our cherished ideals would lose half their validity were they put bodily into the mouths of the less fortunate. But if irony destroys some ideals it builds up others. It tests ideals by their social validity, by their general inter-changeability among all sorts of people and the world, but if it leaves the foundations of many in a shaky condition and renders more simply provisional, those that it does leave standing are imperishably founded in the common democratic experience of all men.

To the ironist it seems that the irony is not in the speaking but in the things themselves. He is a poor ironist who would con-sciously distort, or attempt to make another's idea appear in any light except its own. Absurdity is an intrinsic quality of so many things that they only have to be touched to reveal it. The dead-liest way to annihilate the unoriginal and the insincere is to let it speak for itself. Irony is this letting things speak for themselves and hang themselves by their own rope. Only, it repeats the words after the speaker, and adjusts the rope. It is the com-manding touch of a comprehending personality that dissolves the seemingly tough husk of the idea. The ironical method might be compared to the acid that develops a photographic plate. It does not distort the image, but merely brings clearly to the light all that was implicit in the plate before. And if it brings the pic-ture to the light with values reversed, so does irony revel in a paradox, which is simply a photographic negative' of the truth, truth with the values reversed. But turn the negative ever so slightly so that the light falls upon it, and the perfect picture ap-pears in all its true values and beauty. Irony, we may say then, is the photography of the soul. The picture goes through certain changes in the hands of the ironist, but without these changes the truth would be simply a blank, unmeaning surface. The photograph is a synonym for deadly accuracy. Similarly the ironist insists always on seeing things as they are. He is a realist, whom the grim satisfaction of seeing the truth compen-sates for any sordidness that it may bring along with it. Things as they are, thrown against the background of things as they ought to be—this is the ironist's vision. I should like to feel that the vision of the religious man is not too often things as they are, thrown against the background of things as they ought not to be.

The ironist is the only man who makes any serious attempt to distinguish between fresh and second-hand experience. Our minds are so unfortunately arranged that all sorts of beliefs can be accepted and propagated quite independently of any rational or even experimental basis at all. Nature does not seem to care very much whether our ideas are true or not, as long as we get on through life safely enough. And it is surprising on what an enormous amount of error we can get along· comfortably. We cannot be wrong on every point or we should cease to live, but so long as we are empirically right in our habits, the truth or falsity of our ideas seems to have little effect upon our comfort. We are born into a world that is an inexhaustible store of ready-made ideas, stored up in tradition, in books, and in every medium of communication between our minds and others. All we have to do is to accept this predigested nourishment, and ask no questions. We could live a whole life without ever making a really individual response, without providing ourselves out of our own experience with any of the material that our mind works on. Many of us seem to be just this kind of spiritual parasites. We may learn and absorb and grow, up to a certain point. But eventually something captures us: we become encased in a suit of armor, and invulnerable to our own experience. We have lost the faculty of· being surprised. It is this encasing that the ironist fears, and it is the ironical method that he finds the best for preventing it. Irony keeps the waters in motion, so that the ice never has a chance to form. The cut-and-dried life is easy to form because it has no sense of contrast; everything comes to one on its own terms, vouching for itself, and is accepted or rejected on its own good looks, and not for its fitness and place in the scheme of things.

This is the courage and this the sympathy of irony. Have they not a beauty of their own comparable in excellence with the paler glow of religious virtue? And the understanding of the ironist although aggressive and challenging has its justification, too. For he is mad to understand the world, to get to the bottom of other personalities. That is the reason for his constant classification. The ironist is the most dogmatic of persons. To understand you he must grasp you firmly, or he must pin you down definitely; if he accidentally nails you fast to a dogma that you indignantly repudiate, you must blame his enthusiasm and not his method. Dogmatism is rarely popular, and the ironist of course suffers. It hurts people's eyes to see a strong light, and the pleasant mist-land of ideas is much more emotionally warming than the clear, sunny region of transmissible phrases. How the average person wriggles and squirms under these piercing attempts to corner his personality! "Tell me what you mean!" or "What do you see in it?" are the fatal questions that the ironist puts, and who shall censure him if he does display the least trace of malicious delight as he watches the half-formed baby ideas struggle towards the light, or scurry around frantically to find some decent costume in which they may appear in public?

The judgments of the ironist are often discounted as being too sweeping. But he has a valid defense. Lack of classification is annihilation of thought. Even the newest philosophy will admit that classification is a necessary evil. Concepts are indispensable—and yet each concept falsifies. The ironist must have as large a stock as possible, but he must have a stock. And even the unjust classification is marvelously effective. The ironist's name for his opponent is a challenge to him. The more sweeping it is, the more stimulus it gives him to repel the charge. He must explain just how he is unique and individual in his attitude. And in this explanation he reveals and discovers all that the ironist wishes to know about him. A handful of epithets is thus the ammunition of the ironist. He must call things by what seem to him to be their right names. In a sense, the ironist assumes the prisoner to be guilty until he proves himself innocent; but it is always in order that justice may be done, and that he may come to learn the prisoner's soul and all the wondrous things that are contained there.

It is this passion for comprehension that explains the ironist's apparently scandalous propensity to publicity. Nothing seems to him too sacred to touch, nothing too holy for him to become witty about. There are no doors locked to him, there is nothing that can make good any claim of resistance to scrutiny. His free and easy manner of including everything within the sweep of his vision is but his recognition, however, of the fact that nothing is really so serious as we think it is, and nothing quite so petty. The ironist will descend in a moment from a discussion of religion to a squabble over a card-game, and he will defend himself with the reflection that religion is after all a human thing and must be discussed in the light of everyday living, and that the card-game is an integral part of life, reveals the personalities of the players—and his own to himself—and being worthy of his interest is worthy of his enthusiasm. The ironist is apt to test things by their power to interest as much as by their nobility, and if he sees the incongruous and inflated in the lofty, so he sees the significant in the trivial and raises it from its low degree. Many a mighty impostor does he put down from his seat. The ironist is the great intellectual democrat, in whose presence and before whose law all ideas and attitudes stand equal. In his world there is no privileged caste, no aristocracy of sentiments to be reverenced, or segregated systems of interests to be tabooed. Nothing human is alien to the ironist; the whole world is thrown open naked to the play of his judgment.

In the eyes of its detractors, irony has all the vices of democracy. Its publicity seems mere vulgarity, its free hospitality seems to shock all ideas of moral worth. The ironist is but a scoffer, they say, with weapon leveled eternally at all that is good and true and sacred. The adoption of another's point of view seems little better than malicious dissimulation—the repetition of others' words, an elaborate mockery; the ironist's eager interest seems a mere impudence or a lack of finer instincts; his interest in the trivial, the last confession of a mean spirit; and his love of classifying, a proof of his poverty of imaginative resource. Irony, in other words, is thought to be synonymous with cynicism. But the ironist is no cynic. His is a kindly, not a sour interest in human motives. He wants to find out how the human machine runs, not to prove that it is a worthless, broken-down affair. He accepts it as it comes, and if he finds it curiously feeble and futile in places, blame not him but the nature of things. He finds enough rich compensation in the unexpected charm that he constantly finds himself eliciting. The ironist sees life steadily and sees it whole; the cynic only a distorted fragment.

If the ironist is not cynic, neither is he merely a dealer in satire, burlesque and ridicule. Irony may be the raw material, innocent in itself but capable of being put to evil uses. But it involves neither the malice of satire, nor the horse-play of burlesque, nor the stab of ridicule. Irony is infinitely finer and more delicate and impersonal. The satirist is always personal and concrete, but the ironist deals with general principles, and broad aspects of human nature. It cannot be too much emphasized that the function of the ironist is not to make fun of people, but to give their souls an airing. The ironist is a judge on the bench, giving men a public hearing. He is not an aggressive spirit who goes about seeking whom he may devour, or a spiritual lawyer who courts litigation, but the judge before whom file all the facts of his experience, the people he meets, the opinions he hears or reads, his own attitudes and prepossessions. If any are convicted they are self-convicted. The judge himself is passive, merciful, lenient. There is judgment, but no punishment. Or rather, the trial itself is the punishment. Now satire is all that irony is not. The satirist is the aggressive lawyer, fastening upon particular people and particular qualities. But irony is no more personal than the sun that sends his flaming darts into the world. The satirist is a purely practical man, with a business instinct, bent on the main chance and the definite object. He is often brutal, and always overbearing; the ironist never. Irony may wound from the very fineness and delicacy of its attack, but the wounding is incidental. The sole purpose of the satirist and the burlesquer is to wound, and they test their success by the deepness of the wound. But irony tests its own by the amount of generous light and air it has set flowing through an idea or a personality, and the broad significance it has revealed in neglected things.

If irony is not brutal, neither is it merely critical and destructive. The world has some reason, it is true, to complain against the rather supercilious judiciousness of the ironist. "Who are you to judge us?" it cries. The world does not like to feel the scrutinizing eyes of the ironist as he sits back in his chair; does not like to feel that the ironist is simply studying it and amusing himself at its expense. It is uneasy, and acts sometimes as if it did not have a perfectly clear conscience. To this uncomfortableness the ironist can retort—"What is it that you are afraid to have known about you?" If the judgment amuses him, so much the worse for the world. But if the idea of the ironist as judge implies that his attitude is wholly detached, wholly objective, it is an unfortunate metaphor. For he is as much part and parcel of the human show as any of the people he studies. The world is no stage, with the ironist as audience. His own personal reactions with the people about him form all the stuff of his thoughts and judgments. He has a personal interest in the case; his own personality is inextricably mingled in the stream of impressions that flows past him. If the ironist is destructive, it is his own world that he is destroying; if he is critical, it is his own world that he is criticizing. And his irony is his critique of life. This is the defense of the ironist against the charge that he has a purely aesthetic attitude towards life. Too often, perhaps, the sparkling clarity of his thought, the play of his humor, the easy sense of superiority and intellectual command that he carries off, make his irony appear as rather the aesthetic nourishment of his life than an active way of doing and being. His rather detached air makes him seem to view people as means, not ends in themselves. With his delight in the vivid and poignant he is prone to see picturesqueness in the sordid, and tolerate evils that he should condemn. For all his interest and activity, it is said that he does not really care. But this aesthetic taint to his irony is really only skin-deep. The ironist is ironical not because he does not care, but because he cares too much. He is feeling the profoundest depths of the world's great beating, laboring heart, and his playful attitude towards the grim and sordid is a necessary relief from the tension of too much caring. It is his salvation from unutterable despair. The terrible urgency of the reality of poverty and misery and exploitation would be too strong upon him. Only irony can give him a sense of proportion, and make his life fruitful and resolute. It can give him a temporary escape, a slight momentary reconciliation, a chance to draw a deep breath of resolve before plunging into the fight. It is not a palliative so much as a perspective. This is the only justification of the aesthetic attitude, that, if taken provisionally, it sweetens and fortifies. It is only deadly when adopted as absolute. The kind of aesthetic irony that Pater and Omar display is a paralyzed, half-seeing, half-caring reflection on life—a tame, domesticated irony with its wings cut, an irony that furnishes a justification and a command to inaction. It is the result not of exquisitely refined feelings, but of social anaesthesia. Their irony, cut off from the great world of men and women and boys and girls and their intricate interweavings and jostlings and incongruities, turns pale and sickly and numb. The ironist has no right to see beauty in things unless he really cares. The aesthetic sense is harmless only when it is both ironical and social.

Irony is thus a cure for both optimism and pessimism. Nothing is so revolting to the ironist as the smiling optimist, who testifies in his fatuous heedlessness to the desirability of this best of all possible worlds. But the ironist has always an incorrigible propensity to see the other side. The hopeless maladjustment of too many people to their world, of their bondage in the iron fetters of circumstance—all this is too glaring for the ironist's placidity. When he examines the beautiful picture, too often the best turns worst to him. But if optimism is impossible to the ironist, so is pessimism. The ironist may have a secret respect for the pessimist—he at least has felt the bitter tang of life, and has really cared—but he feels that the pessimist lacks. For if the optimist is blind, the pessimist is hypnotized. He is abnormally suggestive to evil. But clear-sighted irony sees that the world is too big and multifarious to be evil at heart. Something beautiful and joyous lurks even in the most hapless—a child's laugh in a dreary street, a smile on the face of a weary woman. It is this saving quality of irony that both optimist and pessimist miss. And since plain common sense tells us that things are never quite so bad or quite so good as they seem, the ironist carries conviction into the hearts of men in their best moments.

The ironist is a person who counts in the world. He has all sorts of unexpected effects on both the people he goes with and himself. His is an insistent personality; he is as troublesome as a missionary. And he is a missionary; for, his own purpose being a comprehension of his fellows' souls, he makes them conscious of their own souls. He is a hard man; he will take nothing on reputation; he will guarantee for himself the qualities of things. He will not accept the vouchers of the world that a man is wise, or clever, or sincere, behind the impenetrable veil of his face. He must probe until he elicits the evidence of personality, until he gets at the peculiar quality which distinguishes that individual soul. For the ironist is after all a connoisseur in personality, and if his conversation partakes too often of the character of cross-examination, it is only as a lover of the beautiful, a possessor of taste, that he inquires. He does not want to see people squirm, but he does want to see whether they are alive or not. If he pricks too hard, it is not from malice, but merely from error in his estimation of the toughness of their skins. What people are inside is the most interesting question in the world to the ironist. And in finding out he stirs them up. Many a petty doubting spirit does he challenge and bully into a sort of self-respect. And many a bag of wind does he puncture. But his most useful function is this of stimulating thought and action. The ironist forces his friends to move their rusty limbs and unhinge the creaking doors of their minds. The world needs more ironists. Shut up with one's own thoughts, one loses the glow of life that comes from frank exchange of ideas with many kinds of people. Too many minds are stuffy, dusty rooms into which the windows have never been opened—minds heavy with their own crotchets, cluttered up with untested theories and conflicting sympathies that have never got related in any social way. The ironist blows them all helter-skelter, sweeps away the dust, and sets everything in its proper place again. Your solid, self-respectful mind, the ironist confesses he can do little with; it is not of his world. He comes to freshen and tone up the stale minds. The ironist is the great purger and cleanser of life. Irony is a sort of spiritual massage, rubbing the souls of men. It may seem rough to some tender souls, but it does not sere or scar them. The strong arm of the ironist restores the circulation, and drives away anaemia.

On the ironist himself the effect of irony is even more invigorating. We can never really understand ourselves without at least a touch of irony. The interpretation of human nature without is a simple matter in comparison with the comprehension of that complex of elations and disgusts, inhibitions and curious irrational impulses that we call ourselves. It is not true that by examining ourselves and coming to an understanding of the way we behave we understand other people, but that by the contrasts and little revelations of our friends we learn to interpret ourselves. Introspection is no match for irony as a guide. The most illuminating experience that we can have is a sudden realization that had we been in the other person's place we should have acted precisely as he did. To the ironist this is no mere intellectual conviction that, after all, none of us are perfect, but a vivid emotional experience which has knit him with that other person in one moment in a bond of sympathy that could have been acquired in no other way. Those minds that lack the touch of irony are too little flexible, or too heavily buttressed with self-esteem to make this sudden change of attitudes. The ironist, one might almost say, gets his brotherhood intuitively, feels the sympathy and the oneness in truth before he thinks them. The ironist is the only man who really gets outside of himself. What he does for other people—that is, picking out a little piece of their souls and holding it up for their inspection—he does for himself. He gets thus an objective view of himself. The unhealthy indoor brooding of introspection is artificial and unproductive, because it has no perspective or contrast. But the ironist with his constant outdoor look sees his own foibles and humiliations in the light of those of other people. He acquires a more tolerant, half-amused, half-earnest attitude toward himself. His self-respect is nourished by the knowledge that whatever things discreditable and foolish and worthless he has done, he has seen them approximated by others, and yet his esteem is kept safely pruned down by the recurring evidence that nothing he has is unique. He is poised in life, ready to soar or to walk as the occasion demands. He is pivoted, susceptible to every stimulus, and yet chained so that he cannot be flung off into space by his own centrifugal force.

Irony has the same sweetening and freshening effect on one's own life that it has on the lives of those who come in contact with it. It gives one a command of one's resources. The ironist practices a perfect economy of material. For he must utilize his wealth constantly and over and over again in various shapes and shadings. He may be poor in actual material, but out of the contrast and arrangement of that slender store he is able, like a kaleidoscope, to make a multifarious variety of wonderful patterns. His current coin is, so to speak, kept bright by constant exchange. He is infinitely richer than your opulent but miserly minds that hoard up facts, and are impotent from the very plethora of their accumulations.

Irony is essential to any real honesty. For dishonesty is at bottom simply an attempt to save somebody's face. But the ironist does not want any faces saved, neither his own nor those of other people. To save faces is to sophisticate human nature, to falsify the facts, and miss a delicious contrast, an illuminating revelation of how people act. So the ironist is the only perfectly honest man. But he suffers for it by acquiring a reputation for impudence. His willingness to bear the consequences of his own acts, his quiet insistence that others shall bear consequences, seem like mere shamelessness, a lack of delicate feeling for "situations." But accustomed as he is to range freely and know no fear nor favor, he despises this reserve as a species of timidity or even hypocrisy. It is an irony itself that the one temperament that can be said really to appreciate human nature, in the sense of understanding it rightly, should be called impudent, and it is another that it should be denounced as monstrously egotistical. The ironical mind is the only truly modest mind, for its point of view is ever outside itself. If it calls attention to itself, it is only as another of those fascinating human creatures that pass ever by with their bewildering, alluring ways. If it talks about itself, it is only as a third person in whom all the talkers are supposed to be eagerly interested. In this sense the ironist has lost his egotism completely. He has rubbed out the line that separates his personality from the rest of the world.

The ironist must take people very seriously, to spend so much time over them. He must be both serious and sincere or he would not persist in his irony and expose himself to so much misunderstanding. And since it is not how people treat him, but simply how they act, that furnishes the basis for his appreciation, the ironist finds it easy to forgive. He has a way of letting the individual offense slide, in favor of a deeper principle. In the act of being grossly misrepresented, he can feel a pang of exasperated delight that people should be so dense; in the act of being taken in, he can feel the cleverness of it all. He becomes for the moment his enemy; and we can always forgive ourselves. Even while he is being insulted, or outraged or ignored, he can feel, "After all, this is what life is! This is the way we poor human creatures behave!" The ironist is thus in a sense vicarious human nature. Through that deep, anticipatory sympathy, he is kept clean from hate or scorn.

The ironist therefore has a valid defense against all the charges of brutality and triviality and irreverence, that the religious man is prone to bring against him. He can care more deeply about things because he can see so much more widely. And he can take life very seriously because it interests him so intensely. And he can feel its poignancy and its flux more keenly because he delivers himself up bravely to its swirling, many-hued current. The inner peace of religion seems gained only at the expense of the reality of living. A life such as the life of irony, lived fully and joyously, cannot be peaceful; it cannot even be happy, in the sense of calm content and satisfaction. But it can be better than either—it can be wise, and it can be fruitful. And it can be good, in a way that the life of inner peace cannot be. For the life of irony having no reserve and weaving itself out of the flux of experience rather than out of eternal values has the broad, honest sympathy of democracy, that is impossible to any temperament with the aristocratic taint. One advantage the religious life has is a salvation in another world to which it can withdraw. The life of irony has laid up few treasures in heaven, but many in this world. Having gained so much it has much to lose. But its glory is that it can lose nothing unless it lose all.

To shafts of fortune and blows of friends or enemies then, the ironist is almost impregnable. He knows how to parry each thrust and prepare for every emergency. Even if the arrows reach him, all the poison has been sucked out of them by his clear, resolute understanding of their significance. There is but one weak spot in his armor, but one disaster that he fears more almost than the loss of his life—a shrinkage of his environment, a running dry of experience. He fears to be cut off from friends and crowds and human faces and speech and books, for he demands to be ceaselessly fed. Like a modern city, he is totally dependent on a steady flow of supplies from the outside world, and will be in danger of starvation, if the lines of communication are interrupted. Without people and opinions for his mind to play on, his irony withers and faints. He has not the faculty of brooding; he cannot mine the depths of his own soul, and bring forth after labor mighty nuggets of thought. The flow and swirl of things is his compelling interest. His thoughts are reactions, immediate and vivid, to his daily experience. Some deep, unconscious brooding must go on, to produce that happy precision of judgment of his; but it is not voluntary. He is conscious only of the shifting light and play of life; his world is dynamic, energetic, changing. He lives in a world of relations, and he must have a whole store of things to be related. He has lost himself completely in this world he lives in. His ironical interpretation of the world is his life, and this world is his nourishment. Take away this environmental world and you have slain his soul. He is invulnerable to everything except that deprivation.

THE EXPERIMENTAL LIFE

It is good to be reasonable, but too much rationality puts the soul at odds with life. For rationality implies an almost superstitious reliance on logical proofs and logical motives, and it is logic that life mocks and contradicts at every turn. The most annoying people in the world are those who demand reasons for everything, and the most discouraging are those who map out ahead of them long courses of action, plan their lives, and systematically in the smallest detail of their activity adapt means to ends. Now the difficulty with all the prudential virtues is that they imply a world that is too good to be true. It would be pleasant to have a world where cause and effect interlocked, where we could see the future, where virtue had its reward, and our characters and relations with other people and the work we wish to do could be planned out with the same certainty with which cooks plan a meal. But we know that that is not the kind of a world we actually live in. Perhaps men have thought that, by cultivating the rational virtues and laying emphasis on prudence and forethought, they could bend the stubborn constitution of things to meet their ideals. It has always been the fashion to insist, in spite of all the evidence, that the world was in reality a rational place where certain immutable moral principles could be laid down with the same certainty of working that physical laws possess. It has always been represented that the correct procedure of the moral life was to choose one's end or desire, to select carefully all the means by which that end could be realized, and then, by the use of the dogged motive force of the will, to push through the plans to completion. In the homilies on success, it has always been implied that strength of will was the only requisite. Success became merely a matter of the ratio between the quantity of effort and will-power applied, and the number of obstacles to be met. If one failed, it was because the proper amount of effort had not been applied, or because the plans had not been properly constructed. The remedy was automatically to increase the effort or rationalize the plans. Life was considered to be a battle, the strategy of which a general might lay out beforehand, an engagement in which he might plan and anticipate to the minutest detail the movement of his forces and the disposition of the enemy. But one does not have to live very long to see that this belief in the power and the desirability of controlling things is an illusion. Life works in a series of surprises. One's powers are given in order that one may be alert and ready, resourceful and keen. The interest of life lies largely in its adventurousness, and not in its susceptibility to orderly mapping. The enemy rarely comes up from the side the general has expected; the battle is usually fought out on vastly different lines from those that have been carefully foreseen and rationally organized. And similarly in life do complex forces utterly confound and baffle our best laid plans.

Our strategy, unless it is open to instant correction, unless it is flexible, and capable of infinite resource and modification, is a handicap rather than an aid in the battle of life. In spite of the veracious accounts of youths hewing their way to success as captains of industry or statesmen, with their eye singly set on a steadfast purpose, we may be sure that life seldom works that way. It is not so tractable and docile, even to the strongest. The rational ideal is one of those great moral hypocrisies which every one preaches and no one practices, but which we all believe with superstitious reverence, and which we take care shall be proven erroneous by no stubborn facts of life. Better that the facts should be altered than that the moral tradition should die!

One of its evil effects is the compressing influence it has on many of us. Recognizing that for us the world is an irrational place, we are willing to go on believing that there are at least some gifted beings who are proving the truth and vindicating the eternal laws of reason. We join willingly the self-stigmatized ranks of the incompetent and are content to shine feebly in the reflected light of those whose master wills and power of effort have brought them through in rational triumph to their ends. The younger generation is coming very seriously to doubt both the practicability and worth of this rational ideal. They do not find that the complex affairs of either the world or the soul work according to laws of reason. The individual as a member of society is at the mercy of great social laws that regulate his fortune for him, construct for him his philosophy of life, and dictate to him his ways of making a living. As an individual soul, he is the creature of impulses and instincts which he does not create and which seem to lie quite outside the reach of his rational will. Looked at from this large social viewpoint, his will appears a puny affair indeed. There seems little room left in which to operate, either in the sphere of society or in his own spiritual life.

That little of free will, however, which there is, serves for our human purposes. It must be our care simply that we direct it wisely; and the rational ideal is not the wisest way of directing it. The place of our free will in the scheme of life is not to furnish driving, but *directing* power. The engineer could never create the power that drives his engine, but he can direct it into the channels where it will be useful and creative. The superstition of the strong will has been almost like an attempt to create power, something the soul could never do. The rational ideal has too often been a mere challenge to attain the unattainable. It has ended in futility or failure.

This superstition comes largely from our incorrigible habit of looking back over the past, and putting purpose into it. The great man looking back over his career, over his ascent from the humble level of his boyhood to his present power and riches, imagines that that ideal success was in his mind from his earliest years. He sees a progress, which was really the happy seizing of fortunate opportunities, as the carrying-out of a fixed purpose. But the purpose was not there at the beginning; it is the crowning touch added to the picture, which completes and satisfies our age-long hunger for the orderly and correct. But we all, rich and poor, successful and unsuccessful, live from hand to mouth. We all alike find life at the beginning a crude mass of puzzling possibilities. All of us, unless we inherit a place in the world—and then we are only half alive—have the same precarious struggle to get a foothold. The difference is in the fortune of the foothold, and not in our private creation of any mystical force of will. It is a question of happy occasions of exposure to the right stimulus that will develop our powers at the right time. The capacity alone is sterile; it needs the stimulus to fertilize it and produce activity and success. The part that our free will can play is to expose ourselves consciously to the stimulus; it cannot create it or the capacity, but it can bring them together.

In other words, for the rational ideal we must substitute the experimental ideal. Life is not a campaign of battle, but a laboratory where its possibilities for the enhancement of happiness and the realization of ideals are to be tested and observed. We are not to start life with a code of its laws in our pocket, with its principles of activity already learned by heart, but we are to discover those principles as we go, by conscientious experiment. Even those laws that seem incontrovertible we are to test for ourselves, to see whether they are thoroughly vital to our own experience and our own genius. We are animals, and our education in life is, after all, different only in degree, and not in kind, from that of the monkey who learns the trick of opening his cage. To get out of his cage, the monkey must find and open a somewhat complicated latch. How does he set about it? He blunders around for a long time, without method or purpose, but with the waste of an enormous amount of energy. At length he accidentally strikes the right catch, and the door flies open. Our procedure in youth is little different. We feel a vague desire to expand, to get out of our cage, and liberate our dimly felt powers. We blunder around for a time, until we accidentally put ourselves in a situation where some capacity is touched, some latent energy liberated, and the direction set for us, along which we have only to move to be free and successful. We will be hardly human if we do not look back on the process and congratulate ourselves on our tenacity and purpose and strong will. But of course the thing was wholly irrational. There were neither plans nor purposes, perhaps not even discoverable effort. For when we found the work that we did best, we found also that we did it easiest. And the outlines of the most dazzling career are little different. Until habits were formed or prestige acquired which could float these successful geniuses, their life was but the resourceful seizing of opportunity, the utilization, with a minimum of purpose or effort, of the promise of the passing moment. They were living the experimental life, aided by good fortune and opportunity.

Now the youth brought up to the strictly rational ideal is like the animal who tries to get out of his cage by going straight through the bars. The duck, beating his wings against his cage, is a symbol of the highest rationality. His logic is plain, simple, and direct. He is in the cage; there is the free world outside; nothing but the bars separate them. The problem is simply to fortify his will and effort and make them so strong that they will overcome the resistance of the cage. His error evidently lies not in his method, but in his estimation of the strength of the bars. But youth is no wiser; it has no data upon which to estimate either its own strength or the strength of its obstacles. It counts on getting out through its own self-reliant strength and will. Like the duck, "impossible" is a word not found in its vocabulary. And like the duck, it too often dashes out its spirit against the bars of circumstance. How often do we see young people, brought up with the old philosophy that nothing was withheld from those who wanted and worked for things with sufficient determination, beating their ineffectual wings against their bars, when perhaps in another direction the door stands open that would lead to freedom!

We do not hear enough of the tragedies of misplaced ambition. When the plans of the man of will and determination fail, and the inexorable forces of life twist his purposes aside from their end, he is sure to suffer the prostration of failure. His humiliation, too, is in proportion to the very strength of his will. It is the burden of defeat, or at best the sting of petty success, that crushes men, and crushes them all the more thoroughly if they have been brought up to believe in the essential rationality of the world and the power of will and purpose. It is not that they have aimed too high, but that they have aimed in the wrong direction. They have not set out experimentally to find the work to which their powers were adapted, they did not test coolly and impartially the direction in which their achievement lay. They forgot that, though faith may remove mountains, the will alone is not able. There is an urgency on every man to develop his powers to the fullest capacity, but he is not called upon to develop those that he does not possess. The will cannot create talent or opportunity. The wise man is he who has the clear vision to discern the one, and the calm patience to await the other. Will, without humor and irony and a luminous knowledge of one's self, is likely to drive one to dash one's brains out against a stone wall. The world is too full of people with nothing except a will. The mistake of youth is to believe that the philosophy of experimentation is enervating. They want to attack life frontally, to win by the boldness of their attack, or by the exceeding excellence of their rational plans and purposes. But therein comes a time when they learn perhaps that it is better to take life not with their naked fists, but more scientifically—to stand with mind and soul alert, ceaselessly testing and criticizing, taking and rejecting, poised for opportunity, and sensitive to all good influences.

The experimental life does not put one at the mercy of chance. It is rather the rational mind that is constantly being shocked and deranged by circumstances. But the dice of the experimenter are always loaded. For he does not go into an enterprise, spiritual or material, relying simply on his reason and will to pull him through. He asks himself beforehand whether something good is not sure to come whichever way the dice fall, or at least whether he can bear the event of failure, whether his spirit can stand it if the experiment ends in humiliation and barrenness. It is surprising how many seeming disasters one finds one can bear in this anticipatory look; the tension of the failure is relieved, anyhow. By looking ahead, one has insured one's self up to the limit of the venture, and one cannot lose. But to the man with the carefully planned campaign, every step is crucial. If all does not turn out exactly as he intends, he is ruined. He thinks he insures himself by the excellence of his designs and the craftiness of his skill. But he insures himself by the strange method of putting all his eggs in one basket. He thinks, of course, he has arranged his plans so that, if they fall, the universe falls with them. But when the basket breaks, and the universe does not fall, his ruin is complete.

Ambition and the rational ideal seem to be only disastrous; if unsuccessful, they produce misanthropists; if successful, beings that prey upon their fellow men. Too much rationality makes a man mercenary and calculating. He has too much at stake in everything he does to know that calm disinterestedness of spirit which is the mark of the experimental attitude towards life. Our attitude towards our personal affairs, material and spiritual, should be like the interest we take in sports and games. The sporting interest is one secret of a healthy attitude towards life. The detached enthusiasm it creates is a real ingredient of happiness. The trouble with the rational man is that he has bet on the game. If his side wins, there is a personal reward for him; if it loses, he himself suffers a loss. He cannot know the true sporting interest which is unaffected by considerations of the end, and views the game as the thing, and not the outcome. To the experimental attitude, failure means nothing beyond a shade of regret or chagrin. Whether we win or lose, something has been learned, some insight and appreciation of the workings of others or of ourselves. We are ready and eager to begin another game; defeat has not dampened our enthusiasm. But if the man who has made the wager loses, he has lost, too, all heart for playing. Or, if he does try again, it is not for interest in the game, but with a redoubled intensity of self-interest to win back what he has lost. With the sporting interest, one looks on one's relations with others, on one's little role in the world, in the same spirit that we look on a political contest, where we are immensely stirred by the clash of issues and personalities, but where we know that the country will run on in about the same way, whoever is elected. This knowledge does not work against our interest in the struggle itself, nor in the outcome. It only insures us against defeat. It makes life livable by endowing us with disinterestedness. If we lose, why, better luck next time, or, at worst, is not losing a part of life?

The experimenter with life, then, must go into his laboratory with the mind of the scientist. He has nothing at stake except the discovery of the truth, and he is willing to work carefully and methodically and even cold-bloodedly in eliciting it from the tangled skein of phenomena. But it is exactly in this cheerful, matter-of-fact way that we are never willing to examine our own personalities and ideas. We take ourselves too seriously, and handle our tastes arfd enthusiasms as gingerly as if we feared they would shrivel away at the touch. We perpetually either underestimate or overestimate our powers and worth, and suffer such losses on account of the one and humiliations on account of the other, as serve to unbalance our knowledge of ourselves, and discourage attempts to find real guiding principles of our own or others' actions. We need this objective attitude of the scientist. We must be self-conscious with a detached self-consciousness, treating ourselves as we treat others, experimenting to discover our possibilities and traits, testing ourselves with situations, and gradually building up a body of law and doctrine for ourselves, a real morality that will have far more worth and power and virtue than all that has been tried and tested before by no matter how much of alien human experience. We must start our quest with no prepossessions, with no theory of what ought to happen when we expose ourselves to certain stimuli. It is our business to see what does happen, and then act accordingly. If the electrical experimenter started with a theory that like magnetic poles attract each other, he would be shocked to discover that they actually repelled each other. He might even set it down to some inherent depravity of matter. But if his theory was not a prejudice but a hypothesis, he would find it possible to revise it quickly when he saw how the poles actually behaved. And he would not feel any particular chagrin or humiliation.

But we usually find it so hard to revise our theories about ourselves and each other. We hold them as prejudices and not as hypotheses, and when the facts of life seem to disprove them, we either angrily clutch at our theories and snarl in defiance, or we pull them out of us with such a wrench that they draw blood. The scientist's way is to start with a hypothesis and then to proceed to verify it by experiment. Similarly ought we to approach life and test all our hypotheses by experience. Our methods have been too rigid. We have started with moral dogmas, and when life obstinately refused to ratify them, we have railed at it, questioned its sincerity, instead of adopting some new hypothesis, which more nearly fitted our experience, and testing it until we hit on the principle which explained our workings to ourselves. The common-sense, rule-of-thumb morality which has come down to us is no more valid than the common-sense, scientific observation that the sun goes round the earth. We can rely no longer on the loose gleanings of homely proverb and common sense for our knowledge of personality and human nature and life.

If we do not adopt the experimental life, we are still in bondage to convention. To learn of life from others' words is like learning to build a steam-engine from books in the class-room. We may learn of principles in the spiritual life that have proven true for millions of men, but even these we must test to see if they hold true for our individual world. We can never attain any self-reliant morality if we allow ourselves to be hypnotized by fixed ideas of what is good or bad. No matter how good our principles, our devotion to morality will be mere lip-service unless each belief is individually tested, and its power to work vitally in our lives demonstrated.

But this moral experimentation is not the mere mechanical repetition of the elementary student in the laboratory, who makes simple experiments which are sure to come out as the law predicts. The laws of personality and life are far more complex, and each experiment discovers something really novel and unique. The spiritual world is ever-creative; the same experiments may turn out differently for different experimenters, and yet they may both be right. In the spiritual experimental life, we must have the attitude of the scientist, but we are able to surpass him in daring and boldness. We can be certain of a physical law that as it has worked in the past, so it will work in the future. But of a spiritual law we have no such guarantee. This it is that gives the zest of perpetual adventure to the moral life. Human nature is an exhaustless field for investigation and experiment. It is inexhaustible in its richness and variety.

The old rigid morality, with its emphasis on the prudential virtues, neglected the fundamental fact of our irrationality. It believed that if we only knew what was good, we would do it. It was therefore satisfied with telling us what was good, and expecting us automatically to do it. But there was a hiatus somewhere. For we do not do what we want to, but what is easiest and most natural for us to do, and if it is easy for us to do the wrong thing, it is that that we will do. We are creatures of instincts and impulses that we do not set going. And education has never taught us more than very imperfectly how to train these impulses in accordance with our worthy desires. Instead of endeavoring to cure this irrationality by directing our energy into the channel of experimentation, it has worked along the lines of greatest resistance, and held up an ideal of inhibition and restraint. We have been alternately exhorted to stifle our bad impulses, and to strain and struggle to make good our worthy purposes and ambitions. Now the irrational man is certainly a slave to his impulses, but is not the rational man a slave to his motives and reasons? The rational ideal has made directly for inflexiblity of character, a deadening conservatism that is unable to adapt itself to situations, or make allowance for the changes and ironies of life. It has riveted the moral life to logic, when it should have been yoked up with sympathy. The logic of the heart is usually better than the logic of the head, and the consistency of sympathy is superior as a rule for life to the consistency of the intellect.

Life is a laboratory to work out experiments in living. That same freedom which we demand for ourselves, we must grant to every one. Instead of falling with our spite upon those who vary from the textbook rules of life, we must look upon their acts as new and very interesting hypotheses to be duly tested and judged by the way they work when carried out into action. Nonconformity, instead of being irritating and suspicious, as it is now to us, will be distinctly pleasurable, as affording more material for our understanding of life and our formulation of its satisfying philosophy. The world has never favored the experimental life. It despises poets, fanatics, prophets, and lovers. It admires physical courage, but it has small use for moral courage. Yet it has always been those who experimented with life, who formed their philosphy of life as a crystallization out of that experimenting, who were the light and life of the world. Causes have only finally triumphed when the rational "gradual progress" men have been overwhelmed. Better crude irrationality than the rationality that checks hope and stifles faith.

In place, then, of the rational or the irrational life, we preach the experimental life. There is much chance in the world, but there is also a modicum of free will, and it is this modicum that we exploit to direct our energies. Recognizing the precariousness and haphazardness of life, we can yet generalize out of our experience certain probabilities and satisfactions that will serve us as well as scientific laws. Only they must be flexible and they must be tested. Life is not a rich province to conquer by our will, or to wring enjoyment out of with our appetites, nor is it a market where we pay our money over the counter and receive the goods we desire. It is rather a great tract of spiritual soil, which we can cultivate or misuse. With certain restrictions, we have the choice of the crops which we can grow. Our duty is evidently to experiment until we find those which grow most favorably and profitably, to vary our crops according to the quality of the soil, to protect them against prowling animals, to keep the ground clear of noxious weeds. Contending against wind and weather and pests, we can yet with skill and vigilance win a living for ourselves. None can cultivate this garden of our personality but our selves. Others may supply the seed; it is we who must plough and reap. We are owners in fee simple, and we cannot lease. None can live my life but myself. And the life that I live depends on my courage, skill, and wisdom in experimentation.

THIS OLDER GENERATION

I

I read with ever-increasing wonder the guarded defenses and discreet apologies for the older generation which keep filtering through the essays of the *Atlantic*. I can even seem to detect a growing decision of tone, a definite assurance of conviction, which seems to imply that a rally has been undertaken against the accusations which the younger generation, in its self-assurance, its irreverence for the old conventions and moralities, its passion for the novel and startling, seemed to be bringing against them. The first faint twinges of conscience felt by the older generation have given place to renewed homily. There is an evident anxiety to get itself put on record as perfectly satisfied with its world, and desirous that its sons and daughters should learn anew of those peculiar beauties in which it has lived. Swept off its feet by the call to social service and social reform, it is slowly regaining its foundation, and, slightly flushed, and with garments somewhat awry, it proclaims again its belief in the eternal verities of Protestant religion and conventional New England morality.

It is always an encouraging sign when people are rendered self-conscious and are forced to examine the basis of their ideals. The demand that they explain them to skeptics always makes for clarity. When the older generation is put on the defensive, it must first discover what convictions it has, and then sharpen them to their finest point in order to present them convincingly. There are always too many unquestioned things in the world, and for a person or class to have to scurry about to find reasons for its prejudices is about as healthy an exercise as one could wish for either of them. To be sure, the reasons are rarely any more than *ex post facto* excuses—supports and justifications for the prejudices rather than the causes thereof. Reason itself is very seldom more than that. The important point is that one should feel the need of a reason. This always indicates that something has begun to slide, that the world is no longer so secure as it was, that obvious truths no longer are obvious, that the world has begun to bristle with question marks.

One of the basic grievances of this older generation against the younger of today, with its social agitation, its religious heresy, its presumptive individuality, its economic restlessness, is that all this makes it uncomfortable. When you have found growing older to be a process of the reconciliation of the spirit to life, it is decidedly disconcerting to have some youngster come along and point out the irreconcilable things in the universe. Just as you have made a tacit agreement to call certain things non-existent, it is highly discommoding to have somebody shout with strident tones that they are very real and significant. When, after much struggling and compromise, you have got your world clamped down, it is discouraging to have a gale arise which threatens to blow over all your structure. Through so much of the current writing runs this quiet note of disapprobation. These agnostic professors who unsettle the faith of our youth, these "intellectuals who stick a finger in everybody's pie in the name of social justice," these sensation-mongers who unveil great masses of political and social corruption, these remorseless scientists who would reveal so many of our reticences—why can't they let us alone? Can they not see that God's in his heaven, all's right with the world?

II

Now I know this older generation which doth protest so much. I have lived with it for the last fifteen years, ever since I began to wonder whether all was for the best in the best of all possible worlds. I was educated by it, grew up with it. I doubt if any generation ever had a more docile pupil than I. What they taught me, I find they still believe, or at least so many of them as have not gone over to the enemy, or been captured by the militant youth of today. Or, as seems rather likely, they no longer precisely believe, but they want their own arguments to convince themselves. It is probable that when we really believe a thing with all our hearts, we do not attempt to justify it. Justification comes only when we are beginning to doubt it.

By this older generation I mean, of course, the mothers and fathers and uncles and aunts of the youth of both sexes between twenty and thirty who are beginning their professional or business life. And I refer of course to the comfortable or fairly comfortable American middle class. Now this older generation has had a religion, a metaphysics, an ethics, and a political and social philosophy, which have reigned practically undisputed until the appearance of the present generation. It has at least never felt called upon to justify itself. It has never been directly challenged, as it is today. In order to localize this generation still further, we must see it in its typical setting of the small town or city, clustered about the institutions of church and family. If we have any society which can be called "American," it is this society. Its psychology is American psychology; its soul is America's soul.

This older generation, which I have known so well for fifteen years, has a religion which is on the whole as pleasant and easy as could be devised. Though its members are the descendants of the stern and rugged old Puritans, who wrestled with the devil and stripped their world of all that might seduce them from the awful service of God, they have succeeded in straining away by a long process all the repellent attitudes in the old philosophy of life. It is unfair to say that the older generation believe in dogmas and creeds. It would be more accurate to say that it does not disbelieve. It retains them as a sort of guaranty of the stability of the faith, but leaves them rather severely alone. It does not even make more than feeble efforts to reinterpret them in the light of modern knowledge. They are useless, but necessary.

The foundation of this religion may be religious, but the superstructure is almost entirely ethical. Most sermons of today are little more than pious exhortations to good conduct. By good conduct is meant that sort of action which will least disturb the normal routine of modern middle-class life: common honesty in business life, faithfulness to duty, ambition in business and profession, filial obligation, the use of talents, and always and everywhere simply human kindness and love. The old Puritan ethics, which saw in the least issue of conduct a struggle between God and the devil, has become a mere code for facilitating the daily friction of conventional life.

Now one would indeed be churlish to find fault with this devout belief in simple goodness, which characterizes the older generation. It is only when these humble virtues are raised up into an all-inclusive program for social reform and into a philosophy of life, that one begins to question, and to feel afar the deep hostility of the older generation to the new faith.

Simple kindness, common honesty, filial obedience, it is evidently still felt, will solve all the difficulties of personal and social life. The most popular novels of the day are those in which the characters do the most good to each other. The enormous success with the older generation of *The Inside of the Cup, Queed,* and *V. V.'s Eyes,* is based primarily on the fact that these books represent a sublimated form of the good old American melodramatic moral sense. And now comes along Mr. Gerald Stanley Lee with his *Crowds*—what a funny, individualized, personal-responsibility crowd he gives us, to be sure—and his panacea for modern social ills by the old solution of applied personal virtue.[1] Never a word about removing the barriers of caste and race and economic inequality, but only an urging to step over them. Never a trumpet-call to level the ramparts of privilege, or build up the heights of opportunity, but only an appeal to extend the charitable hand from the ramparts of heaven, or offer the kindly patronage to the less fortunate, or—most dazzling of all—throw away, in a frenzy of abandonment, life and fortune. Not to construct a business organization where dishonesty would be meaningless, but to be utopianly honest against the business world. In other words, the older generation believes in getting all the luxury of the virtue of goodness, while conserving all the advantages of being in a vicious society.

If there is any one characteristic which distinguishes the older generation, it is this belief that social ills may be cured by personal virtue. Its highest moral ideals are sacrifice and service. But the older generation can never see how intensely selfish these ideals are, in the most complete sense of the word selfish. What they mean always is, "I sacrifice myself for you," "I serve you," not, "We cooperate in working ceaselessly toward an ideal where all may be free and none may be served or serve." These ideals of sacrifice and service are utterly selfish, because they take account only of the satisfaction and moral consolidation of the doer. They enhance his moral value; but what of the person who is served or sacrificed for? What of the person who is done good to? If the feelings of sacrifice and service were in any sense altruistic, the moral enhancement of the receiver would be the object sought. But can it not be said that for every individual virtuous merit secured by an act of sacrifice or service on the part of the doer, there is a corresponding depression on the part of the receiver? Do we not universally recognize this by calling a person who is not conscious of this depression, a parasite, and the person who is no longer capable of depression, a pauper? It is exactly those free gifts, such as schools, libraries, and so forth, which are impersonal or social, that we can accept gratefully and gladly; and it is exactly because the ministrations of a Charity Organization Society are impersonal and businesslike that they can be received willingly and without moral depression by the poor.

The ideal of duty is equally open to attack. The great complaint of the younger against the older generation has to do with the rigidity of the social relationships into which the younger find themselves born. The world seems to be full of what may be called canalized emotions. One is "supposed" to love one's aunt or one's grandfather in a certain definite way, at the risk of being "unnatural." One gets almost a sense of the quantitative measurement of emotion. Perhaps the greatest tragedy of family life is the useless energy that is expended by the dutiful in keeping these artificial channels open, and the correct amount of current running. It is exactly this that produces most infallibly the rebellion of the younger generation. To hear that one ought to love this or that person; or to hear loyalty spoken of, as the older generation so often speaks of it, as if it consisted in an allegiance to something which one no longer believes in—this is what soonest liberates those forces of madness and revolt which bewilder spiritual teachers and guides. It is those dry channels of duty and obligation through which no living waters of emotion flow that it is the ideal of the younger generation to break up. They will have no network of emotional canals which are not brimming, no duties which are not equally loves.

But when they are loves, you have duty no longer meaning very much. Duty, like sacrifice and service, always implies a personal relation of individuals. You are always doing your duty to somebody or something. Always the taint of inequality comes in. You are morally superior to the person who has duty done to him. If that duty is not filled with good-will and desire, it is morally hateful, or at very best, a necessary evil—one of those compromises with the world which must be made in order to get through it at all. But duty without good-will is a compromise with our present state of inequality, and to raise duty to the level of a virtue is to consecrate that state of inequality forevermore.

III

It is the same thing with service. The older generation has attempted an insidious compromise with the new social democracy by combining the words "social" and "service." Under cover of the ideal of service it tries to appropriate to itself the glory of social work, and succeeds in almost convincing itself and the world that its Christianity has always held the same ideal. The faithful are urged to extend their activities. The assumption is that, by doing good to more individuals, you are thereby becoming social. But to speak of "social democracy," which of course means a freely cooperating, freely reciprocating society of equals, and "service," together, is a contradiction of terms. For, when you serve people or do good to them, you thereby render yourself unequal with them. You insult the democratic ideal. If the service is compulsory, it is menial and you are inferior. If voluntary, you are superior. The difference, however, is only academic. The entire Christian scheme is a clever but unsuccessful attempt to cure the evils of inequality by transposing the values. The slave serves gladly instead of servilely. That is, he turns his master into a slave. That is why good Christian people can never get over the idea that Socialism means simply the triumph of one class over another. Today the proletarian is down, the capitalist up. Tomorrow the proletarian will be up and the capitalist down. To pull down the mighty from their seats and exalt them of low degree is the highest pitch to which Christian ethics ever attained. The failure of the older generation to recognize a higher ethic, the ethic of democracy, is the cause of all the trouble.

The notorious Victorian era, which in its secret heart this older generation still admires so much, accentuated all the latent individualism of Christian ethics, and produced a code which, without the rebellion of the younger generation, would have spiritually guaranteed forever all moral caste divisions and inequalities of modern society. The Protestant Church, in which this exaggerated ethic was enshrined, is now paying heavily the price of this debauch of ethical power. Its rapidly declining numbers show that human nature has an invincible objection to being individually saved. The Catholic Church, which saves men as members of the Beloved Community, and not as individuals, flourishes. When one is saved by Catholicism, one becomes a democrat, and not a spiritual snob and aristocrat, as one does through Calvinism. The older generation can never understand that superb loyalty which is loyalty to a community,—a loyalty which, paradoxical as it may seem, nourishes the true social personality in proportion as the individual sense is lessened. The Protestant Church in its tenacious devotion to the personal ideal of a Divine Master—the highest and most popular Christian ideal of today—shows how very far it still is away from the ideals and ethics of a social democracy, a life lived in the Beloved Community.

The sense of self-respect is the very keystone of the personality in whose defence all this individualistic philosophy has been carefully built up. The Christian virtues date from ages when there was a vastly greater number of morally depressed people than there is now. The tenacious survival of these virtues can be due only to the fact that they were valuable to the moral prestige of some class. Our older generation, with its emphasis on duty, sacrifice, and service, shows us very clearly what those interests were. I deliberately accuse the older generation of conserving and greatly strengthening these ideals, as a defensive measure. Morals are always the product of a situation; they reflect a certain organization of human relations which some class or group wishes to preserve. A moral code or set of ideals is always the invisible spiritual sign of a visible social grace. In an effort to retain the *status quo* of that world of inequalities and conventions in which they most comfortably and prosperously live, the older generation has stamped, through all its agencies of family, church and school, upon the younger generation, just those seductive ideals which would preserve its position. These old virtues upon which however, the younger generation is already making guerrilla warfare are simply the moral support with which the older generation buttresses its social situation.

The natural barriers and prejudices by which our elders are cut off from a freely flowing democracy are thus given a spiritual justification, and there is added for our elders the almost sensual luxury of leaping, by free grace, the barriers and giving themselves away. But the price has to be paid. Just as profits, in the socialist philosophy, are taken to be an abstraction from wages, through the economic power which one class has over another, so the virtues of the older generation may be said to be an abstraction from the virtue of other classes less favorably situated from a moral or personal point of view. Their swollen self-respect is at the expense of others.

How well we know the type of man in the older generation who has been doing good all his life! How his personality has thriven on it! How he has ceaselessly been storing away moral fat in every cranny of his soul! His goodness has been meat to him. The need and depression of other people has been, all unconsciously to him, the air which he has breathed. Without their compensating misfortune or sin, his goodness would have wilted and died. If good people would earnestly set to work to make the world uniformly healthy, courageous, beautiful, and prosperous, the field of their vocation would be constantly limited, and finally destroyed. That they so stoutly resist all philosophies and movements which have these ends primarily in view is convincing evidence of the fierce and jealous egoism which animates their so plausibly altruistic spirit. One suspects that the older generation does not want its vocation destroyed. It takes an heroic type of goodness to undermine all the foundations on which our virtue rests.

If then I object to the ethical philosophy of the older generation on the ground that it is too individualistic, and, under the pretense of altruism, too egoistic, I object to its general intellectuality as not individual enough. Intellectually the older generation seems to me to lead far too vegetative a life. It may be that this life has been lived on the heights, that these souls have passed through fires and glories, but there is generally too little objective evidence of this subjective fact. If the intuition which accompanies experience has verified all the data regarding God, the soul, the family, and so forth—to quote one of the staunchest defenders of the generation—this verification seems to have been obtained rather that the issues might be promptly disposed of and forgotten. Certainly the older generation is rarely interested in the profounder issues of life. It never speaks of death—the suggestion makes it uncomfortable. It shies in panic at hints of sex-issues. It seems resolute to keep life on as objective a plane as possible. It is no longer curious about the motives and feelings of people. It seems singularly to lack the psychological sense. If it gossips, it recounts actions, effects; it rarely seeks to interpret. It tends more and more to treat human beings as moving masses of matter instead of as personalities filled with potent influence, or as absorbingly interesting social types, as I am sure the younger generation does.

The older generation seems no longer to generalize, although it gives every evidence of having once prodigiously generalized, for its world is all hardened and definite. There are the good and the criminal, and the poor, the people who can be called nice, and the ordinary people. The world is already plotted out. Now I am sure that the generalizations of the truly philosophical mind are very fluid and ephemeral. They are no sooner made than the mind sees their insufficiency and has to break them up. A new cutting is made, only in turn to be shaken and rearranged. This keeps the philosopher thinking all the time, and it makes his world a very uncertain place. But he at least runs no risk of hardening, and he has his eyes open to most experience.

I am often impressed with the fact that the older generation has grown weary of thinking. It has simply put up the bars in its intellectual shop-windows and gone off home to rest. It may well be that this is because it has felt so much sorrow that it does not want to talk about sorrow, or so much love that to interpret love tires it, or repulsed so many rude blows of destiny that it has no interest in speaking of destiny. Its flame may be low for the very reason that it has burned so intensely. But how many of the younger generation would eagerly long for such interpretations if the older would only reveal them! And how little plausible is that experience when it is occasionally interpreted! No, enthusiasm, passion for ideas, sensuality, religious fervor—all the heated weapons with which the younger generation attacks the world, seem only to make the older generation uneasy. The spirit, in becoming reconciled to life, has lost life itself.

As I see the older generation going through its daily round of business, church, and family life, I cannot help feeling that its influence is profoundly pernicious. It has signally failed to broaden its institutions for the larger horizon of the time. The church remains a private club of comfortable middle-class families, while outside there grows up without spiritual inspiration a heterogeneous mass of people without ties, roots, or principles. The town changes from a village to an industrial center, and church and school go through their time-honored and listless motions. The world widens, society expands, formidable crises appear, but the older generation does not broaden, or if it does, the broadening is in no adequate proportion to our needs. The older generation still uses the old ideas for the new problem. Whatever new wine it finds must be poured into the old bottles.

Where are the leaders among the older generation in America who, with luminous faith and intelligence, are rallying around them the disintegrated numbers of idealistic youth, as Bergson and Barrès and Jaurès have done in France? A few years ago there seemed to be a promise of a forward movement toward Democracy, led by embattled veterans in a war against privilege. But how soon the older generation became wearied in the march! What is left now of that shining army and its leader? Must the younger generation eternally wait for the sign?

The answer is, of course, that it will not wait. It must shoulder the gigantic task of putting into practice its ideals and revolutionary points of view as wholeheartedly and successfully as our great-grandfathers applied theirs and tightened the philosophy of life which imprisons the older generation. The shuddering fear that we in turn may become weary, complacent, evasive, should be the best preventive of that stagnation. We shall never have done looking for the miracle, that it shall be given us to lighten, cheer, and purify our "younger generation," even as our older has depressed and disintegrated us.

---

[1] Compare Van Wyck Brooks: *America's Coming of Age* (N.Y., 1915). Chapter IV, with the title "Apotheosis of the Lowbrow" is devoted to Gerald Stanley Lee. Bourne is referring to the latter's book: *Crowds: A Moving-Picture of Democracy* (1913), while Brooks is criticizing *Inspired Millionaires: A Forecast*, which had appeared in 1908.

OLD TYRANNIES

When you come as an inhabitant to this earth, you do not have the pleasure of choosing your dwelling or your career. You do not even have the privilege like those poor little shivering souls in *The Blue Bird,* of sitting about, all aware and wondering, while you are chosen, one by one to take up your toilsome way on earth. You are a helpless victim of your parents' coming together. There is denied you even the satisfaction of knowing that they created you, in their own bungling fashion, after some manner of a work of art, or of what they imagined an adequate child should be. On the contrary, you may be merely an accident, unintentioned, a species of catastrophe in the life of your mother, a drain upon the resources that were none too great already. And your parents have not only not conceived you as a work of art, but they are wholly incapable after you are born of bringing you up like a work of art.

The last indignity perhaps is that of being born unconscious, like a drugged girl who wakes up naked in a bed, not knowing how she got there. For by the time you do dimly begin to apprehend your relation to things and an intelligible world begins to clarify out of the buzz and the darting lights and dull sensations, you are lost, a prisoner of your surroundings inextricably tangled up with your mother's soul and all the intimate things around you. Your affections have gotten away from your control and attached themselves to things that you in later life discover you never intended them to touch. You depend for comfort on attitudes of your mother or father or nurse or brothers and sisters, that may be taken away from you, leaving you shivering and forlorn. Your impulses have had no intuition of reality. They have leaped forth blindly and have recoiled against or been satisfied with things of which you did not have the choosing, and which only very partially seem to concern themselves with your desires. For a few years, with infinite tribulation, you have to dodge and butt and back your way through the little world of other people and things that surround you, until you are a little worn down to its shape and are able to predict its reactions.

Everything about you is given, ready, constituted, rigid, set up when you arrive. You always think that some day you are going to catch up to this givenness, that you will dominate instead of falling in line. Fortunate you are if you ever come to dominate! Usually as your world broadens out more and more around you, you merely find a tougher resistance to your desires. Your world at home is simple, personal, appealed to by all sorts of personal manifestations. You can express intense resentment and affect it, or you can express intense joy and affect it. Mother and father have an invincible strength over your feebleness, but your very feebleness is a weapon to break their harsh domination. Their defenses melt against your scream or your chuckle. As you grow older you become stronger to manipulate the world. But just in proportion does the world become stronger to manipulate you. It is no longer susceptible to your scream or your smile. You must use less personal instruments. But that requires subtlety and knowledge. You have still painfully to ferret out the ways of this world, and learn how to use all sorts of unsuspected tools to gain your ends.

For there stands your old world, wary, wily, parrying easily all your childish blows, and beating you down to your knees, so that you must go back and learn your long apprenticeship. By the time you have learned it, and have become master, behold! Your life is inextricably knotted into it. As you learned your apprenticeship, you did as the world did, you learned the tricks in order that you might get your revenge on this world and dominate it as it has tantazingly held you off and subjugated you. But by the time you have learned, are you not yourself firmly established as a part of the world yourself, so that you dominate nothing? Rather are you now a part of that very flaming rampart against which new youth advances. You cannot help being a part of that very rampart without extinguishing your own existence.

So you have never overtaken the given. Actually you have fallen farther and farther behind it. You have not affected the world you live in; you have been molded and shaped by it yourself. Your moral responsibility has been a myth, for you were never really free enough to have any responsibility. While you thought you were making headway, you were really being devoured. And your children are as casually begotten as you were, and born into a world as tight and inelastic as was yours. You have a picture of great things achieved, but Time laughs his ironical laugh and rolls you in the dust.

You would perhaps the more easily become free and strong if

you could choose your qualities, or regulate the strength of your impulses. But you cannot even do that. Your ancestors have implanted in you impulses which very seriously inhibit you and impede you in your grappling with the world. There is anger which makes you misinterpret people's attitudes toward you, and makes you resist when you often should accept. There is fear, which makes you misinterpret the unfamiliar and haunts you with its freezing power all through life. There is love, which ties you irrationally and too strongly first to your mother and your father, and then to people who have no real part with you. And there is the swift revulsion into hatred, when the loved one resists or refuses you. These impulses, which are yours just because you are an animal, soon become your masters, and further tie your hands in your response to the bewildering world into which you have come.

We grow up in the home that society has shaped or coerced our parents into accepting, we adopt the customs and language and utensils that have established themselves for our present through a long process of survival and invention and change. We take the education that is given us, and finally the jobs that are handed out to us by society. As adults, we act in the way that society expects us to act; we submit to whatever regulations and coercions society imposes on us. We live almost entirely a social life, that is, a life as a constituted unit in society, rather than a free and personal one. Most people live a life which is little more than a series of quasi-official acts. Their conduct is a network of representations of the various codes and institutions of society. They act in such a way in order that some institutional or moral scripture may be fulfilled, rather than that some deep personal direction of growth should be realized. They may be half aware that they are not arrived at the place toward which their ardors pointed. They may dimly realize that their outward lives are largely a compulsion of social habit, performed, even after so many years, with a slight grudgingness. This divorce between social compulsion and personal desire, however, rarely rises to consciousness. Their conscious life is divided between the mechanical performance of their task, the attainment of their pleasures, and the wholly uncriticized acceptance and promulgation of the opinions and attitudes which society provides them with.

The normal, or the common, relation between society and the

individual in any society that we know of is that the individual scarcely exists. Those persons who refuse to act as symbols of society's folk ways, as counters in the game of society's ordainings, are outlawed, and there exists an elaborate machinery for dealing with such people. Artists, philosophers, geniuses, tramps, criminals, eccentrics, aliens, freelovers and freethinkers, and persons who challenge the most sacred taboos are treated with great concern by society, and in the hue and cry after them all, respectable and responsible men unanimously and universally join. Some are merely made uncomfortable, the light of society's countenance being drawn from them; others are deprived of their liberty, placed for years in foul dungeons, or even executed. The heaviest penalties in modern society fall upon those who violate any of the three sacred taboos of property, sex, and the State. Religion, which was for so many centuries the most exigent and ubiquitous symbol of society's demand for conformity, has lapsed in these later days and bequeathed most of its virus to the State. Society no longer demands conformity of opinion in religion, even in those countries where nominal adherence is still required.

There is nothing fixed about the objects to which society demands conformity. It is only the quantity that seems to be constant. So much conformity, like the conservation of physical energy in the universe, but the manners in which people shall think alike, or behave, or what objects they shall consider sacred, differ in myriad ways throughout different social groupings and in different eras. Diametrically opposite ideas are held in two social groups with the same vigor and fury; diametrically opposite conduct is considered equally praiseworthy and necessary; two social groups will visit with the same punishment two diametrically opposite actions. To any student of primitive societies or of the history of Western civilization these facts are commonplaces. But the moral is not as commonplace as yet. Yet it must be evident that most of the customs and attitudes of these societies were almost wholly irrational, that is, they were social habits which persisted solely through inertia and the satisfaction they gave the gregarious impulse. The latter had to be satisfied, so that anything which cost the least in invention or reasoning or effort would do. The customs, therefore, of primitive tribes seem to practically everybody in a modern Western society outlandish and foolish. What evidence is there that our codes and conformities which perform exactly the same role, and are mostly traditional survivals, are any the less outlandish and irrational? May they not be tainted with the same purposelessness? Is not the inference irresistible that they are? They seem to us to be intelligent and necessary not because we have derived them or invented them for a clearly imagined and desired end, but because they satisfy our need for acting in a herd, just as the primitive savage is satisfied.

The most important fact we can realize about society is that to every one of us that comes into the world it is something given, irreducible. We are as little responsible for it as we are for our own birth. From our point of view it is just as much a non-premeditated, noncreated, irrational portion of our environment as is the weather. Entering it in the closing years of the nineteenth century, we find it as it exists and as it has developed through the centuries of human change. We had nothing whatever to do with its being as it is, and by the time we have reached such years of discretion as dimly to understand the complex of institutions around us, we are implicated in it and compromised by it as to be little able to effect any change in its irresistible bulk. No man who ever lived found himself in a different relation to society from what we find ourselves. We all enter as individuals into an organized herd-whole in which we are as significant as a drop of water in the ocean, and against which we can about as much prevail. Whether we shall act in the interests of ourselves or of society is, therefore, an entirely academic question. For entering as we do a society which is all prepared for us, so toughly grounded and immalleable that even if we came equipped with weapons to assail it and make good some individual preference, we could not in our puny strength achieve anything against it. But we come entirely helpless.

THE MYSTIC TURNED RADICAL[1]

The mystical temperament is little enough popular in this work-a-day modern world of ours. The mystic, we feel, comes to us discounted from the start; he should in all decency make constant apologies for his existence. In a practical age of machinery he is an anomaly, an anachronism. He must meet the direct challenge of the scientist, who guards every approach to the doors of truth and holds the keys of its citadel. Any thinker who gets into the fold by another way is a thief and a robber.

The mystic must answer that most heinous of all charges—of being unscientific. By tradition he is even hostile to science. For his main interest is in wonder, and science by explaining things attacks the very principle of his life. It not only diminishes his opportunities for wonder, but threatens to make him superfluous by ultimately explaining everything.

The scientist may say that there is no necessary connection between explanation and that beautiful romance of thought we call wonder. The savage, who can explain nothing, is the very creature who has no wonder at all. Everything is equally natural to him. Only a mind that has acquaintance with laws of behavior can be surprised at events.

The wonder of the scientist, however, although it be of a more robust, tough-minded variety, is none the less wonder. A growing acquaintance with the world, an increasing at-homeness in it, is not necessarily incompatible with an ever-increasing marvel both at the beautiful fitness of things and the limitless field of ignorance and mystery beyond. So the modern mystic must break with his own tradition if he is to make an appeal to this generation, and must recognize that the antithesis between mystic and scientific is not an eternally valid one.

It is just through realization of this fact that Maeterlinck, the best of modern mystics, makes his extraordinary appeal. For, as he tells us, the valid mystery does not begin at the threshold of knowledge but only after we have exhausted our resources of knowing. His frank and genuine acceptance of science thus works out a *modus vivendi* between the seen and the unseen. It allows many of us who have given our allegiance to science to hail him gladly as a prophet who supplements the work of the wise men of scientific research, without doing violence to our own consciences. For the world is, in spite of its scientific

clamor, still far from ready really to surrender itself to prosaic-
ness. It is still haunted with the dreams of the ages—dreams of
short roads to truth, visions of finding the Northwest passage to
the treasures of the Unseen. Only we must go as far as possible
along the traveled routes of science.

Maeterlinck is thus not anti-scientific or pseudo-scientific, but
rather sub-scientific. He speaks of delicately felt and subtle influences and aspects of reality that lie beneath the surface of
our lives, of forces and shadows that cannot be measured quan-
titatively or turned into philosophical categories. Or we may say
that he is post-scientific. As science plods along, opening up
the dark wilderness, he goes with the exploring party, throwing a
search-light before them; flickering enough and exasperatingly
uncertain at times, but sufficiently constant to light up the way,
point out a path, and give us confidence that the terrors before
us are not so formidable as we have feared. His influence on
our time is so great because we believe that he is a seer, a man
with knowledge of things hidden from our eyes. We go to him as
to a spiritual clairvoyant,—to have him tell us where to find the
things our souls have lost.

But the modern mystic must not only recognize the scientific
aspect of the age—he must feel the social ideal that directs the
spiritual energies of the time. It is the glory of Maeterlinck's mysticism that it has not lingered in the depths of the soul, but has
passed out to illuminate our thinking in regard to the social life
about. The growth of this duality of vision has been with him a
long evolution. His early world was a shadowy, intangible thing.
As we read the early essays, we seem to be constantly hovering
on the verge of an idea, just as when we read the plays we
seem to be hovering on the verge of a passion. This long brooding away from the world, however, was fruitful and momentous.
The intense gaze inward trained the eye, so that when the mists
cleared away and revealed the palpitating social world about
him, his insight into its meaning was as much more keen and
true than our own as had been his sense of the meaning of the
individual soul. The light he turns outward to reveal the meaning
of social progress is all the whiter for having burned so long
within.

In the essay on "Our Social Duty," the clearest and the con-
summate expression of this new outward look, there are no con-
taminating fringes of vague thought; all is clear white light. With

the instinct of the true radical, the poet has gone to the root of the social attitude. Our duty as members of society is to be radical, he tells us. And not only that, but an excess of radicalism is essential to the equilibrium of life. Society so habitually thinks on a plane lower than is reasonable that it behooves us to think and to hope on an even higher plane than seems to be reasonable. This is the overpoweringly urgent philosophy of radicalism. It is the beautiful courage of such words that makes them so vital an inspiration.

It is the sin of the age that nobody dares to be anything to too great a degree. We may admire extremists in principle, but we take the best of care not to imitate them ourselves. Who in America would even be likely to express himself as has Maeterlinck in this essay? Who of us would dare follow the counsel? Of course we can plead extenuation. In Europe the best minds are thinking in terms of revolution still, while in America our radicalism is still simply amateurish and incompetent.

To many of us, then, this call of Maeterlinck's to the highest of radicalisms will seem irrelevant; this new social note which appears so strongly in all his later work will seem a deterioration from the nobler mysticism of his earlier days. But rather should it be viewed as the fruit of matured insight. There has been no decay, no surrender. It is the same mysticism, but with the direction of the vision altered. This essay is the expression of the clearest vision that has yet penetrated our social confusion, the sanest and highest ideal that has been set before progressive minds. It may be that its utter fearlessness, its almost ascetic detachment from the matter-of-fact things of political life, its clear cold light of conviction and penetration, may repel some whose hearts have been warmed by Maeterlinck's subtle revelations of the spiritual life. They may reproach him because it has no direct bearings on the immediate practical social life; it furnishes no weapon of reform, no tool with which to rush out and overthrow some vested abuse. But to the traveler lost in the wood the one thing needful is a pole-star to show him his direction. The star is unapproachable, serene, cold, and lofty. But although he cannot touch it, or utilize it directly to extend his comfort and progress, it is the most useful of all things to him. It fills his heart with a great hope; it coordinates his aimless wanderings and gropings, and gives meaning and purpose to his course.

So a generation lost in a chaos of social change can find in these later words of Maeterlinck a pole-star and a guide. They do for the social life of man what the earlier essays did for the individual. They endow it with values and significances that will give steadfastness and resource to his vision as he looks out on the great world of human progress, and purpose and meaning to his activity as he looks ahead into the dim world of the future.

[1] Compare John Dewey: "Maeterlinck's Philosophy of Life," *The Hibbert Journal,* July, 1911.

2
EDUCATION AND POLITICS

Civilized life is really one aesthetic challenge after another, and no training in appreciation of art is worth anything unless one has become able to react to forms and settings. The mere callousness with which we confront our ragbag city streets is evidence enough of the futility of the Arnold ideal. To have learned to appreciate a Mantegna and a Japanese print, and Dante and Debussy, and not to have learned nausea at Main street, means an art education which is not merely worthless but destructive.
Randolph Bourne

All education can ever do is to provide the experience, and stimulate, guide, organize interests. Anything else may produce, at its best, a trained animal. It will not be education, and it will not produce men and women.
Randolph Bourne

EDUCATION AND POLITICS

When Herbert Croly asked Bourne to contribute to the newly founded *New Republic,* he offered him the fields of urban planning, education, and religion. On all these subjects, Bourne had already published articles in the *Columbia Monthly* and, more importantly, in the *Atlantic Monthly.* His Master's thesis, "A Study of the 'Suburbanizing' of a Town and its effects upon its Social Life"—written with the aid of a grant—dealt with the development of his hometown Bloomfield. During his trip to Europe, Bourne not only visited public buildings and workers' settlements but also studied the secondary school system in Denmark, among other things. In line with progressivist thought, he saw in architecture, urban planning, and education possibilities of a meliorist social policy.

It is not surprising that problems of education should ultimately have become his greatest interest. As early as 1899, Dewey had written his pamphlet *School and Society.* And in collaboration with his daughter Evelyn he had published *Schools for Tomorrow* in 1915. This material provided Bourne with the understanding that progressive thought and an insistence on the developmental possibilities of the individual could be easily combined when discussing the problem of education.

Within two years, Bourne brought out two books which were collections of his articles: *The Gary Schools* (1916), and *Education and Living* (1917). The first volume gives a positive account of the reforms William Wirt had attempted to bring to the Gary school system. Bourne had criticized the separation between the educational and the learning process both in and out of school and felt that this plan might eliminate it. In Bourne's words: "The ideal of the Wirt plan is that the child should have every day, in some form or other, contact with all the different activities which influence a well-rounded human being, instead of meeting them perfunctorily once or twice a week, as in the ordinary school." Bourne's commitment to Wirt's reform program increased when the City of New York commissioned Wirt to analyze its school system and he became the target of violent criticism on the part of conservative opponents. In addition, Bourne also studied the situation at the universities. He always saw education as an extremely fragile process whose success rested essentially on the growth and stabilization of the subject's autonomy. For this reason, Bourne's criticism directed itself against all those influences which might interrupt or interfere with this process. He detected such influences not only in politically motivated interventions such as the dismissal of professors James McKeen Cattell and Henry Wadsworth Longfellow Dana because they opposed U.S. entry into the war. He also had a keen insight into the indifference and uncertainty of teachers and the protective mechanisms students develop as a reaction to them. Bourne protested that both were the consequences of an educational ideal which was more interested in discipline than in the liberation of the intelligence.

Bourne's essays on the conception and implementation of Wirt's plan require no detailed analysis. They are to be understood chiefly as an attempt to familiarize a wider public with Dewey's educational theory and its practice.

The essay "The Undergraduate" and those following it make it clear that Bourne was also able to combine theoretical considerations and personal experiences and that he sometimes did so in a satirical manner, as in "The Professor."

The commitment evident in the articles on problems of education expresses itself in a style which shows that it was difficult for Bourne to maintain an analytical distance to his subject. One would therefore also neutralize his fundamental intentions, were one to look at his articles on educational questions entirely in the context of the historical debate concerning the necessity and possibility of progressive teaching and learning methods. These articles transcend that framework and are intimately connected with his ideas about the general conditions which make individuality possible, expounded in the early essays on the subject of "Youth," and they must be understood as complementing them.

Sources of First Publication

With few exceptions these articles were taken from *Education and Living* (1917), a collection of slightly revised essays that first appeared in the *New Republic*. "The College: An Undergraduate View" first appeared in the *Atlantic Monthly*, (VIII, November 1911);

"The Professor"	*New Republic*, III (July 10, 1915)
"One of our Conquerors"	N.R. IV (Sept. 4, 1915)
"Those Columbia Trustees"	N.R. XII (Oct. 20, 1917)

IN A SCHOOLROOM

The other day I amused myself by slipping into a recitation at the suburban high school where I had once studied as a boy. The teacher let me sit, like one of the pupils, at an empty desk in the back of the room, and for an hour I had before my eyes the interesting drama of the American school as it unfolds itself day after day in how many thousands of classrooms throughout the land. I had gone primarily to study the teacher, but I soon found that the pupils, after they had forgotten my presence, demanded most of my attention.

Their attitude towards the teacher, a young man just out of college and amazingly conscientious and persevering, was that good-humored tolerance which has to take the place of enthusiastic interest in many of our American schools. They seemed to like the teacher and recognize fully his good intentions, but their attitude was a delightful one of all making the best of a bad bargain, and cooperating loyally with him in slowly putting the hour out of its agony. This good-natured acceptance of the inevitable, this perfunctory going through by its devotees of the ritual of education, was my first striking impression, and the key to the reflections that I began to weave.

As I sank down to my seat I felt all that queer sense of depression, still familiar after ten years, that sensation, in coming into the schoolroom, of suddenly passing into a helpless, impersonal world, where expression could be achieved and curiosity asserted only in the most formal and difficult way. And the class began immediately to divide itself for me, as I looked around it, into the artificially depressed like myself, commonly called the "good" children, and the artificially stimulated, commonly known as the "bad," and the envy and despair of every "good" child. For to these "bad" children, who are, of course, simply those with more self-assertion and initiative than the rest, all the careful network of discipline and order is simply a direct and irresistible challenge. I remembered the fearful awe with which I used to watch the exhaustless ingenuity of the "bad" boys of my class to disrupt the peacefully dragging recitation; and behold, I found myself watching intently, along with all the children in my immediate neighborhood, the patient activity of a boy who spent his entire hour in so completely sharpening a lead-pencil that there was nothing left at the end but the lead. Now what normal boy would do so silly a thing or who would look at him in real life? But here, in this artificial atmosphere, his action had a sort of symbolic quality; it was assertion against a stupid authority, a sort of blind resistance against the attempt of the schoolroom to impersonalize him. The most trivial incident assumed importance; the chiming of the town-clock, the passing automobile, a slip of the tongue, a passing footstep in the hall, would polarize the wandering attention of the entire class like an electric shock. Indeed, a large part of the teacher's business seemed to be to demagnetize, by some little ingenious touch, his little flock into their original inert and static elements.

For the whole machinery of the classroom was dependent evidently upon this segregation. Here were these thirty children, all more or less acquainted, and so congenial and sympathetic that the slightest touch threw them all together into a solid mass of attention and feeling. Yet they were forced, in accordance with some principle of order, to sit at these stiff little desks, equidistantly apart, and prevented under penalty from communicating with each other. All the lines between them were supposed to be broken. Each existed for the teacher alone. In this incorrigibly social atmosphere, with all the personal influences playing around, they were supposed to be, not a network or a group, but a collection of things, in relation only with the teacher.

These children were spending the sunniest hours of their whole lives, five days a week, in preparing themselves, I assume by the acquisition of knowledge, to take their places in a modern world of industry, ideas and business. What institution, I asked myself, in this grownup world bore resemblance to this so carefully segregated classroom? I smiled, indeed, when it occurred to me that the only possible thing I could think of was a State Legislature. Was not the teacher a sort of Speaker putting through the business of the session, enforcing a sublimated parliamentary order, forcing his members to address only the chair and avoid any but a formal recognition of their colleagues? How amused, I thought, would Socrates have been to come upon these thousands of little training-schools for incipient legislators! He might have recognized what admirably experienced and docile Congressmen such a discipline as this would make, if there were the least chance of any of these pupils ever reaching the House, but he might have wondered what earthly connection it had with the atmosphere and business of workshop and factory and office and store and home into which all these children would so obviously be going. He might almost have convinced himself that the business of adult American life was actually run according to the rules of parliamentary order, instead of on the plane of personal intercourse, of quick interchange of ideas, the understanding and the grasping of concrete social situations.

It is the merest platitude, of course, that those people succeed who can best manipulate personal intercourse, who can best express themselves, whose minds are most flexible and most responsive to others, and that those people would deserve to succeed in any form of society. But has there ever been devised a more ingenious enemy of personal intercourse than the modern classroom, catching, as it does, the child in his most impressionable years? The two great enemies of intercourse are bumptiousness and diffidence, and the classroom is perhaps the most successful instrument yet devised for cultivating both of them.

As I sat and watched these interesting children struggling with these enemies, I reflected that even with the best of people, thinking cannot be done without talking. For thinking is primarily a social faculty; it requires the stimulus of other minds to excite curiosity, to arouse some emotion. Even private thinking is only a conversation with one's self. Yet in the classroom the child is evidently expected to think without being able to talk. In such a rigid and silent atmosphere, how could any thinking be done, where there is no stimulus, no personal expression?

While these reflections were running through my head, the hour dragged to its close. As the bell rang for dismissal, a sort of thrill of rejuvenation ran through the building. The "good" children straightened up, threw off their depression and took back their self-respect, the "bad" sobered up, threw off their swollen egotism, and prepared to leave behind them their mischievousness in the room that had created it. Everything suddenly became human again. The brakes were off, and life, with all its fascinations of intrigue and amusement, was flowing once more. The school streamed away in personal and intensely interested little groups. The real world of business and stimulations and rebounds was thick again here.

If I had been a teacher and watched my children going away, arms around each other, all aglow with talk, I should have been very wistful for the injection of a little of that animation into the dull and halting lessons of the classroom. Was I a horrible "intellectual," to feel sorry that all this animation and verve of life should be perpetually poured out upon the ephemeral, while thinking is made as difficult as possible, and the expressive and intellectual child made to seem a sort of monstrous pariah?

Now I know all about the logic of the classroom, the economies of time, money, and management that have to be met. I recognize that in the cities the masses that come to the schools require some sort of rigid machinery for their governance. Hand-educated children have had to go the way of hand-made buttons. Children have had to be massed together into a schoolroom just as cotton looms have had to be massed together into a factory. The difficulty is that, unlike cotton looms, massed children make a social group, and that the mind and personality can only be developed by the freely inter-stimulating play of minds in a group. Is it not very curious that we spend so much time on the practice and methods of teaching, and never criticize the very framework itself? Call this thing that goes on in the modern schoolroom schooling, if you like. Only don't call it education.

THE WASTED YEARS

Only one child out of fourteen in our school system ever reaches the high school; whatever education ninety per cent of American children are to have they must acquire before they are fourteen years old. So elementary a fact as this, it would seem, should be at the background of every discussion and criticism of the public schools. Yet the most cursory inspection of the average city public school shows that its significance has only recently and very dimly been realized.

Indeed, as the average city public school is at present organized, there is every reason to believe that most of the children get practically all their education before their tenth year. Limited as this schooling is, they do not by any means get the full advantage of what is supposed to be given them. One can hardly come from a study of the everyday classroom work of the average city school without a conviction that there is disastrous intellectual leakage which has been strangely ignored by educators.

This leakage is not in the primary school and the high school. For the teaching of "the three R's" American normal schools and training colleges in recent years have worked out many admirable techniques, which seem to have been generally adopted. The younger generation of teachers is doing efficiently its work of giving the child a mastery of these essentials of civilized intercourse. The present primary school on its intellectual side is an efficient institution.

Similarly the high school has had a large amount of attention and skill lavished upon it. Its administrative peculiar problems have been studied and met. The best high schools have been made to approximate elementary colleges, with well-rounded courses of languages and sciences, of artistic, manual and physical work. For the highly selected group which reaches the high school it provides an excellent purely intellectual curriculum, both for higher study and for social orientation.

Between the primary school and the high school, however, there lies a desert waste of four years, the significance and possibilities of which seem to have been scarcely considered. They are the most urgent years of all, for in them the educator must give compensation to the children who are forced to leave school for the opportunities they are to miss. Yet these middle years of what used to be called the "grammar school" are now left not only unmotivated, but without any genuine educational function. Instead of being prophetic of the future they merely drag along the relics of the past. Some schools, it is true, have timidly brought down the beginning of high school studies into the lower grades, but in general the "grammar school" merely continues the interests of the primary school on substantially the same lines.

Fifteen years ago, when I went to school, there may have been some excuse for this system. Teachers may have been correct in their belief that it took the average child eight years to learn arithmetic, reading, writing, spelling, and a smattering of history and geography. Today such an assumption is ridiculous. I have seen children in large classes in an ordinary city school system learn all the elements of "the three R's" in less than six months. The clear writing and accurate reading of little children in the first grade who have only been going to school for a few months is astonishing. It suggests that Mme. Montessori could scarcely have known of the excellence of elementary methods in this country when she urged her ideas as revolutionary. For these small children, as for the Montessori child, the competitive number-work, the writing from dictation, the oral reading, the spelling, seemed not drudgery but interesting activity. Astonishing, too, was the uniform excellence of the results.

Now it is little more than a truism to say that "the three R's" have not really been learned until they have become automatic, that reading, writing and arithmetic are not ends in themselves but merely the tools for work. To give command of the tools is the peculiar task of the primary school, and of the primary school only. If children can be given an acquaintance with "the three R's" in six months, it does not seem too much to expect them to acquire this automatic command in two or three years. It is incredible that the child should have to study eight years for this. Yet our elementary schools continue to assume that every child is thus mentally backward. In the higher grades we find the same subjects, formal reading lessons, formal penmanship lessons, formal arithmetic and spelling. But something has happened to these children. They are distinctly less interested, less interesting, and even less capable than the smaller children. It is depressing to realize that the elementary school has existed only to turn first-grade children into seventh-grade children, and to realize that most of the latter are nearing the end of their school-days and will pass out into the world with that intellectual listlessness and lack of command.

Let me suggest what has happened to these children. Formal work, the learning of any technique, is apt to be pleasurable as long as we can feel ourselves gradually acquiring a command over our instrument. But after we have acquired the technique and can rely upon our skill, there is no gain in continuing formal exercises. There is only gain in using our skill in real work, the work for which we have studied. If we have studied a language, we do not keep mulling over rules of grammar and vocabularies, but we try as soon as possible to read. The means now gives way to the end.

We can understand one cause for that situation of which employers complain when children come to them from the public schools unprepared in the very elements of education. In the bad memories, flimsy information, inability to write or spell or figure accurately, is found the very common indictment of the public school. The criticism is usually that the groundwork has been poor, that the children have not been trained in the fundamentals. If my thesis is correct, the groundwork has not been poor. Of recent years, it has, on the contrary, been unusually excellent and thorough. The leakage has come in the middle years, which have simply disintegrated the foundations. The school has sharpened the mind, and then, by providing only a repetition of formal work instead of practical opportunity for use of the acquired technique, has proceeded to dull it. Grammar has been studied, literature in a curiously desiccated fashion, political history, esoteric branches of arithmetic. Subjects like these have filled the time that might have been given to copious individual reading, to writing about what is read or experienced, to practical number-work in simple statistics or accounting. Time which might have been given, through use of pictures and newspapers, to the cultivation of an imaginative historical and geographical background, has gone into aimless memorizing, or into a glib use of words and phrases.

This situation is all the more preposterous because both the high school and college are full of studies that could be begun by the intelligent child as soon as a technical proficiency in "the three R's" was once obtained. What psychological law declares that before fourteen a human being is incapable of learning languages, the sciences, or even the sociological studies, but that after fourteen he is capable of learning all these things? As a matter of fact, most of these "higher" studies could be much more easily assimilated by the quick and curious mind of the younger child than by the older. And for the worker in any field, acquaintance with elementary science and the organization of society is so emphatically important that we cannot afford to let the vast majority of our citizens remain all their lives ignorant of their very terms. In the four years of the "grammar school" an intelligent interest could be awakened in these fields, and the main outlines grasped. This would not mean the addition of many new subjects to an already crowded curriculum. It would merely mean the dropping of "the three R's" back into their rightful place in the primary school. It would lighten rather than overburden the school. We should then have a fair division of labor and function between the schools, to the profit of both.

If there is one criticism of the public school system on its intellectual side that can justly be made general, it is this of the wasted years. The school has found itself in this paradoxical situation, that the more excellent became its primary methods the poorer became the product at the end of the system. This paradox is explained. Educators have simply failed to recognize that the sharper they made the elementary tools and the better the facilities of obtaining skill in their use, the more varied and immediate should be the work upon which the tools are to be exercised. They have failed to provide this work. They have left a leakage in public education which has almost defeated its own ends.

THE CULT OF THE BEST

A valuable inventory of our American ideals of taste and culture should result from the request of the American Federation of Arts that the Carnegie Foundation undertake an investigation of the teaching of art in this country. We have devoted much attention to importing aesthetic values and works of art from Europe, and to providing museums, libraries and art courses for the public. But we have scarcely asked ourselves what is to come of it all. A survey of what is being done "in the schools and colleges and universities as well as in the professional art schools of the country to promote the knowledge, appreciation and production of art in America" will be of little value, however, if it is to concern itself merely with discovering how many art schools and how many students there are; how many courses on art are given in the colleges, and the credits which each course counts towards the degree. What we need to know is the direction of the studies. We must not feel relieved in spirit if we find there is "enough," and correspondingly depressed if we find there is "not enough" being done for art in America. We must clear up our ideas as to what a genuine art education would be for the layman, and then ask whether the present emphases are the ones to produce it.

Artistic appreciation in this country has been understood chiefly as the acquiring of a familiarity with "good works of art," and with the historical fields of the different arts, rather than as the cultivating of spontaneous taste. The millionaire with his magnificent collections has only been doing objectively what the anxious college student is doing who takes courses in the history and appreciation of art, music or literature, or the women's clubs that follow standard manuals of criticism and patronize bureaus of university travel. Everywhere the emphasis is on acquisition. A great machinery for the extension of culture has grown up around us in the last generation, devoted to the collection, objectively or imaginatively, of masterpieces. The zealous friends of art in and out of the schools have been engaged in bringing before an ever-widening public a roster of the "best." Art education has been almost entirely a learning about what is "good." "Culture" has come to mean the jacking-up of one's appreciations a notch at a time until they have reached a certain standard level. To be cultured has meant to like masterpieces.

Art education has, in other words, become almost a branch of moral education. We are scarcely out of that period when it was a moral obligation upon every child to learn to play the piano. There is still a thoughtful striving after righteousness in our attendance at the opera. And this moral obligation is supported by quasi-ecclesiastical sanctions. Each art, as taught in our schools and colleges, has its truly formidable canon of the "best," and its insistent discrimination between the sanctified and the apocryphal scriptures. The teaching of English literature in the colleges is a pure example of this orthodoxy. Criticism and expression are neglected in favor of absorption and reverence of the classics. The student enters college on a ritual of examination in them. He remains only through his susceptibility to their influence. Examine what passes for cultural education in other fields, and you will find that it is historical, lexicographical, encyclopaedic, and neither utilitarian nor aesthetic. It is prompted by the scholarly ideal rather than by an ideal of taste. The prize goes to those who can acquire the most of these goods. No one is challenged to spontaneous taste any more than the monk is asked to create his own dogmas.

To me this conception of culture is unpleasantly undemocratic. I am not denying the superlative beauty of what has come to be officially labeled "the best that has been thought and done in the world." But I do object to its being made the universal norm. For if you educate people in this way, you only really educate those whose tastes run to the classics. You leave the rest of the world floundering in a fog of cant, largely unconscious perhaps, trying sincerely to squeeze their appreciations through the needle's eye. You get as a result hypocrites or "lowbrows," with culture reserved only for a few. All the rest of us are left without guides, without encouragement, and tainted with original sin.

An education in art appreciation will be valueless if it does not devote itself to clarifying and integrating natural taste. The emphasis must be always on what you do like, not on what you ought to like. We have never had a real test of whether bad taste is positive or merely a lack of consciousness. We have never tried to discover strong spontaneous lines of diversified taste. To the tyranny of the "best" which Arnold's persuasive power imposed upon this most inquisitive, eager and rich American generation, can be laid, I think, our failure to develop the distinctive styles and indigenous art spirit which the soil should have brought forth abundantly. For as long as you humbly follow the best, you have no eyes for the vital. If you are using your energy to cajole your appreciations, you have none left for unforced aesthetic emotion. If your training has been to learn and appreciate the best that has been thought and done in the world, it has not been to discriminate between the significant and the irrelevant that the experience of every day is flinging up in your face. Civilized life is really one aesthetic challenge after another, and no training in appreciation of art is worth anything unless one has become able to react to forms and settings. The mere callousness with which we confront our ragbag city streets is evidence enough of the futility of the Arnold ideal. To have learned to appreciate a Mantegna and a Japanese print, and Dante and Debussy, and not to have learned nausea at Main street, means an art education which is not merely worthless but destructive.

I know that such complaints are met by the plea that the fight has been so hard in this country to get any art education at all that it is idle to talk of cultivating public taste until this battle is won. Mr. Edward Dickinson still pleads in a recent book the cause of music to the stony educationists of the land. Let us get a foothold in the colleges with our music courses, these defenders seem to say, and your taste will evolve from them. But the way to reach a goal is not to start off in the opposite direction, and my thesis is that education in the appreciation of art has been moving exactly in this wrong direction. Widespread artistic taste would have had a better chance to develop in this country if we had not been so much concerned with knowing what we ought to know and liking what we ought to like. The movement has caught those whose taste happened to coincide with the canons. It has perverted a much larger host who have tried to pretend that their taste coincided. And it has left untouched the joyous masses who might easily, as in other countries, have evolved a folk-culture if they had not been outlawed by this ideal.

The ideal still dominates, although it becomes every day more evident that its effect has been disastrous. A younger generation of architects has filled our cities with sepulchral neo-classicism and imitative débris of all the ages. We get its apotheosis in the fantasy of Washington, where French chateaux snuggle up close to colonial mansions, and the great lines of the city are slashed by cheap and tawdry blocks. All this has been done with the best will in the world, by men curious and skilful, well instructed in the "best" of all time. It has been a conscientious following of an ideal of beauty. We are just beginning to discover uneasily how false that ideal is. Art to most of us has come to mean painting instead of the decoration and design and social setting that would make significant our objective life. Our moral sense has made us mad for artistic "rightness." What we have got out of it is something much worse than imitation. It is worship.

This effort to follow the best, which even our revolutionists engage in, has the effect of either closing the appreciation to new styles or leaving it open to passing winds of fashion. That we are fashion-ridden is the direct result of an education which has made acquisition and not discrimination the motive. The cult of the best is harmless only if it has been superimposed on the broadest basis of personal discrimination, begun in earliest years. Let us admit that the appreciations of the Brahmins marvelously coincide with what Matthew Arnold has stamped as right. But perhaps for most of us there has not been the environment to produce that happy coincidence. Our education has forced us all to be self-made men in artistic appreciation. Our tastes suffer from hiatuses and crotchetinesses and color-blindnesses because no effort has been made to integrate our sincere likes and dislikes and focus and sharpen our reactions. Until the present ideal is overthrown, we have no chance of getting a sincere and general public taste. We can have only the mechanics of art education. I do not mean that America has been unique in this. We have only been a little worse than other countries because we have been more conscientious.

WHAT IS EXPERIMENTAL EDUCATION?

At a time when more people are thinking intelligently about American education than ever before, it is unfortunate that there should be any confusion between the widely diverse trails that experimentation is opening up to the modern school. It is becoming increasingly evident that the "experimental" in education does not at all mean the same thing to educational administrators as it does to educational idealists. "Experimental education" has not yet been pitted in competition against the "experimental school," but it is not unlikely that the different techniques which they suggest may come to seem hostile to each other, and so the real values of both be lost. At present the two seem to be developing in a fairly complete disregard of each other. It would be dangerous for American education to tangle itself in the dilemma of choosing between them. On the other hand, it would be even more disastrous to confuse them. If we attempt to apply the quantitative standards of the new "experimental education" to the life of the "experimental school," or to infuse the qualitative ideals of the "experimental school" into the technique of "experimental education," we run the risk of spoiling that modern and socially-adjusted school towards which we are all feeling our way.

When the inventive school superintendent or professor of education speaks of "experimental education," he is thinking, not of the "model school," but of the new standard tests in the fundamental subjects by which the work of large masses of public school children is being regularly measured and compared. The city school survey has elaborated a technique of intellectual measurements which is giving us very rapidly a genuine quantitative science of education. A report like Professor Judd's in the "Cleveland Survey"—"Measuring the Work of the Public Schools"—is a storehouse of suggestiveness for all who like to see how mathematics can be fruitfully applied to living. These statistical studies measure accurately the performance of children in the different grades and at different ages in the specific literate skills which everybody needs even to start fairly in the race of opportunity. The standard tests have been worked out experimentally with great numbers of school-children so that average norms of accomplishment can be set for any class or any individual. Rates of speed and quality of handwriting, and their relation to each other; ability to spell common words; rate and capacity of accurate figuring; rate and quality of silent and oral reading;—these are the aptitudes that are rigidly measured by the tests. The children are treated as segregated arithmetical minds, reading minds, spelling minds, as units of intellectual behavior. The tests are not "examinations," for they do not aim to show any absolute attainment of "knowledge." Their value is in the comparison they afford of individual skill, and of deviations from a norm of effectiveness. In the mass of scores you have an intellectual relief map of your class, your school, your city system.

Now nothing could apparently be more deadly and mechanical than this treating of living children as if they were narrowly isolated minds. In this "experimental education" we are evidently in another world from the "experimental school." Yet out of these tests emerge the most important implications for modern education. Out of this "experimental education" we at last get a scientific basis for the "modern school." For we have irrefutable proof of the enormous diversity of minds and aptitudes. We have a demonstration of the utter foolishness of subjecting children to a uniform educational process. We have accurate proof of the fallacy of the "average" in education. These tests are added proof of the unscientific character of the typical public school on that very technical and administrative side which has been most carefully developed. The graded school was a brilliant invention for its time, but the bases of classification are shown by these new tests to be absurd. Children are now classified, for purposes of education, largely by age and average standing. The tests show that neither category has the slightest relevance for effective learning. We classify things for the purpose of doing something to them. Any classification which does not assist manipulation is worse than useless. But mere numerical age is no clue whatsoever to mental or even physiological age, and minds with the same average may plot out very differently for every individual one of the various skills and interests that elementary training involves. Our educational grading has been as sentimental and sterile as the ancient philosophers' classification of matter into earth, water, fire, air. Such a conception of the world was interesting, but there was nothing you could do with it. All the school has done with its classifying has been to get the children into groups where they could be dosed with an orderly sequence of lessons. There has been no handle by which their heterogeneous minds and wills could be taken hold of and directed. The rule of the classroom is necessarily military, because such diverse people could only be unified in the most objective and external and coercive way. No internal control would be possible. So the teacher must devote a large part of her educational energy to the mere business of policing. When she actually "taught," it was only the average child that she could really address—the fairly bright mediocrity. The other pupils wasted their time almost in direct proportion to their deviation above or below that average. Children passed up through their educational life on the basis of an "average mark," which represented nothing whatever but a number. The standard tests have shown repeatedly that ability is so unevenly distributed that the brightest fourth-year children overlap the poorest eighth-year children. However children may average, scarcely two children in the same class will ever be found to have the identical capacity in the different subjects. The tests reveal not only that children differ, but just how curiously and widely they do differ.

The traditional classification is enough to wreck any educational system, even without the deadness of the curriculum. With the progressive congestion of the public schools, teaching has become more and more impossible. The traditional system of grading has successfully resisted most improvement in teaching, and vitiated the newer values that have been brought into the school. If children, clearly not defective, cannot learn arithmetic, read slowly and unintelligently, spell chaotically and write a slovenly hand, question the grading system. Never have there been such admirable techniques for teaching these fundamental things. But the classification defies them. The "class" gives the teacher no leverage for improving the children's skill. An unscientific grading is as much a barrier to altering minds as it is to changing materials.

These truths seem elementary and obvious, yet we had to wait for this "experimental education" to shake complacency in the "graded school." Now if we accept these tests we have to conclude that it is useless to grade children for education unless those "grades" correspond accurately and specifically to the capacities of the children. Work must be done in each specific subject with—and only with—those who have approximately the same capacity. The "average" is totally unknown in that "real life" which we are constantly forced to set up in antithesis to the school. In no function of life is any one going to be judged by a composite ability to read, write, spell, figure. One succeeds not through any average skill or average information, but through the ability to throw all one's skill and all one's intelligence where it is demanded. A measurement of intelligence by averages will always produce just that ineffectiveness and vagueness for which the products of the public school are censured at present.

The fallacy of the educational "average" involves another fallacy, equally obvious but equally prevalent. This is the fallacy of the "partially perfect." The school ranks the seventy per cent child equal to the hundred per cent child. Children pass to more difficult work on an admitted basis of imperfect accomplishment. But for any real effectiveness in the world it is not enough to be habitually only seventy per cent right. Whenever you need to be literate, the world demands that you be actually literate. If you have information, you are either useless or dangerous unless your information is accurate. It is better not to know arithmetic at all than persistently to make only seven hits out of ten. For all practical purposes your child is as much a failure at seventy per cent as he is at zero per cent. It will avail him little to be able to read and write and figure at a rate and an excellence only seventy per cent of the standard. In any situation which requires these elementary skills he will be almost as much handicapped as if he were entirely illiterate. It is time that the school faced the bitter truth that life demands an approximate perfection in whatever one tries to do. Education must shape all its technique towards this approximate perfection. It is not necessary that all should do the same thing. But it is necessary that what one pretends to do one should succeed gradually in doing. The individual who is allowed to persist continuously on a level of imperfect accomplishment is not being educated. For him education is a failure. He should either drop his technique, or ways should be found to improve him towards mastery. What children are learning at any one time they should be learning with a sense of control. The more difficult should not be confronted till the less difficult has been absorbed. And this controlled progress will be possible only in a school where children work with their equals. Classification in education should be based only on specific proficiency.

The new "experimental education" is engaged in making dramatic in the schools these truths. It is a force even more revolutionary than the idealism of the "experimental school." The situation suggested by the "curve of distribution" is one of the most momentous facts to be reckoned with by us of today. It is making over our theories of democracy, social reform and social progress. To work out its manifold implications in the school is to touch the very nerve of our democratic future.

THE DEMOCRATIC SCHOOL

A recent article in the *New York Times* (Oct. 17, 1915) by Dr. Thomas S. Baker, Headmaster of the Tome School, contains an able pedagogical criticism of the Gary school which is typical of the general attitude towards the Gary idea on the part of conservative schoolmen. Nothing could bring out more clearly the difference in educational values between this professional teaching opinion and the broad social vision of Superintendent Wirt. Dr. Baker admits the impressive social effectiveness of the plan. It is "the last development in socializing the schools." Mr. Wirt is "not only an educator, but also a social reformer, a city worker." But Dr. Baker's argument is really the specialized pedagogical one against the social. Where Mr. Wirt sees the school as a community center, a children's world, Dr. Baker sees it as an educational factory. "The social value of the Gary schools," he says, "is beyond question. Its pedagogic excellence has still to be determined." From this point of view, a school is not so much a place to train effective citizens as to make "thorough scholars." He questions whether "these side issues in the scheme of child-training"—the gymnasia, shops, laboratories, which the Gary school contains—"are really essential in mental development." He is afraid that the young citizens of Gary learn more from their industrial shops and science laboratories than from their books.

Dr. Baker's guarded argument is really a glorification of "intellectual discipline" as against an intelligent capacity to lead an organic life in a modern society which needs above all things resourceful adaptation and social appreciations. It is a question of ideals, and no more important issue was ever put to a people than this one of how we want our next generation trained. The school is not only the one institution which assimilates all the people, but it is the most easily modifiable. It is not only the easiest lever of social progress but the most effective, for it deals with relatively plastic human material. To decide what kind of a school we want is almost to decide what kind of a society we want.

If we only want that kind of a school which would "make hard-working and accurate scholars and produce thoughtful men," we must resign ourselves to a progressive softening of the fiber and capacity of the mass of our people. The average educator acts as if he thought of his child-world as a level plain of capacities. There is the mass of unskilled, unawakened minds; here is the level of scholarship, knowledge, civic virtue, appreciations. Education is to him the process of lifting up the mass from their primitive level to the higher one. The public school is the elevator into which all are to be shoveled and transported to the upper story. And the American public school in the last fifty years has been faithfully following this ideal.

The truth is, of course, that mental aptitude is not any such level desert, but rather a series of inclined planes. When we try to educate all the children of all the people, we are not dealing with a homogeneous mass, but with sliding scales of capacity. A mental test of the school-children of a state would reveal an incline extending in orderly gradation from the genius down to the imbecile. A physical test would give us a different slant, a test for artistic or mechanical capacity another. Stand at the center of divine average and try to lever any of these slopes into a horizontal position and you find half of your society squatting heavily at the lower end. You may ascribe it to race capacity, personal heredity, social environment, malnutrition, defective nervous organization or anything you please, but the fact remains that the greater part of the human raw material will be permanently resistive to or only dully appreciative of any attempts to elevate them to a level. This is true of any capacity you may choose. The outstanding truth of society seems to be the heterogeneous distribution of capacities. And the irony of it is that after artistic capacity true intellectual capacity is probably the rarest. For the public school to try to make intellectualists of all its children is a sheer defiance of sociological reality.

Some educators, while they recognize this diversity, yet insist on uniform standards, uniform curricula, uniform discipline, on the ground that social order in a democracy is imperiled unless the highest degree of like-mindedness prevails. Such a democracy would be the stagnant democracy of China. The result of these attempts at standardization have been the automatic centrifugal flinging off into space of the children whose interests were not intellectual, who were no more capable of being made into "accurate scholars" than they were into artists and poets. And from those who did not get quite flung off, but clung on with their teeth, we get most of our prevailing pseudo-culture. To keep on trying to "develop the mind" and produce "thorough scholarship" in those whom we force to submit to educational processes, means simply to go on creating a nerveless and semi-helpless mass of boys and girls who will never take their effective and interested place in the world because they have no mental tools which they can wield. Such a course is coming to be generally recognized as a kind of slow national suicide, a slow suffocation of industrial and social progress.

The schools do change, but the schoolmen yield grudgingly. Nothing could be more naïve than the test which Dr. Baker proposes for evaluating the Gary plan. Submit, he says, the highest class in the Gary schools to an examination by the College Examining Board. If the students pass, the Gary system will be justified of its children. Was ever a more patent assertion of the professional bias? Let the children drop out of the lower grades untrained except in the rudiments, but if the small minority in the highest class passes its Vergil and algebra and English literature and German with marks as high as the graduates of the Tome School, then the Gary system will cease to be considered a "mere experiment." If this is what the critics of the Gary plan mean when they plead for an "evaluation of this novel experiment," we may well hope that it will escape the peril.

Such a conception of educational values cannot become too speedily obsolete. A public school is a mockery unless it educates the public. It cannot make the rarefied and strained product at the top the test of its effectiveness. And the public is not ideally educated unless its individuals—all of them—are intelligent, informed, skilled, resourceful, up to the limit of their respective capacities. Life itself can no longer be trusted to provide this education; the school must substitute. The Gary school deliberately sets such an ideal. Democracy does not mean uniformity, but it does mean equality of opportunity. A democratic school would be one where every child had the chance to discover and develop aptitude. The Gary school, with its harmonious activities of intellectual, manual, artistic and scientific work, physical education and play, gives just this chance. Democratic education does not mean the provision of separate schools for different kinds of children, or even separate courses in the same school, as the movement for industrial education is now threatening to bring. This is to create at once invidious distinctions, and fasten class education upon us. To say that children are different does not mean that some are fitted to be scholars and others to be manual workers, some to be artists and some to be scientists. The differences are differences of focus and not of quality.

To most children will appear in the course of school life some dominant interest, and it is upon the cultivation of that interest that the child's chance of being more than a nerveless mediocrity will depend. It is upon that training that his chance of being absorbed out of the school into the social and industrial world will depend. At the same time, without a common· background with his fellows he will be alien and adrift in the world. Interest and skill in one's work, whether it be making automobiles or teaching Greek, an acquaintance with the contemporary world, an alert intelligence which is always seeking to diminish the area of things human that are alien to one—a man or woman with this would be truly educated in any society. But both focus and background are supremely necessary. The present educational system does not really set itself to provide either. Only in a school organized on some such plan as the Gary plan will such education be possible.

This does not mean that every child is to marvelously blossom into ideally alert and skilled intelligence. But we can be sure that a school which gives opportunity for the development of the most varied aptitudes in the free play of a child-community life will have done all that it could. No one pretends that the Gary education is the intrinsically ideal education for all time. But we can say that, given the best social demands of America today, this school will make for the most robust, effective, intelligent citizenship of which we are at present capable.

CLASS AND SCHOOL[1]

The proposed experimental school which the General Education Board is to found in conjunction with Teachers' College in New York has sent a shiver through the conservative schoolmen of America. It is assumed that the policy of the new school will follow Dr. Flexner's manifesto of the "Modern School," that adroit and uncompromising crystallization of the radical philosophy of our new American education. Dr. Flexner has proved himself to be an admirable agitator, for he has succeeded, with doctrines that public-school educators have been discussing for ten years and which experimental schools all through the country have been testing out, in rousing the slumberous camp of private secondary schoolmasters to a sense of what is going on in the educational world. The private secondary school is the last stronghold of educational conservatism. Enlightenment has to proceed upward through thick layers of prejudice and smugness. Dr. Flexner's voice seems to have broken in the walls and gotten a hearing for the new education even in the walls of the traditional New England academy. It is for these people that the "Modern School" was written, for only those will find its proposals "revolutionary and dangerous" who have never read a line of Dewey or G. Stanley Hall, never read a copy of an educational journal, never visited an experimental school, or even the newer plants of the best public schools in American cities. There is irony in the location of the new school at Teachers' College. For the latter has been one of the most persistently experimental educational centers in the country. If its "model" schools have felt in the course of time the blighting touch of conventionality, at least in the Speyer course of industrial arts there has been developed a method of permanent value. There is no more accurate application of Dr. Flexner's demand that "children should begin by getting acquainted with objects," "follow the life-cycles of plants and animals," "the observation and execution of industrial and commercial processes," and so forth. In this industrial arts course the children are concerned from the beginning with food-products and clothing and building and the way different peoples make their living. Out of this handling of homely things grow the geography and science and history and mathematics. It seems only a question of time before there will be scarcely an elementary school untouched by this practical approach to knowledge through objects and projects and concrete facts.

Dr. Flexner's tilting is not against our rapidly improving public elementary school so much as it is against the private secondary school, with its sub-college, classical, formal curriculum, and its obsolete educational theory of formal discipline and salvation through drudgery. It is as an object-lesson for this branch of American education that the new school will have permanent value. It will be the heaviest assault which has yet had to be met by that vested, educational interest which we know as the private secondary school. The private school has made it its function to prepare the sons and daughters of the well-to-do for college, and so keep up the tradition of leisured and cultured wealth. This is the ideal at the bottom of the hearts of the conservative schoolmen. A knowledge which is useless, like the formal classics and mathematics, is only a sharpened tool of exclusiveness, for only the younger generation of a ruling class can afford to give its time to it. In a growing industrial society such an education becomes ever more and more a dividing line between classes. That the public high school has been largely controlled by the same ideals does not mean at all that this kind of education has been democratized, but merely that the unthinking and clambering middle classes have been hypnotized by vague aspirations of "culture" and "intellectual training" into imitation of the traditional ruling-class education. Some of the strongest opposition to vocational education in the public schools comes even from the ranks of the ambitious wage-earners who "want their children to have the educational advantages they were denied." They resent what they misinterpret as an attempt to keep their younger generation in a subordinate labor class. What they do not see is that the traditional education which they admire is no real education for the modern world. We find the industrious proletarian and the exclusive Tory joining hands in opposing the new democratic education which is meant to have the effects of freeing both classes and making them fit together to administer a free society. The Tory wants to keep for his children his privileged status; the wage-earner wants to obtain for his children this privileged status. "Book" education, innocent of practicality and use, is still an accepted mark of this geniality. Neither class has any real sense yet of a democratic attitude that finds both the "utilitarian" and the "cultural" irrelevant terms, and demands only effective activity and imaginative understanding from every citizen up to the limit of his capacity.

The "old" education then is a class-education, and therefore has no place in a society which is trying to become democratic. How much class-feeling is behind the current allegiance to the education of discipline and drudgery is shown in a paper by Miss Edith Hamilton of the Bryn Mawr School in the *New Republic* for February 10, 1917. She pleads for the "old" education in behalf of her girls. But when she says "school" she has in the back of her mind an institution for the training of the well-to-do classes. Her argument against a change in education seems to be based on the idea that change would be prejudicial to the life which she accepts as worthiest for those fortunate classes with which she is best acquainted. Her argument is that life will make no stern demands upon the sheltered, economically endowed leisure which most of her girls will enjoy. Without external standards their fiber must deteriorate unless they have learned the joy of work by the doing of things because they are hard. Without impersonal intellectual interests, their personal energy, she says, will waste away in futility or in a meddlesome control of their own daughters. The boy is harnessed into some kind of self-discipline by the exigencies of business life. But for the girl, the substitution in the "modern school" of domestic science for "elegant accomplishments" is only an illusory discipline. Not only are these arts of housekeeping too easy to provide discipline, but they will never be demanded from the upper-class girl. Only the traditional curriculum, therefore, impersonal, cultural, laborious, will give her the needed stimulus to play her leisured rôle worthily.

At first sight nothing could be more ironic than this gospel of strenuous effort preached in the name of a sheltered class. Why should a girl be disciplined, trained to do things "*because* they are hard," for a life which becomes "easier and easier," unless her teachers wish to provide her with some kind of moral and intellectual justification for her social rôle? The "old" education combines uselessness and effort, and it is just this combination which would maintain leisure-class functions and yet leave the individuals morally justified. The uselessness makes you exclusive and the effort satisfies your moral sense. It is a little curious to find Miss Hamilton using the "utilitarian" argument against domestic science, that is, that it will never be used by her girls. Yet she wishes them to acquire "impersonal intellectual interests," which they can never use except in not very real "cultural" dabblings and social work.

Miss Hamilton's argument for tradition is the orthodox one that is now being repeated by all those who oppose the new Rockefeller school. "The old education is superior to any training which makes interest not discipline, efficiency not knowledge, the standard." Now this point at issue between interest and discipline has been so thoroughly discussed by John Dewey in his "Interest as Related to Will" and other writings, that one is surprised at this late day to find responsible educators who are willing to give the impression that they are unacquainted with Dewey's arguments. Even if disciples like Dr. Flexner and myself in our enthusiasm unconsciously caricature him, the philosophy is there in its classic form in Dewey for all to read. The curious notion of the "old" educator that interest makes work "easy," instead of intensifying the effort, is only possible, of course, to minds soaked in a Puritan tradition. Dewey shows that interest and discipline are not antagonistic to efficiency and knowledge, but that knowledge is merely information effectively used and manipulated, and discipline is willed and focused interest. Each has an element of the other. It is meaningless to talk of interest *vs.* discipline when all real interest has an organizing effect on one's activity, and any real discipline is built up on a foundation of interest. Indeed in one of my articles to which Miss Hamilton takes exception, I define discipline as "willed skill," which is as far from any conception of "making things easy," of "smattering and superficiality," as could well be imagined. It is a superstition, of course, as Miss Hamilton says, to suppose that all children burn with a hard gem-like flame of curiosity to know, but it is equally a superstition to suppose that with all children strenuous drudgery flowers into the immense joy of work and creation, or that effort taken consistently against the grain of interest can suddenly be transmuted into spontaneous activity. A certain habit, a mechanical routine spirit, may be evolved by drudgery, but not imaginative skill. All true discipline comes from overcoming obstacles beyond which one is conscious of a goal in itself worth while. It is only a feeble spirit which can be drugged by effort in and for itself. In those admired cases where facility comes after conscientious but uninteresting effort, let the old-fashioned educator ask herself whether the child gained the satisfaction of accomplishment *because* he went through the discipline, or whether it was not only *because* he liked the satisfaction of accomplishment that he was willing to go through the drudgery. If you admit the latter, then you have admitted the case for the new education. Temperaments, impulses, interests—or, if you like, the lack of interests—will insist on dominating, on determining the way each child takes his experience. All education can ever do is to provide the experience, and stimulate, guide, organize interests. Anything else may produce, at its best, a trained animal. It will not be education, and it will not produce men and women.

The task of the democratic school is to provide just this general experience and stimulation. Miss Hamilton's paper shows that such a school would be a challenge to the kind of institution she has in mind when she speaks of education. When leisure-class functions and leisure-class education clasp in a perfect circle, a new sociological and industrial emphasis, such as the "Modern School" suggests, might make the leisure-class pupils uneasy, restless, questioning. If you began emphasizing interest instead of drudgery, you might find yourself calling into question the sincerity of those "impersonal intellectual interests." If you emphasized efficiency instead of knowledge, you might make uncomfortably evident the unreality of much of what passes for culture in society today. You would be making insecure the moral and intellectual justifications of caste. But that is exactly the critical and undermining work which a democratic education is designed to stimulate.

These new educators are seeking a type of school which shall provide for children as human beings and not as members of any one social class. They want a school which creates a common sympathy, a common intimacy with the various activities and expressions of the modern well-rounded personality, just so far as each individual is capable, with his endowments and intelligence, of acquiring such an intimacy. The "Modern School" would turn the child's attention to the projects, objects, processes, facts, of the active world about him, not because they are good in themselves, but because they are the common stock of all classes. The development of communal functions and services forces every family more or less into touch with the active world out of which the "Modern School's" curriculum grows. It is in the study of these "real things," rather than in the logical systems of text-books, the predigested ideals of literature or a leisured class, the technical manipulation of dead languages and official science, that common interest and the sense of common possession will arise. The expectation is that interpretations and ideals which grow out of such a study will be more vital and sound because they will have come out of the child's own experience, and not have been merely shoveled into his memory. It is expected that the "strenuous effort" of the past, which was so much an effort of memory and routine, will become, in a curriculum harnessed to occupational life, an effort of interest and intelligent enthusiasm. Out of such a spirit and such a school should issue the self-sustained discipline by which all good work is done in the world.

[1] In the article later cited by Bourne, E. Hamilton, among other things, wrote:

. . . leave the boys altogether to life for the sterner training; they will not be able to escape the adamantine nails of the dread goddess Necessity. But give to the girls, denied that exacting education, schools where the central idea is work that results in discipline, whether of the mind or the will must be left to the psychologists, but at all events in some power to make oneself do thoroughly the task that lies at hand; where it is recognized that the best preparation for life in the "real" world is the habit of not shirking what is hard, and that only through steady, strenuous effort, yes, and through drudgery too, can the immense joy of work ever be tasted.

THE UNDERGRADUATE

In these days of academic self-analysis, the intellectual caliber of the American undergraduate finds few admirers or defenders. Professors speak resignedly of the poverty of his background and imagination. Even the undergraduate himself in college editorials confesses that the student soul vibrates reluctantly to the larger intellectual and social issues of the day. The absorption in petty gossip, sports, class politics, fraternity life, suggests that too many undergraduates regard their college in the light of a glorified preparatory school where the activities of their boyhood may be worked out on a grandiose scale. They do not act as if they thought of the college as a new intellectual society in which one acquired certain rather definite scientific and professional attitudes, and learned new interpretations which threw experience and information into new terms and new lights. The average undergraduate tends to meet studies like philosophy, psychology, economics, general history, with a frankly puzzled wonder. A whole new world seems to dawn upon him, in its setting and vocabulary alien to anything in his previous life. Every teacher knows this baffling resistance of the undergraduate mind.

It is not so much that the student resists facts and details. He will absorb trusts and labor unions, municipal government and direct primaries, the poems of Matthew Arnold, and James's theory of the emotions. There is no unkindliness of his mind towards fairly concrete material. What he is more or less impervious to is points-of-view, interpretations. He seems to lack philosophy. The college has to let too many undergraduates pass out into professional and business life, not only without the germ of a philosophy, but without any desire for an interpretative clue through the maze. In this respect the American undergraduate presents a distinct contrast to the European. For the latter does seem to get a certain intellectual setting for his ideas which makes him intelligible, and gives journalism and the ordinary expression of life a certain tang which we lack here. Few of our undergraduates get from the college any such intellectual impress.

The explanation is probably not that the student has no philosophy, but that he comes to college with an unconscious philosophy so tenacious that the four years of the college in its present technique can do little to disintegrate it. The cultural background of the well-to-do American home with its "nice" people, its sentimental fiction and popular music, its amiable religiosity and vague moral optimism, is far more alien to the stern secular realism of modern university teaching than most people are willing to admit. The college world would find itself less frustrated by the undergraduate's secret hostility if it would more frankly recognize what a challenge its own attitudes are to our homely American ways of thinking and feeling. Since the college has not felt this dramatic contrast, or at least has not felt a holy mission to assail our American mushiness of thought through the undergraduate, it has rather let the latter run away with the college.

It is a trite complaint that the undergraduate takes his extracurricular activities more seriously than his studies. But he does this because his homely latent philosophy is essentially a sporting philosophy, the good old Anglo-Saxon conviction that life is essentially a game whose significance lies in terms of winning or losing. The passion of the American undergraduate for intercollegiate athletics is merely a symbol of a general interpretation for all the activities that come to his attention. If he is interested in politics, it is in election campaigns, in the contests of parties and personalities. His parades and cheerings are the encouragement of a racer for the goal. After election, his enthusiasm collapses. His spiritual energy goes into class politics, fraternity and club emulation, athletics, every activity which is translatable into terms of winning and losing. In Continental universities this energy would go rather into a turbulence for causes and ideas, a militant radicalism or even a more militant conservatism that would send Paris students out into the streets with a "Cail-laux as-sas-sin!" or tie up an Italian town for the sake of Italia Irredenta. Even the war, though it has called out a fund of antimilitarist sentiment in the American colleges, still tends to be spoken of in terms of an international sporting event. "Who will win?" is the question here.

Now this sporting philosophy by which the American undergraduate lives, and which he seems to bring with him from his home, may be a very good philosophy for an American. It is of the same stuff with our good-humored contempt for introspection, our dread of the "morbid," our dislike of conflicting issues and insoluble problems. The sporting attitude is a grateful and easy one. Issues are decided cleanly. No irritating fringes are left over. The game is won or lost. Analysis and speculation seem superfluous. The point is that such a philosophy is as different as possible from that which motivates the intellectual world of the modern college, with its searchings, its hypotheses and interpretations and revisions, its flexibility and openness of mind. In the scientific world of the instructor, things are not won or lost. His attitude is not a sporting one.

Yet the college has allowed some of these sporting attitudes to be imposed upon it. The undergraduates' gladiatorial contests proceed under faculty supervision and patronage. Alumni contribute their support to screwing up athletic competition to the highest semi-professional pitch. They lend their hallowing patronage to fraternity life and other college institutions which tend to emphasize social distinction. And the college administration, in contrast to the European scheme, has turned the college course into a sort of race with a prize at the goal. The degree has become a sort of honorific badge for all classes of society, and the colleges have been forced to give it this quasi-athletic setting and fix the elaborate rules of the game by which it may be won—rules which shall be easy enough to get all classes competing for it, and hard enough to make it a sufficient prize to keep them all in the race. An intricate system of points and courses and examinations sets the student working for marks and the completion of schedules rather than for a new orientation in important fields of human interest.

The undergraduate can scarcely be blamed for responding to a system which so strongly resembles his sports, or for bending his energies to playing the game right, rather than assimilating the intellectual background of his teachers. So strongly has this sporting technique been acquired by the college that even when the undergraduate lacks the sporting instinct and does become interested in ideas, he is apt to find that he has only drawn attention to his own precocity and won amused notice rather than respect. In spite of the desire of instructors to get themselves over to their students, in spite of a real effort to break down the "class-consciousness" of teacher and student, the gulf between their attitudes is too fundamental to be easily bridged. Unless it is bridged, however, the undergraduate is left in a sort of Peter Pan condition, looking back to his schoolboy life and carrying along his schoolboy interests with him, instead of anticipating his graduate or professional study or his active life. What should be an introduction to professional or business life in a world of urgent political and social issues, and the acquiring of intellectual tools with which to meet their demands, becomes a sort of sequestered retreat out of which to jump from boyhood into a badly prepared middle age.

The college will not really get the undergraduate until it becomes more conscious of the contrast of its own philosophy with his sporting philosophy, and tackles his boyish Americanisms less mercifully, or until it makes college life less like that of an undergraduate country club, and more of an intellectual workshop where men and women in the fire of their youth, with conflicts and idealisms, questions and ambitions and desire for expression, come to serve an apprenticeship under the masters of the time.

WHO OWNS THE UNIVERSITIES

The marked and immediate reaction of the thinking public to the Scott Nearing case shows a growing conviction that all is not well within the conventional forms of university control. It implies a sense that universities, whether supported by the state or privately, are becoming too vitally institutions of public service to be much longer directed on the plan of a private corporation. University trustees are generally men of affairs, and as men of affairs they naturally tend to hold the same attitude towards the university that they do to the other institutions—the churches and railroads and corporations—they may direct. The university officers whom they appoint seem to have exactly the same duties of upholding the credit of the institution, of securing funds to meet its pressing needs, of organizing the administrative machinery, which their corporation officers would have. Professors are engaged by contract as any highly-skilled superintendent would be engaged in a factory. If a well-paid subordinate of a mining corporation could not get along with his colleagues and his men, or if he consorted with the I. W. W. or made revolutionary speeches in the streets, his services would be dispensed with as readily as the Pennsylvania trustees rid themselves of the unpleasantness of Professor Nearing. Trustees may respect a professor more than they do intrinsically a fourth vice-president. They may tend to err, as Chancellor Day has suggested, on the side of "merciful consideration." But they cannot see that the amenities of the case materially alter the professor's status.

This would be the case of university trustees stated in its rawest terms. That they tend so often to act as if they were a mere board of directors of a private corporation gives rise to endless suspicion that they consult their own interests and the interests of the donors of the vested wealth they represent as trustees of the university, just as they would protect, as faithful corporation directors, the interests of the shareholders of the company. It is just this attitude which the thinking public is no longer inclined to tolerate. We are acquiring a new view of the place of the university in the community. When the American college was no more than an advanced boys' academy, there may have been some excuse for this form of control by self-perpetuating and irresponsible boards of trustees. But many things have changed since Harvard and Yale, Princeton, Pennsylvania and Columbia, were founded.

Now this determined autocracy may not have worked so badly when most of the trustees and practically all of the instructors were ministers of the Gospel, although even in those days faculties sometimes complained that their careful plans were overridden by men ignorant of collegiate business and little interested in educational policy. The demand that trustees' functions should be limited to the management of funds, leaving the faculties to regulate administration and control appointments is a hoary one. But with the passing of control from the ghostly to the moneyed element, the gulf between trustee and professor has become extreme. Professors have fallen into a more and more subordinate place, and the president, who used to be their representative, has now become almost entirely the executive agent of the trustees, far removed in power and purse and public distinction from the professor. The university president in this country has become a convenient symbol for autocratic power, but even when he has become a "mayor of the palace" and professors may not approach their governors except through him, the real autocracy still lies in the external board behind him.

This absentee and amateur form of university control is being constantly ratified by our American notions of democracy, and that folkway, which runs so omnipresently through our institutional life, of giving the plain ultimate citizen control, in order that we may be protected from the tyranny of the bureaucrat. The newer state universities are controlled in exactly the same spirit. Regents, elected by legislatures, have shown themselves quite as capable as the most private trustees of representing vested political interests. Nor has democracy been achieved by the cautious admission, in recent years, of alumni trustees, as in the case of Columbia, or, as in the case of Harvard and Yale, by the substitution of alumni for the former state officials. Self-perpetuating boards will always propagate their own kind, and even if alumni trustees were ever inclined to be anything but docile, their minority representation would always be ineffective for democracy.

The issues of the modern university are not those of private property but of public welfare. Irresponsible control by a board of amateur notables is no longer adequate for the effective scientific and sociological laboratories for the community that the universities are becoming. The protests in the most recent case imply a growing realization that a professor who has a dynamic and not a purely academic interest in social movements is an asset for the whole community. The latest controversy between trustees and professors seems to have been very definitely an issue between interested policy and accurate, technical fact. It seems to have been clearly a case of old tradition against new science, the prejudiced guesses of corporation officials against the data of a scientific student of economics. Any form of university control which gives the prejudiced guess the power over the scientific research is thus a direct blow at our own social knowledge and effectiveness. The public simply cannot afford to run this risk of having the steady forging ahead of social and economic research curtailed and hampered. We cannot afford to depend wholly on the tempering of trustees by the fear of the clamor of public opinion. It is wholly undesirable that trustees should be detained only by "merciful consideration" from discharging professors whom they find uncongenial or who they feel are spreading unsound doctrine. Make university trustees directors of a private corporation and you give them the traditional right of terminating contracts with their employees without giving reasons or any form of trial. But if the university is not to be a mere degree-manufactory, or a pre-vocational school representing the narrow interests of a specialized economic class, but is to be that public intellectual and scientific service that we all want it to be, the governance must be different from that of a mining company, and the status of the professor different from that of a railroad employee. Professors should have some security of office.

An interested public which feels this way will demand that the faculties be represented strongly in the determination of all university policy and in the selection and dismissal of the instructors. It may even demand that the community itself be represented. Trustees who really envisage the modern university as a public service, as a body of scientific and sociological experts, will gladly share their power. If they do not, they will demonstrate how radically their own conception of a university differs from the general one, and it will be the duty of professors to assert their rights by all those forms of collective organization whereby controlled classes from the beginning of time have made their desires effective.

ONE OF OUR CONQUERORS[1]

When Dr. Alexander Mackintosh Butcher was elected to the presidency of Pluribus University ten years ago, there was general agreement that in selecting a man who was not only a distinguished educator but an executive of marked business ability the trustees had done honor to themselves and their university as well as to the new president. For Dr. Butcher had that peculiar genius which would have made him as successful in Wall Street or in a governor's chair as in the classroom. Every alumnus of Pluribus knows the story told of the young Alexander Mackintosh Butcher, standing at the age of twenty-two at the threshold of a career. Eager, energetic, with a brilliant scholastic record behind him, it was difficult to decide into what profession he should throw his powerful talents. To his beloved and aged president the young man went for counsel. "My boy," said the good old man, "remember that no profession offers nobler opportunities for service to humanity than that of education." And what should he teach? "Philosophy is the noblest study of man." And a professor of philosophy the young Butcher speedily became.

Those who were so fortunate as to study philosophy under him at Pluribus will never forget how uncompromisingly he preached absolute idealism, the Good, the True and the Beautiful, or how witheringly he excoriated the mushroom philosophies which were springing up to challenge the eternal verities. I have heard his old students remark the secret anguish which must have been his when later, as president of the university, he was compelled to entertain the famous Swiss philosopher, Monsfilius, whose alluring empiricism was taking the philosophic world by storm.

Dr. Butcher's philosophic acuteness is only equaled by his political rectitude. Indeed, it is as philospher-politician that he holds the unique place he does in our American life, injecting into the petty issues of the political arena the immutable principles of Truth. Early conscious of his duty as a man and a citizen, he joined the historic party which had earned the eternal allegiance of the nation by rescuing it from slavery. By faithful service to the chiefs of his state organization, first under the powerful Flatt, and later under the well-known Harnes, himself college-bred and a political philosopher of no mean merit, the

young Dr. Butcher worked his way up through ward captain to
the position of district leader. The practical example of Dr.
Butcher, the scholar and educator, leaving the peace of his
academic shades to carry the banner in the service of his party
ideals of Prosperity and Protection has been an inspiration to
thousands of educated men in these days of civic cowardice.
When, three years ago, his long and faithful services were rewarded by the honor of second place on the Presidential ticket
which swept the great states of Mormonia and Green Mountain,
there were none of his friends and admirers who felt that the distinction was undeserved.

President Butcher is frequently called into the councils of the
party whenever there are resolutions to be drawn up or statements of philosophic principle to be issued. He is in great demand also as chairman of state conventions, which his rare
academic distinction lifts far above the usual level of such affairs. It was at one of these conventions that he made the
memorable speech in which he drew the analogy between the
immutability of Anglo-Saxon political institutions and the multiplication table. To the applause of the keen and head-headed
business men and lawyers who sat as delegates under him, he
scored with matchless satire the idea of progress in politics, and
demonstrated to their complete satisfaction that it was as absurd
to tinker with the fundamentals of our political system as it would
be to construct a new arithmetic. In such characteristic wisdom
we have the intellectual calibre of the man.

This brilliant and profound address came only as the fruit of a
lifetime of thought on political philosophy. President Butcher's
treatise on "Why We Should Never Change Any Form of Government" has been worth more to thoughtful men than
thousands of sermons on civic righteousness. No one who has
ever heard President Butcher's rotund voice discuss in a public
address "those ideas and practices which have been tried and
tested by a thousand years of experience" will ever allow his
mind to dwell again on the progressive and disintegrating tendencies of the day, nor will he have the heart again to challenge
on any subject the "decent respect for the common opinions of
mankind."

President Butcher's social philosophy is as sound as his political. The flexibility of his mind is shown in the fact that, although
an immutabilist in politics, he is a staunch Darwinian in sociol-

ogy. Himself triumphantly fit, he never wearies of expressing his robust contempt for the unfit who encumber the earth. His essay on "The Insurrection of the Maladjusted" is already a classic in American literature. The trenchant attack on modern social movements as the impudent revolt of the unfit against those who, by their personal merits and industry, have, like himself, achieved success, has been a grateful bulwark to thousands who might otherwise have been swept sentimentally from their moorings by those false guides who erect their own weakness and failure into a criticism of society.

Dr. Butcher's literary eminence has not only won him a chair in the "American Academy of All the Arts, Sciences, and Philosophies," but has made him almost as well known abroad as at home. He has lectured before the learned societies of Lisbon on "The American at Home," and he has a wide circle of acquaintances in every capital in Europe. Most of the foreign universities have awarded him honorary degrees. In spite of his stout Americanism, Dr. Butcher has one of the most cosmopolitan of minds. His essay on "The Cosmopolitan Intellect" has been translated into every civilized language. With his admired friend, Owen Griffith, he has collaborated in the latter's endeavor to beat the swords of industrial exploitation into the ploughshares of universal peace. He has served in numerous capacities on Griffith's many peace boards and foundations, and has advised him widely and well how to distribute his millions so as to prevent the recurrence of war in future centuries.

Let it not be thought that, in recounting President Butcher's public life and services, I am minimizing his distinction as a university administrator. As executive of one of the largest universities in America, he has raised the position of college president to a dignity surpassed by scarcely any office except President of the United States. The splendid $125,000 mansion which President Butcher had the trustees of Pluribus build for him on the heights overlooking the city, where he entertains distinguished foreign guests with all the pomp worthy of his high office, is the precise measure both of the majesty with which he has endowed the hitherto relatively humble position, and the appreciation of a grateful university. The relations between President Butcher and the trustees of Pluribus have always been of the most beautiful nature. The warm and profound intellectual sympathy which he feels for the methods and practices of the

financial and corporate world, and the extensive personal affilia-
tions he has formed with its leaders, have made it possible to
leave in his hands a large measure of absolute authority. Huge
endowments have made Pluribus under President Butcher's rule
one of the wealthiest of our higher institutions of learning. With a
rare intuitive response to the spirit of the time, the President has
labored to make it the biggest and most comprehensive of its
kind. Already its schools are numbered by the dozens, its buildings by the scores, its instructors by the hundreds, its students
by the thousands, its income by the millions, and its possessions by the tens of millions.

None who have seen President Butcher in the commencement
exercises of Pluribus can ever forget the impressiveness of the
spectacle. His resemblance to Henry VIII is more marked now
that he has donned the crimson gown and flat hat of the famous
English university which gave him the degree of LL.D. Seated in
a high-backed chair—the historic chair of the first colonial president of Pluribus—surrounded by tier upon tier of his retinue of
the thousand professors of the university, President Alexander
Mackintosh Butcher presents the degrees, and in his emphatic
voice warns the five thousand graduates before him against everything new, everything untried, everything untested.

Only one office could tempt President Butcher from his high
estate. Yet even those enthusiastic alumni and those devoted
professors who long to see him President of the United States
have little hope of tempting him from his duties to his alma ma-
ter. Having set his hand to the plough, he must see Pluribus
through her harvest season, and may God prosper the work! So,
beloved of all, alumni and instructors alike, the idol of the undergraduates, a national oracle of Prosperity and Peace, President Butcher passes to a green old age, a truly Olympian figure
of the time.

---

[1] The satirical portrait is of Nicholas Murray Butler, who became president
of Columbia University at age thirty-nine. This portrait was to confirm Bourne
particularly with his unequivocal limitation of academic freedom after the
American entry into World War I. In 1912 Butler was a candidate for vice
president under Taft.

3
POLITICS, STATE, AND SOCIETY

... we stand for ideal interests solely, for we have no corporate selfishness and wield no powers of corruption. We ought to have our own class consciousness, "Les Intellectuels"!

WILLIAM JAMES

American intelligence has still to issue its Declaration of Independence. It has still to proclaim that in a democratic system the intelligence has a discipline, an interest, and a will of its own, and that this special discipline and interest call for a new conception both of individual and of national development.

HERBERT CROLY

The American intellectual class, having failed to make the higher syntheses, regresses to ideas that can issue in quick, simplified action. Thought becomes any easy rationalization of what is actually going on or what is to happen inevitably tomorrow.

RANDOLPH BOURNE

POLITICS, STATE, AND SOCIETY

Randolph Bourne's social criticism testifies to an individualistic style of thought. It is not theoretically anchored and does not have the character of a blueprint. But the lack of systematic rigor is offset by a greater persuasiveness and precision. Because general applicability is an inherent claim, large designs often put up with colorless arguments. In Bourne's case, however, we observe a preference for detail. This tendency does not result from intellectual resignation but from Bourne's understanding that social reality can be experienced and that its complexity might invalidate the comprehensive system. Recognition of the concrete thus takes the place of abstract conceptualization. Bourne was certainly far from setting great store by this polarity or from seeing it as necessary. The opposite is the case. Because he believed that subjective experience is in principle capable of truth, he attempted to express the general in the particular. It is also true, however, that after the event he often noted that he had failed; in retrospect, he sharply criticized his book *Youth and Life,* for example, saying that it was not an adequate expression of his personality.

The rhetorical structure of texts such as "A Mirror of the Middle West," "Emerald Lake," "What is Exploitation?" and "The Scientific Manager" corresponds to this fundamental ambivalence in Bourne's thought. The argument always progresses from the expression of subjective participation to a definition of the general situation. This strategy of the argument is also indicative of a dilemma, however. For Bourne's ability to argue politically always encounters its limits where it would be necessary to deal with political organizations. But Bourne avoids that. Although a concept of class used increasingly in the Marxist sense crystallized in the writings of his final years, reflection upon problems of organization is almost entirely absent. In part, this is due to the fact that Bourne's ideas about the movement of thought cannot be harmonized with its organization. His call for "desperate spiritual outlaws" was meant seriously, indeed literally. Besides, Bourne bases his notion of intellectual radicalism on the rejection of any and every pressure to conform. A *necessary* connection of whatever kind between thought and class was something Bourne could see only as a way of rationalizing a lack of freedom. The essay "What is Exploitation?" shows how Bourne breaks through the context described—a discussion with a factory owner concerning the problems of the strike—because he wants to deal with the question of exploitation from the perspective of his own experience. The ambivalence referred to and the dilemma that results from it become apparent where Bourne says of his discussion partner: "He recognizes only individuals, I recognize classes." But then he himself insists on the necessity of individual experience: "One has to feel exploitation perhaps before one understands it."   The ambivalence in the structure of the argument in this essay signals Bourne's problem: how does one mediate between individual and collective experience? In "The Price of Radicalism," he bemoans his insufficient knowledge of the thoughts of the working class. But he also warns young intellectuals of the dangers of socialist organization.

Because he lacked a concept of ideology in the Marxist sense, Bourne occasionally develops a notion of radicalism which is specific to a particular class and not altogether free of elitist and leadership elements. Yet these are irreconcilable with his insistence on the right to autonomous experience. But this gives him a chance to reflect about the possibilities the middle class may have to take on leadership tasks because it is intellectually radical. "The only way by which middle-class radicalism can serve is by being fiercely and concentratedly intellectual."

What Bourne had in mind were both engagement and the kind of analytical dispassionateness Bertrand Russell embodied. They were qualities which appeared to naturally entitle the intellectual to claim leadership roles.

Further thought about the role of the intellectual would have been necessary, had Bourne had the opportunity to reflect carefully about this dilemma. But historical developments forced his political speculations and his social criticism into the opposite direction at whose terminal point we find his thoughts about the treason of the intellectuals. Under the impact of the First World War and the consequences of the United States' entry into it, the critical motive for Bourne's hopes in the intellectuals paled: the society was becoming irrational. Ultimately, even critics could only be defined negatively. Bourne uses the concept "intellectual" primarily to refer to the liberals on the staff of the *New Republic*. But those from whom he expected a critical position in the emphatic sense he called "malcontents."

Only in the beginning did Bourne see the treason of the intellectuals solely in their support for America's entry into the war. As he pondered their responsibility, he also attempted to understand the *causes* of their failure. This failure had occurred on several planes: it lay in the advocacy of barbarism, of strategies of rationalization which had no logical coherence but merely served those ruling elites which have always proven themselves fundamentally undemocratic, in the backsliding from a developed to a more primitive level of thought, and finally in the regression to a phase of political and cultural colonialism, the dependence on Great Britain. The principal reason for the failure of the intellectuals, in Bourne's view, was their inability to endure contradictory situations, the weakness that lies in wanting to retreat to safer positions. He complains that critical reflection inadequately resists its own conditions, i.e., the paradoxical nature of reality itself. There is the further assumption that the intellectual always feels inferior to the man of action.

Starting with the principle that intellectual conflicts must either be resolved in a synthesis—i.e., a qualitative leap—or by the return to ideas which were believed to be obsolete, Bourne writes: "The American intellectual class, having failed to make the higher syntheses, regresses to ideas that can issue in quick, simplified action. Thought becomes an easy rationalization of what is actually going on or what is to happen inevitably tomorrow".

Not only have the intellectuals become rationalizers, they also suffer from the illusion that they have an influence on the course of things. What really happens is that intellect is sacrificed on the altar of the factual. Critique, which requires vision, is absorbed in the mere description and justification of what is. The intellectual becomes the mouthpiece of things as they are.

In his denunciation of the intellectual as being corrupted by

historical events, Bourne occasionally attains a precision of language whose unyielding moralistic tone is reminiscent of a famous European contemporary who formulated the same insights, Karl Kraus. Both articulate not only their horror at the War
itself but also at the levity and opportunism with which the intellectuals accepted it. Bourne's sentence "War is the health of the
state" reads like the sum of all the denunciatory descriptions of
those who profited from the war in both a spiritual and a material
sense and who are presented to us in Karl Kraus' *The Last Days
of Mankind.*

How justified Bourne's attacks were can easily be reconstructed. In the *New Republic,* on April 14, 1917, in an unsigned
editorial entitled "Who Willed American Participation," Bourne
could read this proud confession: "The bankers and the
capitalists have favored war, but they have favored it without
realizing the extent to which it would injure their own interest,
and their support has been one of the most formidable political
obstacles to American participation. The effective and decisive
work on behalf of war has been accomplished by an entirely different class—a class which must be comprehensively but
loosely described as the 'intellectuals.' "

Sources of first publication

"The Doctrine of the Rights of Man Ms.
as Formulated by Thomas Paine"

"Trans-National America"	*Atlantic Monthly,* July, 1916
"A Mirror of the Middle West"	*Dial,* November, 1918
"Emerald Lake"	*New Republic,* January, 1917
"Our Unplanned Cities"	NR., June, 1915
"The Architect"	NR., January, 1916
"The Night-Court"	Ms.
"What is Exploitation?"	NR., November, 1916
"The 'Scientific' Manager"	Ms.
"New Ideals in Business"	D., February, 1917
"The Price of Radicalism"	NR., March, 1916
"The Puritan's Will to Power"	NR., April, 1917
"The War and the Intellectuals"	NR., June, 1917
"A War Diary"	NR., September, 1917
"John Dewey's Philosophy"	NR., March, 1915

"Twilight of Idols"	NR., October, 1917
"Practice vs. Product"	Ms.
"Law and Order"	*Masses,* March, 1912
"The State"	*Untimely Papers* (1919)
"The Disillusionment"	Ms.
"The Artist in Wartime"	Ms.

THE DOCTRINE OF THE RIGHTS OF MAN AS FORMULATED BY THOMAS PAINE[1]

The doctrine of the Rights of Man, of which Thomas Paine was so eloquent an exponent, is perhaps the most important in result and influence of those leit-motives that run through the political philosophy of the centuries of intellectual awakening and speculation that followed the Italian Renaissance. In the writings of Thomas Paine, we have its culmination—the first account of a great political laboratory experiment attempting to put into practice in the reorganization of a modern State a theory that for two hundred years had been a fancy in the minds of philosophers. Paine's discussion of the Rights of Man shows the doctrine at last loose in the world, doing work—deposing kings, overturning classes, and altering long-established social habits. In its origin, however it had had little of this revolutionary character; it had been merely an effort of the advanced thinkers of the intellectual class of Western Europe to discover a new basis for civil society and a new authority for the government of men. They had been loth to watch the ideal hope of a great World-Empire fade slowly away from their sight—an empire which should control all temporal things, unite all peoples and confer upon all men an indestructible citizenship. The rise of nationalities, however, with their hopelessly conflicting claims and rivalries, had given the coup de grâce to this political ideal, and the Reformation came to deal a similar blow to the spiritual Empire—the Church Universal through which all men were united to God and derived spiritual authority from him. The old bases for authority seemed to be irrevocably gone, and the acutest philosophers began to look for a new unshakable foundation that would appeal with axiomatic force to the moral and spiritual nature of every intelligent man. This new basis they found, as they found so many of their ideas, in the Roman Law. Taking an old conception of Roman equity, which had gradually come to lend a symbolic meaning to what was at first simply the common law of the Mediterranean peoples, and to be thought of as an abstract extra-human law of Nature, as impregnable in the moral realm as were the laws of God in the spiritual—taking this conception, they deduced the natural rights of man, which postulated his original equality in a state of Nature and a social compact as the bond which had joined individuals together and still united them. From this law came the authority and justification of government and of the relations of individuals to each other and to the State. The doctrine did away at once with the need of a spiritual Vicar, through whom temporal princes derived their authority from God, of a Church which controlled the spiritual life of men and gave meaning to his social customs and his family and class relations, and of a World-Empire to confer universal citizenship.

From this original source, then, did Paine and his fellow-radicals of thought and action derive their philosophy. The doctrine, however, before it came to them had passed through a curious evolution. From a justification of authority, it became a justification and even incitement to revolution. From its original purpose of providing a secular basis for existing legitimate government, it became the platform of a revolutionary republic. To Grotius, writing about 1625, the doctrine of Natural Rights had meant a tacit and implied promise on the part of the members of society to obey the majority, or the organ of society to whom power had been delegated. Hobbes, writing a little later, deduced from the pristine equality of men, an absolute government as the only way to curb the anarchic spirits of individual and lawless men. Equality and independence, he said, though the original state of nature, mean hopeless anarchy and war; in order to put an end to the intolerable strife, men contract together and surrender as much of their natural right as is inconsistent with their living in peace. The rights of freedom are surrendered for security. Mere agreement, however, will not control them; there must be a common power to whom they surrender their rights, and who will keep them in awe and direct their actions towards the common benefit. An equality of dependence is therefore necessary. The natural rights of man lead infallibly to an autocracy, but an autocracy tempered by revolution. For Hobbes admits that the original right to make their existence good cannot be surrendered. The ethics of revolution is success, but rebellion against authority is an impious crime.

With Locke, however, who wrote at the time of the English Revolution of 1688, and whose purpose was to justify that very conservative change, the implications of the doctrine begin to veer away from autocracy. The State, to Locke, is a joint-stock company; men, free, equal and independent, had voluntarily es

tablished government, not for their own control, but for the pres-
ervation of their lives, liberties, and estates. Men in the state of
nature, he says, are subject to the law of reason, which teaches
all mankind, who will but consult it, that, all being equal, no one
ought to harm another in his life, health, liberty, and possessions. Society, then, is not a mutual surrender, but a mutual
compact of its original members, perpetually renewed by each
generation which gives its allegiance to the State. In contract,
Locke finds the foundation and nature of the civil state.

Rousseau, in his *Social Contract,* continues the process and
goes practically the whole way towards democracy. His State
purports to be a common sovereign power, and yet to leave
every contracting party as free as he was before, still owing
obedience only to himself. The common power to which rights
were surrendered—which to Hobbes could mean only an
autocrat—signifies to Rousseau the whole of society. Each of us,
he says, puts his person and faculties in a common stock under
the sovereign direction of the general will. The right of all men to
be free, equal, and independent postulates a society formed by
contract to be a partnership of equals and not an equality in the
sense that all are equally subjected to a sovereign power. The
ideal is a covenant of social brotherhood, not a covenant of
mutual subjection. The attempt of Rousseau to combine the perfect sovereignty of society with the perfect freedom of the individual, however, left the doctrine very much up in the air. Its attractive paradoxes have given political philosophers a problem
to wrestle with which might better have been recognized at once
as insoluble. The mass of men, feeling dimly the hollowness and
lack of grip in this attempt to reconcile perfect individual freedom with perfect social control, rightly accepted his theories as
destructive of society. It was not Rousseau's specious analysis
of the sovereignty of the people that attracted them, but the
phrase with which he opened his *Social Contract*—"Man is born
free, and is everywhere in chains." To Hobbes, the natural state
of man was anarchic and intolerable—a state to be transcended
as soon as possible. To Locke, society was desirable from a
utilitarian point of view, as the pooling of interests, in the same
manner that a business corporation is more effective than a single business man. But to Rousseau, filled with an emotional revulsion at the artificialities of civilization, the freedom and equal-

ity of man was a bright pristine social state from which we had drifted disastrously far, and to which it was imperative that we return. Thus the doctrine of the Rights of Man, which at first had been a mere theory to fill the intellectual gap caused by the passing of the old authorities, developing into a satisfactory juristic explanation of the origin and evolution of society and a justification of legitimate government, became in Rousseau's mouth a revolutionary cry, calling society back to sounder and primitive bases. In his pleading persuasive voice, he called upon all men to throw off their chains and become human and natural again.

Shall we say that the French Revolution was the answer to that call? It is true that great social forces reck little of the writings of philosophers or of the thoughts of men. The true causes of the Revolution we shall find rather in the rise of the middle class in France after the commercial revolution of the seventeenth century, without a corresponding advance in political rights, and in the expensive and unwieldy administration which was driving France on towards bankruptcy—in other words, in the economic factors of the time. Without the bankruptcy, the economic crises, and the suffering of the people, there seems no reason to believe that the Revolution might not have been postponed for decades, just as the revolution in Russia is being postponed today. The effect of the political philosophy was rather to mellow the popular mind, to create an expectant attitude and prepare social opinion for the great change. And its chief function was to furnish a channel into which all sentiment ran when once the change had begun. It was the most potent factor in dictating the course that events took then, and in sweeping away the old abuses that had festered for centuries. The social philosophy was, as spiritual forces always are, the indispensable ally of social progress, preparing the way and backing it up with a set of definite principles, rather than actually forcing and accomplishing the change.

The work of Rousseau was to do this preparing, and it was the work of Paine to defend and fortify the actual movement in its early concrete stages. It is this that gives Paine's formulation of the Rights of Man its unique interest. Here is something more than a body of a priori reasoning, based—as Rousseau was forced to base his speculations, because he could find no modern democratic States that corroborated him—on the legendary accounts of lawgivers and republics of antiquity. Paine had all the advantage of a working model before him. He imagined that he was witnessing in the early years of the Revolution the formation of the very social compact about which the philosophers had written, and the direct exercises of that sovereignty and foundation of civil rights which they had discovered in original society. The concrete embodiment of the Rights of Man, the transmutation of philosophy into political institutions, was working itself out before his very eyes. He could find illustration for his principles in the stirring events that succeeded the meeting of the National Assembly. He writes in a fresh flood of enthusiasm that was natural in those early days of innocence when the Revolution seemed like a peaceful and orderly change in government by a great people in full command of their reason, and with a consistent purpose of embodying in a national Constitution the most idealistic social philosophy of the age. But because he could not see the growing storm—the welter of foreign invasion, private ambition, and class struggle, that drew France rapidly through a reign of terror into despotism, his point of view and enthusiasm is not thereby invalidated. For through all the vicissitudes of post-revolutionary France, the great political achievements of the French Revolution did stand unscathed. Its work did endure, and it was thorough and healing.

However inadequate for permanent *social* regeneration we may judge the doctrine of the Rights of Man, looking at the Revolution in the broad perspective of a century, that Revolution still remains the most amazing thing in history. A great nation, trained for centuries to absolutism, did deliberately, in the face of the counter-revolution of the monarch, the active hostility of all Europe, economic distress at home, defy all laws of social inertia, social conservatism, and social timidity, and alter its form of government in accord with abstract and idealistic principles. In comparison, our own boasted Revolution, by reason of our small population, the distance from the mother country, our already semi-independent status, was no more of a feat or a political achievement than the leaving home of a big boy who has outgrown parental control. But the Revolution in France was analogous to the self-reformation of a drunkard, the conscious and willed alteration of a nation's habits of life. It was this aspect of it that caused the passionate enthusiasm, the hope, the delirious joy, that swept through the youth of Europe at the sight.

"Good was it in that day to be alive, And to be young was very heaven!" It was Paine's *Rights of Man* that carried the first lucid account of the Revolution and the principles on which it was founded to English-speaking peoples. His story of the events of the first two years of the Revolution, which to readers of today seems so just and balanced, came as a shock to the conservatively inclined, who had been fed by Burke and others on distorted tales of horror and carnage and treason and blasphemy which were ruining France. Even in republican America the good John Quincy Adams took it upon himself to answer Paine in a defense of "law and order," while in England Paine had to answer to a charge of treason on account of his inevitable comparisons of the prerogative-ridden British Constitution with the legislation of the National Assembly. The logic and candor of the book only served to inflame the bigoted conservatives in both countries, and only a fortunate escape to France saved the author from serious consequences in London. In the United States, the disfavor with which the book and all similar literature were greeted by the wealthy classes, coupled with enthusiasm for the French, caused a wave of popular democratic sentiment that rocked the Federalist Administration to its foundations. It may be a salutary thing for an American to pause now and then and wonder what would have been the character of our Federal Constitution if the Philadelphia Convention had met five years later than it did. It is safe to say that after 1791 our oligarchic Constitution could never have been ratified in a single State of the Union. The people would have insisted that the Declaration of the Rights of Man and the measures of the National Assembly be taken as our model, rather than Montesquieu's misconception of the British Constitution, and the aristocratic philosophy of Hamilton and Madison. It might not then have been still necessary in the year 1912 to be fighting the wearisome struggle for political democracy, and Thomas Paine might be our political oracle, rather than the authors of the *Federalist* and Edmund Burke. For it was Burke, of course, whose *Reflections on the Revolution in France* had driven Paine to his defense of the Rights of Man, in which he so thoroughly exposed Burke that the latter's nineteenth century apologists could only save his reputation by ascribing the incredible *Reflections* to senility or hysteria. But there was no senility; there was no hysteria. Burke was simply a reactionary unmasked—a reactionary like hundreds of "liberty-loving" Englishmen and Americans, whose reverence for Anglo-Saxon institutions and the palladia of English freedom always stops just short of any attempt to make that freedom vital and significant instead of a superstition. Our strongest modern exponents of the rights of "freedom" and "property," oppose all attempts to extend the sphere of freedom and make it potent in our social life and to change our social system, where the majority of men are economically unfree in everything but a Pickwickian sense, and in which only a minority own any property at all. Conservatives, however, will always prefer to hear the doctrines of English freedom expounded by Edmund Burke rather than Thomas Paine. For to Burke freedom meant freedom to be governed by a representative class.

To Paine, however, it meant the equal exercise of civil rights in society. His exposition of the Rights of Man follows in its general outline the theories of Natural Rights and the Social Compact that we have sketched above. He differs from Rousseau in giving a religious twist to the explanation of the equality of men. His Quakerism leads him to base it on the fact that every man is a child of God. For authority as to the Rights of Man, he says, we must go back to the time when Man first came from the hand of his Maker. "What was he then? Man. Man was his high and only title, and a higher cannot be given." This original generation of men had equal natural rights, since all derived their existence equally from God; in the same manner, posterity has equal rights with them, just as if the race had been continued by creation and not by generation. Paine riddles Burke's contention that the Parliament of 1688 in England was able to submit not only its own generation, but all posterity forever to the Crown, and thus make a change of government forever illegitimate and impious. This tyranny of the dead hand, Paine says rightly, is worse than the tyranny of the living; and we of America today, whose desires for social reform are blocked by a sacredly archaic Constitution may say Amen to his plea that each generation is competent to deal with its own affairs and formulate anew the political and social principles that shall guide it. Men must never lose sight of their divine unity and equality, says Payne. "Only when he forgets his divine origin, his birth and family, so to speak, does he become dissolute. Not Nature, but an artificial chasm, filled up with barriers and turnpike-gates of kings, priests and nobility, through which man has to pass, has broken down this unity. Since his origin, artificial government has been presumptuously working to unmake him."

His natural rights are based on this equality. Paine quotes them from the famous Declaration of the Rights of Man, adopted August, 1789, by the National Assembly. Men are born and continue free and equal in respect to their rights, it runs, which are liberty, property, security, and resistance of oppression. All men in society are entitled to honors and rewards according to their different abilities, without other distinction than their own virtues and talents. But Man could not depend on his natural rights alone, which he receives by reason of his existence as man; he has certain civil rights, which are his by right of his being a member of society, and which grow out of his natural rights. For man did not enter society to become worse than he was before; not to have fewer rights, but to have those rights better secured. But here Paine parts company with Rousseau. The State is not based on an impossible combination of perfect civil freedom with perfect individual freedom, as Rousseau fondly believed, but by a frank exchange by the individual on entering society of certain of his natural rights for civil rights. The natural rights which he retains are all those in which the power to execute is as perfect as the right itself. Such are all rights of the mind, and of individual action where no one is concerned but the person himself. Those rights which are exchanged are those in which, although the right is perfect in the individual, the power to execute is defective. Such, for instance is the right of judging one's own cause. Each has that right, but it avails him little, since he has no power in himself to make redress. He therefore deposits this right in the common stock of society, and takes the arm of society of which he is a part, in preference to, and in addition to, his own. But he obtains this assistance as a civil right, and not as the grant of society. He draws on the capital of society as a proprietor and not as a pensioner.

Every civil right, then, in Paine's theory, grows out of a natural right, is a natural right exchanged. "The civil power is made up of an aggregate of that class of natural rights which becomes defective in point of power and answers not the individual's purpose, but when collected to a focus becomes competent to the purpose of every one." But this civil power cannot be made to invade those natural rights which are retained by the individual

and in which the power to exercise is as perfect as the right itself.

In his theory of rights Paine seems to make a sort of synthesis
of Hobbes and Rousseau. He agrees with Hobbes that there is
a surrender of rights to society, but with Rousseau that this society is a common power and not a central sovereign to which
all the members are subject. For government, as the institution
of the social compact, is, to Paine, not a compact between
those who govern and those who are governed, as Hobbes implied, but a compact between the individuals themselves, who
each in his own personal sovereign right enters into a compact
to create a government, founded on the common interest of society and the common rights of man. What is government but
the management of the affairs of a nation? says Paine, not the
property of any particular man, but of the whole community.
Sovereignty appertains to the nation only, and not to any individual. The nation is the source of all sovereignty, and no individual or body of men can be entitled to any authority which is
not expressly derived from it.

In his illustration of these principles Paine compares the English government, which, he says, arose by conquest *over* the
people, with the new French government arising *out of* the
people. The new National Assembly he sees as the people in
the act of expressing the social compact; its members are delegates of the nation in its original character. Its duty is to formulate a Constitution which shall embody the social union and the
social will and found a true government whose authority shall be
derived straight from the people. Paine jeers at the English government as no government, because it has no Constitution and
derives its authority not from the people but from the original
Norman conquest. The fancied English love of freedom is but an
empty word, for England's enthronement of aristocracy denies
equality, and there can be no real freedom without equality. Aristocracy cannot exist with the free exercise of man's natural
rights. Titles, Paine says, are like circles drawn by the magi-
cian's wand to contract the sphere of man's felicity. The French
people have abolished aristocracy, because it has meant family
tyranny and injustice; because of the unfitness of aristocrats to
be legislators, since their ideas of inequality corrupt justice at its
very source; because a body of men holding themselves ac-

countable to nobody ought not to be trusted by anybody. It might be said here in parenthesis that our universal American practice of organizing our institutional life in every department with Boards of Governors, Directors, and Trustees, ruling in many instances rather by divine right than by the direct authority of those whose actions they control, and responsible in only a perfunctory fashion to those dependent upon them, shows how little our inherently oligarchic "spirit of American government" has recognized the truth of this last great principle. Paine insists justly that government must never lose sight of the common interest for whose protection it is founded, or of the responsibility those in power have primarily to those below—the people whose sovereignty the government is expressing and from whom it derives its authority.

This is the formulation of the origin and nature of the natural and civil Rights of Man, according to Thomas Paine, and he seems to have had no doubt that it constituted a true historical picture and a valid philosophical basis, for the relations of men to each other and to the State. In a modern critique of these principles, it is necessary that both the history and the philosophy be seriously questioned. In the light of modern knowledge, the theory of the original freedom of man and the formation of a Social Compact is far different from what we know of early man, and in the light of the nineteenth century and modern ideals, the philosophy is inadequate.

For, far from its being true that in their original state, men were free and independent, and combined into societies in order to increase their security and prosperity, modern science is convinced that the most primitive state of man is actually the social state. Primitive man is found everywhere highly socialized with an elaborate system of social customs controlling the individual—a state utterly unlike Hobbes' autocracy or Rousseau's free-and-easy democracy. There is equality but little individuality, for all are bound by tradition and custom which has grown up on lines of evolutionary selection to secure the safety and welfare of the group *as a social group,* and not *as a collection of individuals.* Most anthropologists, moreover, agree that man's first appearance was in a horde, which with the passing of barbarism split into tribes, tribes into clans, and clans into families. The progress of society, then, consisted in a dissipation of social control and the individualization of the members of the group, and not a combination and compact; Man was not social because he willed it but because if he was not he perished. He was social by an evolutionary process of selection, and not by any contract. The only rights of primitive man were social rights, so he could not have made the exchange which Paine imagined. Individual rights would be a much later development and only possible after a toilsome period of civilizing.

This historical error of the Natural Rights philosophers entails a more serious one in methods of reform. Paine and Rousseau are filled with the idea that the French people are somehow repeating an eternally right and consecrated program for the reformation of a society, for they are proceeding along the same lines on which society was originally organized. And this idea is fundamentally unscientific. For it means the forcing of society into harmony with a preconceived plan or scheme, and reverses the practicable process. Instead of investigating actual conditions and then asking what can be built out of them by rational direction of social forces and development of institutions in the direction that makes for the general welfare of all, it starts with the finished plan and then asks how can the social conditions as they are be forced into the mould. Of this discredited type of social philosophizing are all those today who argue against a change in our form of government, not on the plea that the present system is adequate to modern conditions, but on the ground that the form of government in existence embodies certain eternal a priori principles to which human society must be made to conform. This is the reason why modern Socialism, so fundamentally scientific in its philosophy, has displaced the old doctrine of Rights as an engine of social change. For Socialism, accepting the scientific demonstration that economic reasons are at the bottom of all social change, and that human nature in its social relations is capable of almost indefinite modification in accordance with the stimuli which institutions and ideals apply to it, seeks to abolish poverty and class hostility and the attendant human ills by controlling the economic order and moulding institutions to secure desirable and fruitful reactions from individuals and social groups. How different is this attitude from the constant assumption of Paine and his fellow reformers that society is composed of units which can be combined and separated like marbles in a box! and from their childlike innocence of the infinite complexity of the social fabric with its interweavings of personal ambition with class antagonisms and variety of cultural and traditional influences. Modern Socialism recognizes society as a process, determined by economic forces; Paine thought of it as a state, determined by the agreement of individuals. This contrast is sufficient to explain the increasing inadequacy that was felt through the nineteenth century by the radical classes who had caught the spirit of the new dynamic industrial age which was being born in England at the time that Paine wrote.

What was actually taking place before Paine's eyes was something far different from what he and his contemporaries imagined it to be. What they saw as the emancipation of man from tyranny proved to be simply the emergence out of the old feudal order of a new industrial order. The contest, as 1848 well showed, was less between oppression and freedom than between an old absurd feudal exploitation and a new rational industrial exploitation. The middle class, which had put through the French Revolution and abolished the aristocracy, became in turn the masters of society, and exploited through the economic organization the classes beneath them. The attainment of political freedom had not prevented the political machinery which the industrial revolution put in the hands of the entrepreneur class from sidetracking that positive and aggressive principle—justice. The working classes soon found that men might be everywhere equal in respect to their rights, and yet that economic disadvantage would render that political freedom valueless to secure for them even a modicum of prosperity and happiness. Freedom to work means little in a social system whose very existence depends on the presence of a reserve army of the unemployed. When the relation of employer and employee in the new system gave one class economic power over the other, the equal rights of men before the law became almost an empty dignity. What avail was the guarantee of life and property to classes whose life and labor were infinitely cheap, and who possessed no property that any one would care to deprive them of? The most perfect political rights could scarcely prevent such classes from falling into a practical economic serfdom, holding their livelihood, as they did, at the mercy of another.

Men of Paine's time were obsessed by the idea that the State and Society were identical. They tended to think of men's civil rights as embracing all his social relations, or at least all those social relations which were vital and significant for his prosperity and happiness. This fatal but fascinating fallacy, which has vitiated the writing of History for so long, will partly explain the failure of political philosophy to extend the conception of equality and freedom to the economic order. Men did not see that the new industrial order was pushing the role of the State more and more into the background, until it has become simply one of the expressions of our institutional life, and in countries like France and America one of the less significant of those expressions. Our interest in the State in this country is rather a sporting interest than a feeling that political institutions play any really vital part in the life of the ordinary citizen. And everywhere in the modern world, the elaborately organized hierarchy of industry—an economic State built up alongside the political State and based on a curious mixture of status and contract—has taken its place as the dominant social element. The State has been reduced to a mere reservoir of armed force; its role has become that of helplessly attempting—as in our American trust laws—to grapple with economic maladjustments, and enforcing contracts made within the economic order. About the status of classes and individuals in that order it has nothing to say; that has been fixed by the struggle of classes. Modern Socialism is simply a movement to make the economic order supreme; although it has been occasionally attracted by the fallacy of the State, its real aim is to absorb the State into the industrial organization, and abolish class antagonisms by thoroughly socializing this joint organization.

Since, then, the doctrine of the Rights of Man has retained this incorrigibly political character, modern Socialism does not derive its philosophy out of those revolutionary principles. It is true that, broadly interpreted, all the principles of democracy, both political and industrial might be derived from them, just as they can be deduced out of the Gospels. But they were not, and perhaps we can find some explanation of this fact in the consideration that Liberty and the Rights of Man are after all negative rather than positive principles. Men appeal to rights as a defensive weapon, as a resistance to aggression rather than as a call to constructive work. We have seen the destructive force of Rousseau's writing. The doctrine was well enough as a war-cry of an intelligent and self-respecting middle class against the lumbering, decaying Old Regime, but with the accomplishment of its overthrow the force was about spent. It is perhaps significant that the great attempts to embody it in political history were in our Declaration of 1776 and the French Declaration of 1789— both proclamations of the *independence* of a nation. The principles were powerful in moving men's minds to a fanatical enthusiasm for throwing off oppression, but left them, when that was done, with no guarantees of positive justice. Can it be that an appeal to Rights is too egotistical to appeal permanently to so complex a bundle of instincts and sentiments as the human spirit? Mazzini felt this failure, and tried to remedy it by an appeal to Duties. Paine had distinctly said that a declaration of rights was by reciprocity a declaration of duties—duties towards God, expressed in religion—"man's bringing to his Maker the fruits of his heart"—and towards one's neighbor, expressed in doing as one would be done by. But a doctrine of Duty as a dynamic engine of social reform makes use of too few of men's desires and tendencies to replace successfully even a doctrine of Rights. A combination of the two doctrines results only in that nerveless sentimentalism which the Christian churches preach today as the solution of social problems. Only some kind of a strong fusion could make a permanent appeal, and this the modern dynamic Socialism which we have suggested above, provides in the ideal of *social justice*. An applied scientific ethics is at the bottom of the Socialist movement today. It extends the ideals of democracy, equality, and fraternity from the political to the economic order, and adds the ideal of Justice, which makes its appeal to men as social beings albeit with personal desires. And Justice provides in addition that slight aesthetic appeal without which no complex ideal ever had dynamic force—the idea that its realization will bring what is rational and beautiful and satisfying. Sublimating all of these ideals is that of both individual and social Self-realization as the end and purpose of all social effort. The modern ethic demands the development of the personal potentialities of every human being, and of the social potentialities of the great age of invention in which we live. The modern radical opposes the present social system not because it does not give him his "rights," but because it warps and stunts the potentialities of society and of human nature. And he finds the social sciences establishing with greater force every day this ethic of Justice and Self-Realization. Whoever has felt the full import of this contrast between the *Rights of Man* and such a modern book as Dickinson's *Justice and Liberty* will have acquired the correct perspective and seen the great principles of the French Revolution in their proper light in the history of social ideals.

[1] Bourne, writing under the pseudonym "J. Lowes," entered this piece in 1912 in an essay competition. He gave as his sources:

The Holy Roman Empire by James Bryce
A History of the Science of Politics by Sir Frederic Pollock
Rousseau by John Morley
The New History by James Harvey Robinson
The Spirit of American Government by J. Allen Smith
A History of Politics by Edward Jenks
Why Should We Change Our Form of Government? by N. M. Butler
The Mind of Primitive Man by Joseph Mazzini
Justice and Liberty by G. Lowes Dickinson

TRANS-NATIONAL AMERICA[1]

No reverberatory effect of the great war has caused American public opinion more solicitude than the failure of the "melting-pot." The discovery of diverse nationalistic feelings among our great alien population has come to most people as an intense shock. It has brought out the unpleasant inconsistencies of our traditional beliefs. We have had to watch hard-hearted old Brahmins virtuously indignant at the spectacle of the immigrant refusing to be melted, while they jeer at patriots like Mary Antin who write about "our forefathers." We have had to listen to publicists who express themselves as stunned by the evidence of vigorous nationalistic and cultural movements in this country among Germans, Scandinavians, Bohemians, and Poles, while in the same breath they insist that the alien shall be forcibly assimilated to that Anglo-Saxon tradition which they unquestioningly label "American."

As the unpleasant truth has come upon us that assimilation in this country was proceeding on lines very different from those we had marked out for it, we found ourselves inclined to blame those who were thwarting our prophecies. The truth became culpable. We blamed the war, we blamed the Germans. And then we discovered with a moral shock that these movements had been making great headway before the war even began. We found that the tendency, reprehensible and paradoxical as it might be, has been for the national clusters of immigrants, as they became more and more firmly established and more and more prosperous, to cultivate more and more assiduously the literatures and cultural traditions of their homelands. Assimilation, in other words, instead of washing out the memories of Europe, made them more and more intensely real. Just as these clusters became more and more objectively American, did they become more and more German or Scandinavian or Bohemian or Polish.

To face the fact that our aliens are already strong enough to take a share in the direction of their own destiny, and that the strong cultural movements represented by the foreign press, schools, and colonies are a challenge to our facile attempts, is not, however, to admit the failure of Americanization. It is not to fear the failure of democracy. It is rather to urge us to an investigation of what Americanism may rightly mean. It is to ask ourselves whether our ideal has been broad or narrow—whether perhaps the time has not come to assert a higher ideal than the "melting-pot." Surely we cannot be certain of our spiritual democracy when, claiming to melt the nations within us to a comprehension of our free and democratic institutions, we fly into panic at the first sign of their own will and tendency. We act as if we wanted Americanization to take place only on our own terms, and not by the consent of the governed. All our elaborate machinery of settlement and school and union, of social and political naturalization, however, will move with friction just in so far as it neglects to take into account this strong and virile insistence that America shall be what the immigrant will have a hand in making it, and not what a ruling class, descendant of those British stocks which were the first permanent immigrants, decide that America shall be made. This is the condition which confronts us, and which demands a clear and general readjustment of our attitude and our ideal.

I

Mary Antin is right when she looks upon our foreign-born as the people who missed the Mayflower and came over on the first boat they could find. But she forgets that when they did come it was not upon other Mayflowers, but upon a "Maiblume," a "Fleur de Mai," a "Fior di Maggio," a "Majblomst." These people were not mere arrivals from the same family, to be welcomed as understood and long-loved, but strangers to the neighborhood, with whom a long process of settling down had to take place. For they brought with them their national and racial characters, and each new national quota had to wear slowly away the contempt with which its mere alienness got itself greeted. Each had to make its way slowly from the lowest strata of unskilled labor up to a level where it satisfied the accredited norms of social success.

We are all foreign-born or the descendants of foreign-born, and if distinctions are to be made between us they should rightly be on some other ground than indigenousness. The early colonists came over with motives no less colonial than the later. They did not come to be assimilated in an American melting-pot. They did not come to adopt the culture of the American Indian. They had not the smallest intention of "giving themselves without reservation" to the new country. They came to get freedom to live as they wanted to. They came to escape from the stifling air and chaos of the old world; they came to make their fortune in a new land. They invented no new social framework. Rather they brought over bodily the old ways to which they had been accustomed. Tightly concentrated on a hostile frontier, they were conservative beyond belief. Their pioneer daring was reserved for the objective conquest of material resources. In their folkways, in their social and political institutions, they were, like every colonial people, slavishly imitative of the mother-country. So that, in spite of the "Revolution," our whole legal and political system remained more English than the English, petrified and unchanging, while in England law developed to meet the needs of the changing times.

It is just this English-American conservatism that has been our chief obstacle to social advance. We have needed the new peoples—the order of the German and Scandinavian, the turbulence of the Slav and Hun—to save us from our own stagnation. I do not mean that the illiterate Slav is now the equal of the New Englander of pure descent. He is raw material to be educated, not into a New Englander, but into a socialized American along such lines as those thirty nationalities are being educated in the amazing schools of Gary. I do not believe that this process is to be one of decades of evolution. The spectacle of Japan's sudden jump from mediaevalism to post-modernism should have destroyed that superstition. We are not dealing with individuals who are to "evolve." We are dealing with their children, who, with that education we are about to have, will start level with all of us. Let us cease to think of ideals like democracy as magical qualities inherent in certain peoples. Let us speak, not of inferior races, but of inferior civilizations. We are all to educate and to be educated. These peoples in America are in a common enterprise. It is not what we are now that concerns us, but what this plastic next generation may become in the light of a new cosmopolitan ideal.

We are not dealing with static factors, but with fluid and dynamic generations. To contrast the older and the newer immigrants and see the one class as democratically motivated by love of liberty, and the other by mere money-getting, is not to illuminate the future. To think of earlier nationalities as culturally assimilated to America, while we picture the later as a sodden and resistive mass, makes only for bitterness and misunderstanding. There may be a difference between these earlier and these later stocks, but it lies neither in motive for coming nor in strength of cultural allegiance to the homeland. The truth is that no more tenacious cultural allegiance to the mother country has been shown by any alien nation than by the ruling class of Anglo-Saxon descendants in these American States. English snobberies, English religion, English literary styles, English literary reverences and canons, English ethics, English superiorities, have been the cultural food that we have drunk in from our mothers' breasts. The distinctively American spirit—pioneer, as distinguished from the reminiscently English—that appears in Whitman and Emerson and James, has had to exist on sufferance alongside of this other cult, unconsciously belittled by our cultural makers of opinion. No country has perhaps had so great indigenous genius which had so little influence on the country's traditions and expressions. The unpopular and dreaded German-American of the present day is a beginning amateur in comparison with those foolish Anglophiles of Boston and New York and Philadelphia whose reversion to cultural type sees uncritically in England's cause the cause of Civilization, and, under the guise of ethical independence of thought, carries along European traditions which are no more "American" than the German categories themselves.

It speaks well for German-American innocence of heart or else for its lack of imagination that it has not turned the hyphen stigma into a "Tu quoque!"[2] If there were to be any hyphens scattered about, clearly they should be affixed to those English descendants who had had centuries of time to be made American where the German had had only half a century. Most significantly has the war brought out of them this alien virus, showing them still loving English things, owing allegiance to the English Kultur, moved by English shibboleths and prejudice. It is only because it has been the ruling class in this country that bestowed the epithets that we have not heard copiously and scornfully of "hyphenated English-Americans." But even our quarrels with England have had the bad temper, the extravagance, of family quarrels. The Englishman of today nags us and dislikes us in that personal, peculiarly intimate way in which he dislikes the Australian, or as we may dislike our younger brothers. He still thinks of us incorrigibly as "colonials." America—official, controlling, literary, political America—is still, as a writer recently expressed it, "culturally speaking, a self-governing dominion of the British Empire."

The non-English American can scarcely be blamed if he sometimes thinks of the Anglo-Saxon predominance in America as little more than a predominance of priority. The Anglo-Saxon was merely the first immigrant, the first to found a colony. He has never really ceased to be the descendant of immigrants, nor has he ever succeeded in transforming that colony into a real nation, with a tenacious, richly woven fabric of native culture. Colonials from the other nations have come and settled down beside him. They found no definite native culture which should startle them out of their colonialism, and consequently they looked back to their mother-country, as the earlier Anglo-Saxon immigrant was looking back to his. What has been offered the newcomer has been the chance to learn English, to become a citizen, to salute the flag. And those elements of our ruling classes who are responsible for the public schools, the settlements, all the organizations for amelioration in the cities, have every reason to be proud of the care and labor which they have devoted to absorbing the immigrant. His opportunities the immigrant has taken to gladly, with almost a pathetic eagerness to make his way in the new land without friction or disturbance. The common language has made not only for the necessary communication, but for all the amenities of life.

If freedom means the right to do pretty much as one pleases, so long as one does not interfere with others, the immigrant has found freedom, and the ruling element has been singularly liberal in its treatment of the invading hordes. But if freedom means a democratic cooperation in determining the ideals and purposes and industrial and social institutions of a country, then the immigrant has not been free, and the Anglo-Saxon element is guilty of just what every dominant race is guilty of in every European country: the imposition of its own culture upon the minority peoples. The fact that this imposition has been so mild and, indeed, semi-conscious does not alter its quality. And the war has brought out just the degree to which that purpose of "Americanizing," that is, "Anglo-Saxonizing," the immigrant has failed.

For the Anglo-Saxon now in his bitterness to turn upon the other peoples, talk about their "arrogance," scold them for not

being melted in a pot which never existed, is to betray the unconscious purpose which lay at the bottom of his heart. It betrays too the possession of a racial jealousy similar to that of
which he is now accusing the so-called "hyphenates." Let the
Anglo-Saxon be proud enough of the heroic toil and heroic sacrifices which moulded the nation. But let him ask himself, if he
had had to depend on the English descendants, where he
would have been living today. To those of us who see in the
exploitation of unskilled labor the strident red *leit-motif* of our
civilization, the settling of the country presents a great social
drama as the waves of immigration broke over it.

Let the Anglo-Saxon ask himself where he would have been if
these races had not come? Let those who feel the inferiority of
the non-Anglo-Saxon immigrant contemplate that region of the
States which has remained the most distinctively "American,"
the South. Let him ask himself whether he would really like to
see the foreign hordes Americanized into such an Americanization. Let him ask himself how superior this native civilization is to
the great "alien" states of Wisconsin and Minnesota, where
Scandinavians, Poles, and Germans have self-consciously labored to preserve their traditional culture, while being outwardly
and satisfactorily American. Let him ask himself how much more
wisdom, intelligence, industry and social leadership has come
out of these alien states than out of all the truly American ones.
The South, in fact, while this vast Northern development has
gone on, still remains an English colony, stagnant and complacent, having progressed culturally scarcely beyond the early
Victorian era. It is culturally sterile because it has had no advantage of cross-fertilization like the Northern states. What has happened in states such as Wisconsin and Minnesota is that strong
foreign cultures have struck root in a new and fertile soil.
America has meant liberation, and German and Scandinavian
political ideas and social energies have expanded to a new potency. The process has not been at all the fancied "assimilation"
of the Scandinavian or Teuton. Rather has it been a process of
their assimilation of us—I speak as an Anglo-Saxon. The foreign
cultures have not been melted down or run together, made into
some homogeneous Americanism, but have remained distinct
but cooperating to the greater glory and benefit, not only of
themselves but of all the native "Americanism" around them.

What we emphatically do not want is that these distinctive

qualities should be washed out into a tasteless, colorless fluid of uniformity. Already we have far too much of this insipidity— masses of people who are cultural half-breeds, neither assimilated Anglo-Saxons nor nationals of another culture. Each national colony in this country seems to retain in its foreign press, its vernacular literature, its schools, its intellectual and patriotic leaders, a central cultural nucleus. From this nucleus the colony extends out by imperceptible gradations to a fringe where national characteristics are all but lost. Our cities are filled with these half-breeds who retain their foreign names but have lost the foreign savor. This does not mean that they have actually been changed into New Englanders or Middle Westerners. It does not mean that they have been really Americanized. It means that, letting slip from them whatever native culture they had, they have substituted for it only the most rudimentary American—the American culture of the cheap newspaper, the "movies," the popular song, the ubiquitous automobile. The unthinking who survey this class call them assimilated, Americanized. The great American public school has done its work. With these people our institutions are safe. We may thrill with dread at the aggressive hyphenate, but this tame flabbiness is accepted as Americanization. The same moulders of opinion whose ideal is to melt the different races into Anglo-Saxon gold hail this poor product as the satisfying result of their alchemy.

Yet a truer cultural sense would have told us that it is not the self-conscious cultural nuclei that sap at our American life, but these fringes. It is not the Jew who sticks proudly to the faith of his fathers and boasts of that venerable culture of his who is dangerous to America, but the Jew who has lost the Jewish fire and become a mere elementary, grasping animal. It is not the Bohemian who supports the Bohemian schools in Chicago whose influence is sinister, but the Bohemian who has made money and has got into ward politics. Just so surely as we tend to disintegrate these nuclei of nationalistic culture do we tend to create hordes of men and women without a spiritual country, cultural outlaws, without taste, without standards but those of the mob. We sentence them to live on the most rudimentary planes of American life. The influences at the centre of the nuclei are centripetal. They make for the intelligence and the social values which mean an enhancement of life. And just because the foreign-born retains this expressiveness is he likely to be a better citizen of the American community. The influences at the fringe, however, are centrifugal, anarchical. They make for detached fragments of peoples. Those who came to find liberty achieve only license. They become the flotsam and jetsam of American life, the downward undertow of our civilization with its leering cheapness and falseness of taste and spiritual outlook, the absence of mind and sincere feeling which we see in our slovenly towns, our vapid moving pictures, our popular novels, and in the vacuous faces of the crowds on the city street. This is the cultural wreckage of our time, and it is from the fringes of the Anglo-Saxon as well as the other stocks that it falls. America has as yet no impelling integrating force. It makes too easily for this detritus of cultures. In our loose, free country, no constraining national purpose, no tenacious folk-tradition and folk-style hold the people to a line.

The war has shown us that not in any magical formula will this purpose be found. No intense nationalism of the European plan can be ours. But do we not begin to see a new and more adventurous ideal? Do we not see how the national colonies in America, deriving power from the deep cultural heart of Europe and yet living here in mutual toleration, freed from the age-long tangles of races, creeds, and dynasties, may work out a federated ideal? America is transplanted Europe, but a Europe that has not been disintegrated and scattered in the transplanting as in some Dispersion. Its colonies live here inextricably mingled, yet not homogeneous. They merge but they do not fuse.

America is a unique sociological fabric, and it bespeaks poverty of imagination not to be thrilled at the incalculable potentialities of so novel a union of men. To seek no other goal than the weary old nationalism—belligerent, exclusive, inbreeding, the poison of which we are witnessing now in Europe—is to make patriotism a hollow sham, and to declare that, in spite of our boastings, America must ever be a follower and not a leader of nations.

II

If we come to find this point of view plausible, we shall have to give up the search for our native "American" culture. With the exception of the South and that New England which, like the

Red Indian, seems to be passing into solemn oblivion, there is no distinctively American culture. It is apparently our lot rather to be a federation of cultures. This we have been for half a century, and the war has made it ever more evident that this is what we are destined to remain. This will not mean, however, that there are not expressions of indigenous genius that could not have sprung from any other soil. Music, poetry, philosophy, have been singularly fertile and new. Strangely enough, American genius has flared forth just in those directions which are least understood [sic] of the people. If the American note is big-ness, action, the objective as contrasted with the reflective life, where is the epic expression of this spirit? Our drama and our fiction, the peculiar fields for the expression of action and objec-tivity, are somehow exactly the fields of the spirit which remain poor and mediocre. American materialism is in some way inhib-ited from getting into impressive artistic form its own energy with which it bursts. Nor is it any better in architecture, the least romantic and subjective of all the arts. We are inarticulate of the very values which we profess to idealize. But in the finer forms—music, verse, the essay, philosophy—the American genius puts forth work equal to any of its contemporaries. Just in so far as our American genius has expressed the pioneer spirit, the adventurous, forward-looking drive of a colonial empire, is it representative of that whole America of the many races and peoples, and not of any partial or traditional enthusiasm. And only as that pioneer note is sounded can we really speak of the American culture. As long as we thought of Americanism in terms of the "melting-pot," our American cultural tradition lay in the past. It was something to which the new Americans were to be moulded. In the light of our changing ideal of Americanism, we must perpetrate the paradox that our American cultural tradi-tion lies in the future. It will be what we all together make out of this incomparable opportunity of attacking the future with a new key.

Whatever American nationalism turns out to be, it is certain to become something utterly different from the nationalisms of twentieth-century Europe. This wave of reactionary enthusiasm to play the orthodox nationalistic game which is passing over the country is scarcely vital enough to last. We cannot swagger and thrill to the same national self-feeling. We must give new edges to our pride. We must be content to avoid the unnumbered woes that national patriotism has brought in Europe, and that fiercely heightened pride and self-consciousness. Alluring as this is, we must allow our imaginations to transcend this scarcely veiled belligerency. We can be serenely too proud to fight if our pride embraces the creative forces of civilization which armed contest nullifies. We can be too proud to fight if our code of honor transcends that of the schoolboy on the playground surrounded by his jeering mates. Our honor must be positive and creative, and not the mere jealous and negative protectiveness against metaphysical violations of our technical rights. When the doctrine is put forth that in one American flows the mystic blood of all our country's sacred honor, freedom, and prosperity, so that an injury to him is to be the signal for turning our whole nation into that clan-feud of horror and reprisal which would be war, then we find ourselves back among the musty schoolmen of the Middle Ages, and not in any pragmatic and realistic America of the twentieth century.

We should hold our gaze to what America has done, not what mediaeval codes of dueling she has failed to observe. We have transplanted European modernity to our soil, without the spirit that inflames it and turns all its energy into mutual destruction. Out of these foreign peoples there has somehow been squeezed the poison. An America, "hyphenated" to bitterness, is somehow non-explosive. For, even if we all hark back in sympathy to a European nation, even if the war has set every one vibrating to some emotional string twanged on the other side of the Atlantic, the effect has been one of almost dramatic harmlessness.

What we have really been witnessing, however unappreciatively, in this country has been a thrilling and bloodless battle of Kulturs. In that arena of friction which has been the most dramatic—between the hyphenated German-American and the hyphenated English-American—there have emerged rivalries of philosophies which show up deep traditional attitudes, points of view which accurately reflect the gigantic issues of the war. America has mirrored the spiritual issues. The vicarious struggle has been played out peacefully here in the mind. We have seen the stout resistiveness of the old moral interpretation of history on which Victorian England thrived and made itself great in its own esteem. The clean and immensely satisfying vision of the war as a contest between right and wrong; the enthusiastic support of the Allies as the incarnation of virtue-on-a-rampage; the fierce envisaging of their selfish national purposes as the ideals of justice, freedom, and democracy—all this has been thrown with intensest force against the German realistic interpretations in terms of the struggle for power and the virility of the integrated State. America has been the intellectual battleground of the nations.

III

The failure of the melting-pot, far from closing the great American democratic experiment, means that it has only just begun. Whatever American nationalism turns out to be, we see already that it will have a color richer and more exciting than our ideal has hitherto encompassed. In a world which has dreamed of internationalism, we find that we have all unawares been building up the first international nation. The voices which have cried for a tight and jealous nationalism of the European pattern are failing. From the ideal, however valiantly and disinterestedly it has been set for us, time and tendency have moved us further and further away. What we have achieved has been rather a cosmopolitan federation of national colonies, of foreign cultures, from whom the sting of devastating competition has been removed. America is already the world-federation in miniature, the continent where for the first time in history has been achieved that miracle of hope, the peaceful living side by side, with character substantially preserved, of the most heterogenous peoples under the sun. Nowhere else has such contiguity been anything but the breeder of misery. Here, notwithstanding our tragic failures of adjustment, the outlines are already too clear not to give us a new vision and a new orientation of the American mind in the world.

It is for the American of the younger generation to accept this cosmopolitanism, and carry it along with self-conscious and fruitful purpose. In his colleges, he is already getting, with the study of modern history and politics, the modern literatures, economic geography, the privilege of a cosmopolitan outlook such as the people of no other nation of today in Europe can possibly secure. If he is still a colonial, he is no longer the colonial of one partial culture, but of many. He is a colonial of the world. Colonialism has grown into cosmopolitanism, and his motherland is no one nation, but all who have anything life-enhancing to offer to the spirit. That vague sympathy which the France of ten years ago was feeling for the world—a sympathy which was drowned in the terrible reality of war—may be the modern American's, and that in a positive and aggressive sense. If the American is parochial, it is in sheer wantonness or cowardice. His provincialism is the measure of his fear of bogies or the defect of his imagination.

Indeed, it is not uncommon for the eager Anglo-Saxon who goes to a vivid American university today to find his true friends not among his own race but among the acclimatized German or Austrian, the acclimatized Jew, the acclimatized Scandinavian or Italian. In them he finds the cosmopolitan note. In these youths, foreign-born or the children of foreign-born parents, he is likely to find many of his old inbred morbid problems washed away. These friends are oblivious to the repressions of that tight little society in which he so provincially grew up. He has a pleasurable sense of liberation from the stale and familiar attitudes of those whose ingrowing culture has scarcely created anything vital for his America of today. He breathes a larger air. In his new enthusiasms for continental literature, for unplumbed Russian depths, for French clarity of thought, for Teuton philosophies of power, he feels himself citizen of a larger world. He may be absurdly superficial, his outward-reaching wonder may ignore all the stiller and homelier virtues of his Anglo-Saxon home, but he has at least found the clue to that international mind which will be essential to all men and women of good-will if they are ever to save this Western world of ours from suicide. His new friends have gone through a similar evolution. America has burned most of the baser metal also from them. Meeting now with this common American background, all of them may yet retain that distinctiveness of their native cultures and their national spiritual slants. They are more valuable and interesting to each other for being different, yet that difference could not be creative were it not for this new cosmopolitan outlook which America has given them and which they all equally possess.

A college where such a spirit is possible even to the smallest degree, has within itself already the seeds of this international intellectual world of the future. It suggests that the contribution of America will be an intellectual internationalism which goes far beyond the mere exchange of scientific ideas and discoveries and the cold recording of facts. It will be an intellectual sympathy which is not satisfied until it has got at the heart of the different cultural expressions, and felt as they feel. It may have immense preferences, but it will make understanding and not indignation its end. Such a sympathy will unite and not divide.

Against the thinly disguised panic which calls itself "patriotism" and the thinly disguised militarism which calls itself "preparedness" the cosmopolitan ideal is set. This does not mean that those who hold it are for a policy of drift. They, too, long passionately for an integrated and disciplined America. But they do not want one which is integrated only for domestic economic exploitation of the workers or for predatory economic imperialism among the weaker peoples. They do not want one that is integrated by coercion or militarism, or for the truculent assertion of a mediaeval code of honor and of doubtful rights. They believe that the most effective integration will be one which coordinates the diverse elements and turns them consciously toward working out together the place of America in the world-situation. They demand for integration a genuine integrity, a wholeness and soundness of enthusiasm and purpose which can only come when no national colony within our America feels that it is being discriminated against or that its cultural case is being prejudged. This strength of cooperation, this feeling that all who are here may have a hand in the destiny of America, will make for a finer spirit of integration than any narrow "Americanism" or forced chauvinism.

In this effort we may have to accept some form of that dual citizenship which meets with so much articulate horror among us. Dual citizenship we may have to recognize as the rudimentary form of that international citizenship to which, if our words mean anything, we aspire. We have assumed unquestioningly that mere participation in the political life of the United States must cut the new citizen off from all sympathy with his old allegiance. Anything but a bodily transfer of devotion from one sovereignty to another has been viewed as a sort of moral treason against the Republic. We have insisted that the immigrant whom we welcomed escaping from the very exclusive nationalism of his European home shall forthwith adopt a nationalism just as exclusive, just as narrow, and even less legitimate because it is founded on no warm traditions of his own. Yet a nation like France is said to permit a formal and legal dual citizenship even at the present time. Though a citizen of hers may pretend to cast off his allegiance in favor of some other sovereignty, he is still subject to her laws when he returns. Once a citizen, always a citizen, no matter how many new citizenships he may embrace. And such a dual citizenship seems to us sound and right. For it recognizes that, although the Frenchman may accept the formal institutional framework of his new country and indeed become intensely loyal to it, yet his Frenchness he will never lose. What makes up the fabric of his soul will always be of this Frenchness, so that unless he becomes utterly degenerate he will always to some degree dwell still in his native environment.

Indeed, does not the cultivated American who goes to Europe practice a dual citizenship, which, if not formal, is no less real? The American who lives abroad may be the least expatriate of men. If he falls in love with French ways and French thinking and French democracy and seeks to saturate himself with the new spirit, he is guilty of at least a dual spiritual citizenship. He may be still American, yet he feels himself through sympathy also a Frenchman. And he finds that this expansion involves no shameful conflict within him, no surrender of his native attitude. He has rather for the first time caught a glimpse of the cosmopolitan spirit. And after wandering about through many races and civilizations he may return to America to find them all here living vividly and crudely, seeking the same adjustment that he made. He sees the new peoples here with a new vision. They are no longer masses of aliens, waiting to be "assimilated," waiting to be melted down into the indistinguishable dough of Anglo-Saxonism. They are rather threads of living and potent cultures, blindly striving to weave themselves into a novel international nation, the first the world has seen. In an Austria-Hungary or a Prussia the stronger of these cultures would be moving almost instinctively to subjugate the weaker. But in America those wills-to-power are turned in a different direction into learning how to live together.

Along with dual citizenship we shall have to accept, I think, that free and mobile passage of the immigrant between America and his native land again which now arouses so much prejudice among us. We shall have to accept the immigrant's return for the same reason that we consider justified our own flitting about the earth. To stigmatize the alien who works in America for a few years and returns to his own land, only perhaps to seek American fortune again, is to think in narrow nationalistic terms. It is to ignore the cosmopolitan significance of this migration. It is to ignore the fact that the returning immigrant is often a missionary to an inferior civilization.

This migratory habit has been especially common with the unskilled laborers who have been pouring into the United States in the last dozen years from every country in southeastern Europe. Many of them return to spend their earnings in their own country or to serve their country in war. But they return with an entirely new critical outlook, and a sense of the superiority of American organization to the primitive living around them. This continued passage to and fro has already raised the material standard of living in many regions of these backward countries. For these regions are thus endowed with exactly what they need, the capital for the exploitation of their natural resources, and the spirit of enterprise. America is thus educating these laggard peoples from the very bottom of society up, awakening vast masses to a new-born hope for the future. In the migratory Greek, therefore, we have not the parasitic alien, the doubtful American asset, but a symbol of that cosmopolitan interchange which is coming, in spite of all war and national exclusiveness.

Only America, by reason of the unique liberty of opportunity and traditional isolation for which she seems to stand, can lead in this cosmopolitan enterprise. Only the American—and in this category I include the migratory alien who has lived with us and caught the pioneer spirit and a sense of new social vistas—has the chance to become that citizen of the world. America is coming to be, not a nationality but a trans-nationality, a weaving back and forth, with the other lands, of many threads of all sizes and colors. Any movement which attempts to thwart this weaving, or to dye the fabric any one color, or disentangle the threads of the strands, is false to this cosmopolitan vision. I do not mean that we shall necessarily glut ourselves with the raw product of humanity. It would be folly to absorb the nations faster than we could weave them. We have no duty either to admit or reject. It is purely a question of expediency. What concerns us is the fact that the strands are here. We must have a policy and an ideal for an actual situation. Our question is, What shall we do with our America? How are we likely to get the more creative America—by confining our imaginations to the ideal of the melting-pot, or broadening them to some such cosmopolitan conception as I have been vaguely sketching?

The war has shown America to be unable, though isolated geographically and politically from a European world-situation, to remain aloof and irresponsible. She is a wandering star in a sky dominated by two colossal constellations of states. Can she not work out some position of her own, some life of being in, yet not quite of, this seething and embroiled European world? This is her only hope and promise. A trans-nationality of all the nations, it is spiritually impossible for her to pass into the orbit of any one. It will be folly to hurry herself into a premature and sentimental nationalism, or to emulate Europe and play fast and loose with the forces that drag into war. No Americanization will fulfill this vision which does not recognize the uniqueness of this trans-nationalism of ours. The Anglo-Saxon attempt to fuse will only create enmity and distrust. The crusade against "hyphenates" will only inflame the partial patriotism of trans-nationals, and cause them to assert their European traditions in strident and unwholesome ways. But the attempt to weave a wholly novel international nation out of our chaotic America will liberate and harmonize the creative power of all these peoples and give them the new spiritual citizenship, as so many individuals have already been given, of a world.

Is it a wild hope that the undertow of opposition to metaphysics in international relations, opposition to militarism, is less a cowardly provincialism than a groping for this higher cosmopolitan ideal? One can understand the irritated restlessness with which our proud pro-British colonists contemplate a heroic conflict across the seas in which they have no part. It was inevitable that our necessary inaction should evolve in their minds into the bogey of national shame and dishonor. But let us be careful about accepting their sensitiveness as final arbiter. Let us look at our reluctance rather as the first crude beginnings of assertion on the part of certain strands in our nationality that they have a right to a voice in the construction of the American ideal. Let us face realistically the America we have around us. Let us work with the forces that are at work. Let us make something of this trans-national spirit instead of outlawing it. Already we are living this cosmopolitan America. What we need is everywhere a vivid consciousness of the new ideal. Deliberate headway must be made against the survivals of the melting-pot ideal for the promise of American life.

We cannot Americanize America worthily by sentimentalizing and moralizing history. When the best schools are expressly renouncing the questionable duty of teaching patriotism by means of history, it is not the time to force shibboleth upon the immigrant. This form of Americanization has been heard because it appealed to the vestiges of our old sentimentalized and moralized patriotism. This has so far held the field as the expression of the new American's new devotion. The inflections of other voices have been drowned. They must be heard. We must see if the lesson of the war has not been for hundreds of these later Americans a vivid realization of their trans-nationality, a new consciousness of what America meant to them as a citizenship in the world. It is the vague historic idealisms which have provided the fuel for the European flame. Our American ideal can make no progress until we do away with this romantic gilding of the past.

All our idealisms must be those of future social goals in which all can participate, the good life of personality lived in the environment of the Beloved Community. No mere doubtful triumphs of the past, which redound to the glory of only one of our trans-nationalities, can satisfy us. It must be a future America, on which all can unite, which pulls us irresistibly toward it, as we understand each other more warmly.

To make real this striving amid dangers and apathies is work for a younger *intelligentsia* of America. Here is an enterprise of integration into which we can all pour ourselves, of a spiritual welding which should make us, if the final menace ever came, not weaker, but infinitely strong.

---

[1] Compare Josiah Royce: "Race Questions, Provincialism and Other American Problems," reissued in Josiah Royce: *Basic Writings,* edited by John J. McDermott (Chicago/London, 1969). Bourne's essay "The Jew and Trans-National America" which he originally gave as a lecture at Harvard (*The Menorah Journal* II, December, 1916) represents a different version of this piece.

[2] Compare "American Use for German Ideals," *New* Republic, IV (Sept. 4, 1915).

A MIRROR OF THE MIDDLE WEST

No Easterner, born forlornly within the sphere of New York, Boston, or Philadelphia, can pass very far beyond the Alleghenies without feeling that American civilization is here found in the full tide of believing in itself. The flat countryside looks more ordered, more farmlike; the Main Streets that flash by the car-windows somehow look more robust and communal. There may be no less litter and scrubbiness; the clustered houses of the towns may look even more flimsy, undistinguished, well-worn; but it is a litter of aspiring order, a chaos which the people are insensitive to because they are living in the light of a hopeful future. The East has pretty much abandoned itself to the tides of immigration and industrial change which have overwhelmed it: no one really believes that anything startling will be done to bring about a new heaven and a new earth. But the intelligence of the West seems to live in apocalyptic sociological—not socialistic, however—dreams. Architects and business men combine half-heartedly to "save New York" from the horrors of the Jewish clothing-trade invasion, but Chicago draws great maps and sketches of a city-planning that shall make it not only habitable but radiant and palatial.

Hope has not vanished from the East, but it has long since ceased to be our daily diet. Europe has infected us perhaps with some of its world-weariness. The East produces more skeptics and spiritual malcontents than the West. For the Middle West seems to have accomplished most of the things, industrial and political, that the East has been trying to do, and it has done them better. The Middle West is the apotheosis of American civilization, and like all successes it is in no mood to be very critical of itself or very examinatory as to the anatomy and physiology of its social being. No Easterner with Meredith Nicholson's human and literary experience would write so complacently and cheerfully about his part of the country as Mr. Nicholson writes about The Valley of Democracy.[1]

His self-confidence is the very voice of the Middle West, telling us what it thinks of itself. This, we say as we read, must be the inner candor which goes with the West that we see with our eyes. So we like Mr. Nicholson's articles not so much for the information they give us as for the attitudes they let slip, the unconscious revelations of what the people he is talking for think important.

It is not a book of justification, although he would rather anxiously have us take not too seriously the political vagaries like Bryanism and Progressivism. And he wishes us to miss none of the symphony orchestras and art institutes that evidently now begin to grow like grasshoppers on the prairies. He treats himself rather as an expositor, and he is explicitly informational, almost as if for a foreign country. He sometimes has an amusing air of having hastily read up and investigated Western wonders and significances that have been not only common material in the Eastern magazines, but matter of despairing admiration on the part of those of us who are general improvers of mankind. He is naive about the greatness of Chicago, the vastness of agricultural production, the ravages of culture among the middle classes. He is almost the professional Westerner showing off his prize human stock.

Mr. Nicholson does well to begin with the folksiness of the West. No one who has experienced that fine open friendliness of the prosperous Middle Westerner, that pleasant awareness of the alert and beneficent world we live in, can deny that the Middle West is quite justified in thinking of itself as the real heart of the nation. That belief in the ultimate good sense, breadth of vision, and devotion to the common good, of the "folks back home," is in itself a guaranty of social stability and of a prosperity which implies that things will never be any different except as they slowly improve. Who can say that we have no Gemutlichkeit in America, when he runs up against this warm social mixability which goes so far to compensate for the lack of intellectual nuances and spontaneous artistic sensibilities?

Of course the Middle West has to pay for its social responsiveness in a failure to create, at least in this day and generation, very vigorous and diverse spiritual types. An excessive amiability, a genius for adaptability will, in the end, put a premium on conformity. The Westerner sincerely believes that he is more averse to conventionality than the Easterner, but the latter does not find him so. The heretic seems to have a much harder time of it in the West. Classes and attitudes that have offended against the "folks' " codes may be actually outlawed. When there are acute differences of opinion, as in the war, society splits into bitter and irreconcilable camps, whereas in the East the undesirable have been allowed to shade off towards limbo in gradual degrees. When hatred and malice, too long starved by too much "niceness," do break out from the natural man, they may produce those waves of persecution and vindictiveness which, coming from a so recently pacific West, astonished an East that was no less densely saturated with aliens but was more conversant with the feeling that it takes all kinds of people to make a world. Folksiness evidently has its dark underlining in a tendency to be stampeded by herd-emotion. "Social conscience" may become the duty to follow what the mob demands, and democracy may come to mean that the individual feels himself somehow expressed—his private tastes and intelligence—in whatever the crowd chooses to do.

I have followed Mr. Nicholson in his speaking of the Middle West as if he thought of the region as a unit. He does speak as if he did, but he does not really mean it. Much as he would like to believe in the substantial equality of the people in the Valley of Democracy, he cannot help letting us see that it is but one class that he has in mind—his own, the prosperous people of the towns. He protests against their being scornfully waved aside as bourgeoisie. "They constitute the most interesting and admirable of our social strata." And he is quite right. Certainly this stratum is by far the most admirable of all the middle classes of the world. It is true that "nowhere else have comfort, opportunity, and aspiration produced the same combination." He marvels at the numbers of homes in the cities that cannot imaginably be supported on less than five thousand a year. And it is these homes, and their slightly more impoverished neighbors, who are for him the "folks," the incarnate Middle West. The proletarian does not exist for him. The working-classes are merely so much cement, filling in the bricks of the temple—or, better, folks in embryo, potential owners of bungalows on pleasant suburban streets. Mr. Nicholson's enthusiasm is for the college-girl wife, who raises babies, attends women's clubs, and is not afraid to dispense with the unattainable servant. It is for the good-natured and public-spirited business man, who goes into politics because politics in the Middle West has always been concerned with the prosperity of the business community. But about the economic foundation of this class Mr. Nicholson sounds as innocent as a babe.

Take his attitude towards the farmer. You gather from these

pages that in the Middle West the farmer is a somewhat unfortunate anomaly, a shadow on the bright scene. Farming is
scarcely even a respectable profession; "the great grandchil-
dren of the Middle Western pioneers are not easily persuaded
that farming is an honorable calling"! He hints darkly at a decay
in fiber. Only one chapter out of six is given to the farmer, and
that is largely occupied with the exertions of state agencies, universities, to lift him out of his ignorance and selfishness. The average farmer has few of the admirable qualities of the Valley of
Democracy. He is not "folksy"; he is suspicious, conservative,
somewhat embittered, little given to cooperation; he even
needed prodding with his Liberty bonds. In Mr. Nicholson's
pages the farmer becomes a huge problem which lies on the
brain and conscience of a Middle West that can only act towards him in its best moments like a sort of benevolent Charity
Organization Society. "To the average urban citizen," says Mr.
Nicholson, "farming is something remote and uninteresting, carried on by men he never meets in regions that he only observes
hastily from a speeding automobile or the window of a limited
train."

It would take whole volumes to develop the implications of
that sentence. Remember that that urban citizen is Mr. Nicholson's Middle West, and that the farmer comprises the huge bulk
of the population. Is this not interesting, the attitude of the prosperous minority of an urban minority—a small but significant
class which has in its hands all the non-productive business and
political power—towards the great productive mass of the
people? Could class division be revealed in plainer terms? This
Middle West of Mr. Nicholson's class sees itself as not only innocent of exploitation, but full of all the personal and social virtues besides. But does the farmer see this class in this light? He
does not. And Mr. Veblen has given us in one of his books an
analysis of this society which may explain why: "The American
country town and small city," he says, "is a business community, that is to say it lives for and by business traffic, primarily of a
merchandising sort. . . . Municipal politics is conducted as in
some sort a public or overt extension of that private or covert
organisation of local interests that watches over the joint
pecuniary benefit of the local businessmen. It is a means . . . of
safe-guarding the local business community against interlopers
and against any evasive tactics on the part of the country popu-

lation that serves as a host. . . . The country town is a product and exponent of the American land system. In its beginning it is located and 'developed' as an enterprise of speculation in land values; that is to say it is a businesslike endeavor to get something for nothing by engrossing as much as may be of the increment of land values due to the increase of population and the settlement and cultivation of the adjacent agricultural area. It never (hitherto) loses this character of real-estate speculation. This affords a common bond and a common ground of pecuniary interest, which commonly masquerades under the name of public patriotism, public spirit, civic pride, and the like."

In other words, Town, in the traditional American scheme of things, is shown charging Country all the traffic will bear. It would be hard to find a member of Mr. Nicholson's Middle West—that minority urban class—who was not owing his prosperity to some form of industrial or real-estate speculation, of brokerage business enterprise, or landlordism. This class likes to say sometimes that it is "carrying the farmer." It would be more like the truth to say that the farmer is carrying this class. Country ultimately has to support Town; and Town, by holding control of the channels of credit and market, can make the farmer pay up to the hilt for the privilege of selling it his product. And does. When the farmers, getting a sense of the true workings of the society they live in, combine in a Non-Partisan League to control the organism of market and credit, they find they have a bitter class war on their hands. And the authentic voice of Mr. Nicholson here scolds them roundly for their restlessness and sedition. In this ferocious reaction of Town against Country's Socialistic efforts to give itself economic autonomy, we get the betrayal of the social malaise of the Middle West, a confession of the cleavage of latent class conflict in a society as exploitative, as steeply tilted, as tragically extreme in its poles of well-being, as any other modern society based on the economic absolutism of property.

A large part of the hopefulness, the spiritual comfort of the Middle West, of its sturdy belief in itself, must be based on the inflexible reluctance of its intelligentsia to any such set of ideas. However thoroughly Marxian ideas may have saturated the thought of Europe and become the intellectual explosive of social change, the Middle West, as in this book, persists in its robust resistance to any such analysis or self-knowledge.

Whenever there is a menace of such an intellectual invasion, as in the recent war, we get typical protests, like the letter of Vachel Lindsay (in *The Dial* of September 5), that troubadour of the bourgeoisie, who would spew out of his mouth all Marxian, even all foreign ideas, and return to the sacred principles of the Tory republicanism of Samuel Adams. It is not that Mr. Nicholson's attitudes are not true. It is that they are so very much less than the whole truth. They need to be supplemented by analyses set in the terms in which the progressive minds of the rest of the world are thinking. The intelligent Middle West needs to sacrifice a certain amount of complacency in exchange for an understanding of the structure of its own society. It would then realize that to read *The Valley of Democracy* in conjunction with pages 315-323 of Veblen's *Imperial Germany and the Industrial Revolution* is to experience one of the most piquant intellectual adventures granted to the current mind.

[1] Meredith Nicholson is better known for his mystery novels *The House of a Thousand Candles* (1905) and *The Siege of the Seven Suitors* (1910). Also compare Bourne's parallel text "Morals and Art from the West," *The Dial*, LXV (December 14, 1918), a review of William A. White's *In the Heart of a Fool* and Willa Cather's *My Antonia*.

EMERALD LAKE

I do not know whether, as a manner of living, Emerald Lake is worse than those Calabrian villages from which so many of its inhabitants come, but as an architectural litter it is almost as desperate as anything our landscape offers. Once the bed of a broad shallow lake, the region is as low as land can be, and its fields are almost perpetually damp. Streets have been cut in long straight lines and left to wallow in their mud. A gaudy sign-board announces the shifty "real-estate development company" which is responsible for the little foreign settlement. Looking down these vapid streets, one sees a broken line of square, flat-roofed houses of brick and stone, like a caricature of the squat earthquake buildings of Caserta, with here and there a balcony and a .touch of color. But in spite of the sprawling space all about, these houses bulge with dark people. A little squalid shop usually darkens the ground floor, and from the apartments above float streamers of bright-colored clothes. Already these streets suggest the time when the combined genius of the land speculator and the Italian padrone will have built Emerald Lake solidly up to the great city which it brushes.

But now the little settlement overflows its streets. The scene is dotted with tiny homesteads, dilapidated shacks of weather-beaten boards thrown together out of old lumber and tar-paper, with a window or two and a stove-pipe chimney. Each little hut is set in its patch of garden and surrounded by its stockade of palings, a brave gesture of an ownership that looks so pitifully clinging and uncertain. On the gaunt and rocky places is tethered the ubiquitous goat against whose marauding these proprietors waste their precious lumber. Black-haired babies and bristly dogs roll in the gutter and on the sidewalks where some bold entrepreneur has already laid his line of "concrete." There are few trees, and the settlement lies in a hot September glare that seems only too grateful to the swarthy, heavy, incorrigibly healthy women who drag themselves to the corner grocery or stand fiercely talking at the doorways. They are all smoothly black-haired, and they all look middle-aged and they all look alike. But for all their clumsiness there is a certain piratical vigor and intensity about them. In my childhood, whenever I rode through Emerald Lake in the car, this was what was most the very essence of "foreign" to me. And as I heard tales of these Italian

neighbors going in so whole-heartedly for the anger or lascivi-
ousness or murder which life elementally seemed to demand of
them, I wondered at our complacent way of hearing them and of
pitying their weak servitude to emotion. These Italians always
looked very determined to me, and illiterate and primitive as I
knew them to be, they insisted, against the gray background of
our town life, upon seeming important as people. Even the
babies have a certain intensity and determination as they totter
on the sidewalks, giving evidence that these broad women are
not middle-aged but the authentic mothers of them and in the
full tide of their prolific career. The young girls you do not see
until six o'clock calls them pouring out of the mills, running and
chattering in a confused babble. The fact that the eternal-
looking mothers were once such ungainly, flimsy, indefinite
young animals is no more mysterious perhaps than the fact that
the cheerfully guttural men who are repairing the electric road
were once like those definite little babies who are bruising themselves on the pavement. For such integrated and elemental
people youth cannot be a protective period of prolonged infancy. It is rather something quick, unpleasant, irrelevant, to
explode quickly into the real business of working and fighting
and breeding. Such people do not fool and fritter away their
passions, but get them somehow conserved for life. Emerald
Lake represents the injection of sudden vitality into our Puritan
town.

The question of what we are going to do with this vitality is so
important that it vaguely stirs our community conscience. And
they with us! What will America do to these babies in their growing up? Will they lose something of that intensity and become
like the painfully collared Domenicoes who stand around the saloon of an evening? If they surrender ditch-digging to some
even more needy race, will there be provided for them or will
they create for themselves work that will keep all that elemental
vigor? Will the girls stay soft and foolish and fail to jump suddenly into eternal-looking mothers? Will they make us gayer, intenser, more primitive, or will our streets merely sophisticate and
corrode their vigor? If they become more like us, what obscure
things will happen to their souls, and if they do not, what things
will happen to ours?

Our town shows its sense of the significance of all these matters by sending Emerald Lake a school, a raw red brick hulk with hideous green shades and a proud and strutting flag-pole. Indeed with characteristic American other-worldliness the school has preceded the sewer. The school is the gift of democracy, while the sewer waits on the demand of property-owners. The town trusts the school to Americanize Emerald Lake, as it pulls the little children from the gutters to the kindergarten and sends around the truant officer to catch those under fourteen. The children sing patriotic songs, and salute the American flag every morning, and learn the varied information which the millions of other American children are learning at the same moment all over our broad land.

As yet Emerald Lake has no church and probably will not have a church. For its people seem to have all the robust atheism of those Latin peoples who at once so much enjoy the voluptuousness of religious devotion and get along so easily without it. But it is our custom to contrast rather unfavorably this churchlessness of Emerald Lake with the Polish settlement at the other end of the town, where the church under a nationalistic priest has made a patriotic Poland out of the invigorated neighborhood.

It is surprising how little we know about the inhabitants of Emerald Lake. We do not know whether they come from the same Italian villages, or whether they have drifted in as isolated families. We do not know what old customs and associations they keep up, how they feel themselves related to each other, what they think of us, their neighbors. Politically, Emerald Lake does not count. Even if there were many more naturalized citizens, its voting would still be a mere ratification of the policy of one or the other of the native local politicians who direct township affairs as retainers of our tight little Puritan aristocracy. Emerald Lake's political activity is likely to be limited for some time to such matters as pulling wires for a new saloon license, getting its thirteen-year-old children out of the clutch of the truant officer, coaxing off some youthful brigand from the Recorder's court. Emerald Lake is not yet aware that its true interests lie in securing well paved streets, well drained land, lights, city water and sewers, sanitary tenements, garden space, protection against exploiting builders and landlords, a modern school. It knows that it is not interested in just which popular fellow of the ward shall be councilman. But our town is as innocent as any other of any machinery for getting the newcomer to feel his interest in these needs of his, and to express it effectively. All we can think of to do is to let him say who shall be councilman, and, if he owns a piece of land, pay a few dollars of taxes. We don't work him into the local freemasonry of politics. We tolerate his coming and settling on unoccupied territory which is geographically within our borders, but it is only geographically that Emerald Lake is a part of us.

The Italian of Emerald Lake forces himself upon our attention, works himself in, through acquiring property. There have been times when he unwittingly did it by crime and disease. Our aesthetic stomach has seemed strong enough to stand almost anything he may give us in the manner of living. But his soundest instinct is property. Italian names dot the tax-rolls of the township. Insusceptible to ugliness, mildly susceptible to pestilence, our Puritan community is impressed by property. The Italian first makes his impression as a propertied man. And this is the road along which Emerald Lake advances. To see it for the first time is to feel a chill of despair. Such squalor, such filth, such gaunt forsaken rubbish of lane and hut. Yet I can remember when Emerald Lake was only hovels, and there were not even palings to protect the garden-patch. These queer little buildings, these gardens, these little shops, represent economic advance. For Emerald Lake was true pioneer territory, without any free homestead land: Even the foothold had to be struggled for. There is something unconquerably robust about Emerald Lake. Its dilapidation is the squalor of hope. It is not the squalor of recession and defeat.

OUR UNPLANNED CITIES

The city club of a great Western town held recently a competitive exhibition of plans for a city neighborhood center. Around the walls of the beautiful corridors and rooms, designed with the last touches of thoughtful taste, were the bold conceptions of the architects of the city. Upon this problem of civic art they had lavished all their imaginative skill. These scores of radiant sketches seemed eloquent of a professional belief that for the building-up of the modern American city nothing too fine could be conceived.

Yet to see this exhibition I had had to travel from a suburban town thirty miles across a flat sandy waste strewn with the surplusage of the monster city's industry and life. We had come in the merciful dusk through an endless chaos of straggling towns, which seemed not so much towns as disgorged fragments of communities. Wilderness of dirty frame houses, gaunt factories, frowzy open spaces and outbuildings, isolated tenements in all stages of decrepitude, were interspersed with trim rows of cottages, shady streets, bright apartment-houses, and here and there an imposing church or school. From the lines of the streets one did get a certain sense of design. Otherwise the mass-effect was as if the heavens had opened and dumped out upon the desolate prairie the architectural garbage of some celestial city.

To pass from this chaotic savagery into the delightful club with its brave designs and its kindly and intelligent professional people, was to get a distinct ironic shock, a sudden sense of how little the repellent form in which the ordinary American city has got itself clothed expresses the individual intelligence and good-will of the citizens whose care should be to attend to that very civic clothing. The quality of these people, and the quality of the city as expressed in brick and wood and stone, bore not the slightest discoverable relation. One of the chief charms of a European country is the way the physical communal body of town and village seems to express the characteristic attitudes and spirit of the people. To say that the American city in its design and styles represented our spiritual capacity would be almost to say that we were a nation of madmen. We could convince a stranger that our churches and country houses were

built by architects, but we could not convince him that our cities
were so built.

About these confident designs there was something almost
pathetic as one came into them fresh from the pervading architectural crassness. These publicists and town-planners, social workers and architects, seemed scarcely out of the magical
stage. They had not yet sensed the legal and economic barriers
to be surmounted for the realization of their ideals. They
scarcely felt even the full incongruity of the American urban
scene, which makes one perpetually wonder at the pleasantness
and gentleness of the people whom one meets upon such di-
shevelled and barbaric streets.

I should have been more inclined to ascribe the peculiar horror of this city to its unmanageable size if I had not just come
from the small capital of a neighboring state, a state which has
the "social sense" if any of our states have it. Yet from a comparison of the two cities I could only conclude that the smaller
had been preserved from chaos by its smallness rather than by
its intelligence. On its hills by its lakes it has a famous and incomparable site, a site for artists to mould and develop. From
the train one alights into an uncertain station-square, which trails
off on one side to a cluster of hovels and boat-houses that
obscure the lake, and on the other past an ugly line of shop-
buildings towards the town. For the tree-lined lake-promenade
that a Swiss town would possess, for the stately avenue to the
capitol, the eye roams in vain. American towns don't have such
things. I thought of the picture of this same town-approach in
the report of one of those experts whom American cities suffering from twinges of town-planning conscience are calling in with
increasing frequency to chide them for their sins. On the opposite page he had printed a picture of the magnificent plaza and
station at San Paolo, Brazil. He had remarked that the comparison was not unfair, because both cities were small provincial
capitals. It was a striking contrast of what Americans and Brazil-
ians consider of civic importance.

Now this stodgy approach to our small Western city was no
mere accident. It was more or less a clue to the town. The
shabby surroundings of the capitol emphasized its showy waste-
fulness rather than its white grandeur. The beautiful university
building on the opposite hill made one mourn the characterless
streets that lay between. The lakes were almost as if they were

not. The town blindly turned its back upon them all. For the lake promenades and vistas, for the stately avenues between the hills, for the harmonious city that might be there, one had to rely on one's imagination. The town straggled out feebly towards the marshes and farms. No ray of civic design or art had shone down from that great university on the hill. No effort would invest these prosaic streets with charm and significance. The people and institutions, yes! But not the civic house in which they reside.

My first city had been a vast incalculable metropolis, desolately situated, without opportunity of natural beauty. The second was the small and self-conscious capital of a self-conscious state, with a natural situation such as few towns possess. Yet apparently the same spirit had gone to the upbuilding of both. Youth and newness will scarcely explain this American idiom. The large German cities have notoriously grown faster in the last fifty years than our own. Yet they are the models of civic art and design.[1] Many of them look in their mass-effect even newer than our American towns. Nor can it be a question of our absorption in selfish commercialism. The German people have not acquired a reputation for altruism, nor has it been the fashion to accuse their governments of Utopian idealism. That German cities are beautiful and nobly planned, and our own more hideous than anybody cares or dares to say, means that the directing and professional classes in Europe have inherited or reacquired a tradition, a town-planning sense, which we have somehow missed. Our eager pioneer development and our immigrant inundation have thrown the attention to individualistic effort, to a competitive race, and the artistic sense seems to have curiously followed. We have remained obsessed with the individual building, while the European has built towns and streets and squares rather than houses and churches and shops. The careless ugliness of the business streets and the outskirts of the American city suggests a veritable blind-spot to civic beauty. If we admitted this blindness we might wonder less frequently why we do not produce more or greater art. Youth growing up in such streets as ours would be the least likely in the world to acquire delicate discriminations, the sense of charm and atmosphere that makes for artistic sense and power.

We often excuse ourselves on the ground that our civic sense is prophetic. Where the visitor sees only the cheap prairie village, the resident sees the vision of the city which is one day to arise. When the city does arise, however, with its gridiron streets and staring blocks, one looks wistfully back to the prairie village. In too many towns this forward vision seems to have become hallucinatory. We are still a pioneer country, sketched over rather than drawn in firm outline. But there is danger of becoming so accustomed to the pioneer stage that we forget there is no more frontier and that most of us are living in the midst of relatively old and dense communities. We have no excuse for preserving, as we do, even throughout the East, the pioneer look as of some temporary encampment. There is little inducement, it is true, to think of our cities as communal homes. Our industrial and even professional population is in constant flux. The city has become a lodging-place. We are all in this sense pioneers, scrapping our cabins, deserting our farms, and moving on to better land and fortune. But the city remains behind us, with a life and integrity of its own, regardless of the individuals who flit through it.

Until architects and engineers, school-children and the average citizen, begin to think of the town or village not merely as a geographical expression or a business enterprise, but as a communal house to be made as well-ordered and beautiful as the citizen would make his home, social effort will lack a focus, and civic good-will and enterprise be shadowy and unreal. To preach town-planning in these days of threatened municipal bankruptcy may seem like Utopianism. To emphasize this order and beauty in the face of destitution and unemployment may seem like a case of hyperaesthesia. But let us not be too sure. In Europe town-planning has gone hand in hand with the alleviation of social ills. From the chaos and ugliness of American cities flows too palpably our economic and human waste. The well-planned city pays immensely from the social point of view. In Europe it has paid immensely from the financial point of view. Perhaps the road out of bankruptcy for the American city is exactly this Utopia.

THE ARCHITECT[1]

It is not so much that he is a member of the architectural profession as that he represents to us, in a sense, architecture itself. In his square head and body, in his broad scholarly face, is something architectonic. He does not suggest, it is true, those Gothic churches with which he and his disciples have strewn our land, and which stand uneasily like shamefaced strangers amid our alien corn. His own construction has a more pleasant solidity, a high good-humor of form, a confidence, both polished and bluff, in the eternal rightness of being mediaeval in this modern age. Or perhaps his appearance does suggest what he is emphatically is, the Gothic strained through the New Hampshire temperament. Something a little rocky and uncouth there is about his great cathedrals which grow into monstrous globes, bloating out their chapels one by one.

The democratic indifference to his Gothic does not in the least disturb him. "Beauty," he has repeatedly said, "is a manifestation of the Absolute," and the Absolute would scarcely be itself were it not derided of the people. Our architect has always lived on the high surfaces of thought. He has never asked himself whether the true secret of the Gothic might not be lost, whether mere imitation could ever bring that delicate balance of thrusts and proportion of varied design which suddenly sets the whole organism in a beautiful equilibrium as one enters a perfect interior like St. Ouen or Chartres. He does not care if our American streets jangle and jar us. Give him a Gothic church on a corner and he is happy. I hate this Teutonic critical spirit, he would say. My churches look like Gothic, anyway, and besides, church-building is the noblest work of man. The function of art is the development of character and perhaps one cannot develop one's moral sense if one is too subtly aesthetic.

It seems a little hard to connect the building of Chartres with the building of character, but it is easy when your artistic pedigree is by Rheims out of Boston, if you happen to be born in New Hampshire you can transmute almost anything into granite morality. Gothic cathedrals and Puritan correctness can be merged into a satisfying system of defence against democracy, industrialism, vocational training, and inductive science. Art for art's sake, and life for the glory of God merge perfectly. The one crime of education becomes the learning to make a living. And so our architect achieves an invigorating blindness which tilts at all the windmills that are grinding out the corn of the world. Young men are drawn after him in droves, fascinated by his masterly idealism. Europe is ransacked with gusto in order that a flamboyant tower may look down on the tawdry brick of Main street. Thus is the pure spirituality of the great Christian ages preserved in the midst of a blighting materialism. Character and art remain very much in the world, but as little as possible of the world.

The architect is the devoutest of Catholics, though strangely disloyal to the Vicar of God and the successor of St. Peter. He keeps all the festivals of the church, lights candles before the altars of the saints, writes with fervid eloquence of the beauty of ceremonial. Authority in church and state he worships, and wears black on the anniversary of the execution of St. Charles the First. Nothing thrills him like the early mass chanted in the dim light of dawn by a proper priest in a Gothic chasuble of splendid brocade wrought with holy figures and symbols in exquisite needlework, while the tall candles flicker before the reredos set with multitudinous saints and the labors of many artificers. He loves a Bishop who knows beauty and the significance of it, and grasps the full moment of tradition, memory, and association. He loves to watch him enter in solemn procession, enveloped in a splendid cope, on his head the mitre of spiritual authority, in his hand the great carved crozier of his pastoral office, before him the professional crucifix with its flanking candles, the sweet incense, the solemn radiance. This is the wine of life, and to what nobler service could one consecrate one's self than to building Gothic chalices for such a wine?

Thus summing up in himself the richness of the great tradition, our architect speaks with full-blooded authority, almost, as I have said, as the voice of architecture itself. He is most notable at conventions of his professional colleagues whom he holds spellbound by his uncompromising idealism. At such occasions he is constantly on his feet, protesting with biting sarcasm against some misrepresentation of himself, or bringing the wandering convention back to the eternal verities. A most cruel irony has made the architect professor in a technological college, and he feels bitterly the degradation of being controlled by faculties of engineers and physicists. The great question of the absolute autonomy of architectural schools within the college or university he fights over at every convention. He thrills his friends with his demands that very sharp notes be written to the presidents demanding that architecture be liberated from this humiliating control of the utilitarian. Architecture must be linked forever with the fine arts and not with mechanics, he says. In his own school he has no means of preventing his students from learning biology and psychology and sociology and all the other Teutonic fads which are the cause of the present war, of the debacle of character, righteousness, and honor, and of all those things which make for the creation and endurance of decent society.

The robust confidence of his thought, the fine flavor of personal success, the note of social resonance which he sounds—all these keep the architect at the very forefront of his profession. One gets from him a comforting sense of a still complacent and cultivated American class which loves the old because it is right and because it is spiritual, which is still interested in the antithesis of spirit and matter, which is still feebly charmed by the wrappings and the clothes after the body that wore them is dead, which still shudders at the encroachments of materialism and the extirpation of culture. Art, says the architect, is the symbolical expression of otherwise inexpressible ideas. In a sense therefore the architect himself is a work of art. He is the symbolical expression of this torpid old vague culture of ours. He is a symbol of our rootlessness, of that cultural colonialism which has so little left but smug comfort and polite aspiration. This idea is very hard to express. We owe gratitude to the architect for symbolizing so perfectly, in his phobias for democracy and vocational training and the new knowledge about ourselves, these passing ideals.

[1] Bourne published this in *The New Republic* under the pseudonym "Juvenis." The satirical attitude is due to Bourne's demand for a functional architecture. The question, whether architecture should be regarded from the point of view of art or that of applied science analogous to the activity of the engineer, had been extensively discussed in Herbert Croly's *Architectural Record*.

THE NIGHT-COURT

The audience, ranged on the stiff long wooden benches, flowed solidly up to the line of lawyers and plain-clothes at the bar. Horrified students, out for a glance at seamy life, social workers and well-dressed women, stood sharply out of the attentive lines of spectators, but as a whole the audience seemed not so much idly curious gazers as a part of the drama which went on under the desk of the judge. At first it seemed horrible that we should be sitting there, staring at these captive animals of the law, but as the monotonous round dragged along towards midnight, one felt caught into a great wheel. Free and safe, we seemed to be witnessing some grotesque parody of our own desires and escapes, and to be vicariously living the sordid experience upon which the law had set its hand. Type for type the faces of the audience became like those behind the bar. Vulgar curiosity left our fascinated gaze. Only the judge remained high, aloof from this slimy network of disorder.

But there were moments of detachment, and then one told one's self that in this human hopper through which passed the endless nightly chain of men and women, justice was being done, the bad being punished, vice corrected, and society rescued from jeopardy. Before one's eyes was being enacted the most austere and majestic function of the State. I looked with breathless attention on these offenders who had put society in jeopardy, and for protection against whom we had all this costly system of policemen and jails. There were some classic types—the old blowze with crooked hat, scarcely sobered, a little expostulatory against her periodic ten days in the workhouse; the pink young street-walker, fat and brazen; the seedy vagrant. These were the people that the city's life seems to manufacture only as meal for the judicial mills to grind, and who enjoy a regular publicity and institutional attention denied to the less flagrantly conventional.

There were many types, however, that were not at all familiar, types that one passes every day in city streets with no other thought than a slight depression at their vacuous faces. There was a stolid and respectable German janitress against whom vast conspiracies were charged, involving three dollars and disorderly conduct, and who raised up a host of incredible people to testify to her decency and honesty. People who could not

have existed outside of Dickens, ancient and corpulent book-
keepers who sent the imagination back to the Irish New York of
the draft-riots, old bonneted women with rich and racy accent,
who suggested an unknown world of lifelong skating on the
edge of respectability. One realized how much life must be to
some people a tissue of complaisances and blinkings.

There was a tastefully dressed girl of twenty-two, with the face
of a child, who wept for a long time and then answered impossible questions as to her virtue with an intelligence and courtesy
that left you no relief of pity for the subnormal. For her was won
a speedy release through the excessive zeal of her plain-clothes
captor, and she slipt out with one wondered what damage or
rectification. Then the janitress appeared again, the coils of the
law inexorably about her head.

There were bare-headed, tragic-faced Italian girls, who might
have led strikes and revolutions, and who told stories of brutality
in low poignant tones that could scarcely be heard. And there
were many stolid-faced simple creatures, who looked merely
bewildered and followed their captors as meekly as dumb animals. What struck one most was the helplessness of the prisoners. There were none of the correct moral and immoral attitudes. There was neither bravado nor terror, violence nor cring-
ing. It was mostly a merely "I am caught. What are you going to
do with me?" There was only apathy, as of human lumps being
shuffled along through a routine process which elicited neither
retrospect, present emotion, or foreboding. One could feel
neither pity nor repulsion, only that curious affinity. One rubbed
one's eyes. Society must be very fragile indeed if it could be
placed in jeopardy by anything these half-formed people could
do. Morality must be a very frail web if it could be assailed by
any of these petty immoralities unveiled to our listening ears.
There was the laughable assumption through it all that this
gowned judge and this swarm of policemen and bailiffs and
plain-clothes men and the jails and Island behind them really
availed to control or reform the vices they pursued. One had to
decide that there was something mystical in it all. In the detec-
tion and punishment of one shameless culprit, justice was
served and into that case, as into a part of infinity, went the full
essence of the majesty of the State.

No peculiar stigma or guilt seemed to fasten on the culprits
from their appearance in court. Most of them faced the spec-

tators with a dull calm, and listened unmoved to the glib tales of
their shamelessness which rolled from the lips of their accusers.
How these helpless and mediocre people could get into such
complications was revealed as the plain-clothes men went on
the stand, and told tale after tale of organized temptation and
betrayal. They gave the whole proceeding a touch of even
higher mysticism. For the State to play this ignoble game of de-
ceit with weak or miserable women must be in the interests of a
higher justice than is apparent to the layman's mind. Perhaps on
the principle of setting a thief to catch a thief the pander is set
to catch the prostitute. But the revolting unctuousness with
which these young men told their tales, and the practised effron-
tery with which they parried the questions, gave a background
against which none of the culprits' guilt could be taken with the
proper seriousness and horror. The whole thing took the form of
a contest of wits, a peculiarly depraved and urban form of the
chase, the last degenerate manifestation of the hunting
psychosis. Most amazing of all was the clumsy chivalry with
which each man escorted his victim in and out of the court-
room. His manner was that of one who, having achieved a pious
consciousness of the rectitude of his position as a servant of the
State, yet wished to show himself sensible to the wrong that he
had officially done her.

The scene was not all black however. There were alleviations.
Matrons and probation officers and institution agents hovered
around. Many of these who passed through the court doubtless
suffered no harm, and were perhaps scared into a little wisdom.
The judge was kindly and dispassionate and indefatigable. At
times there was a curious air of moral surgery about, as of hurt-
ing you only for your own good. The hateful young men even
wore a sober air at times as of entrapping the girls only for a
higher moral end. Perhaps this was not all hypocrisy. Sordid as
it all was, and motivated by a kind of grotesque unintelligence, it
was not inhumane. We seemed all too much a part of a system
of things to make revolted indignation really possible. One felt
the first faint murmur of days that should take a robuster view of
the jeopardies of society, decide more intelligently what really offends us, and work out new ways of attacking the factors of offence at their root.

WHAT IS EXPLOITATION?[1]

My western friend who runs a prosperous stove-factory has been finding fault with my insistent use of the word "exploitation." My outlook on life is not sufficiently cheerful, and I am inclined to see malevolence where everything is, as they say at college, healthy, hearty, and happy. Our quarrel rose over the Mesaba strike, and my acceptance of an I. W. W. pamphlet as a plausible account of what was going on there. The accounts of the insecurity of pay, the petty robberies, the reeking houses, the bigoted opposition to labor organization, seemed to me to smell of truth, because I had read the maddening tales of Colorado and West Virginia, and seen with my own eyes in Scranton and Gary and Pittsburgh the way workers live, not in crises of industrial war but in brimming times of peace.

My friend, however, is more robust. He would make no such hasty impassioned judgments. He would judge nothing without "going to the mines, working in them for a year or two, being one of the men, getting their free confidence, then working for a couple of years as confidential auditor for the company." Such Olympian judiciality fills me with envy and dismay. I feel that his serenity is the normal mood of healthy activity, facing the modern world. Could he find anything but scorn for those of us who go around with the vestiges of what it is now priggish to call a "social conscience"? To him an industrial strike is like an exciting political contest or the recriminations between "two kid baseball terms." Both sides, he says, "squawk a good deal about the raw stuff the other side is trying to pull off," but deep down, his experience convinces him, "they are very uniformly a pretty human bunch." He hasn't been to Mesaba, but his friend the Duluth bread-dealer assures him that agitators were the cause of all the trouble. They always are. Trouble, to my friend, is a personal matter. He sees individuals, laboring as happily as they can expect to labor on this far from perfumed earth. He sees their contentment disturbed by "outsiders," individuals, bitter envious mischievous men who make a business of setting workmen against their employers. He sees the "outsiders" deluding, persuading, intimidating honest workers into stopping work and engaging in careers of lawlessness. He sees the individual employer in natural self-defense fighting for his rights, defending his property, ousting the agitators, carrying the war into his laborers' camp. From the busy office of his stove-factory, it all looks like a personal quarrel between free and equal individuals. When the state interferes with its militia and its injunctions, it is not flouting individuality, but merely doing its business of maintaining order and defending private property.

Our argument really hinges on whether to the workman all this excitement and deprivation and delusion is not part of the daily business of living. I am too tender-minded. What is at the back of my confused hints that there is "something shameful, something consciously brutal" about industrial relations? My friend admits that he has in his shop men who work in places that are noisy and dusty, in hot places, in rooms where paint is being sprayed. He has workmen who do their work at night the year round. He is sorry. He wishes these things did not have to be, and he is remedying them as fast as he can. What he will not admit is that any one is "specifically to blame." He does not imprison his men. They come freely to him and ask for employment. He "gives them such compensation as makes the jobs attractive to them, in competition with all other jobs in city and country." He is fair and scrupulous. His company is in business to produce goods at such cost that people can afford to buy them. He cannot make his plant a sanatorium—and when he says this the faintest note of irony steals into his robust voice—for his wage-earners. The stockholders have built a factory and not a philanthropic institution. If the workers did not like his factory, would they send for their brothers and cousins from the old country across the sea? If these "hunkies" in stove-factory and iron mine were being "exploited," would they not drift speedily away to jobs where they were content? My friend cannot imagine a man being willingly exploited. There are, no doubt, heartless employers; workmen here and there are perhaps subject to oppression. But systematic, prevalent industrial exploitation—and he has worked in all parts of the country and at every level of skill—my stove-factory friend has never seen. And he turns aside from my abstract philosophy to the daily manipulation of stoves and men.

What then do I mean by exploitation? And I have to remind my friend that my very first industrial experience was one of those rudimentary patterns of life which, if they are imprinted on your mind early enough, remain to fix the terms in which you interpret the world. The experience was leaving school to work for a musician who had an ingenious little machine on which he cut perforated music-rolls for the players which were just then becoming popular. His control of the means of production consisted in having the machine in his house, to which I went every morning at eight and stayed till five. He provided the paper and the music and the electric power; I worked as a wage-earner, serving his skill and enterprise. I was on piece-work, and everything suggested to my youthful self that it depended only upon my skill and industry how prosperous I should become. But what startled me was my employer's lack of care to conceal from me the fact that for every foot of paper which I made he received fifteen cents from the manufacturer with whom he had his contract. He paid me five, and while I worked, spent his time composing symphonies in the next room. As long as I was learning the craft, I had no more feeling about our relation than that there was a vague injustice in the air. But when I began to be dangerously clever and my weekly earnings mounted beyond the sum proper for a young person of eighteen who was living at home, I felt the hand of economic power. My piece-rate was reduced to four and a half cents. My innocence blazed forth in rebellion. If I was worth five cents a foot while I was learning, I was worth more, not less, after I had learned. My master folded his arms. I did not have to work for him. There were neighbors who would. I could stay or go. I was perfectly free. And then fear smote me. This was my only skill, and my timorous inexperience filled the outside world with horrors. I returned cravenly to my bench, and when my employer, flushed with his capitalistic ardor, built another machine and looked about for a young musician to work it, I weakly suggested to an old playmate of mine that he apply for the position.

Enlarge my musician into the employing class of owners and managers and shareholders of factory and mine and railroad, and myself into the class of wage-earners in all these enterprises, and you have the picture of the industrial system which the I. W. W. agitator has in his mind when he writes the Mesaba pamphlet to which my friend took such exception. With my five cents making that huge differential of profit for my employer, and with my four and a half cents giving his enterprise a productiveness which, if he had incorporated himself, he could have turned into additional capitalization, I was a crude symbol of the industrial system as my mind gradually took in the fact that there was an industrial system. This was my first experience in "exploitation." If there had been fewer musicians available I should have gotten more pay, and if there had been more available I should probably have had even less. But there would always have been a surplus, and I should have always felt the power of my employer to skim it, to pull it towards himself. As long as I continued at work, nothing could have removed my sense of helplessness. Any struggle I might have made would have been only towards weakening his pull, and lessening the amount he was able to skim. He was not robbing me, and no person of sense would have said he was, but our very relation was an exploitation. There was no medium way between exploitation and philanthropy.

My stove-factory friend, however, will have none of this theory. If it is a question of power, he says, then Mike Solomon exploits the stove company when he is able to get three dollars a day, on account of the present demand for labor, when two dollars was wealth to him a year ago. Then I admit that local groups of workers are able—either through lack of competition or clever politics or display of force—to exercise temporarily a decisive pull on the surplus and divert most of it to themselves. It is all a question of power. But as long, I tell him, as the employer is entrenched in property rights with the armed state behind him, the power will be his, and the class that does the diverting will not be labor. My friend, however, does not like these Nietzschean terms. He is sure that his workmen have just as much power to exploit him as he has of exploiting them. This is where we differ, and this is why thought will buzz in an angry murky haze over eight-hour bills and individual contracts and collective bargaining as long as millions agree with him. He trusts rights, I trust power. He recognizes only individuals, I recognize classes.

That is why I can never make him understand what I mean by "exploitation." He thinks of it as something personally brutal. He does not see it inherent in a system, for which no one is "specifically to blame" only because all are equally guilty of short vision and flimsy analysis. And yet as I read his letters and clippings, I wonder if he is not the realist and I the mystic. He punctures my phrases of power and class with a coarse satisfied hunky to whom work and disease and riot are all in the day's work and who would despise the philosophy which I am so anxiously weaving for him. It seems a long way from my dainty music-bench to the iron range, or the stove-factory. One has to feel exploitation perhaps before one understands it. I console myself with the thought that power is itself mystic, and that my friend will have to get hit with some invisible threat of class-force, as some of his frightened friends are now getting hit, before he will analyze any deeper that industrial system of which he is so efficient and loyal an officer.

---

[1] This essay is a slightly dramatized representation of a childhood experience. Compare John Adam Moreau oo. cit.

THE "SCIENTIFIC" MANAGER.[1]

The scientific manager whom I know is very fond of distinguishing himself from the horde of mere "efficiency" men who are everywhere imposing themselves upon the credulous industrialist of today. My friend is, in fact, one of the seven picked men, he tells us—mystic number—whom the great Founder left as disciples to carry on the work. This authority gives my scientific manager a certain bland impressiveness, and makes his tall, black, and uncouth form tower among us in a way that perhaps neither his speech nor his personality would tend to make him tower. He has a fine quality of prevalence. He is not merely in a room, he pervades it. That little group of serious thinkers which he frequents when he is in town he manages to straddle and absorb. Scientific management *oozes from his lips* and gradually the occasion is full of it. It jumps into every discussion. Our friend is a walking evangel, an insistent, reiterate note of a new thing that is to dominate mankind.

I often try to get the scientific manager to tell me what Scientific Management really is. But whenever I try, I get a new sense of the inadequacy of words to express ideas. I get a sense of living in a different intellectual world from that in which business and industry operate. The scientific manager seems to come up out of a country where personal attitudes rather than ideas are the counters of life. He is used to impressing people. His object in life is to make men efficient but to make them purr while doing it. His manner is large and broad. It says to you, "Please rub away all the little sharp points of criticism which may tend to protrude from you, and submit to the pervasive geniality of my influence." The scientific manager makes you feel that his thought is not devoted chiefly to clear formulation or clear technical exposition, and certainly not to the interpretation of industrial processes and the handling of labor, but to the personal lubrication of institutional wheels. He is the oil-can of the industrial establishment, rather than the real scientist of the industrial laboratory. You do not expect him to thresh out problems with employers and employees, but you know that he will be very kind in showing them exactly how things ought to be done. You feel that he is not so much interested in pouring general comprehension around him as he is in greasing the human machinery of management in the industrial plants where he is engaged.

He seems, in short, an industrial charmer. As he talks to us in his loud, full way, I conceive his intellectual technique to consist in the breaking down of resistance, so that scientific absolutism may come into its own. He has an impartial and healthy contempt for both the stubborn and archaic employer and the uppish and suspicious employe. Both must yield to the man of science. Now these are often difficult to manage. I get very vividly from his words how childish and silly their opposition is to the new gospel. But they amuse rather than annoy him. The scientific manager does not intrude history upon you, but these resistive manufacturers and bigoted labor-unions seem to him as foolish as the obscurantists who opposed Galileo.

But if my friend is grieved at the benightedness of the interested classes with whom he directly deals, what does he not think of the general ignorant public? Whenever I see him talking with a friend I know that his very next sentence is likely to be— "But my dear man, you don't seem to know in the least what scientific management really is!" And when you ask him, he tends to dismiss you with a wave of his hand, humorously. You are struck at once with the enormous difficulty of getting over to your untrained mind the complexity of the new science. The analytic burden under which the scientific manager staggers is too heavy to transfer in a short conversation to your puny shoulders.

If you follow his talk, however—and he is always talking about peace and war and education in an easy authoritative roll—you somehow suspect that science to him does not mean so much a method of tested and checked hypotheses as a more specialized and more exact way of getting results. Being scientific seems to mean taking a long time to find out about a thing. Scientific management, he tells us, is only in its infancy. It will take years and years of analyzing processes before there will be discovered the one right and quick way of doing each little separate task. If it took Mr. Taylor twenty years to find the best way of cutting metals, shall we complain at the lapse of centuries which may be necessary to complete the analysis of our thousands of industries? He suggests a vision of thousands of professional descendants from the scientific loins of himself and his six so authorized and documented colleagues. I once pointed out to him the fact that scientists could afford to discover things slowly because they had a reasonable reliance on

the stability of natural phenomena. The Universe would wait for
them and be just as dependable as if they had discovered it
immediately. But I questioned whether industry was in this respect like the Universe. Didn't processes change constantly,
and mightn't it be that after the scientific manager had spent ten
years analyzing his process, he would find there wasn't any
process left to operate? But he seemed to think there was a
quibble hidden somewhere, and gave me little satisfaction.

I wanted to know also whether science didn't depend on reliable factors as well as upon a generally reliable Universe. I
asked him how reliable his human labor factor was. He seemed
to have no doubts about it. There was first the continual magic
of his personality—perhaps he does not put it in just this way,
but one cannot be long with him in the same room without feeling his tactful pervasiveness, which one knows, even when one
evades the glamor one's self, is working cheerfully and daily in a
realer world. If this did not propitiate and melt together the wills
of employer and employe into cooperation, there was then the
motive of scientific passion that would come to the worker himself. If there is only one right way of doing a task, the worker will
feel ennobled in performing it that one right way. Even though
his task is analyzed and delimited until he becomes a mere part
of the machine or a mere handle to his tool, yet he will feel a
responsible glow from his participation in so vast and perfect an
enterprise. His very humility will lend him awe. He will become a
kind of industrial Marcus Aurelius, surveying the matchless and
uncontrollable system with Stoic calm.

My friend, however, does not rely entirely on motives so
exalted. His psychology is cleverer than that. It is the bonuses
given for the completion of the task that are to maintain the
equilibrium. Bonuses applied with scientific precision to the
workers will not only reward them justly in proportion to their
output, but will automatically adjust any little temperamental friction or discontent of theirs. The worker, then, his egoistic and altruistic impulses played upon like an instrument, will give forth
the musical sounds of perfect efficiency and perfect contentment. Scientific disinterestedness and personal ambition will fertilize each other. Scientific management will become, for the
worker, a course in character-building.

I have no way at all of testing my friend's scientific attainment.
I only know that he is both official and sure. In fact, his broad

and beaming face expresses nothing but assurance. I know that such ideas as those of the class-struggle, of labor and capital contending for the power of distributing the product, of the wild hopes of labor and the grim hardness of capital, of collective bargaining, and the different potentials of labor classes, are simply not in his head. Exploitation is an unknown word to him, and industrial democratic organization means nothing. Democracy, it is true, flows freely from his lips. What could be more democratic than a system which brings both employer and employe docilely before the bar of stern and immutable fact and measurement? In his vision they are subjugated to himself, the expert. Of vast social and economic forces he cares little. He has much of Mr. Carnegie's perfectly happy quality. One recalls those stories which the ironmaster tells with such glee how he settled great strikes with a pun or a nickname opportunely applied. My friend radiates the same optimisms. Like the Laird of Skibo, there are no storms for him.

---

[1] This unpublished manuscript represents Bourne's clearest position on the "Scientific Management" movement fathered by F. W. Taylor. A thorough examination of this movement can be found in Samuel Haber's *Efficiency and Uplift, Scientific Management in the Progressive Era, 1890-1920* (Chicago/London, 1964).

NEW IDEALS IN BUSINESS

New Ideals in Business, by Ida M. Tarbell. (Macmillan Co.; $1.75.)
An Approach to Business Problems, by A. W. Shaw. (Harvard University press; $2.)
America and the New Epoch, by Charles P. Steinmetz. (Harper & Bros.; $1.)

Mild English satirists like Mr. G. Lowes Dickinson tell us that business has become the American religion, with its own creed and its distinct evangelistic flavor of utterance. There is always a tendency for the successful to expand into a cult. And American business, more than any other activity, has had the glamour of success. Daring, swift, clean strokes of organizing and inventive genius brought their quick and exceeding great reward. The colossal booms, the mushroom growths of industrial plants, the expansion of trade, the sudden cataclysms, have touched American business with a sense of the miraculous. And now the original ruthless struggle for growth and survival has given place, with the integration of the big industries, to a milder era. The improvement of technique has been accompanied by a new idealism. Disdain for the public, when the hand of every business man was against every man, has changed into concern for the public's good will. A number of prophets have arisen to fortify and justify that sense of ubiquitous goodness which the business man of today seems to need around him as the fish needs water.

Of these prophets Miss Tarbell is one of the most industrious and comforting. She does not ask how far the new idealism has been forced by the pressure of government, by the fear of social unrest, by the desire for sweeter and subtler forms of control over the lives of the industrially subject classes. She accepts at its face value this new and anxious solicitude for the welfare of employees, for the conservation of their health and intelligence. She makes a wide sweep of industry, and strains out all the good intentions from the chaotic, elemental, pig-headed American industrial life that we see out of our car windows. These she presents to us with so evangelistic an ardor that our perspectives are quite destroyed. Her observation, she tells us, has been exhaustive, but one is skeptical about so unanimous a demonstration that American industry is finding the Golden Rule synonymous with business profits. An idealism must surely be false when it is most impressive for what it glaringly ignores. One of the unhappiest days of Miss Tarbell's life was the occasion when she appeared before the Industrial Relations Commission in New York, and had her easy optimism remorselessly probed about the things she hadn't seen in those industrial communities that she had visited. Her method was "to see at their work all the men and women in a plant from those with the shovel or scrubbing brush to those in the head offices; to look at their conditions, to see them in their homes, to learn from their lips what they thought and felt about it all." But she brought away none of the impressions that disturb other idealists among us—the subtle corrosion of the workers' power of self-defence through corporation philanthropy, the destruction of collective effort through scientific management. Anyone who heard Miss Tarbell's revealing testimony understood that she had gone out, not as a scientific investigator or even as an understanding idealist, but as a detective to find the Golden Rule. The matter of her personal sincerity is irrelevant. The fact is that the model workshops and houses, the safety and anti-alcohol crusades, the health insurance and pension schemes, the profit-sharing, education, scientific management that she found, she advertises to the glory of business and not to the glory of growing democracy and social responsibility. I do not mean to sneer at ideals in business. But I do insist that the value in reporting them must lie in a scrutiny whether such ideals are not inhibiting broader and more crucial visions. Is not this autocratic regimentation of the workers a handicap to democracy? Should not the workers' welfare be the concern of the community at large rather than of the individual corporation, to which it means only a more powerful instrument for control of the habits, ideals, attitudes of the worker, and for his ultimate feudalization? Miss Tarbell, as a prophet of enlightened capitalism, does not even pose this question. She therefore befuddles her idealism and is an intellectual darkener of counsel rather than a bringer of light.

One turns to the more appealing Mr. Shaw, editor of "System," lecturer on Business Policy in Harvard University, whose scheme of business idealism is scientific rather than evangelistic. For if American business has been a religion it is rapidly becoming a science. The business man approaches his problems of production, distribution, and management in the same spirit of analysis and experimentation as the chemist in his laboratory.

Such an idealism is one of efficiency and integration. To the layman Mr. Shaw's analysis will seem very obvious, business science the most elementary of all techniques. If success in business is not the lot of all of the even moderately intelligent, it must be because there are external factors over which one has no control. The particular approach which Mr. Shaw outlines seems lined only with the most truistic common sense. His science suggests the disquieting thought that American energy in its flood of enthusiasm and conviction has gone into a profession which makes little strain upon the intellect or imagination. It is not that ideals of efficiency and wastelessness are "low," it is that they are so easy. The effect of many more such books on "business science" would be to destroy all our sense of the peculiar mystery, genius, and arduousness of the enterprise. Our current American imagination might slip away and begin to fasten itself on the really intricate problems of personal and class relations. Welfare work, harmonious organization of labor force, Mr. Shaw sees rightly as part of the technique of efficiency. In our present industrial system it is far more fruitful to idealize the "betterment" forces in this way than in Miss Tarbell's prophetic strain. As long as we have our present class rule in industry, it will be healthier for the worker to be treated as an implement of production than as a laboratory for the working out of the Golden Rule.

If class rule passes in a socialist reorganization of industry, then these ideals of welfare and efficiency might both find their proper meaning. Welfare would become a series of minimum standards maintained by the industrial state impersonally for the benefit of all. Efficiency would become a spontaneously lived technique. Such a scheme Dr. Steinmetz presents. His vision of American social reconstruction is so magnificent and far-flung in its implications that it should challenge the attention of prophets, experts, and laymen alike. The discussion and appreciation which these ideas create will almost be a test of the intellectual vitality which American socialism has left in its bones. For Dr. Steinmetz has that rare and suggestive vision of the socialist who is at the same time a great inventive engineer and an active officer in one of our most advanced and successful industrial corporations. He is personally engaged in fashioning the corporation out of which he hopes the industrial state will be built. His socialism might be called a "corporation syndicalism," for what he outlines is a union of huge corporations into whose hands will be entrusted the productive work of the nation. The corporation type of organization has demonstrated its permanent administrative superiority over any form of political machinery. The state of the future must be built out of the corporation rather than out of the present political organization. Politically organized, the nation would have only veto and referendum power over general policy. The dual state, with parallel industrial and political organization (which we already virtually have, though the relations are disguised and infinitely disordered), will be publicly recognized. A national organism, stable, flexible, effective, will be achieved where efficiency and democracy will at last strike their proper balance and undertake the functions they can best perform. It is a grandiose conception, and quite the most plausible of all the Utopias. America drives straight to such an ideal, and into it can be fitted all other business and political idealisms. Dr. Steinmetz turns prophet, too, and fears our slow decadence, in competition with the State socialism of Europe, unless we develop our policy toward this dual government. The new epoch will drive us hard. Our slow democracy, striving to throw chains of control over the embryo industrial state, must fail. The new epoch forces this corporation socialism upon us. Business ideals which are to be fruitful must point toward this goal.

THE PRICE OF RADICALISM

The Pillar of Fire, by Seymour Deming. Boston: Small, Maynard and Co. $1.00 net.

Mr. Seymour Deming follows his eloquent "Message to the Middle Class" with an assault upon the colleges. His book he calls "a profane baccalaureate," and it rips along as from one who is overturning the altars of Baal. No one has a style quite like this, with its mixture of Greek classicism and Broadway slang, with its cheap sardonic kicks and its sudden flashes of insight. Mr. Deming moves you, but he leaves you in the end more entertained than persuaded. His prophetic fire is so much fire and so little light. The first part of the book is devoted to picturesque denunciation of the colleges for not training a man to make a living. The second glorified the radical as the man who scorns success, and has turned from everything which the world thinks of value. Such logic dims the force of his blast.

I quite agree with Mr. Deming that the object of an education is to know a revolution when you see one. Colorado, Calumet, and West Virginia should make the college sky much more lurid than they do. But something more is needed for this "class unconscious of class-consciousness" than clarion calls summoning it to be radical. Mr. Deming has too much of the martyr-complex. He talks as if the radical of today occupied the position of social outlawry that the Abolitionist of 1850 occupied. To be radical, he says, is to be thrust out of the society of cultivated men, and to seek one's companionship among the meek and lowly. He speaks too always as if this little group of early Christians living in catacombs were all of the saintliest breed, the foolish who have confounded the sayings of the wise. Most of us used to believe both of these things. But most of us have given up looking on ourselves as heroes and martyrs because we blaspheme the "property-god of Things-As-They-Are." We have climbed out of the catacombs, and we find many radicals disillusioning. We have either grown up or the world has moved on.

The real trouble with middle-class radicalism in this country today is that it is too easy. It is becoming too popular. It is not the heroic abnegation which Mr. Deming pictures, but something which almost anybody can encompass. The ranks are full of the unfocused and the unthinking. Let the college man or girl who listens to Mr. Deming's sermon join the Intercollegiate Socialist Society or some similar institution, and discover how discouragingly respectable they are. The only way by which middle-class radicalism can serve is by being fiercely and concentratedly intellectual. This is something which these organizations have so far failed to do. The labor movement in this country needs a philosophy, a literature, a constructive socialist analysis and criticism of industrial relations. How very far even the most intelligent accredited representatives of labor are still from such a goal is shown by the Manly report. Labor will scarcely do this thinking for itself. Unless middle-class radicalism threshes out its categories and interpretations and undertakes this constructive thought it will not be done. Mr. Deming must add to his message of fire the clear cold determination to be intolerantly intellectual.

Given the prophetic fire, the young middle-class radical to whom Mr. Deming appeals should be able to find himself in an intellectual movement which is struggling to clarify its ideas and use them as tools for turning up the layers and interpreting the changes in the social world about them. Intellectual radicalism should not mean repeating stale dogmas of Marxism. It should not mean "the study of socialism." It had better mean a restless, controversial criticism of current ideas, and a hammering out of some clear-sighted philosophy that shall be this pillar of fire. The young radical today is not asked to be a martyr, but he is asked to be a thinker, an intellectual leader. So far as the official radicals deprecate such an enterprise they make their movement sterile. Yet how often when attempts are made to group radicals on an intellectual basis does not some orthodox elder of the socialist church arise and solemnly denounce such intellectual snobbishness. Let these young men and women, he will say, go down into the labor unions and the socialist locals and learn of the workingman. Let them touch the great heart of the people. Let them put aside their university knowledge and hear that which is revealed unto babes. Only by humbly working up through the actual labor movement will the young radical learn his job. His intellectualism he must disguise. The epithet "intellectual" must make him turn pale and run.

And so this middle-class radicalism tends to drift, destitute of intellectual light. The pugnacious thinkers who want to thresh things out find themselves labelled heterodox and esoteric.

There is little controversy because nobody will quarrel about ideas. The workers must not be offended and the movement must not be split. The young radical soon learns to be ashamed of his intellectual bias, and after an ineffectual effort to squeeze himself into the mind of the workingman drifts away disillusioned from his timid collegiate radicals. His energy evaporates, because intellectual radicalism was afraid to be itself.

Mr. Deming ignores this practical postlude to his challenges. The pillar of fire was not an exciting alarm but a guide which led the way towards the Promised Land. A cloud by day, its mission by night was to give forth not heat but light. Just so far as such messages as Mr. Deming's are real pillars of fire they are the needfullest we could have.

THE PURITAN'S WILL TO POWER

To the modern young person who tries to live well there is no type so devastating and harassing as the puritan. We cannot get away from him. In his sight we always live. We finish with justifying our new paganism against him, but we never quite lose consciousness of his presence. Even Theodore Dreiser, who always revolted from the puritan clutch, finds it necessary now and then to tilt a lance against him. If there were no puritans we should have to invent them. And if the pagan Mr. Dreiser has to keep on through life fighting puritans, how much more intrigued must we be who are only reformed puritans, and feel old dangers stirring at every aggressive gesture of righteousness? For the puritan is the most stable and persistent of types.[1] It is scarcely a question of a puritanical age and a pagan age. It is only a question of more puritans or less puritans. Even the most emancipated generation will find that it has only broken its puritanism up into compartments, and balances sexual freedom—or better perhaps a pious belief in sexual freedom—with a cult of efficiency and personal integrity which is far more coercive than the most sumptuary of laws. Young people who have given up all thought of "being good" anxiously celebrate a cult of "making good." And a superstition like eugenics threatens to terrorize the new intelligentsia.

Every new generation, in fact, contrives to find some new way of being puritanical. Every new generation finds some new way of sacrifice. Every new triumphant assertion of life is counterbalanced by some new denial. In Europe this most proud and lusty young generation goes to its million-headed slaughter, and in America the social consciousness arises to bewilder and deflect the *essor* towards life. Just when convention seemed to be on the run, and youth seemed to be facing a sane and candid attitude towards sex, we find idealistic girls and men coming out of the colleges to tell us of our social responsibility towards the race. This means not only that our daily living is to be dampened by the haunting thought of misery that we cannot personally prevent, but that our thirst towards love-experience is to be discouraged and turned aside into a concern for racial perfection. That is, we are subtly persuaded against merely growing widely and loving intensely. We become vague and mystified means toward nebulous and unreal ends. This new puritanism will not let us be ends in ourselves, or let personality be the chief value in life. It will almost let us sometimes. But it always pulls us up somewhere. There is always a devil of inhibition to interpose before our clean and naive grasping of life. (You see, my puritanism takes the form of a suspicion that there may be a personal devil lurking in the universe.)

This is why the puritan always needs to be thoroughly explained and exposed. We must keep him before our eyes, recognize him as the real enemy, no matter in what ideal disguise he lurks. We must learn how he works, and what peculiar satisfactions he gets from his activity. For he must get satisfaction or he would not be so prevalent. I accept the dogma that to explain anybody we have to do little more than discover just what contentment people are getting from what they do, or from what they are permitting to have happen to them, or even from what they are flinging their will into trying to prevent have happen to them. For, if life is anything positive, it is the sense of control. In the puritan, of course, we have the paradox how he can get satisfaction from ruggedly and sternly subjecting himself and renouncing the world, the flesh and the devil. There is a popular superstition that the puritan has an extra endowment of moral force, that he reverses the natural current of life, that he resists the drag of carnality down toward hell, that his energy is thrown contra-satisfaction, that his control is a real straddling of the nefarious way. But, of course, it is just this superstition that gives the puritan his terrific prestige. In the light of the will-to-power dogma, however, this superstition fades. The puritan becomes just as much of a naturalistic phenomenon as the most carnal sinner. Instincts and impulses, in the puritan, are not miraculously cancelled, but have their full play. The primitive currents of life are not blocked and burned back on their sources, but turned into powerful and usually devastating channels. The puritan is just as much of a "natural" man as you or I.

But we still have to explain how this lustful, headstrong creature called man, spilling with greed, could so unabatedly throughout the ages give up the primitive satisfactions of sex and food and drink and gregariousness and act the ascetic and the glumly censorious. How could an animal whose business was to feel powerful get power from being in subjection and deprivation? Well, the puritan gets his sense of power from a very cunningly organized satisfaction of two of his strongest impulses—the self-conscious personal impulses of being re-garded and being neglected. The puritan is no thwarted and depleted person. On the contrary, he is rather a complete per-son, getting almost the maximum of satisfaction out of these two apparently contradictory sentiments—the self-regarding and self-abasing. The pure autocrat would feed himself wholly on the first, the pure slave would be only a human embodiment of the second. But the pure puritan manages to make the most power-ful amalgam of both.

What we may call the puritan process starts with the satisfac-tion of the impulse for self-abasement, (an impulse as primitive as any, for in the long struggle for survival, it was often just as necessary for life to cower as it was to fight). It is only the puri-tan's prestige that has attached moral values to self-sacrifice, for there is nothing intrinsic in it that makes it any more praisewor-thy than lust. But its pragmatic value is immense. When the puri-tan announces himself as the least worthy of men, he not only predisposes in his favor the naturally slavish people around him, but he neutralizes the aggressive and self-regarding who would otherwise be moved to suppress him. He renounces, he puts on meekness, he sternly regiments himself, he makes himself un-happy in ways that are just not quite severe enough to excite pity and yet run no risk of arousing any envy. If the puritan does all this unconsciously, the effect is yet the same as if he were deliberately plotting. To give his impulses of self-abasement full play, he must, of course, exercise a certain degree of control. This control, however, gives him little of that sense of power that makes for happiness. Puritan moralists have always tried to make us believe in this virtue of self-control. They forget to point out, however, that it does not become a virtue until it has be-come idealized. Control over self gives us little sense of control. It is the dreariest of all satisfactions of the will-to-power. Not until we become *proud* of our self-control do we get satisfaction. The puritan only begins to reap his satisfaction when the self-regarding impulse comes into play.

Having given his self-abasing impulse free rein, he is now in a position to exploit his self-regard. He has made himself right with the weak and slavish. He has fortified himself with their al-liance. He now satisfies his self-regard by becoming proud of his humility and enjoining it on others. If it were self-control alone that made the puritan, he would not be as powerful as he is. Indeed he would be no more than the mild ascetic, who is all abnegation because his self-regarding mechanism is weak. But in the puritan, both impulses are strong. It is control over others that yields him his satisfactions of power. He may stamp out his sex-desire, but his impulse to shatter ideas that he does not like will flourish wild and wanton. To the true puritan the beauty of unselfishness lies in his being able to enforce it on others. He loves virtue not so much for its own sake as for its being an instrument of his terrorism.

The true puritan is at once the most unselfish and the most self-righteous of men. There is nothing he will not do for you, give up for you, suffer for you. But at the same time there is no cranny of your world that he will not illuminate with the virtue of this doing of his. His real satisfaction comes not from his action of benevolence but from the moral of the tale. He need not boast about his renunciation or his altruism. But in any true puritan atmosphere, that pride will be prevalent. Indeed, it is the oxygen of that atmosphere. Wherever you come across that combination of selfless devotion with self-righteousness, you have the essence of the puritan. Should you come across the one without the other you would find not the puritan but the saint.

The puritan then gets the satisfaction of his will-to-power through the turning of his self-abasement into purposes of self-regard. Renunciation is the raw material for his positive sense of power. The puritan gets his satisfaction exactly where the most carnal of natural men gets his, out of the stimulation of his pride. And in a world where renunciation has to happen to us whether we want it or not, the puritan is in the most impressive strategic position. In economy of energy he has it all over the head that is bloody but unbowed. For the puritan is so efficient morally that he can bow his head and yet extract control both out of the bowing and out of the prestige which his bowing gives him, as well as out of the bowing which he can enforce on others. The true puritan must become an evangelist. It is not enough to renounce the stimulus to satisfaction which is technically known as a "temptation." The renouncing must be made into an ideal, the ideal must be codified, promulgated, and, in the last analysis, enforced. In the compelling of others to abstain, you have the final glut of puritanical power. For in getting other people to renounce a thing, you thereby get renewed justification for your

own renouncing. And so the puritan may go on inexhaustibly roll-
ing up his satisfaction, one impulse reinforcing the other. The
simultaneous play of these two apparently inconsistent personal
impulses makes the puritan type one of the stables in society.
While the rest of us are longing for power, the puritan is enjoying
his. And because the puritan is so well integrated, he almost always rules. The person whose satisfactions of control are more
various and more refined is on the defensive against him.

The puritan gets his sense of power not in the harmless way
of the artist or the philosopher or the lover or the scientist, but in
a crude assault on that most vulnerable part of other people's
souls, their moral sense. He is far more dangerous to those he
converts than to those he intimidates. For he first scares them
into abandoning the rich and sensuous and expressive impulses
in life, and then teaches them to be proud of having done so.
We all have the potentiality of the puritan within us. I remember
suffering agonies at the age of ten because my aunt used to
bring me candy that had been wickedly purchased on the Sabbath day. I forget whether I ate it or not, but that fact is irrelevant. What counted was the guilt with which the whole universe
seemed to be stained. I need no other evidence for the irrational
nature of morality than this fact that children can be such dogged little puritans, can be at the age of ten so sternly and intuitively righteous.

The puritan is a case of arrested development. Most of us do
grow beyond him and find subtler ways of satisfying our desire
for power. And we do it because we never can quite take that
step from self-abasement to self-regard. We never can quite become proud of our humility. Renunciation remains an actual
going without, sacrifice a real thwarting. If we value an experience and deliberately surrender it, we are too naive to pretend
that there are compensations. There *is* a loss. We are left with a
vacuum. There is only depression and loss of control. Our self-
regard is not quite elemental enough to get stimulation from
wielding virtue over others. I never feel so degraded as when I
have renounced. I had rather beat my head rhythmically and
endlessly against an unyielding wall. For the pagan often breaks
miraculously through the wall. But the puritan at his best can
only strut outside.

Most of us, therefore, after we have had our puritan fling,
sown our puritan wild oats as it were, grow up into devout and

progressing pagans, cultivating the warmth of the sun, the deliciousness of love-experience, the high moods of art. The puritans remain around us, a danger and a threat. But they have value to us in keeping us acutely self-conscious of our faith. They whet our ardor. Perhaps no one can be really a good appreciating pagan who has not once been a bad puritan.

---

[1] Anti-Puritanism—used not so much historically but as a socially critical metaphor—had already been articulated in a milder form by Van Wyck Brooks in 1908 in *The Wine of the Puritans*.

THE WAR AND THE INTELLECTUALS

To those of us who still retain an irreconcilable animus against war, it has been a bitter experience to see the unanimity with which the American intellectuals have thrown their support to the use of war-technique in the crisis in which America found herself. Socialists, college professors, publicists, new-republicans, practitioners of literature, have vied with each other in confirming with their intellectual faith the collapse of neutrality and the riveting of the war-mind on a hundred million more of the world's people. And the intellectuals are not content with confirming our belligerent gesture. They are now complacently asserting that it was they who effectively willed it, against the hesitation and dim perceptions of the American democratic masses. A war made deliberately by the intellectuals! A calm moral verdict, arrived at after a penetrating study of inexorable facts! Sluggish masses, too remote from the world-conflict to be stirred, too lacking in intellect to perceive their danger! An alert intellectual class, saving the people in spite of themselves, biding their time with Fabian strategy until the nation could be moved into war without serious resistance! An intellectual class, gently guiding a nation through sheer force of ideas into what the other nations entered only through predatory craft or popular hysteria or militarist madness![1] A war free from any taint of self-seeking, a war that will secure the triumph of democracy and internationalize the world! This is the picture which the more self-conscious intellectuals have formed of themselves, and which they are slowly impressing upon a population which is being led no man knows whither by an indubitably intellectualized President. And they are right, in that the war certainly did not spring from either the ideals or the prejudices, from the national ambitions or hysterias, of the American people, however acquiescent the masses prove to be, and however clearly the intellectuals prove their putative intuition.

Those intellectuals who have felt themselves totally out of sympathy with this drag toward war will seek some explanation for this joyful leadership. They will want to understand this willingness of the American intellect to open the sluices and flood us with the sewage of the war spirit. We cannot forget the virtuous horror and stupefaction which filled our college professors when they read the famous manifesto of their ninety-three German colleagues in defence of their war. To the American academic mind of 1914 defence of war was inconceivable. From Bernhardi it recoiled as from a blasphemy, little dreaming that two years later would find it creating its own cleanly reasons for imposing military service on the country and for talking of the rough rude currents of health and regeneration that war would send through the American body politic. They would have thought anyone mad who talked of shipping American men by the hundreds of thousands—conscripts—to die on the fields of France. Such a spiritual change seems catastrophic when we shoot our minds back to those days when neutrality was a proud thing. But the intellectual progress has been so gradual that the country retains little sense of the irony. The war sentiment, begun so gradually but so perseveringly by the preparedness advocates who came from the ranks of big business, caught hold of one after another of the intellectual groups. With the aid of Roosevelt, the murmurs became a monotonous chant, and finally a chorus so mighty that to be out of it was at first to be disreputable and finally almost obscene. And slowly a strident rant was worked up against Germany which compared very creditably with the German fulminations against the greedy power of England. The nerve of the war-feeling centred, of course, in the richer and older classes of the Atlantic seaboard, and was keenest where there were French or English business and particularly social connections. The sentiment then spread over the country as a class-phenomenon, touching everywhere those upper-class elements in each section who identified themselves with this Eastern ruling group. It must never be forgotten that in every community it was the least liberal and least democratic elements among whom the preparedness and later the war sentiment was found. The farmers were apathetic, the small business men and workingmen are still apathetic towards the war. The election was a vote of confidence of these latter classes in a President who would keep the faith of neutrality. The intellectuals, in other words, have identified themselves with the least democratic forces in American life. They have assumed the leadership for war of those very classes whom the American democracy has been immemorially fighting. Only in a world where irony was dead could an intellectual class enter war at the head of such illiberal cohorts in the avowed cause of world-liberalism and world-democracy. No one is left to point out the undemocratic nature of this war-liberalism. In a time of faith, skepticism is the most intolerable of all insults.

Our intellectual class might have been occupied, during the last two years of war, in studying and clarifying the ideals and aspirations of the American democracy, in discovering a true Americanism which would not have been merely nebulous but might have federated the different ethnic groups and traditions. They might have spent the time in endeavoring to clear the public mind of the cant of war, to get rid of old mystical notions that clog our thinking. We might have used the time for a great wave of education, for setting our house in spiritual order. We could at least have set the problem before ourselves. If our intellectuals were going to lead the administration, they might conceivably have tried to find some way of securing peace by making neutrality effective. They might have turned their intellectual energy not to the problem of jockeying the nation into war, but to the problem of using our vast neutral power to attain democratic ends for the rest of the world and ourselves without the use of the malevolent technique of war. They might have failed. The point is that they scarcely tried. The time was spent not in clarification and education, but in a mulling over of nebulous ideals of democracy and liberalism and civilization which had never meant anything fruitful to those ruling classes who now so glibly used them, and in giving free rein to the elementary instinct of self-defence. The whole era has been spiritually wasted. The outstanding feature has been not its Americanism but its intense colonialism. The offence of our intellectuals was not so much that they were colonial—for what could we expect of a nation composed of so many national elements?—but that it was so one-sidedly and partisanly colonial. The official, reputable expression of the intellectual class has been that of the English colonial. Certain portions of it have been even more loyalist than the King, more British even than Australia. Other colonial attitudes have been vulgar. The colonialism of the other American stocks was denied a hearing from the start. America might have been made a meeting-ground for the different national attitudes. An intellectual class, cultural colonists of the different European nations, might have threshed out the issues here as they could not be threshed out in Europe. Instead of this, the English colonials in university and press took command at the start, and we became an intellectual Hungary where thought was subject to an effective process of Magyarization. The reputable opinion of the American intellectuals became more and more either what could be read pleasantly in London, or what was written in an earnest effort to put Englishmen straight on their war-aims and war-technique. This Magyarization of thought produced as a counter-reaction a peculiarly offensive and inept German apologetic, and the two partisans divided the field between them. The great masses, the other ethnic groups, were inarticulate. American public opinion was almost as little prepared for war in 1917 as it was in 1914.

The sterile results of such an intellectual policy are inevitable. During the war the American intellectual class has produced almost nothing in the way of original and illuminating interpretation. Veblen's *Imperial Germany*; Patten's *Culture and War,* and addresses; Dewey's *German Philosophy and Politics*; a chapter or two in Weyl's *American Foreign Policies*;—is there much else of creative value in the intellectual repercussion of the war? It is true that the shock of war put the American intellectual to an unusual strain. He had to sit idle and think as spectator not as actor. There was no government to which he could docilely and loyally tender his mind as did the Oxford professors to justify England in her own eyes. The American's training was such as to make the fact of war almost incredible. Both in his reading of history and in his lack of economic perspective he was badly prepared for it. He had to explain to himself something which was too colossal for the modern mind, which outran any language or terms which we had to interpret it in. He had to expand his sympathies to the breaking-point, while pulling the past and present into some sort of interpretative order. The intellectuals in the fighting countries had only to rationalize and justify what their country was already doing. Their task was easy. A neutral, however, had really to search out the truth. Perhaps perspective was too much to ask of any mind. Certainly the older colonials among our college professors let their prejudices at once dictate their thought. They have been comfortable ever since. The war has taught them nothing and will teach them nothing. And they have had the satisfaction, under the rigor of events, of seeing prejudice submerge the intellects of their younger colleagues. And they have lived to see almost their entire class, pacifists and democrats too, join them as apologists for the "gigantic irrelevance" of war.

We have had to watch, therefore, in this country the same

process which so shocked us abroad—the coalescence of the intellectual classes in support of the military programme. In this country, indeed, the socialist intellectuals did not even have the grace of their German brothers and wait for the declaration of war before they broke for cover. And when they declared for war they showed how thin was the intellectual veneer of their socialism. For they called us in terms that might have emanated from any bourgeois journal to defend democracy and civilization, just as if it was not exactly against those very bourgeois democracies and capitalist civilizations that socialists had been fighting for decades. But so subtle is the spiritual chemistry of the "inside" that all this intellectual cohesion—herd-instinct become herd-intellect—which seemed abroad so hysterical and so servile, comes to us here in highly rational terms. We go to war to save the world from subjugation! But the German intellectuals went to war to save their culture from barbarization! And the French went to war to save their culture from barbarization! And the French went to war to save their beautiful France! And the English to save international honor! And Russia, most altruistic and self-sacrificing of all, to save a small State from destruction! Whence is our miraculous intuition of our moral spotlessness? Whence our confidence that history will not unravel huge economic and imperialist forces upon which our rationalizations float like bubbles? The Jew often marvels that his race alone should have been chosen as the true people of the cosmic God. Are not our intellectuals equally fatuous when they tell us that our war of all wars is stainless and thrillingly achieving for good?

An intellectual class that was wholly rational would have called insistently for peace and not for war. For months the crying need has been for a negotiated peace, in order to avoid the ruin of a deadlock. Would not the same amount of resolute statesmanship thrown into intervention have secured a peace that would have been a subjugation for neither side? Was the terrific bargaining power of a great neutral ever really used? Our war followed, as all wars follow, a monstrous failure of diplomacy. Shamefacedness should now be our intellectuals' attitude, because the American play for peace was made so little more than a polite play. The intellectuals have still to explain why, willing as they now are to use force to continue the war to absolute exhaustion, they were not willing to use force to coerce the world to a speedy peace.

Their forward vision is no more convincing than their past rationality. We go to war now to internationalize the world! But surely their League to Enforce Peace is only a palpable apocalyptic myth, like the syndicalists' myth of the "general strike." It is not a rational programme so much as a glowing symbol for the purpose of focusing belief, of setting enthusiasm on fire for international order. As far as it does this it has pragmatic value, but as far as it provides a certain radiant mirage of idealism for this war and for a world-order founded on mutual fear, it is dangerous and obnoxious. Idealism should be kept for what is ideal. It is depressing to think that the prospect of a world so strong that none dare challenge it should be the immediate ideal of the American intellectual. If the League is only a makeshift, a coalition into which we enter to restore order, then it is only a description of existing fact, and the idea should be treated as such. But if it is an actually prospective outcome of the settlement, the keystone of American policy, it is neither realizable nor desirable. For the programme of such a League contains no provision for dynamic national growth or for international economic justice. In a world which requires recognition of economic internationalism far more than of political internationalism, an idea is reactionary which proposes to petrify and federate the nations as political and economic units. Such a scheme for international order is a dubious justification for American policy. And if American policy had been sincere in its belief that our participation would achieve international beatitude, would we not have made our entrance into the war conditional upon a solemn general agreement to respect in the final settlement these principles of international order? Could we have afforded, if our war was to end war by the establishment of a league of honor, to risk the defeat of our vision and our betrayal in the settlement? Yet we are in the war, and no such solemn agreement was made, nor has it even been suggested.

The case of the intellectuals seems, therefore, only very speciously rational. They could have used their energy to force a just peace or at least to devise other means than war for carrying through American policy. They could have used their intellectual energy to ensure that our participation in the war meant the international order which they wish. Intellect was not so used. It was used to lead an apathetic nation into an irresponsible war, without guarantees from those belligerents whose cause we were saving. The American intellectual, therefore, has been rational neither in his hindsight nor his foresight. To explain him we must look beneath the intellectual reasons to the emotional disposition. It is not so much what they thought as how they felt that explains our intellectual class. Allowing for colonial sympathy, there was still the personal shock in a world-war which outraged all our preconceived notions of the way the world was tending. It reduced to rubbish most of the humanitarian internationalism and democratic nationalism which had been the emotional thread of our intellectuals' life. We had suddenly to make a new orientation. There were mental conflicts. Our latent colonialism strove with our longing for American unity. Our desire for peace strove with our desire for national responsibility in the world. That first lofty and remote and not altogether unsound feeling of our spiritual isolation from the conflict could not last. There was the itch to be in the great experience which the rest of the world was having. Numbers of intelligent people who had never been stirred by the horrors of capitalistic peace at home were shaken out of their slumber by the horrors of war in Belgium. Never having felt responsibility for labor wars and oppressed masses and excluded races at home, they had a large fund of idle emotional capital to invest in the oppressed nationalities and ravaged villages of Europe. Hearts that had felt only ugly contempt for democratic strivings at home beat in tune with the struggle for freedom abroad. All this was natural, but it tended to over-emphasize our responsibility. And it threw our thinking out of gear. The task of making our own country detailedly fit for peace was abandoned in favor of a feverish concern for the management of the war, advice to the fighting governments on all matters, military, social, and political, and a gradual working up of the conviction that we were ordained as a nation to lead all erring brothers towards the light of liberty and democracy. The failure of the American intellectual class to erect a creative attitude toward the war can be explained by these sterile mental conflicts which the shock to our ideals sent raging through us.

Mental conflicts end either in a new and higher synthesis or adjustment, or else in a reversion to more primitive ideas which have been outgrown but to which we drop when jolted out of our attained position. The war caused in America a recrudescence of nebulous ideals which a younger generation was fast outgrowing because it had passed the wistful stage and was discovering concrete ways of getting them incarnated in actual institutions. The shock of the war threw us back from this pragmatic work into an emotional bath of these old ideals. There was even a somewhat rarefied revival of our primitive Yankee boastfulness, the reversion of senility to that republican childhood when we expected the whole world to copy our republican institutions. We amusingly ignored the fact that it was just that Imperial German regime, to whom we are to teach the art of self-government, which our own Federal structure, with its executive irresponsible in foreign policy and with its absence of parliamentary control, most resembles. And we are missing the exquisite irony of the unaffected homage paid by the American democratic intellectuals to the last and most detested of Britain's tory premiers as the representative of a "liberal" ally, as well as the irony of the selection of the best hated of America's bourbon "old guard" as the missionary of American democracy to Russia.

The intellectual state that could produce such things is one where reversion has taken place to more primitive ways of thinking. Simple syllogisms are substituted for analysis, things are known by their labels, our heart's desire dictates what we shall see. The American intellectual class, having failed to make the higher syntheses, regresses to ideas that can issue in quick, simplified action. Thought becomes any easy rationalization of what is actually going on or what is to happen inevitably tomorrow. It is true that certain groups did rationalize their colonialism and attach the doctrine of the inviolability of British seapower to the doctrine of a League of Peace. But this agile resolution of the mental conflict did not become a higher synthesis, to be creatively developed. It gradually merged into a justification for our going to war. It petrified into a dogma to be propagated. Criticism flagged and emotional propaganda began. Most of the socialists, the college professors and the practitioners of literature, however, have not even reached this high-water mark of synthesis. Their mental conflicts have been resolved much more simply. War in the interests of democracy! This was almost the sum of their philosophy. The primitive idea to which they regressed became almost insensibly translated into a craving for action. War was seen as the crowning relief of their indecision. At last action, irresponsibility, the end of anxious and torturing attempts to reconcile peace-ideals with the drag of the world towards Hell. An end to the pain of trying to adjust the facts to what they ought to be! Let us consecrate the facts as ideal! Let us join the greased slide towards war! The momentum increased. Hesitations, ironies, consciences, considerations—all were drowned in the elemental blare of doing something aggressive, colossal. The new-found Sabbath "peacefulness of being at war"! The thankfulness with which so many intellectuals lay down and floated with the current betrays the hesitation and suspense through which they had been. The American university is a brisk and happy place these days. Simple, unquestioning action has superseded the knots of thought. The thinker dances with reality.

With how many of the acceptors of war has it been mostly a dread of intellectual suspense? It is a mistake to suppose that intellectuality necessarily makes for suspended judgments. The intellect craves certitude. It takes effort to keep it supple and pliable. In a time of danger and disaster we jump desperately for some dogma to cling to. The time comes, if we try to hold out, when our nerves are sick with fatigue, and we seize in a great healing wave of release some doctrine that can be immediately translated into action. Neutrality meant suspense, and so it became the object of loathing to frayed nerves. The vital myth of the League of Peace provides a dogma to jump to. With war the world becomes motor again and speculation is brushed aside like cobwebs. The blessed emotion of self-defense intervenes too, which focused millions in Europe. A few keep up a critical pose after war is begun, but since they usually advise action which is in one-to-one correspondence with what the mass is already doing, their criticism is little more than a rationalization of the common emotional drive.

The results of war on the intellectual class are already apparent. Their thought becomes little more than a description and justification of what is going on. They turn upon any rash one who continues idly to speculate. Once the war is on, the conviction spreads that individual thought is helpless, that the only way one can count is as a cog in the great wheel. There is no good holding back. We are told to dry our unnoticed and ineffective tears and plunge into the great work. Not only is everyone forced into line, but the new certitude becomes idealized. It is a noble realism which opposes itself to futile obstruction and the cowardly refusal to face facts. This realistic boast is so loud and sonorous that one wonders whether realism is always a stern and intelligent grappling with realities. May it not be sometimes a mere surrender to the actual, an abdication of the ideal through a sheer fatigue from intellectual suspense? The pacifist is roundly scolded for refusing to face the facts, and for retiring into his own world of sentimental desire. But is the realist, who refuses to challenge or criticise facts, entitled to any more credit than that which comes from following the line of least resistance? The realist thinks he at least can control events by linking himself to the forces that are moving. Perhaps he can. But if it is a question of controlling war, it is difficult to see how the child on the back of a mad elephant is to be any more effective in stopping the beast than is the child who tries to stop him from the ground. The ex-humanitarian, turned realist, sneers at the snobbish neutrality, colossal conceit, crooked thinking, dazed sensibilities, of those who are still unable to find any balm of consolation for this war. We manufacture consolations here in America while there are probably not a dozen men fighting in Europe who did not long ago give up every reason for their being there except that nobody knew how to get them away.

But the intellectuals whom the crisis has crystallized into an acceptance of war have put themselves into a terrifyingly strategic position. It is only on the craft, in the stream, they say, that one has any chance of controlling the current forces for liberal purposes. If we obstruct, we surrender all power for influence. If we responsibly approve, we then retain our power for guiding. We will be listened to as responsible thinkers, while those who obstructed the coming of war have committed intellectual suicide and shall be cast into outer darkness. Criticism by the ruling powers will only be accepted from those intellectuals who are in sympathy with the general tendency of the war. Well, it is true that they may guide, but if their stream leads to disaster and the frustration of national life, is their guiding any more than a preference whether they shall go over the right-hand or the left-hand side of the precipice? Meanwhile, however, there is comfort on board. Be with us, they call, or be negligible, irrelevant. Dissenters are already excommunicated. Irreconcilable radicals, wringing their hands among the debris, become the most despicable and impotent of men. There seems no choice for the intellectual but to join the mass of acceptance. But again the terrible dilemma arises—either support what is going on, in which case you count for nothing because you are swallowed in the mass and great incalculable forces bear you on; or remain aloof, passively resistant, in which case you count for nothing because you are outside the machinery of reality.

Is there no place left, then, for the intellectual who cannot yet crystallize, who does not dread suspense, and is not yet drugged with fatigue? The American intellectuals, in their preoccupation with reality, seem to have forgotten that the real enemy is War rather than imperial Germany. There is work to be done to prevent this war of ours from passing into popular mythology as a holy crusade. What shall we do with leaders who tell us that we go to war in moral spotlessness, or who make "democracy" synonymous with a republican form of government? There is work to be done in still shouting that all the revolutionary by-products will not justify the war, or make war anything else than the most noxious complex of all the evils that afflict men. There must be some to find no consolation whatever, and some to sneer at those who buy the cheap emotion of sacrifice. There must be some irreconcilables left who will not even accept the war with walrus tears. There must be some to call unceasingly for peace, and some to insist that the terms of settlement shall be not only liberal but democratic. There must be some intellectuals who are not willing to use the old discredited counters again and to support a peace which would leave all the old inflammable materials of armament lying about the world. There must still be opposition to any contemplated "liberal" world-order founded on military coalitions. The "irreconcilable" need not be disloyal. He need not even be "impossibilist." His apathy towards war should take the form of a heightened energy and enthusiasm for the education, the art, the interpretation that make for life in the midst of the world of death. The intellectual who retains his animus against war will push out more boldly than ever to make his case solid against it. The old ideals crumble; new ideals must be forged. His mind will continue to roam widely and ceaselessly. The thing he will fear most is premature crystallization. If the American intellectual class rivets itself to a "liberal" philosophy that perpetuates the old errors, there will then be need for "democrats" whose task will be to divide, confuse, disturb, keep the intellectual waters constantly in motion to prevent any such ice from ever forming.

[1] Compare the unsigned editorial in *The New Republic,* April 14, 1917:

The American nation is entering this war under the influence of a moral verdict reached after the utmost deliberation of the more thoughtful members of the community. . . . The United States might have blundered into the war at any time during the past two years, but to have entered, as it is now doing, at the right time and in the clear interest of a purely international program required the exercise of an intellectualized and imaginative leadership.

A WAR DIARY[1]

I

Time brings a better adjustment to the war. There had been so
many times when, to those who had energetically resisted its
coming, it seemed the last intolerable outrage. In one's wilder
moments one expected revolt against the impressment of unwilling men and the suppression of unorthodox opinion. One conceived the war as breaking down through a kind of intellectual
sabotage diffused through the country. But as one talks to
people outside the cities and away from ruling currents of opinion, one finds the prevailing apathy shot everywhere with acquiescence. The war is a bad business, which somehow got fastened on us. They· won't want to go, but they've got to go. One
decides that nothing generally obstructive is going to happen
and that it would make little difference if it did. The kind of war
which we are conducting is an enterprise which the American
government does not have to carry on with the hearty cooperation of the American people but only with their acquiescence. And that acquiescence seems sufficient to float an indefinitely protracted war for vague or even largely uncom-
prehended and unaccepted purposes. Our resources in men
and materials are vast enough to organize the war-technique
without enlisting more than a fraction of the people's conscious
energy. Many men will not like being sucked into the actual
fighting organism, but as the war goes on they will be sucked in
as individuals and they will yield. There is likely to be no element
in the country with the effective will to help them resist. They are
not likely to resist of themselves concertedly. They will be licked
grudgingly into military shape, and their lack of enthusiasm will
in no way unfit them for use in the hecatombs necessary for the
military decision upon which Allied political wisdom still apparently insists. It is unlikely that enough men will be taken from
the potentially revolting classes seriously to embitter their spirit.
Losses in the well-to-do classes will be sustained by a sense of
duty and of reputable sacrifice. From the point of view of the
worker, it will make little difference whether his work contributes
to annihilation overseas or to construction at home. Temporarily,
his condition is better if it contributes to the former. We of the

middle classes will be progressively poorer than we should otherwise have been. Our lives will be slowly drained by clumsily levied taxes and the robberies of imperfectly controlled private enterprises. But this will not cause us to revolt. There are not likely to be enough hungry stomachs to make a revolution. The materials seem generally absent from the country, and as long as a government wants to use the war-technique in its realization of great ideas, it can count serenely on the human resources of the country, regardless of popular mandate or understanding.

II

If human resources are fairly malleable into the war-technique, our material resources will prove to be even more so, quite regardless of the individual patriotism of their owners or workers. It is almost purely a problem of diversion. Factories and mines and farms will continue to turn out the same products and at an intensified rate, but the government will be working to use their activity and concentrate it as contributory to the war. The process which the piping times of benevolent neutrality began, will be pursued to its extreme end. All this will be successful, however, precisely as it is made a matter of centralized governmental organization and not of individual offerings of good-will and enterprise. It will be coercion from above that will do the trick rather than patriotism from below. Democratic contentment may be shed over the land for a time through the appeal to individual thoughtfulness in saving and in relinquishing profits. But all that is really needed is the co-operation with government of the men who direct the large financial and industrial enterprises. If their interest is enlisted in diverting the mechanism of production into war-channels, it makes not the least difference whether you or I want our activity to count in aid of the war. Whatever we do will contribute toward its successful organization, and toward the riveting of a semi-military State-socialism on the country. As long as the effective managers, the "big men" in the staple industries remained loyal, nobody need care what the millions of little human cogs who had to earn their living felt or thought. This is why the technical organization for this American war goes on so much more rapidly than any corresponding popular sentiment for its aims and purposes. Our war is teaching us that patriotism is really a superfluous quality in war. The government of a modern organized plutocracy does not have to ask whether the people want to fight or understand what they are fighting for, but only whether they will tolerate fighting. America does not cooperate with the President's designs. She rather feebly acquiesces. But that feeble acquiescence is the all-important factor. We are learning that war doesn't need enthusiasm, doesn't need conviction, doesn't need hope, to sustain it. Once manoeuvred, it takes care of itself, provided only that our industrial rulers see that the end of the war will leave American capital in a strategic position for world-enterprise. The American people might be much more indifferent to the war even than they are and yet the results would not be materially different. A majority of them might even be feebly or at least unconcertedly hostile to the war, and yet it would go gaily on. That is why a popular referendum seems so supremely irrelevant to people who are willing to use war as an instrument in the working-out of national policy. And that is why this war, with apathy rampant, is probably going to act just as if every person in the country were filled with patriotic ardor, and furnished with a completely assimilated map of the League to Enforce Peace. If it doesn't, the cause will not be the lack of popular ardor, but the clumsiness of the government officials in organizing the technique of the war. Our country in war, given efficiency at the top, can do very well without our patriotism. The non-patriotic man need feel no pangs of conscience about not helping the war. Patriotism fades into the merest trivial sentimentality when it becomes, as so obviously in a situation like this, so pragmatically impotent. As long as one has to earn one's living or buy tax-ridden goods, one is making one's contribution to war in a thousand indirect ways. The war, since it does not need it, cannot fairly demand also the sacrifice of one's spiritual integrity.

III

The "liberals" who claim a realistic and pragmatic attitude in politics have disappointed us in setting up and then clinging wistfully to the belief that our war could get itself justified for an idealistic flavor, or at least for a world-renovating social purpose, that they had more or less denied to the other belligerents. If these realists had had time in the hurry and scuffle of events to turn their philosophy on themselves, they might have seen how thinly disguised a rationalization this was of their emotional undertow. They wanted a League of Nations. They had an un-analyzable feeling that this was a war in which we had to be, and be in it we would. What more natural than to join the two ideas and conceive our war as the decisive factor in the attain-ment of the desired end! This gave them a good conscience for willing American participation, although as good men they must have loathed war and everything connected with it. The realist cannot deny facts. Moreover, he must not only acknowledge them but he must use them. Good or bad, they must be turned by his intelligence to some constructive end. Working along with the materials which events give him, he must get where and what he can, and bring something brighter and better out of the chaos.

Now war is such an indefeasible and unescapable Real that the good realist must accept it rather comprehensively. To keep out of it is pure quietism, an acute moral failure to adjust. At the same time, there is an inexorability about war. It is a little unbri-dled for the realist's rather nice sense of purposive social con-trol. And nothing is so disagreeable to the pragmatic mind as any kind of an absolute. The realistic pragmatist could not rec-ognize war as inexorable—though to the common mind it would seem as near an absolute, coercive social situation as it is pos-sible to fall into. For the inexorable abolishes choices, and it is the essence of the realist's creed to have, in every situation, al-ternatives before him. He gets out of his scrape in this way: Let the inexorable roll in upon me, since it must. But then, keeping firm my sense of control, it will somehow tame it and turn it to my own creative purposes. Thus realism is justified of her chil-dren, and the "liberal" is saved from the limbo of the wailing and irreconcilable pacifists who could not make so easy an adjust-ment.

Thus the "liberals" who made our war their own preserved their pragmatism. But events have shown how fearfully they im-perilled their intuition and how untameable an inexorable really is. For those of us who knew a real inexorable when we saw one, and had learned from watching war what follows the loos-ing of a war-technique, foresaw how quickly aims and purposes would be forgotten, and how flimsy would be any liberal control of events. It is only we now who can appreciate *The New*

Republic—the organ of applied pragmatic realism—when it complains that the League of Peace (which we entered the war to guarantee) is more remote than it was eight months ago; or that our State Department has no diplomatic policy (though it was to realize the high aims of the President's speeches that the intellectuals willed American participation); or that we are subordinating the political management of the war to real or supposed military advantages, (though militarism in the liberal mind had no justification except as a tool for advanced social ends). If, after all the idealism and creative intelligence that were shed upon America's taking up of arms, our State Department has no policy, we are like brave passengers who have set out for the Isles of the Blest only to find that the first mate has gone insane and jumped overboard, the rudder has come loose and dropped to the bottom of the sea, and the captain and pilot are lying dead drunk under the wheel. The stokers and engineers however, are still merrily forcing the speed up to twenty knots an hour and the passengers are presumably getting the pleasure of the ride.

IV

The penalty the realist pays for accepting war is to see disappear one by one the justifications for accepting it. He must either become a genuine Realpolitiker and brazen it through, or else he must feel sorry for his intuition and be regretful that he willed the war. But so easy is forgetting and so slow the change of events that he is more likely to ignore the collapse of his case. If he finds that his government is relinquishing the crucial moves of that strategy for which he was willing to use the technique of war, he is likely to move easily to the ground that it will all come out in the end the same anyway. He soon becomes satisfied with tacitly ratifying whatever happens, or at least straining to find the grain of unplausible hope that may be latent in the situation.

But what then is there really to choose between the realist who accepts evil in order to manipulate it to a great end, but who somehow unaccountably finds events turn sour on him, and the Utopian pacifist who cannot stomach the evil and will have none of it? Both are helpless, both are coerced. The Utopian, however, knows that he is ineffective and that he is coerced, while the realist, evading disillusionment, moves in a twilight

zone of half-hearted criticism and hoping for the best, where
he does not become a tacit fatalist. The latter would be the man-
lier position, but then where would be his realistic philosophy of
intelligence and choice? Professor Dewey has become impatient
at the merely good and merely conscientious objectors to war
who do not attach their conscience and intelligence to forces
moving in another direction. But in wartime there are literally no
valid forces moving in another direction. War determines its own
end—victory, and government crushes out automatically all
forces that deflect, or threaten to deflect, energy from the path
of organization to that end. All governments will act in this way,
the most democratic as well as the most autocratic. It is only
"liberal" naïveté that is shocked at arbitrary coercion and suppression. Willing war means willing all the evils that are organically bound up with it. A good many people still seem to believe
in a peculiar kind of democratic and antiseptic war. The pacifists
opposed the war because they knew this was an illusion, and
because of the myriad hurts they knew war would do the promise of democracy at home. For once the babes and sucklings
seem to have been wiser than the children of light.

V

If it is true that the war will go on anyway whether it is popular or
not or whether its purposes are clear, and if it is true that in wartime constructive realism is an illusion, then the aloof man, the
man who will not obstruct the war but who cannot spiritually accept it, has a clear case for himself. Our war presents no more
extraordinary phenomenon than the number of the more creative
minds of the younger generation who are still irreconcilable toward the great national enterprise which the government has
undertaken. The country is still dotted with young men and women, in full possession of their minds, faculties, and virtue, who
feel themselves profoundly alien to the work which is going on
around them. They must not be confused with the disloyal or the
pro-German. They have no grudge against the country, but their
patriotism has broken down in the emergency. They want to see
the carnage stopped and Europe decently constructed again.
They want a democratic peace. If the swift crushing of Germany
will bring that peace, they want to see Germany crushed. If the

embargo on neutrals will prove the decisive coup, they are willing to see the neutrals taken ruthlessly by the throat. But they
do not really believe that peace will come by any of these
means, or by any use of our war-technique whatever. They are
genuine pragmatists and they fear any kind of an absolute, even
when bearing gifts. They know that the longer a war lasts the
harder it is to make peace. They know that the peace of exhaustion is a dastardly peace, leaving enfeebled the morale of the
defeated, and leaving invincible for years all the most greedy
and soulless elements in the conquerors. They feel that the
greatest obstacle to peace now is the lack of the powerful
mediating neutral which we might have been. They see that war
has lost for us both the mediation and the leadership, and is
blackening us ever deeper with the responsibility for having prolonged the dreadful tangle. They are skeptical not only of the
technique of war, but also of its professed aims. The President's
idealism stops just short of the pitch that would arouse their
own. There is a middle-aged and belated taint about the best
ideals which publicist liberalism has been able to express. The
appeals to propagate political democracy leave these people
cold in a world which has become so disillusioned of democracy in the face of universal economic servitude. Their ideals
outshoot the government's. To them the real arena lies in the international class-struggle, rather than in the competition of artificial national units. They are watching to see what the Russian
socialists are going to do for the world, not what the timorous
capitalistic American democracy may be planning. They can
feel no enthusiasm for a League of Nations, which should solid-
ify the old units and continue in disguise the old theories of international relations. Indispensable, perhaps? But not inspiring;
not something to give one's spiritual allegiance to. And yet the
best advice that American wisdom can offer to those who are
out of sympathy with the war is to turn one's influence toward
securing that our war contribute toward this end. But why would
not this League turn out to be little more than a well-oiled
machine for the use of that enlightened imperialism toward
which liberal American finance is already whetting its tongue?
And what is enlightened imperialism as an international ideal as
against the anarchistic communism of the nations which the new
Russia suggests in renouncing imperialist intentions?

VI

Skeptical of the means and skeptical of the aims, this element of the younger generation stands outside the war, and looks upon the conscript army and all the other war-activities as troublesome interruptions on its thought and idealism, interruptions which do not touch anywhere a fibre of its soul. Some have been much more disturbed than others, because of the determined challenge of both patriots and realists to break in with the war-obsession which has filled for them their sky. Patriots and realists can both be answered. They must not be allowed to shake one's inflexible determination not to be spiritually implicated in the war. It is foolish to hope. Since the 30th of July, 1914, nothing has happened in the arena of war-policy and war-technique except for the complete and unmitigated worst. We are tired of continued disillusionment, and of the betrayal of generous anticipations. It is saner not to waste energy in hope within the system of war-enterprise. One may accept dispassionately whatever changes for good may happen from the war, but one will not allow one's imagination to connect them organically with war. It is better to resist cheap consolations, and remain skeptical about any of the good things so confidently promised us either through victory or the social reorganization demanded by the war-technique. One keeps healthy in wartime not by a series of religious and political consolations that something good is coming out of it all, but by a vigorous assertion of values in which war has no part. Our skepticism can be made a shelter behind which is built up a wider consciousness of the personal and social and artistic ideals which American civilization needs to lead the good life. We can be skeptical constructively, if, thrown back on our inner resources from the world of war which is taken as the overmastering reality, we search much more actively to clarify our attitudes and express a richer significance in the American scene. We do not feel the war to be very real, and we sense a singular air of falsity about the emotions of the upper-classes toward everything connected with war. This ostentatious shame, this grovelling before illusory Allied heroisms and nobilities, has shocked us. Minor novelists and minor poets and minor publicists are still coming back from driving ambulances in France to write books that nag us into an appreciation of the "real meaning." No one can object to the generous emotions of service in a great cause or to the horror and pity at colossal devastation and agony. But too many of these prophets are men who have lived rather briskly among the cruelties and thinnesses of American civilization and have shown no obvious horror and pity at the exploitations and the arid quality of the life lived here around us. Their moral sense had been deeply stirred by what they saw in France and Belgium, but it was a moral sense relatively unpractised by deep concern and reflection over the inadequacies of American democracy. Few of them had used their vision to create literature impelling us toward a more radiant American future. And that is why, in spite of their vivid stirrings, they seem so unconvincing. Their idealism is too new and bright to affect us, for it comes from men who never cared very particularly about great creative American ideas. So these writers come to us less like ardent youth, pouring its energy into the great causes, than like youthful mouthpieces of their strident and belligerent elders. They did not convert us, but rather drove us farther back into the rightness of American isolation.

VII

There was something incredibly mean and plebeian about that abasement into which the war-partisans tried to throw us all. When we were urged to squander our emotion on a bedevilled Europe, our intuition told us how much all rich and generous emotions were needed at home to leaven American civilization. If we refused to export them it was because we wanted to see them at work here. It is true that great reaches of American prosperous life were not using generous emotions for any purpose whatever. But the real antithesis was not between being concerned about luxurious automobiles and being concerned about the saving of France. America's "benevolent neutrality" had been saving the Allies for three years through the ordinary channels of industry and trade. We could afford to export material goods and credit far more than we could afford to export emotional capital. The real antithesis was between interest in expensively exploiting American material life and interest in creatively enhancing American personal and artistic life. The fat and earthy American could be blamed not for not palpitating more richly about France, but for not palpitating more richly about America and her spiritual drouths. The war will leave the country spiritually impoverished, because of the draining away of sentiment into the channels of war. Creative and constructive enterprises will suffer not only through the appalling waste of financial capital in the work of annihilation, but also in the loss of emotional capital in the conviction that war overshadows all other realities. This is the poison of war that disturbs even creative minds. Writers tell us that, after contact with the war, literature seems an idle pastime, if not an offense, in a world of great deeds. Perhaps literature that can be paled by war will not be missed. We may feel vastly relieved at our salvation from so many feeble novels and graceful verses that khaki-clad authors might have given us. But this noble sounding sense of the futility of art in a world of war may easily infect conscientious minds. And it is against this infection that we must fight.

VIII

The conservation of American promise is the present task for this generation of malcontents and aloof men and women. If America has lost its political isolation, it is all the more obligated to retain its spiritual integrity. This does not mean any smug retreat from the world, with a belief that the truth is in us and can only be contaminated by contact. It means that the promise of American life is not yet achieved, perhaps not even seen, and that, until it is, there is nothing for us but stern and intensive cultivation of our garden. Our insulation will not be against any great creative ideas or forms that Europe brings. It will be a turning within in order that we may have something to give without. The old American ideas which are still expected to bring life to the world seem stale and archaic. It is grotesque to try to carry democracy to Russia. It is absurd to try to contribute to the world's store of great moving ideas until we have a culture to give. It is absurd for us to think of ourselves as blessing the world with anything unless we hold it much more self-consciously and significantly than we hold anything now. Mere negative freedom will not do as a twentieth-century principle. American ideas must be dynamic or we are presumptuous in offering them to the world.

IX

The war—or American promise: one must choose. One cannot be interested in both. For the effect of the war will be to impoverish American promise. It cannot advance it, however liberals may choose to identify American promise with a league of nations to enforce peace. Americans who desire to cultivate the promises of American life need not lift a finger to obstruct the war, but they cannot conscientiously accept it. However intimately a part of their country they may feel in its creative enterprises toward a better life, they cannot feel themselves a part of it in its futile and self-mutilating enterprise of war. We can be apathetic with a good conscience, for we have other values and ideals for America. Our country will not suffer for our lack of patriotism as long as it has that of our industrial masters. Meanwhile, those who have turned their thinking into war-channels have abdicated their leadership for this younger generation. They have put themselves in a limbo of interests that are not the concerns which worry us about American life and make us feverish and discontented.

Let us compel the war to break in on us, if it must, not go hospitably to meet it. Let us force it perceptibly to batter in our spiritual walls. This attitude need not be a fatuous hiding in the sand, denying realities. When we are broken in on, we can yield to the inexorable. Those who are conscripted will have been broken in on. If they do not want to be martyrs, they will have to be victims. They are entitled to whatever alleviations are possible in an inexorable world. But the others can certainly resist the attitude that blackens the whole conscious sky with war. They can resist the poison which makes art and all the desires for more impassioned living seem idle and even shameful. For many of us, resentment against the war has meant a vivider consciousness of what we are seeking in American life.

This search has been threatened by two classes who have wanted to deflect idealism to the war—the patriots and the realists. The patriots have challenged us by identifying apathy with disloyalty. The reply is that war-technique in this situation is a matter of national mechanics rather than national ardor. The realists have challenged us by insisting that the war is an instrument in the working-out of beneficent national policy. Our

skepticism points out to them how soon their "mastery" becomes "drift," tangled in the fatal drive toward victory as its own
end, how soon they become mere agents and expositors of
forces as they are. Patriots and realists disposed of, we can
pursue creative skepticism with honesty, and at least a hope
that in the recoil from war we may find the treasures we are looking for.

[1] Together with "Twilight of Idiols," "A War Diary" represents Bourne's most
clear-sighted analysis of the failure of pragmatism and liberalism as he saw
them vouchsafed by the leading personalities of *The New Republic*. The
several references to "the American promise" are to Croly's *The Promise of
American Life*.

JOHN DEWEY'S PHILOSOPHY[1]

Nothing is more symbolic of Professor Dewey's democratic attitude towards life than the disintegrated array of his published writings. Where the neatly uniform works of William James are to be found in every public library, you must hunt long and far for the best things of the man who, since the other's death, is the most significant thinker in America. Pamphlets and reports of obscure educational societies; school journals, university monographs and philosophical journals, limited to the pedant few; these are the burial-places of much of this intensely alive, futuristic philosophy. For the best educational essays one has to look until very recently to a little compilation made by an unknown London house. The "Educational Creed," in style and conciseness and spirit the most admirably popular of all his writings, is, I think, still lost in an out-of-print cheap bulletin in some innocuous series for elementary teachers. "School and Society," with some of the wisest words ever set to paper, frightens one away with its infantile cover and its university chaperonage. Only some heterogeneous essays, brilliant but not holding the exact kernel of his thought, and his "How We Think," in which is shown that scientific method is simply a sublimely well-ordered copy of our own best and most fruitful habits of thought, have been launched in forms that would reach a wide public. No man, I think, with such universally important things to say on almost every social and intellectual activity of the day, was ever published in forms more ingeniously contrived to thwart the interest of the prospective public.

Professor Dewey's thought is inaccessible because he has always carried his simplicity of manner, his dread of show or self-advertisement, almost to the point of extravagance. In all his psychology there is no place for the psychology of prestige. His democracy seems almost to take that extreme form of refusing to bring one's self or one's ideas to the attention of others. On the college campus or in the lecture-room he seems positively to efface himself. The uncertainty of his silver-gray hair and drooping mustache, of his voice, of his clothes, suggests that he has almost studied the technique of protective coloration. It will do you no good to hear him lecture. His sentences, flowing and exact and lucid when read, you will find strung in long festoons of obscurity between pauses for the awaited right word. The whole business of impressing yourself on other people, of getting yourself over to the people who want to and ought to have you, has simply never come into his ultra-democratic mind.

This incapacity of imagining his own distinction has put him in the paradoxical situation of a revolutionist with an innate contempt for propaganda. His philosophy of "instrumentalism" has an edge on it that would slash up the habits of thought, the customs and institutions in which our society has been living for centuries. He allies himself personally with every democratic movement, yet will not preach. As we discover in the essay on Maeterlinck, where he shows himself poet as well as philosopher, his tolerant democracy loves all human values, and finds nothing so intolerable as artificial inequality. He hates nothing so much as the preacher who tells others how bad they are and what they must do to reform. Yet his philosophy is a great sermon, challenging in every line, in spite of his discreet style, our mechanical habits of thought, our mechanical habits of education, our mechanical morality. A prophet dressed in the clothes of a professor of logic, he seems almost to feel shame that he has seen the implications of democracy more clearly than anybody else in the great would-be democratic society about him, and so been forced into the unwelcome task of teaching it.

Orthodox philosophical thinking has usually gone along on the comfortable assumption that words always have the same meaning, and that they stand for real things, that logic is the science of thinking correctly, that reason is eternal, that if you can only get your ideas consistent you have then a true picture of what you are trying to interpret. We have taken for granted the old view, which goes back to Aristotle's logic, that our mental life was a receiving and combining and storing of certain dead inert sensations and ideas of which words were the true symbols.

Professor Dewey's fundamental thesis has been that thinking is not like this. The mind is not a looking-glass, reflecting the world for its private contemplation, not a logic-machine for building up truth, but a tool by which we adjust ourselves to the situations in which life puts us. Reason is not a divinely appointed guide to eternal truth, but a practical instrument by which we solve problems. Words are not invariable symbols for invariable things, but clues to meanings. We think in meanings, not in words, and a meaning is simply a sign-post pointing towards our doing something or feeling something or both. The words are the handles by which we take hold of these meanings which our intercourse with people and things presents to us. Our life is a constant reaction to a world which is constantly stimulating us. We are in situations where we must do something, and it is for the purpose of guiding this doing from the point of view of what has happened or what is likely to happen, that we think. We are not bundles of thoughts and feelings so much as bundles of attitudes or tendencies. We act usually before we "perceive"; the perception is only important as it enables us to act again. We remember what we use, and we learn what we occupy ourselves with. Our minds are simply the tools with which we forge out our life.

If we are to live worthily and happily, it is not necessary that we should "be" anything or "know" anything, so much as that we should be able to meet the situation in which developing life places us, and express our capacities in our activity. Our social problem as well as our personal problem is to understand what we are doing. This is almost the whole law and the prophets. In the ideal home we should have learned as children, through social converse and the household occupations and solution of the problems which our curiosity and our work brought us, how to adjust ourselves to the demands of life. But the home can no longer effect this and the school must step in. But the school is only really educative if it is helping the child to understand the social situations in which he finds and is to find himself, and to regulate his impulses so that he can control these situations. The ideal school would be an embryonic community life, where the child would sense the occupations and interests of the larger society into which he is to enter and so have his curiosity and practical skill awakened to meet and conquer them.

In its larger social implications, Professor Dewey's philosophy challenges the whole machinery of our world of right and wrong, law and order, property and religion, the old techniques by which society is still being managed and regulated. Our institutions have been made as scales and measures to which we bring our actions, rigid standards by whose codes we are judged, frameworks to whose lines we strive to mould ourselves. All the revolutionary strivings of the past have been away from these institutional authorities towards greater freedom. But in spite of all the freedom we have won, society was probably never more deeply unhappy than it is today. For freedom is not happiness; it is merely the first negative step towards happiness. Happiness is control, and society, now intensely self-conscious of its imperfections, is still very helpless towards controlling its destiny. Life, Professor Dewey says, is a modification of the present with reference to the conditions of the future, a conflict between the habits engendered in the past and the new aims and purposes, clearly envisaged, to be worked for.

It is in showing the unity of all the democratic strivings, the social movement, the new educational ideals, the freer ethics, the popular revolt in politics, of all the aspects of the modern restless, forward-looking personal and social life, and the applicability to all of them of scientific method, with its hypotheses and bold experimentation, that Professor Dewey has been the first thinker to put the moral and social goal a notch ahead. His philosophy has the great advantage of making nonsensical most of the writing and thinking that has been done in the old terms. See how much of this can be truthfully called anything else than a "juggling with the symbols of learning." See how much of the energy of the moulders of opinion in politics, industry, education, religion, morality, goes to the squaring up of the activity of individuals and groups with certain principles which, however much they may once have been solutions of genuine problems and interpretations of genuine situations, are now mere caked and frozen barricades to activity and understanding.

Professor Dewey has given us a whole new language of meanings. After reading him, you can see nothing again in the old terms. And when I see college presidents and publicists who have cultivated the arts of prestige, expressing their views on every question of the day in the old caked and frozen language, thinking along the old lazy channels, I feel a savage indignation that Professor Dewey should not be out in the arena of the concrete, himself interpreting current life. I am conscious of his horror of having his ideas petrified into a system. He knows that it will do no good to have his philosophy intellectually believed unless it is also thought and lived. And he knows the uncanny propensity of stupid men to turn even the most dynamic ideas into dogmas. He has seen that in his school world. Meanwhile his influence goes on increasing to an extent of which he is almost innocently unconscious.

[1] This article, published in 1915, shows the extent of the disappointment and criticism that Bourne uttered in "Twilight of Idols." It shows how positively Bourne once felt about Dewey's instrumentalism.

TWILIGHT OF IDOLS[1]

I

Where are the seeds of American promise? Man cannot live by politics alone, and it is small cheer that our best intellects are caught in the political current and see only the hope that America will find her soul in the remaking of the world. If William James were alive would he be accepting the war-situation so easily and complacently? Would he be chiding the over-stimulated intelligence of peace-loving idealists, and excommunicating from the ranks of liberal progress the pitiful remnant of those who struggle "above the battle"? I like to think that his gallant spirit would have called for a war to be gallantly played, with insistent care for democratic values at home, and un-equivocal alliance with democratic elements abroad for a peace that should promise more than a mere union of benevolent imperialisms. I think of James now because the recent articles of John Dewey's on the war suggest a slackening in his thought for our guidance and stir, and the inadequacy of his pragmatism as a philosophy of life in this emergency. Whether James would have given us just that note of spiritual adventure which would make the national enterprise seem creative for an American future—this we can never know. But surely that philosophy of Dewey's which we had been following so uncritically for so long, breaks down almost noisily when it is used to grind out interpretation for the present crisis. These articles on "Conscience and Compulsion," "The Future of Pacifism," "What America Will Fight For," "Conscription of Thought," which *The New Republic* has been printing, seem to me to be a little off-color. A philosopher who senses so little the sinister forces of war, who is so much more concerned over the excesses of the pacifists than over the excesses of military policy, who can feel only amusement at the idea that any one should try to conscript thought, who assumes that the war-technique can be used without trailing along with it the mob-fanaticisms, the injustices and hatreds, that are organically bound up with it, is speaking to another element of the younger intelligentsia than that to which I belong. Evidently the attitudes which war calls out are fiercer and more incalculable than Professor Dewey is accustomed to take into his hopeful and intelligent imagination, and the pragmatist mind, in trying to adjust itself to them, gives the air of grappling, like the pioneer who challenges the arid plains, with a power too big for it. It is not an arena of creative intelligence our country's mind is now, but of mob-psychology. The soldiers who tried to lynch Max Eastman showed that current patriotism is not a product of the will to remake the world. The luxuriant releases of explosive hatred for which peace apparently gives far too little scope cannot be wooed by sweet reasonableness, nor can they be the raw material for the creation of rare liberal political structures. All that can be done is to try to keep your country out of situations where such expressive releases occur. If you have willed the situation, however, or accepted it as inevitable, it is fatuous to protest against the gay debauch of hatred and fear and swagger that must mount·and mount, until the heady and virulent poison of war shall have created its own anti-toxin of ruin and disillusionment. To talk as if war were anything else than such a poison is to show that your philosophy has never been confronted with the pathless and the inexorable, and that, only dimly feeling the change, it goes ahead acting as if it had not got out of its depth. Only a lack of practice with a world of human nature so raw-nerved, irrational, uncreative, as an America at war was bound to show itself to be, can account for the singular unsatisfactoriness of these later utterances of Dewey. He did have one moment of hesitation just before the war began, when the war and its external purposes and unifying power seemed the small thing beside that internal adventure which should find our American promise. But that perspective has now disappeared, and one finds Dewey now untainted by skepticism as to our being about a business to which all our idealism should rally. That failure to get guaranties that this country's efforts would obligate the Allies to a democratic world-over Dewey blames on the defection of the pacifists, and then somehow manages to get himself into a "we" who "romantically," as he says, forewent this crucial link of our strategy. Does this easy identification of himself with undemocratically controlled foreign policy mean that a country is democratic when it accepts what its government does, or that war has a narcotic effect on the pragmatic mind? For Dewey somehow retains his sense of being in the controlling class, and ignores those anxious questions of democrats who have been his disciples but are now resenters of the war.

What I come to is a sense of suddenly being left in the lurch, of suddenly finding that a philosophy upon which I had relied to carry us through no longer works. I find the contrast between the idea that creative intelligence has free functioning in wartime, and the facts of the inexorable situation, too glaring. The contrast between what liberals ought to be doing and saying if democratic values are to be conserved, and what the real forces are imposing upon them, strikes too sternly on my intellectual senses. I should prefer some philosophy of War as the grim and terrible cleanser to this optimism-haunted mood that continues unweariedly to suggest that all can yet be made to work for good in a mad and half-destroyed world. I wonder if James, in the face of such disaster, would not have abandoned his "moral equivalent of war" for an "immoral equivalent" which, in swift and periodic saturnalia, would have acted as vaccination against the sure pestilence of war.

II

Dewey's philosophy is inspiring enough for a society at peace, prosperous, and with a fund of progressive good-will. It is a philosophy of hope, of clear-sighted comprehension of materials and means. Where institutions are at all malleable, it is the only clue for improvement. It is scientific method applied to "uplift." But this careful adaptation of means to desired ends, this experimental working out of control over brute forces and dead matter in the interests of communal life, depends on a store of rationality, and is effective only where there is strong desire for progress. It is precisely the school, the institution to which Dewey's philosophy was first applied, that is of all our institutions the most malleable. And it is the will to educate that has seemed, in these days, among all our social attitudes the most rationally motivated. It was education, and almost education alone, that seemed susceptible to the steady pressure of an "instrumental" philosophy. Intelligence really seemed about to come into conscious control of an institution, and that one the most potent in moulding the attitudes needed for a civilized society and the aptitudes needed for the happiness of the individual.

For both our revolutionary conceptions of what education means, and for the intellectual strategy of its approach, this country is immeasurably indebted to the influence of Professor Dewey's philosophy. With these ideas sincerely felt, a rational nation would have chosen education as its national enterprise. Into this it would have thrown its energy though the heavens fell and the earth rocked around it. But the nation did not use its isolation from the conflict to educate itself. It fretted for three years and then let war, not education, be chosen, at the almost unanimous behest of our intellectual class, from motives alien to our cultural needs, and for political ends alien to the happiness of the individual. But nations, of course, are not rational entities, and they act within their most irrational rights when they accept war as the most important thing the nation can do in the face of metaphysical menaces of imperial prestige. What concerns us here is the relative ease with which the pragmatist intellectuals, with Professor Dewey at the head, have moved out their philosophy, bag and baggage, from education to war. So abrupt a change in the direction of the national enterprise, one would have expected to cause more emotion, to demand more apologetics. His optimism may have told Professor Dewey that war would not materially demoralize our growth—would, perhaps, after all, be but an incident in the nation's life—but it is not easy to see how, as we skate toward the bankruptcy of war-billions, there will be resources available for educational enterprise that does not contribute directly to the war-technique. Neither is any passion for growth, for creative mastery, going to flourish among the host of militaristic values and new tastes for power that are springing up like poisonous mushrooms on every hand.

How could the pragmatist mind accept war without more violent protest, without a greater wrench? Either Professor Dewey and his friends felt that the forces were too strong for them, that the war had to be, and it was better to take it up intelligently than to drift blindly in; or else they really expected a gallant war, conducted with jealous regard for democratic values at home and a captivating vision of international democracy as the end of all the toil and pain. If their motive was the first, they would seem to have reduced the scope of possible control of events to the vanishing point. If the war is too strong for you to prevent, how is it going to be weak enough for you to control and mould to your liberal purposes? And if their motive was to shape the war firmly for good, they seem to have seriously miscalculated the fierce urgencies of it. Are they to be content, as the materialization of their hopes, with a doubtful League of Nations

and the suppression of the I. W. W.? Yet the numbing power of
the war-situation seems to have kept them from realizing what
has happened to their philosophy. The betrayal of their first
hopes has certainly not discouraged them. But neither has it
roused them to a more energetic expression of the forces
through which they intend to realize them. I search Professor
Dewey's articles in vain for clues as to the specific working-out
of our democratic desires, either nationally or internationally,
either in the present or in the reconstruction after the war. No
programme is suggested, nor is there feeling for present vague
popular movements and revolts. Rather are the latter chided, for
their own vagueness and impracticalities. Similarly, with the
other prophets of instrumentalism who accompany Dewey into
the war, democracy remains an unanalyzed term, useful as a
call to battle, but not an intellectual tool, turning up fresh sod for
the changing future. Is it the political democracy of a plutocratic
America that we are fighting for, or is it the social democracy of
the new Russia? Which do our rulers really fear more, the
menace of Imperial Germany, or the liberating influence of a
socialist Russia? In the application of their philosophy to politics,
our pragmatists are sliding over this crucial question of ends.
Dewey says our ends must be intelligently international rather
than chauvinistic. But this gets us little distance along our way.

In this difficult time the light that has been in liberals and radicals has become darkness. If radicals spend their time holding
conventions to attest their loyalty and stamp out the "enemies
within," they do not spend it in breaking intellectual paths, or
giving us shining ideas to which we can attach our faith and
conscience. The spiritual apathy from which the more naive of
us suffer, and which the others are so busy fighting, arises
largely from sheer default of a clear vision that would melt it
away. Let the motley crew of ex-socialists, and labor radicals,
and liberals, and pragmatist philosophers, who have united for
the prosecution of the war, present a coherent and convincing
democratic programme, and they will no longer be confronted
with the skepticism of the conscientious and the impossibilist.
But when the emphasis is on technical organization, rather than
organization of ideas, on strategy rather than desires, one begins to suspect that no programme is presented because they
have none to present. This burrowing into war-technique hides
the void where a democratic philosophy should be. Our intellec-

tuals consort with war-boards in order to keep their minds off the question what the slow masses of the people are really desiring, or toward what the best hope of the country really drives. Similarly the blaze of patriotism on the part of the radicals serves the purpose of concealing the feebleness of their intellectual light.

Is the answer that clear formulation of democratic ends must be postponed until victory in the war is attained? But to make this answer is to surrender the entire case. For the support of the war by radicals, realists, pragmatists, is due—or so they say—to the fact that the war is not only saving the cause of democracy, but is immensely accelerating its progress. Well, what are those gains? How are they to be conserved? What do they lead to? How can we further them? Into what large idea of society do they group? To ignore these questions, and think only of the war-technique and its accompanying devotions, is to undermine the foundations of these people's own faith.

A policy of "win the war first" must be, for the radical, a policy of intellectual suicide. Their support of the war throws upon them the responsibility of showing inch by inch the democratic gains, and of laying out a charter of specific hopes. Otherwise they confess that they are impotent and that the war is submerging their expectations, or that they are not genuinely imaginative and offer little promise for future leadership.

III

It may seem unfair to group Professor Dewey with Mr. Spargo and Mr. Gompers, Mr. A. M. Simons, and the Vigilantes. I do so only because in their acceptance of the war, they are all living out that popular American "instrumental!" philosophy which Professor Dewey has formulated in such convincing and fascinating terms. On an infinitely more intelligent plane, he is yet one with them in his confidence that the war is motivated by democratic ends and is being made to serve them. A high mood of confidence and self-righteousness moves them all, a keen sense of control over events that makes them eligible to discipleship under Professor Dewey's philosophy. They are all hostile to impossibilism, to apathy, to any attitude that is not a cheerful and brisk setting to work to use the emergency to consolidate the gains of democracy. Not, Is it being used? but, Let us make a flutter about using it! This unanimity of mood puts the resenter of war out of the arena. But he can still seek to explain why this philosophy which has no place for the inexorable should have adjusted itself so easily to the inexorable of war, and why, although a philosophy of the creative intelligence in using means toward ends, it should show itself so singularly impoverished in its present supply of democratic values.

What is the matter with the philosophy? One has a sense of having come to a sudden, short stop at the end of an intellectual era. In the crisis, this philosophy of intelligent control just does not measure up to our needs. What is the root of this inadequacy that is felt so keenly by our restless minds? Van Wyck Brooks has pointed out searchingly the lack of poetic vision in our pragmatist "awakeners." Is there something in these realistic attitudes that works actually against poetic vision, against concern for the quality of life as above machinery of life? Apparently there is. The war has revealed a younger intelligentsia, trained up in the pragmatic dispensation, immensely ready for the executive ordering of events, pitifully unprepared for the intellectual interpretation or the idealistic focusing of ends. The young men in Belgium, the officers' training corps, the young men being sucked into the councils at Washington and into war-organization everywhere, have among them a definite element, upon whom Dewey, as veteran philosopher, might well bestow a papal blessing. They have absorbed the secret of scientific method as applied to political administration. They are liberal, enlightened, aware. They are touched with creative intelligence toward the solution of political and industrial problems. They are a wholly new force in American life, the product of the swing in the colleges from a training that emphasized classical studies to one that emphasized political and economic values. Practically all this element, one would say, is lined up in service of the war-technique. There seems to have been a peculiar congeniality between the war and these men. It is as if the war and they had been waiting for each other. One wonders what scope they would have had for their intelligence without it. Probably most of them would have gone into industry and devoted themselves to sane reorganization schemes. What is significant is that it is the technical side of the war that appeals to them, not the interpretative or political side. The formulation of values and ideals, the production of articulate and suggestive thinking, had not, in their education, kept pace, to any extent whatever, with their technical aptitude. The result is that the field of intellectual formulation is very poorly manned by this younger intelligentsia. While they organize the war, formulation of opinion is left largely in the hands of professional patriots, sensational editors, archaic radicals. The intellectual work of this younger intelligentsia is done by the sedition-hunting Vigilantes, and by the saving remnant of older liberals. It is true, Dewey calls for a more attentive formulation of war-purposes and ideas, but he calls largely to deaf ears. His disciples have learned all too literally the instrumental attitude toward life, and, being immensely intelligent and energetic, they are making themselves efficient instruments of the war-technique, accepting with little question the ends as announced from above. That those ends are largely negative does not concern them, because they have never learned not to subordinate idea to technique. Their education has not given them a coherent system of large ideas, or a feeling for democratic goals. They have, in short, no clear philosophy of life except that of intelligent service, the admirable adaptation of means to ends. They are vague as to what kind of a society they want, or what kind of society America needs, but they are equipped with all the administrative attitudes and talents necessary to attain it.

To those of us who have taken Dewey's philosophy almost as our American religion, it never occurred that values could be subordinated to technique. We were instrumentalists, but we had our private utopias so clearly before our minds that the means fell always into its place as contributory. And Dewey, of course, always meant his philosophy, when taken as a philosophy of life, to start with values. But there was always that unhappy ambiguity in his doctrine as to just how values were created, and it became easier and easier to assume that just any growth was justified and almost any activity valuable so long as it achieved ends. The American, in living out this philosophy, has habitually confused results with product, and been content with getting somewhere without asking too closely whether it was the desirable place to get. It is now becoming plain that unless you start with the vividest kind of poetic vision, your instrumentalism is likely to land you just where it has landed this younger intelligentsia which is so happily and busily engaged in the national enterprise of war. You must have your vision and you must have your technique. The practical effect of Dewey's philosophy has evidently been to develop the sense of the latter at the expense of the former. Though he himself would develop them together, even in him there seems to be a flagging of values, under the influence of war. *The New Republic* honorably clamors for the Allies to subordinate military strategy to political ends, technique to democratic values. But war always undermines values. It is the outstanding lesson of the whole war that statesmen cannot be trusted to get this perspective right, that their only motto is, first to win and then grab what they can. The struggle against this statesmanlike animus must be a losing one as long as we have not very clear and very determined and very revolutionary democratic ideas and programmes to challenge them with. The trouble with our situation is not only that values have been generally ignored in favor of technique, but that those who have struggled to keep values foremost, have been too bloodless and too near-sighted in their vision. The defect of any philosophy of "adaptation" or "adjustment," even when it means adjustment to changing, living experience, is that there is no provision for thought or experience getting beyond itself. If your ideal is to be adjustment to your situation, in radiant co-operation with reality, then your success is likely to be just that and no more. You never transcend anything. You grow, but your spirit never jumps out of your skin to go on wild adventures. If your policy as a publicist reformer is to take what you can get, you are likely to find that you get something less than you should be willing to take. Italy in the settlement is said to be demanding one hundred in order to get twenty, and this machiavellian principle might well be adopted by the radical. Vision must constantly outshoot technique, opportunist efforts usually achieve less even than what seemed obviously possible. An impossibilist élan that appeals to desire will often carry further. A philosophy of adjustment will not even make for adjustment. If you try merely to "meet" situations as they come, you will not even meet them. Instead you will only pile up behind you deficits and arrears that will some day bankrupt you.

We are in the war because an American Government practised a philosophy of adjustment, and an instrumentalism for minor ends, instead of creating new values and setting at once a large standard to which the nations might repair. An intellectual attitude of mere adjustment, of mere use of the creative intelligence to make your progress, must end in caution, regression, and a virtual failure to effect even that change which you so clear-sightedly and desirously see. This is the root of our dissatisfaction with much of the current political and social realism that is preached to us. It has everything good and wise except the obstreperous vision that would drive and draw all men into it.

IV

The working-out of this American philosophy in our intellectual life then has meant an exaggerated emphasis on the mechanics of life at the expense of the quality of living. We suffer from a real shortage of spiritual values. A philosophy that worked when we were trying to get that material foundation for American life in which more impassioned living could flourish no longer works when we are faced with inexorable disaster and the hysterias of the mob. The note of complacency which we detect in the current expressions of this philosophy has a bad taste. The congruous note for the situation would seem to be, on the contrary, that of robust desperation—a desperation that shall rage and struggle until new values come out of the travail, and we see some glimmering of our democratic way. In the creation of these new values, we may expect the old philosophy, the old radicalism, to be helpless. It has found a perfectly definite level, and there is no reason to think that it will not remain there. Its flowering appears in the technical organization of the war by an earnest group of young liberals, who direct their course by an opportunist programme of State-socialism at home and a league of benevolently imperialistic nations abroad. At their best they can give us a government by prudent, enlightened college men instead of by politicians. At their best, they can abolish war by making everybody a partner in the booty of exploitation. That is all, and it is technically admirable. Only there is nothing in the outlook that touches in any way the happiness of the individual, the vivifying of the personality, the comprehension of social forces, the flair of art—in other words, the quality of life. Our intellectuals have failed us as value-creators, even as value-emphasizers. The allure of the martial in war has passed only to be succeeded by the allure of the technical. The allure of fresh and true ideas, of free speculation, of artistic vigor, of cultural styles, of intelligence suffused by feeling, and feeling given fibre and outline by intelligence, has not come, and can hardly come, we see now, while our reigning philosophy is an instrumental one.

Whence can come this allure? Only from those who are thorough malcontents. Irritation at things as they are, disgust at the continual frustrations and aridities of American life, deep dissatisfaction with self and with the groups that give themselves forth as hopeful—out of such moods there might be hammered new values. The malcontents would be men and women who could not stomach the war, or the reactionary idealism that has followed in its train. They are quite through with the professional critics and classicists who have let cultural values die through their own personal ineptitude. Yet these malcontents have no intention of being cultural vandals, only to slay. They are not barbarians, but seek the vital and the sincere everywhere. All they want is a new orientation of the spirit that shall be modern, an orientation to accompany that technical orientation which is fast coming, and which the war accelerates. They will be harsh and often bad-tempered, and they will feel that the break-up of things is no time for mellowness. They will have a taste for spiritual adventure, and for sinister imaginative excursions. It will not be Puritanism so much as complacency that they will fight. A tang, a bitterness, an intellectual fibre, a verve, they will look for in literature, and their most virulent enemies will be those unaccountable radicals who are still morally servile, and are now trying to suppress all free speculation in the interests of nationalism. Something more mocking, more irreverent, they will constantly want. They will take institutions very lightly, indeed will never fail to be surprised at the seriousness with which good radicals take the stated offices and systems. Their own contempt will be scarcely veiled, and they will be glad if they can tease, provoke, irritate thought on any subject. These malcontents will be more or less of the American tribe of talent who used either to go immediately to Europe, or starved submissively at home. But these people will neither go to Europe, nor starve submissively. They are too much entangled emotionally in the possibilities of American life to leave it, and they have no desire whatever to starve. So they are likely to go ahead beating their heads at the wall until they are either bloody or light appears. They will give offense to their elders who cannot see what all the concern is about, and they will hurt the more middle-aged sense of adventure upon which the better integrated minds of the younger generation will have compromised. Optimism is often compensatory, and the optimistic mood in American thought may mean merely that American life is too terrible to face. A more skeptical, malicious,·desperate, ironical mood may actually be the sign of more vivid and more stirring life fermenting in America today. It may be a sign of hope. That thirst for more of the intellectual "war and laughter" that we find Ñietzsche calling us to may bring us satisfactions that optimism-haunted philosophies could never bring. Malcontendedness may be the beginning of promise. That is why I evoked the spirit of William James, with its gay passion for ideas, and its freedom of speculation, when I felt that slightly pedestrian gait into which the war had brought pragmatism. It is the creative desire more than the creative intelligence that we shall need if we are ever to fly.

[1] Like "Conscience and Intelligence in War," this article refers primarily to John Dewey's positive feelings about America's entry into the war. Dewey had expressed his opinion in the series of articles in *The New Republic* listed below:

"Conscience and Compulsion," NR. XI (July 14, 1917)
"The Future of Pacifism," NR. XI (July 28, 1917)
"What America Will Fight For," NR. XII (August 18, 1917)
"Conscription of Thought." NR, XII (September 1, 1917)

PRACTICE VS. PRODUCT

Americans are thought to be a very practical people, but it is in the sense that our real interest is in practice rather than in what the practice achieves as an end. It is the game we like rather than the winning of it. That often-quoted defence of the American business man that it is the activity and adventure of business that he cares for rather than the money he makes is quite valid. Whether it be baseball or business, we have a passion for the game. If we are not playing it, at least we are fascinatedly watching others play it. It is the thrills that count, and the profits are only stakes for a new game, with new thrills and a new struggle. Winning has no point of its own; it is merely the signal for a new deal. Why are we so essentially a nation of poker-players, advertisers, and lawyers? Because each of these vocations stresses practice as against product, is primarily activity for its own sake. The interminable poker-game is perhaps the classic symbol for this attitude, but it is only an attitude that runs through all the businesses and professions. Of all the professions the law contains the purest essence of the game. For here the rules are known with a precision and detail unknown in any other department of human life outside of sport. From beginning to end, the lawyer has only to practice. He is called upon at no time to criticize the game with any reference to the end; he has no call to judge the machine with any reference to the product. He need have no other standard than its continuing to run smoothly and noiselessly. Considerations of product, human and social considerations only cause friction. To elderly lawyers controversy over legal principles or proposals for change in the legal or judicial system must seem as senseless as suggestions to amend the rules of chess.

Contrary to our impression, pragmatism is not at all an easy philosophy for our American mind to grasp. The insistence on the end of the road rather than the journey, the winning rather than the game, its demand that practice shall be judged by results, machinery by its product—this is not really our common attitude towards life. An amazing amount of our intellectual energy goes into advertising, speculation, business organization, and ingenious machinery which produces nothing at all. We have a perfect passion for organizing and systematizing things within an inch of their lives. But then we are inclined to sit back and contemplate fondly the spinning around of the machinery, instead of criticizing the products it turns out. It may be pragmatism to be satisfied with things that work but it is a very shallow one. We do have an eagerness for results, but by "results" we do not mean "products." The business man is satisfied with his "results" if his business does not actually stop going. One achieves "results" when the machine goes on operating, not when it turns out a desirable product. By prosperity we do not mean any essential improvement in the human or technical product, but simply that the great social and industrial machine is whirling a little faster, and more men are engaged in tending it. The fact that we are inclined to speak of "prosperity" as the last goal of the desired shows how habitually we tend to think in terms of practice rather than product.

With such an attitude we come to look upon the world as a gigantic play-room. There can be no doubt that the constructive labor of workmen and foremen and superintendents in factory and workshop and railroad is "work." It is carried on in terms of the product to be turned out, in terms of achievement of the goal. We seldom realize what an entirely different psychology modern "business" enlists. Business has become almost entirely a matter of bargaining, and the obtaining and manipulating of capital. It is a game of skill, played according to rules, but with a large dependence upon personal prowess for success. It is essentially "play," where the great players play with real railroads instead of toy ones, securities instead of toy money, and toss corporations about as a child tosses ping-pong balls. Indeed, by the old system of interlocking directorates, business could even play at store with itself, and be both storekeeper behind the counter and customer in front of it. "Success in business" means simply the ability to buy more toys to play with.

In a sense, this play-attitude is the least mercenary or materialistic of things. It seems, indeed, almost innocently free from ulterior motive. What the public have called the predatory activity of capitalists and corporations has been only incidentally predatory. If small competitors and the consumer have been injured, it was only as the unfortunate spectators who got in the way of the ball. Or they are considered as a kind of impersonal counters, pawns in a great game. This produces that curious irony which makes our business civilization a byword with other nations. No industrial system is apparently more ruthless, so little

mitigated by the social sense and social protection. Yet in no
country does public opinion display more genuine humanitarian
interest; in none do the business leaders show more amiable
personal qualities. This incongruity can only arise from the fact
that in the wider group-life of business and politics and industry,
everybody is playing a game, while in everything that can be
put into terms of the personal life, it is individuals that are being
dealt with, that is, living persons seriously regarded as ends in
themselves, whose happiness is a product to be worked for. We
tend to keep the work-attitude for our private life, and indulge
the play-attitude in the public life. We have not yet learned to
take social classes and social conditions as personal ends, or
general prosperity and large situations as products to be
worked for too. Just as we "tinker" with the tariff, we tinker with
our civilization. Our public activity is too much a perpetual
patching up of the old machine so that it will run smoothly. What
we always try to do is to get rid of friction, rather than to improve
the product. We are too accustomed to admiring enterprises
which merely intensify the speed or improve the practice. Conservatives and radicals are equally inclined to think in terms of
practice rather than product. New political ideas are advocated
almost solely on the ground of improved methods, rather than
the improved product to be turned out by the new machinery.
And the conservative defence of the old is placed on the same
ground of correct practice. The old ways are more in harmony
with sound principles of government, is the cry. We still feel the
novelty and the danger of any program which contemplates the
realization of certain clearly envisaged social ends, to be
worked for with all the political and economic resources in our
power.

   Our attitude is as different as possible from that of either the
scientist or the artist. The latter works for a finished product
which he may contemplate and enjoy. He expresses some impression of his, embodies some vision. This does not mean that
his goal is perfect. He is always dissatisfied with the result. His
expression only serves to suggest new ideas to be realized,
another goal to be reached, from which new breath is taken.
American civilization lacks these halting-places, lacks these
realizations of clearly seen ideas.

   Similarly, the scientist's experimentation is based on a
hypothesis, that is an idea imagined and tested. To this testing,

he sets all his technical skill, apparatus, ingenuity, and imagination. Like the artist, he uses machinery only as means to an end. Neither are engaged in activity for its own sake. Both are constantly thinking in terms of product and not of practice.

In this play-attitude of ours we are not alone. We inherit it from our Anglo-Saxon mother across the sea. But let us not complacently assure ourselves that it is a necessarily human attitude. In the last few decades some of the Continental countries have been acting exactly as if they were bending their resources towards very definite social ends, as if they had human and cultural products which they wished to realize. To urge upon ourselves the envisaged goal, and decry the play-attitude is not to repeat the Jesuitical adage that the end justifies the means. But it is to insist that means are only means, that the journey is not the goal. It is to insist that it is childish to take such delight in watching the wheels go round that we fail to observe whether or not our watch is keeping time with the clock of civilization.

LAW AND ORDER

No incident of recent years has served to bring out so much crude thinking among supposedly educated men as the now happily ended McNamara case. A wave of hysterical passion for "law and order" seems suddenly to have swept over the land, a passion which one would like to believe is entirely sincere and ready to carry itself through to logical conclusions. It looks a little too much like a sudden scare, a purely physical timidity on the part of the comfortable classes, to be quite convincing. The gallant and well-worn phrase, "law and order," has been worked overtime to conceal a very real fear on the part of the dominant classes for their lives and property.

The "law and order" which they reverence is one in which society minds its own business as far as they are concerned, and attends with drastic severity to any violent interference with their peaceful rule of things. Now "law and order" is a very admirable ideal. It is the highest ideal for a society with the exception of one—and that is, justice. The neglect of this important fact has made it very difficult to secure any impartial discussion on the question. Those who have insisted on analyzing the concept of "law and order" and have kept before their minds the ideal of justice, have been instantly denounced as defenders of dynamiting, champions of murder, and enemies of the human race.

Now, it is one thing to defend a deed; it is another to explain it. Because Socialists have kept their heads and tried to explain this remarkable and unprecedented incident, they have had to face a torrent of abuse and vilification which in too many cases has caused an ignominious retreat of Socialist thinkers to cover and a surrender of their logical position. This position is not one of defense or indictment; it is a coldly scientific one of explanation. And the fact that in this overheated atmosphere of prejudice and recrimination, there is a set of principles and a body of facts which will give that scientific explanation, speaks volumes for the truth, accuracy and wisdom of the Socialist philosophy.

Socialists see in the dynamiting incident a symptom of the class-struggle, and in this they are absolutely right. The violence of the labor-unions is simply a pawn in the great game they are waging against the employers' organizations, and the retaliations of the employers are as ruthless, though not perhaps so sensational. It is a real state of war, little as our God-fearing citizens like to acknowledge it. To be sure, the unions are not actuated by any motives of sympathy for the working-class as a whole. They are out simply for the aggrandizement of their own interests. They are the cleverest, most aggressive and most determined portion of the working class, just as the big employers they fight are the most intelligent and aggressive of the capitalistic class.

It is inevitable that the unions should adopt the same methods of organization as do the industrial corporations; that graft and corruption and lobbying should permeate their organization just as it does "big business." We can best understand the situation by picturing the labor unions and the corporations as the respective advance guards of two hostile armies. Their contact represents the point where the smouldering hostility breaks out into open warfare. The rest of the army we can see straggling back in the rear; on one side the unorganized workers, the unskilled laborers, clerks, etc.; on the other, small merchants, salaried officers and professional men. But the essential, never-closing gulf remains, based on different economies of life, on absolutely opposed interests—a gulf that will never be filled up, except in one way, and that is, of course, Socialism.

This idea of industrial war and the open conflict of a submerged and eternal class-hostility is no mere figure of speech. It is the only sane interpretation of this complex situation. The dynamiting, just as the strikes and riots, is a social phenomenon, not an individual. To speak of murder in this connection is irrelevant. Murder is the wilful taking of the life of a definite individual or individuals. Malice is a necessary accompaniment to murder. The dynamiting was, we will admit, a reckless and absurd attempt to further the material interests of the labor unions, but its intent was this ultimate political end, not the taking of the life of individuals, any more than the death of the employees in a badly ventilated mine can be called murder. Indeed, both deeds—the blowing up of the men in Los Angeles, and the mine explosion in Tennessee—are similar in character. Neither expresses malice, but both express a cynical and ruthless disregard for human life, a "class-carelessness," rather than an individual carelessness. It does little good to hold the individual responsible. Punishing the individual does not change the class ethics and the class practices. You have to change the class attitudes towards each other. And here again, of course, the Socialists have the solution. Abolish this hostile attitude of classes towards each other by abolishing the class-struggle. Abolish class-struggle by abolishing classes. Abolish classes by merging the classes into one.

The part of the government in this case seems perhaps the most unjust of all. We have seen that the labor union system and the corporation system are, to all intents and purposes, each a State revolving in the larger State. Each has its political organization and its control over its members which are the characteristics of a State. These two States are the antagonists in the industrial war. Now the crucial question is, what shall be the position of the governmental State in this struggle? It can throw its governmental machinery of courts and law on the side of the corporations, or on the side of the labor unions, or it can remain neutral and let the contestants fight it out.

Of course, every one recognizes that in actual practice our governmental system is at the disposal of the corporation class. The common law, injunctions, and the entire machinery of the courts is set in motion against the offences perpetrated by the labor unions against the corporations, and but seldom, and that unsystematically, against corporations for their wrongs to labor. Now it is manifest that this is as unfair as it would be for the governmental machinery to be turned over exclusively to the labor unions. And the third alternative—that the State remain neutral—while theoretically fair, would, of course, result in intolerable anarchy, and besides would abrogate the State's claim to authority as the political expression of the whole people. The only thing left then is that the State become either the arbitrator between the two sides (a function for which it is badly fitted), or that it should become progressively Socialistic and devote all its efforts to the abolition of the class-war.

Thus we see that all the morals of this incident of the McNamaras lead to Socialism. It is imperative that college men should think clearly on this subject and not let themselves be carried away by traditional phrases which they have never stopped to analyze. We have a new situation to interpret, and we must think of it in new terms. The Socialist philosophy gives the only intelligible analysis and interpretation of this as of so many other situations. Without it, one has only confusions and absurdities of thought.

THE STATE[1]

I

To most Americans of the classes which consider themselves
significant the war brought a sense of the sanctity of the State
which, if they had had time to think about it, would have seemed
a sudden and surprising alteration in their habits of thought. In
times of peace, we usually ignore the State in favor of partisan
political controversies, or personal struggles for office, or the
pursuit of party policies. It is the Government rather than the
State with which the politically minded are concerned. The state
is reduced to a shadowy emblem which comes to consciousness only on occasions of patriotic holiday.

Government is obviously composed of common and un-
sanctified men, and is thus a legitimate object of criticism and
even contempt. If your own party is in power, things may be assumed to be moving safely enough; but if the opposition is in,
then clearly all safety and honor have fled the State. Yet you do
not put it to yourself in quite that way. What you think is only that
there are rascals to be turned out of a very practical machinery
of offices and functions which you take for granted. When we
say that Americans are lawless, we usually mean that they are
less conscious than other peoples of the august majesty of the
institution of the State as it stands behind the objective government of men and laws which we see. In a republic the men who
hold office are indistinguishable from the mass. Very few of them
possess the slightest personal dignity with which they could
endow their political role; even if they ever thought of such a
thing. And they have no class distinction to give them glamour.
In a Republic the Government is obeyed grumblingly, because it
has no bedazzlements or sanctities to gild it. If you are a good
old-fashioned democrat, you rejoice at this fact, you glory in the
plainness of a system where every citizen has become a king. If
you are more sophisticated you bemoan the passing of dignity
and honor from affairs of State. But in practice, the democrat
does not in the least treat his elected citizen with the respect
due to a king, nor does the sophisticated citizen pay tribute to
the dignity even when he finds it. The republican State has almost no trappings to appeal to the common man's emotions.
What it has are of military origin, and in an unmilitary era such
as we have passed through since the Civil War, even military

trappings have been scarcely seen. In such an era the sense of
the State almost fades out of the consciousness of men.

With the shock of war, however, the State comes into its own
again. The Government, with no mandate from the people, without consultation of the people, conducts all the negotiations, the
backing and filling, the menaces and explanations, which slowly
bring it into collision with some other Government, and gently
and irresistibly slides the country into war. For the benefit of
proud and haughty citizens, it is fortified with a list of the intolerable insults which have been hurled toward us by the other nations; for the benefit of the liberal and beneficent, it has a convincing set of moral purposes which our going to war will
achieve; for the ambitious and aggressive classes, it can gently
whisper of a bigger role in the destiny of the world. The result is
that, even in those countries where the business of declaring
war is theoretically in the hands of representatives of the people,
no legislature has ever been known to decline the request of an
Executive, which has conducted all foreign affairs in utter pri-
vacy and irresponsibility, that it order the nation into battle.
Good democrats are wont to feel the crucial difference between
a State in which the popular Parliament or Congress declares
war, and the State in which an absolute monarch or ruling class
declares war. But, put to the stern pragmatic test, the difference
is not striking. In the freest of republics as well as in the most
tyrannical of empires, all foreign policy, the diplomatic negotiations which produce or forestall war, are equally the private
property of the Executive part of the Government, and are
equally exposed to no check whatever from popular bodies, or
the people voting as a mass themselves.

The moment war is declared, however, the mass of the
people, through some spiritual alchemy, become convinced that
they have willed and executed the deed themselves. They then,
with the exception of a few malcontents, proceed to allow themselves to be regimented, coerced, deranged in all the environments of their lives, and turned into a solid manufactory of destruction toward whatever other people may have, in the appointed scheme of things, come within the range of the Government's disapprobation. The citizen throws off his contempt
and indifference to Government, identifies himself with its purposes, revives all his military memories and symbols, and the
State once more walks, an august presence, through the imagi-

nations of men. Patriotism becomes the dominant feeling, and produces immediately that intense and hopeless confusion between the relations which the individual bears and should bear toward the society of which he is a part.

The patriot loses all sense of the distinction between State, nation, and government. In our quieter moments, the Nation or Country forms the basic idea of society. We think vaguely of a loose population spreading over a certain geographical portion of the earth's surface, speaking a common language, and living in a homogeneous civilization. Our idea of Country concerns itself with the non-political aspects of a people, its ways of living, its personal traits, its literature and art, its characteristic attitudes toward life. We are Americans because we live in a certain bounded territory, because our ancestors have carried on a great enterprise of pioneering and colonization, because we live in certain kinds of communities which have a certain look and express their aspirations in certain ways. We can see that our civilization is different from contiguous civilizations like the Indian and Mexican. The institutions of our country form a certain network which affects us vitally and intrigues our thoughts in a way that these other civilizations do not. We are a part of Country, for better or for worse. We have arrived in it through the operation of physiological laws, and not in any way through our own choice. By the time we have reached what are called years of discretion, its influences have molded our habits, our values, our ways of thinking, so that however aware we may become, we never really lost the stamp of our civilization, or could be mistaken for the child of any other country. Our feeling for our fellow countrymen is one of similarity or of mere acquaintance. We may be intensely proud of and congenial to our particular network of civilization, or we may detest most of its qualities and rage at its defects. This does not alter the fact that we are inextricably bound up in it. The Country, as an inescapable group into which we are born, and which makes us its particular kind of a citizen of the world, seems to be a fundamental fact of our consciousness, an irreducible minimum of social feeling.

Now this feeling for country is essentially noncompetitive; we think of our own people merely as living on the earth's surface along with other groups, pleasant or objectionable as they may be, but fundamentally as sharing the earth with them. In our simple conception of country there is no more feeling of rivalry with other peoples than there is in our feeling for our family. Our interest turns within rather than without, is intensive and not belligerent. We grow up and our imaginations gradually stake out the world we live in, they need no greater conscious satisfaction for their gregarious impulses than this sense of a great mass of people to whom we are more or less attuned, and in whose institutions we are functioning. The feeling for country would be an uninflatable maximum were it not for the ideas of State and Government which are associated with it. Country is a concept of peace, of tolerance, of living and letting live. But State is essentially a concept of power, of competition; it signifies a group in its aggressive aspects. And we have the misfortune of being born not only into a country but into a State, and as we grow up we learn to mingle the two feelings into a hopeless confusion.

The State is the country acting as a political unit, it is the group acting as a repository of force, determiner of law, arbiter of justice. International politics is a "power politics" because it is a relation of States and that is what States infallibly and calamitously are, huge aggregations of human and industrial force that may be hurled against each other in war. When a country acts as a whole in relation to another country, or in imposing laws on its own inhabitants, or in coercing or punishing individuals or minorities, it is acting as a State. The history of America as a country is quite different from that of America as a State. In one case it is the drama of the pioneering conquest of the land, of the growth of wealth and the ways in which it was used, of the enterprise of education, and the carrying out of spiritual ideals, of the struggle of economic classes. But as a State, its history is that of playing a part in the world, making war, obstructing international trade, preventing itself from being split to pieces, punishing those citizens whom society agrees are offensive, and collecting money to pay for all. . . .

Government on the other hand is synonymous with neither State nor Nation. It is the machinery by which the nation, organized as a State, carries out its State functions. Government is a framework of the administration of laws, and the carrying out of the public force. Government is the idea of the State put into practical operation in the hands of definite, concrete, fallible men. It is the visible sign of the invisible grace. It is the word made flesh. And it has necessarily the limitations inherent in all practicality. Government is the only form in which we can envisage the State, but it is by no means identical with it. That the State is a mystical conception is something that must never be forgotten. Its glamour and its significance linger behind the framework of Government and direct its activities.

Wartime brings the ideal of the State out into very clear relief, and reveals attitudes and tendencies that were hidden. In times of peace the sense of the State flags in a republic that is not militarized. For war is essentially the health of the State. The ideal of the State is that within its territory its power and influence should be universal. As the Church is the medium for the spiritual salvation of men, so the State is thought of as the medium for his political salvation. Its idealism is a rich blood flowing to all the members of the body politic. And it is precisely in war that the urgency for union seems greatest, and the necessity for universality seems most unquestioned. The State is the organization of the herd to act offensively or defensively against another herd similarly organized. The more terrifying the occasion for defense, the closer will become the organization and the more coercive the influence upon each member of the herd. War sends the current of purpose and activity flowing down to the lowest level of the herd, and to its most remote branches. All the activities of society are linked together as fast as possible to this central purpose of making a military offensive or a military defense, and the State becomes what in peacetimes it has vainly struggled to become—the inexorable arbiter and determinant of men's business and attitudes and opinions. The slack is taken up, the crosscurrents fade out, and the nation moves lumberingly and slowly, but with ever accelerated speed and integration, toward the great end, toward the "peacefulness of being at war," of which L. P. Jacks has so unforgettably spoken.[2]

The classes which are able to play an active and not merely a passive role in the organization for war get a tremendous liberation of activity and energy. Individuals are jolted out of their old routine, many of them are given new positions of responsibility, new techniques must be learned. Wearing home ties are broken and women who would have remained attached with infantile bonds are liberated for service overseas. A vast sense of rejuvenescence pervades the significant classes, a sense of new importance in the world. Old national ideals are taken out, readapted to the purpose and used as universal touchstones, or molds into which all thought is poured. Every individual citizen who in peacetimes had no function to perform by which he could imagine himself an expression or living fragment of the State becomes an active amateur agent of the Government in reporting spies and disloyalists, in raising Government funds, or in propagating such measures as are considered necessary by officialdom. Minority opinion, which in times of peace, was only irritating and could not be dealt with by law unless it was conjoined with actual crime, becomes, with the outbreak of war, a case for outlawry. Criticism of the State, objections to war, lukewarm opinions concerning the necessity or the beauty of conscription, are made subject to ferocious penalties, far exceeding in severity those affixed to actual pragmatic crimes. Public opinion, as expressed in the newspapers, and the pulpits and the schools, becomes one solid block. "Loyalty," or rather war orthodoxy, becomes the sole test for all professions, techniques, occupations. Particularly is this true in the sphere of the intellectual life. There the smallest taint is held to spread over the whole soul, so that a professor of physics is *ipso facto* disqualified to teach physics or to hold honorable place in a university—the republic of learning—if he is at all unsound on the war. Even mere association with persons thus tainted is considered to disqualify a teacher. Anything pertaining to the enemy becomes taboo. His books are suppressed wherever possible, his language is forbidden. His artistic products are considered to convey in the subtlest spiritual way taints of vast poison to the soul that permits itself to enjoy them. So enemy music is suppressed, and energetic measures of opprobrium taken against those whose artistic consciences are not ready to perform such an act of self-sacrifice. The rage for loyal conformity works impartially, and often in diametric opposition to other orthodoxies and traditional conformities, or even ideals. The triumphant orthodoxy of the State is shown at its apex perhaps when Christian preachers lose their pulpits for taking in more or less literal terms the Sermon on the Mount, and Christian zealots are sent to prison for twenty years for distributing tracts which argue that war is unscriptural.

War is the health of the State. It automatically sets in motion throughout society those irresistible forces for uniformity, for passionate cooperation with the Government in coercing into obedience the minority groups and individuals which lack the larger herd sense. The machinery of government sets and enforces the drastic penalties; the minorities are either intimidated into silence, or brought slowly around by a subtle process of persuasion which may seem to them really to be converting them. Of course, the ideal of perfect loyalty, perfect uniformity is never really attained. The classes upon whom the amateur work of coercion falls are unwearied in their zeal, but often their agitation instead of converting, merely serves to stiffen their resistance. Minorities are rendered sullen, and some intellectual opinion bitter and satirical. But in general, the nation in wartime attains a uniformity of feeling, a hierarchy of values culminating at the undisputed apex of the State ideal, which could not possibly be produced through any other agency than war. Loyalty—or mystic devotion to the State—becomes the major imagined human value. Other values, such as artistic creation, knowledge, reason, beauty, the enhancement of life, are instantly and almost unanimously sacrificed, and the significant classes who have constituted themselves the amateur agents of the State are engaged not only in sacrificing these values for themselves but in coercing all other persons into sacrificing them.

War—or at least modern war waged by a democratic republic against a powerful enemy—seems to achieve for a nation almost all that the most inflamed political idealist could desire. Citizens are no longer indifferent to their Government, but each cell of the body politic is brimming with life and activity. We are at last on the way to full realization of that collective community in which each individual somehow contains the virtue of the whole. In a nation at war, every citizen identifies himself with the whole, and feels immensely strengthened in that identification. The purpose and desire of the collective community live in each person who throws himself wholeheartedly into the cause of war. The impeding distinction between society and the individual is almost blotted out. At war, the individual becomes almost identical with his society. He achieves a superb self-assurance, an intuition of the rightness of all his ideas and emotions, so that in the suppression of opponents or heretics he is invincibly strong; he feels behind him all the power of the collective community. The individual as social being in war seems to have achieved almost his apotheosis. Not for any religious impulse could the American nation have been expected to show such devotion *en masse,* such sacrifice and labor. Certainly not for any secular good, such as universal education or the subjugation of nature, would

it have poured forth its treasure and its life, or would it have
permitted such stern coercive measures to be taken against it,
such as conscripting its money and its men. But for the sake of
a war of offensive self-defense, undertaken to support a difficult
cause to the slogan of "democracy," it would reach the highest
level ever known of collective effort.

For these secular goods, connected with the enhancement of
life, the education of man and the use of the intelligence to
realize reason and beauty in the nation's communal living, are
alien to our traditional ideal of the State. The State is intimately
connected with war, for it is the organization of the collective
community when it acts in a political manner, and to act in a
political manner towards a rival group has meant, throughout all
history—war.

There is nothing invidious in the use of the term "herd" in
connection with the State. It is merely an attempt to reduce
closer to first principles the nature of this institution in the
shadow of which we all live, move, and have our being.
Ethnologists are generally agreed that human society made its
first appearance as the human pack and not as a collection of
individuals or of couples. The herd is in fact the original unit,
and only as it was differentiated did personal individuality develop. All the most primitive surviving tribes of men are shown to
live in a very complex but very rigid social organization where
opportunity for individuation is scarcely given. These tribes remain strictly organized herds, and the difference between them
and the modern State is one of degree of sophistication and variety of organization, and not of kind.

Psychologists recognize the gregarious impulse as one of the
strongest primitive pulls which keeps together the herds of the
different species of higher animals. Mankind is no exception.
Our pugnacious evolutionary history has prevented the impulse
from ever dying out. This gregarious impulse is the tendency to
imitate, to conform, to coalesce together, and is most powerful
when the herd believes itself threatened with attack. Animals
crowd together for protection, and men become most conscious
of their collectivity at the threat of war. Consciousness of collectivity brings confidence and a feeling of massed strength, which
in turn arouses pugnacity and the battle is on. In civilized man,
the gregarious impulse acts not only to produce concerted action for defense, but also to produce identity of opinion. Since

thought is a form of behavior, the gregarious impulse floods up into its realms and demands that sense of uniform thought which wartime produces so successfully. And it is in this flooding of the conscious life of society that gregariousness works its havoc.

For just as in modern societies the sex instinct is enormously oversupplied for the requirements of human propagation, so the gregarious impulse is enormously oversupplied for the work of protection which it is called upon to perform. It would be quite enough if we were gregarious enough to enjoy the companionship of others, to be able to cooperate with them, and to feel a slight malaise at solitude. Unfortunately, however, this impulse is not content with these reasonable and healthful demands, but insists that like-mindedness shall prevail everywhere, in all departments of life. So that all human progress, all novelty, and nonconformity, must be carried against the resistance of this tyrannical herd instinct which drives the individual into obedience and conformity with the majority. Even in the most modern and enlightened societies this impulse shows little sign of abating. As it is driven by inexorable economic demand out of the sphere of utility, it seems to fasten itself ever more fiercely in the realm of feeling and opinion, so that conformity comes to be a thing aggressively desired and demanded.

The gregarious impulse keeps its hold all the more virulently because when the group is in motion or is taking any positive action, this feeling of being with and supported by the collective herd very greatly feeds that will to power, the nourishment of which the individual organism so constantly demands. You feel powerful by conforming, and you feel forlorn and helpless if you are out of the crowd. While even if you do not get any access of power by thinking and feeling just as everybody else in your group does, you get at least the warm feeling of obedience, the soothing irresponsibility of protection.

Joining as it does to these very vigorous tendencies of the individual—the pleasure in power and the pleasure in obedience—this gregarious impulse becomes irresistible in society. War stimulates it to the highest possible degree, sending the influences of its mysterious herd-current with its inflations of power and obedience to the farthest reaches of the society, to every individual and little group that can possibly be affected. And it is these impulses which the State—the organization of the entire herd, the entire collectivity—is founded on and makes use of.

There is, of course, in the feeling toward the State a large element of pure filial mysticism. The sense of insecurity, the desire for protection, sends one's desire back to the father and mother, with whom is associated the earliest feelings of protection. It is not for nothing that one's State is still thought of as Father or Motherland, that one's relation toward it is conceived in terms of family affection. The war has shown that nowhere under the shock of danger have these primitive childlike attitudes failed to assert themselves again, as much in this country as anywhere. If we have not the intense Father-sense of the German who worships his Vaterland, at least in Uncle Sam we have a symbol of protecting, kindly authority, and in the many Mother-posters of the Red Cross, we see how easily in the more tender functions of war service, the ruling organization is conceived in family terms. A people at war have become in the most literal sense obedient, respectful, trustful children again, full of that naïve faith in the all-wisdom and all-power of the adult who takes care of them, imposes his mild but necessary rule upon them and in whom they lost their responsibility and anxieties. In this recrudescence of the child, there is great comfort, and a certain influx of power. On most people the strain of being an independent adult weighs heavily, and upon none more than those members of the significant classes who have had bequeathed to them or have assumed the responsibilities of governing. The State provides the convenientest of symbols under which these classes can retain all the actual pragmatic satisfaction of governing, but can rid themselves of the psychic burden of adulthood. They continue to direct industry and government and all the institutions of society pretty much as before, but in their own conscious eyes and in the eyes of the general public, they are turned from their selfish and predatory ways, and have become loyal servants of society, or something greater than they—the State. The man who moves from the direction of a large business in New York to a post in the war management industrial service in Washington does not apparently alter very much his power or his administrative technique. But psychically, what a transfiguration has occurred! His is now not only the power but the glory! And his sense of satisfaction is directly proportional not to the genuine amount of personal sacrifice that may be involved in the change but to the extent to which he retains his industrial prerogatives and sense of command.

From members of this class a certain insuperable indignation arises if the change from private enterprise to State service involves any real loss of power and personal privilege. If there is to be pragmatic sacrifice, let it be, they feel, on the field of honor, in the traditionally acclaimed deaths by battle, in that detour to suicide, as Nietzsche calls war. The State in wartime supplies satisfaction for this very real craving, but its chief value is the opportunity it gives for this regresion to infantile attitudes. In your reaction to an imagined attack on your country or an insult to its government, you draw closer to the herd for protection, you conform in word and deed, and you insist vehemently that everybody else shall think, speak, and act together. And you fix your adoring gaze upon the State, with a truly filial look, as upon the Father of the flock, the quasi-personal symbol of the strength of the herd, and the leader and determinant of your definite action and ideas.

The members of the working classes, that portion at least which does not identify itself with the significant classes and seek to imitate it and rise to it, are notoriously less affected by the symbolism of the State, or, in other words, are less patriotic than the significant classes. For theirs is neither the power nor the glory. The State in wartime does not offer them the opportunity to regress, for, never having acquired social adulthood, they cannot lose it. If they have been drilled and regimented, as by the industrial regime of the last century, they go out docilely enough to do battle for their State, but they are almost entirely without that filial sense and even without that herd-intellect sense which operates so powerfully among their "betters." They live habitually in an industrial serfdom, by which, though nominally free, they are in practice as a class bound to a system of machine-production the implements of which they do not own, and in the distribution of whose product they have not the slightest voice, except what they can occasionally exert by a veiled intimidation which draws slightly more of the product in their direction. From such serfdom, military conscription is not so great a change. But into the military enterprise they go, not with those hurrahs of the significant classes whose instincts war so powerfully feeds, but with the same apathy with which they enter and continue in the industrial enterprise.

From this point of view, war can be called almost an upper-class sport. The novel interests and excitements it provides, the inflations of power, the satisfaction it gives to those very tenacious human impulses—gregariousness and parent-regression—endow it with all the qualities of a luxurious collective game which is felt intensely just in proportion to the sense of significant rule the person has in the class division of his society. A country at war—particularly our own country at war—does not act as a purely homogeneous herd. The significant classes have all the herd-feeling in all its primitive intensity, but there are barriers, or at least differentials of intensity, so that this feeling does not flow freely without impediment throughout the entire nation. A modern country represents a long historical and social process of disaggregation of the herd. The nation at peace is not a group, it is a network of myriads of groups representing the cooperation and similar feeling of men on all sorts of planes and in all sorts of human interests and enterprises. In every modern industrial country, there are parallel planes of economic classes with divergent attitudes and institutions and interests—bourgeois and proletariat, with their many subdivisions according to power and function, and even their interweaving, such as those more highly skilled workers who habitually identify themselves with the owning and the significant classes and strive to raise themselves to the bourgeois level, imitating their cultural standards and manners. Then there are religious groups with a certain definite, though weakening sense of kinship, and there are the powerful ethnic groups which behave almost as cultural colonies in the New World, clinging tenaciously to language and historical tradition, though their herdishness is usually founded on cultural rather than State symbols. There are even certain vague sectional groupings. All these small sects, political parties, classes, levels, interests, may act as foci for herd-feelings. They intersect and interweave, and the same person may be a member of several different groups lying at different planes. Different occasions will set off his herd-feeling in one direction or another. In a religious crisis he will be intensely conscious of the necessity that his sect (or sub-herd) may prevail; in a political campaign, that his party shall triumph.

To the spread of herd-feeling, therefore, all these smaller herds offer resistance. To the spread of that herd-feeling which arises from the threat of war, and which would normally involve the entire nation, the only groups which make serious resistance are those, of course, which continue to identify themselves with the other nation from which they or their parents have come. In times of peace they are for all practical purposes citizens of their new country. They keep alive their ethnic traditions more as a luxury than anything. Indeed these traditions tend rapidly to die out except where they connect with some still unresolved nationalistic cause abroad, with some struggle for freedom, or some irredentism. If they are consciously opposed by a too invidious policy of Americanism, they tend to be strengthened. And in time of war, these ethnic elements which have any traditional connection with the enemy, even though most of the individuals may have little real sympathy with the enemy's cause, are naturally luke-warm to the herd-feeling of the nation which goes back to State traditions in which they have no share. But to the natives inbued with State-feeling, any such resistance or apathy is intolerable. This herd-feeling, this newly awakened consciousness of the State, demands universality. The leaders of the significant classes, who feel most intensely this State compulsion, demand a 100 per cent Americanism, among 100 per cent of the population. The State is a jealous God and will brook no rivals. Its sovereignty must pervade every one, and all feeling must be run into the stereotyped forms of romantic patriotic militarism which is the traditional expression of the State herd-feeling.

Thus arises conflict within the State. War becomes almost a sport between the hunters and the hunted. The pursuit of enemies within outweighs in psychic attractiveness the assault on the enemy without. The whole terrific force of the State is brought to bear against the heretics. The nation boils with a slow insistent fever. A white terrorism is carried on by the Government against pacifists, socialists, enemy aliens, and a milder unofficial persecution against all persons or movements that can be imagined as connected with the enemy. War, which should be the health of the State, unifies all the bourgeois elements and the common people, and outlaws the rest. The revolutionary proletariat shows more resistance to this unification, is, as we have seen, psychically out of the current. Its vanguard, as the I.W.W., is remorselessly pursued, in spite of the proof that it is a sympton, not a cause, and its persecution increases the disaffection of labor and intensifies the friction instead of lessening it.

But the emotions that play around the defense of the State do not take into consideration the pragmatic results. A nation at war, led by its significant classes, is engaged in liberating certain of its impulses which have had all too little exercise in the past. It is getting certain satisfactions, and the actual conduct of the war or the condition of the country are really incidental to the enjoyment of new forms of virtue and power and aggressiveness. If it could be shown conclusively that the persecution of slightly disaffected elements actually increased enormously the difficulties of production and the organization of the war technique, it would be found that public policy would scarcely change. The significant classes must have their pleasure in hunting down and chastizing everything that they feel instinctively to be not imbued with the current State enthusiasm, though the State itself be actually impeded in its efforts to carry out those objects for which they are passionately contending. The best proof of this is that with a pursuit of plotters that has continued with ceaseless vigilance ever since the beginning of the war in Europe, the concrete crimes unearthed and punished have been fewer than those prosecutions for the mere crime of opinion or the expression of sentiments critical of the State or the national policy. The punishment for opinion has been far more ferocious and unintermittent than the punishment of pragmatic crime. Unimpeachable Anglo-Saxon Americans who were freer of pacifist or socialist utterance than the State-obsessed ruling public opinion, received heavier penalties and even greater opprobrium, in many instances, than the definitely hostile German plotter. A public opinion which, almost without protest, accepts as just, adequate, beautiful, deserved, and in fitting harmony with ideals of liberty and freedom of speech, a sentence of twenty years in prison for mere utterances, no matter what they may be, shows itself to be suffering from a kind of social derangement of values, a sort of social neurosis, that deserves analysis and comprehension.

On our entrance into the war, there were many persons who predicted exactly this derangement of values, who feared lest democracy suffer more at home from an America at war than could be gained for democracy abroad. That fear has been amply justified. The question whether the American nation would act like an enlightened democracy going to war for the sake of high ideals, or like a State-obsessed herd, has been decisively answered. The record is written and cannot be erased. History will decide whether the terrorization of opinion and the regimentation of life were justified under the most idealistic of democratic administrations. It will see that when the American nation had ostensibly a chance to conduct a gallant war, with scrupulous regard to the safety of democratic values at home, it chose rather to adopt all the most obnoxious and coercive techniques of the enemy and of the other countries at war, and to rival in intimidation and ferocity of punishment the worst governmental systems of the age. For its former unconsciousness and disrespect of the State ideal, the nation apparently paid the penalty in a violent swing to the other extreme. It acted so exactly like a herd in its irrational coercion of minorities that there is no artificiality in interpreting the progress of the war in terms of the herd psychology. It unwittingly brought out into the strongest relief the true characteristics of the State and its intimate alliance with war. It provided for the enemies of war and the critics of the State the most telling arguments possible. The new passion for the State ideal unwittingly set in motion and encouraged forces that threaten very materially to reform the State. It has shown those who are really determined to end war that the problem is not the mere simple one of finishing a war that will end war.

For war is a complicated way in which a nation acts, and it acts so out of a spiritual compulsion which pushes it on, perhaps against all its interests, all its real desires, and all its real sense of values. It is States that make wars and not nations, and the very thought and almost necessity of war is bound up with the ideal of the State. Not for centuries have nations made war; in fact the only historical example of nations making war is the great barbarian invasions into southern Europe, the invasions of Russia from the East, and perhaps the sweep of Islam through northern Africa into Europe after Mohammed's death. And the motivations for such wars were either the restless expansion of migratory tribes or the flame of religious fanaticism. Perhaps these great movements could scarcely be called wars at all, for war implies an organized people drilled and led; in fact, it necessitates the State. Ever since Europe has had any such organization, such huge conflicts between nations— nations, that is, as cultural groups—have been unthinkable. It is preposterous to assume that for centuries in Europe there would have been any possibility of a people *en masse,* (with their own leaders, and not with the leaders of their duly constituted State), rising up and overflowing their borders in a war raid upon a neighboring people. The wars of the Revolutionary armies of France were clearly in defense of an imperiled freedom, and, moreover, they were clearly directed not against other peoples, but against the autocratic governments that were combining to crush the Revolution. There is no instance in history of a genuinely national war. There are instances of national defenses, among primitive civilizations such as the Balkan peoples, against intolerable invasion by neighboring despots or oppression. But war, as such, cannot occur except in a system of competing States, which have relations with each other through the channels of diplomacy.

War is a function of this system of States, and could not occur except in such a system. Nations organized for internal administration, nations organized as a federation of free communities, nations organized in any way except that of a political centralization of a dynasty, or the reformed descendant of a dynasty, could not possibly make war upon each other. They would not only have no motive for conflict, but they would be unable to muster the concentrated force to make war effective. There might be all sorts of amateur marauding, there might be guerrilla expeditions of group against group, but there could not be that terrible war *en masse* of the national State, that exploitation of the nation in the interests of the State, that abuse of the national life and resource in the frenzied mutual suicide, which is modern war.

It cannot be too firmly realized that war is a function of States and not of nations, indeed that it is the chief function of States. War is a very artificial thing. It is not the naïve spontaneous outburst of herd pugnacity; it is no more primary than is formal religion. War cannot exist without a military establishment, and a military establishment cannot exist without a State organization. War has an immemorial tradition and heredity only because the State has a long tradition and heredity. But they are inseparably and functionally joined. We cannot crusade against war without crusading implicitly against the State. And we cannot expect, or take measures to ensure, that this war is a war to end war, unless at the same time we take measures to end the State in its traditional form. The State is not the nation, and the State can be modified and even abolished in its present form, without harming the nation. On the contrary, with the passing of the dominance of the State, the genuine life-enhancing forces of the nation will be liberated. If the State's chief function is war, then the State must suck out of the nation a large part of its energy for its purely sterile purposes of defense and aggression. It devotes to waste or to actual destruction as much as it can of the vitality of the nation. No one will deny that war is a vast complex of life-destroying and life-crippling forces. If the State's chief function is war, then it is chiefly concerned with coordinating and developing the powers and techniques which makes for destruction. And this means not only the actual and potential destruction of the enemy, but of the nation at home as well. For the very existence of a State in a system of States means that the nation lies always under a risk of war and invasion, and the calling away of energy into military pursuits means a crippling of the productive and life-enhancing processes of the national life.

All this organization of death-dealing energy and technique is not a natural but a very sophisticated process. Particularly in modern nations, but also all through the course of modern European history, it could never exist without the State. For it meets the demands of no other institution, it follows the desires of no religious, industrial, political group. If the demand for military organization and a military establishment seems to come not from the officers of the State but from the public, it is only that it comes from the State-obsessed portion of the public, those groups which feel most keenly the State ideal. And in this country we have had evidence all too indubitable how powerless the pacifically minded officers of State may be in the face of a State obsession of the significant classes. If a powerful section of the significant classes feels more intensely the attitudes of the State, then they will most infallibly mold the Government in time to their wishes, bring it back to act as the embodiment of the State which it pretends to be. In every country we have seen groups that were more loyal than the king—more patriotic than the Government—the Ulserites in Great Britain, the Junkers in Prussia, L'Action Française in France, our patrioteers in America. These groups exist to keep the steering wheel of the State straight, and they prevent the nation from ever veering very far from the State ideal.

Militarism expresses the desires and satisfies the major impulse only of this class. The other classes, left to themselves, have too many necessities and interests and ambitions, to concern themselves with so expensive and destructive a game. But the State-obsessed group is either able to get control of the machinery of the State or to intimidate those in control, so that it is able through use of the collective force to regiment the other grudging and reluctant classes into a military program. State idealism percolates down through the strata of society; capturing groups and individuals just in proportion to the prestige of this dominant class. So that we have the herd actually strung along between two extremes, the militaristic patriots at one end, who are scarcely distinguishable in attitude and animus from the most reactionary Bourbons of an Empire, and unskilled labor groups, which entirely lack the State sense. But the State acts as a whole, and the class that controls governmental machinery can swing the effective action of the herd as a whole. The herd is not actually a whole, emotionally. But by an ingenious mixture of cajolery, agitation, intimidation, the herd is licked into shape, into an effective mechanical unity, if not into a spiritual whole. Men are told simultaneously that they will enter the military establishment of their own volition, as their splendid sacrifice for their country's welfare, and that if they do not enter they will be hunted down and punished with the most horrid penalties; and under a most indescribable confusion of democratic pride and personal fear they submit to the destruction of their livelihood if not their lives, in a way that would formerly have seemed to them so obnoxious as to be incredible.

In this great herd machinery, dissent is like sand in the bearings. The State ideal is primarily a sort of blind animal push toward military unity. Any difference with that unity turns the whole vast impulse toward crushing it. Dissent is speedily outlawed, and the Government, backed by the significant classes and those who in every locality, however small, identify themselves with them, proceeds against the outlaws, regardless of their value to the other institutions of the nation, or to the effect their persecution may have on public opinion. The herd becomes divided into the hunters and the hunted, and war enterprise becomes not only a technical game but a sport as well.

It must never be forgotten that nations do not declare war on each other, nor in the strictest sense is it nations that fight each other. Much has been said to the effect that modern wars are wars of whole peoples and not of dynasties. Because the entire nation is regimented and the whole resources of the country are levied on for war, this does not mean that it is the country *qua* country which is fighting. It is the country organized as a State that is fighting, and only as a State would it possibly fight. So literally it is States which make war on each other and not peoples. Governments are the agents of States, and it is Governments which declare war on each other, acting truest to form in the interests of the great State ideal they represent. There is no case known in modern times of the people being consulted in the initiation of a war. The present demand for "democratic control" of foreign policy indicates how completely, even in the most democratic of modern nations, foreign policy has been the secret private possession of the executive branch of the Government.

However representative' of the people Parliaments and Congresses may be in all that concerns the internal administration of a country's political affairs, in international relations it has never been possible to maintain that the popular body acted except as a wholly mechanical ratifier of the Executive's will. The formality by which Parliaments and Congresses declare war is the merest technicality. Before such a declaration can take place, the country will have been brought to the very brink of war by the foreign policy of the Executive. A long series of steps on the downward path, each one more fatally committing the unsuspecting country to a warlike course of action, will have been taken without either the people or its representatives being consulted or expressing its feeling. When the declaration of war is finally demanded by the Executive, the Parliament or Congress could not refuse it without reversing the course of history, without repudiating what has been representing itself in the eyes of the other States as the symbol and interpreter of the nation's will and animus. To repudiate an Executive at that time would be to publish to the entire world the evidence that the country had been grossly deceived by its own Government, that the country with an almost criminal carelessness had allowed its Government to commit it to gigantic national enterprises in which it had no heart. In such a crisis, even a Parliament, which in the most democratic States represents the common man and not the significant classes who most strongly cherish the State ideal, will cheerfully sustain the foreign policy which it understands even less than it would care for if it understood, and will vote almost unanimously for an incalculable war, in which the nation may be brought well nigh to ruin. That is why the referendum which was advocated by some people as a test of American sentiment in entering the war was considered even by thoughtful democrats to be something subtly improper. The die had been cast. Popular whim could only derange and bungle monstrously the majestic march of State policy in its new crusade for the peace of the world. The irresistible State ideal got hold of the bowels of men. Whereas up to this time, it had been irreproachable to be neutral in word and deed, for the foreign policy of the State had so decided it, henceforth it became the most arrant crime to remain neutral. The Middle West, which had been soddenly pacifistic in our days of neutrality, became in a few months just as soddenly bellicose, and in its zeal for witch-burnings and its scent for enemies within gave precedence to no section of the country. The herd mind followed faithfully the State mind and, the agitation for a referendum being soon forgotten, the country fell into the universal conclusion that, since its Congress had formally declared the war, the nation itself had in the most solemn and universal way devised and brought on the entire affair. Oppression of minorities became justified on the plea that the latter were perversely resisting the rationally constructed and solemnly declared will of a majority of the nation. The herd coalescence of opinion which became inevitable the moment the State had set flowing the war attitudes became interpreted as a prewar popular decision, and disinclination to bow to the herd was treated as a monstrously antisocial act. So that the State, which had vigorously resisted the idea of a referendum and clung tenaciously and, of course, with entire success to its autocratic and absolute control of foreign policy, had the pleasure of seeing the country, within a few months, given over to the retrospective impression that a genuine referendum had taken place. When once a country has lapped up these State attitudes, its memory fades; it conceives itself not as merely accepting, but of having itself willed, the whole policy and technique of war. The significant classes, with their trailing satellites, identify themselves with the State, so that what the state, through the agency of the Government, has willed, this majority conceives itself to have willed.

All of which goes to show that the State represents all the autocratic, arbitrary, coercive, belligerent forces within a social group, it is a sort of complexus of everything most distasteful to the modern free creative spirit, the feeling for life, liberty, and the pursuit of happiness. War is the health of the State. Only when the State is at war does the modern society function with that unity of sentiment, simple uncritical patriotic devotion, cooperation of services, which have always been the ideal of the State lover. With the ravages of democratic ideas, however, the modern republic cannot go to war under the old conceptions of autocracy and death-dealing belligerency. If a successful animus for war requires a renaissance of State ideals, they can only come back under democratic forms, under this retrospective conviction of democratic control of foreign policy, democratic desire for war, and particularly of this identification of the democracy with the State. How unregenerate the ancient State may be, however, is indicated by the laws against sedition, and by the Government's unreformed attitude on foreign policy. One of the first demands of the more farseeing democrats in the democracies of the Alliance was that secret diplomacy must go. The war was seen to have been made possible by a web of secret agreements between States, alliances that were made by Governments without the shadow of popular support or even popular knowledge, and vague, half-understood commitments that scarcely reached the stage of a treaty or agreement, but which proved binding in the event. Certainly, said these democratic thinkers, war can scarcely be avoided unless this poisonous underground system of secret diplomacy is destroyed, this system by which a nation's power, wealth, and manhood may be signed away like a blank check to an allied nation to be cashed in at some future crisis. Agreements which are to affect the lives of whole peoples must be made between peoples and not by Governments, or at least by their representatives in the full glare of publicity and criticism.

Such a demand for "democratic control of foreign policy" seemed axiomatic. Even if the country had been swung into war by steps taken secretly and announced to the public only after they had been consummated, it was felt that the attitude of the American State toward foreign policy was only a relic of the bad old days and must be superseded in the new order. The American President himself, the liberal hope of the world, had demanded, in the eyes of the world, open diplomacy, agreements freely and openly arrived at. Did this mean a genuine transference of power in this most crucial of State functions from Government to people? Not at all. When the question recently came

to a challenge in Congress, and the implications of open discussion were somewhat specifically discussed, and the de-
sirabilities frankly commended, the President let his disapproval
be known in no uncertain way. No one ever accused Mr. Wilson
of not being a State idealist, and whenever democratic aspirations swung ideals too far out of the State orbit, he could be
counted on to react vigorously. Here was a clear case of conflict
between democratic idealism and the very crux of the concept
of the State. However unthinkingly he might have been led on to
encourage open diplomacy in his liberalizing program, when its
implication was made vivid to him, he betrayed how mere a tool
the idea had been in his mind to accentuate America's redeem-
ing role. Not in any sense as a serious pragmatic technique had
he thought of a genuinely open diplomacy. And how could he?
For the last stronghold of State power is foreign policy. It is in
foreign policy that the State acts most concentratedly as the organized herd, acts with fullest sense of aggressive-power, acts
with freest arbitrariness. In foreign policy, the State is most itself.
States, with reference to each other, may be said to be in a continual state of latent war. The "armed truce," a phrase so familiar
before 1914, was an accurate description of the normal relation
of States when they are not at war. Indeed, it is not too much to
say that the normal relation of States is war. Diplomacy is a disguised war, in which States seek to gain by barter and intrigue,
by the cleverness of wits, the objectives which they would have
to gain more clumsily by means of war. Diplomacy is used while
the States are recuperating from conflicts in which they have
exhausted themselves. It is the wheedling and the bargaining of
the worn-out bullies as they rise from the ground and slowly restore their strength to begin fighting again. If diplomacy had
been a moral equivalent for war, a higher stage in human progress, an inestimable means of making words prevail instead of
blows, militarism would have broken down and given place to it.
But since it is a mere temporary substitute, a mere appearance
of war's energy under another form, a surrogate effect is almost
exactly proportioned to the armed force behind it. When it fails,
the recourse is immediate to the military technique whose thinly
veiled arm it has been. A diplomacy that was the agency of
popular democratic forces in their non-State manifestations
would be no diplomacy at all. It would be no better than the
Railway or Education commissions that are sent from one coun-

try to another with rational constructive purpose. The State, acting as a diplomatic-military ideal, is eternally at war. Just as it must act arbitrarily and autocratically in time of war, it must act in time of peace in this particular role where it acts as a unit. Unified control is necessarily autocratic control. Democratic control of foreign policy is therefore a contradiction in terms. Open discussion destroys swiftness and certainty of action. The giant State is paralyzed. Mr. Wilson retains his full ideal of the State at the same time that he desires to eliminate war. He wishes to make the world safe for democracy as well as safe for diplomacy. When the two are in conflict, his clear political insight, his idealism of the State, tells him that it is the naïver democratic values that must be sacrificed. The world must primarily be made safe for diplomacy. The State must not be diminished.

What is the State essentially? The more closely we examine it, the more mystical and personal it becomes. On the Nation we can put our hand as a definite social group, with attitudes and qualities exact enough to mean something. On the Government we can put our hand as a certain organization of ruling functions, the machinery of lawmaking and law-enforcing. The Administration is a recognizable group of political functionaries, temporarily in charge of the government. But the State stands as an idea behind them all, eternal, sanctified, and from it Government and Administration conceive themselves to have the breath of life. Even the nation, especially in times of war—or at least, its significant classes—considers that it derives its authority and its purpose from the idea of the State. Nation and State are scarcely differentiated, and the concrete, practical, apparent facts are sunk in the symbol. We reverence not our country but the flag. We may criticize ever so severely our country, but we are disrespectful to the flag at our peril. It is the flag and the uniform that make men's heart beat high and fill them with noble emotions, not the thought of and pious hopes for America as a free and enlightened nation.

It cannot be said that the object of emotion is the same, because the flag is the symbol of the nation, so that in reverencing the American flag we are reverencing the nation. For the flag is not a symbol of the country as a cultural group, following certain ideals of life, but solely a symbol of the political State, inseparable from its prestige and expansion. The flag is most intimately connected with military achievement, military memory. It represents the country not in it intensive life, but in its far-flung challenge to the world. The flag is primarily the banner of war; it is allied with patriotic anthem and holiday. It recalls old martial memories. A nation's patriotic history is solely the history of its wars, that is, of the State in its health and glorious functioning. So in responding to the appeal of the flag, we are responding to the appeal of the State, to the symbol of the herd organized as an offensive and defensive body, conscious of its prowess and its mystical herd strength.

Even those authorities in the present Administration, to whom has been granted autocratic control over opinion, feel, though they are scarcely able to philosophize over, this distinction. It has been authoritatively declared that the horrid penalties against seditious opinion must not be construed as inhibiting legitimate, that is, partisan criticism of the Administration. A distinction is made between the Administration and the Government. It is quite accurately suggested by this attitude that the Administration is a temporary band of partisan politicians in charge of the machinery of Government, carrying out the mystical policies of State. The manner in which they operate this machinery may be freely discussed and objected to by their political opponents. The Governmental machinery may also be legitimately altered, in case of necessity. What may not be discussed or criticized is the mystical policy itself or the motives of the State in inaugurating such a policy. The President, it is true, has made certain partisan distinctions between candidates for office on the ground of support or nonsupport of the Administration, but what he means was really support or nonsupport of the State policy as faithfully carried out by the Administration. Certain of the Administration measures were devised directly to increase the health of the State, such as the Conscription and the Espionage laws. Others were concerned merely with the machinery. To oppose the first was to oppose the State and was therefore not tolerable. To oppose the second was to oppose fallible human judgment, and was therefore, though to be depreciated, not to be wholly interpreted as political suicide.

The distinction between Government and State, however, has not been so carefully observed. In time of war it is natural that Government as the seat of authority should be confused with the State or the mystic source of authority. You cannot very well injure a mystical idea which is the State, but you can very well interfere with the processes of Government. So that the two become identified in the public mind, and any contempt for or opposition to the workings of the machinery of Government is considered equivalent to contempt for the sacred State. The State, it is felt, is being injured in its faithful surrogate, and public emotion rallies passionately to defend it. It even makes any criticism of the form of Government a crime.

The inextricable union of militarism and the State is beautifully shown by those laws which emphasize interference with the Army and Navy as the most culpable of seditious crimes. Pragmatically, a case of capitalistic sabotage, or a strike in war industry would seem to be far more dangerous to the successful prosecution of the war than the isolated and ineffectual efforts of an individual to prevent recruiting. But in the tradition of the State ideal, such industrial interference with national policy is not identified as a crime against the State. It may be grumbled against; it may be seen quite rationally as an impediment of the utmost gravity. But it is not *felt* in those obscure seats of the herd mind which dictate the identity of crime and fix their proportional punishments. Army and Navy, however, are the very arms of the State; in them flows its most precious lifeblood. To paralyze them is to touch the very State itself. And the majesty of the State is so sacred that even to attempt such a paralysis is a crime equal to a successful strike. The will is deemed sufficient. Even though the individual in his effort to impede recruiting should utterly and lamentably fail, he shall be in no wise spared. Let the wrath of the State descend upon him for his impiety! Even if he does not try any overt action, but merely utters sentiments that may incidentally in the most indirect way cause someone to refrain from enlisting, he is guilty. The guardians of the State do not ask whether any pragmatic effect flowed out of this evil will or desire. It is enough that the will is present. Fifteen or twenty years in prison is not deemed too much for such sacrilege.

Such attitudes and such laws, which affront every principle of human reason, are no accident, nor are they the result of hysteria caused by the war. They are considered just, proper, beautiful by all the classes which have the State ideal, and they express only an extreme of health and vigor in the reaction of the State to its nonfriends.

Such attitudes are inevitable as arising from the devotees of the State. For the State is a personal as well as a mystical symbol, and it can only be understood by tracing its historical origin. The modern State is not the rational and intelligent product of modern men desiring to live harmoniously together with security of life, property, and opinion. It is not an organization which has been devised as pragmatic means to a desired social end. All the idealism with which we have been instructed to endow the State is the fruit of our retrospective imaginations. What it does for us in the way of security and benefit of life, it does incidentally as a by-product and development of its original functions, and not because at any time men or classes in the full possession of their insight and intelligence have desired that it be so. It is very important that we should occasionally lift the incorrigible veil of that *ex post facto* idealism by which we throw a glamor of rationalization over what is, and pretend in the ecstasies of social conceit that we have personally invented and set up for the glory of God and man the hoary institutions which we see around us. Things are what they are, and come down to us with all their thick encrustations of error and malevolence. Political philosophy can delight us with fantasy and convince us who need illusion to live that the actual is a fair and approximate copy—full of failings, of course, but approximately sound and sincere—of that ideal society which we can imagine ourselves as creating. From this it is a step to the tacit assumption that we have somehow had a hand in its creation and are responsible for its maintenance and sanctity.

Nothing is more obvious, however, than that every one of us comes into society as into something in whose creation we had not the slightest hand. We have not even the advantage, like those little unborn souls in *The Blue Bird,* of consciousness before we take up our careers on earth.[3] By the time we find ourselves here we are caught in a network of customs and attitudes, the major directions of our desires and interests have been stamped on our minds, and by the time we have emerged from tutelage and reached the years of discretion when we might conceivably throw our influence to the reshaping of social institutions, most of us have been so molded into the society and class we live in that we are scarcely aware of any distinction between ourselves as judging, desiring individuals and our social environment. We have been kneaded so successfully that we approve of what our society approves, desire what our society desires, and add to the group our own passionate inertia against change, against the effort of reason, and the adventure of beauty.

Every one of us, without exception, is born into a society that is given, just as the fauna and flora of our environment are given. Society and its institutions are, to the individual who enters it, as much naturalistic phenomena as is the weather itself. There is, therefore, no natural sanctity in the State any more than there is in the weather. We may bow down before it, just as our ancestors bowed before the sun and moon, but it is only because something in us unregenerate finds satisfaction in such an attitude, not because there is anything inherently reverential in the institution worshiped. Once the State has begun to function, and a large class finds its interest and its expression of power in maintaining the State, this ruling class may compel obedience from any uninterested minority. The State thus becomes an instrument by which the power of the whole herd is wielded for the benefit of a class. The rulers soon learn to capitalize the reverence which the State produces in the majority, and turn it into a general resistance toward a lessening of their privileges. The sanctity of the State becomes identified with the sanctity of the ruling class, and the latter are permitted to remain in power under the impression that in obeying and serving them, we are obeying and serving society, the nation, the great collectivity of all of us.

II

An analysis of the State would take us back to the beginnings of society, to the complex of religious and personal and herd impulses which has found expression in so many forms. What we are interested in is the American State as it behaves and as Americans behave toward it in this twentieth century, and to understand that, we have to go no further back than the early English monarchy of which our American republic is the direct descendant. How straight and true is that line of descent almost nobody realizes. Those persons who believe in the sharpest distinction between democracy and monarchy can scarcely appreciate how a political institution may go through so many transformations and yet remain the same. Yet a swift glance must show us that in all the evolution of the English monarchy, with all its broadenings and its revolutions, and even with its jump across the sea into a colony which became an independent nation and then a powerful State, the same State functions and attitudes have been preserved essentially unchanged. The changes have been changes of form and not of inner spirit, and the boasted extension of democracy has been not a process by which the State was essentially altered to meet the shifting of classes, the extension of knowledge, the needs of social organization, but a mere elastic expansion by which the old spirit of the State easily absorbed the new and adjusted itself successfully to its exigencies. Never once has it been seriously shaken. Only once or twice has it been seriously challenged, and each time it has speedily recovered its equilibrium and proceeded with all its attitudes and faiths reenforced by the disturbance.

The modern democratic State, in this light, is therefore no bright and rational creation of a new day, the political form under which great peoples are to live healthfully and freely in a modern world, but the last decrepit scion of an ancient and hoary stock, which has become so exhausted that it scarcely recognizes its own ancestor, does, in fact repudiate him while it clings tenaciously to the archaic and irrelevant spirit that made that ancestor powerful, and resists the new bottles for the new wine that its health as a modern society so desperately needs. So sweeping a conclusion might have been doubted concerning the American State had it not been for the war, which has provided a long and beautiful series of examples of the tenacity of the State ideal and its hold on the significant classes of the American nation. War is the health of the State, and it is during war that one best understands the nature of that institution. If the American democracy during wartime has acted with an almost incredible trueness to form, if it has resurrected with an almost joyful fury the somnolent State, we can only conclude that that tradition from the past has been unbroken, and that the American republic is the direct descendant of the early English State.

And what was the nature of this early English State? It was first of all a medieval absolute monarchy, arising out of the feudal chaos, which had represented the first effort at order after the turbulent assimilation of the invading barbarians by the Christianizing Roman civilization. The feudal lord evolved out of the invading warrior who had seized or been granted land and held it, souls and usufruct thereof, as fief to some higher lord whom he aided in war. His own serfs and vassals were exchanging faithful service for the protection which the warrior with his organized band could give them. Where one invading chieftain retained his power over his lesser lieutenants, a petty kingdom would arise, as in England, and a restless and ambitious king might extend his power over his neighbors and consolidate the petty kingdoms only to fall before the armed power of an invader like William the Conqueror, who would bring the whole realm under his heel. The modern State begins when a prince secures almost undisputed sway over fairly homogeneous territory and people and strives to fortify his power and maintain the order that will conduce to the safety and influence of his heirs. The State in its inception is pure and undiluted monarchy; it is armed power, culminating in a single head, bent on one primary object, the reducing to subjection, to unconditional and unqualified loyalty of all the people of a certain territory. This is the primary striving of the State, and it is a striving that the State never loses, through all its myriad transformations.

When this subjugation was once acquired, the modern State had begun. In the King, the subjects found their protection and their sense of unity. From his side, he was a redoubtable, ambitious, and stiff-necked warrior, getting the supreme mastery which he craved. But from theirs, he was a symbol of the herd, the visible emblem of that security which they needed and for which they drew gregariously together. Serfs and villains, whose safety under their petty lords had been rudely shattered in the constant conflicts for supremacy, now drew a new breath under the supremacy, that wiped out all this local anarchy. King and people agreed in the thirst for order, and order became the first healing function of the State. But in the maintenance of order, the King needed officers of justice; the old crude group-rules for dispensing justice had to be codified, a system of formal law worked out. The King needed ministers, who would carry out his will, extensions of his own power, as a machine extends the power of a man's hand. So the State grew as a gradual differentiation of the King's absolute power, founded on the devotion of his subjects and his control of a military band, swift and sure to smite. Gratitude for protection and fear of the strong arm sufficed to produce the loyalty of the country to the State.

The history of the State, then, is the effort to maintain these personal prerogatives of power, the effort to convert more and more into stable law the rules of order, the conditions of public vengeance, the distinction between classes, the possession of privilege. It was an effort to convert what was at first arbitrary usurpation, a perfectly apparent use of unjustified force, into the taken for granted and the divinely established. The State moves inevitably along the line from military dictatorship to the divine right of Kings. What had to be at first rawly imposed becomes through social habit to seem the necessary, the inevitable. The modern unquestioning acceptance of the State comes out of long and turbulent centuries when the State was challenged and had to fight its way to prevail. The King's establishment of personal power—which was the early State—had to contend with the impudence of hostile barons, who saw too clearly the adventitious origin of the monarchy and felt no reason why they should not themselves reign. Feuds between the King and his relatives, quarrels over inheritance, quarrels over the devolution of property, threatened constantly the existence of the new monarchial State. The King's will to power necessitated for its absolute satisfaction universality of political control in his dominions, just as the Roman Church claimed universality of spiritual control over the whole world. And just as rival popes were the inevitable product of such a pretension of sovereignty, rival kings and princes contended for that dazzling jewel of undisputed power.

Not until the Tudor regime was there in England an irresponsible absolute personal monarchy on the lines of the early State ideal, governing a fairly well-organized and prosperous nation. The Stuarts were not only too weak-minded to inherit this fruition of William the Conqueror's labors, but they made the fatal mistake of bringing out to public view and philosophy the idea of Divine Right implicit in the State, and this at a time when a new class of country gentry and burghers were attaining wealth and self-consciousness backed by the zeal of a theocratic and individualistic religion. Cromwell might certainly, if he had continued in power, revised the ideal of the State, perhaps utterly transformed it, destroying the concepts of personal power, and universal sovereignty, and substituting a sort of Government of Presbyterian Soviets under the tutelage of a celestial Czar. But the Restoration brought back the old State under a peculiarly frivolous form. The Revolution was the merest change of monarchs at the behest of a Protestant majority which insisted on guarantees against religious relapse. The intrinsic nature of the monarchy as the symbol of the State was not in the least altered. In place of the inept monarch who could not lead the State in person or concentrate in himself the royal prerogatives, a coterie of courtiers managed the State. But their direction was consistently in the interest of the monarch and of the traditional ideal, so that the current of the English State was not broken.

The boasted English Parliament of lords and commoners possessed at no time any vitality which weakened or threatened to weaken the State ideal. Its original purpose was merely to facilitate the raising of the King's revenues. The nobles responded better when they seemed to be giving their consent. Their share in actual government was subjective, but the existence of Parliament served to appease any restiveness at the autocracy of the King. The significant classes could scarcely rebel when they had the privilege of giving consent to the King's measures. There was always outlet for the rebellious spirit of a powerful lord in private revolt against the King. The only Parliament that seriously tried to govern outside of and against the King's will precipitated a civil war that ended with the effectual submission of Parliament in a more careless and corrupt autocracy than had yet been known. By the time of George III Parliament was moribund, utterly unrepresentative either of the new bourgeois classes or of peasants and laborers, a mere frivolous parody of a legislature, despised both by King and people. The King was most effectively the State and his ministers the Government, which was run in terms of his personal whim, by men whose only interest was personal intrigue. Government had been for long what it has never ceased to be—a series of berths and emoluments in Army, Navy and the different departments of State, for the representatives of the privileged classes.

The State of George III was an example of the most archaic ideal of the English State, the pure, personal monarchy. The great mass of the people had fallen into the age-long tradition of loyalty to the crown. The classes that might have been restive for political power were placated by a show of representative government and the lucrative supply of offices. Discontent showed itself only in those few enlightened elements which could not refrain from irony at the sheer irrationality of a State managed on the old heroic lines for so grotesque a sovereign and by so grotesque a succession of courtier-ministers. Such discontent could by no means muster sufficient force for a revolution, but the Revolution which was due came in America where even the very obviously shadowy pigment of parliamentary representation was denied the colonists. All that was vital in the political thought of England supported the American colonists in their resistance to the obnoxious government of George III.

The American Revolution began with certain latent hopes that it might turn into a genuine break with the State ideal. The Declaration of Independence announced doctrines that were utterly incompatible not only with the century-old conception of the Divine Right of Kings, but also with the Divine Right of the State. If all governments derive their authority from the consent of the governed, and if a people is entitled, at any time that it becomes oppressive, to overthrow it and institute one more nearly conformable to their interests and ideals, the old idea of the sovereignty of the State is destroyed. The State is reduced to the homely work of an instrument for carrying out popular policies. If revolution is justifiable, a State may be even criminal sometimes in resisting its own extinction. The sovereignty of the people is no mere phrase. It is a direct challenge to the historic tradition of the State. For it implies that the ultimate sanctity resides not in the State at all or in its agent, the government, but in the nation, that is, in the country viewed as a cultural group and not specifically as a king-dominated herd. The State then becomes a mere instrument, the servant of this popular will, or of the constructive needs of the cultural group. The Revolution had in it, therefore, the makings of a very daring modern experiment—the founding of a free nation which should use the State to effect its vast purposes of subduing a continent just as the colonists' armies had used arms to detach their society from the irresponsible rule of an overseas king and his frivolous ministers. The history of the State might have ended in 1776 as far as the American colonies were concerned, and the modern nation which is still striving to materialize itself have been born.

For a while it seemed almost as if the State were dead. But men who are freed rarely know what to do with their liberty. In each colony the fatal seed of the State had been sown; it could not disappear. Rival prestiges and interests began to make themselves felt. Fear of foreign States, economic distress, discord between classes, the inevitable physical exhaustion and prostration of idealism which follows a protracted war—all combined to put the responsible classes of the new States into the mood for a regression to the State ideal. Ostensibly there is no reason why the mere lack of a centralized State should have destroyed the possibility of progress in the new liberated America, provided the interstate jelousy and rivalry could have been destroyed. But there were no leaders for this anti-State nationalism. The sentiments of the Declaration remained mere sentiments. No constructive political scheme was built on them. The State ideal, on the other hand, had ambitious leaders of the financial classes, who saw in the excessive decentralization of the Confederation too much opportunity for the control of society by the democratic lower-class elements. They were menaced by imperialistic powers without and by democracy within. Through their fear of the former they tended to exaggerate the impossibility of the latter. There was no inclination to make the new State a school where democratic experiments could be worked out as they should be. They were unwilling to give reconstruction the term that might have been necessary to build up this truly democratic nationalism. Six years is a short time to reconstruct an agricultural country devastated by a six-year war. The popular elements in the new States had time only to show their turbulence; they were given no time to grow. The ambitious leaders of the financial classes got a convention called to discuss the controversies and maladjustments of the States, which were making them clamor for a revision of the Articles of Confederation, and then, by one of the most successful *coups d'état* in history, turned their assembly into the manufacture of a new government on the strongest lines of the old State ideal.

This new constitution, manufactured in secret session by the leaders of the propertied and ruling classes, was then submitted to an approval of the electors which only by the most expert manipulation was obtained, but which was sufficient to override the indignant undercurrent of protest from those popular elements who saw the fruits of the Revolution slipping away from them. Universal suffrage would have killed it forever. Had the liberated colonies had the advantage of the French experience before them, the promulgation of the Constitution would undoubtedly have been followed by a new revolution, as very nearly happened later against Washington and the Federalists. But the ironical ineptitude of Fate put the machinery of the new Federalist constitutional government in operation just at the moment that the French Revolution began, and by the time those great waves of Jacobin feeling reached North America, the new Federalist State was firmly enough on its course to weather the gale and the turmoil.

The new State was therefore not the happy political symbol of a united people, who in order to form a more perfect union, etc., but the imposition of a State on a loose and growing nationalism, which was in a condition of unstable equilibrium and needed perhaps only to be fertilized from abroad to develop a genuine political experiment in democracy. The preamble to the Constitution, as was soon shown in the hostile popular vote and later in the revolt against the Federalists, was a pious hope rather than actuality, a blessedness to be realized when by the force of government pressure, the creation of idealism, and mere social habit, the population should be welded and kneaded into a State. That this is what has actually happened is seen in the fact that the somewhat shockingly undemocratic origins of the American State have been almost completely glossed over and the unveiling is bitterly resented, by none so bitterly as the significant classes who have been most industrious in cultivating patriotic myth and legend. American history, as far as it has entered into the general popular emotion, runs along this line: The Colonies were freed by the Revolution from a tyrannous King and became free and independent States; there follow six years of impotent peace, during which the Colonies quarrel among themselves and reveal the hopeless weakness of the principle under which they are working together; in desperation the people then create a new instrument, and launch a free and democratic republic, which was and remains—especially since it withstood the shock of civil war—the most perfect form of democratic government known to man, perfectly adequate to be promulgated as an example in the twentieth century to all people, and to be spread by propaganda, and, if necessary, the sword, in all unregenerately Imperial regions.

Modern historians reveal the avowedly undemocratic personnel and opinions of the Convention. They show that the members not only had an unconscious economic interest but a frank political interest in founding a State which should protect the propertied classes against the hostility of the people. They show how, from one point of view, the new government became almost a mechanism for overcoming the repudiation of debts, for putting back into their place a farmer and small trader class whom the unsettled times of reconstruction had threatened to liberate, for reestablishing on the securest basis of the sanctity of property and the State, their class supremacy menaced by a democracy that had drunk too deeply at the fount of Revolution. But all this makes little impression on the other legend of the popular mind, because it disturbs the sense of the sanctity of the State, and it is this rock to which the herd-wish must cling.

Every little schoolboy is trained to recite the weaknesses and inefficiencies of the Articles of Confederation. It is taken as axiomatic that under them the new nation was falling into anarchy and was only saved by the wisdom and energy of the Convention. These hapless articles have had to bear the infamy cast upon the untried by the radiantly successful. The nation had to be strong to repel invasion, strong to pay to the last loved copper penny the debts of the propertied and the provident ones, strong to keep the unpropertied and improvident from ever using the government to ensure their own prosperity at the expense of moneyed capital. Under the Articles the new States were obviously trying to reconstruct themselves in an alarming tenderness for the common man impoverished by the war. No one suggests that the anxiety of the leaders of the heretofore unquestioned ruling classes desired the revision of the Articles and labored so weightily over a new instrument not because the nation was failing under the Articles but because it was succeeding only too well. Without intervention from the leaders, reconstruction threatened in time to turn the new nation into an agrarian and proletarian democracy. It is impossible to predict what would have been worked out in time, whether the democratic idealism implicit in the Declaration of Independence would have materialized into a form of society very much modified from the ancient State. All we know is that at a time when the current of political progress was in the direction of agrarian and proletarian democracy, a force hostile to it gripped the nation and imposed upon it a powerful form against which it was never to succeed in doing more than blindly struggle. The liberating virus of the Revolution was definitely expunged, and henceforth if it worked at all it had to work against the State, in opposition to the armed and respectable power of the nation.

The propertied classes, seated firmly in the saddle by their Constitutional *coup d'état* have, of course, never lost their ascendancy. The particular group of Federalists who had engineered the new machinery and enjoyed the privilege of setting it in motion, were turned out in a dozen years by the "Jeffersonian democracy" whom their manner had so deeply offended. But the Jeffersonian democracy never meant in practice any more than the substitution of the rule of the country gentleman for the rule of the town capitalist. The true hostility between their interests was small as compared with the hostility of both toward the common man. When both were swept away by the irruption of the western democracy under Andrew Jackson and the rule of the common man appeared for a while in its least desirable forms, it was comparatively easy for the two propertied classes to form a tacit coalition against them. The new West achieved an extension of suffrage and a jovial sense of having come politically into its own, but the rule of the ancient classes was not seriously challenged. Their squabbles over the tariff were family affairs, for the tariff could not materially affect the common man of either East or West. The eastern and northern capitalists soon saw the advantage of supporting southern country-gentleman slave power as against the free-soil pioneer. Bad generalship on the part of this coalition allowed a western free-soil minority President to slip into office and brought on the Civil War, which smashed the slave power and left northern capital in undisputed possession of a field against which the pioneer could make only sporadic and ineffective revolts.

From the Civil War to the death of Mark Hanna, the propertied capitalist industrial classes ran a triumphal career in possession of the State. At various times, as in 1896, the country had to be saved for them from disillusioned, rebellious hordes of small farmers and traders and democratic idealists, who had in the overflow of prosperity been squeezed down into the small end of the horn. But except for these occasional menaces, business, that is to say, aggressive expansionist capitalism, had nearly forty years in which to direct the American republic as a private preserve, or laboratory, experimenting, developing, wasting, subjugating, to its heart's content, in the midst of a vast somnolence of complacency such as has never been seen and contrasts strangely with the spiritual dissent and constructive revolutionary thought which went on at the same time in England and the Continent.

That era ended in 1904 like the crack of doom, which woke a

whole people into a modern day which they had far overslept, and for which they had no guiding principles or philosophy to conduct them about. They suddenly became acutely and painfully aware of the evils of the society in which they had slumbered and they snatched at one after the other idea, program, movement, ideal, to uplift them out of the slough in which they had slept. The glory of those shining figures—captains of industry—went out in a sulphuric gloom. The head of the State, who made up in dogmatism what he lacked in philosophy, increased the confusion by reviving the Ten Commandments for political purposes, and belaboring the wicked with them. The American world tossed in a state of doubt, of reawakened social conscience, of pragmatic effort for the salvation of society. The ruling classes—annoyed, bewildered, harassed—pretended with much bemoaning that they were losing their grip on the State. Their inspired prophets uttered solemn warnings against political novelty and the abandonment of the tried and tested fruits of experience.

These classes actually had little to fear. A political system which had been founded in the interests of property by their own spiritual and economic ancestors, which had become ingrained in the country's life through a function of 120 years, which was buttressed by a legal system which went back without a break to the early English monarchy was not likely to crumble before the anger of a few muckrakers, the disillusionment of a few radical sociologists, or the assaults of proletarian minorities. Those who bided their time through the Taft interregnum, which merely continued the Presidency until there could be found a statesman to fill it, were rewarded by the appearance of the exigency of a war in which business organization was imperatively needed. They were thus able to make a neat and almost noiseless coalition with the Government. The mass of the worried middle classes, riddled by the campaign against American failings, which at times extended almost to a skepticism of the American State itself, were only too glad to sink back to a glorification of the State ideal, to feel about them in war the old protecting arms, to return to the old primitive robust sense of the omnipotence of the State, its matchless virtue, honor, and beauty, driving away all the foul old doubts and dismays.

That the same class which imposed its Constitution on the

nascent proletarian and agrarian democracy has maintained itself to this day indicates how slight was the real effect of the
Revolution. When that political change was consolidated in the
new government, it was found that there had been a mere transfer of ruling-class power across the seas, or rather that a ruling
commercial class in the colonies had been able to remove
through a war fought largely by the masses a vexatious over-
lordship of the irresponsible coterie of ministers that surrounded
George III. The colonies merely exchanged a system run in the
interest of the overseas trade of English wealth for a system run
in the interest of New England and Philadelphia merchanthood,
and later of southern slavocracy. The daring innovation of get-
ing rid of a King and setting up a kingless State did not apparently impress the hardheaded farmers and small traders with as
much force as it has their patriotic defenders. The animus of the
Convention was so obviously monarchical that any executive
they devised could be only a very thinly disguised king. The
compromise by which the presidency was created proved but to
be the means by which very nearly the whole mass of traditional
royal prerogatives was brought over and lodged in the new
State.

The President is an elected King, but the fact that he is
elected has proved to be of far less significance in the course of
political evolution than the fact that he is pragmatically a king. It
was the intention of the founders of the Constitution that he be
elected by a small body of notables, representing the ruling
propertied classes, who could check him up every four years in
a new election. This was no innovation. Kings have often been
selected in this way in European history, and the Roman Em-
peror was regularly chosen by election. That the American President's term was limited merely shows the confidence which the
founders felt in the buttressing force of their instrument. His election would never pass out of the hands of the notables, and so
the office would be guaranteed to be held by a faithful representative of upper-class demands. What he was most obviously
to represent was the interests of that body which elected him,
and not the mass of the people who were still defranchised. For
the new State started with no quixotic belief in universal suffrage. The property qualifications which were in effect in every
colony were continued. Government was frankly a function of
those who held a concrete interest in the public weal, in the

shape of visible property. The responsibility for the security of property rights could safely lie only with those who had something to secure. The "stake" in the commonwealth which those who held office must possess was obviously larger.

One of the larger errors of political insight which the sage founders of the Constitution committed was to assume that the enfranchised watchdogs of property and the public order would remain a homogeneous class. Washington, acting strictly as the mouthpiece of the unified State ideal, deprecated the growth of parties and of factions which horridly keep the State in turbulence or threaten to rend it asunder. But the monarchical and repressive policies of Washington's own friends promptly generated an opposition democratic party representing the landed interests of the ruling classes, and the party system was fastened on the country. By the time the electorate had succeeded in reducing the Electoral College to a mere recorder of the popular vote, or, in other words, had broadened the class of notables to the whole property-holding electorate, the parties were firmly established to carry on the selective and refining and securing work of the Electoral College. The party leadership then became, and has remained ever since, the nucleus of notables who determine the presidency. The electorate, having won an apparently democratic victory in the destruction of the notables, finds itself reduced to the role of mere ratification or selection between two or three candidates, in whose choice they have only a nominal share. The Electoral College which stood between even the propertied electorate and the executive with the prerogatives of a King, gave place to a body which was just as genuinely a bar to democratic expression, and far less responsible for its acts. The nucleus of party councils which became, after the reduction of the Electoral College, the real choosers of the Presidents, were unofficial, quasi-anonymous, utterly unchecked by the populace whose rulers they chose. More or less self-chosen, or chosen by local groups whom they dominated, they provided a far more secure guarantee that the State should remain in the hands of the ruling classes than the old electoral college. The party councils chould be loosely organized entirely outside of the governmental organization, without oversight by the State or check from the electorate. They could be composed of the leaders of the propertied classes themselves or their lieutenants, who could retain their power indefinitely, or at least until they were unseated by rivals within the same charmed domain. They were at least entirely safe from attack by the officially constituted electorate, who, as the party system became more and more firmly established, found they could vote only on the slates set up for them by unknown councils behind an imposing and all-powerful "party."

As soon as this system was organized into a hierarchy extending from national down to state and county politics, it became perfectly safe to broaden the electorate. The clamors of the unpropertied or the less propertied to share in the selection of their democratic republican government could be graciously acceded to without endangering in the least the supremacy of those classes which the founders had meant to be supreme. The minority were now even more effectually protected from the majority than under the old system, however indirect the election might be. The electorate was now reduced to a ratifier of slates, and as a ratifier of slates, or a chooser between two slates, both of which were pledged to upper-class domination, the electorate could have the freest, most universal suffrage, for any mass desire for political change, any determined will to shift the class balance, would be obliged to register itself through the party machinery. It could make no frontal attack on the government. And the party machinery was directly devised to absorb and neutralize this popular shock, handing out to the disgruntled electorate a disguised stone when it asked for political bread, and effectually smashed any third party which ever avariciously tried to reach government except through the regular two-party system.

The party system succeeded, of course, beyond the wildest dreams of its creators. It relegated the founders of the Constitution to the role of doctrinaire theorists, political amateurs. Just because it grew up slowly to meet the needs of ambitious politicians and was not imposed by ruling-class fiat, as was the Constitution, did it have a chance to become assimilated, worked into the political intelligence and instinct of the people, and be adopted gladly and universally as a genuine political form, expressive both of popular need and ruling-class demand. It satisfied the popular demand for democracy. The enormous sense of victory which followed the sweeping away of property qualifications of suffrage, the tangible evidence that now every citizen was participating in public affairs, and that the entire manhood democracy was now self-governing, created a mood of political complacency that lasted uninterruptedly into the twentieth century. The party system was thus the means of removing political grievance from the greater part of the populace, and of giving to the ruling classes the hidden but genuine permanence of control which the Constitution had tried openly to give them. It supplemented and repaired the ineptitudes of the Constitution. It became the unofficial but real government, the instrument which used the Constitution as its instrument.

Only in two cases did the party system seem to lose its grip, was it thrown off its base by the inception of a new party from without—in the elections of Jackson and of Lincoln. Jackson came in as the representative of a new democratic West which had no tradition of suffrage qualifications, and Lincoln as a minority candidate in a time of factional and sectional strife. But the discomfiture of the party politicians was short. The party system proved perfectly capable of assimilating both of these new movements. Jackson's insurrection was soon captured by the old machinery and fed the slavocracy, and Lincoln's party became the property of the new bonanza capitalism. Neither Jackson nor Lincoln made the slightest deflection in the triumphal march of the party system. In practically no other contests has the electorate had for all practical purposes a choice except between two candidates, identical as far as their political role would be as representatives of the significant classes in the State. Campaigns such as Bryan's, where one of the parties is captured by an element which seeks a real transference of power from the significant to the less significant classes, split the party, and sporadic third-party attacks merely throw the scale one way or the other between the big parties, or, if threatening enough, produce a virtual coalition against them. . . .

[1] Of all Bourne's texts, the fragment "The State" exerted the greatest fascination; partly, of course, because it provoked speculation about how Bourne might have ended it, whether in the sense of a Marxist theory of the state or not. It was first published by James Oppenheim in *Untimely Papers* (1919), then by Carl Resek in *War and the Intellectuals* (1964) in a corrected sequence. The present text follows the once-more corrected version by Lillian Schlissel in *The World of Randolph Bourne* (1965).

[2] Compare L. P. Jacks, "The Peacefulness of Being at War," *New Republic*, IV (Sept. 11, 1915).

[3] Compare Maurice Meeterlinch, *L'Oiseau Bleu* (1908)

THE DISILLUSIONMENT:[1]

They told us that war was becoming economically impossible. They said that the great European nations were on the verge of bankruptcy, riding to a colossal fall, for they could neither stop the mad competitive race, nor continue it without having the whole system crash into ruin. They said that the all-powerful coterie of international bankers who held in their hands the leading strings of the nations would never permit their resources to be plundered and their credits shattered by a Welt-Krieg. They showed us indubitably that, in these days of international economic dependence, of inextricably interlacing communications, and financial obligations, the very instinct of self-protection would keep the most belligerent nation from making the suicidal assault upon its own life and prosperity that war would be; that the more the world became one vast market and the more each nation's economic interests became definitely implicated in those of the others, just so much the more unready would be any government that had the welfare and greatness of the nation at heart to cut all these implicating arteries of life and drain its prosperity to death. They showed us conclusively that the most triumphant trampling down of the despised enemy could bring no economic gain to the conqueror, and that the utmost tribute that could be exacted would be more costly and less profitable than the income from the international trade that now flowed voluntarily across the borders.

They said that our world would be saved by the very materiality of our twentieth-century civilization. These lusty nations, with their growing wealth, their love of pleasure, their increasing scorn for ideals, would be unnerved by lease and become ever more averse to the sacrifices of war. The prosperous classes would refuse to sanction offensive war, and luxury, though it might sap our vitality and expose us to the assaults of barbarian invaders, would yet be our salvation from the horrors of internecine war: So that this materiality which seemed to be bruising so many of the world's old lovelinesses, seemed yet to be generating within itself the power to abolish this most hideous of the world's afflictions. If wars did come, however, they were very sure that they could only come as the result of commercial quarrels, and could only be waged where the prospective market seemed worth the cost. The old wars for prestige and territory would give place to competitive commercial wars, but we should be saved from these by business prudence. And we who had bravely accepted the new naturalism and had come to see in the new industrialism the promise of mighty things to be, felt renewed hope. Was it not worth the loss of many old ideals to have received this preventive of this worst of scourges,—war and the grim spectre of war?

They told us that war was becoming physically impossible. The very magnitude of the armaments was making their employment hazardous. It seemed incredible that any modern government would take the initiative of letting loose these incalculable engines of destruction. The more formidable and complicated the armaments became, the safer were we in reality from their use. The invention of the submarine, the aeroplane, the mine, the meeting of each new and menacing form of attack by some ingenious counter-stroke of defense seemed an ever-growing guarantee of armed peace. Science with its inexhaustible fecundity of invention seemed actually to be lifting the war-game to a level where only supermen could play it. Slowly the bristling navies and ports began to take on for us the aspect of mere symbols. Perpetually waiting, they became for our imaginations, frozen symbols of power, grim, menacing and tragically costly, yet little more than graphic expressions, in a language that all the world could understand, of the strength and prestige of the nations. For their utilization the world was beginning to lose its imagination. Genuine military ardor was becoming transformed into childish pleasure in the spectacle of parade and manoeuvre, and even that delight seemed to be flagging. In the sentiment of the people, war was beginning to become almost physically unthinkable.

And they said—and here we believed them with an enthusiastic belief—that war was becoming morally impossible. The nations, armed to the teeth, disclaimed nevertheless any offensive intention. Hypocritical as this might seem, it was yet the tribute which vice pays to virtue, and gave evidence that militarism was being placed on the defensive. After the recent wars—the Spanish-American, the Boer War, the Tripolitan—we seemed to see a slow canker of remorse spread over the victorious country. The victors tried to forget what they had done. Offensive war began to feel the need of apologies to itself.

They pointed to the vast growth of international travel and intellectual intercourse; this continued interest and mutual contact, stimulated by so many varying motives, could only produce an understanding and sympathy that would make it ever more difficult for the most warlike of governments to set their peoples at each other's throats. The "international mind" was becoming more and more universal, so that an inter-European war would be dreaded with the horror of a civil conflict.

There was the Peace propaganda, which could not have extended so rapidly if the world had not been well disposed towards peace. There was the Hague Court and the Commissions for international arbitration, and it seemed incredible that the sentiment of the nations would not crystallize about these institutions, functioning, ready, suggestive. There was the growing body of international law, and the steady growth of an international public opinion, which should keep the nations to their obligations through the fear of ostracism in the same way that individuals are kept to their orderly track in society. No nations would dare, men said, risk the universal condemnation that would be visited upon the initiator of a world-war. They said, and we almost believed, that a new international morality was arising with a social control of the national sentiments through the agency of customs, agreements and the pressure of opinion. This new morality had only to be codified to become the constitution of a veritable Federation of the World.

We saw crises arise whose causes we could discern as economic, whose lines we could clearly trace as in harmony with the predicted motives of twentieth-century warfare. We saw these crises—Morocco, Persis, Turkey—settled through peaceful diplomatic negotiation. We watched the universal sobriety and restraint in the midst of the Balkan crises, and we saw the dawning of a new day in this imperturbability of the great Powers, while all Southeastern Europe was being devasted. We seemed to see in all this a symptom of the growing avoidance of war, a guarantee that the governments were desirous of preventing war at any cost. We came to believe almost that it was true, as the nations said, that these vast armaments were mainly preventive, a costly form of insurance, until the machinery of international relations was perfected. All the moral sense of the world seemed to be drawing away from war.

But mostly we relied on the organized working-classes of Europe to tie the hands of those who would menace world-peace. The peace movement might be the work of sentimentalists, out of touch with the grim realities of life, a literary expression of mere hopes and ideals, with no attitude strongly rooted in the war of classes and the economic maladjustments of society. But the international Socialist movement, with its record of revolutions and battles behind it, faced with clearest eye and steadiest head the militaristic state—the common enemy of all workers and democrats, no matter under what patriotic shibboleth of "nationality" it paraded. Eternal war against war: If the "bourgeois" States fought, it would have to be without the proletariat. It was to throw off the chains of war that the workers of the world were to unite; while the governments were brandishing their arms, the rank and file of the working-classes would be fraternising with the "enemy." Militarism would be impotent in the grip of this world-shaking international brotherhood. The general strike would beat the warring governments to their knees. We were to be saved by these cohorts of the battle-line of society, who would free the world from the menace of war at the same time that they freed themselves from the domination of the capitalisitic State. In their freedom we were all to be free.

All this menacing "armed camp" of Europe I had just been seeing with my own eyes, and had taken renewed hope in finding it bristle in less sharply defined lines when viewed nearly. In England I had watched the persistent hostility to Compulsory Service, the gnawing compunction at the Boer War, the subsidence of the panic over German invasion. In France I had seen the unyielding opposition to the new three years' military service, the superb irony of the journals over the Zabern affair, the strong resistive tendency to the new note of chauvinism and "*revanche*." In Italy I had seen the wild outburst of reaction against the Tripolitan War, which culminated in the general strike. And even in Germany all the talk had been of defense against some gigantic slow-moving Slavic pressure and invasion, and not of the blatant world-defiance that I had expected. The ceaseless machinery and preparing went on everywhere, it is true; uniforms sprinkled the sidewalks, wagon-trains littered the streets. But never had press and people seemed so soothing. Was I deluded into feeling everywhere a vast overspreading weariness for war and for all this ceaseless soaring preparation? This lulling quietude of the peoples that seemed to augur a gradual emergence from the black nightmare that had weighed for so long a time—was it nothing but the last breathless hush before the impending horror? And what a deluded fancy that all these colossal armaments were perhaps a necessary stage in the development of our civilization in order that their very excesses might weary and disgust men with the whole idea of war, and it might consume itself in the slow fire of the peoples' own contempt!

But all Europe seemed to be on the verge of a Twentieth-century Renaissance. Regeneration seemed to be everywhere at hand. The pessimism and restlessness of the Weltschmerz seemed to have given place everywhere to an outburst of elan. Everywhere a vast impatience with the old mean ways of living, an anger at squalor and muddle. Everywhere an outburst of expansion, a discontent with the shabbiness that we in America still so complacently suffer; a desire for more air, more light, more expression: The new passion for social reform in England, the disgust with the old cramped and festering cities; in France the new morality, the new passion for athletics, the campaign against the sapping national vices; in Italy the outburst of democratic and idealistic expression, freed from the old trammels of Northern conceptualism, the industrial energy, the projects of social reform; in Germany the passion for order and cleanliness and diffused well-being and the astonishing splendor and originality of the new architecture and household art which, in its contrast with the deadly depression of the age of the first scientific and industrial advance, is so telling a symbol of the new rejuvenation of taste and endeavor. It seemed to see all lines conveying towards a civilization of this century, opulent, free, daring, and clear-sighted, set on a basis of material prosperity and scientific control of resources that was to develop gradually a state of diffused well-being far beyond what the world had ever hoped.

War on squalor and ugliness was being waged on every hand. The amazing development of civic art, town-planning, the brilliant and fecund progress of industrial and decorative arts, all the more impressive against the degradation of painting and music, seemed to mean the establishment of new social values and social taste. And taste is, after all, the only morality.

Certain long-fought-for values seemed to have been definitely won—sex-equality, freedom of speech, secular control of education. In every country the ecclesiastical power had been mortally defeated and was in full retreat. But the new years of the century were not a mere working out of the tendencies of the old. There were new ideals, new philosophies, new sensitivenesses. Both the old Christian civilization, with its taint of defeat and sacrifice, and the new scientific civilization with its hard and uninspired crassness seemed to be giving way to a new social and pragmatic civilization with direction and purpose and élan. Something in the early years of the twentieth century seemed to have suddenly opened the eyes of Europe on an infinitely wider horizon. The fight with the old was not over, but men believed they had found the track, and began to press forward with conviction and courage.

But along that track they had not gone far enough to spike the guns of that Welt-Krieg which should sureliest check or even wreck that budding civilization whose inspiration and hope we were beginning to feel.

For the collapse has come, crashing down across the full swing of our beliefs and hopes. Just as men were ready to believe that it was all a dreary hallucination, the spectre assumed horrible form and precipitated all its ghastly horror upon them. No power on earth can put us back now into those golden hours each of which made us less ready to believe that the horror would ever be upon us. In those first sickening moments, the long vista of the forty years of militarism, which had seemed the heavy, straining emergence from a nightmare towards peace in a rational world, loomed up in their true light as years of breathless waiting for the blow to fall. In the torpor that militarism had thrown upon the world, the social reform and the achievements of the new civilization had been things wrested by main force from the power that was dragging down towards hell. They began now to assume the guise of the audacious challenges of a Prometheus in the face of inevitable despair. Was the gasp that went up from the world one of relief at the snapping of the intolerable tension, which we ourselves had struggled against feeling, because we had not wanted to feel it?

In the first shock of disillusionment, when the world seemed to turn black and sick around us, all this civilization that we had been so hopefully watching, turned a ghastly mockery in the presence of this grim superhuman power, so eternal, so indomitable. Once more we had to learn that it had conquered. We had to taste all the bitterness of the truth that this incredible, which everybody feared and nobody expected, had happened. The precise combination of all the evil coincidences had occurred, and in the presence of the opportunity, this militarism, which for forty years had been playing with the fate of nations was to be like adamant against all those human and rational considerations that our hopes and good wills had been creating below it. One had only to hear the Kaiser speak to "his people" on that historic day in Berlin, and see that sinister, helmeted figure, the very personification of nonhuman, irrational force, to realize how little weight all those notions of personal, social, or even national welfare would have against the grandiose ideals of prestige, aggrandizement, and imperialism incarnated in him. We realized with a shock that all through the years of this blossoming new civilization there had been left—either through negligence or fear or ignorance—in control of the destinies of great peoples powers which had their roots in ages that considered death more glorious than life, empty honor more desirable than material well-being, conquest and destruction more splendid than conservation. The nations had allowed themselves to be left in the clutch of topsy-turvey valuations that rated all these things that we considered precious and desirable—the prosperity and wealth, spiritual and material, of the countries—as mere ammunition and rations for predatory war rather than anything in themselves excellent and life-enhancing.

We had not really believed that there existed in the world an initiative capable of willing the World War, and we had to learn not only that there was such a power, but also the persistent ruthlessness of its initiative. Living in a world that seemed to have been removed so materially from the edge of urgency, we had to learn anew of the infinite resourcefulness of desperate men. We had to learn that in the antique topsy-turvey valuation that obsessed the Emperors economic prudences would weigh no more than would social ideals. The delicate structure of international finance and credit would be brushed contemptuously aside like cobwebs, while they went direct to the material resources of their countries, which they were prepared to drain and bleed to the point of exhaustion.

No sordid question of cost or even gain seemed to have tainted the initiative in this most irrational of all wars. No arguments or appeals that the modern world could present would be of any avail, for the archaic international military caste is not of this world. It is as unchanging as the Church. Its rules are as eternal as the dogmas of the creed. It knows no morality except the few rules it lays down for war. It takes seriously no life but that mad welter of the last extremities, the last violences, the last desperations that is war.

Our fallacy in trusting to either labor or capital to save civilized Europe from a world-war lay in ignoring the isolated persistence of this third power—the military caste, to whom both were merely means to an end, the one as food for powder, the other as sinews of war. The *Défaillance* of one was no worse than the other. In our disillusionment and chagrin, we must recognize that the attitudes of the Socialists and of the Great-Illusionists were equally sentimental. While they were educating the people, the Emperors were drilling their soldiers. Proletarians, bankers, scientists, poets, business men—all the numberless classes that did not want war—these had the sentiments. The Emperors had the guns.

Yet this is no time to talk about responsibility, futile enough in any case after the mischief is done. The world always loves the task and feels that it has done something when it has fixed responsibility. What were all those wearisome, diplomatic negotiations which pretended to have as their aim the prevention of a war that was inevitable, but the attempt of every party to push off a measure of responsibility upon everybody else? And each succeeded in driving everybody into a position of defending the Fatherland. What a bitter irony that all should have been drawn into a conflict in which all were on the defensive! Responsibility lies always on the shoulders of those who failed to prevent. Here it lies upon the cowardly middle classes who failed to curb militarism. Oh, they had their chance—in France, in Germany! But always after a little bluster, they yielded and postponed the inevitable issue. European intellect and commerce, science and religion, are paying and will pay in bitter tears for their faint-hearted negligence in leaving mediaeval constitutions thrashing about loose in a modern world.

In our first disillusionment, as we struggled to rally and interpose some protection against this universal shattering, we asked ourselves—"What has gone down in the crash? What may we hope will survive?"

There has gone down with so many ideals all that complacent nineteenth-century philosophy of progress upon which the peace movement was based, that illusion, which has hallucinated us so long, that the world is moving in solid phalanx onward and upward forever. We must learn the stern truth now that there is no such thing as automatic progress, that determinism is perhaps nowhere so ridiculous a theory as when used in interpretations of society. We have been obsessed with Evolution, Moral Evolution, Political Evolution. We had believed that a certain level had been reached, that permanent acquisitions had been made, that they had been rendered relatively safe. This colossal shock has opened our eyes to the instability of our world of today. Neither in political nor moral nor social values were we safely secured. Where the world improves—we must learn—it improves in spots. It is a kaleidoscope where the same elements make strangely different combinations and a movement disarranges the pattern. "Progress" is always local, empirical. It is always on the defensive. The keynote of social "progress" is not evolution but the overlapping of the generations, with their stains and traces of the past; it is the struggle of the old to conserve, of the new to adapt.

All this our disillusionment has taught us, and in addition that morality is not a mere acquirement but the reflecting of situations, and that men who are fighting for their lives and believe they are being betrayed will become savages, even in the midst of civilization. It is to the situations that we must look, and not expect amiable sentiments to guarantee the world. The collapse of the peace movement will teach the world at heavy cost the folly of expecting sentiment to do the work of organized machinery or to compete with it. Men will behave well when their environment tempts them to behave well, and all the sentiment and good-will in the world will not avail against a power, which, with its hands on the machinery, is able to defy or hypnotize loosely floating "public opinion." If good causes and movements are ever to triumph they must be hard, stern, unyielding. Militarism should have been attacked directly by political means. All the feeble well-wishing of the masses did not hurt it. All the sentiment of the Socialists, millions strong, did not insulate them against that electric thrill of panic and patriotism, which the military caste, with its superior initiative, was able to send through them. Not the least of our disillusionments and chagrins is the realization how thoroughly worsted in the attack upon militarism we have been. Discarded must be the theories and methods of that failure, if never the ideals.

I no longer let my hopes build out bridges of prediction into the future. Military autocracy destroyed, democracy came to its own in Europe? Perhaps. But democracy was already smashingly defeated by the very act of war. Can it rally and seize the leadership in the exhaustion that will surely follow the issue of the war, no matter what it may be? That international Socialist movement which seemed to be approaching its maturity turned out to be in its mere infancy too weak to stand against the old ingrained traditional fears and jealousies, and that insane suspicion of every people that they are living in a world of enemies. The people of Germany seem really to believe that their national existence is threatened. So they attack France and thereby threaten *her* national existence. In the weary circle of reasonings and responsibilities there seems to be no resting-place. And the various democratic elements having implicated themselves in the fight, will not find it easy to disentangle themselves from their unnatural allies. For whichever wins, the democracy of the victorious side will find itself bound with an ally more deadly and genuinely fearful than all the enemies it has been fighting.

The final solution will neither be short nor soon. There are too many old crimes unpunished, too many spoliations unrecompensed, to make this struggle anything but the prelude to a long series of laborious adjustments. There is no indication that the monarchies will learn reason and justice. Again that fearful responsibility of the democracies, and the heartbreak at their momentary defection!

Preparing for the worst outcome, what may we expect? From the prospect of German hegemony, we can at least foreshadow the Pax Romana, with its lulling truce, its shelter for the recuperation of the world, its enforced learning of the ideals of order, neatness, prosperity, to which the British and Latin civilizations seem as yet so relatively indifferent. A Germanized England and France would be an England and France immensely furbished, immensely modernized. Germanization would be the rough massage that would bring the red blood to the surface and a new glow of health to these two nations, which, with all their virtues, show a tendency to falter and fiddle a little in this modern world.

A German defeat or a drawn contest, on the other hand, might be much less decisive. There might be perhaps a sharp reaction from internationalism, a rush to make each country self-sustaining so that the shock of war would not shatter the social system so carefully built up. Will there arise perhaps a sort of Socialistic Nationalism, formed by a coalition between the most virile elements of the governing classes and the Socialist elements, for the purpose of dragooning the individualistic, property-loving middle classes into an intensive cultivation of the national resources, material and spiritual—a regimentation of the nation into an economic independence and an aggressive spiritual self-consciousness, with the paramount ideal of diffused prosperity and intelligence for all?

Either outcome suggests the confident hope that this twentieth-century civilization upon whose threshold we seemed to stand, will, in some fashion, survive. She is not dead, but sleepeth. The currents of the French Revolution and the Industrial Revolution, buried in 1815, worked their way painfully through the debris to the vast expansion of the scientific and democratic age just ended. The longer the war lasts, the more eager will be the heartsick world to restore and revive that life whose infinite impossibilities for a sane, intelligent, forward-springing social welfare it has learned to realize. The very incongruity and unreason of the war into which the world was so suddenly plunged will make all the more strenuous the efforts to put society back on a safe and rational basis. And what we have seen of our new civilization will have convinced the world that it will never be safe until it has learned a high and brave materiality that will demand cleanliness, order, comfort, beauty, and welfare as the indispensable soil in which the virtues of mutual respect, intelligence, and good will may flourish.

All the chaos and suffering will not have been useless if it brings a new seriousness into the heart of western society, teaches it the precariousness of social life, and how incessant must be the struggle against dirt, disease, vulgarity, caste feeling, unreason, if our world is ever to be made a safe place to live in; if it teaches us the insane peril of leaving about loose and omnipotent in the world antiquated institutions to shatter at any moment the order and beauty we are realizing; if it shakes us out of our fatuous complacency of shibboleths and creeds, and makes us long for a clear and radiant civilization as a lover desires his bride. I will have nothing to do with those who would say that such a lesson would justify the war. This is not a world where things are justified. But such reflections may serve to lighten a little these hours of disillusionment and permit us to meet with faith and hope whatever darker hours are yet to come.

[1] This previously unpublished manuscript, written in the form of intellectual stock-taking, is Bourne's most thorough presentation of his early hopes and their coming to nought.

THE ARTIST IN WARTIME

Clement writes novels, plunging ahead, throwing off a dozen sheets a day. I interrupt him in the middle of a sultry April afternoon. He is tacitly grateful, I am tacitly depressed. He is too shockingly industrious. My own days are tantalizing messengers whom I am always running breathlessly to catch, in the hope that they may have some accomplishment for me. But they always leave me behind. Clement's are his slaves. War has not affected their servitude. Today I find him sad. What war could not do to his exuberance, the thought of money has done. He wants reassurance as to the value of Art. When he had finished his work, did he have anything left but a heap of scribbled paper? Would any one remember him? Did his friends who praised have real knowledge and authority? Is greatness only something that happens to the artist after he is dead? If he was great already, how would he ever know it? If his novel sold, it might be because it stirred the very heart of the people? Or it might be because it was only their congenial trash? If it did not sell, it might be because his work was too feeble to be more than still-born. Or it might be that it was so dazzling that it had to wait its slow day of immortality. Who could tell? Even if they praised him astonishingly, behind the scenes Time might be laughing at him through all eternity.

Didn't war make art look like something shaky and filmy? There was the business man. Clement envying the business man! Clement, who built up block by block his massive novel so that America should see that literary art was just as honorable and active a pursuit as banking! But now suppose in cold-blooded business you make six thousand a year. Have you not something wonderfully solid? You can feel it behind you, rounded experience, its own justification, its own reward. Clement glows; I see that six thousand in all its mystical beauty. Money does not haunt you. It suggests no thought of fame. Yet it is your creation. It is yours. And there are no upsetting various judgments about it either. No worry about what people will think of your work. All will agree as to its worth. You do not need eternity's assistance. Only one possible comment, now and forever after—that you had made six thousand. Nothing filmy and shaky about that!

I remind Clement of Arthur Symons, weary with eating the thin air of spiritual love, and of his descent "only the good firm flesh to hold." Clement descending to hold the good firm flesh of money, not for lust of it, but for sheer discontent with art! Why don't you make your six thousand by your novel, I ask him? But this would never do. For you still had your quandary about fame, and you had your guilt of earning money by art. The bedrock you needed was just that irresponsible sense of having done something which your artistic conscience didn't have to approve.

The pale thick sunlight pours in the window and shows up each taudry line of the room. Clement wants me to restore his faith at once. Or else to excuse him, sympathize with his skepticism, console him with the thought perhaps that war has made grey many things that were of deathless import. I have a vision of Clement, as a neatly dressed young business man, "making," with a stern gesture of the arm and a look of infinite decision, that six thousand. The heap of manuscript makes no defensive gesture for art. Rather it seems to cower and shrink. Perhaps art *is* only a heap of scribbled paper. I cannot defend her.

So we go out to walk on the avenue, and the first person we meet is Sebert who turns and idles along with us. Sebert is the ideal *flâneur.* Some call him lazy, but we admire him too much to allow such a word to be used with his graceful flaunting of leisure. He has at least the air of always having important business which he will be about later. At the time you never find him doing anything. Yet he never looks bored with life. You would not take him for a bohemian, for he is too serious and conventional in his looks. And yet you could never mistake him for a business man, for there is a languor about his movements that betrays a slower tempo of the soul. He combines a pleasing poverty with an untedious leisure, avoiding both the responsibility and guilt of wealth and the burden of labor. Sebert is the only person I know who wears the air of freedom. Do you wonder we admire him? If he wrote more we should call him a literary artist. As it is, I always think of him when I hear that slightly priggish phrase. Compared with Clement's bustle, his art is that of the droning bee. Yet when Sebert does get anything printed, it has the air of having been dashed off spontaneously. Yet the quality is there.

Was art a futility? Sebert takes our question with his usual composure, and replies that perhaps it is the war that bothers

Clement. With that he begins to talk about himself. He says that
he has had to do a lot of thinking about the relation of the artist
to the war. He had decided that they are mutually incompatible.
If you are interested in creating and expressing or in what others
create and express, you can't be very much allured by the
wholesale business of destruction. And if you have the artist in
you, it will always seem to you more important to create that
which has to be created than destroy that which has to be destroyed.

"The war has had the strangest perverse effect on me," he
says as we walk along. "When I was younger, my imagination
always took the most belligerent forms in the cause of righteousness. I saw my future to be that of riding at the head of
crusades and revolutions, on a white horse. I was a sort of fusion of Lloyd George, Scott Nearing, and Joan of Arc. I was as
eloquent in my idealism as I was uncompromising in my politics.
I was to be as bold in battle as I was inflaming in my speech. It
never occurred to me that if the world fell into any cataclysm I
would not be in the front ranks, leading the hosts of light to victory. And I admire those who go, believing that they are leading
the hosts of light. Now I don't know whether it is my skepticism or
my timidity or my artistic temperament that makes me walk here
with such equanimity in the sunlight. I am not leading revolutionists against barricades. I am not agitating for the oppressed proletariat. I am not even exciting the liberals of the
world with a plan to end war. Instead I am trying to write a
novel, showing the enticing charm of all the desirable people I
know. I remain in a hibernating state, waiting for the world to
stop its raging, and become interested again, if it ever was
such, in life, liberty, and the pursuit of happiness."

Here Clement gives him a severe look, and says, "And are
you doing nothing in the service of Art? Are you content simply
to hibernate?" He was forgetting how ready he had been to renounce the service of Art himself for the solidity of six thousand
a year.

"No," says Sebert, "not exactly nothing. But the war has made
me a sybarite. I used to have what they call a social conscience, but I can find little trace of it now. I felt keenly my duty
towards society to remove its terrible evils and enlighten its terrible stupidities. In its guilt of littering the world with poverty and

disease and ugliness I suffered too, feeling myself an accomplice in the crime. I was enraged at institutions for not being perfect. Any world which I was brought to live in should be fundamentally perfect, and these deviations maddened me. Yet at bottom I never doubted that these evils of society were committed by well-meaning people, and were errors rather than examples of original sin. They were like the shameful weaknesses of a member of one's family, whom one was always trying to reform. One continued to love even when one was most staggered by the enormity of the offense. And down in one's heart there was even some respect. There was kinship with this world struggling towards improvement and so constantly falling down. Society was in my mind a potentially repentant sinner who in his heart of hearts really wanted to be good.

"Even the war I felt to be a momentary aberration. But as it went on, I realized that, in the eloquent words of Mr. Stuart P. Sherman, man 'at the present moment, with the utmost deliberateness, with all the energy of his will, with all the resources of his intellect, is seeking, in all quarters of the globe, to multiply pain beyond all recorded precedent—pain to the body and pain to the heart—disease, dismemberment and death, to body, mind and spirit.' In view of this fact, I came to feel myself no longer a big brother to society. I have not decided yet whether to call it original sin or insanity, this new affliction of my era. It feels to me more like insanity, based on an almost incurable neurosis of herd-fear. Society turns out to be not a slowly repenting sinner, but a hysterical mob. As long as your friend is struggling with his faults and errors, you feel sympathy rather than pity. He intrigues you, challenges your interest, makes you almost live with him in his absorbing experience. But when his conflicts have proven too much for him and he has really become a lunatic, impossible to argue with, insusceptible any longer to rational appeal, unmoved by the simplest human considerations, then you find your sympathy deserting you. You retain an infinite pity for him, you regret, you grieve, but there is a gulf between you. The things he now, in his delusion, considers it important to do and to say are too alien from what you know to be reasonable and effective. You are lucky if your regret is not shot through at times with a cold disdain. There is a hollow now in your life where your former warm friendly devotion lay. You resent the misfortune which has taken your friend out of your life. If there is hope of his recovery, you can only sit bitterly and helplessly by while the madness runs its course.

"This," says Sebert, as we dodge a screeching taxi, "is the way I feel now about society. This is the way the new era in which I am living affects me. My social conscience no longer operates to make me feel a part of this society. So I turn aside and find life significant where it is exhilarating and amusing. I look around and find almost every institution, every group, every social engine, enthusiastic for this multiplication of pain. I see individuals cooperating, either delightedly or under coercion, in the myriad branches of this enterprise. And my heart turns sour within me. The effect is to send me back to my personal satisfactions with a good conscience that I never had before. If my society insists on engaging itself in what is either destructive or futile, I feel a sort of moral holiday to follow my own pleasurable designs. . . ."

Here, knowing Sebert's harmlessness, I interject—"oh, they can't be very wicked, those pleasurable designs of yours!"

And he frowns a little, and says, "In my social conscience days I used to think almost everything unjustified that took my mind away from the amelioration of society. Now I can cultivate my tastes without being haunted with remorse. I can loaf and speculate freely on the nature of things, follow music and philosophy. I can even get a fierce perverse joy out of idleness and out of my conviction of the corruption of the world. I have time even for the development of certain sins which previously would have seemed to me wasteful and anti-social. My new sybaritism is rather sharply limited, it is true, by my poverty, but in my new sense of the surpassing value of beautiful and living things, I can enjoy with a new keenness and warmth that are in themselves riches. I live in an ivory tower, I know, but it is good ivory, and I have not thrown away the key. With battling armies and intolerant superstitions filling the air to the horizon, I have no more view. Everything of value is within. I owe to this warlike era a new worship of life and beauty. I want to enjoy, and I do get a profound satisfaction from the passing moments with their little freights of happiness. When I feel active and powerful, all I want to do is to write something which will collide with and challenge that enterprise of pain in which the world is engaged. I want. . . ."

But at this point Sebert sees on the other side of the street a brown-haired girl whom he knows, and he forsakes us without another word, intent, as we suppose, upon the exhilaration and little freight of happiness which will be his as he snatches an hour with her from the lunacy of the era. He leaves us a little disturbed. Broken as it was by the roll of motor-buses, the shrieking of horns and our wary skipping over cross-streets, Sebert's discourse has had a certain impressive continuity about it. We are impressed, but are we converted? At least Clement's particular doubts disappear in the face of this scorching egoism. But is it only to leave us with the final crushing evidence as to the futility of the artist in wartime? How could we excuse the terrible contentment of Sebert's aerial convictions? Here is Clement, uneasy and depressed because artistic striving seems useless when the world is engaged in action, either selfishly or with blatant sacrifice. But here is Sebert, pretending to find his artistic conscience exactly in wartime when the world goes about a business in which he has no part.

Is he a fool or a prophet? Is it proof of virility and right feeling to banish all artistic effort or appreciation from the world until a democratic law and order is obtained among the nations? Is Sebert a cold monster, cultivating his miserable little sense, deaf to the colossal demands of the time? Is he a fiend fiddling while civilization burns? Is he a weakling and an incredible spiritual snob, who makes art a reproach? Or is he with his talk about creation and his ivory tower an inspired seer, with the unearthly aim of an early Christian, announcing a new evangel from the caves? Clement and I discuss him yet without avail. Occasionally we shudder at his blasphemies. At times we thrill to his candor. Suppose all the world agreed with him! Would it be safe for anything, even for Sebert himself?

4
PORTRAITS, CRITICISM AND THE ART OF REVIEWING

If our literary criticism is always impelled sooner or later to become social criticism, it is certainly because the future of our literature and art depends upon the wholesale reconstruction of a social life all the elements of which are as if united in a sort of conspiracy against the growth and freedom of the spirit.

VAN WYCK BROOKS

Criticism is the attempt to express that appreciation, constantly conscious, however, of its limitations, and indeed its impossibilities. It is struggling heroically and resolutely up a path to a goal that it knows it will never achieve. And yet somehow that march, predestined as it is to failure, aids countless wayfarers, whose eyes would be otherwise fixed stonily on the ground, to see the vision at the goal and be glad.

RANDOLPH BOURNE

PORTRAITS, CRITICISM AND THE ART OF REVIEWING

Literary criticism in the narrow sense has only a relatively modest share in the total output of Randolph Bourne. This is understandable for he did not look on literature as something distinct from the more inclusive whole of a many-sided national culture. Besides, it was difficult to assign literature a place in the canon of the "social arts." Bourne could certainly experience the immanent esthetic quality of literature, but his ability to judge it by literary categories was considerably more limited. At a very early date, an essay of his published in the *Columbia Monthly* which dealt with Joel E. Spingarn expressed a view concerning the necessary divorce of criticism and literature. He never really revised this position. His ability to reflect on literature thus hinged on his doing so within a more comprehensive and coherent contest. The style of Bourne's reviews therefore expressed a methodically controlled intellectual disposition. In *The Armed Vision*, Stanley Hyman has correctly pointed out that Bourne's critical method belongs to a tradition whose principle it is to bring a considerable amount of knowledge to the subject being discussed. Under the most favorable circumstances, this principle contributes to a fuller understanding of the matter at hand. In the worst case, the subject shrivels; it becomes the isolated occasion for reflections irrelevant to it. To be sure, this was not the way Bourne thought, yet it seems plausible to feel that he was in danger of using such occasions as a springboard for his arguments. For it was not only the previously mentioned intellectual disposition that stamped Bourne's style in his reviews. There was the additional fact that the greater part of the reviews Bourne published in the *Dial* owed their existence to a predicament which had resulted from historical developments. It had become difficult if not impossible to publish other writings of his. His notorious antiwar essays in *The Seven Arts,* the early demise of that journal which was largely their result, and Dewey's hostility caused the editors of the *Dial* to feel—nolens volens—that it was only as a reviewer that Bourne would be acceptable. But as one reads the reviews from this period, it becomes clear that Bourne frequently and successfully freed himself from the straitjacket of political silence. He took certain books as the occasion to say something about the historical conditions which had visibly stamped their origin. The tenor of these reviews was determined by the attempts to understand the consequences of the war and the reactions of the literary intellectuals to it.

If one thinks about the conditions that gave rise to Bourne's literary criticism such as we described them; if one realizes that Bourne came to literature via a detour or, more precisely, returned to it—the first steps of this path are set forth in the posthumously published *The History of a Literary Radical*—the abundance of reflections after his death concerning the possibilities of his further development as a literary critic prove to be projective speculations. The question whether he would have become a sociological or Marxist critic cannot be answered because it raises the issue of a methodological division of labor that was alien to Bourne. This is not to say that he would have been methodologically naive. On the contrary, he frequently criticized impressionistic arguments for being arbitrary. But at least by the time of his dispute with Dewey, he knew that there is also an arbitrariness of vigor.

Bourne was aware that literature, and art generally, cannot be viewed outside of a social context. But what distinguishes him is the insight that while literature and art must be judged immanently, it is also true that they will be understood as little when they are seen as autonomous as when they are judged by normative criteria. For these reasons, Bourne could only evaluate literature by his image of society, in that tension between a condition he found and criticized and one he thought was worth striving for. But at the same time, he insisted that creativity cannot be subsumed under sociological categories. To what extent he felt that that element which resists definition by categories was the real characteristic of successful art and literature; how he saw the relationship between literature, criticism and a general audience is expressed in the sentences: "The artist writes for that imagined audience of perfect comprehenders. . . . The critic must judge for that audience too." The knowledge Bourne brings to the subject ultimately serves that imaginary community of "perfect comprehenders." It is not an end in itself but attempts to introduce the conceptual through contemplation and expression. Although Bourne strongly criticized the arbitrary "I know what I like," he was convinced that it was essential that one's subjectivity come to grips with its object.

This is also apparent in the portraits which testify to both Bourne's capacity for empathy and his ability to maintain a critical distance. It is apparent that his own painful experiences entered into these portraits to some extent, as did his ability to give form to those experiences. Here, subjectivity does not block what it confronts and to which it owes its existence but gives expression to it. "Although Josella no longer speaks to me..." is the beginning of a portrayal in the course of which both the dimensions of subjective reaction and the development of Josella are reconstructed. The style is reminiscent of Bourne's observations on friendship, for in spite of the opening of this portrayal, Josella continues to be surrounded by that aura which arises in a form of implicit conversation and negates the past tense. To speak about Josella is the occasion for reconstructing her as a vis-à-vis so that a dialogue may be continued. To use Bourne's categories: in the medium of the portrayal, Josella is still a "friend" and has not become a pale "type" that belongs to the past.

What distinguishes his own portraiture becomes, for Bourne, the yardstick of criticism. "Sociological Fiction" and "A Little Thing of Brunelleschi's" are examples. In both cases, his objections have the identical structure: there is the attempt to categorize, not the effort of a sensibility to come to terms with the complexity of its object. In one case, we have sociological classification; in the other, the use of the tape measure. In both, the price is the same. The relation to the object is lost. It remains part of a cultural nexus as Bourne described it: "Culture as a living effort, a driving attempt both at sincere expression and at the comprehension of sincere expression wherever it was found."

Sources of first publication

"The History of a Literary Radical"   *Yale Review,* April, 1919
"Mon Amie"   *Atlantic Monthly,* March, 1915

"From an Older Time"	*New Republic,* September, 1916
"Traps for the Unwary"	N.R., May, 1915
"Chivalry and Sin"	Ms.
"An Examination of Eminences"	N.R., supplement, April, 1915
"The Uses of Infallibility"	*Dial,* June, 1917
"The Light Essay"	N.R., April, 1916
"Sociologic Fiction"	N.R., November, 1917
"Pageantry and Social Art"	D., November, 1918
"A Sociological Poet"	D., March, 1918
"A Little Thing of Brunelleschi's"	Ms.
"The American Adventure"	D., December, 1918
"A Vanishing World of Gentility"	*History of a Literary Radical* (1920)
"Karen: A Portrait"	D., November, 1918
"Fergus"	N.R., October, 1917
"Suffrage and Josella"	Ms.
"Theodore Dreiser"	Ms.
"The Art of Theodore Dreiser"	Ms.
"Paul Elmer More"	N.R., October, 1917
"H. L. Mencken"	D., March, 1918

THE HISTORY OF A LITERARY RADICAL[1]

For a man of culture, my friend Miro began his literary career in a singularly unpromising way. Potential statesmen in log-cabins might miraculously come in touch with all the great books of the world, but the days of Miro's young school life were passed in innocence of Homer or Dante or Shakespeare, or any of the other traditional mind-formers of the race. What Miro had for his nourishment, outside the Bible, which was a magical book that you must not drop on the floor, or his school-readers, which were like lightning flashes of unintelligible scenes, was the literature that his playmates lent him—exploits of British soldiers in Spain and the Crimea, the death-defying adventures of young filibusters in Cuba and Nicaragua. Miro gave them a languid perusing, and did not criticize their literary style. Huckleberry Finn and Tom Sawyer somehow eluded him until he had finished college, and no fresher tale of adventure drifted into his complacent home until the era of "Richard Garvel" and "Janice Meredith" sharpened his wits and gave him a vague feeling that there was such a thing as literary art. The classics were stiffly enshrined behind glass doors that were very hard to open—at least Hawthorne and Irving and Thackeray were there, and Tennyson's and Scott's poems—but nobody ever discussed them or looked at them. Miro's busy elders were taken up with the weekly *Outlook* and *Independent* and *Christian Work,* and felt they were doing much for Miro when they provided him and his sister with *St. Nicholas* and *The Youth's Companion.* It was only that Miro saw the black books looking at him accusingly from the case, and a rudimentary conscience, slipping easily over from calvinism to culture, forced him solemnly to grapple with *The Scarlet Letter* or *Marmion.* All he remembers is that the writers of these books he browsed among used a great many words and made a great fuss over shadowy offences and conflicts and passions that did not even stimulate his imagination with sufficient force to cause him to ask his elders what it was all about. Certainly the filibusters were easier.

At school Miro was early impressed with the vast dignity of the literary works and names he was compelled to learn. Shakespeare and Goethe and Dante lifted their plaster heads frowningly above the teacher's, as they perched on shelves about the room. Much was said of the greatness of literature. But the art of phonetics and the complications of grammar swamped Miro's early school years. It was not until he reached the High School that literature began really to assume that sacredness which he

had heretofore felt only for Holy Scripture. His initiation into culture was made almost a religious mystery by the conscientious
and harassed teacher. As the Deadwood Boys and Henty and
David Harum slipped away from Miro's soul in the presence of
Milton's "Comus" and Burke's "On Conciliation," a cultural dev-
outness was engendered in him that never really died. At first it
did not take Miro beyond the stage where your conscience is
strong enough to make you uncomfortable, but not strong
enough to make you do anything about it. Miro did not actually
become an omnivorous reader of great books. But he was filled
with a rich grief that the millions pursued cheap and vulgar fiction instead of the best that has been thought and said in the
world. Miro indiscriminately bought cheap editions of the English
classics and read them with a certain patient uncomprehend-
ingness.

As for the dead classics, they came to Miro from the hands of
his teachers with a prestige even vaster than the books of his
native tongue. No doubt ever entered his head that four years of
Latin and three years of Greek, an hour a day, were the important preparation he needed for his future as an American citizen.
No doubt ever hurt him that the world into which he would pass
would be a world where, as his teacher said, Latin and Greek
were a solace to the aged, a quickener of taste, a refreshment
after manual labor, and a clue to the general knowledge of all
human things. Miro would as soon have doubted the rising of
the sun as have doubted the wisdom of these serious, puckered
women who had the previous manipulation of his cultural upbringing in their charge. Miro was a bright, if a rather vague, little
boy, and a fusion of brightness and docility gave him high
marks in the school where we went together.

No one ever doubted that these marks expressed Miro's assimilation of the books we pored over. But he told me later that
he had never really known what he was studying. Caesar, Virgil,
Cicero, Xenophon, Homer, were veiled and misty experiences to
him. His mind was a moving present, obliterating each day what
it had read the day before, and piercing into a no more com-
prehended future. He could at no time have given any intelligible account of Aeneas's wanderings or what Cicero was really
inveighing against. The *Iliad* was even more obscure. The only
thing which impressed him deeply was an expurgated passage,
which he looked up somewhere else and found to be about

Mars and Venus caught in the golden bed. Caesar seemed to be at war, and Xenophon wandering somewhere in Asia Minor, with about the same lengthiness and hardship as Miro suffered in reading him. The trouble, Miro thought afterwards, was that these books were to his mind flickering lights in a vast jungle of ignorance. He does not remember marvelling at the excessive dullness of the stories themselves. He plodded his faithful way, using them as his conscientious teachers did, as exercises in language. He looked on Virgil and Cicero as essentially problems in disentangling words which had unaccountably gotten into a bizarre order, and in recognizing certain rather amusing and ingenious combinations, known as "constructions." Why these words took so irritating an order Miro never knew, but he always connected the problem with those algebraic puzzles he had elsewhere to unravel. Virgil's words were further complicated by being arranged in lines which one had to "scan." Miro was pleased with the rhythm, and there were stanzas that had a roll of their own. But the inexorable translating that had to go on tore all this fabric of poetry to pieces. His translations were impeccable, but, as he never wrote them down, he had never before his eyes the consecutive story.

Translations Miro never saw. He knew that they were implements of deadly sin that boys used to cheat with. His horror of them was such as a saint might feel towards a parody of the Bible. Just before Miro left school, his sister in a younger class began to read a prose translation of the *Odyssey,* and Miro remembers the scorn with which he looked down on so sneaking an entrance into the temple of light. He knew that not everyone could study Latin and Greek, and he learned to be proud of his knowledge. When at last he had passed his examinations for college—his Latin composition and grammar, his syntax and his sight-reading, and his Greek composition and grammar, his Greek syntax and sight-reading, and his translation of Gallic battles and Anabasian frosts, and Dido's farewell and Cicero's objurgations—his zealous rage did not abate. He even insisted on reading the Bucolics, while he was away on his vacation, and a book or two in the *Odyssey.* His family was a little chilled by his studiousness, but he knew well that he was laying up cultural treasures in heaven, where moth and rust do not corrupt, neither do thieves break through and steal.

Arrived at college, Miro expanded his cultural interests on the approved lines. He read Horace and Plato, Lysias and Terence, impartially, with faithful conscience. Horace was the most exciting because of the parodies that were beginning to appear in the cleverer newspapers. Miro scarcely knew whether to be amused or shocked at "Odi Persicos" or "Integer Vitae" done into current slang. The professors, mild-mannered men who knew their place and kept it, never mentioned these impudent adventures, but for Miro it was the first crack in his Ptolemaic system of reverences. There came a time when his mind began to feel replete, when this heavy pushing through the opaque medium of dead language began to fatigue him. He should have been able to read fluently, but there were always turning up new styles, new constructions, to plague him. Latin became to him like a constant diet of beefsteak, and Greek like a constant diet of fine wheaten bread. They lost their taste. These witty poets and ostentatious orators—what were they all about? The professors knew some history but what did that history mean? Miro found himself surfeited and dissatisfied. He began to look furtively at translations to get some better English than he was able to provide. The hair-splittings of Plato began to bore him when he saw them in crystal-clear English, and not muffled in the original Greek. His apostasy had begun.

It was not much better in his study of English literature. Miro was given a huge anthology, a sort of press-clipping bureau of *belles-lettres,* from Chaucer to Arthur Symons. Under the direction of a professor who was laying out a career for himself as poet—or "modern singer," as he expressed it—the class went briskly through the centuries sampling their genius and tasting the various literary flavors. The enterprise reminded Miro of those books of woolen samples which one looks through when one is to have a suit of clothes made. But in this case, the student did not even have the pleasure of seeing the suit of clothes. All that was expected of him, apparently, was that he become familiar, from these microscopic pieces, with the different textures and patterns. The great writers passed before his mind like figures in a crowded street. There was no time for preferences. Indeed the professor strove diligently to give each writer his just due. How was one to appreciate the great thoughts and the great styles if one began to choose violently between them, or attempted any discrimination on grounds of the peculiar congeniality for one's own soul? Criticism had to spurn such subjectivity, scholarship could not be wilful. The neatly arranged book of "readings," with its medicinal doses of inspiration, became the symbol of Miro's education.

These early years of college did not deprive Miro of his cultural loyalty, but they deadened his appetite. Although almost inconceivably docile, he found himself being bored. He had come from school a serious boy, with more than a touch of priggishness in him, and a vague aspiration to be a "man of letters." He found himself becoming a collector of literary odds-and-ends. If he did not formulate this feeling clearly, he at least knew. He found that the literary life was not as interesting as he had expected. He sought no adventures. When he wrote, it was graceful lyrics or polite criticisms of William Collins or Charles Lamb. These canonized saints of culture still held the field for Miro, however. There was nothing between them and that popular literature of the day that all good men bemoaned. Classic or popular, "highbrow" or "lowbrow," this was the choice, and Miro unquestioningly took the orthodox heaven. In 1912 the most popular of Miro's English professors had never heard of Galsworthy, and another was creating a flurry of scandal in the department by recommending Chesterton to his classes. It would scarcely have been in college that Miro would have learned of an escape from the closed dichotomy of culture. Bored with the "classic," and frozen with horror at the "popular," his career as a man of culture must have come to a dragging end if he had not been suddenly liberated by a chance lecture which he happened to hear while he was home for the holidays.

The literary radical who appeared before the Lyceum Club of Miro's village was none other than Professor William Lyon Phelps, and it is to that evening of cultural audacity Miro thinks he owes all his later emancipation. The lecturer grappled with the "modern novel," and tossed Hardy, Tolstoi, Turgenev, Meredith, even Trollope, into the minds of the charmed audience with such effect that the virgin shelves of the village library were ravished for days to come by the eager minds upon whom these great names dawned for the first time. *Jude the Obscure* and *Resurrection* were of course kept officially away from the vulgar, but Miro managed to find *Smoke* and *Virgin Soil* and *Anna Karenina* and *The Warden* and *A Pair of Blue Eyes* and *The Return of the Native*. Later at college he explored the forbidden realms. It was as if some devout and restless saint had suddenly been introduced to the Apocrypha. A new world was opened to Miro that was neither "classic" nor "popular," and yet which came to one under the most unimpeachable auspices. There was, at first, it is true, an air of illicit adventure about the enterprise. The lecturer who made himself the missionary of such vigorous and piquant doctrine had the air of being a heretic, or at least a boy playing out of school. But Miro himself returned to college a cultural revolutionist. His orthodoxies crumbled. He did not try to reconcile the new with the old. He applied pick and dynamite to the whole structure of the canon. Irony, humor, tragedy, sensuality, suddenly appeared to him as literary qualities in forms that he could understand. They were like oxygen to his soul.

If these qualities were in the books he had been reading, he had never felt them. The expurgated sample-books he had studied had passed too swiftly over the Elizabethans to give him a sense of their lustiness. Miro immersed himself voluptuously in the pessimism of Hardy. He fed on the poignant torture of Tolstoi. While he was reading *Resurrection,* his class in literature was making an "intensive" study of Tennyson. It was too much. Miro rose in revolt. He forswore literary courses forever, dead rituals in which anemic priests mumbled their trite critical commentary. Miro did not know that to naughtier critics even Mr. Phelps might eventually seem a pale and timid Gideon, himself stuck in moral sloughs. He was grateful enough for that blast of trumpets which made his own scholastic walls fall down.

The next stage in Miro's cultural life was one of frank revolt. He became as violent a heretic as he had been docile a believer. Modern novels merely started the rift that widened into modern ideas. The professors were of little use. Indeed, when Miro joined a group of radicals who had started a new college paper, a relentless vendetta began with the teachers. Miro and his friends threw over everything that was mere literature. Social purpose must shine from any writing that was to rouse their enthusiasm. Literary flavor was to be permissible only where it made vivid high and revolutionary thought. Tolstoi became their god, Wells their high priest. Chesterton infuriated them. They wrote violent assaults upon him which began in imitation of his cool paradoxicality and ended in incoherent ravings. There were so many enemies to their new fervor that they scarcely knew where to begin. There were not only the old tables of stone to destroy, but there were new and threatening prophets of the eternal verities who had to be exposed. The nineteenth century which they had studied must be weeded of its nauseous moralists. The instructors consulted together how they might put down the revolt, and bring these sinners back to the faith of cultural scripture.

It was of no avail. In a short time Miro had been converted from an aspiration for the career of a cultivated "man of letters" to a fiery zeal for artistic and literary propaganda in the service of radical ideas. One of the results of this conversion was the discovery that he really had no standards of critical taste. Miro had been reverential so long that he had felt no preferences. Everything that was classic had to be good to him. But now that he had thrown away the books that were stamped with the mark of the classic mint, and was dealing with the raw materials of letters, he had to become a critic and make selection. It was not enough that a book should be radical. Some of the books he read, though impeccably revolutionary as to ideas, were clearly poor as literature. His muffled taste began to assert itself. He found himself impressionable where before he had been only mildly acquisitive. The literature of revolt and free speculation fired him into a state of spiritual explosiveness. All that he read now stood out in brighter colors and in sharper outlines than before. As he reached a better balance, he began to feel the vigor of literary form, the value of sincerity and freshness of style. He began to look for them keenly in everything he read. It was long before Miro realized that enthusiasm not docility had made him critical. He became a little proud of his sensitive and discriminating reactions to the modern and the unsifted.

This pursuit had to take place without any help from the college. After Miro graduated, it is true that it became the fashion to study literature as the record of ideas and not merely as a canon of sacred books to be analyzed, commented upon, and absorbed. But no dent was made upon the system in Miro's time, and, the inventory of English criticism not going beyond Stevenson, no college course went beyond Stevenson. The Elizabethans had been exhumed and fumigated, but the most popular attention went to the gallery of Victorians, who combined moral soundness with literary beauty, and were therefore considered wholesome food for young men. The instructors all remained in the state of reverence which saw all things good that had been immemorially taught. Miro's own teacher was a fragile, earnest young man, whose robuster parents had evidently seized upon his nature as a fortunate pledge of what the family might produce in the way of an intellectual flower that should surpass in culture and gentility the ambitions of his parents. His studiousness, hopeless for his father's career as grocer, had therefore been capitalized into education.

The product now shone forth as one of the most successful and promising younger instructors in the department. He knew his subject. Card-indexes filled his room, covering in detail the works, life, and death of the illustrious persons whom he expounded, as well as everything that had been said about them in the way of appreciation or interpretation. An endless number of lectures and courses could be made from this bountiful store. He never tried to write himself, but he knew all about the different kinds of writing, and when he corrected the boys' themes he knew infallibly what to tell them to avoid. Miro's vagaries scandalized his teacher all the more because during his first year in college Miro had been generally noticed as one with the proper sobriety and scholarly patience to graduate into a similar priestly calling. Miro found scant sympathy in the young man. To the latter, literary studies were a science not an art, and they were to be treated with somewhat the same cold rigor of delimitation and analysis as any other science. Miro felt his teacher's recoil at the idea that literature was significant only as the expression of personality or as interpretation of some social movement. Miro saw how uneasy he became when he was confronted with current literature. It was clear that Miro's slowly growing critical sense had not a counterpart in the scholastic mind.

When Miro and his friends abandoned literary studies, they followed after the teachers of history and philosophy, intellectual arenas of which the literary professor seemed scandalously ignorant. At this ignorance Miro boiled with contempt. Here were the profitable clues that would give meaning to dusty literary scholarship, but the scholars had not the wits to seize them. They lived along, playing what seemed to Miro a rather dreary game, when they were not gaping reverently at ideas and forms which they scarcely had the genuine personality to appreciate. Miro felt once and for all free of these mysteries and reverences. He was to know the world as it has been and as it is. He was to put literature into its proper place, making all "culture" serve its apprenticeship for him as interpretation of things larger than it-self, of the course of individual lives and the great tides of soci-ety.

Miro's later cultural life is not without interest. When he had finished college and his architectural course, and was making headway in his profession, his philosophy of the intellectual life began to straighten itself out. Rapid as his surrender of or-thodoxy had been, it had taken him some time to live down that early education. He found now that he would have to live down his heresies also, and get some coherent system of tastes that was his own and not the fruit of either docility or propaganda zeal.

The old battles that were still going on helped Miro to realize his modern position. It was a queer, musty quarrel, but it was enlisting minds from all classes and of all intellectual fibres. The "classics" were dying hard, as Miro recognized whenever he read, in the magazines, attacks on the "new education." He found that professors were still taken seriously who declared in passion that without the universal study of the Latin language in American schools all conceptions of taste, standards, criticism, the historic sense itself, would vanish from the earth. He found that even as late as 1917 professional men were gathering to-gether in solemn conclave and buttressing the "value of the classics" with testimonials from "successful men" in a variety of vocations. Miro was amused at the fact that the mighty studies once pressed upon him so uncritically should now require, like the patent medicines, testimonials as to their virtue. Bank presi-dents, lawyers, and editors had taken the Latin language regu-larly for years, and had found its effects painless and invigorat-ing. He could not escape the unconscious satire that such plump and prosperous Americans expressed when they thought it admirable to save their cherished intellectual traditions in any such fashion.

Other conservatives Miro saw to be abandoning the line of opposition to science, only to fall back on the line of a defensive against "pseudo-science," as they seemed to call whatever intel-lectual interests had not yet become indubitably reputable. It was a line which would hold them rather strongly for a time, Miro thought, because so many of the cultural revolutionists agreed with them in hating some of these arrogant and mechanical psychologies and sociologies that reduced life to figures or or-

ganisms. But Miro felt also how obstructive was their fight. If the
"classics" had done little for him except hold his mind in an uncomprehending prison, and fetter his spontaneous taste, they
seemed to have done little more for even the thorough scholars.
When professors had devoted scholarly lives to the "classics"
only to exhibit in their own polemics none of the urbanity and
intellectual command which were supposed by the believer
somehow to rub off automatically on the faithful student, Miro
had to conclude an absence of causal connection between the
"classics" and the able modern mind. When, moreover, critical
power or creative literary work became almost extinct among
these defenders of the "old education," Miro felt sure that a revolution was needed in the materials and attitudes of "culture."

The case of the defenders was all the weaker because their
enemies were not wanton infidels, ignorant of the holy places
they profaned. They were rather cultural "Modernists," reforming
the church from within. They had the classic background, these
young vandals, but they had escaped from its flat and un-
oriented surface. Abreast of the newer objective, impersonal
standards of thinking, they saw the weakness of these archaic
minds which could only appeal to vested interests in culture and
testimonials from successful men.

The older critics had long since disavowed the intention of
discriminating among current writers. These men, who had to
have an Academy to protect them, lumped the younger writers
of verse and prose together as "anarchic" and "naturalistic,"
and had become, in these latter days, merely peevish and
querulous, protesting in favor of standards that no longer represented our best values. Every one, in Miro's time, bemoaned
the lack of critics, but the older critics seemed to have lost all
sense of hospitality and to have become tired and a little spite-
fully disconsolate, while the newer ones were too intent on their
crusades against puritanism and philistinism to have time for a
constructive pointing of the way.

Miro had a very real sense of standing at the end of an era.
He and his friends had lived down both their old orthodoxies of
the classics and their new orthodoxies of propaganda. Gone
were the priggishness and self-consciousness which had
marked their teachers. The new culture would be more personal
than the old, but it would not be held as a personal property. It
would be democratic in the sense that it would represent each

person's honest spontaneous taste. The old attitude was only speciously democratic. The assumption was that if you pressed your material long enough and winningly enough upon your culturable public, they would acquire it. But the material was something handed down, not grown in the garden of their own appreciations. Under these conditions the critic and appreciator became a mere impersonal register of orthodox opinion. The cultivated person, in conforming his judgments to what was authoritatively taught him, was really a member of the herd—a cultivated herd, it is true, but still a herd. It was the mass that spoke through the critic and not his own discrimination. These authoritative judgments might, of course, have come—probably had come—to the herd through discerning critics, but in Miro's time judgment in the schools had petrified. One believed not because one felt the original discernment, but because one was impressed by the weight and reputability of opinion. At least so it seemed to Miro.

Now just as the artists had become tired of conventions and were breaking through into new and personal forms, so Miro saw the younger critics breaking through these cultural conventions. To the elders the result would seem mere anarchy. But Miro's attitude did not want to destroy, it merely wanted to rearrange the materials. He wanted no more second-hand appreciations. No one's cultural store was to include anything that one could not be enthusiastic about. One's acquaintance with the best that had been said and thought should be encouraged—in Miro's ideal school—to follow the lines of one's temperament. Miro, having thrown out the old gods, found them slowly and properly coming back to him. Some would always repel him, others he hoped to understand eventually. But if it took wisdom to write the great books, did it not also take wisdom to understand them? Even the Latin writers he hoped to recover, with the aid of translations. But why bother with Greek when you could get Euripides in the marvellous verse of Gilbert Murray? Miro was willing to believe that no education was complete without at least an inoculation of the virus of the two orthodoxies that he was transcending.

As Miro looked around the American scene, he wondered where the critics were to come from. He saw, on the one hand, Mr. Mencken and Mr. Dreiser and their friends, going heavily forth to battle with the Philistines, glorying in pachydermous vulgarisms that hurt the polite and cultivated young men of the old school. And he saw these violent critics, in their rage against puritanism, becoming themselves moralists, with the same bigotry and tastelessness as their enemies. No, these would never do. On the other hand, he saw Mr. Stuart P. Sherman, in his youthful if somewhat belated ardor, revolting so conscientiously against the "naturalism" and crude expression of current efforts that, in his defense of *belles-lettres,* of the fine traditions of literary art, he himself became a moralist of the intensest brand, and as critic plumped for Arnold Bennett, because that clever man had a feeling for the proprieties of human conduct. No, Mr. Sherman would do even less adequately. His fine sympathies were as much out of the current as was the specious classicism of Professor Shorey. He would have to look for the critic among the young men who had an abounding sense of life, as well as a feeling for literary form. They would be men who had not been content to live on their cultural inheritance, but had gone out into the modern world and amassed a fresh fortune of their own. They would be men who were not squeamish, who did not feel the delicate differences between "animal" and "human" conduct, who were enthusiastic about Mark Twain and Gorki as well as Romain Rolland, and at the same time were thrilled by Copeau's theatre.

Where was a better programme for culture, for any kind of literary art? Culture as a living effort, a driving attempt both at sincere expression and at the comprehension of sincere expression wherever it was found! Appreciation to be as far removed from the "I know what I like!" as from the textbook impeccability of taste! If each mind sought its own along these lines, would not many find themselves agreed? Miro insisted on liking Amy Lowell's attempt to outline the tendencies in American poetry in a form which made clear the struggles of contemporary men and women with the tradition and against "every affectation of the mind." He began to see in the new class-consciousness of poets the ending of that old division which "culture" made between the chosen people and the gentiles. We were now to form little pools of workers and appreciators of similar temperaments and tastes. The little magazines that were starting up became voices for these new communities of sentiment. Miro thought that perhaps at first it was right to adopt a tentative superciliousness towards the rest of the world, so that both Mr. Mencken with his shudders at the vulgar Demos and Mr. Sherman with his obsession with the sanely and wholesomely American might be shut out from influence. Instead of fighting the Philistine in the name of freedom, or fighting the vulgar iconoclast in the name of wholesome human notions, it might be better to write for one's own band of comprehenders, in order that one might have something genuine with which to appeal to both the mob of the "bourgeois" and the ferocious vandals who have been dividing the field among them. Far better a quarrel among these intensely self-conscious groups than the issues that have filled *The Atlantic* and *The Nation* with their dreary obsolescence. Far better for the mind that aspired towards "culture" to be told not to conform or worship, but to search out its group, its own temperamental community of sentiment, and there deepen appreciations through sympathetic contact.

It was no longer a question of being hospitable towards the work of other countries. Miro found the whole world open to him, in these days, through the enterprise of publishers. He and his friends felt more sympathetic with certain groups in France and Russia than they did with the variegated "prominent authors" of their own land. Winston Churchill as a novelist came to seem more of an alien than Artzybachev. The fact of culture being international had been followed by a sense of its being. The old cultural attitude had been hospitable enough, but it imported its alien culture in the form of "comparative literature." It was hospitable only in trying to mould its own taste to the orthodox canons abroad. The older American critic was mostly interested in getting the proper rank and reverence for what he borrowed. The new critic will take what suits his community of sentiment. He will want to link up not with the foreign canon, but with that group which is nearest in spirit with the effort he and his friends are making. The American has to work to interpret and portray the life he knows. He cannot be international in the sense that anything but the life in which he is soaked, with its questions and its colors, can be the material for his art. But he can be international—and must be—in the sense that he works with a certain hopeful vision of a "young world," and with certain ideal values upon which the younger men, stained and revolted by war, in all countries are agreeing.

Miro wonders sometimes whether the direction in which he is tending will not bring him around the circle again to a new classicism. The last stage in the history of the man of culture will be that "classic" which he did not understand and which his mind spent its youth in overthrowing. But it will be a classicism far different from that which was so unintelligently handed down to him in the American world. It will be something worked out and lived into. Looking into the future he will have to do what Van Wyck Brooks calls "invent a usable past." Finding little in the American tradition that is not tainted with sweetness and light and burdened with the terrible patronage of bourgeois society, the new classicist will yet rescue Thoreau and Whitman and Mark Twain and try to tap through them a certain eternal human tradition of abounding vitality and moral freedom and so build out the future. If the classic means power with restraint, vitality with harmony, a fusion of intellect and feeling, and a keen sense of the artistic conscience, then the revolutionary world is coming out into the classic. When Miro sees behind the minds of *The Masses* group a desire for form and for expressive beauty, and sees the radicals following Jacques Copeau and reading Chekov, he smiles at the thought of the American critics, young and old, who do not know yet that they are dead.[2]

[1] This autobiographically based text was published post-humously in 1919. A second autobiographical fragment appeared in January, 1920, in *The Dial* under the title "An Autobiographica Chapter."

MON AMIE[1]

I

She was French from the crown of her head to the soles of her feet, but she was of that France which few Americans, I think, know or imagine. She belonged to that France which Jean-Christophe found in his friend Olivier, a world of flashing ideas and enthusiasms, a golden youth of ideals.

She had picked me out for an exchange of conversation, as the custom is, precisely because I had left my name at the Sorbonne as a person who wrote a little. I had put this bait out, as it were, deliberately, with the intention of hooking a mind that cared for a little more than mere chatter, but I had hardly expected to find it in the form of a young girl who, as she told me in her charmingly polished note, was nineteen and had just completed her studies.

These studies formed a useful introduction when she received me in the little old-fashioned apartment in the Batignolles quarter on my first visit. She had made them ever since she was five years old in a wonderful old convent at Bourges; and in the town had lived her grandmother, a very old lady, whom she had gone lovingly to see as often as she could be away from the watchful care of the nuns. In her she had found her real mother, for her parents had been far away in Brittany. When the old lady died, my friend had to face an empty world, and to become acquainted all over again with a mother whom she confessed she found "little sympathetic." But she was a girl of *devoir*, and she would do nothing to wound her.

She told me one afternoon as we took our first walk through the dusky richness of the Musée Cluny, that the shock of death had disclosed to her how fleeting life was, how much she thought of death, and how much she feared it. I used the lustiness of her grandmother's eighty-four years to convince her as to how long she might have to postpone her dread, but her fragile youth seemed already to feel the beating wings about her. As she talked, her expression had all that wistful seriousness of the French face which has not been devitalized by the city, that sense of the nearness of unutterable things which runs, a golden thread, through their poetry. Though she had lived away from Brittany, in her graver moments there was much in her of the patient melancholy of the Breton. For her father's people had been seafolk—not fishermen, but pilots and navigators on those misty and niggardly shores—and the long defeat and ever-trustful suffering was in her blood. She would interpret to me the homely pictures at the Luxembourg which spoke of coast and peasant life; and her beautiful articulateness brought the very soul of France out of the canvases of Cottet and Breton and Carrière. She understood these people.

But she was very various, and, if at first we plumbed together the profoundest depths of her, we soon got into shallower waters. The fluency of her thought outran any foreign medium, and made anything but her flying French impossible. Her meager English had been learned from some curious foreigner with an accent more German than French, and we abandoned it by mutual consent. Our conversation became an exchange of ideas and not of languages. Or rather her mind became the field where I explored at will.

I think I began by assuming a Catholic devotion in her, and implied that her serious outlook on life might lead her into the church. She scoffed unmitigatedly at this. The nuns were not unkindly, she said, but they were hard and narrow and did not care for the theater and for books, which she adored.

She believed in God. *"Et le théâtre!"* I said, which delighted her hugely. But these Christian virtues made unlovely characters and cut one off so painfully from the fascinating moving world of ideas outside. But surely after fourteen years of religious training and Christian care, did she not believe in the Church, its priesthood and its dogmas?

She repudiated her faith with indescribable vivacity. A hardened Anglo-Saxon agnostic would have shown more diffidence in denying his belief in dogma or the Bible. As for the latter, she said, it might do for children of five years. And the cutting sweep of that *"enfants de cinq ans"* afforded me a revealing glimpse of that lucid intelligence with which the French mind cuts through layers and strata of equivocation and compromise.

Most Frenchmen, if they lose their faith, go the swift and logical road to atheism. Her loss was no childish dream or frenzy; she still believed in God. But as for the Church and its priesthood—she told me, with malicious irony, and with the intelligence that erases squeamishness, of a friend of hers who was the daughter of the priest in charge of one of the largest Parisian churches. Would she confess to a member of a priestly caste which thus broke faith? Confession was odious anyway. She had been kept busy in school inventing sins. She would go to church on Easter, but she would not take the Eucharist, though I noticed a charming lapse when she crossed herself with holy water as we entered Notre Dame one day.

Where had she ever got such ideas, shut up in a convent?— Oh, they were all perfectly obvious, were they not? Where would one not get them? This amazing soul of modern France!—which pervades even the walls of convents with its spirit of free criticism and its terrible play of the intelligence; which will examine and ruthlessly cast aside, just as my vibrant, dark-haired, fragile friend was casting aside, without hypocrisy or scruple, whatever ideas do not seem to enhance the clear life to be lived.

II

Accustomed to grope and flounder in the mazes of the intellect, I found her intelligence well-nigh terrifying. I would sit almost helplessly and listen to her sparkle of talk. Her freedom knocked into pieces all my little imagined world of French conventionalities and inhibitions. How could this pale, dignified mother, to whom I was presented as she passed hurriedly through the room one day, allow her to wander so freely about Paris parks and museums with a foreign young man? Her answer came superbly, with a flare of decision which showed me that at least in one spot the eternal conflict of the generations had been settled: "*Je me permets!*"—I allow myself. She gave me to understand that for a while her mother had been difficult, but that there was no longer any question of her "living her life"—*vivre sa vie.* And she really thought that her mother, in releasing her from the useless trammels, had become herself much more of an independent personality. As for my friend, she dared, she took risks, she played with the adventure of life. But she knew what was there.

The motherly Anglo-Saxon frame of mind would come upon me, to see her in the light of a poor ignorant child, filled with fantastic ideals, all so pitifully untested by experience. How ignorant she was of life, and to what pitfalls her daring freedom must expose her in this unregenerate France! I tried and gave it up. As she talked—her glowing eyes, in which ideas seemed to well up brimming with feeling and purpose, saying almost more than her words—she seemed too palpably a symbol of luminous youth, a flaming militant of the younger generation, who by her courage would shrivel up the dangers that so beset the timorous. She was French, and that fact by itself meant that whole layers of equivocation had been cut through, whole sets of intricacies avoided.

In order to get the full shock of her individuality, I took her one afternoon to a model little English tea-room on the rue de Rivoli, where normal Britishers were reading *Punch* and the *Spectator* over their jam and cake. The little flurry of disapprobation and the hostile stare which our appearance elicited from the wellbred families and discreet young men at the tables, the flaring incongruity of her dark, lithe, inscrutable personality in this bland, vacuous British atmosphere, showed mé as could nothing else how hard was the gem-like flame with which she burned.

As we walked in the Luxembourg and along the quays, or sat on the iron chairs in the gardens of the Parc Monceau or the Trocadéro, our friendship became a sort of intellectual orgy. The difficulty of following the pace of her flying tongue and of hammering and beating my own thoughts into the unaccustomed French was fatiguing, but it was the fascinating weariness of exploration. My first idle remarks about God touched off a whole battery of modern ideas. None of the social currents of the day seemed to have passed her by, though she had been immured so long in her sleepy convent at Bourges. She had that same interest and curiosity about other classes and conditions of life which animates us here in America, and the same desire to do something effective against the misery of poverty.

I had teased her a little about her academic, untried ideas, and in grave reproof she told me, one afternoon, as we stood— of all places!—on the porch of the Little Trianon at Versailles, a touching story of a family of the poorest of the Parisian poor, whom she and her mother visited and helped to get work. She did not think charity accomplished very much, and flamed at the word "Socialism," although she had not yet had its program made very clear to her.

But mostly she was feminist—an ardent disciple in that singularly uncomplicated and happy march of the Frenchwomen, already so practically emancipated, toward a definite social recognition of that liberation. The normal French woman, in all but the richer classes, is an economic asset to her country. And economic independence was a cardinal dogma in my friend's faith. She was already taking a secretarial course, in order to ensure her ability to make her living; and she looked forward quite eagerly to a career.

Marriage was in considerable disfavor; it had still the taint of the Church upon it, while the civil marriage seemed, with the only recently surrendered necessary parental consent, to mark the subjection of the younger to the older generation. These barriers were now removed, but the evil savor of the institution lingered on. My friend, like all the French intellectuals, was all for the *"union libre,"* but it would have to be loyal unto death. It was all the more inspiring as an ideal, because it would be perhaps hard to obtain. Men, she was inclined to think, were usually *malhonnête*, but she might find some day a man of complete sympathy and complete loyalty. But she did not care. Life was life, freedom was freedom, and the glory of being a woman in the modern world was enough for her.

The French situation was perhaps quite as bad as it was pictured. Friendship between a girl and a young man was almost impossible. It was that they usually wished to love her. She did not mind them on the streets. The students—oh, the students!—were frightfully annoying; but perhaps one gave a *gifle* and passed rapidly on. Her parents, before she had become genuinely the captain of her soul, had tried to marry her off in the orthodox French way. She had had four proposals. Risking the clean candor of the French soul, I became curious and audacious. So she dramatized for me, without a trace of self-consciousness, a wonderful little scene of provincial manners. The stiff young Frenchman making his stilted offer, her self-possessed reluctance, her final refusal, were given in inimitable style. These incidents, which in the life of a little American *bourgeoise* would have been cries or triumphs, and, at any rate, unutterably hoarded secrets, were given with a cold frankness which showed refreshingly to what insignificance marriage was relegated in her life. She wished, she said, to *vivre sa vie*—to live her life. If marriage fitted in with her living of her life, it might take her. It should never submerge or deflect her. Countless Frenchwomen, in defiance of the strident Anglo-Saxon belief, were able both to keep a household and to earn their own living; and why not she also? She would always be free; and her black eyes burned as they looked out so fearlessly into a world that was to be all hers, because she expected nothing from it.

About this world, she had few illusions. To its worldliness and glitter she showed really a superb indifference. I brutally tried to trap her into a confession that she spurned it only because it might be closed to her through lack of money or prestige. Her eloquent eyes almost slew me with vivacious denial. She despised these "dolls" whose only business in life was to wear clothes. Her own sober black was not affectation, but only her way of showing that she was more than a *poupée*. She did not say it, but I quite appreciated, and I knew well that she knew, how charming a *poupée* she might have made.

Several of her friends were gay and worldly. She spoke of them with charming frankness, touching off, with a tone quite clean of malice, all their little worthlessnesses and futilities. Some of this world, indeed, shaded off into unimaginable *nuances,* but she was wholly aware of its significance. In the inimitable French way, she disdained to use its errors as a lever to elevate her own virtues.

III

Her blazing candor lighted up for me every part of her world. We skirted abysses, but the language helped us wonderfully through. French has worn tracks in so many fields of experience where English blunders either boorishly or sentimentally. French is made for illumination and clear expression; it has kept its purity and crispness and can express, without shamefacedness or bungling, attitudes and interpretations which the Anglo-Saxon fatuously hides.

My friend was dimly sensible of some such contrast. I think she had as much difficulty in making me out as I had in making her out. She was very curious as to how she compared with American girls. She had once met one but had found her, though not a doll, yet not *sympathique* and little understandable. I had to tell my friend how untranslatable she was. The Anglo-Saxon, I had to tell her, was apt to be either a school-child or a middle-aged person. To the first, ideas were strange and disturbing. To the second, they were a nuisance and a bore. I almost assured her that in America she would be considered a quite horrible portent. Her brimming idealism would make everybody uncomfortable. The sensual delight which she took in thinking, the way her ideas were all warmly felt and her feelings luminously expressed, would adapt her badly to a world of school-children and tired business men. I tried to go over for her the girls of her age whom I had known. How charming they were to be sure, but, even when they had ideas, how strangely inarticulate they sometimes were, and, if they were articulate, how pedantic and priggish they seemed to the world about them! And what forests of reticences and exaggerated values there were, and curious illogicalities. How jealous they were of their personalities, and what a suspicious and individualistic guard they kept over their candor and sincerities! I was very gay and perhaps a little cruel.

She listened eagerly, but I think she did not quite understand. If one were not frankly a doll, was not life a great swirl to be grappled with and clarified, and thought and felt about? And as for her personality, the more she gave the more she had. She would take the high risks of friendship.

To cross the seas and come upon my own enthusiasms and ideals vibrating with so intense a glow seemed an amazing fortune. It was like coming upon the same design, tinted in novel and picturesque colors of a finer harmony. In this intellectual flirtation, carried on in *musée* and garden and on quay throughout that cloudless April, I began to suspect some gigantic flattery. Was her enthusiasm sincere, and her clean-cutting ideas, or had she by some subtle intuition anticipated me? Did she think, or was it to be expected of me, that I should fall in love with her? But perhaps there was a touch of the too foreign in her personality. And if I had fallen in love, I know it would not have been with herself. It would have been with the Frenchness of her, and perhaps was. It would have been with the eternal youth of France that she was. For she could never have been so very glowing if France had not been full of her. Her charm and appeal were far broader than herself. It took in all that rare spiritual climate where one absorbs ideas and ideals as the earth drinks in rain.

She was of that young France with its luminous understanding, its personal verve, its light of expression, its way of feeling its ideas and thinking its emotions, its deathless loyalty which betrays only at the clutch of some deeper loyalty. She adored her country and all its mystic values and aspirations. When she heard I was going to Germany, she actually winced with pain. She could scarcely believe it. I fell back at once to the position of a vulgar traveler, visiting even the lands of the barbarians. They were her country's enemies, and some day they would attack. France awaited the onslaught fatalistically. She did not want to be a man, but she wished that they would let women be soldiers. If the war came, however, she would enlist at once as a Red Cross nurse. She thrilled at the thought that perhaps there she could serve to the uttermost.

And the war has come, hot upon her enthusiasms. She must have been long since in the field, either at the army stations, or moving about among the hospitals of Paris, her heart full of pride and pity for the France which she loved and felt so well, and of whose deathless spirit she was, for me, at least, so glowing a symbol.

[1] This portrait describes an acquaintance that Bourne made on his trip to Paris. "Karen," "Sophronisba," and "Suffrage and Josella" are also biographically based presentations whose ambivalence between romanticizing admiration and analytically founded understanding provide an adequate picture of Bourne's relation to women. Also compare "In Search of a Golden Person" in J. A. Moreau op. cit.

KAREN: A PORTRAIT

Karen interested more by what she always seemed about to say and be than by anything she was at the moment. I could never tell whether her inscrutability was deliberate or whether she did not know how to be articulate. When she was pleased she would gaze at you benignly but there was always a slight uneas-iness in the air as if the serenity were only a resultant of tumultuous feelings that were struggling to appreciate the situation. She was always most animated when she was annoyed at you. At those times you could fairly feel the piquant shafts of evilheartedness hitting your body as she contended against your egoism or any of the personal failings that hurt her sense of your fitness. These moments took you into the presence of the sombre irascibility of that northern land from which she came, and you felt her foreignness brush you. Her smooth, fair, parted hair would become bristly and surly; that face, which looked in repose like some Madonna which a Swedish painter would love, took on a flush; green lights glanced from her eyes. She was as inscrutable in anger as she was in her friendliness. You never knew just what strange personal freak of your villainy had set it off, though you often found it ascribed to some boiling fury in your own placid soul. You were not aware of this fury, but her intuition for it made her more inscrutable than ever.

I first met Karen at a state university in the West where she had come for some special work in literature, after a few years of earning her living at browbeaten stenography. She never went to her classes, and I had many long walks with her by the lake. In that somewhat thin intellectual atmosphere of the college, she devoted most of her time to the fine art of personal relations, and as nobody who ever looked at her was not fascinated by her blond inscrutability and curious soft intensity, she had no difficulty in soon enmeshing herself in several nebulous friendships. She told us that she hoped eventually to write novels, but there was never anything to show that her novels unfolded anywhere but in her mind as they interpreted the richly exciting detail of her daily personal contacts. If you asked her about her writings, you became immediately thankful that looks could not slay, and some witch-fearing ancestor crossed himself shudderingly in your soul. Intercourse with Karen was not very concrete. Our innumerable false starts at understanding, the violence and exact quality of my interest, the technique of getting just that smooth and silky rapport between us which she was always anticipating—this seemed to make up the fabric of her thoughts. At that time she was reading mostly George Moore and Henry James, and I think she hoped we would all prove adequate for a subtly interwoven society. This was a little difficult in a group that was proud of its modernities, of its dizzy walking over flimsy generalizations, of its gifts of exploding in shrapnels of epigram. Karen loathed ideas and often quoted George Moore on their hideousness. The mere suggestion of an idea was so likely to destroy the poise of her mood, that conversation became a strategy worth working for. Karen did not think, she felt—in slow, sensuous outlines. You could feel her feelings curiously putting out long streamers at you, and, if you were in the mood, a certain subterranean conversation was not impossible. But if you did not happen to guess her mood, then you quarreled.

When I met Karen, she was twenty-five, and I guessed that she would always be twenty-five. She had personal ideals that she wished for herself, and if you asked what she was thinking about, it was quite likely to be the kind of noble woman she was to be, or feared she would not be, at forty. But she was too insistent upon creating her world in her own image to remain sensitive to the impressions that make for growth. As the story of her life came out, the bitter immigrant journey, the despised house work, the struggle to get an education, the office drudgery, the lack of roots and a place, you came to appreciate this personal cult of Karen's. She was so clearly finer and intenser than the people who had been in the world about her, that her starved soul had to find nourishment where it could. Even if she was insensible to ideas, her soft searching at least allured. It was perhaps her starved condition which made her friendships so subject to sudden disaster. Karen's notes were always a little more brightly intimate than her personal resources were able to support. She seemed to start with a plan of the conversation in her head. If you bungled, and with her little retreats and evasions you were always bungling, you could feel her spirit stamp its feet in vexation. She would plan pleasant soliloquies, and you would find yourself in a fiercely cross-examinatory mood. She loathed your probing of her mood, and parried you in a helpless way which made you feel as if you were tearing tissue. You always seemed with Karen to be in a laboratory of personal relations where priceless things were being discovered, but you felt her more as an alchemist than a modern physicist of the soul, and her method rather that of trial and error than real experiment.

I am quite sure that Karen's system of personal relations was platonic. She never seemed to get beyond that laying of the broad foundation of the Jamesian tone that would have been necessary to make the thing an "affair." She was often lovely and she was not unloved. She was much interested in men, but it was more as co-actors in a personal drama of her own devising than as lovers or even as men. The most she ever hoped for, I think, was to be the sacred fount, and to have her flow copious and manifold. You felt the immense qualifications a man would have to have in the subtleties of rapport to make him even a candidate for loving. For Karen, men seemed to exist only as they brought a touch of ceremonial into their personal relations. I think Karen never quite intended to surround herself with the impenetrable armor of vestal virginity, and yet she did not avoid it. However glowing and mysterious she might look as she lay before the fire in her room, so that to an impatient friend nothing might seem more important than to catch her up warmly in his arms, he would have been an audacious brigand who violated the atmosphere. Karen always so much gave the impression of playing for higher and nobler stakes that no brigand ever appeared. Whether she deluded herself as to what she wanted or whether she had a clearer insight than most women into the predatoriness of my sex, her relations with men were rarely smooth. Caddishness seemed to be breaking out repeatedly in the most unexpected places.

Some of the most serious of my friends got dark inadequacies charged against them by Karen. I was a little in her confidence, but I could rarely gather more than that the men of today had no sensitiveness and were far too coarse for the fine and decent friendships which she spent so much of her time and artistic imagination on arranging for them with herself. I was constantly undergoing, at the hands of Karen, a course of discipline myself, for my ungovernable temper or my various repellant "tones" or my failure to catch just the quality of certain people we discussed. I understood dimly the lucklessness of her "cads." They had perhaps not been urbanely plastic, they had perhaps been impatiently adoring. They had at least not offended in any of the usual ways. She would even forgive them sometimes with surprising suddenness. But she never so far forgot her principles as to let them dictate a mood. She never recognized any of the naïve collisions of men and women.

Karen often seemed keenly to wonder at this unsatisfactoriness of men. She cultivated them, walking always in her magic circle, but they slipped and grew dimmer. She had her fling of feminism towards the end of her year. She left the university to become secretary for a state suffrage leader. Under the stress of public life she became fierce and serious. She abandoned the picturesque peasant costumes which she had affected, and made herself hideous in mannish skirts and waists. She felt the woes of women, and saw everywhere the devilish hand of the exploiting male. If she ever married, she would have a house separate from her husband. She would be no parasite, no man's woman. She spoke of the "human sex," and set up its norms for her acquaintanceships.

When I saw Karen later, however, she was herself again. She had taken up again the tissue of personal relations. But in that reconstituted world all her friends seemed to be women. Her taste of battle had seemed to fortify and enlighten that ancient shrinking; her old annoyance that men should be abruptly different from what she would have them. She was intimate with feminists whose feminism had done little more for their emotional life than to make them acutely conscious of the cloven hoof of the male. Karen, in her brooding way, was able to give this philosophy a far more poetical glamor than any one I knew. Her woman friends adored her, even those who had not acquired that mystic sense of "loyalty to woman" and did not believe that no man was so worthy that he might not be betrayed with impunity. Karen, on her part, adored her friends, and the care that had been spent on unworthy men now went into toning up and making subtle the women around her. She did a great deal for them, and was constantly discovering godlike creatures in shop and street and bringing them in to be mystically mingled with her circle.

Naturally it is Karen's married friends who cause her greatest concern. Eternal vigilance is the price of their salvation from masculine tyranny. In the enemy's country, under at least the nominal yoke, these married girls seem to Karen subjects for her prayer and aid. She has become exquisitely sensitive to any aggressive gestures on the part of these creatures with whom her dear friends have so inexplicably allied themselves, and she is constantly in little subtle intrigues to get the victim free or at least armisticed. She broods over her little circle, inscrutable, vigilant, a true vestal virgin on the sacred hearth of woman. Husbands are doubtless better for that silent enemy whom they see jealously adoring their wives.

Karen still leaves trails of mystery and desire where she goes, but it is as a woman's woman that I see her now, and, I am ashamed to say, ignore her. Men could not be crowded into her Jamesian world and she has solved the problem by obliterating them. She will not live by means of them. Since she does not know how to live with them she lives without them.

FERGUS[1]

My friend Fergus has all the characteristics of genius except the divine fire. The guardian angel who presided at his birth and set in order all his delicate appreciations just forgot to start flowing the creative current. Fergus was born to suffer the pangs of artistic desire without the gushing energy that would have moulded artistic form. It was perhaps difficult enough to produce him as it was. There is much that is clearly impossible about him. His father is a bluff old Irish newspaper compositor, with the obstinately genial air of a man who cannot believe that life will not some day do something for him. His mother is a French-Canadian, jolly and stout, who plays old Irish and French melodies on the harp, and mothers the young Catholic girls of the crowded city neighborhood in which they live. She has the slightly surprised background of never realized prosperity. Fergus is an old child, and moves in the dark little flat, with its green plush furniture, its prints of the Great Commoner and Lake Killarney, its Bible texts of the Holy Name, with the detached condescension of an exiled prince. He is very dark and finely formed, of the type that would be taken for a Spaniard in France and an Italian in Spain, and his manners have the distinction of the born aristocrat.

The influences of that close little Catholic society in which he was brought up he has shed as a duck sheds water. His mother wished him to be a Jesuit. The quickness of his mind, the refinement and hauteur of his manner, intoxicated her with the assurance of his priestly future. His father, however, inclined towards the insurance business. Fergus himself viewed his future with cold disinterestedness. When I first met him he had just emerged from a year of violin study at a music school. The violin had been an escape from the twin horrors that had menaced him. On his parents' anxiety that he "make something of himself" he looked with some disdain. He did, however, feel to a certain extent their chagrin at finding so curious and aristocratic a person in their family, and he allowed himself, with a fine stoicism as of an exiled prince supporting himself until the revolution was crushed and he was reinstated in his possessions, to be buried in an insurance broker's office. At this time he spent his evenings in the dim vaulted reading-room of a public library composing music, or in wandering in the park with his friends, discussing philosophy. His little music notebook and Gomperz's "Greek Thinkers" were rarely out of his hand.

Harmony and counterpoint had not appealed to him at the Conservatory, but now the themes that raced and rocketed through his head compelled him to composition. The bloodless scherzos and allegros which he produced and tried to play for me on his rickety piano had so archaic a flavor as to suggest that Fergus was inventing anew the art of music, somewhat as our childhood is supposed to pass through all the stages of the evolution of the race. As he did not seem to pass beyond a pre-Bachian stage, he began to feel at length, he told me, that there was something lacking in his style. But he was afraid that routine study would dull his inspiration. It was time that he needed, and not instruction. And time was slipping so quickly away. He was twenty-two, and he could not grasp or control it.

When summer was near he came to me with an idea. His office work was insupportable. Even accepting that one dropped eight of the best hours of one's every day into a black and bottomless pit in exchange for the privilege of remaining alive, such a life was almost worse than none. I had friends who were struggling with a large country farm. He wished to offer them his services as farmhand on half-time in exchange for simple board and lodging. Working in the morning, he would have all the rest of his pastoral day for writing music.

Before I could communicate to him my friends' reluctance to this proposal, he told me that his musical inspiration had entirely left him. He was now spending all his spare time in the Art Museum, discovering tastes and delights that he had not known were in him. Why had not some one told him of the joy of sitting and reading Plato in those glowing rooms? The Museum was more significant when I walked in it with Fergus. His gracious bearing almost seemed to please the pictures themselves. He walked as a princely connoisseur through his own historic galleries.

When I saw Fergus next, however, a physical depression had fallen upon him. He had gone into a vegetarian diet and was enfeebling himself with Spartan fare. He was disturbed by loneliness, the erotic world gnawed persistently at him, and all the Muses seemed to have left him. But in his gloominess, in the fine discrimination with which he analyzed his helplessness, in the noble despair with which he faced an insoluble world, he was more aristocratic than ever. He was not like one who had never attained genius, fame, voluptuous passion, riches, he was rather as one who had been bereft of all these things.

Returning last autumn from a year abroad, during which I had not heard a word of Fergus, I found he had turned himself into a professional violin-teacher. The insurance job had passed out, and for a few weeks he had supported himself by playing the organ in a small Catholic church. There was jugglery with his salary, however, and it annoyed him to be so intimate a figure in a ritual to which he could only refer in irony. Priests whose "will to power" background he analyzed to me with Nietzschean fidelity always repelled him.

He was saved from falling back on the industrious parents who had so strangely borne him by an offer to play the harmonium in the orchestra of a fashionable restaurant. To this opportunity of making eighteen dollars a week he had evidently gone with a new and pleasurable sense of the power of wealth. It was easy, he said, but the heat and the lights, the food and the long evening hours fairly nauseated him, and he gave the work up.

All this time, I gathered, his parents had been restive over a certain economic waste. They seemed to feel that his expensive musical education should be capitalized more profitably. His mother had even deplored his lack of ambition. She had explored and had discovered that one made much money as a "vaudeville act." He had obtained a trial at an Upper Bronx moving-picture vaudeville theater. Fergus told me that the nervous girl who had gone on the stage before him had been cut short in the middle of her "Fox-Trot Lullaby," or whatever her song was, by hostile yells from the audience. Fergus himself went on in rather a depressed mood, and hardly did himself justice. He played the Bach air, and a short movement from Brahms. He did not, however, get that rapport with his audience which he felt the successful vaudeville artist should feel. They had not yelled at him, but they had refused to applaud, and the circuit manager had declined to engage him.

After this experience it occurred to Fergus that he liked to teach, and that his training had made him a professional musician. His personality, he felt, was not unfavorable. By beginning modestly he saw no reason why he should not build up a clientele and an honorable competence. When I saw him a week later at the Music Settlement, he told me that there was no longer any doubt that he had found his lifework. His fees are very small and his pupils are exacting. He has practised much besides. He told me the other day that teaching was uninspiring drudgery. He had decided to give it up, and compose songs.

Whenever I see Fergus I have a slight quickening of the sense of life. His rich and rather somber personality makes all ordinary backgrounds tawdry. He knows so exactly what he is doing and what he is feeling. I do not think he reads very much, but he breathes in the air around him certain large aethestic and philosophical ideas. There are many philosophies and many artists, however, that he never heard of and this ignorance of the concrete gives one a fine pleasure of impressing him. One can pour into receptive ears judgments and enthusiasms that have long ago been taken for granted by one's more sophisticated friends. His taste in art as in music is impeccable, and veers strongly to the classics—Rembrandt and the Greeks, as Bach and Beethoven.

Fergus has been in love, but he does not talk much about it. A girl in his words is somewhat dark and inscrutable. She always has something haunting and finely-toned about her, whoever she may be. I always think of the clothed lady in the flowing silks, in Titian's *Sacred and Profane Love.* Yet withal Fergus gives her a touch of the allurement of her nude companion. His reserve, I think, always keeps these persons very dusky and distant. His chastity is a result of his fineness of taste rather than of feeble desire or conscious control. That impersonal passion which descends on people like Fergus in a sultry cloud he tells me he contrives to work off into his violin. I sometimes wonder if a little more of it with a better violin would have made him an artist.

But destiny has just clipped his wings so that he must live a life of noble leisure instead of artistic creation. His unconscious interest is the art of life. Against a background of Harlem flats and stodgy bourgeois prejudices he works out this life of *otium cum dignitate,* calm speculation and artistic appreciation that Nietzsche glorified. On any code that would judge him by the seven dollars a week which is perhaps his average income he looks with cold disdain. He does not demand that the world give him a living. He did not ask to come into it, but being here he will take it with candor. Sometimes I think he is very patient with

life. Probably he is not happy. This is not important. As his candor and his appreciations refresh me, I wonder if the next best
thing to producing works of art is not to be, like Fergus, a work
of art one's self.

---

[1] Bourne spent some time at an artists' colony in Dublin, New Hampshire,
with "Fergus," i. e., Edward Murray, a friend from his Columbia days. There
he also came to know Amy Lowell.

SUFFRAGE AND JOSELLA

Although Josella no longer speaks to me, there was a time when she was my very good friend. She first came across my consciousness during the suffrage campaign of five years ago when she was spending her days assailing frightened barbers and florists and haberdashers in their shops. She was the apparition of woman militant going forth into the arena to wrest the vote from the triumphant male. This was wearying work, and she would fling down her gloves by her fireside, as I stopped for tea, with imprecations upon the obstructive sex against whose stupidity she was wearing out her life. I was accepted at that time because I was less blatant than this tough world with which her political zeal collided. And I liked her integrity and her intensity for the cause. There was something racy in her small Irish head and her harsh metallic tongue. The male world took on a grotesque air when it was seen through her scornful eyes. She overflowed with stories of the fatuous American man, and her truculence became a vivid taste in my world that was too much flavored with the tame piousness of altruistic causes. Not being in business, I was all sympathy for her attacks. It pleased me to see the mangled remains of my well-meaning acquaintances after they had been strained through Josella's intellect. It was instructive to keep seeing my sex as a blundering caste, monopolizing political power only because no one had challenged us. It was refreshing to find a foe who wanted the vote, first, because she was an idealist for woman, and secondly, because she wanted to put the men in a hole.

As the campaigns went on, however, and suffrage was twice defeated in our State, Josella's mood changed. She was working at some not very rewarding position in the organization, and I saw her less often. But now her imprecations were grimmer, her violence had lost its satirical tone. She said the same things but she began to mean them now. She felt a brute wall of male perversity against her, which she was not able to coerce. The times had changed from the gay days when it was a mere matter of accosting shopmen and carrying a banner in a parade. Hope deferred wore rapidly on her nerves. Out came one by one the issues that were making a battleground of Josella's soul. She was the least reticent of women, and she let you see just what votelessness had really done to her through the years.

Josella, it seems, had been one of those belated sheltered daughters who are well on towards thirty before they fling themselves out on the world. For a father she had had a hearty old tyrant who had apparently incarnated in himself all the worst blatancies of drink and women, and who ruled his terrified brood of daughters with the rigor of a Roman patriarch. Women were to know their place, and of all of them it seemed to have been only Josella who didn't. Women were fit for nothing but to weep and adore, and Josella did neither. So the fierce and eager battle raged, and it was partly just because of the sport of warfare that Josella stayed on in her devastating home. To be brutally tyrannized over and yet to be obstreperous was almost as good as to be free and serene. Her father would not hear of educating her beyond the toning-off process of the convent. Her energy had to go into tennis and golf and canoeing and long tramps in the hills. She rebelled against society, and yet she could not help acquiring from her sisters a certain social manner which often made an odd contrast with her truculence. She loathed the foolish ways of woman, the triviality of gossip and "social duties," and yet her own tongue was scandalous and prevalent in our circle, and she entertained with a feverish zest that suggested a secret fascination.

I knew Josella only after she had fled her oppression, but her soul was very patchy and unexpected. Out of that youth of hers she had brought an enthusiasm for men as "good sports," as athletic comrades, as efficiency experts. She loathed them as lovers, as politicians, as artists. They were always infuriating her by passing out of some role in which she had placed them. She had nothing but scorn for sex manifestations, and yet one could at times detect in her a lurking softness for some more than usually humane man. She talked a great deal about ideal human relations, but she was always smashing her own. Her personal ideal seemed to be a union that was at once perfectly eugenic and perfectly platonic. If Josella were ever to take a lover, it would have to be some soft and submissive, yet immensely virile-looking youth, who would be able to alternate rapidly between the platonic comrade and the eugenic mate. He would have to misinterpret her nerves as vitality, her truculence as power, and her egotism as character.

For Josella this last year or two has worked herself into a state where she is a very bad advertisement for feminism. Out of that hectic, tyrannized, frustrated life of hers has come a peculiar code of "loyalty to woman," with the corresponding irresponsibility towards man. Her experience she begins to see as vicariously concentrating the wrongs of her sex. She is intensely vocal about it all, and has become the undisputed high-priestess of a circle. In her protegees, who are striving to become noble women under her experienced tutelage, she inculcates fiercely irrational ideals of "character" and "efficiency" which would turn them into tenth-rate imitations of the most unpleasing types of American business man. On the other hand, she encourages a recklessness in personal relations which would reverse the historic role of wickedness which men have played towards women. It must have been after my protest against some particularly atrocious betrayal of some friend of mine that I was excommunicated. Protest made my feminism suspect. Through my mild philosophy there began to show through the claws of the predatory male. Josella has become a very unfortunate advertisement for feminism. Just when it should convert men she makes it seem hateful and partial. If her feminist friends were wise who are in the vanguard of progress, they would suppress her activities, or at least very frowningly discountenance her codes and philosophies.

But if Josella is the worst prophet for feminism she is the best argument for suffrage. In a State where the twenty-one year-old daughter voted I should suppose that a primitive Roman household such as Josella grew up in would be impossible. Even a whiskied Irish tyrant would get a novel conception of women when he saw politicians bidding for their votes. If Josella had been voting for fifteen years, I think her feminism would not be the queer distorted thing it is. She would scarcely have gotten her chance to develop all those complexes against man's oppressiveness. She might have remained a rebel, but she would have been able too to struggle towards the sense of being a freewoman. Now she is that destructive hybrid, the rebel who is not a freewoman. All her old battles she has to be continually fighting over again. As long as women are without the vote, the old conflict with her tyrant father is as vivid as ever it was. It springs out at her perpetually as a symbol of the general suppression of women, and when she looks at their fruitless struggle to get some dramatic expression of freedom, she is in turn reminded of her own bitter personal experience. So the two interact always breeding more bitterness and more nerves. The more she throws herself into the thwarted fight, the more deranged become her impulses.

Thus I interpret Josella when I am in a philosophic mood. She stands out as a sign of the pathology of woman's votelessness. I remember her personal crimes and my heart hardens. I think of her neurotic outbursts and I am cruel again. But if she had been caught young, would not suffrage have saved her? She must surely have been one of those intense and single-hearted ones for whom the only cure is victory.

THEODORE DREISER[1]

It is becoming more and more embarrassing to read an American novel. Periodically I return to those writers like Robert Herrick, Mrs. Watts, Winston Churchill, Henry Sydnor Harrison, Albert Edwards, who are, I am assured by the unanimity of current opinion, the best we have, only to come away with a slight feeling of shame, the embarrassment of accidentally intruding upon things that might better be hidden. I could not help blushing, for instance, when in Mr. Herrick's latest story I discovered, a few pages ahead, that the stone-mason was the long-lost cousin of Adelle. I knew immediately that she would have to be redeemed and share her wealth. And she did. Cally's sacrifice in *V.V.'s Eyes* bothered me a good deal too, the funeral made me drop my eyes, and even Mr. Churchill's *John Hodder* made me feel indelicate. Now I do not like to have novels embarrass me, or cause me to cast down my eyes in shame. I cannot blame the authors. I can merely wonder at the current American psychology of life.

I suspect myself of almost a morbid eye for that theme of redemption which no excellent American novelist seems able to resist. One may start bravely enough with an uncompromisingly real person, playful, selfish, lustful, or ambitious, set firmly in the American scene. After a few hundred pages, the author's incorrigible itch to make over the character gets the better of him. The *idée fixe* of American fiction roughly intrudes itself, and before our astonished eyes the moral transformation takes place under various virile and inspiring influences of ideas and personalities. The eyes of the blind are opened, the crooked are made straight. The author's "best" inevitably prevails, whether it be his sense of the futility of riches, the triumph of social ideals, or the power of noble love. People awaken to the barrenness of their lives, and find purpose and meaning before the novelist allows us to part from them. The only trouble is that these metamorphosed personalities have long since ceased to be interesting.

Possibly we Americans really have this astonishing talent and habit of redemption in the proportion which our fiction would incline us to believe. Yet, though I see vastly interesting life going on about me, a richness of charming, mediocre and repellent types, I do not seem to witness this process of creating a new heart. Human nature, on the contrary, seems to move in un-commonly definite channels, the roots of people's interests and dominant impulses to lie very far down. Experience may strengthen or attenuate their outward-reaching attitudes and lines of endeavor, but it rarely alters them, except as it comes in some volcanic shock that has far pathological reverberations. In their hasty desire to get that fulfilled which was spoken by the prophets, our serious American novelists usually let slip through their fingers the stuff of life itself.

Mr. Dreiser can scarcely be appreciated unless he is con-trasted with the hearty unanimity of this American thirst for re-demption. It is still incredible that if he was really only *A Traveler at Forty*, he should have remained untouched by this pervading tradition. How is it that you can read him without shame and embarrassment, with your head straight? It must be his foreign psychology that English critics feel when they call *Sister Carrie* the best novel written in America. His coarse, common American life even has a certain Continental flavor. His Chicago and Philadelphia get something of the exotic touch that "New-York" has in the pages of a French play. His long gallery of women in the *Titan* is more seductive, richer in timbre, than the women of his contemporaries.

To say that he has a Continental quality is not only to say that he has a more universal psychology, but that he suggests that life is somewhat warmer and clearer than it is usually presented to us at home, a stream of desire both more intelligent and less critical. Our America may be still young, but it cannot be said that radiance and daring, charm and desire, shine out of our fic-tion. Those who wish to find in Continental senility and de-crepitude the secret of Continental charm are welcome to their interesting observation. It seems more likely that those Continen-tal peoples who produce great fiction today have somehow kept their lives and attitudes truer to some of the elementary currents of life. They have escaped some of the blight of Puritan op-timism that has fallen on us, and the sentimentality which is the fine flower of the attempt to make a kind of seedless orange of man. Anglo-Saxon civilization seems to have been slowly starved to some of the emotional values which Europe has con-served, to both its woe and glory. We are spiritually anaemic, but it is not because we are young, but because we have cut ourselves off from certain nourishments which, primitive though the raw materials may be, the finer souls of Europe have known how to refine and enjoy. It is as if we had said that because we can't eat sugar-cane we shall have no sugar, and then gone on to prove that stones and acorns and Easter lilies and bobbins were good and nourishing food.

Mr. Dreiser reinstated some of these values with such emphasis in his first book that the outraged and repentant publisher withdrew it from circulation. The American public had to wait twelve years until the success of *Jennie Gerhardt* forced a reprinting of *Sister Carrie*. The recent "Trilogy of Desire," with its *Financier* and *Titan,* to be completed by a volume in the autumn, seems to take a long stride towards popular taste. But Mr. Dreiser does the familiar hero, the captain of industry, with his steel-grey eyes and indomitable will, his captive shoals of aldermen and legislatures, and his colossal coups, rather better than his contemporaries. Although American taste since 1900 has grown up to and indeed far beyond the frankness of *Sister Carrie,* still his books have too few of the old moral and immoral landmarks to attract a public which can now find far spicier fare. And the elect are likely to leave him for the hard glitter of more sophisticated work.

Sister Carrie continues to occupy a position of enviable isolation. Mr. Dreiser, uninterested in redemption, excites no competition. His psychology of desire is still too new. This language of the perpetual eagerness of life, of dominant impulse that pounds away at environment, of desire in which sexual hunger is only the deepest current, still falls strangely on American ears. To a public that delights in "Queed," it must still seem shocking that Carrie should not have been redeemed. To follow this aimless and alluring soul as she passes from sphere to sphere, in quest of the warmth and light that she craves, and then to leave her still wistful and unrepentant, is to offend our sense of righteousness. If she is not to be redeemed, most of us would prefer that she be degraded. Mr. Dreiser, however, paints her career actually as growth and not demoralization. She emerges enhanced, a richer personality, elemental but genuinely unspotted, rather poetically human. It is all the more incredible because on page 357 the novelist had an opportunity for redemption of a kind that comes to few American novelists. The unformed country girl, coming to Chicago for work, has passed from the dullness of her sister's industrious flat and the disgusting factory to life with a genial salesman, and then, with an almost vegetative sureness, to the New York scene with a man who offers her a bigger and a warmer world. Here she meets a young man who suggests a still wider horizon to which she vaguely responds, books, music, more interesting persons, and surer and more refined judgments than she has ever felt. What other American novelist could have resisted the appeal to her "better nature" and the opportunity slowly to improve her character through this steady and elevating influence? Mr. Herrick, I fear, would have jumped at the chance. But Mr. Dreiser, apparently innocent of the greatness of his renunciation, lets the young Ames pass into oblivion, while Carrie saves herself in a less appealing way from her husband's degradation and falling fortune.

Sister Carrie is one of those rare stories that present not only lives but a rudimentary pattern of life itself. Too many American novels resemble an amateur play acted against a background of very bad scenery. In them persons and environment are far too sharply distinct. Life is over-individualized. The naïve assumption seems to be that as persons we are primarily rational beings of free will, possessed of a collection of ticketed sentiments and ideas. To such beings, of course, redemption would be ridiculously easy. It would involve nothing more than rearranging, adding or subtracting elements. Mr. Dreiser's world is much more fused. Sister Carrie fairly soaks in environment. One cannot too much admire those early chapters where the country girl seeps in the sights and sounds that flow from the glittering, ugly city. She is sensitive, breathing, scarcely conscious where herself leaves off and the rest of the world begins. You feel impressions impinging upon her. In such a world there is neither character nor static scenery, only flowing life; but this is the world in which the well-intentioned, not very wise, not very controlling persons that most of us are, actually live.

Mr. Dreiser's later work is coarser and rougher. It lacks the freshness and unpretentiousness that makes *Sister Carrie* beautiful, and that inevitable air of almost having written itself—though Mr. Dreiser's poetical chapter headings show that he was not unconscious of what he was doing. *Jennie Gerhardt* is almost too much an attempt to do it again; but *Sister Carrie* is one of those things that are not done again. One wonders if the caricature of redemption which Lester performs in leaving Jennie for an orthodox marriage with an heiress was the true reason for the wider public acclaim which the book received. But even *Jennie Gerhardt* can be read with self-respect. One does not need to blush. Here, as in almost all of Mr. Dreiser's pages, one can follow the pattern of life, sincere, wistful and unredeemed.

[1] Dreiser describes his acquaintance with Bourne in "Appearance and Reality" (*The American Spectator, 1933*). It was reprinted in *Twice-A-Year* I, 1938.

THE ART OF THEODORE DREISER

Theodore Dreiser has had the good fortune to evoke a peculiar quality of pugnacious interest among the younger American intelligentsia such as has been the lot of almost nobody else writing today unless it be Miss Amy Lowell. We do not usually take literature seriously enough to quarrel over it. Or else we take it so seriously that we urbanely avoid squabbles. Certainly there are none of the vendettas that rage in a culture like that of France. But Mr. Dreiser seems to have made himself, particularly since the suppression of *The Genius,* a veritable issue. Interesting and surprising are the reactions to him. Edgar Lee Masters make him a "soul-enrapt demiurge, walking the earth, stalking life"; Harris Merton Lyon saw in him a "seer of inscrutable mien"; Arthur Davison Ficke sees him as master of a passing throng of figures, "labored with immortal illusion, the terrible and beautiful, cruel and wonder-laden illusion of life"; Mr. Powys makes him an epic philosopher of the "life-tide"; H. L. Mencken puts him ahead of Conrad, with "an agnosticism that has almost passed beyond curiosity." On the other hand, an unhappy critic in *The Nation* last year gave Mr. Dreiser his place for all time in a neat antithesis between the realism that was based on a theory of human conduct and the naturalism that reduced life to a mere animal behavior. For Dreiser this last special hell was reserved, and the jungle-like and simian activities of his characters were rather exhaustively outlined. At the time this antithesis looked silly. With the appearance of Mr. Dreiser's latest book, *A Hoosier Holiday,* it becomes nonsensical. For that wise and delightful book reveals him as a very human critic of very common human life, romantically sensual and poetically realistic, with an artist's vision and a thick, warm feeling for American life.

This book gives the clue to Mr. Dreiser, to his insatiable curiosity about people, about their sexual inclinations, about their dreams, about the homely qualities that make them American. His memories give a picture of the floundering young American that is so typical as to be almost epic. No one has ever pictured this lower middle-class American life so winningly, because no one has had the necessary literary skill with the lack of self-consciousness. Mr. Dreiser is often sentimental, but it is a sentimentality that captivates you with its candor. You are seeing this vacuous, wistful, spiritually rootless, Middle-Western life through the eyes of a naïve but very wise boy. Mr. Dreiser seems queer only because he has carried along his youthful attitude in unbroken continuity. He is fascinated with sex because youth is usually obsessed with sex. He puzzles about the universe because youth usually puzzles. He thrills to crudity and violence because sensitive youth usually recoils from the savagery of the industrial world. Imagine incorrigible, sensuous youth endowed with the brooding skepticism of the philosopher who feels the vanity of life, and you have the paradox of Mr. Dreiser. For these two attitudes in him support rather than oppose each other. His spiritual evolution was out of a pious, ascetic atmosphere into intellectual and personal freedom. He seems to have found himself without losing himself. Of how many American writers can this be said? And for this much shall be forgiven him—his slovenliness of style, his lack of *nuances,* his apathy to the finer shades of beauty, his weakness for the mystical and the vague. Mr. Dreiser suggests the over-sensitive temperament that protects itself by an admiration for crudity and cruelty. His latest book reveals the boyhood shyness and timidity of this Don Juan of novelists. Mr. Dreiser is complicated, but he is complicated in a very understandable American way, the product of the uncouth forces of small-town life and the vast disorganization of the wider American world. As he reveals himself, it is a revelation of a certain broad level of the American soul.

Mr. Dreiser seems uncommon only because he is more naïve than most of us. It is not so much that his pages swarm with sexful figures as that he rescues sex for the scheme of personal life. He feels a holy mission to slay the American literary superstition that men and women are not sensual beings. But he does not brush this fact in the sniggering way of the popular magazines. He takes it very seriously, so much so that some of his novels become caricatures of desire. It is, however, a misfortune that it has been Brieux and Freud and not native Theodore Dreiser who has saturated the sexual imagination of the younger American intelligentsia. It would have been far healthier to absorb Mr. Dreiser's literary treatment of sex than to go hysterical over its pathology. Sex has little significance unless it is treated in personally artistic, novelistic terms. The American tradition had tabooed the treatment of those infinite gradations and complexities of love that fill the literary imagination of a sensitive people. When curiosity became too strong and reticence was repealed in America, we had no means of articulating ourselves except in a deplorable pseudo-scientific jargon that has no more to do with the relevance of sex than the chemical composition of orange paint has to do with the artist's vision. Dreiser has done a real service to the American imagination in despising the underworld and going gravely to the business of picturing sex as it is lived in the personal relations of bungling, wistful, or masterful men and women. He seemed strange and rowdy only because he made sex human, and American tradition had never made it human. It had only made it either sacred or vulgar, and when these categories no longer worked, we fell under the dubious and perverting magic of the psychoanalysts.

In spite of his looseness of literary gait and heaviness of style Dreiser seems a sincere groper after beauty. It is natural enough that this should so largely be the beauty of sex. For where would a sensitive boy, brought up in Indiana and in the big American cities, get beauty expressed for him except in women? What does Mid-Western America offer to the starving except its personal beauty? A few landscapes, an occasional picture in a museum, a book of verse perhaps! Would not all the rest be one long, flaunting offense of ugliness and depression? *The Genius,* instead of being that mass of pornographic horror which the Vice Societies repute it to be, is the story of a groping artist whose love of beauty runs obsessingly upon the charm of girlhood. Through different social planes, through business and manual labor and the feverish world of artists, he pursues this lure. Dreiser is refreshing in his air of the moral democrat, who sees life impassively, neither praising nor blaming, at the same time that he realizes how much more terrible and beautiful and incalculable life is than any of us are willing to admit. It may be all *apologia,* but it comes with the grave air of a mind that wants us to understand just how it all happened. *Sister Carrie* will always retain the fresh charm of a spontaneous working-out of mediocre, and yet elemental and significant, lives. A good novelist catches hold of the thread of human desire. Dreiser does this, and that is why his admirers forgive him so many faults.

If you like to speculate about personal and literary qualities that are specifically American, Dreiser should be as interesting as any one now writing in America. This becomes clearer as he writes more about his youth. His hopelessly unorientated, half-educated boyhood is so typical of the uncritical and careless society in which wistful American talent has had to grope. He had to be spiritually a self-made man, work out a philosophy of life, discover his own sincerity. Talent in America outside of the ruling class flowers very late, because it takes so long to find its bearings. It has had almost to create its own soil, before it could put in its roots and grow. It is born shivering into an inhospitable and irrelevant group. It has to find its own kind of people and piece together its links of comprehension. It is a gruelling and tedious task, but those who come through it contribute, like Vachel Lindsay, creative work that is both novel and indigenous. The process can be more easily traced in Dreiser than in almost anybody else. *A Hoosier Holiday* not only traces the personal process, but it gives the social background. The common life, as seen throughout the countryside, is touched off quizzically, and yet sympathetically, with an artist's vision. Dreiser sees the American masses in their commonness and at their pleasure as brisk, rather vacuous people, a little pathetic in their innocence of the possibilities of life and their optimistic trustfulness. He sees them ruled by great barons of industry, and yet unconscious of their serfdom. He seems to love this countryside, and he makes you love it.

Dreiser loves, too, the ugly violent bursts of American industry—the flaming steel-mills and gaunt lakesides. *The Titan* and *The Financier* are unattractive novels, but they are human documents of the brawn of a passing American era. Those stenographic conversations, webs of financial intrigue, bare bones of enterprise, insult our artistic sense. There is too much raw beef, and yet it all has the taste and smell of the primitive business-jungle it deals with. These crude and greedy captains. of finance with their wars and their amours had to be given some kind of literary embodiment, and Dreiser has hammered a sort of raw epic out of their lives.

It is not only his feeling for these themes of crude power and sex and the American common life that makes Dreiser interesting. His emphases are those of a new America which is latently expressive and which must develop its art before we shall really have become articulate. For Dreiser is a true hyphenate, a product of that conglomerate Americanism that springs from other roots than the English tradition. Do we realize how rare it is to find a talent that is thoroughly American and wholly un-English? Culturally we have somehow suppressed the hyphenate. Only recently has he forced his way through the unofficial literary censorship. The vers-librists teem with him, but Dreiser is almost the first to achieve a largeness of utterance. His outlook, it is true, flouts the American canons of optimism and redemption, but these were never anything but conventions. There stirs in Dreiser's books a new American quality. It is not at all German. It is an authentic attempt to make something artistic out of the chaotic materials that lie around us in American life. Dreiser interests because we can watch him grope and feel his clumsiness. He has the artist's vision without the sureness of the artist's technique. That is one of the tragedies of America. But his faults are those of his material and of uncouth bulk, and not of shoddiness. The interest he evokes is part of the eager interest we feel in that growth.

PAUL ELMER MORE

Aristocracy and Justice, by Paul Elmer More. Boston and New York: Houghton Mifflin Co. $1.50 net.

The author of *Aristocracy and Justice* is more than an essayist, more than a critic. He is an American institution, the ablest spokesman for the idealism of our intellectual plutocracy. If his books are not read, at least his ideas are thought, and if our plutocracy has become too timid in the face of a growling Demos to express itself so uncompromisingly, at least it continues to act just as if it had this social and moral philosophy which Mr. More expounds.

Human life, says Mr. More, is a very primitive thing, prone without control to degenerate into savagery. In preventing society from crumbling beneath the aggressive passions of the present, artificial institutions are required to curb the restive and self-seeking nature of man. These institutions make up civilization, and property is its bulwark. In the struggle for life and goods, the strong and cruel will conquer, and nature will not gainsay their irrational victory. Order requires that a controlling power over will and appetite be placed somewhere. Man must recognize nature's rigid hierarchy and subordination of her creatures, but sublimate it into justice, which is right distribution of power and privilege. Society must seek justice after the pattern of the moral individual soul, in which the reason and feelings are reconciled. The strong must have the privilege of imposing their will upon those who are inferior to them, but only in a way that at once satisfied the distinctions of reason among the superior, and does not outrage the feelings of the inferior. This is social justice, and its operation requires a natural aristocracy. This natural aristocracy will be found in the class whose views are broadened by the inherited possession of privilege and honors. In a democracy inherited wealth replaces aristocracy. Property is the symbol and instrument of these privileges, and is therefore the very foundation of society. The dollar must always be more than the man and the right to property more sacred than the right to life.

A natural aristocracy is spiritually supported through the exercise of the moral imagination working in all classes of society. This moral imagination which accepts the powerful everywhere as the good and wise, if an illusion, is a most pleasing and beneficent one, for it makes power gentle and obedience liberal and harmonizes the different shades of life. Church and university are ever the strongest stimulators of this imagination, the strongest reactionaries against innovations which threaten the intrenched rights of property, and this not because of greed of possession, but because the safety and usefulness of institutions is bound up with the inviolability of property by which a leisure class, by character destined more specifically to be the creators and transmitters of the world's intellectual and spiritual heritage, retains its stability and its capacity for governing the masses.

That training of the disciplined mind by which a natural aristocracy cultivates this heritage is one of the most important tasks of society. Only the liberal studies—Greek, Latin, philosophy, mathematics—perform this office of discipline. On these the college must concentrate. Any attempt to make education an industrial social training for the masses stabs deep at the vitals of society. The true aim of a state is to make possible the high friendship of those who have raised themselves to a vision of the supreme good. To care for mediocrity is to destroy that just inequality of Nature, and open the gates to warring class-passions and the revolt of the unfit.

To the neglect of these principles, Mr. More attributes our present discontents. Under the rising tide of democracy, our intellectual plutocrats themselves have faltered and paled. A new morality has arisen which renounces personal responsibility in favor of social responsibility. We have become enfeebled by humanitarianism. We give full liberty to human nature to follow its own impulsive desire of expansion. Sympathy in place of justice saps the fibre of character and gives free rein to egoistic impulses. The release of the inhibitions of reason and conscience have plunged us into the savagery of a world war. The envious many have broken down the securities of property rights, and imperiled social order. Even Mr. Rockefeller and the New York *Sun* have come to defending the right to work, rather than the inalienable right of property. In the new social ideals the intellectual class has been guilty of a moral treason. Unless it return to the eternal principles of justice, restoring harmony in the individual breast and a just and contented subordination in society, our civilization is doomed.

Such a philosophy is, of course, its own best self-satirization.

A piece of *a priori* reasoning in the classic style, it is a mere apologia for the modern legal reactionary. The calm of Mr. More's style cannot keep the claws of class-exploitation from showing through.

Granting the power of his classic social analysis, he makes two gratuitous assumptions. One assumption, that modern America, before it was sapped by the new morality, was a Platonic Republic, betrays the extent of his inductive studies. The other is that the only choice is between a contented plutocracy and anarchy.

His misunderstanding of modern radicalism is complete. His major premises are exactly those of that modern social and psychological science which he so deplores, and of the modern pragmatic philosophy. Any book of statistics or sociological survey would show him curves of distribution which are nothing more or less than his "inequality of nature" made graphic and explicit. And any modern philosopher of force from Nietzsche to Dewey will show him our full appreciation of the philosophy of will-to-power. It is not in his premises but in his conclusions that Mr. More is flatly out of touch with the driving and creative thought of the day. He assumes the very question he ought to prove—that a "natural aristocracy" of inherited wealth does produce in society that harmony of reason and emotion which is justice. He has canonized the particular denouement of a nonmoral struggle of group wills-to-power which our time most passionately rebels against, and which has been most productive of disorder and intellectual chaos—the rule of an industrial plutocracy.

For what we have learned in our American experience is that property rights cannot be put above human rights unless humanity itself become property. Mr. More's ideal is a slave-society, as the Greek state to which he always reverts was a slave-state. Any society which works towards such a social goal works towards a society based on slavery or on serfdom.

What Mr. More sees as a sentimental humanitarianism is really a growing general disinclination to live longer in a semi-servile society. What he sees as the materializing of life is rather a determined effort to understand the forces and goods of nature so that they may become the tools of a genuine all-nourishing humanism such as has never before been remotely possible in the world.

To have missed all this, and to have seen the modern democratic movement as merely an invidious mob-desire to level life to
mediocrity or as the mere drift of sentiment, is to have betrayed
a dearth of imagination far more sinister than that want of the
Burkian reverence for the established which Mr. More so much
deplores in us. This continuing to live in the America of 1915
among the political and moral problems of an Attic Deme would
be comic if it were not pathetic. Mr. More is ignorant of the fact
that we live in a new age of surplus value, economic and
spiritual. The kernel of our problems is the use of that surplus
energy. It is this changed orientation that has destroyed the old
antithesis. Equilibrium can no longer be the ideal. We find that
we are not dealing with economic or social forces which can be
balanced against each other, and society and the individual reduced to a harmonious and static design. Our psychology
shows us life not as an arrangement of emotions, sensations,
judgments, which can be treated kaleidoscopically to produce
certain effects of character. We see life now rather as an incalculable and importunate stream of desire, which rises in the
adult to a will-to-power. The problem of the soul becomes the
direction of this desire and energy into creative channels, not its
suppression or even control by that reason which is so often a
mere disguise of another and more acceptable desire. In such a
world, personality becomes more desirable than character, creative expressiveness than self-control, cooperation than justice,
social freedom than rights. Mr. More's ethics is the ethics of a
parsimonious world. It has no place in a world of surplus energy
or of possible surplus energy. Only by repressing this energy,
only by turning it back to its latent state, could the modern world
be put back to the tight little Greek frame in which Mr. More and
his friends would find themselves most at home and their rights
and privileges least disturbed. And that would mean a serfdom,
of both person and group, for which the time is too late.

The social purpose no longer means the sentimentality of a
social conscience which is mere sympathy, but work towards a
creative, imaginative and inter-stimulating community life, in
which personality and expressiveness shall flourish as they cannot flourish under present institutions. The enterprises which
seem to the conservative mere enervating fads and fancies are
experimental means towards this end. This readjustment, this
progressive re-shaping, is the work of the modern radical
movements. It is an audacious and Promethean task, as far as

possible removed from drift or vagueness. At its lowest, it stems "the amorous and vehement drift of man's herd to hell." At its best, it tones up society, giving to great masses vigor, skill and outlook, endowing institutions with new purpose, adjusting them to the best wills and powers of the men and women affected by them. Industrial education, town-planning, labor legislation, social insurance and the rest are not ends in themselves, but means of social technique toward this great social end.

Mr. More met this century in its childish years, and he has neglected to observe its growing up. His misinterpretation of the modern spirit which is so bold in desire to substitute mastery for drift betrays either an ignorance or a callousness. It is probably both, for his philosophy was hammered together in its perfect form fifteen years ago, and no word of the movement of men and minds has since penetrated his studied isolation. It is not only an insensitiveness that he betrays, but since the modern political and social vision is so largely an aesthetic one, a genuine anesthesia. His narrow preoccupation with the Greek classics has prevented him from seeing the color and forms of that sociological world which men are now eagerly studying and in which they seem to find all the imaginative lift and intellectual discipline which their fathers get from the classics. If he looked about the world, he would find his orthodox classical scholars the stalest and most stagnant of men, their fire passed to pragmatic philosophers or the realistic publicists. He would find Gilbert Murray, the greatest Greek scholar of his age, gone with all his students over into the sociological camp, delving into mana and initiation ceremonies and primitive magic in order to explain his Greek tragedy, or else making the abhorrent classical compromise by popularizing Euripides in English verse. One wonders of what classics and of what discipline Mr. More is talking when his greatest scholars, his natural aristocracy, are finding his lovely archaic poems a tangled tissue of social myth rather than the naive outpourings of the human heart.

The world has grown too wide and too adventurous for Mr. More's tight little categories. We are becoming too conscious of vast economic forces which control the destinies of society. We cannot believe that our salvation lies in the resolution of Mr. More and his anxious friends to put a harsh stop to those dangerous modern ideas that are undermining the sober virility of our minds.

H. L. MENCKEN

Mr. Mencken gives the impression of an able mind so harried and irritated by the philistinism of American life that it has not been able to attain its full power. These more carefully worked-over critical essays are, on the whole, less interesting and provocative than the irresponsible comment he gives us in his magazine. How is it that so robust a hater of uplift and puritanism becomes so fanatical a crusader himself? One is forced to call Mr. Mencken a moralist, for with him appraisement has constantly to stop while he tilts against philistine critics and outrageous puritans. In order to show how good a writer is, he must first show how deplorably fatuous, malicious or ignorant are all those who dislike him. Such a proof is undoubtedly the first impulse of any mind that cares deeply about artistic values. But Mr. Mencken too often permits it to be his last, and wastes away into a desert of invective. Yet he has all the raw material of the good critic—moral freedom, a passion for ideas and for literary beauty, vigor and pungency of phrase, considerable reference and knowledge. Why have these intellectual qualities and possessions been worked up only so partially into the finished attitude of criticism? Has he not let himself be the victim of that paralyzing Demos against which he so justly rages? As you follow his strident paragraphs, you become a little sorry that there is not more of a contrast in tone between his illumination of the brave, the free, and the beautiful, and the peevish complaints of the superannuated critics of the old school. When are we going to get anything critically curative done for our generation, if our critical rebels are to spend their lives cutting off hydra-heads of American stodginess?

Mr. Mencken's moralism infects the essay on Conrad perhaps the least. With considerable effort the critic shakes himself loose from the clutches of his puritan enemies and sets Conrad very justly in relation to his time. "What he sees and describes in his books," Mr. Mencken says, "is not merely this man's aspiration or that woman's destiny, but the overwhelming sweep and devastation of universal forces, the great central drama that is at the heart of all other dramas, the tragic struggles of the soul of man under the gross stupidity and obscene joking of the gods." He likes Dreiser for the same reason, because "he puts into his novels a touch of the eternal Weltschmerz. They get below the drama that is of the moment and reveal the greater drama that is without end." Mr. Mencken discusses Dreiser with admirable balance, and his essay is important because it criticizes him more harshly and more searchingly than many of us dare to do when we are defending him against the outrageous puritan. The essay on Huneker is perhaps the most entertaining. If "to be a civilized man in America is measurably less difficult, despite the war, than it used to be, say, in 1890" (when Mr. Mencken, by the way, was ten years old), it is to Mr. Huneker's gallant excitement that part of the credit is due.

Dreiser and Huneker Mr. Mencken used with the utmost lustiness, as Samson used the jaw -bone, to slay a thousand Philistines, and his zeal mounts to a closing essay on Puritanism as a Literary Force, which employs all the Menckenian artillery. Here Mr. Mencken, as the moralist contra moralism, runs amuck. It is an exposure that should stir our blood, but it is so heavily documented and so stern in its conviction of the brooding curtain of bigotry that hangs over our land, that its effect must be to throw paralyzing terror into every American mind that henceforth dares to think of not being a prude. Mr. Mencken wants to liberate, but any one who took his huge concern seriously would never dare challenge in any form that engine of puritanism which derives its energy from the history and soul of the American people. Mr. Mencken is much in earnest. His invective rises above the tone of scornful exaggeration. But his despair seems a little forced. I cannot see that the younger writers—particularly the verse-writers—are conscious of living under any such cultural terrorism as he describes. Mr. Mencken admits that the puritan proscription is irrational and incalculable in its operation. Surely as long as there are magazines and publishers—as there are in increasing numbers—who will issue vigorous and candid work, comstockery in art must be seen as an annoying but not dominating force. Mr. Mencken queerly shows himself as editor, bowing meekly under the puritan proscription, acting as censor of "a long list of such things by American authors, well-devised, well-imagined, well-executed, respectable as human documents and as works of art—but never to be printed in mine or any other American magazine." But what is this but to act as busy ally to that very comstockery he denounces? If the Menckens are not going to run the risk, in the name of freedom, they are scarcely justified in trying to infect us with their own caution.

The perspective is false that sees this persecution as peculiar to America. Was not Lemonnier prosecuted in Paris? Did not Baudelaire, Flaubert, Zola suffer? Did not Zola's publisher in England die in prison? Has not D. H. Lawrence's latest novel been suppressed in England before it had even a chance to be prosecuted here? It is England not America that has an official censorship of plays. Comstockery is not so much a function of American culture as it is of the current moralism of our general middle-class civilization. The attack must be, as Nietzsche made it, on that moralism rather than on its symptoms. But Mr. Mencken is not particularly happy in his understanding of Nietzsche. He wrote the book from which a majority of the Americans who know about Nietzsche seem to have gotten their ideas. How crude a summary it is may be seen by comparing it with the recent study of Nietzsche by another American, W. M. Salter. One wishes Mr. Mencken had spent more time in understanding the depth and subtleties of Nietzsche, and less on shuddering at puritanism as a literary force, and on discovering how the public libraries and newspaper reviewers are treating Theodore Dreiser.

Mr. Mencken's mode of critical attack thus plays into the hands of the philistines, demoralizes the artist, and demoralizes his own critical power. Why cannot Demos be left alone for a while to its commercial magazines and its mawkish novels? All good writing is produced in serene unconsciousness of what Demos desires or demands. It cannot be created at all if the artist worries about what Demos will think of him or do to him. The artist writes for that imagined audience of perfect comprehenders. The critic must judge for that audience too.

FROM AN OLDER TIME

Those of us who began our reading careers after 1900 are inclined, perhaps unjustly, to neglect the school of excellent writers who delighted the youth of our fathers and mothers. The eighties and nineties saw a very deliberate and serious attempt to found a "national" American literature, and that attempt deserves far more respect and investigation from those of us who pretend to be still wanting that very thing than we usually give it. The approach to this enterprise was sectional but not separatist, sectional in the sense that if each great region—New England, Virginia, the Tennessee mountains, Louisiana, California, the Western plains—were fittingly embodied in fiction, their distinctive types of personality and ways of speech artistically presented, the federated picture would produce us a veritable American contemporary literature, comparable in depth of life and beauty of pattern to the French and Russian material that we were beginning to admire. With this motive more or less at the bottom of their hearts, writers like Miss Jewett, Miss Wilkins, G. W. Cable, Bret Harte, Hamlin Garland, Thomas Nelson Page, and James Lane Allen worked conscientiously to catch and fix the distinctiveness of the life that each one knew. And over this school presided with unquestioned authority Mr. Howells, that incredible genius who had come from humble Ohio to capture the Brahmin citadel itself, and—when the kings had been gathered to their fathers—to reign in royal Cambridge himself. Mr. Howells himself was never consciously sectional; he conveyed the simple homeliness of that naive middle-class age which got itself recognized everywhere as broadly and pervasively "American." But it was in his mellow art and under his pontifical blessing that the school felt itself sustained and encouraged.

Of all these writers, Mr. Cable is the only one who continues to produce novels of the same quality and with the same motive. Those of his school who are not dead, have earned an honorable retirement in other fields. *Lovers of Louisiana* (Scribner; $1.50) comes to us from this fine veteran of seventy-five, with his unmistakable characteristics, after a literary career of much more than forty years. And, as if to show his perennial vigor, he has not gone lazily back to his Creole life of the past, but writes his romance about a very modern New Orleans of the last three

or four years. This gives him the opportunity to show the Creole
life in all its unfading charm, in the beautiful flower of a Rosalie
Durel, in the courtliness and finesse of her banker father, and
even in the wickedness of her wonderfully named cousin
Zéphire. And it enables him to confront and then to mingle with
this inexhaustible Creole theme the other molding element of
modern New Orleans, the rather stiffly admirable Philip Castleton, with his sociological modernity and his critical love for the
South. It is rather an astonishing thing for so veteran a novelist
to do—to keep so much of the old flavor of romance and yet
pour so much intellectuality into his work. The interest of the feat
almost disarms our criticism of the artistic creation.

Mr. Cable has always blended his romance and sociology.
From many of his contemporaries we could excusably have acquired our current legend that his generation was serenely oblivious of "social problems." But we could never have got it from
him. From the very first he seems to have seen the South as an
impartially criticizable society as well as the beloved Dixie of romance. And it was the South's very energetic dislike to be
looked at in any such light that sent him long ago to make his
home in Massachusetts. If it was his upbringing in ante-bellum
New Orleans that gave him his tender love of her picturesque
life, it must have been his Northern, and perhaps his partly
German heritage, that gave him a fatally critical sense of the
poisons that continued to beset the South's convalescence of
reconstruction. To my Northern mind he seems the fairest of critics, with a justice that is sincerely tempered by love. His defense of the freedman, those pamphlets he wrote in the eighties
about the "silent South" and the post-slavery problems, are re-
strained in tone and earnest with a high-minded persuasiveness.
Only a South that would stand for nothing but a servile adulation
of its ways could resist such a prophet. He spoke as a lover of
Dixie, but it was just that plea Dixie would not listen to—that only
through political fairness to the Negro would the South be released from the clutch of its "Negro problem."

In this latest novel Philip Castleton is Mr. Cable's attitude personified. Those Southerners who do not complain about Mr. Cable's strictures on the South put their complaints against him on
the ground that he is too much the sociologist at all times and
too little the artist. I do not know whether he wrote *John March,
Southerner* (1894) to prove his impartiality. But it happens that

this story, with its pugnacious and chivalrous young hero of reconstruction and its rascally Negro politicians, is one of his best novels. Mr. Cable was artist enough to draw vivid portraits which were the reverse of special pleading for the sociological idealisms he had been expressing. Into that book he got pretty nearly the entire life of a turbulent and proud Southern community in its welter of personal and political feuds and aspirations to develop its suddenly discovered resources. No mere apologia could have been so convincing.

But in *Lovers of Louisiana* the reader who missed the artist in Mr. Cable would have a better case. Philip rarely becomes more than an abstraction. If he is not exactly priggish, he is little more than a voice calling upon his great city to lead the South to modernity. He comes back from Princeton to take his place in the public life of the city. He gives a course at Tulane in political history. He delivers before a Negro society an address which is taken by his proud Creole rival for the hand of Rosalie as an apology for being a white man. He heads the Grand Jury, and menaces the mysteries of Creole clairvoyants and quadroon girls. In his high-minded courtship of Rosalie he invades the precincts of the finest Creole families closed till then to ideas, and not only saves her father from bankruptcy but wins him to a larger tolerance. Philip is always less a lover, less even a reformer, than he is a walking idea of what Mr. Cable would like the effective modern Louisianan young man to be. Even when he secures his Rosalie Durel—her whom he has once identified with his city, and his city with her—our romantic interest is less stirred by their union than by that of the two touching old figures behind them, the grandmère and the Judge, who find their belated happiness after forty years.

The romance that is embodied in Rosalie and her family scarcely compensates for the abstractions of Philip and the Castletons. Of course she is utterly charming, and charming in a more vigorous and intelligent way than Mr. Cable's other Creole heroines, such as the Nancanous. Her creator spares us much of the enormity of dialect, and is thus able to save both her and her really admirably drawn father from that belittling and patronage which seems the inevitable effect of dialect on the modern taste. In this book Mr. Cable's phonetic atrocities are so much milder than usual and his conversations so much briefer as to bring his story completely within the range of what, I take it, is our demand today. Nothing cuts off his school from us quite so much as that lavish cultivation of dialect. Our eye simply balks at untangling the paragraphs of a character like Narcisse in *Dr. Sevier,* so that that youth, who is so obviously intended to be a most amusing and winning figure, falls as flat as a Petrouchka who has lost his sawdust. Mr. Cable seems well aware of this change of taste. *Lovers of Louisiana* is brief and pointed in its style. It has few of those leisurely wastes of conversation which that school copied Mr. Howells in pouring out upon us. Mr. Howells himself was saved by the fact that even in his most prairie-like stretches there is always a faint amusingness, in its transcript, of the literal banality of life. The other writers are seldom so fortunate. When they use dialect they produce books which will, I think, become progressively unreadable.

Mr. Cable's romance is still old-fashioned, however modern his literary manner may have become. His generation also followed Mr. Howells in what H. L. Mencken calls a "kittenishness" in all references to love. *Lovers of Louisiana* sounds stilted; deprived of the flow of conversation, the romance is a little bare and angular. For a short book, it has a bewildering ingenuity of plot. So short a story will scarcely carry so much interweaving of themes without fatiguing the reader, and fatiguing him justifiably. At times the meaning almost sinks out of sight under the weight of the financial intrigue, and of the influence of the young people's romance upon the shy reunion of their elders. Here are not only a Creole grandmother and an "English" grandfather who should have married years before, but were kept apart by social prejudice. There is also a broken love-match between Rosalie's father and Philip's mother, which was prevented by the same beloved Aunt Castleton who now works against Philip's suit. Add to this a financial complication in which the Castletons rather quixotically attempt to make up to the Durels the losses suffered by the embezzlements of the wicked cousin Zéphire, rival suitor for Rosalie's hand, and get the aid of an ex-slave of the Durels as well as a Scotch banker who intrigues ceaselessly to bring Rosalie and Philip together. Weave into this the realization that this indebtedness stands between Rosalie and Philip, and you produce a network that at times baffles your intelligence. To the author these intricacies of property and family pride have a significance that a younger novelist would be inclined to yawn over. For the mere situation of these two families (not hostile, still unmingling, though each represents its kind of aristocratic best in the fascinating life of New Orleans) would have been motif enough. He would not have felt so much the need of elaboration. There would have been more to understand of the people themselves and less of the too neat intermingling of their objective fortunes.

Lovers of Louisiana therefore helps us to understand, I think, the limitations of that "national" school of fiction. For our interest today is vaguely in "life" itself rather than in the distinctive trappings of life, picturesque as they may be. We like to understand characters from their cradles to their graves. We pry around the intimacies of their souls in a way that seems almost ribald in the light of these scrupulous older novelties. It is not even "American" life we are after. We are on a restless search for "human life," almost as the thing in itself. We feel a craving to look beyond and through the particular type or the odd individual to some calm, immemorial current of personal truth. Any deliberately sectional portrayal comes to seem dangerously near an exploitation. The novelist is exploiting his material, digging out his marketable ore instead of making his human landscape reveal some significant veracity. This is the difference between books like *John March, Southerner* and *The Grandissimes*. In the latter one feels the exploiting touch. But fundamentally, to Mr. Cable's honor, it must be said that he does not deserve that stigma. He has felt deeply enough about his land to be its sound and bravely passionate counselor. And he has been artist enough not to let either this idealism nor his own very strict personal moralism impede his portrayal of all the sweetness and gayety of that life which his youth loved.

TRAPS FOR THE UNWARY[1]

What place is there to be for the younger American writers who have broken the "genteel" tradition with a sudden violence that elicits angry cries of pain from the critics, so long regarded by the significant classes as guardians of our cultural faith? Read Mr. Brownell on standards and see with what a bewildered contempt one of the most vigorous and gentlemanly survivals from the genteel tradition regards the efforts of the would-be literary artists of today. Read Stuart P. Sherman on contemporary literature, and see with what a hurt panic a young gentleman, perhaps the very last brave offshoot of the genteel tradition, regards those bold modern writers from whom his contemporaries derive. One can admire the intellectual acuteness and sound moral sense of both these critics, and yet feel how quaintly irrelevant for our purposes is an idea of the good, the true, and the beautiful, which culminates in a rapture for Thackeray (vide Mr. Brownell), or is a literary aesthetic (vide Mr. Sherman) which gives Mr. Arnold Bennett first place as an artist because of his wholesome theories of human conduct. Mr. Sherman has done us the service of showing us how very dead is the genteel tradition in our hearts, how thoroughly the sense of what is desirable and absorbing has shifted in our younger American life.

But he has also shown us how gentility in literary attitude lingers on. Professors of literature still like it, and those pioneer rebels who hate it have tended to hate it not wisely but too well. Crusaders like Mr. Dreiser and Mr. Mencken have dealt loud enough blows, but they beat at a straw man of puritanism which, for the younger generation, has not even the vitality to be interesting. Art always has to struggle with the mob, and Mr. Mencken's discovery that it has to struggle in America is a little naïve. The philistine and the puritan are troublesome, though never decisive, and in America today they seem less decisive than ever. Mr. Sherman, an arrant philistine, in that he defends the life lived through the conventions, is dangerous because he makes philistinism sound like belles-lettres. Mr. Mencken, on the other hand, deserves everything Mr. Sherman says about him, because in his rather self-conscious bluster he makes literary art sound like vulgarity. The best thing that can be done to these contending critics is to persuade them to kill each other off. Both are moralists before they are critics of literary art. Both have an exaggerated respect for Demos, which one expresses by means of a phobia, the other by a remarkable process of idealization. Mr. Mencken is as much a product of the genteel tradition as is Mr. Sherman, for he represents a moralism imperfectly transcended.

Let us look for the enemy of the literary artist in America today not among the philistines or the puritans, among the animal-obsessed novelist or the dainty professors who make Mr. Mencken profane. The real enemy is still the genteel tradition which tends to smother the timid experiments of a younger generation that is not satisfied with husks. For the deadly virus of gentility is carried along by an up-to-date cultivated public— small perhaps, but growing—who are all the more dangerous because they are so hospitable. The would-be literary artist needs to be protected not so much from his enemies as from his friends. Puritan and professor may agree in their disgust at the creative imagination at work in America, but it is not their hostility which keeps it from being freer and more expressive. The confusing force is rather an undiscriminating approval on the part of a public who want the new without the unsettling. The current popularity of verse, the vogue of the little theatres and the little magazines reveal a public that is almost pathetically receptive to anything which has the flavor or the pretension of literary art. The striving literary artist is faced by no stony and uncomprehending world. Almost anyone can win recognition and admiration. But where is the criticism that will discriminate between what is fresh, sincere, and creative and what is merely stagy and blatantly rebellious? The Brownells profess to find no nuances in this mob of young literary anarchists. The Shermans cannot degrade themselves to the level of treating seriously a crowd of naughty children. A new criticism has to be created to meet not only the work of the new artists but also the uncritical hospitality of current taste. If anything more than ephemeral is to come out of this younger school, outlawed by the older criticism, the new critic must intervene between public and writer with an insistence on clearer and sharper outlines of appreciation by the one, and the attainment of a richer artistry by the other.

That is why a study such as Miss Amy Lowell's on recent tendencies in American verse is so significant. The intelligent reviewers who saw in the book only a puff for Imagism disclosed how very novel is an intelligent attempt to place our current literary art not merely against the spiritual background of tradition, but in the terms and in the spirit of the contemporary imagination itself. Her very tone is revolutionary. She is neither sentimental nor apologetic. Poetry appears for the first time on our critical horizon as neither a refined dessert to be consumed when the day's work is done, nor as a private hobby which the business man will deride if he hears about it, but as a sound and important activity of contemporary American life. Some people who habitually patronize Miss Lowell complain that in her book she patronizes Carl Sandburg. Actually she makes him a powerful figure, with his brave novelty of the America that is in the making. Her sound intuition gets the better of her class-feeling even in her attitude towards the war. For, having orthodoxly registered her sense of the complete *bouleversement* which it is making in the spiritual life of the world, she calmly proceeds as if it were not. Neither in her criticism nor in her verse is the slightest evidence that into the domain of literary art has the war penetrated, or will it penetrate. Nothing shows better than her attitude how very far the younger generation is beyond those older counselors who hope that the war will "get under our skins"— perhaps to make a few bad poets write worse poems, and to give many mediocre writers a momentary patriotic and social glamor, but not to touch a "young world" which has its treasures for other heavens!

The problem of the literary artist is how to obtain more of this intelligent, pertinent, absolutely contemporaneous criticism, which shall be both severe and encouraging. It will be obtained when the artist himself has turned critic and set to work to discover and interpret in others the motives and values and efforts he feels in himself. The "high seriousness" of Miss Lowell's own critical attitude towards the artistic problems of the six poets suggests, I think, that there is a promise of a rich and vibrant literary era before us. No one pretends to be satisfied with the novels and plays and interpretations now being turned out by the younger intellectuals. Least of all must they themselves be satisfied. After all, very little of their work really gives voice to the ambitions, desires, discontents, and spiritual adventures of the all too self-conscious young American world. Moreover, there is for this healthy dissatisfaction an insidious trap—the terrible glamor of social patronage which so easily blunts idealism in the young prophet. The other day, reading *My Literary Friends and*

Acquaintances, I shuddered at Howells's glee over the impeccable social tone of Boston and Cambridge literary life. He was playful enough about it, but not too playful to conceal the enormity of his innocence. He does not see how dreadful it is to contrast Cambridge with ragged vagabonds and unpresentable authors of other ages. To a younger generation which feels that the writer ought to be at least a spiritual vagabond, a de-classed mind, this gentility of Mr. Howells and his friends has come to seem more alien than Sologub. We are acquiring an almost Stendhalian horror for those correctnesses and tacts which wield such hypnotic influence over our middle-class life. "Society," we say, whether it be in the form of the mob or the cultivated dinner-circle, is the deadly enemy of the literary artist. Literary promises can be seen visibly fading out in the warm beams of association with the refined and the important. And social glamor was never so dangerous as it is today when it is anxious to be enlightened and liberal. Timidity is still the reigning vice of the American intellect, and the terrorism of "good taste" is yet more deadly to the creation of literary art than is sheer barbarism. The literary artist needs protection from the liberal audience that will accept him though he shock them, but that subtly tame him even while they appreciate.

If this literary promise does not fulfill itself, it will be because our younger writers have pleased a public too easy to please. As we look around at those who have ideas, our proper mood is not pleasure that their work is so good, but discontent that it is not better. It will not be better unless certain values are felt more intensely. Those Americans who are fortunate enough to see Copeau's theatre seem to remark there a fusion of fervor and simplicity with finished workmanship, a sort of sensuous austerity of tone—an effort of creative novelty working with all that is vital in a tradition. Do we not want these values in our American effort? Should we not like to see from this younger generation a literary art which will combine a classical and puritan tradition with the most modern ideas? Do we not want minds with a touch of the apostolic about them and a certain edge—a little surly, but not embittered—with an intellectual as well as an artistic conscience, with a certain tentative superciliousness towards Demos and an appalling hatred for everything which savors of the bourgeois or the sentimental? Now while everything that is respectable in America seems to be putting its effort, with a sort of joyful perversity, into the technique of destruction, are there no desperate spiritual outlaws with a lust to create?

[1] Bourne's article resulted in a discussion. Harriet Monroe replied with "Mr. Bourne on Traps" in *Poetry*, 12 (April, 1918). In September, 1918, there appeared in *Poetry* a reply by Bourne and Van Wyck Brooks, "The Reply Courteous," whereupon Harriet Monroe retorted with "The Static Social Criticism" in October of the same year.

CHIVALRY AND SIN

**The Cry of Youth, by Harry Kemp. New York: Mitchell Kennerley.
Americans, by John Curtis Underwood. New York: G.P.Putnam's
Sons.**

There is something admirable in the way our younger American
poets are coming to the rescue of our lady of poetry. Her
somewhat bedraggled condition after a too long wandering in
the maze of the popular magazine appeals to all the chivalric
instincts of their souls. Chivalry in the ordinary sense transforms
every feminine human being into a lady and then makes her uncomfortable or illegitimately flattered by reverencing her. Mr.
Harry Kemp's chivalry consists in turning a number of his ordinary ideas and feelings into verse, and then making us uncomfortable by getting himself hailed as a poet. His "cry of youth"
seems scarcely commensurate with that romantic career of his
which began, according to his veracious publisher, when "he
discovered Keats, and began to take short tramping expeditions" in the adventurous country around Arlington, New Jersey.
Those of us who live a pokey, untitillated life may be excused for
painting our world gray or a pale yellow, but we have a right to
express our exasperation with a poet who has tramped it, sailed
it, starved it, studied it, Roycrofted it, and finally Greenwich-
Villaged it, and then lets so little of the color and slam and lift of
life shoot out of his words at us. Does such a life breed only
interest in bread-lines and Christian fable and the other stock
themes of the little modern poet? When one has apparently
made a glorious, racing mistress of life, one can only be described as chivalric who respectfully takes her gloved hand as
he lifts his—perhaps indeed sufficiently Bohemian—soft hat to
her on the city street.

Mr. Underwood's chivalry is of a different pattern. Poetry to
him is not a hot and passionate paramour met, for propriety's
sake, gallantly upon the street, but a plain and dowdy damsel in
distress. It is the typical American life which he is after; he
wishes to give a "fairly comprehensive criticism up-to-date." I
like the poetical touch of that "up-to-date." It implies that our
damsel is neither periled nor old maidish, but merely neglected.
The poet announces himself as "insurgent." Perhaps he has
been looking for some more resonant and far-flinging American
spirit to sing. But failing to find it, he has courageously fallen

back on what is vouchsafed us. Let us look in our cultural heart and write, about Gouverneur Morris, Owen Johnson, and Robert W. Chambers instead of new Whitmans and James's, let us not superciliously sniff aside, but accept them as the interpreters of the racy, indigenous American Kultur of the day. It may cost us a wry face for the moment, but after all the only way to attain a virtuous peace of mind is to fall in love with your own vices.

What makes significant these hundred monologues of "Americans," representing all types, and expressed in the choicest language of the moment, is the old Puritan sense of sin which crops up in a thousand unexpected ways. We are supposed to have buried it in this sophisticated generation, but it persists even in the most daring and popular magazine fiction. It is the undercurrent of Gouverneur Morris's adored and chastely passionate stories, of Owen Johnson's precocious world, of Chambers' precarious situations. These lovers are constantly suggesting—"How wicked we'd be if we were doing anything different from what we are doing!" The sinister and desperate beauties who stalk through so many of the worldly novels of the day all seem to say, "We know we're bad, but what are we going to do about it? Aha!" and then they turn and take another glass or stalk one more step towards their ruin. If you are to be a character in American fiction you must still be either good or bad, or at least selfish or unselfish. And you must be conscious of your goodness or your badness, and your author must be conscious of it too, and be always pointing it out to the reader—never grossly, but in a thousand shades of regret and irony and justification and blame. Each of Mr. Underwood's Americans is trying to suck out a grain of moral truth from his experience, justifying his own existence, exculpating his wickedness, or beating his breast in cynical despair. Everything is grist to our moral mill. To the cool and scientific truth that human beings are largely the resultant of sociological and economic forces we must give the twist that people are innocent victims of their environment. A cold-blooded program of national conservation and social reorganization could not be accepted until "Onward, Christian Soldiers" had been sung over it. Socialism has to appear as the Law of Love, Penrose not as a wasteful and foolish politician but a crook. We are all fearfully self-conscious morally, but hardly self-conscious in any other way. Instead of putting our energy, therefore, into economic and social reconstruction, it goes into castigation of malefactors, and pity for the victims. Energy which might go into clarifying our ideas and our desires goes into "being and doing good."

All this comes to a refusal to see life vividly in any but moral terms. We act as if we were afraid to look at it in other terms. Our literary poverty is due to a sort of fear of the dark, a dread of grappling with the stuff of life, which men and women actually experience—their half-understood motives and feelings, the groping ache of their desires, their unrecognized bestialities, their fixed ideas, their irritations, their illusory imaginings. Any real literature is, of course, impossible without a democratic attitude towards experience, without a tendency to find the things that people think and feel, *interesting* before we consign them to a moral heaven, purgatory, or hell. We seem uneasy in the presence of fervent personalities, unconventional relations, dangerous emotions, unhappinesses, spiritual struggles and despairs. Even the rawly sexual has a better chance in our drama and fiction than the obscure interweavings of real sex-feeling. As a rule, if we must have strong emotions, we prefer to have them shifted off to the Klondike or the wilderness, by a Rex Beach or a Jack London. We want them in the form of the lure of gold or ambition, or the love of a strong man for a woman. We want our emotions turned into "red blood." We don't want them lying around in people of everyday life. It makes us uneasy to read of people living an interior life of struggle and feeling, caught perhaps in coils of desire and personal issues. We shun the irrevocable, the insoluble. We are afraid of feeling deeply, or looking boldly at the obscure and sinister forces at the background of human life. We would flee in terror from such Continental implications that this background might be ennui or thwarted desire.

Our literature tends always to create an impossibly idealized and ladylike world, where feelings get somehow diluted into sentimentality—a world of selfishness and altruism, of dutiful filial relations, ambition, kindness, pity, chaste love. The framework is of reason, goodness, and justification. The malign appears only as assaults upon this framework. Now this may be the world towards which all human life should tend, but it is certainly not the world in which we live. And literature has some other function than being clumsy poetry.

Our American attitude towards life is, in other words, a chivalric one. It is caddish to insinuate that a woman is not a perfect lady. It is caddish to shock her reticence and modesty. It is caddish to speak of her in other terms than reverence or affection. So it would be unchivalric to imply that life was not respectable or only casually and externally so. Chivalry was originally a sort of protective magic directed by man against woman to keep her from suddenly springing the unpleasant fact on him that she was also a equally valid personality, to be accounted for. Our literary chivalry is exactly this attempt to prevent ourselves suddenly becoming convinced that life has vast, unmanageable depths and complexities and hopeless incompatibilities, which perhaps cannot be resolved, but which ought to be seriously felt and understood. Such a realization would, of course, require us to reorganize too many codes, too many relations. It would make life an adventure rather than a ride in a suburban train.

AN EXAMINATION OF EMINENCES

For making a younger generation of rebels and malcontents the Victorian Age gets and deserves a good deal of reproach. Its descendants have not desired to find it so unsatisfactory. They would much prefer to have sprung from a society which they could really reverence. It is easier and altogether pleasanter to love your parents than to dislike them; and one's days would have been all the fairer in the land if the commandment could have been obeyed by their children with a joyous heart and a clear conscience. But it was not so to be. A budding young middle class in England and America found itself too tightly encased in tastes and values that did not at all accord with the pushings within or the faint but tantalizing interests without. In a world where everything was becoming public, where everyone was being enjoined to take his place in the world's work, the young person feeling the oats of his intelligence found that he was still being kept by family, school, and church in a state of tutelage. Parents to whose timid souls the confines of conventionality had been extremely grateful found themselves giving birth to amazing prodigies of reluctance and self-will. The turbulence of old submerged ancestors seemed to break out rather generally in this younger generation; and contempt, disdain, irreverence, flightiness, bumptiousness, and rebellion raised their horrid heads. The vigorous and the wicked got easily free, but on the more sensitive youth the divine right of parents and of the small-town sanctities often bore so heavily that a large part of their golden youth was spent in mere disentanglement.

The mournful inadequacies of religion, the urgency of socialism, sex-expression, and worthy work all served as rationalizations for the wild impulsive need of escape. But the fashion became gradually for us to roll our resentments into a blanket indictment of the Victorian Age. This happy way of taking the offensive-defensive has almost driven the Victorians from the field. It has been almost too successful. Not content with turning the dear Queen into a sort of perpetual wetnurse to a civilization, it has made of all the notables—political, literary, religious—a cluster of priggish children about her skirts. Even Wells still pursues her relentlessly in his last novel as "that little old German woman." The anti-Victorian rebellion long since got into the play and the novel, but biography has been left untouched. No one has dared to touch the sacred personalities themselves. One could flash sharp little nips at them; but to take a life and turn it inside out, letting all the modern irony and youthful disdain play upon it, was an enterprise which has surpassed the genius of this younger generation.

Until now. Mr. Lytton Strachey, in *Eminent Victorians* has done that very thing—just at the time when the fun of hitting the Victorian Age over the head, the delight of referring all our spiritual disorders, bonds, and tensions back to the innocent maleficence of what was after all a varied and vivid time, is becoming a little stale. With a cruelly masterful hand he has gone below the surface and turned up its paradoxes. We gloat over that "eminent." Not Gladstone or Tennyson or Browning or Disraeli are his samples; but Cardinal Manning, Florence Nightingale, Dr. Thomas Arnold, and General Gordon—people of no permanent influence, but revealing because their contemporaries became excited about them. They had the luck to set vibrating the peculiar reverences and interests which that society took with the most unquestioning sobriety and satisfaction. Mr. Strachey is the young man looking his elders and betters for the first time full in the face, sizing them up in the complete poise of a modern self-assurance. From them he squeezes the last drop of the glorious juice which they so unexpectedly have to give forth. They live under his hand as no mere solitary targets for his depreciations. They trail along with themselves other figures— Newman, Gladstone, Clough, Sir Evelyn Baring, and typical Englishmen like Lord Hartington—in etched portraits that bring a surprisingly large part of the political and religious tendencies of the time before us.

Mr. Strachey's preface is disarming and entrancing:

> The history of the Victorian Age will never be written; we know too much about it. For ignorance is the first requisite of the historian—ignorance which simplifies and clarifies, which selects and omits, with a placid perfection unattainable by the highest art. Concerning the age which has just passed, our fathers and our grandfathers have poured forth and accumulated so vast a quantity of information that the industry of a Ranke would be submerged by it, and the perspicacity of a Gibbon would quail before it. It is not by the direct method of a scrupulous narration that the explorer of the past

can hope to depict that singular epoch. If he is wise, he will adopt a subtler strategy. He will attack his subject in unexpected places; he will fall upon the flank or the rear; he will shoot a sudden, revealing searchlight into obscure recesses, hitherto undivined. He will row out over that great ocean of material, and lower down into it, here and there, a little bucket, which will bring up to the light of day some characteristic specimen from these far depths, to be examined with a careful curiosity.

That subtler strategy Mr. Strachey has adopted, with a mind so keenly tempered, a skill so deadly, that it is no wonder that the tough Victorian remnant is reported to be in consternation over this book which has created a stir in England even in wartime. This man has them at his mercy because he does not rant he does not wring his hands or rail at Victorian obtuseness and middle-class stodginess. Up till now our anti-Victorianism has been evangelistic. He improves on the evangelists by presenting not an argument, or a gospel, but the clear, cool, and always joyous truth. He tells the revealing facts, and he lets his heroes perform all their own malice for him in their own words: Gladstone congratulating Manning gleefully on his promotion to an Archdeaconship, only to catch himself up with a reminder of "the great principle of communion in the body of Christ"; Dr. Arnold saying that the "one thing needful for a Christian and an Englishman to study is Christian and moral and political philosophy"; and the Royal approbation falling with exquisite timeliness on the exploits of Miss Nightingale and revealing in the inimitable style of the Queen's own letters the origin of the immortal Hermione.

Mr. Strachey is formidable. He escapes smartness, even when he says that "when Newman was a child he wished he could believe the Arabian nights were true. When he came to be a man, his wish seems to have been granted"; or that "one has the impression that Miss Nightingale has got the Almighty too into her clutches, and that, if He is not careful, she will kill Him with overwork." All his cleverness is substantiated. He treats his subjects, no matter how playful he sounds—and the book is dotted with delicious anecdotes—with a fine seriousness. But his tact has the vigor of a generation that has at last come into its intellectual own and has its ancient hinderers on the run. Bumptious youth can usually be discounted on the ground of its hopeless ignorance, its smattering scholarship, its lack of experience, and its eloquence that is mere raw egoism. But what can be done with a mind of this terrifying competency, who builds up an unassailable structure of facts, and writes a racy narrative in the clearest and most rhythmical of styles? His irreverences are not mere insubordination but a genuine transvaluation of values. Froude and Clough "went through an experience which was more distressing in those days than it has since become; they lost their faith." He has only to outline the great hubbub about the Gorham Judgment—"the questions at issue were taken very seriously by a large number of persons"—or the questions of Church and State that Dr. Arnold and others ground the edges of their minds upon, to relegate the Age almost to the medievality of the angelic doctors.

Manning's scruples deepened with his desires, and he could satisfy his most exorbitant ambitions in a profundity of self-abasement.

He traces lightly the intricate thread of personal ambition that played through a society which had almost completely succeeded in translating every human purpose into terms of exalted altruism, or Christian casuistry. We see the surprising tenacity of Christian metaphysics in lives of the most worldly adventure. He is able to present very human figures without ever losing the sense of their social role in some great conflict of ideas or parties. The indomitable will and strident personality of Miss Nightingale, that early wrecker of a parental home, is as living as her decisive effect on the English War Office. Dr. Arnold's majesty slips into a biting paragraph (as from the pen of one who has suffered but restrains himself) about the influence of Rugby on English education:

The earnest enthusiast who strove to make his pupils Christian gentlemen and who governed his school according to the principles of the Old Testament has proved to be the founder of the worship of athletics and the worship of good form.

In the end of General Gordon we read the weird story of a British Imperialism that did not know its own interests and had to break through, by a sort of animal push, the wavering passions of statesmen to attain its ends.

At any rate it all ended very happily in a glorious slaughter of twenty thousand Arabs, a vast addition to the British Empire, and a step in the peerage for Sir Evelyn Baring.

The book runs over with good things. One closes it with a new sense of the delicious violence of sheer thought. If there were more Gideons like this, at the sound of such trumpets all the walls of the Victorian Jerichos would certainly fall.

THE USES OF INFALLIBILITY[1]

I

Few people read Newman today. The old anxious issues have been drowned in a flood of social problems, and that world of liberal progress which to him was the enemy at the gates has long ago broken in and carried everything before it. Newman's persuasive voice sounds thin and remote, and his ideas smell of a musty age. Yet that title of his, *Apologia Pro Vita Sua,* always intrigues one with its modern and subjective sound. It is so much what all of us are itching to write. Its egotism brushes with a faint irony that absorption in the righteousness most emphatically not ourselves with which Newman's life was mingled. In that call upon him to interpret his life, one feels an unquenchable ego which carries him over to these shameless and self-centered times. Fortunately placed for a week in a theological household, I plunged into the slightly forbidding pages of the wistful cardinal. What I found in him must be very different from what he found in himself or what anybody else found in him at the time. Newman in 1917 suggests less a reactionary theology than a subtle and secret sympathy with certain veins of our modern intellectual radicalism. The voice was faint, but what I heard made Newman significant for me. For it implied that if faith is eternal, so is skepticism, and that even in the most pious mind may be found the healthy poison of doubt.

Superficially seen, Newman appeared to have abolished doubt. His faith was more conservative than that of the orthodox. He surrendered all that Victorian life for the narrowest of obscurantisms. The reasons he found for his course only riveted him impregnably to the rock of unreason. What my mind fastened on, however, was the emotional impulse that led him his tortuous way. One detected there in him that same sinister note one feels in Pascal. It is a reasonableness that eats away at belief until it finally destroys either it or you. It is an uncanny honesty of soul which, struggling utterly for faith, saves it only by unconsciously losing it. For if you win your way through to belief by sheer intellectual force, you run the risk of over-reaching your belief. You do not know that you have passed it, but you have really dispensed with its use. If you are honest in mind and religious in temperament, you find yourself reduced to the naked reality of religion. You are left with only the most primitive mysticism of feeling. You are one with the primitive savage group. Ineffable feeling, ecstatic union with the universe—this is your state. The more religious you become, the more you tear the fabric of your dogma. Belief is only for the irreligious. Intellectuality in religion, under the guise of fortifying faith, only destroys its foundations. Newman's approach towards the certitude of dogma was really only an approach towards the certitude of mysticism. When he thought he was satisfying his intellectual doubts, he was satisfying his emotional cravings. Intending to buttress dogma, he only assured for himself the mystic state.

How far he really attained mysticism is a fascinating problem for the reader of the *Apologia*. Popular impression is probably right that he bore to his incredibly lengthened age a pathos of uneasiness and sadness. But popular impression is probably wrong in ascribing this to lingering remorse or regret. If there was any uncertainty, it was not for having left his Anglican position, but for not having seen the thing wholly through. Intellectuality still clung aorund him like a cold swathing garment. He probably never attained that pure mysticism which his soul craved. One has the impression that Newman's pathos lay in the fact that he never quite became a saint. The official world seemed to hang about him hamperingly. One wonders sometimes if he could not almost as easily have become a wan sweet pagan as a saint. The tragedy of Pascal was that intrinsically he was a pagan. The kind of Christianity to which he drove himself was for him the most virulent form of moral suicide. The terrible fascination of his *Pensées* lies in that relentless closing in of the divine enemy on his human "pride," which might have been, with his intellectual genius, so lusty an organ of creativeness and adventure. It was not disease that killed him but Christianity. Pascal is an eternal warning from the perils of intellectual religion.

Dogma did not kill Newman, but it did not save him. He was not a pagan, but he never became a saint. He never quite got rid of dogma. And that is what so fascinates us in his religious technique. For his *Apologia* is really a subtle exposure of infallibility. It shows us what the acute intellectuality of a mystic finds to do with dogma. The goal towards which he tends is the utter bankruptcy of articulate religion. And involved in it is the bankruptcy of institutional religion. It is a religious bankruptcy that acts like modern commercial bankruptcy. All material assets are relinquished, and you start again in business on the old footing. You throw over your dogma but keep the mystic experience, which can never be taken away from you. In this way the Catholic Church becomes, or could become, eternal. Newman shows a way just short of relinquishment. He uses infallibility to liquidate his intellectual debts, and then becomes free of his creditors.

II

How these attitudes are implied in the *Apologia* I can only suggest through the surprises that a reading brought. The contention had always been that Newman's apostasy was due to feebleness of will, to a fatigue in the search for certitude that let him slip into the arms of Mother Church. My protestant training had persistently represented every going over to Rome as a surrender of individual integrity. For the sake of intellectual peace, one became content to stultify the intellect and leave all thinking to the infallible Church. There is nothing of intellectual fatigue, however, in Newman. His course did not spring from weariness of thinking. He had a most fluent and flexible mind, and if he seemed to accept beliefs at which Protestants thrilled with frightened incredulity, it was because such an acceptance satisfied some deeper need, some surer craving. Read today, Newman interests not because of the beliefs but because of this deeper desire. He had a sure intuition of the uses of infallibility and intellectual authority, and of their place in the scheme of things. This is his significance for the modern mind. And he is the only one of the great religious writers who seems to reach out to us and make contact with our modern attitude.

Newman loved dogma, but it was not dogma that he loved most. It was not to quiet a heart that ached with doubt that he passed from the Anglican to the Roman Church. As an Anglican Catholic he was quite as sure of his doctrine as he was as a Roman Catholic. His most primitive craving was not so much for infallibility as for legitimacy. It was because the Roman Church was primitive, legitimate, authorized, and the Anglican Church yawned in spots, that he made his reluctant choice. His Anglican brothers would not let him show them the catholicity of the Articles. They began to act schismatically, and there was nothing to do but join the legitimate order and leave them to their vulgar insufficiencies. This one gets from the *Apologia*. But this craving, one feels, sprang not from cowardice but from a sense of proportion. Newman was frankly a conservative. Here was a mind that lived in the most exciting of all intellectual eras, when all the acuteness of England was passing from orthodoxy to liberalism. Newman deliberately went in the other direction. But he went because he valued certain personal and spiritual things to which he saw the new issues would be either wholly irrelevant or fatally confusing. One of the best things in the *Apologia* is the appendix on Liberalism, where Newman, with the clarity of the perfect enemy, sums up the new faith. Each proposition outrages some aspect of legitimacy which is precious to him, yet his intuition—he wrote it not many years after the Reform Bill—has put in classic form what is the Nicene Creed of liberal religion. No liberal ever expressed liberalism so justly and concisely. Newman understands this modern creed as perfectly as he flouts it. So Pascal's uncanny analysis of human pride led him only to self-prostration.

Why did Newman disdain liberalism? He understood it, and he did not like it. His deathless virtue lies in his disconcerting honesty. The air was full of strange new cries that he saw would arrest the Church. She would have to explain, defend, interpret, on a scale far larger than had been done for centuries. She would have to make adjustment to a new era. Theology would be mingled with sociology. The church of the spirit would be challenged with social problems, would be called down into a battling arena of life. Newman's intuition saw that the challenge of liberalism meant a worried and harassed Church. He was not interested in social and political questions. The old order had a fixed charm for him. It soothed and sustained his life, and it was in his own life that he was supremely interested. He loved dogma, but he loved it as a priceless jewel that one does not wear. His emotion was not really any more entangled in it than it was in social problems. Given an established order that made his personal life possible, what he was interested in was mystical meditation, the subtle and difficult art of personal relations, and the exquisite ethical problems that arise out of them.

Newman's position was one of sublime common sense. He saw that the Protestant Church would be engaged for decades in the doleful task of reconciling the broadening science with the old religious dogma. He knew that this was ludicrous. He saw that liberalism was incompatible with dogma. But mostly he saw that the new social and scientific turn of men's thinking was incompatible with the mellowed mystical and personal life where lay his true genius. So, with a luminous sincerity, following the appeal of his talents, he passed into the infallible Church which should be a casket for the riches of his personal life. He was saved thus from the sin of schism, and from the sin of adding to that hopeless confusion of intellectual tongues which embroiled the English world for the rest of the century. The Church guaranteed the established order beneath him, blotted out the sociological worries around him, and removed the incubus of dogma above him. Legitimacy and infallibility did not imprison his person or his mind. On the contrary, they freed him, because they abolished futilities from his life. Nothing is clearer from the *Apologia* than Newman's sense of the hideous vulgarity of theological discussion. He uses infallibility to purge himself of that vulgarity. He uses it in exactly the way that it should rightly be employed. The common view is that dogma is entrusted to the Church because its truth is of such momentous import as to make fatal the risk of error through private judgment. Through ecclesiastical infallibility dogma becomes the letter and spirit of religion, bony structure and lifeblood.

But Newman's use of infallibility was as a storage vault in which one puts priceless securities. They are there for service when one wishes to realize on their value. But in the business of daily living one need not look at them from one year to another. Infallibility is the strong lock of the safety-vault. It is a guarantee not of the value of the wealth but of its protection. The wealth must have other grounds for its valuableness, but one is assured that it will not be tampered with. By surrendering all your dogmas to the keeper-Church, you win, not certitude—for your treasures are no more certain inside the vault than they are in your pocket—but assurance that you will not have to see your life constantly interrupted by the need of defending them against burglars, or of proving their genuineness for the benefit of inquisitive and incredulous neighbors. The suspicion is irresistible that Newman craved infallibility not because dogma was so supremely significant to him, but because it was so supremely irrelevant. Nothing could be more revealing than his acceptance of the doctrine of the Immaculate Conception. He has no trouble whatever in believing this belated and hotly-disdained dogma.

Because it is essential to his understanding of heaven and hell, eternity and the ineffable God? On the contrary, because it is so quintessentially irrelevant to anything that really entangles his emotions. His tone in acknowledging his belief is airy, almost gay. He seems to feel no implications in the belief. It merely rounds off a logical point in his theology. It merely expresses in happy metaphor a poetical truth. To him there is no tyranny in the promulgation of this new dogma. Infallibility, he seems to suggest, removes from discussion ideas that otherwise one might be weakly tempted to spend unprofitable hours arguing about.

And nothing could be more seductive than his belief in Transubstantiation. Science, of course, declares this transmutation of matter impossible. But science deals only with phenomena. Transubstantiation has to do not with phenomena but with things-in-themselves. And what has science to say about the inner reality of things? Science itself would be the first to disclaim any such competence. Why, therefore, should not the Church know as much as anybody about the nature of this thing-in-itself? Why is it not as easy to believe the Church's testimony as to the nature of things as it is to believe any testimony? Such dogma is therefore unassailable by science. And if it cannot be criticized it might just as well be infallible. The papal guarantee does not invade science. It merely preempts an uncharted region. It infringes no intellectual rights. It steps in merely to withdraw from discussion ideas which would otherwise be misused. Infallibility Newman uses as a shelf upon which to store away his glowing but pragmatically sterile theological ideas, while down below in the arena are left for discussion the interesting aspects of life. He is at great pains to tell us that the Church is infallible only in her expressly declared doctrine. It is only over a few and definite dogmas that she presides infallibly. You surrender to infallibility only those cosmic ideas it would do you no good to talk of anyway. In the vast overflowing world of urgent practical life you are free to speculate as you will. Underneath the eternal serene of dogma is the darting vivid web of casuistry. Relieved of the inanity of theological discussion, the Catholic may use his intellect on the human world about him. That is why we are apt to find in the Catholic the acute psychologist, while the Protestant remains embroiled in weary dialectics.

Such a use of infallibility as Newman implies exposes the fallacy of the Protestant position. For as soon as you have removed this healthy check to theological embroilment you have opened the way to intellectual corruption. As soon as you admit the right of individual judgment in theological matters you have upset the balance between dogma and life. The Catholic consigns his dogmas to the infallible Church and speculates about the pragmatic issues of the dynamic moral life. The Protestant on the other hand, encases himself in an iron-bound morality and gives free rein to his fancy about the eternal verities. The Catholic is empirical in ethics and dogmatic in theology. The Protestant is dogmatic in ethics and more and more empirical in theology. He speculates where it is futile to speculate, because in supernatural matters you can never come by evidence to any final, all-convincing truth. But he refuses to speculate where a decent skepticism and a changing adjustment to human nature would work out attitudes towards conduct that make for flowering and growth. The Protestant infallibility of morals is the cruellest and least defensible of all infallibilities. Protestantism passes most easily into that fierce puritan form which constrains both conduct and belief.

The Protestant inevitably gravitates either towards puritanism or towards unitarianism. The one petrifies in a harsh and narrow moral code, the ordering of conduct by the most elderly, least aesthetic, dullest and gloomiest elements in the community. The other mingles in endless controversy over the attributes of deity, the history of its workings in the world, and the power of the supernatural. Religion becomes a village sewing-society, in which each member's life is lived in the fearful sight of all the others, while the tongues clack endlessly about rumors that can never be proved and that no one outside will ever find the slightest interest in having proved.

If the Catholic Church had used infallibility in the way that Newman did, its influence could never have been accused of oppression. There need never have been any warfare between theology and science. Infallibility affords the Church an adroit way of continuing its spiritual existence while it permits free speculation in science and ethics to go on. Suppose the Church in its infallibility had not stuck to dogma. Suppose the reformers had been successful, and the Church had accepted early scientific truth. Suppose it had refused any longer to insist on correctness in theological belief but had insisted on correctness in scientific belief. Suppose the dogmas of the Resurrection had made way for the first crude imperfect generalizations in physics. Imagine the hideousness of a world where scientific theories had been declared infallible by an all-powerful Church! Our world's safety lay exactly in the Church's rejection of science. If the Church had accepted science, scientific progress would have been impossible. Progress was possible only by ignoring the Church. Knowledge about the world could only advance through accepting gratefully the freedom which the Church tacitly offered in all that fallible field of the technique of earthly living. What progress we have we owe not to any overcoming or converting of the Church but to a scrupulous ignoring of her.

In punishing heresy the Church worked with a sound intuition. For a heretic is not a man who ignores the Church. He is one who tries to mix his theology and science. He could not be a heretic unless he were a victim of muddy thinking, and as a muddy thinker he is as much a nuisance to secular society as he is to the Church against which he rebels. He is the officious citizen who tries to break into the storage-vault with the benevolent intention of showing that the jewels are paste. But all he usually accomplishes is to set the whole town by the ears. The constructive daily life of the citizens is interrupted in a flood of idle gossip. It is as much to the interest of the intelligent authorities, who have important communal projects on hand, to suppress him as it is to the interest of the owner of the jewels. Heresy is fundamentally the error of trying to reconcile new knowledge with old dogma. The would-be heretic could far more wisely ignore theology altogether and pursue his realistic knowledge in the aloofness which it requires. If there is still any theological taint in him, he should not dabble in science at all. If there is none, the Church will scarcely feel itself threatened and he will not appear as a heretic. On the pestiferousness of the heretic both the Church and the most modern realist can agree. Let theology deal with its world of dogma. Let science deal with its world of analyzable and measurable fact. Let them never touch hands or recognize even each other's existence.

The intellectual and spiritual chaos of the nineteenth century was due to the prevalence of heresy which raged like an epidemic through Europe. Minds which tried to test their new in-

dubitable knowledge by the presuppositions of faith were bound
to be disordered and to spread disorder around them. Faith and
science tap different planes of the soul, elicit different emotional
currents. It is when the Church has acted from full realization of
this fact that it has remained strong. Protestantism, trying to live
in two worlds at the same time, has swept thousands of excellent minds into a spiritual limbo where, in their vague twilight
realm of a modernity which has not quite sacrificed theology,
they have ceased to count for intellectual or spiritual light.

Perhaps the most pathetic of heresies is the "modernism"
which is spreading through the French and Italian Church. For
this effort to bring unitarian criticism into Catholic theology, to
make over the dogmas from within, to apply reason to the un-
reasonable, is really the least "modern" of enterprises. It is only
a belated Protestant reformation, and if it succeeds it could do
little more than add another Protestant sect to the existing mul-
titude. It would not in the least have modernized Catholicism, for
the most modern attitude which one can take towards the
Church is to ignore it entirely, to cease to feel its validity in the
new humane, democratic world that is our vision. In other words,
to take towards it exactly the attitude which it takes towards itself. This is its strength. It has never hesitated to accept pragmatic truth that was discovered by others. The Catholic makes
use of whatever scientific, industrial, political, sociological development works, and adjusts himself without discomfort to a
dynamic world. He makes no attempt at reconciliation with the
supernatural. A Catholic hospital uses all the latest medical science without exhibiting the least concern over its infallible
"truth." It is doubtful whether the Church ever attempted to prevent Catholics from adopting anything as long as they did not
bother whether it was "true" or not. This is the real mischief, to
get your infallible divine truth confused with your pragmatic
human truth. The "modernist" in setting about this confusion
simply counts that expulsion which is his.

All this seemed to me implicit in the *Apologia*. But if the use
Newman made of infallibility destroys the Protestant position, it
no less destroys the Catholic. For if you use infallibility as a
technique for getting dogmas into a form in which they are easy
to forget, you reduce the Church from a repository of truth to a
mere political institution. When dogma is removed from discussion, religious truth becomes irrelevant to life as it is commonly

lived. The Church, therefore, can touch life only through its political and organizing power, just as any human institution touches life. It no longer touches it through the divinely inspiring quality of its thought. Intellectually the Church will only appeal to those cowed minds which have no critical power and demand absolutism in thought. Spiritually it will appeal only to temperaments like Newman's which crave a guarantor for their mystic life. Politically it will appeal to the subtle who want power through the devious control over human souls. To few other types will it appeal.

Newman unveils the true paradox of dogma. If, on the one hand, you throw it open to individual judgment, you destroy it through the futile wranglings of faith which can never be objectively solved. If, on the other hand, you declare it infallible, you destroy it by slowly sending it to oblivion. Infallibility gets rid of dogma just as surely as does private judgment. Under the pretense of consolidating the Church in its cosmic role, Newman, therefore, has really put it in its proper parochial place as a pleasant grouping of souls who are similarly affected by a collection of beautiful and vigorous poetic ideas. Fundamentally, however, this grouping has no more universal significance than any other, than a secret society or any religious sect.

Thus Newman unconsciously anticipates the most modern realistic agnostic. For the latter would agree that to relegate dogma to the storage-vault of infallibility is exactly what ought to be done with dogma. At such an infallible as Newman pictures no modern radical need balk. Newman's argument means little more than that infallibility is merely the politest way of sending an idea to Nirvana. What more can the liberal ask who is finished with theology and all its works? He can accept this infallible in even another sense. For there is not a single Christian doctrine in which he does not feel a kind of wild accuracy. Every Christian dogma has a poetic vigor about it which might just as well be called "true" because to deny its metaphorical power would certainly be to utter an untruth. Indeed is not poetry the only "truth" that can be called infallible? For scientific truth is constantly being developed, revised, re-applied. It is only poetry that can think in terms of absolutes. Science cannot because it is experimental. But poetry may, because each soul draws its own meaning from the words. And dogma is poetry.

To render dogma infallible is to make it something that no

longer has to be fought for. This attitude ultimately undermines the whole structure for belief. If it is only infallible ideas that we are to believe, then belief loses all its moral force. It is no longer a fierce struggle to maintain one's intellectual position. Nothing is at stake. One is not braced in faith with the hosts of hell assailing one's citadel. To the puritan, belief meant something to be gloweringly and tenaciously held against the world, the flesh and the devil. But Catholic belief, in the Newman atmosphere, is too sheltered, too safely insured, to count excitingly. One only yawns over it, as his own deep soul must have secretly yawned over it, and turns aside to the genuine issues of life. But this is just what we should do with belief. We are passing out of the faith era, and belief, as an intellectual attitude, has almost ceased to play an active part in our life. In the scientific attitude there is no place whatever for belief. We have no right to "believe" anything unless it has been experimentally proved. But if it has been proved, then we do not say we "believe" it, because this would imply that an alternative was possible. All we do is to register our common assent to the new truth's incontrovertibility. Nor has belief any place in the loose, indecisive issues of ordinary living. We have to act constantly on insufficient evidence, on the best "opinion" we can get. But opinion is not belief, and we are lost if we treat it so. Belief is dogmatic, but opinion has value only when it is tentative, questioning. The fact is that in modern thinking the attitude of belief has given place to what may be called the higher plausibility. Stern, rugged conviction which has no scientific background behind it is coming to be dealt with impatiently by the modern mind. We have difficulty in distinguishing it from prejudice. There is no hostility to faith, if by "faith" we only mean an emotional core of desire driving towards some ideal. But idealism is a very different thing from belief. Belief is impelled from behind; it is sterile, fixed. Belief has no seeds of progress, no constructive impulse. An ideal, on the other hand, is an illumined end towards which our hopes and endeavors converge. It looks forward and pulls us along with it. It is ideals and not beliefs that motivate the modern mind. It is meaningless to say that we "believe" in our ideals. This separates our ideals from us. But what they are is just the push of our temperaments towards perfection. They are what is most inseparable and intrinsically ourselves. The place of a belief which put truth outside of us and made virtue a hard clinging to it has been taken by the idealism which merges us with the growing end we wish to achieve.

Newman illustrates the perpetual paradox of ecclesiasticism, that the more devoutly you accept the Church the less important you make it. As you press closer to its mystic heart, its walls and forms and ideas crumble and fade. The better Catholic you are, the more insidious your vitiation of Catholicism. So that the Church has remained strong only through its stout politicians and not through its saints. As a casket for the precious jewel of mysticism, it cannot die. But shorn of its political power it shrinks to a poetical society of mystics, held together by the strong and earthly bond of men who enjoy the easy expression of power over the least intelligent and intellectually assertive masses in Western society. The Church declines towards its natural limits. No attack on it, no undermining of it from within, can destroy religious feeling, for that is an organization of sentiments that are incarnate in man. Newman's emotion, whatever his mind may have done, reached through to this eternal heart. Implicit in his intellect, however, is that demolition of religious intellectuality which has freed our minds for the work of the future. He was an unconscious pioneer. Ostensibly reactionary, he reveals in his own *Apologia* an anticipation of our modern outlook. His use of infallibility insidiously destroys the foundations of belief.

[1] This was first published in 1920 in *The History of a Literary Radical.*

THE LIGHT ESSAY

Perhaps it is hardly fair to relegate the light essay to the less creative forms of literature, to see it as journalism dressed up, as it were, for a literary party. Yet when you have begun to identify "creative" writing with novels, verse, and drama you find yourself belittling the essay as scarcely more than a subterfuge, an illegitimate method of securing the literary sensation without doing the genuine literary work. You suspect that the light essayist is a person who was born without the narrative style and the poetic gift, who has not had enough adventures or does not understand life well enough to write stories, and lacks the divine fire for verse. In spite of the august examples of the essay which our professors slowly brought us to admire, most of us would rather be a Maxim Gorky than a Lamb, or have written *The Brook Kerith* than the *Sketchbook* of Washington Irving. American writers especially seem to be compensating for their lack of novelistic talent by a striking artistic capacity for the light essay. They do not, like the protean Mr. Chesterton, simply toss it in as one of the many things they can do. They found whole literary careers on it. But you always feel something lacking, even in the piquant petulance of Miss Repplier, the sly charm of Dr. Crothers, the urbanity of Mr. Sedgwick, and even the inexhaustibly witty fooling of Simeon Strunsky. Just the last vivifying touch is absent. You feel that it is proper that most of these writers are middle-aged, and most of their readers too.

The youthful light essayist is usually a painful phenomenon. He is apt to be ostentatiously bright. The middle-aged mind is legitimately mellow, and its self-consciousness is rather pleasant. We know that it has ruminated over and is aware of a lot of things that happened before we were born. But vivid green shoots can't be mellow. The young essayist is afraid you will think he is unsophisticated, while the middle-aged doesn't much care if you do. And youth's idea of being whimsical is usually to nose about among the irrelevant, and be very bold with the trivial. The youthful essayist usually develops into the professional anecdotalist, with an active mind that is harnessed up to no real thinking but can only stream off from itself a futile current of amusing incident.

When Mr. Robert Cortes Holliday, therefore, in his *Walking-Stick Papers,* describes himself as a "pale, spectacled, middle-aged young man" you are prepossessed in his favor. A middle-aged young man ought to write pretty good light essays. He ought to be mellow without giving you the impression that life has no more adventures, and he ought to be as diverting as his youth and naivete will let him. The first requirement of the light essay is that it should amuse you. To be amused is to experience one of the really great pieces of good fortune in life. The trouble with most pretended amusement is the suddenness of your deflation. Mere wit and anecdote go out like a candle in the wind. But the good essay does not stale. You leave it refreshed and in a nice glow of pleasedness, and its flavor follows you. So that it is this quality of amusingness that finally saves the light essay from the non-creative reproach. But all the more ghastly are the efforts that fail. The light essay is a truly perilous thing.

Mr. Holliday does not fail. Almost every page is amusing, and amusing in so simple a way that it rather astonishes you. He does not overload like Strunsky, and yet he is not thin. When you find yourself turning back to get the exact words in which he describes the departure of the Whartons and Henry James from the Scribner shop, or the call of Chesterton, or the expensive girls at the art exhibition, you decide that it was no mistake to capture these papers from the journals for which they were written, and put them between the covers of a book. To be sure, Mr. Holliday gives your mind no run for your money. He seems to have no particular convictions, and he has not a touch of scholarliness. His motto is: "It is a very pleasant thing to go about in the world and see all the people." Scrubwomen and "bartenders in very low places," as well as policemen, are among those people whose conversation he values. He shares with you the romance of the fish-reporter's life. He delights in the thunder of the trucks on Hudson Street. He loiters on upper Broadway, hunts lodgings, and takes you behind the scenes of the book reviewer's sorry life. And with all his informality of language and mood he always manages to escape both cheapness and self-consciousness.

I don't know how much of Mr. Holliday's appeal comes from the fact that he is so charmingly one of the submerged, observing the world from behind the counter of a bookshop or a reporter's desk, or from the anonymous sidewalk. Here is no respectability to maintain. He is neither a gentleman nor a preacher nor a maiden lady nor even a playgoer, as most American essayists are. He is not dignity unbending and rather obviously in the act of play. This irresponsible obscurity has so many advantages that you wish he had endowed his papers occasionally with more mind. Not the least amusing touch is his dedication to "three fine men"—Brownell, Belloc, and Cortissoz, three tough knights of reaction if there ever were any. Mr. Holliday is the cat looking at these kings. He admires them because "they represent to my mind the best things going; the pure milk of the word." Well, it is fortunate for him that the mysterious processes of animal chemistry transform the purest milk into strange new forms of tissue and blood. In these papers there is not the faintest trace of the style, attitudes, or opinions of these "fine men." Is this the adorable naivete of a young man who admired without in the least comprehending, or who is so genuinely humble that he does not even imitate? So perhaps it is lucky he has left out the mind, and given us his diverting pictures of celebrities in the solemn business of buying books, and of succumbing to his Literary Levities in London.

Mr. Holliday is not one of those writers who believe that to do a light essay all one needs is a light subject. Mr. Carl Van Vechten is. So in *The Merry-Go-Round* he writes on Music and Cooking, De Senectute Cantorum, and then stuffs his pages with the most deplorably indigestible facts and anecdotes imaginable. For he is of that school of which James Huneker is the grandfather and H. L. Mencken the honored immediate sire. They are a curious crowd. They combine the utmost ferocity of conviction against the academic and the puritanical with a pedantic fondness for the ragbag of facts. They are, or have been, most of them, musical and theatrical critics or inveterate reviewers. And it is, of course, good for critics to be erudite. As reviewers their minds require and receive continual fertilization of after-the-play suppers and convivial glasses. Their paradise is Munich, that dowdy city of heavenly beer, bad art, good music, and a German king's idea of Greek architecture. In their friendly intercourse there must be much barter of facts and anecdotes. And one cannot write description, or praise and blame, interminably. So into their writing, little by little, the facts do creep, the mere historical rubbish of the profession, and you get light essays like those of Mr. Van Vechten, delineating every instance where musicians and food have come into contact, or reciting lists of the musical comedies he saw in his younger days. Or you get pages strewn with felicities like this: "Sophie Arnould; one of the most celebrated actresses of the Eighteenth century, died in poverty at the age of 63, and there is no record of her burial place."

There are, of course, minds like that. But to read their work is as uncomfortable as taking out the stuffing of a sofa-pillow to rest your head against. And yet Mr. Van Vechten's intentions are evidently all for the light essay—for the bright unconventional sauntering about the musical, dramatic, and literary fair. But like the others of his school, his gustatory capacities are too enormous. He can swallow any amount of bad plays, and any number of pseudo-decadents like Edgar Saltus and Erik Satie. When he chooses out Feydeau and Mirbeau and Avery Hopwood and Philip Moeller to praise in the theater, you feel that hatred of puritanism has thrown his taste, as it has that of Mencken's, askew. His essay "In Defense of Bad Taste" argues in favor of sincerity, and that is good. But the trouble with his school, with the Menckens and the Nathans, is not that their taste is bad but that it is all disintegrated. They mire themselves in facts because their learning is not assimilated to their tastes. Neither are their tastes harmonious with each other. These critics appreciate the second-rate, not because they do not know any better, but because the whole slant of their judgment has tended to take up the defense of whatever the puritan mind most violently objects to. They have, one feels, let their taste be determined rather by negativing the puritan than by positively asserting a strong modern harmony of appreciation.

Mr. Van Vechten however deserves some mitigation of these strictures. He is always as sprightly as his intellectual dough will allow him to be. Where he can resist the clutch of facts, as in the little piece called "Au Bal Musette," he is graphic and amusing. Here he has the light essay trembling on the very verge of the short story, and you find him writing with a power that you wish he would oftener avail himself of. He leaves the impression elsewhere of a talent that has been somewhat coarsened either by too much use or by a following of minor prophets. What saves him in the end is the freshness and warmth of his appreciations. The "Impressions of the Theater," the notes on Mimi Aguglia, Isadora Duncan, and the Spanish dancers of "The

Land of Joy" are fine pieces of discerning admiration. In a merry-go-round of criticism it is, after all, this fine cordiality of liking that the reader himself warms to. Just as Mr. Holliday wins us by his sense of the pleasantness of the world, so Mr. Van Vechten wins us by his feeling, all theories put aside, for the downright delight of dramatic genius. And at their best both of these young American writers do lift the light essay out of that disparaged level of non-creation, and make it not only truly amusing but imaginatively artistic as well.

SOCIOLOGIC FICTION

King Coal, by Upton Sinclair. New York: The Macmillan Company. $1.50.

You must judge the American sociological novelist by standards of sociological pertinency rather than of literary art. Whether it is Winston Churchill exposing the capitalistic taint in the church, or Ernest Poole extending the family into the Gary school, or Upton Sinclair revealing the bestialities of the stockyards, you never look for those subtleties of personal life or for those living and breathing people that make the good novelist's art. The sociological raconteur uses people, but only as bricks to build his institutional edifice. It is the family, church, industry, that the story is really about. It is the institution that is the hero or villain, and the institution either in process of reformation or in shrieking need of it. The purpose of the story is to "show conditions," and the significance is frankly the message that something ought to be done about it. Where the literary artist would let the institution and its "message" play insistently out of the palpitating life of the individuals, caught in the struggle with it and busy with a thousand personal desires and adjustments, the sociological novelist sharply isolates institutional consciousness and denies his people thoughts and feelings that do not contribute directly to the missionary effect he wants to produce. Zola still lives because, though the master of the sociological novelist, he laboriously painted in every segment of his canvas, documenting sensual impression and confused aspiration, as well as institutional circumstance, so as to produce, through sheer massiveness and breadth, a feeling of personal life.

The Americans are less industrious, and consequently they are under a certain responsibility of showing that their work "shows conditions" better than would a sober report or generalized narrative. The theory is, of course, that the fictional form will make them more widely read. So they throw their material into dramatic shape, arrange the incidents cumulatively, give their characters fictitious names, endow them with conversation, and presumably get a more brilliant effect. All we have a right to ask, therefore, of such a novel is that its sociology be sound and true, and its "message" urgent. Such a story should not pretend to be more than a movie transcription of life. It is sociological observation "filmed." There is no claim to artistic value, and we do not ask for any. All we say is, Does the novel make visible conditions as they are and as they ought to be speedily altered?

Judged from this standard, I should say that Upton Sinclair's *King Coal* was a most satisfactory effort at fictional sociology. Technically it reads like a stenographic report run through the mould of a melodrama. All the same, it is far superior to a book like Ernest Poole's *His Family*, which, although constructed with more literary tact, had its sociology of both education and the family so lamentably strained and off the key. Ernest Poole erred in attempting art. You have the irritating task of disentangling the sociology from the well meant but clumsy personal characterization, and when you get it disentangled you find it is neither sound nor true. Upton Sinclair pleases because he makes it so easy to unwarp the melodrama from this picture of the servitude of unorganized labor in a great mining camp of the American West. The soundness and truth of the sociology are fortified by "eight million words of evidence" collected in the investigations of the great Colorado coal strike of 1913-14. Upton Sinclair slaps melodrama and sociology together so honestly as to make it easy for you to believe that "practically all the characters are real persons, and every incident which has social significance is not merely a true incident but a typical one."

You discard the rich young hero who, fresh from his sociological courses at college, goes to work incognito in a coal mine to test out what he has learned, but you retain the brutal intrigue, the almost Turkish oppression, the terrorism of suspicion and fear which compose life within the armed camp of the "Pine Creek Coal Co." You discard his sensational escape into the private car of his friend, the son of the owner of the mines, and the ineptitude of the little plutocratic party, but you retain a sense of the callous indifference with which the owners hand over labor troubles to the slave driving foremen. You discard the decayed gentility of the company official to whom the hero, in disgrace, makes appeal, but you retain a vivid insight into that crew of petty helots, and provocateurs into whose hands these industrial helots, the mine workers, are delivered. You discard the amorous troubles of Red Mary and her confrontation with the dainty capitalistic sweetheart, but you do not lose the horror of the crushing out of hope in these grim and terrible camps. Throughout the book, the "social significance" of the incidents seems as impressive as the dramatic invention is unconvincing.

You smile at the plot, but you say, These are conditions as they are, in all their almost incredible detail of exploitation.

Upton Sinclair does his work so well, however, as to leave you undecided whether an honest generalized summary of the labor camp life, such as that Colorado judicial decision which he prints in his postscript as proof of the accuracy of his work, would not have carried just as much dramatic conviction. Yet *King Coal* is an exceedingly vivacious narrative, boyishly sincere. If it proves to carry its "message" further than did the "eight million words," it will have to be preferred to any unfictional account. Other writers, however, might not strike so good a balance, might not make their fiction so easy to unwind. Their invention might grotesquely distort the conditions they were trying to render vivid. We are left with the question whether there is really any place for anything between the straightforward social document and the work of literary art in which the writer not only keeps the faith towards his sociological material, but creates also a drama of personal life. But if we are to have something else, *King Coal* is perhaps as good a compromise as we are likely ever to get.

The "message" needs no paraphrasing. The total impression the reader gets is one of outraged wonder that Assyrian centers of iniquity like these camps should have grown up in a country with any intuition whatever for democracy. Where political boundaries have been made to coincide with the limits of corporation property, these camps have become actual little industrial principalities within the state, armed and barricaded against the world, and "justified" in any oppression by the plea of an "industrial necessity" which parodies the "military necessity" of the state. These camps represent the systematic squeezing of the worker almost to the last detail that human ingenuity could suggest. The system shows the will-to-exploit almost gone insane and run amuck. Scruple, legality, tradition, humaneness, have collapsed, and brutal power acts unrestrained. *King Coal* shows step by step the ingenuity of extortion, the difficulty of protest or revolt, the organized espionage which crushes any effort at organization. The direction of the industrially subjugated has become an engineering task like the mining of coal. The workers are so much wood and stone to be manipulated into the mine, and so much human slag to be destroyed with the other refuse. Only because the human instrument shows animal perversity and resistance has this technique of subjugation been turned over by corporations not to engineers but to the terrorism of criminaloid foremen. Will the war do anything to this terrible industrial slavery? *King Coal* provides a lurid but convincing background against which to understand the present industrial revolt.

PAGEANTRY AND SOCIAL ART.

The plans for a great community festival such as the pageant which the Shakespeare Celebration Committee is to produce in New York during the last week of May register the sudden popularizing of freer forms of artistic and social expression than an earlier generation ever knew. Surely those of us who fifteen years ago were still in school can look back to no touch of the dramatic work which is now a commonplace in the schools. No one thought of having us dramatize the stories we read. No one ever thought of turning play and gymnastics into the boisterous and delightful folkdancing that one sees now in city playgrounds. Physical education meant the dullest of calisthenic exercises, or mechanical manipulation of bars and rings. The free and joyous expression of the body which we are now so eager for in interpretative dancing had not gotten beyond the languid posturing of "delsarte." In no kindergarten could you come upon little bare-legged children flitting about like rhythmic birds in naive response to some tune on the phonograph. People were not creating such things as a beautiful neighborhood festival I recently saw at the settlement house, where the lines of grave and half-nude dancers wound their way with gifts to the altar, and in the interludes delicious little bare children, who must have incredibly come out of the cluttered streets with their bulging houses, capered in absolute abandon and joy. Such simple and artless expressiveness, so graceful and liberating, this inexhaustible fertility of childhood and youthful flesh and movement and color and music, simply wasn't in our world of that time. If our starved and Pagan soul responds to these appeals now, it is because they are set against a background which contained so little expression that was not either tame or vulgar.

Our elders were not getting excited over any Vachel Lindsays with their chanted rhapsodies. The only way they heard poetry was through some ghastly manifestation of the professional elocutionist in a sophisticated technique which demanded nothing of the personal quality of the speaker. Amateur drama and dancing existed as a mere society setting for village relationships. Most modes of artistic expression seem to have been regarded as the plutocracy is said to regard the opera, as contributory to social functions. The passion and emotional liberation for which we are now making these things vehicles were shamefacedly disguised. The sex-taboo was really an art taboo, or at least a social-art taboo. A bare-legged dancer jumping into America of 1900 would have caused a moral panic. Our growing-up was in an atmosphere that was afraid of personal and aesthetic expressiveness unless it was carefully justified and decently clothed. We scarcely realize how vividly the interests of today record the immense loosening-up of that stiff old America which so long had the manner of a maiden-aunt. The outburst of Pagan expressiveness is far more revolutionary than any other social change we have been making. It is a New Freedom that really liberates and relaxes the spirit from the intolerable tensions of an over-repressed and mechanicalized world.

This liberation is seen in the current rage for the theatre. But this interest is not for the village intrigue and cheap social photography that we are used to calling drama, but for broader and more symbolic representation. Pantomime and decoration become important. Clean design takes the place of the old fussy over-loaded concreteness. The appeal is to the imagination. The motives are social and allegorical. The individual is transcended. The jealous old individual arts with their formal techniques and their tight little categories of critical norms get broken up. We look for spectacles as well as dramas. We like great wholes where music, gesture, declamation, decoration, the dance, fuse together into a living and exciting impression. These drama societies and "little theatres" which are springing up in which the group writes its own plays, designs and makes its costumes and scenes, produces and acts its own efforts, are symptoms of this synthetic emphasis. We feel an urge to get into the game. The solitary artist bores. We like group-art. And we are tired of seeing artistic expression stereotyped, sophisticated, artificially segregated into subjects. We want to get expressiveness in some sort of thick whole, not by making the arts imitate each other, but by making them co-operate and blend until the spectator forgets what each art is contributing to the joy of the whole. Already we see painting committing suicide by imitating music, and music by imitating poetry. Individual genius is fast becoming subservient to the larger social purpose and design. The newest creative composers write not symphonic poems but music for pantomimes and ballets and masques. The artists do stage-setting and civic design. The poets are writing masques and lyric rhapsodies. Dancing the primitive social art comes to its own again.

Now the significance of pageantry is that it is exactly this fusing social art that we crave, the pulling together into a gorgeous whole of all these isolated expressions upon which we stumble everywhere today in school, and theatre and settlement and home. The dancing children, the pantomime, the gesticulating rhapsodist, the new decoration, the dramatic interpretation of ideas, the exciting color of post-modern music—all are caught together into a genuine community theatre which involves hundreds of actors and thousands of appreciators. The Shakespeare pageant will be a landmark of this social art in America. A supreme dramatist will be commemorated who had above all the pageant sense, whose plays were decorative settings of personal and social situations rather than the petty ingrowing conflicts and ironies of the drama of today, and who used our language for its high and bold decorative beauty. And Shakespeare will be commemorated in a festival which will impress on the spectators' consciousness the art of the civic theatre throughout the ages.

Mr. Percy MacKaye's masque, "Caliban of the Yellow Sands," weaves these motives together in a remarkable way. He has produced what is really a pageant of pageants. Caliban is the uncouth, seeking, failing, base but pathetically aspiring people, ever dragged down by Lust and Death and War, yet slowly freeing itself through climbing imagination and social expression. The Community-Theatre, in which the arts merge in social expressiveness and popular enthusiasm, is represented as the goal of his striving. The interludes of the masque present dramatically scenes of social expression throughout the ages and the different civilizations. Ritual and war, festivity and worship, royal meetings and popular uprisings, are threaded together, with appropriate scenes from Shakespeare as commentary. The pageant, staged by the magic of Prospero in the cave of Setebos before the astonished and allured Caliban, makes a social drama of civilization, with the devilish spirits of Setebos every now and then putting to rout the constructive forces. The Great War finally seems to crush the toilsome creation to the ground, yet there emerges at the end unconquerable this vision of the Civic Theatre which shall turn into creative expression that craving for relaxation and release from the tension of overwork which drives the world so madly along and finds only lust and drunkenness and war to satisfy it.

Pageant-makers like Mr. MacKaye are the Prosperos of today, conjuring up by their magic all the latent charm and beauty that is among us. For a brilliant enterprise like this Celebration will organize, as have never before been organized, these various isolated artistic expressions. Scarcely a neighborhood will be unaffected, and no school or settlement. Nationalistic groups will contribute their characteristic dances and cultural skill. Local societies representing all classes in the community will give their time and talent to the numberless details of the festival. The whole city will come to see the spectacle given at night in the great Stadium. For pageantry is a taste shared by the most diverse classes. The rhythm, the color, the music, the group-excitement, appeals to the most primitive emotions. The unsophisticated expressiveness demands no technique of appreciation. Yet in satisfying elemental cravings every aspect of such a pageant sublimates into imagination the impulses that it satisfies. Even the most poverty-stricken intellect and imagination can hardly resist some glow, and every fine pageant has innumerable details which vivify even the most delicate taste.

A community festival not only uses all this diverse individual and group talent but it unlocks new resources. People cannot spend months on working up the dances and the scenes and the music without becoming conscious of that immense liberation which is ours today. Any enterprise which enlists the capacities and talents of such large groups of people will produce a new attitude towards art. It will make the term "social art" mean something. The private and individual arts, such as painting, music, literature, sculpture, must always be dependent on rarefied talent. No democratic delusion must let down the standards there. The world will always be sparsely settled with the genius that creates beauty in those fields. But a social art is possible which calls for what may be called group-talent, in dancing, athletic exhibition, choral singing, spectacle, and so forth. We shall always find many more people who possess group-talent than individual genius. And this is exactly as it should be. The pageant, which is our developing social art at its best, involves a small corps of directing genius and great masses of co-operating actors. The little increments of talent in the crowd actually combine into an artistic whole of overpowering force and genius. Vistas of social expressiveness are opened that we have scarcely yet begun to realize here in America. Who that saw the Paterson Strike Pageant in 1913 can ever forget that thrilling evening when an entire labor community dramatized its wrongs in one supreme outburst of group-emotion? Crude and rather terrifying, it stamped into one's mind the idea that a new social art was in the American world, something genuinely and excitingly new. The cities like St. Louis that have had great communal pageants within recent years must have had this same new sense of social expressiveness. The coming celebration in New York will bring this self-consciousness to millions more.

A SOCIOLOGICAL POET

Contemporary students of the psychology and customs of primitive peoples—a science that has been much enriched and developed during very recent years—and is now one of the most fascinating in the world—cannot fail to be impressed by the imaginative vistas opened by these revelations of the earliest responses which the soul of man made to this confusing and variegated world of ours. These newer studies of the religion and magic of the most primitive peoples remaining today seem to indicate an origin of religion not at all similar to what our naively individualistic English philosophers of the last century imagined they had established. The first religion, the first feeling and thinking, originated not at all in the fear and awe experienced before the powers of nature, or in the desire to explain the mysteries of things, but rather in an intense social consciousness, in a mystical sense of the unity and power of living things, non-human as well as human. It was the group that came first, the collective thinking and feeling that was the first reality. The Group-Will, the Group-Desire, the Group-Action, were the first gods, the reverberation of these collective representations was the first thinking, and only very slowly did the individual mind and consciousness and logical thought emerge from this fused and intense tribal life. Religion, in this interpretation, comes to be seen as fundamentally the sense of social unity, the social consciousness, rather than any individual relation of a man to his Creator, or a reverence before the grandeur of inanimate Nature.

Such an interpretation would have been almost incomprehensible before this twentieth century; indeed it must be incomprehensible even now to those minds who have not felt the stirrings of the social conscience which is the most characteristic spiritual sign of our age. For it is only in recent years that our civilization, so chaotically individualized in the middle ages, has begun to weld for itself, through the growth of industry and the spread of communications, a new cohesion, accompanied by consciousness and sympathy. Those who have the eyes to see may witness everywhere this new spirit of the time. It comes to some of us with almost appalling power, in the vivid realization of its two aspects—one, what Nietzsche calls the "herd instinct," the blind compressing forces of conventionality; the other, the liberating forces of democratic camaraderie, the common life without whose nourishment and support we should be infinitely less than human. We feel both the tyranny of the herd, and the social hunger for the larger collective life, the straining out of our sympathy to fill the immensely widened world that has been revealed by the science and invention of the last century.

In this revivifying of these immemorial social instincts, we seem to feel the world that our primitive ancestors felt—a world of group-beings, outside and above the world of Nature, which the poets have so long idealized, and the world of Man, which individualistic humanitarianism has been teaching us to idealize. We are just beginning to realize the infinite power for good and evil, which these beings, vague and formless as they are but very real, actually exercise over our attitudes and feelings. We are beginning to understand that our individual souls are little more than focus-points of the life of these larger collective persons. The individual, which our western morality and philosophy has for so long glorified, begins to seem to us somehow less real than the mass-life in which we live and move and have our being, which unconsciously both compresses and enlarges us. We are becoming very restless in the isolation that caste and class and sect and fortune have imposed upon us; the social appeal leaps all these barriers and demands a vivid consciousness of that vast collective enterprise that modern life has become, a consciousness of the new mass-forces that are overwhelming the old ideals, which were born out of the breaking-up and specialization of the primitive tribal group and the narrow and selfish interests and exclusions of the social morsels which resulted.

This new social consciousness demands its poetry. The old gods are dead, men say, and new gods have not been born. They cannot be born out of materialistic science, though the world has been making a brave effort these latter years to deliver deities of Force and Matter. But just as the first gods were crystallized out of the desires and collective rhythms of the primitive group, so we may expect to see emerge from the new social conscience new gods of a collective humanity, which will be very real because they will be incarnations of our deepest and most universal instincts. But if this new social religion has on the one hand its elevated sentiments of democracy and a restored Christianity, it also has down in the heart of the people its Pagan side, vague, formless, terrible, the stirrings of an incalculable force. Who can walk the lighted streets of a city at night and watch the flowing crowds, the shining youthful faces, the eager exhilaration of the sauntering life, or who can see the surge of humanity on a holiday or Sunday, without feeling the strange power of this mass-life? This mysterious power of the city which sucks out the life of the countryside, which welds individuals into a co-operative life, is not this the basal force of the age, and does it not suggest the stirrings of a new civilization, socialized and purified? In this garish, vulgar, primitive flow of Broadway, are not new gods being born? This exaltation of the flowing crowd, is it not one with the mystic thrill of the dancing savage, a new affirmation of life? To millions of our fellow-beings, is not the life of the city the real religion, the daily toil the real sacrifice, the evening saunter and amusement the real worship? Is not the god the city, and the merging of one's petty individuality and cares into his throbbing dynamic life the mystic union with him?

These are the questions suggested by the work of a young French poet, M. Jules Romains, who to me is one of the most significant literary figures of the time. While we have been vaguely wishing for the new poetry and wondering how we could ever idealize our factories and our railroads, our aeroplanes and our electric wires, M. Romains, and his followers, who call themselves "unanimistes," have been feeling the basal mass-enthusiasms of the time, crude and barbarous as they are, but hot with vitality. If poetry is an interpretation, in terms of beauty, of the real, if it is a vista opening up past the brute facts of existence and revealing the significances behind them, then this poetry, with its feeling for the common soul, the thrill of personality, the vigor of industry, the wonder of work, the reverberation of the electric exciting modern life in the individual consciousness, must be the genuine poetry of our industrial and socializing age. There is much in the work of M. Romains that suggests Walt Whitman, divinest of poets, and the "unanimistes" do acknowledge his influence. But he is a Whitman industrialized, and, if I may say it, sociologized; for besides the push of industrial invention and energy that throbs through his poetry, there is a strong intellectual fibre running through him, the fibre of sociological science which Whitman of course could not have. To us Americans this poetry—and one sees so clearly the same drift in many of our very young writers at home—should come as a ful-

fillment of Whitman, who, prophetic before his time, was submerged in our cult of an individualistic capitalism. That day,
however, is definitely over; we are breaking our idols, and are
ready for a new worship. Contemporary sociologists are showing
us how the Olympian gods represent the last individualistic crystallization out of a long process of the incarnation of the group-
desires. Having completely externalized and personified the
god, the Greek genius felt his insufficiency, and fell back to a
more social and primitive paganism. So, I take it, we Americans,
having achieved our millionaires, and crystallized them out of
our throbbing pioneer life, feel the coldness and deadness of
their perfect individuality, and are ready to return to a more
satisfying and nourishing social idealism. This poetry, which is
only French in the sense that France always responds more
sensitively and quickly to the social and democratic currents of
an age than do the Anglo-Saxons, shows the way to that return.

M. Romains sings of "La Vie Unanime," the life of the common
soul; he is the poet of the crowd and not of the "cultivated persons" whom Whitman so much deprecated. He does not preach
the social religion which is merely a mild extension of the orthodox Christianity to embrace and assist the poorer classes.
His theme is much more elemental—the group-life of the city, the
surge of the mass. In his rugged lines, there is something that
thrills us back to the early tribal life with its passionate dancing,
its overpowering sense of the unity and sacredness of living
things. And these group gods he chants as follows:

> We desire a god! There must be gods for us!
> Not gods lost in heaven, pale first causes,
> But fleshly living gods, who are ourselves,
> Whose substance we can taste—
> Gods who suffer in our body and see with our eyes,
> Creatures divine of whom we are the members,
> Who hold all things, our bodies, space, our dwellings,
> Enclosed in their real and palpable unity
> Some day there must be a god who shall personify Human-
> ity.

> The great creatures stir—the theatre, the barracks,
> The churches, the streets and the cities—
> The great divine creatures, conscienceless and naked,

Who will become the real gods,
Because they are our dream,
Because they are what we have willed.

    To each of these group-creatures, the poet devotes a poem—
"La Caserne," a poignant picture of the life of the barracks with
the young recruits, torn from their employment or studies for
three years' military training in their barren and brutalizing prison; one feels here all the horror of this brute, irrational soul of
the military institution, preparing blindly, inexorably, for a war
which no individual will have willed: "Le Theatre," with its picture
of the group-soul enlarging, exalting the individual, during its little span of life during which

    The limbs and nerves and muscles of all
Labor to forge the one common enjoyment.
The individual is dissolved.
No one any longer thinks of the morsel of flesh and soul that
he was.
Trampling under foot his sorrows, his desires and his hates,
His ephemeral personality and his puny will,
Each soul feels the uplift and mounts out of himself.

    The theme of "L'Eglise" gives the poet opportunity for a strik-
ing contrast between the slow senility of this immemorially rich collective life which

    In former times was the grandest of the collective crea-
tures
And the whole city transfused its life with its own,

and the new dynamic vibrant life of the industrial city.

    But now they have arisen, the factories,
The young factories, with their muscular life.
Their smoke rises higher than the churchbells sound.
They do not fear to hide the sun, for
They make the sun with their machines.

And in sharp ironic strokes he draws the comparison of the
somnolent worship of the faithful, the petty individuality of their
prayers to a god whom they think of as existing only for them-

selves, and the common aspirations of the workers outside, with the infinite potency for good or evil of their co-operating mass-life.

In "Le Cafe," "La Ville," "Dimanche," "La Groupe contre La Ville," the poet analyzes, in haunting metaphors, the psychology of the group, as it flows together motivated by a holiday or a funeral procession, or the desire for amusement, and then as it disperses again into its houses and chambers, all mysteriously linked by this subtle social force. The mystery and glamor of railroad yards at night, the surge of the tugs and barges on the river, the heave and strain of great steel buildings in course of erection, the bells and dissonances of the cars and engines, the variegated flow of the boulevards—these are the new spiritual milieus of the poet. Wherever people are working or thinking or feeling together, there is being created a social personality, whose life is an appeal to the interpretation of the "unanimiste" poet.

In "La Vie Unanime" of M. Romains, we have not only successfully poetized social psychology—a thrilling demonstration that poetry has still the unconquerable power to make significant even our most abstract knowledge—but we have also, in the progress of the poet's thought, the whole drama of individual and society. Beginning as individual, in a blind searching, he feels the reverberations of the city life in his heart. As he sits in the room, the noises of the house, the suffering child upstairs, the wheels in the street, the faces he sees from his window, all strike vibrations through him, "in great strokes that embrace all the emotions of the city" he draws towards him its life.

The forces from outside flow through my hands.
Oh! what shall I do with these unknown guides?

He feels the pain and strain of his expanding consciousness, the strain that so many of us feel who try to find our bearings in life—

I can never enlarge my living unity
Up to the point where this vast outside could enter into it.
At least if I could only remain the heart of this room!
At least if I could only remain the heart of this room!

If my pulsations, like the wings of the eagle,
Would only keep beating down upon it and master it!
If I could only think my room alone!

He passes out into the street and finds himself immersed in the
collective wave of the city—

The step of the passers-by is something scarcely physi-
cal;
There are no longer movements, there are rhythms,
And I have no longer need of my eyes to see them.
The air that I breathe has a sort of mental taste.
The men resemble ideas which pass along through a mind.

He begins to feel this group-mind in which the men are ideas,
and in a burst of surrender he cries

I do not love myself any longer, Unanime,
I love you.
It is no longer myself that thinks in my soul;
But your thought appears above mine like drops of oil
In each of which there shines the sun.
Some one who is not myself becomes God where I am.

The poet begins to see "Dieu le long des maisons," the gods
that he is searching, in the group that so compels him.
But there comes a second act of the drama, a reaction
against the crowd, a weariness of the insistent clamor on the
spirit:

I am no longer a being engulfed in a group,
I have drawn the nails that riveted my spirit,
I have acquired again the august attitude
Of the living being who resumes and completes his life.
My individual consciousness is clarified and extends,
And my isolation makes me illimitable.

But not for long; the poet feels the hollowness of this isolation.
He finds his soul refusing to be merged with the grass and the
flowers, the pine trees and the wheat, in the unconscious
splendor of Nature. The social that is in him demands the

human milieu, "worthy of his thought"; he must have the city, "unanime et condensée." The final reconciliation comes, in a burst of virile verse; Nature and the individual soul are resolved into the "nous." The reconciliation comes, as it must come to all of us in these latter days, in recognition that the highest reality of the world is not Nature or the Ego, but the Beloved Community. What is the Universe, cries the poet, but one vast city? Spreading out by means of the social personality that is in him and through him, he reaches the uttermost bounds of the stars. Not to live in awed contemplation of the impersonal grandeur of Nature, or to worship any individual power outside himself, but to feel surging through him the social forces, to be co-operating with them in the making of the ideal Universe—this is the religion of the "unanimiste," as it was of the earliest human group that looked upon the world—he flings

"la terre unanime au front du monde."

"A LITTLE THING OF BRUNELLESCHI'S"[1]

As I walk on Fifth Avenue and come upon the million staring windows of one of those gaunt new office-buildings that are replacing the old mansions, obtruding themselves impudently into the centre of some of the finest blocks, my mind goes back to that confident young American student of architecture that I met in Florence last Spring. He must have been of no common clay, for he was in Europe as a prize pupil, sent over by a famous school to the Academy in Rome, and his studies had taken him through every nook and cranny of Italy. When I met him he had just come in from measuring "a little thing of Brunelleschi's." His indefatigable tape-measure had been busy, one felt, in every little church that was worth while in Italy. How all this was to be absorbed and assimilated, and into what American things it was to be "converted," as Henry James would say, I was very eager to know. Certainly to little degree into that revision of beautiful Fifth Avenue to meet the needs of Jewish clothing manufacturers—a revision which seems to go on with so impressive a Tolstoyan non-resistance on the part of the architectural world of New York.

His point-of-view about all this turned out to be very curious and interesting. As an architect he seemed to feel little of the unpleasantness and irritation with the process that I did, as an amateur lover of civic art and design. A faintly accusing implication in my tone that the architects of America were somehow responsible for the bedlam which our city streets presented and the vulgarizing and defacing that I deplored, annoyed him greatly. He rushed to the defence of his masters. I expected to hear the plea that they were helpless, that their hands were tied, that art had become commercialized, that owing to the rush of business and the low standards of public taste, the building-up of our streets fell into the hands of little fellows who were a disgrace to their profession. Not at all. What he said was—and he said it with a flare of professional hauteur—that nowadays no decent architect—I am sure he said "decent"—would so much as touch a small office-building or apartment-house or any of the common varieties of architecture with which our workaday cities must be filled. All their glories of taste and skill must be reserved, he implied, for the big "jobs," for the heroic feats of the art, for churches, public buildings, great skyscrapers, perhaps even millionaires' country-houses. For the common humdrum building which must go up in endless profusion about our cities and make or mar the whole quality and style and character of the civic house which our communities build for themselves, that prosaic business must be left to the "canaille" of the profession.

I should not have taken this utterance as one of oracular force were it not that my friend was so full of the current orthodoxies on every other subject that I could only assume that here too he was but repeating, with the enthusiasm of a disciple, the code and philosophy of his teachers and of the general architectural world of America in its higher artistic reaches. And this philosophy, as presented by him, seemed to contemplate with equanimity the building-up and making-over of our cities with patient, cheerful industry by people either without taste or with the weirdest ideas of originality, while all the learning and talent, and the skill acquired by a long cosmopolitan education such as my friend was acquiring, were to be reserved for the isolated, individual things. When I suggested that the city scheme was the thing, that the quality of the street or block or plaza as a whole was the thing to be considered, he looked at me, in the startled way of one who senses a paradox or catches the first faint distant halloo of a joke. He took me, I think, for some kind of a dull, pestilential reformer, instead merely as an ingenuous person, who had come to find a large measure of aesthetic delight in well-designed towns and stately streets and picturesque open places, who took them all as composed pictures and demanded the same qualities of distinction and design and significance in a square or street vista that he would demand in a painting. I tried to present this new art, for which we have no better word than town-planning, but I could not arouse enthusiasm in my friend's mind, trained as he was in the best principles of contemporary America's architectural science and art. There seemed simply to be no peg in him on which to hang my amateurish words. Was he really oblivious, in his wanderings about Europe, to the caressing quality of the silver-grey quais of Paris, to the full-blooded opulence of Charlottenburg, to the mediaeval elegance of the curving and gabled streets of Nordlingen, to the friendly arcades of Bern's tower-closed "gassen," to the orange and yellow charm of the Piazza Navona in Rome? Was his eye trained only to see the individual Palazzo or Chiesa, with its definite architectural design and character, and not at all the broad composition of the scene? Was he to spend his time measuring little things of Brunelleschi's and not in analyzing the effect of massed gable and towers, and marketplace, and subtle perfection of curving street? Of course he was not actually oblivious of these latter beauties, but he did not give them the values of the famous and splendid masterpieces of distinct buildings. Squares and streets might be charming, but they did not "count," as did Santa Croce or the Palazzo Strozzi to this American student as something enormously to be understood and appreciated and made dynamic and creative in his own art. The absurd little yellow houses he would not take seriously, any more than he would take seriously the undistinguished mass of people he met in the streets. For me, of course, the houses would count, for they would compose into a design or picture, and the tower or church to which my friend gave his enthusiasm would be for me but the glory of the mass, the larger part of whose distinction came from the charm of the setting and juxtaposition.

In working out my own attitude against his background, I could not help finding in his philosophy a high moral distinction. To study so carefully and eclectically the masterpieces of the ages, to acquire this sense for the fineness of individual craftmanship, to wish to put one's best art and skill into a big enterprise rather than cheapen it in mercenary work, seemed to argue an admirable artistic allegiance in my friend. He seemed to have, much more than I, a vivid sense of what was worth doing and what was not. But then I seemed suddenly to find in his tone a note of aristocratic contempt for the earthy, plebeian character of office-buildings and apartment-houses, and their uninspired builders. And then as suddenly came a curious note of democracy. This willingness to leave such work to the chance builder or commercial architect or humblest clerk in the offices, seemed almost to indicate that same willingness we show in our political life—that all shall have an equal chance. Skill and talent, should not be allowed to monopolize everything. There should be a fair division of labor. Talent educated abroad, with the opportunities to observe and study the genius of past centuries, should do our great monuments. Those people who like to or must build houses and offices should be left to do the rest. We should even have a sense of outraged democracy at the suggestion that, in the interests of the beauty or welfare of the community, men should be prevented from putting up the kind of building they like. Everything seemed to conspire to give my friend the highest moral, artistic, and democratic justification for his individualistic philosophy of architecture.

And how American such an inconsistent jumble of artistic earnestness and aristocratic jealousy for good things and easygoing democratic tolerance of taste and insensitiveness to mass-effects! Our fantastic individualism draws us all the time in two opposite directions, towards an aristocratic cult of the "best," and towards a democratic tolerance of the average. One becomes amazed at what we complacently suffer in matters of taste. We have our aesthetic feelings under marvellous control. We complacently leave our novels to be written by the Chambers and the Churchills and our plays by the Sheldons, and make no savage criticism or betray any violent reactions of disgust. We say nothing about the shabbiness in which America clothes so much of its community life. The architects, like my friend, who should be the first to shudder and revolt, and who could make the loudest murmurs, murmur the least of all. I can only admire the unperturbed serenity with which my friend will return to walk our streets, content and happy at one fine individual work which would replace for him, though it might be in isolation, all the architectural glories of Europe.

[1]Compare Bourne's article "The Architect."

THE AMERICAN ADVENTURE

A Son of the Middle Border, by Hamlin Garland. New York: The Macmillan Company. $1.60.

Mr. Howells has written a criticism of Hamlin Garland's story which must make as memorable a mark in the literature of appreciation as *A Son of the Middle Border* will make in the literature of American autobiography. Thirty years ago, when Mr. Garland, a pioneer from Dakota to Boston, was feeling for his literary sincerity, it was Mr. Howells as he tells us in this book, whom he revered as master and pursued in and out of season. What charm, therefore, in this mellow benediction bestowed on the disciple, himself no longer young, with his career already largely behind him! To a younger generation, Mr. Howells and Mr. Garland seem almost like contemporaries, and their issues of a national literature, which should spring out of a conscientious sectional interpretation, seem faded and old. Cable, Harris, Miss Jewett, and Miss Wilkins, whom the young radical put into an American literary scheme for Mr. Howells' approving ears, have not had quite the staying power for a national literature. From their graceful fading, however, Mr. Garland has rescued himself, and in this beautiful and virile book seized a theme which makes his story not only that personal document which Mr. Howells could not pinnacle too high but perhaps also the most sensitive interpretation that has been written of the later pioneer life in America.

Mr. Garland's best work, like *Main-Travelled Roads,* was built directly out of the stones of his autobiographical quarry. But how much more vivid and alluring is the quarry than the constructed short stories and novels. How much more significant this dramatic landscape of his struggling life than the little huts his talent has built on it. The inventive writer, after long struggling with stiff fictional forms, suddenly discovers himself as his own best artistic form and material and bursts out into the freshest of self-revelations, without self-consciousness and yet with an insight that makes silly the legend that the American has no talent for introspection and resents its expression. Thus it was with Mr. Dreiser's happy and unlabored *A Hoosier Holiday,* and thus it is with Mr. Garland's more finished and significant reminiscence. These two books are not only better literature than anything either novelists have written, but better than almost any novel or short story of their fellows. I mean, there is more flavor of life, more appreciation of beauty, greater sincerity of pathos, greater simplicity, and even a more convincing sense of form.

In a country which lacks a strong literary tradition or a uniform and vigorous training in expression, we must expect writers, with the exception of those born luckily into a milieu of literary taste, always to cope more or less unsuccessfully with literary construction. Men of talent, but of hampered education, would suffer a long handicap from not starting with the cultural capital with which a mind in a more intensive civilization is endowed. They would have years of just such work as Mr. Garland had in even getting their bearings. They would have almost to create for themselves the standards, preferences, techniques of expression. At first they would work for the conventional forms as the only package in which a conventional public would receive their gifts. Only much later would they find that their chance to make a permanent impression lay not so much in a paraphrasing of their experience into arbitrary plots and narratives as in an interpretation of the very experience itself. Thus they would gradually attain the true sincerity of their talent, and feel themselves as significant, so that their story, when it came, would be much more than a mere personal record, it would be a drama of a social movement or a struggling class. Out of themselves would have come a great and revealing book, where they could not have created a great book out of the world on which they looked objectively. But that fight to get their bearings and make a living, however much it might impede their mastery of literary art, would give these books a glamor that the more fortunate writer could never attain. Introspection would work out an artistic form that they never could have invented. So this first book of Mr. Garland's reminiscences has the artistic charm that comes from spontaneity with a sustained reflective mood. And the story has a plot that only life could have invented for him. No novelist could have provided such motives and meanings as the excitements and ironies of pioneer life have provided.

What irony, for instance, in the fact that his commencement oration at the Academy in the little Iowa village to which the Garlands had come from the "Middle Border" was on the theme of Going West, to be immediately followed by a hungry pilgrimage back to that very New England from which his father had set out on the pioneering march! Penniless and bare-handed, the young

Garland was a true pioneer back to the culture which the pioneers' war with the plains had crowded out of their life, so that all his work on the land and his response to the freedom and beauty of the West had left him with nothing but yearning. As he was carried along from homestead to homestead by his father's restlessness, he only lived until he could find some place where his starving imagination, which had clutched at every scrap of print that floated into homestead or village, could find a more bountiful fare. Those travels through the Massachusetts country and his struggle for a foothold in Boston are adventures that thrill us as much as any western career. And what irony in the closing of the book with the return of the broken, if undaunted, father and mother from the parched Dakota plains to the very Wisconsin village from which their pioneering twenty-five years before had begun!

Under his romantic feeling and sympathy, Mr. Garland does not conceal the grim mischief that this pioneering worked. The early chapters show the "Middle Border" in the late sixties, settled into a vigorous civilization, which had not appreciably drained the New England from which it had sprung, nor yet become itself attenuated. In this western Wisconsin where Mr. Garland was born, the wine of the Puritans was still sweet and ruddy. The life was rough but left a margin. Climate and soil were favorable, and there was bounty. Mr. Garland gives a vivid picture of a society of much personality and charm. Little official culture had come with them perhaps, but among the uncles and aunts and neighbors there was music and gaiety and a certain sturdy raciness of legend and homely philosophy. Would this life have all been conserved, if the Mississippi that bounded the "Middle Border" had been an impassable iron wall, or if the men had only doubted their ability to grapple with the endless plains that lured them from their wooded hills? One gets hints in these pages of the kind of mature and intensive democracy that Whitman prophesied out of the vigorous America he looked upon. But the war made men restless, and this American life was so much diverted from its course that Whitman reads quaintly today, as a visionary who made his democratic dreams out of his desires. But Mr. Garland brings back a conviction that his America of Whitman's visions was really there, or at least there in the raw for the building of his democracy of great personalities.

The "farther on," however, gnawed at the lives of the Garlands and the other men of the "Middle Border," and the pioneer songs bedeviled them. They ripped their civilization up by the roots, and scattered it over the boundless plains. This vigorous communal life was shattered into a thousand isolated homesteads and wan hamlet outposts. Through Minnesota and Iowa to Dakota, the Garlands made their way, harried by drought and blizzards and insect pests in the impossible single-handed fight. The doggedness which assumed that mere intensity of will could overcome the pitiless climate, and the pride that would never admit a return, took the pioneers ever farther from possible prosperity, and strewed the plains with shriveled lives and communities that scarcely ever even began to live. The "Middle Border" scarcely recovered from this ripping away of its best vigor, and the life that was taken withered in this relentless West. That is a memorable chapter in which Mr. Garland describes his return years later to the village and the wistful boyhood friends eating out their hearts in an arid life from which only talent like his or bravado could have rescued them. New immigration saved the deserted land, but nothing could save the sturdy old American fabric. In the later chapters, those passionate and daring uncles of his boyhood are seen as disappointed, unfulfilled wanderers. The pioneer spirit is shown as blighting successively the borders which it was always restlessly passing beyond, until in this progressive thinning it vanished in defeat by invincible wind and dryness and cold. A colonizing civilization, going out in companies, with science as well as heroism, might have conquered. Mr. Garland shows the wrecking of a civilization to the tune of all the braveries and virtues.

In this struggle which he understood so well, he feels all the honorable shame of the deserter. Saved by contact with a still vitalizing Boston, he could help the radicals and reformers in their political war on the business interests that were always ready to cooperate with pitiless nature in the slaughter of the pioneer. In these old wars he played a manful part, and what seems now a little old-fashioned in his reminiscence is that he should have so little bitterness left. If there is a defect in his art, it is the romantic treatment which at times almost approaches obstinacy. His romantic attitude never sounds anything but sincere, but it is not the tone of today. We are no longer so amiable. We begin to feel the huge deficit that must be put to the pioneering account, and we have the resentment of enterprising sons towards the father who has squandered the family substance. Still we are not yet so shrill as not to appreciate with a personal warmth this admirable book, the revealing drama, not only of brave and sensitive youth, but also of the ironic tragedy of the later American pioneering, told with more genius than America has yet been able to muster. It is a story that the mellowest critic will smilingly commend, and the rawest young malcontent read with enthusiasm and delight.

A VANISHING WORLD OF GENTILITY

These Many years, by Brander Matthews. Scribners: $3.

What more cordial welcome could the reviewer ask than this *"Que pensez-vous de cette comédie?"* from the bookplate designed for Mr. Matthews by Abbey, and reproduced on the cover of these "recollections"? The bookplate, symbolizing Mr. Matthews as "an American interested in the drama," represents an Indian gazing into the face of a Greek mask. Our author will scarcely realize how much better a joke this is than any contained within the cover of his book. For anything less Indian or less Greek than the particular comedy of his life cannot well be imagined.

Deliberately and expensively bred to follow the profession of millionaire, he was released, just as he came of age, by the wiping-out of his father's fortune, for the profession that his heart craved—that of writing plays and seeing them acted on the stage. His unexpected translation to the professorial sphere did not transform him from being about the most naively worldly soul who ever got himself recognized as a man of letters. He gazed at life with no Indian hauteur, but with a never sated enjoyment in the pleasant comedy of clubs and theatres and literary associations—equally at home in London, Paris, and New York—incorrigibly anecdotal, genial, and curious. And it was no Sophoclean tragedy upon which he gazed, but the second-rate imitations of Scribe and Augier, and the cleverly turned short-story, and the wittiness of familiar verse. Sarcey, Coquelin divided his worship with Austin Dobson, Bunner, and Locker-Lampson. How fortunate he was to live in the era of well-made plays, and of ballades and rondeaux! He took to them all like a fish to water. And he recalls his own half-dozen acted plays with a justifiable pleasure that is undimmed by the realization that no one now remembers that at least two of them had long and popular successes.

In his youth, he had a significant era of skill as an acrobat and gymnast, and he tells with glee of his being invited to go out on the road "under canvas." It was always the acrobatics of literature that Mr. Matthews responded to, and always the circus of the social and literary world which enthralled him. He achieved a wide acquaintance among the lions, and he practiced all the tricks, in verse and play and story. But he is so completely objective that scarcely one of the writers whom he knew is characterized with any precision whatever, except perhaps Andrew Lang, for whom he had a prodigious admiration, and W. E. Henley, for whose attack on Stevenson he has an unexpectedly sympathetic word. Otherwise the contacts and occasions pass before our eyes like dates in Mr. Matthews's diaries, carried along by his own pleasure in their abundance and their notability. There is plenty of mild gossip, and we are present at the founding of innumerable clubs, and at least one Academy. His anecdotes sound better in the classroom. The compulsion to autobiography sprang, in Mr. Matthews's case, less from a sense of personal flavor and distinctive quality in what he saw than from a boyish desire to get down a record of his passing life.

Anyone so completely extroverted as Mr. Matthews could not be immodest. He is as little interested in the processes of his own soul as in those of the brilliant and complex personalities whom he has known. He does not think of himself as an absorbing person, to be detachedly studied and analyzed as a type of man, nor as a person of romantic significance to be interpreted from the innermost core of his soul. His diary treatment of life is so pure as almost to make these "recollections" interesting. But there are too many passages such as this, where he reflects on his university life:

So far as I have been able to form an opinion, there is no university in the United States where the position of the professor is pleasanter than it is at Columbia. The students, graduate and undergraduate, are satisfactory in quality; and their spirit is excellent. The teaching staff is so large that it is generally possible for each of us to cover that part of his field in which he is most keenly interested. Our relations with each other and with the several deans and the president and the trustees are ever friendly. So long as we do our work faithfully we are left alone to do it in our own fashion. And we have all of us the Lernfreiheit and the Lehrfreiheit, the liberty of the soul and of the mind, which was once the boast of the German universities, but which has been lost of late under the rigidity of Prussian autocracy.

"God bless us every one!" said little Tim.

Anyone who gets the full flavor of this passage, recalling all there is to be said on these matters, will be near the secret of that American race of men of letters of whom Mr. Matthews is one of the naiver specimens, a race to whom literature was a gesture of gentility and not a comprehension of life. There is a fascination about that brilliant literary world of the seventies and eighties when the *Nation* and the New York *Tribune* and *World* monopolized the younger generation of critical talent. But what on earth can a younger generation of today do with the remains of this gentility? In his account of the atrocious college education that the best of money could buy in America in 1868, Mr. Matthews gave me a guess at the secret of the continuance of this genteel tradition. Was it because you could get no education at all unless you got it from foreign travel or from cultivated relatives? Only the genteel, apparently, had these opportunities, so that the creation of a proletarian man of letters in America became automatically impossible, until universities and libraries improved and diffused the raw materials of the spirit.

What do I think of this comedy? I like the slight pugnacity with which Mr. Matthews went into the contest for the copyright bill and for simplified spelling. I like the candor with which he confesses his relief at being freed from the dread possibilities of practicing the profession of millionaire. But if there was ever a man of letters whose mind moved submerged far below the significant literary currents of the time, that is the man revealed in this book. He seems to have known everybody, and to have felt nothing. His genial youthfulness is infectious. But it is not the youth of idealism and aspiration, but of Peter Pan, writing stories of treasure-trove for *St. Nicholas.* I know there's the "Molière," and the "Shakespeare," and the critical essays. But that's not the mind that writes *These Many Years.* Turned on itself, it creates a tell-tale commentary of a literary era that never grew up. The puzzle to us now is that these *bons viveurs* have not made life more exciting, that these dear old romancers and realists of Mr. Matthews's generation have not made life more romantic and realistic. What on earth, I repeat, are we going to do with these people who blissfully never even knew what a world of horizons and audacities they lived in?

BIBLIOGRAPHY

BOOKS

Youth and Life. Boston: Houghton Mifflin, 1913.
The Gary Schools. Boston: Houghton Mifflin, 1916.
Education and Living. New York: The Century Company, 1917.
Untimely Papers, ed. James Oppenheim. New York: B. W. Huebsch, 1919.
History of a Literary Radical, ed. Van Wyck Brooks. New York: B. W. Huebsch, 1920.
History of a Literary Radical, ed. Van Wyck Brooks. New York: S. A. Russell, 1956. This collection is different from the Huebsch edition.
Towards an Enduring Peace, symposium ed. R. Bourne. New York: American Association for International Conciliation, 1916.
Vagabonds of the Sea, by Maurice Larrouy. Trans. from the French by R. Bourne. New York: E. P. Dutton, 1919.

UNDERGRADUATE WRITINGS

[*Columbia Monthly*] "Some Aspects of Good Talk," VII (January, 1910), 92–97; "Chesterton's Orthodoxy," VII (March, 1910), 170–172; "On Hero-Making," VII (April, 1910), 178–81; "The Function of a College Literary Magazine," VIII (November, 1910), 3-7; "The Bluebird of Happiness," VIII (December, 1910), 61–64; "On Playing at Five Hundred," VIII (January, 1911), 105–10; "The Prayer of a Materialist," VIII (February, 1911), under the pseudonym Aurelius Bloomfield; "The Suicide of Criticism," VIII (March, 1911), 188–92; review of S. N. Patten, *The Social Basis of Religion,* VIII (April, 1911), 269–70; review of J. G. Hibben, *A Defense of Prejudice,* VIII (May, 1911), 313–15; "Over the Quadrangle," VIII (August, 1911); "Individuality and Education," IX (January, 1912), 88–90; "Seeing, We See Not," IX (February, 1912), 132–36; "Poker and Veronica," IX (April, 1912), 175–79; "Some Thoughts on Religion," IX (May, 1912), 229–32; "Socialism and the Catholic Ideal," X (November, 1912), 11–19; "The Next Revolution," X (May, 1913), 221–27; "Sabotage," XI (November, 1913), under the pseudonym Aurelius Bloomfield.

PAMPHLETS

[for the American Association of International Conciliation] *Arbitration and International Politics,* No. 70, September, 1913. *The Tradition of War,* No. 79, June, 1914.

ARTICLES

[*The Atlantic Monthly*]

"The Two Generations," CVII (May, 1911), 591–98.
"The Handicapped," CVIII (September, 1911), 320–39.
"The College: An undergraduate view," CVIII (November, 1911), 667–74.
"Mystic Turned Radical," CIX (February, 1912), 236–38.
"Youth," CIX (April, 1912), 433–41.
"The Excitement of Friendship," CX (December, 1912), 795–800.
"The Social Order in an American Town," CXI (February, 1913), 227–36.
"The Life of Irony," CXI (March, 1913), 357–67.

"In the Mind of the Worker," CXIII (March, 1914), 375.
"An Experiment in Cooperative Living," CXIII (June, 1914), 823–31.
"An Hour in Chartres," CXIV (August, 1914), 214–17.
"Maurice Barrès and the Youth of France," CXIV (September, 1914), 394–99.
"Our Cultural Humility," CXIV (October, 1914), 503–7.
"Mon Amie," CXV (March, 1915), 354–59.
"This Older Generation," CXVI (September, 1915), 385–91.
"Housekeeping for Men," CXVII (March, 1916), 430–32.
"Smoking," CXVII (April, 1916), 573–75.
"Trans-National America," CXVIII (July, 1916), 86–97.
"Ernest, or, a parent for a day," CXIX (June, 1917), 778–86.

[*The New Republic*]

"In a Schoolroom," I (November 7, 1914), 23–24.
"Holy Poverty," I (November 14, 1914), 25.
"Maeterlinck and the Unknown," I (November 21, 1914), 26.
"Bumptious Psychology," I (November 28, 1914), 27.
"Sincerity in the Making," I (December 5, 1914), 26–27.
"Town Planning and the Law," I (December 19, 1914), 27–28.
"Good People," I (December 26, 1914), 18.
"Puzzle Education," I (January 2, 1915), 10–11.
"Continental Cultures," I (January 6, 1915), 14–16.
"A Substitute for Schools," II (February 6, 1915), 25–26.
"When We Went to School," II (February 27, 1915), 101–3.
"The Class Struggle in Education," II (March 6, 1915), 135.
"John Dewey's Philosophy," II (March 13, 1915), 154–56.
"Schools in Gary," II (March 27, 1915), 198–99.
"Communities for Children," II (April 3, 1915), 233–34.
"Really Public Schools," II (April 10, 1915), 259–61.
"Theodore Dreiser," II supplement (April 17, 1915), 7–8.
"Map of the Public," II (April 17, 1915), 11–12.
"Apprentices to the School," II (April 24, 1915), 302–3.
"Natural Schools," II (May 1, 1915), 326–28.
"Failing Church," III (May 15, 1915), 49.
"Fergus—a portrait," III (May 22, 1915), 62–64.
"Wasted Years," III (June 5, 1915), 120–22.
"Platitude," III (June 19, 1915), 183–84.
"Our Unplanned Cities," III (June 26, 1915), 202.
"The Issue of Vocational Education," III (June 26, 1915), 191–92.
"Heart of the People," III (July 3, 1915), 233.
"The Professor," III (July 10, 1915), 257–58.
"Who Owns the Universities?" III (July 17, 1915), 269–70.
"Studies in Tone Poetry," IV (August 7, 1915), 26–27.
"The Organic School," IV (August 21, 1915), 64.
"Medievalism in the Colleges," IV (August 28, 1915), 87–88.
"American Use for German Ideals," IV (September 4, 1915), 117–19.
"One of Our Conquerors," IV (September 4, 1915), 121–23.
"Mental Unpreparedness," IV (September 11, 1915), 143–44.
"The Undergraduate," IV (September 25, 1915), 197–98.
"Fortress of Belief," IV (October 16, 1915), 283–84.
"The Democratic School," IV (October 16, 1915), 297–98.
"Sophronisba," V (November 13, 1915), 41–43.
"Desire as Hero," V (November 20, 1915), 5–6.

"What Is College For?" V (December 4, 1915), 127–28.
"The Architect," V (January 1, 1916), 222–23.
"The Portland School Survey," V (January 8, 1916), 238–39.
"Cult of the Best," V (January 15, 1916), 275–77.
"The School Situation in New York," VI (February 5, 1916), 6–8.
"Parents and Children," VI (February 19, 1916), 81–82.
"Education in Taste," VI (March 4, 1916), 122–24.
"Education for Work," VI (March 11, 1916), 145–46.
"The Price of Radicalism," VI (March 11, 1916), 161.
"Paul Elmer More," VI (April 1, 1916), 245–47.
"Self-Conscious School," VI (April 8, 1916), 260–61.
"Learning to Write," VI (April 22, 1916), 326.
"Organized Labor on Education," VII (May 6, 1916), 8–9.
"On Discussion," VII (May 27, 1916), 87–89.
"Continuation Schools," VII (June 10, 1916), 143–45.
"The World's Second Worst Failure," VII (June 17, 1916), 177–78.
"A Moral Equivalent for Universal Military Service," VII (July 1, 1916), 217–19.
"Very Long and Sunny," VII (July 15, 1916), 283–84.
"Education as Living," VIII (August 5, 1916), 10–12.
"Making One's Contribution," VIII (August 26, 1916), 91–92.
"Karen, a portrait," VIII (September 23, 1916), 187–88.
"Americanism," VIII (September 23, 1916), 197.
"Heroics," VIII (October 7, 1916), 249–50.
"What is Exploitation?" IX (November 4, 1916), 12–14.
"Magic and Scorn," IX (December 2, 1916), 130–31.
"France of Yesterday," IX (December 9, 1916), 156–58.
"Emerald Lake," IX (January 6, 1917), 267–68.
"Extending the University," IX (January 6, 1917), 259–60.
"Joseph Fels," X (February 3, 1917), 28–29.
"Do the People Want War?" an advertisement, X (March 3, 1917), 145.
"The Charm of Distance," X (March 10, 1917), 170–173.
"An Epic of Labor," X supplement (April 21, 1917), 8–10.
"Experimental Education," X (April 21, 1917), 345–47.
"Two Amateur Philosophers," X (April 28, 1917), 383–84.
"A Reverberation of War," XI (May 19, 1917), 86–87.
"Thinking at Seventy-six," XII (August 25, 1917), 111–12.
"The American Adventure," XII (October 20, 1917), 333–34.
"Those Columbia Trustees," a letter to the editor, XII (October 20, 1917), 328–29.
"Sociologic Fiction," XII (October 27, 1917), 359–60.
"Gorky's Youth," XIII (November 3, 1917), 26–27.
"H. L. Mencken," XIII (November 24, 1917), 102–3.
"Mr. Huneker's Zoo," XIII (December 1, 1917), 130–31.
"Americans in the Making," XIV (February 2, 1918), 30–32.
"The Guild Idyl," XIV (March 2, 1918), 151–52.
"Adventures in Miniature," XIV (March 9, 1918), 180–82.
"Making Over the Body," XV (May 4, 1918), 28–29.
"Other Messiahs," a letter to the editor, XV (May 25, 1918), 117.

[Seven Arts]

"The Puritan's Will to Power," I (April, 1917), 631–37.
"The War and the Intellectuals," II (June, 1917), 133–46.
"Below the Battle," II (July, 1917), 270–77.

"The Collapse of American Strategy," II (August, 1917), 409–24.
"Conspirators," II (August, 1917), 528–30.
"A War Diary," II (September, 1917), 535–47.
"Twilight of Idols," II (October, 1917), 688–702.

[*The Dial*]

"Seeing It Through," LXI (December 28, 1916), 563–65.
"New Ideals in Business," LXII (February 22, 1917), 133–34.
"A Modern Mind," LXII (March 22, 1917), 239–40.
"A Stronghold of Obscurantism," LXII (April 5, 1917), 303–5.
"International Dubieties," LXII (May 3, 1917), 387–88.
"The Art of Theodore Dreiser," LXII (June 14, 1917), 507–9.
"Immanence of Dostoevsky," LXIII (June 28, 1917), 24–25.
"The Later Feminism," LXIII (August 16, 1917), 103–4.
"An American Humanist," LXIII (August 30, 1917), 148–50.
"Conscience and Intelligence in War," LXIII (September 13, 1917), 193–95.
"Belgian Carthage," LXIII (October 11, 1917), 343–44.
"Denatured Nietzsche," LXIII (October 25, 1917), 389–91.
"The Idea of a University," LXIII (November 22, 1917), 509–10.
"Industrial Revolution," LXIII (December 20, 1917), 642.
"A Primer of Revolutionary Idealism," LXIV (January 17, 1918), 69.
"Quadrangles Paved with Good Intentions," LXIV (February 14, 1918), 151–52.
"A Vanishing World of Gentility," LXIV (March 14, 1918), 234–35.
"Traps for the Unwary," LXIV (March 28, 1918), 277–79.
"Clipped Wings," LXIV (April 11, 1918), 358.
"The Brevity School in Fiction," LXIV (April 25, 1918), 405–7.
"An Imagist Novelist," LXIV (May 9, 1918), 451–52.
"Our Enemy Speaks," LXIV (May 23, 1918), 486–87.
"Purpose and Flippancy," LXIV (June 6, 1918), 540–41.
"Mr. Bennett Is Disturbed," LXV (July 18, 1918), 72.
"Two Scandinavian Novelists," LXV (September 5, 1918), 167–68.
"The Relegation of God," LXV (September 19, 1918), 215–16.
"The Morality of Sacrifice," LXV (October 19, 1918), 309–10.
"From an Older Time," LXV (November 2, 1918), 363–64.
"The Light Essay," LXV (November 16, 1918), 419–20.
"A Mirror of the Middle West," LXV (November 30, 1918), 480–82
"Morals and Art from the West," LXV (December 14, 1918), 556–57.
"An Examination of Eminences," LXV (December 18, 1918), 603–4.

[*Miscellaneous*]

Review of *The Moral Life*, by W. R. Sorley, *Journal of Philosophy, Psychology and Scientific Methods*, IX (May 9, 1912), 277; review of *Nietzsche*, by P. E. More, IX (August 15, 1912), 471; review of *The Desire for Qualities*, by S. M. Bligh, IX (September 12, 1912), 530–31.
"College Life Today," *North American Review* (September, 1912), 365–72.
"College Lecture Course as the Student Sees It," *Educational Review*, XLVI (June, 1913), 60–70.
"A Glance at German Culture," *Lippincott's Monthly Magazine*, XCV (February 7, 1915), 22–27.
"Impressions of Europe, 1913–1914," *Columbia Quarterly*, XVII (March, 1915), 109–26.
"Democracy and University Administration," *Educational Review*, XLIX (May, 1915), 455–59.

"Gary Public Schools," *Scribner's Magazine,* LX (September, 1916), 371–80.

"The Jew and Trans-National America," *The Menorah Journal,* II (December, 1916), 277–84.

"The Vampire," *The Masses,* IX (June, 1917), 35–38.

"The Cult of Convention," *The Liberator,* I (June, 1918), 38–39.

[*Posthumous works*]

"History of a Literary Radical," *The Yale Review,* VIII (April, 1919), 468–84.

"Old Tyrannies," *Untimely Papers* (New York: B. W. Huebsch, 1919).

"The State," *Untimely Papers* (New York: B. W. Huebsch, 1919).

"Autobiographic Chapter," *The Dial* LXVIII (January, 1920), 1–21; reprinted as "Fragment of a Novel," in *History of a Literary Radical* (New York: B. W. Huebsch, 1920).

"Randolph Bourne: Some Pre-War Letters (1912–14)," *Twice-A-Year,* II (Spring–Summer, 1939), 79–102.

"Randolph Bourne: Letters (1913–14)," *Twice-A-Year,* V–VI (Fall–Winter, 1940, Spring–Summer, 1941), 79–88.

"Randolph Bourne: Diary for 1901," *Twice-A-Year,* V–VI (Fall–Winter, 1940, Spring–Summer, 1941), 89–98.

"Randolph Bourne: Letters (1913–16)," *Twice-A-Year,* VII (Fall–Winter, 1941), 76–90.

IMPORTANT BIOGRAPHICAL DATA:

1886   May 30th is Bourne's birth-date. He is the first son of Sarah Bourne (née Barrett) and Charles R. Bourne. As a result of forceps-delivery, his face remains twisted.

1890   Bourne becomes ill with spinal tuberculosis. Further deformities result.

1903   Bourne graduates from high school (June 28th), but family finances prohibit college. After the separation of his parents, the family becomes financially dependent on Sarah Bourne's brother, the lawyer Halsey Barrett, who refuses to pay college tuition.

1909   After a six-year interval marked by futile attempts to find an appropriate activity (cf. "The Handicapped," and "What is Exploitation?"), Bourne receives a scholarship and registers at Columbia University. His teachers include Felix Adler, Charles S. Baldwin, Charles Beard, John Dewey, W. L. Dana, John Erskine, F. H. Giddings, and Frederick Woodbridge. During his college years, Bourne turns to socialism.

1911   Bourne published his first article, "The Two Generations," in the *Atlantic Monthly.*

1913   Publication of *Youth and Life,* a collection of essays which had appeared in the *Columbia Monthly* and the *Atlantic Monthly.*

1913/14 A grant makes it possible for Bourne to travel through Europe. He visits England, France, Italy, Germany, and Denmark, and returns home from Sweden. After the founding of the *New Republic,* the first issue of which appeared on November 7, 1914, Bourne becomes a contributor and writes articles on education, urban planning, and literature. Bourne opposes U.S. entry into the war while the editorial board supports it.

1916   *The Gary Schools* is published. The first issue of *The Seven Arts* appears in November of this year. It was here that Bourne later published most of his antiwar articles, which finally were partly responsible for the stopping of further funding.

1917   *Education and Living* appears. Bourne writes his best essays: "The War and the Intellectuals" (June), "A War

Diary" (September), and "Twilight of Idols" (October). *Seven Arts* ceases publication. At the same time, Bourne begins writing reviews for the *Dial* on a regular basis.

1918   Bourne dies on December 23rd during an influenza epidemic. The essay "The State" and an autobiographical text remain fragments. Bourne's life and early death become the material for legend.

ACKNOWLEDGEMENTS:

Without the general help of the Special Collections Section of Columbia University Library in the use of the Randolph Bourne Collection in 1970 and 1975, this anthology would not have been possible. Of the earlier works on the subject, two were especially helpful. Lillian Schlissel's *The World of Randolph Bourne* (New York, 1965) and particularly her bibliography which required only minor additions. And John Adam Moreau's biography, *Randolph Bourne, Legend and Reality* (Washington, D.C., 1966). The reprint of Bourne's letters in *Twice-A-Year* and the essay by Max Lerner, "Randolph Bourne and Two Generations," also published there, significantly contributed to rounding out the image of Randolph Bourne.

OTHER BOOKS OF INTEREST PUBLISHED BY URIZEN

LITERATURE

Bresson, Robert
Notes on Cinematography,
132 p. / Cloth $6.95 / paper $3.50

Brodsky, Michael
Detour, novel,
350 p. / Cloth $8.95

Cohen, Marvin
The Inconvenience of Living, fiction,
200 p. / Cloth $8.95 / paper $4.95

Ehrenburg, Ilya
The Life of the Automobile, novel,
192 p. / Cloth $8.95 / paper. $4.95

Enzensberger, Hans Magnus
Mausoleum, poetry,
132 p. / Cloth $10.00 / paper $4.95

Hamburger, Michael
German Poetry 1910-1975,
576 p. / Cloth $17.50 / paper $6.95

Handke, Peter
Nonsense & Happiness, poetry,
80 p. / Cloth $7.95 / paper $3.95

Innerhofer, Franz
Beautiful Days, novel,
228 p. / Cloth $8.95 / paper $4.95

Kroetz, Franz Xaver
Farmyard & Other Plays,
192 p. / Cloth $12.95 / paper $4.95

Montale, Eugenio
Poet In Our Time, essays,
96 p. / Cloth $5.95 / paper $2.95

Shepard, Sam
*Angel City, Curse of the Starving Class,
& Other Plays,*
300 p. / Cloth $15.00 / paper $4.95

Sternberger, Dolf
Preface by Erich Heller
Panorama of the 19th Century
Cloth $15.00

PSYCHOLOGY

Borneman, Ernest (Ed.)
The Psychoanalysis of Money,
420 p. / Cloth $15.00 / paper $5.95

Elias, Norbert
The Civilizing Process, Vol. I,
400 p. / Cloth $15.00

Fuller, Peter
*The Champions: The Secret Motives
in Games & Sports*,
260 p. / Cloth $10.95

Patrick C. Lee and Robert S. Stewart
Sex Differences,
500 p. / Cloth $17.50 / paper $5.95

Moser, Tilmann
Years of Apprenticeship on the Couch
240 p. / Cloth $10.00

ECONOMICS

De Brunhoff, Suzanne
Marx on Money,
192 p. / Cloth $10.00 / paper $4.95

Linder, Marc
Anti-Samuelson Vol. I,
400 p. / Cloth $15.00 / paper $5.95
Anti-Samuelson Vol. II,
440 p. / Cloth $15.00 / paper $5.95

CONTEMPORARY AFFAIRS

Andrew Arato / Eike Gebhardt (Eds.)
The Essential Frankfurt School Reader,
554 p. / Cloth $17.50 / paper $6.95

Augstein, Rudolf
Preface by Gore Vidal
Jesus Son of Man,
420 p. / Cloth $12.95

Burchett, Wilfred
Grasshoppers & Elephants,
260 p. / Cloth $12.95 / paper $4.95

Kristeva, Julia
About Chinese Women,
250 p. / Cloth $8.95

Steele, Jonathan
Inside East Germany,
300 p. / Cloth $12.95

Stern, August
The USSR vs. Dr. Mikhail Stern,
300 p. / Cloth $9.95

Write for a complete catalog to:
Urizen Books, Inc., 66 West Broadway, New York, N.Y. 10007
212-962-3413